CASES IN INTERNATIONAL MARKETING

KU-258-043

. 1290927

CHESTER COLLEGE

ACC. No.	DEPT.
01 0 56246	OWL
CLASS No.	
658 -848 JEA	

LIBRARY

Second Edition

Jean-Pierre Jeannet

Professor of Marketing and International Business
Walter H. Carpenter Chairholder, Babson College, Wellesley, MA
Professor of Marketing
International Institute for Management Development (IMD), Lausanne, Switzerland

Christopher Gale

Professor of Business Administration
The Colgate Darden Graduate School of Business Administration
The University of Virginia

Kamran Kashani

Professor of Marketing
International Institute for Management Development (IMD), Lausanne, Switzerland

Dominique Turpin

Professor of Marketing
Egon Zehnder International Fellow
International Institute for Management Development (IMD), Lausanne, Switzerland

Prentice Hall, Englewood Cliffs, New Jersey 07632

Library of Congress Cataloging-in-Publication Data

CASES IN INTERNATIONAL MARKETING / Jean Pierre Jeannet . . . [et al.].—
2nd ed.

p. cm.
Rev. ed. of: Cases in international marketing / Christopher Gale.
c1986.
Includes bibliographical references.
ISBN 0-13-037474-1
1. Export marketing—Case studies. I. Jeannet, Jean-Pierre.
II. Gale, Christopher. Cases in international marketing.
HF1009.5.C343 1995
382′.6—dc20

94-5927
CIP

Acquisitions editor: *Sandra Steiner*
Editorial/production supervision: *Kim Gueterman*
Cover design: *William McLoskey*
Buyer: *Marie McNamara*

 ©1995, 1986 by Prentice-Hall, Inc.
A Simon & Schuster Company
Englewood Cliffs, New Jersey 07632

All rights reserved. No part of this book may be
reproduced, in any form or by any means,
without permission in writing from the publisher.

Printed in the United States of America
10 9 8 7 6 5 4 3 2 1

ISBN 0-13-037474-1

Prentice-Hall International (UK) Limited, *London*
Prentice-Hall of Australia Pty. Limited, *Sydney*
Prentice-Hall Canada Inc., *Toronto*
Prentice-Hall Hispanoamericana, S.A., *Mexico*
Prentice-Hall of India Private Limited, *New Delhi*
Prentice-Hall of Japan, Inc., *Tokyo*
Simon & Schuster Asia Pte. Ltd., *Singapore*
Editora Prentice-Hall do Brasil, Ltda., *Rio de Janeiro*

CASES
IN
INTERNATIONAL
MARKETING

Accession no.
01056246

WITHDRAWN

University of
Chester

CHESTER CAMPUS
LIBRARY
01244 513301

This book is to be returned on or before the last date stamped
below. Overdue charges will be incurred by the late return of
books.

25 MAR 2008   CANCELLED

21 JUN 2008 CANCELLED

WITHDRAWN

2007

One
Week
Loan

One Week
Loan

To the global managers of the 21st century

Contents

SECTION 3.   MARKETING IN EASTERN EUROPEAN MARKETS   116

SECTION 4.   THE CHALLENGE TO MARKET IN JAPAN   167

SECTION 5.   THE PAN-EUROPEAN CHALLENGE   231

SECTION 6. THE GLOBAL CHALLENGE   285

SECTION 7. THE MANAGERIAL CHALLENGE: IMPLEMENTING INTERNATIONAL MARKETING PROGRAMS   385

Preface

Since our first edition was published in 1986, the world of business has changed in ways many of us would not have believed possible. With the collapse of the communist regimes in Eastern Europe, a vast part of the world has been opened up to international business, and marketing in particular. The boom of developing economies in the Asia Pacific Basin has opened up new frontiers. Not only has Japan established itself as one of the strongest economies in the world, but other Asian countries such as China, Taiwan, Korea, Singapore, Thailand, Indonesia, and India are developing rapidly. Economic, business, and marketing activities of international firms have globalized in such a way that the international marketing landscape has completely changed. With such sweeping changes, it should only be normal to expect that our new edition is completely revamped.

We have retained our first edition the features of a selective amount of text in the form of short section introductions and, of course, a collection of attractive, current, real-life cases. This book is still intended as an accompanying book for classes in international or global marketing. We hope that some teachers will find the text features sufficient to provide a framework for students without access to full-fledged textbooks. The cases are broad enough that they may also serve to supplement regular marketing strategy classes that are in need of international material.

While some features have been retained, it should be pointed out that this is an entirely new book. All cases included are new, with none held over from the first edition. The number of cases has been significantly increased, providing greater flexibility to the instructor. The cases have been grouped into several specific areas of concerns, or challenges, which make it also different from the typical international case book and from our first edition. In particular, the new regional focus on Europe, Eastern Europe, Japan, and developing countries with corresponding short cases allows students access to contemporary international marketing problems. The cases continue to cover different industries, countries, and complexities, allowing the instructor to tailor the case selection to the skill, interest, and experience of the audience.

THE ORGANIZATION OF THIS BOOK

This text is organized into seven sections, each consisting of a short introductory section and several cases. The purpose of the introductory sections is to frame the issues conceptually for the reader. They are not meant to contain exhausting background that might bear directly on the approach to any of the cases contained in the book.

Section 1: The International Marketing Environment

This section deals with the difference between the domestic or home country environment and international marketing environment and is meant to sensitize students to differences in order to provide a framework that will help them understand, appreciate, and spot differences encountered in the cases in this book. This section is closely patterned after a successful earlier version from the first edition, although the second edition's version has been shortened and focuses more on the analytical aspects of understanding and appreciating differences in domestic and international marketing. The Skisailer, Porsche, and Dow Ziploc™ cases introduce students to the different complexities of the international environment, including physical, economic, and cultural differences.

Section 2: Challenges in Emerging Markets

The international marketing challenges in emerging or developing markets are in some important aspects different from those in the already developed Western economies. This section outlines these differences and sensitizes the reader to the immense potential in these areas. We have selected two very different cases for this section, taking the reader to Indonesia (P.T. Food Specialties Indonesia), India (Wiltech India), and Brazil (Ericsson Do Brasil).

Section 3: Challenges in Eastern Europe

The spotlight has been on Eastern Europe ever since the breakup of the Soviet Union and the vast liberalization of the Eastern European countries (with prior state-run economies). During the past few years, this area has become a new frontier for international marketing with enormous new markets suddenly opened to the rest of the world. However, political and economic barriers to true internationalization remain, and, as recent events in several of the Eastern European countries have shown, political stability has not yet returned. This section contains brief summaries of the recently formed countries in Eastern Europe and their economic potential and of the challenges faced by international firms. The cases contained in this section were all written after the liberalization drive and take us to Slovenia (a part of former Yugoslavia), Poland, and Russia. The cases cover both the challenges of local firms expanding or even exporting and the decisions faced by western firms entering these markets.

Section 4: The Japanese Challenge

This section deals with the particular challenges faced both by Japanese firms marketing locally and international firms entering the Japanese market. The introductory section gives the reader a background in the particular features of marketing as practiced by major firms in Japan. The

Kirin Brewery case is an excellent example of the tough local competition prevalent in Japan, pitting a Japanese firm against Japanese firm. The Philip Morris case intends to show the challenges faced by a foreign, but largely established, firm, whereas the Lestra Design and Delissa cases are typical for smaller foreign firms entering the Japanese market.

Section 5: The Pan-European Challenge

Since our first edition, much has been written and speculated about the developments surrounding pan-European integration. With the 1992 initiative and the Maastricht Treaty, the European business environment has been substantially changed, challenging all businesses who compete there. This section gives a brief background on the content and form of European integration, the key acts, and an overview of the major markets. The cases selected cover a range of truly pan-European issues faced by European-based firms who are struggling with different ways to integrate their operations. The examples from the computer industry (Nokia Data) and pharmaceutical industry (Pharma Swede) take the reader right into the integration debate. How to handle the managerial challenge is the context of the third case (Alto Chemicals).

Section 6: The Global Challenge

Since our first edition, the conceptual development of global marketing has proceeded at a rapid pace. While we had no such material in our first edition, we are now providing new material, some never before published in textbook form, to give the reader a strong sense of the nature of global marketing. The conceptual material in the brief introductory section is intended to frame the debate on globalization. Black & Decker serves as an introduction to the debates waged in many firms about the meaning of globalization. The section also contains two sets of materials, one on the robotics industry and the other on the paint industry worldwide, and each consisting of a global industry overview and accompanying cases on companies, to develop an understanding of how global industries shape global marketing and strategy.

Section 7: The Managerial Challenge

This section, adapted from our first edition, features the particular challenges of managing an international marketing operation. The cases deal with issues such as developing marketing strategies, organization, and planning, as well as the perennial debate as to where a company should locate marketing decision making. The cases include both shorter ones (Pakkasakku, Mediquip, and Club Med España) and more challenging and complex cases (Libby's Beverages and Alliance ANDIV) that may be used as capstones for an international marketing course.

ACKNOWLEDGMENTS

The development and publication of this collection of cases would not have been possible without the generous support of a great number of people and institutions. First and foremost we would like to thank the many companies and executives who spent their valuable time with us, confiding some of their most important decisions and thus contributing the learning of future generations of managers. We are also grateful to our home institutions for supporting the development of case teaching materials, in particular IMD Institute (International Management Development Institute) in Lausanne, Switzerland, where all the case authors have spent important time either on full-time assignments or as visiting professors, Babson College at Wellesley, Massachusetts, and the Colgate Darden Graduate School of Business Administration at the University of Virginia. We are particularly grateful to a number of our colleagues who have contributed cases to this book: Steve Allen at Babson College and Bill Fisher, Bob Collins, and Per Jenster, all from IMD. They have enriched this collection of cases with their own very special contributions. And finally we owe our gratitude to IMD and Colgate Darden School for allowing us to publish this unique set of cases.

Behind the case authors, however, there were a great many number of talented professionals who made these cases possible. We acknowledge our indebtedness to our case writers who have toiled endless hours over many of the cases included in this book. Furthermore, we would like to acknowledge the invaluable assistance received from Faith Towle, who in her role as case editor at IMD has improved the readability and clarity of all IMD cases immeasurably. And finally we all acknowledge a special amount of gratitude to Silvia Farmanfarma, who has managed the IMD case collection for many years and has carefully maintained the case records and handled all permissions and preproduction requirements in the most prompt manner.

The authors also thank the reviewers whose valuable comments helped make this a better book: Dan Rajaratnam at Baylor University, William Frech at Ramapo College, Peter Gordon at South East Missouri State University, Rosemary Purser at the College of Notre Dame, Joseph Miller at Indiana University, MaryAnn McGrath at Loyola University–Chicago, Lalita Manrai at the University of Delaware, and Massoud Saghafi at San Diego State University.

Jean-Pierre Jeannet
Christopher Gale
Kamran Kashani
Dominique Turpin

Note to the Reader

Case material of IMD (International Institute for Management Development), Babson College, and the Colgate Darden Graduate School of Business Administration, University of Virginia is made possible by the kind cooperation of various corporations only for the purposes of class discussion. In some instances, the names of individuals and certain data have been disguised, but in the opinion of the executives involved, the cases fairly represent the situation and issues they were facing. These cases are not intended to represent an effective or ineffective handling of these situations.

In order to develop and maintain the cooperation of corporations in the development of case material, we have assured them that only material that they reviewed and approved in writing will be published. In addition, they have been assured that STUDENTS WILL BE TOLD NOT TO CONTACT THE EXECUTIVES OR COMPANY INVOLVED in any way when they are assigned these cases. Not only would this be an inappropriate way for students to prepare these cases, it would as well subject us to the risk of severely straining our relationships with cooperating companies in the future.

CASES
IN
INTERNATIONAL
MARKETING

1

The International Marketing Environment

The first step in international marketing begins with a commitment to find opportunities that exist outside one's home market. The cases in this section focus on the first step—examining potential new markets in other countries for the economic, cultural, and other environmental factors that will fit a corporation's strengths.

One way to begin the analysis of where to market abroad is to determine which are our most successful products at home and why. One should then ask in which markets would their marketing strategies work best. These seductively simple questions involve some important assumptions: One is that a company is better off exporting its domestically successful products and strategies rather than its less successful products. Another is that there are other markets in which these products will be successful, albeit with some adjustments in the strategy. A product may be successful in only one or a few countries due to some very local peculiarities. For example, baseball—America's national pastime—turns out to be a very poor export. On the other hand, basketball has turned out to be a far better export performer as demonstrated by the popularity of the United States' "Dream Team" during the 1992 Olympics in Barcelona.

For most marketers, however, the prevailing assumption is that a company's best opportunities for international success begin with its domestic "winners." The studies of successful domestic companies indicate that there is a strong relationship between high market shares and profitability. This can be explained largely by the superior accumulation of power, experience, and consumer wisdom enjoyed by the leading market shareholders. The logical instinct for a domestically successful company is to extend its experience to other markets. This *assumes* that there *are* opportunities to transfer marketing strategies and that there *are* similar (or sufficiently similar) economies, cultures, and therefore markets abroad where the strategy can be applied. To determine where domestic strategies will work and where and how strategies may need to be changed, a manager must have ways of sizing up international markets in both economic and cultural terms.

THE ECONOMIC ENVIRONMENT

Two aspects of the global environment affect international marketing: the world economy and the economies of individual nations. The cases in this section involve both. The reader is referred to general textbooks for discussions of such aspects of the global economy as the historical development of world trade, trade patterns, international trade agreements, and regional economic and trade associations.

The economic structure of an individual country affects whether a marketing program can be successfully transferred from another environment. Analysis of these structures requires, first, gathering of economic data and, second, interpreting the types of data relevant to the proposed marketing plan.

Regarding data collection, in recent years there has been tremendous growth in the availability of all kinds of economic data for the world's approximately 200 countries. Japan and the United States are probably unexcelled in providing a marketer with an incredible wealth of information on all aspects of their economies, including population and income data, sales by various industrial and product sectors, trends, and international trade.

Most published economic data are directed at such *macro* statistics as population, gross national product, and income per household. However, marketers are also very interested in learning about marketing and infrastructural information, such as what kinds of retail outlets carry a particular kind of product, the number of these outlets, the levels of distribution, and the discount structure at each level. They may also want to know about the cost and availability of various communications media or what the price points are for a product line. This information is not readily available in published data banks, and while it could be supplied by personnel in the company's foreign subsidiary, that resource is, of course, not usually available to the firm or division considering going abroad for the first time. Data could also be researched by a local advertising agency or consultant in the foreign market, but this alternative is often not appropriate for marketers who are in the preliminary planning or feasibility stages of investigation and not yet ready to commission any such formal research.

There is no substitute for a personal visit to the candidate countries, but often marketers have made the serious error of allowing that contact to be the primary or only source of data they gather on a new market. The problem is that the visits are usually short, given the executive's busy schedule, and, more significantly, the executive does not always know what to look for or what questions to ask. The collective wisdom of many different sources of information may help an executive learn about the infrastructure of his or her target market, as well as some of its cultural oddities. Such intelligence makes personal visits much more informative and valid.

THE ROLE OF CULTURE

The word *culture* evokes all the mysteries and obsessions about things foreign that many novices associate with international marketing. It is a difficult concept to define and one that is difficult to work with constructively in the building of a multinational business plan. Vern Terpstra reports that

> after surveying no less than 164 definitions of culture, [two Harvard scholars found] that the consensus of social scientists is that "culture consists of patterns, explicit and implicit, of behavior acquired and transmitted by symbols, constituting the distinctive achievements of human groups. . . . the essential core of culture consists of traditional ideas and especially their attached values."[1]

---

[1] Material from *The Cultural Environment of International Business* by Vern Terpstra, published by South-Western Publishing Co., 1978. Reprinted by permission.

Culture consists of the learned values and perceptual biases passed on from one generation to the next; while difficult to describe, you know a new culture by the behavior around you; you know, in short, that you are in a different place.

For international marketers, culture can be an "elephant trap"—large but hidden and unforgiving when it captures unsuspecting prey.[2] The trap can lie in two dimensions: You can unwittingly ignore cultural differences and make the usual or "classical" international marketing blunders, or you can overplay those differences, ignoring major opportunities for economies of scale and true global standardization of product, distribution strategy, or advertising message. When are you likely to make either of these two mistakes, and which one would you make? How can you capitalize on similarities without being ambushed by differences? There are plenty of opportunities to address such questions in the case studies that follow.

The first trap—forgetting to take local culture into account—has been historically the most common cause of unsuccessful international marketing. While most people have an intellectual understanding that "culture is important" and that they should "look out" for the differences, they still make decisions that fly in the face of those differences.

Why does this problem persist? The answer probably involves the way most marketing decisions are made. In the end, all marketing plans must involve an in-depth analysis of consumer segments and their needs and wants, yet unfortunately most marketers do this critical analysis implicitly. That is, they make decisions based on their intuitive, but *unspoken*, feelings about what consumers want and how the company will satisfy these needs. Unless their analysis is made very explicit—written down in black and white—marketers do not realize that their intuitions are based on experience in their own culture. (And, of course, lack of an explicit, detailed analysis invites disaster in the home market as well.) Perhaps the danger is greatest when a marketer least expects it, especially in countries that seem to be more similar to one's own. For example, a U.S. manager may feel very much at home with the idea of selling in Canada, the United Kingdom, or Australia, since there is the comfortable feeling that everyone speaks English. The greater the seeming similarity, however, the deeper the possible trap of being caught off guard.

But failure has befallen even the marketers who write out explicit statements or hypotheses about how their customers behave, based either on their own experience or on market research studies. Here, again, their explicit statements have failed to account for cultural differences, even though they were trying to understand those very differences and take them into account. This sometimes happens when, by their very nature, the differences are hidden to the foreigner who does not know where to look for them. Even where research has been conducted by persons native to the area, these individuals may not be consciously aware of the differences, or they may be reluctant to point them out. After all, many famous blunders in international marketing, while designed by outsiders, were still executed by local executives. Why were they so silent when these gaffes were being committed? Being a "native" does not make a person any better as a marketer in his or her own country than being an American makes a person a good marketer in the United States. There is a need, then, for both the "foreigner" and the "local" to discuss each point in the marketing program explicitly: Who is the target consumer, how does he or she behave in finding out about and shopping for a product, and what marketing methods are available and appropriate in that area? Through such discussion, one

---

[2] For some graphic examples of how marketers can be blinded by cultural biases, see David A. Ricks, *Big Business Blunders—Mistakes in Multinational Marketing* (Homewood, Ill.: Dow Jones-Irwin, 1983).

has the best chance of uncovering the cultural market differences that otherwise would sabotage a program.

There is also the risk of looking too hard for differences when there might be universal human needs that can be satisfied by a more or less standard offering. Certainly, the Coca-Cola and Gillette companies have offered the same basic products around the world for years (with some local variations, to be sure, but the similarities far outweigh the differences). Certain "status" products such as expensive watches, perfumes, or sports cars appeal to a common set of attributes in an upscale market that exists in every country, regardless of whether official economic or political doctrine in that country would admit it.

The key to avoiding cultural traps is to realize that good marketers in a foreign environment do not really behave any differently than they would in a domestic market; they simply add a "cultural lookout" to the analysis of consumer needs and segments.

THE COMPARATIVE–ANALYTIC APPROACH

One framework for analyzing where and how to market abroad has been called the *comparative–analytic method.*[3] (For ease of communicating this idea, only the transfer to one other country is considered.) This approach finds a direct relationship between a country's environment (E) and the resulting marketing process (P). Here the term *process* can mean the total marketing infrastructure (or marketing practices that can be found in the environment), or it can refer to a specific marketing mix that a company has developed for a product in that environment. Clearly, no matter how a product is originally introduced, a successful marketing program is the result of an evolutionary process in which the marketing mix is adjusted and fine-tuned as the marketer continually responds to changes in the environment. This relationship between marketing process (P) and the environment (E) can be stated as

$$E_1 = P_1$$

and only emphasizes the important point that environment leads to marketing structures and successful marketing plans, and not vice versa.

International marketing requires an investigation of other environments (E_2 through E_n) and a determination of what marketing infrastructures (P_2 through P_n) result from them. This analysis is done at the country, or macro, level and is undertaken mostly as a rigorous way to help the marketer understand both the distinctive characteristics of a country's environment and how marketing works in that environment. The next step is to ask how or whether the marketing mix ($MMix_1$) in one country (E_1) can be transferred to another country (E_2), or

$$E_1 = MMix_1 : E_2 = MMix_2$$

where $MMix_2$ is the unknown. The closer $MMix_1$ is to $MMix_2$, the more transferable the strategy. The relevant considerations are pictured in Figure 1.

This analysis forces marketers to reassess the environmental variables in their own coun-

---

[3] See Jean-Pierre Jeannet, "International Marketing Analysis: A Comparative–Analytic Approach," Working Paper, 1981.

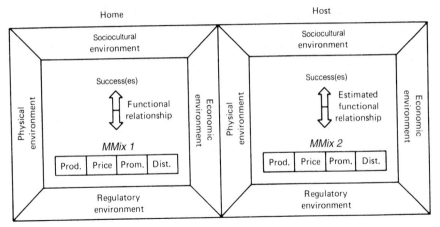

FIGURE 1   Transferring Strategy from Home to Host Environment

try that allowed the company's success and to inquire which of those necessary factors are in place in the new environment. For example, McDonald's fast-food chain has been so successful in the United States that it created a new segment in the restaurant industry; success in this segment depends heavily on a highly organized and well-managed service operation, which McDonald's has pioneered. The product policy is to offer a limited variety of high-quality products with very high consistency; the price is low relative to fuller-service restaurants and gives the impression of a good bargain, even vis-à-vis home cooking. The outlets are placed in areas of high population concentrations and are similar in design. Large advertising budgets, used mainly for television, stress the high product quality and service (convenience) attributes of the chain. In the early 1970s, the company was looking at several possible sites for foreign expansion. The decisions to be made were (1) in which countries and (2) with what products. The ethnocentric view of marketing would have argued that the success of McDonald's was due to its unique service and price features, that is, its marketing mix ($MMix_1$), which should therefore work well anywhere. Although such thinking would appear to be arrogant and insensitive to what is cause and what is effect, this kind of thinking has been common and has led to innumerable international marketing failures.

The comparative–analytic approach warns the marketer that the McDonald's marketing mix works in the United States because it fills a hole in a particular market that other competitors in that market had failed to see, and that it was environmental factors (E_1) that created that hole in the market. That is,

$$E_1 = MMix_1$$

The environmental variables can be grouped into four major categories; physical, sociocultural, economic, and legal-regulatory. The relevant physical variables allowing McDonald's to take the radical step of cooking hamburgers in anticipation of demand might be the number of urban and suburban areas with sufficient population within driving distance of a restaurant to make reliable prediction of demand possible. The sociocultural variables that favored McDonald's included Americans' preoccupation with time and a fast pace of living (and eating), the trend toward eating out (and thus a decreased formality associated with mealtime), and the American love of the hamburger. All this was coincident, in the 1960s, with a rapidly expanding youth market. Of course, drive-in restaurants were made possible by an increasing disposable income that allowed for multicar ownership in a family and money to spend on the perceived luxury of eating out. There are probably other factors one could postulate to explain the McDonald's phenomenon.

Having isolated and identified the elements in the American environment that made McDonald's strategy workable (and that were exploited through superb marketing and operations executions), the international marketer would now ask whether enough of these same conditions exist elsewhere to transfer the strategy, whether it is necessary to modify the strategy somewhat, or whether it would have to be modified drastically. Analysis of various other environments (E_2 through E_n) would lead to various marketing strategies ($MMix_2$ through $MMix_n$), and the search would be for those $MMix_n$'s that are as close as possible to the American strategy, $MMix_1$.

The searching process itself is not trivial, since data have to be obtained for a number of countries to conduct this analysis. The initial choice of countries to screen is itself a difficult step and is often made through intuitive notions based on the home marketer's personal experience in other countries or based on the advice of outside consultants. Gathering data on the physical variables necessary for success (for example, population densities and disposable income) is relatively easy, subject to the usual problems of obtaining accurate data. However, determining certain cultural norms (for example, attitude toward the meal as a family event and attitudes toward time) is more difficult, and the data here may be less reliable.

As it turns out, McDonald's has made entries into many foreign markets with what is basically the identical store layout and design and an identical menu (even down to the English names for the products). In many markets, the availability of television advertising was severely limited, and growth in some markets was slow at first. Some early units were located near tourist attractions, and business was often dependent on American tourists. In certain markets, changes were made (for example, wine is served in France, beer in Germany, sake in Japan), which led to a substantial improvement in sales. In some countries, the hamburger not at first well accepted. But it can be argued that enough of the environmental factors (E_n) were sufficiently similar to the United States so that transfer of the strategy was successful.

In the search for new markets, it may turn out that there are very few situations in which the new environments are similar to the home environment (E_1). In that case, the new strategy ($Mmix_{new}$) must be significantly different from that for the home environment ($MMix_1$). Then the question becomes one of whether current management, which is so successful in its home environment, can be as successful with both a new strategy and a new environment. For example, one of the most successful fast-food chains in Japan is Kentucky Fried Chicken, since chicken is a favorite dish in that country. The question would then be whether McDonald's should place a heavier emphasis on chicken than on hamburger in Japan, which would be a major departure for that company. (McDonald's has successfully introduced a chicken product in the United States, but the company's marketing emphasis is still largely on hamburgers.) There are no easy answers about how far a company can shift its area of expertise when entering a new market and still maximize its chances for success. As in all important marketing decisions, this calls for intensive investigation and thinking, but the comparative–analytic framework described here should provide a basis for asking intelligent questions. A very similar challenge was faced by Disney with the construction of EuroDisney near Paris. Built largely along the Disney World model in Florida, the property is performing below expectations since its opening in 1992.

SUMMARY

This section has presented a brief overview of a procedure for analyzing opportunities in foreign markets. This much should be clear: When a manager thinks about exporting a product, he or she makes a serious mistake in thinking only in terms of the product, rather than in terms of the entire mix or strategy that is needed to make the new venture successful. If the manager employs a more holistic approach, his or her thinking will be considerably sharpened.

These basic ideas may not seem to contribute to what a good marketer already knows when planning for the introduction of a new product or service. However, if that is the case, then we need to explain why these important steps have not been observed in the past. The reason may be that, when a manager plans for export of an existing product to another environment, he or she may be taking the product's current success for granted, forgetting the hard work, the fine tuning, and the time the current strategy represents. The transfer of strategy takes the same commitment to "begin at the beginning" that a manager would naturally make for a new product. If he or she starts out afresh, developing a total package of consumer research, product design, promotional message, media allocation, and appropriate channels of distribution will necessitate analyzing what worked well in the home environment and why, finding opportunities that match those conditions, and making necessary adaptations.

In your approach to the cases that follow, consider the following questions:

1. What do I know about the product's marketing strategy at home? Who needs the product and why?
2. What do I know about the need for the product in the target market? Who needs it and why?
3. How do environmental or cultural forces affect this analysis? Where are the traps? Where can I safely ignore cultural differences and thus enjoy economies of international scale?
4. How does my analysis affect my marketing strategy in the new environment? How much will I have to change my current strategy, and if this change is considerable, how well can I adapt my organization to make it work?

For the cases in this section, we suggest that students spend most of their analysis time on the environment and the cultural fit between the product in its home environment and the target foreign environment. Managers who have learned to begin at the beginning have come a long way in developing their talent as international marketers.

The Skisailer (R)

Early in 1987, David Varilek was given the bad news about the worldwide sales of his invention, the Skisailer. The management at Mistral, the company that had invested in David's innovation, informed him that the first-year sales of Skisailer had failed to match the target and that the future of the product was in doubt. Only 708 Skisailers had been sold in the first season the product was on sale. Mistral, who manufactured and marketed the product worldwide, had already invested more than half a million dollars in the project. The management was seriously considering dropping the product from its line next year.

Realizing that such an initial setback could jeopardize the future of his 4-year-old invention, in March 1987 David asked a group of MBA students at a leading international school of management in Switzerland to study the market potential for Skisailer and recommend what needed to be done to revive sales. The students had recently completed the first phase of the project. They had presented David with their findings and the 23-year-old inventor was reviewing the information.

The Invention

Skisailer was based on a concept that combined downhill skiing and windsurfing in a new sport: skisailing. As a Swiss native, David Varilek considered himself "born on skis."

However, he had always been frustrated by not being able to ski on the flat snow fields that surrounded his home in the winter season.

In 1983, in his own garage, David invented a connection bar that could be fixed onto regular skis while still allowing them to be directed with great flexibility. A windsurfing rig, consisting of a connecting bar and a sail, could then be installed on the connection bar and, with enough wind, flat snow surfaces could become great fun for skiing. The idea was subsequently patented under the Swiss law. A major feature of the invention was that the Skisailer's unique design also allowed "windskiers" to use regular downhill skis and almost any type of windsurfing rig, an innovation that limited the buyer's expense. The connection bar and the sail were easy to install. Lateral clamps used for attaching the connection bar to the skis did not damage them in any way except for small grooves on the side of each ski. Only 5 centimeters (2 inches) of the ski's length were held rigid and the rest retained normal flexibility. Safety had also been an important consideration when developing the Skisailer; three self-releasing safety mechanisms were installed on the product (refer to Exhibit 1 for an illustration of the Skisailer).

The Skisailer could be used on either smooth slopes or flat surfaces. The ideal surface for skisailing was on the kind of hard-packed snow usually found on groomed ski

This case was written by Professors Dominique Turpin and Kamran Kashani as a basis for class discussion rather than to illustrate either effective or ineffective handling of an administrative situation. Copyright © 1991 by the International Institute for Management Development (IMD), Lausanne, Switzerland. IMD retains all rights. Not to be used or reproduced without permission directly from IMD.

mistral

PRESENTS

A NEW WAY OF SKIING

The **SKISAILER** ™

Invented by David Varilek and developed in conjunction
with Mistral Windsurfing AG, Bassersdorf, Switzerland

Contact

Mistral Windsurfing A.G.
CH - 8303 Bassersdorf/Zürich
Switzerland
Telephone 01/836-8922
Telex 59 266 MWAG CH

EXHIBIT 1   Illustration of Skisailer from Product Brochure

slopes, but the Skisailer could also be used on ice, where it could achieve speeds of up to 100 km/h.[1] Skisailing in deep snow or slightly up-hill required stronger wind. For use at high speeds, a safety helmet was recommended.

According to David Varilek, skisailing was as much fun as windsurfing even though it had to be done in cold weather. "For identical sensations, skisailing is easier to learn and handle than windsurfing," David claimed. "You can get on and get off the Skisailer easily, and you are always on your feet. Another great thing with the Skisailer is that you can take advantage of the terrain to perform the same kind of loopings as on sea waves. The Skisailer is a great vehicle for discovering variety in the surroundings."

Mistral Windsurfing AG

In 1987, Mistral Windsurfing AG was a company affiliated with the ADIA Group. ADIA, a $1 billion conglomerate with headquarters in Lausanne, Switzerland, had its activities centered around ADIA Interim, a company providing temporary personnel to companies around the world.

In 1980, ADIA had acquired Mistral as part of its diversification strategy. The acquisition was seen as an opportunity to enter a rapidly growing industry. Consistency in marketing and product policy over the past 10 years had made Mistral a leader in the worldwide windsurfing industry. This success was grounded in technological competence, permanent innovation, high quality standards, a selective international distribution policy, and strong financial backing. Thus, in a fiercely competitive market for windsurfing equipment, characterized by the rise and fall of brands and manufacturers, Mistral was occupying a leading position. To Martin Pestalozzi, the president of Adia, the Skisailer represented a good opportunity to extend Mistral's product line at a time when Mistral management was increasingly concerned about the future of the windsurf market.

---

[1] 1 kilometer = 0.62 mile.

MISTRAL AND THE WINDSURF MARKET

The fathers of the modern windsurf were two Californians, Hoyle Schweitzer and James Drake, who had developed the concept and registered the Windsurfer brand. They had applied for and received a patent in 1970 for their device, which was a cross between a surfboard and a sailboat.

In the early 1970s, Schweitzer bought out Drake and developed his firm, Windsurfing International, from a living-room operation into a multimillion dollar corporation with branches in six countries. Due to its North American patents, Windsurfing International was able to hold a virtual monopoly in the United States and Canada until 1979 when a number of other firms entered the market.

Meanwhile, competition in the European windsurfing equipment market was years ahead of North America. First introduced to the European market by Ten Cate, a Dutch firm, windsurfing enjoyed an unprecedented growth, particularly in France and Germany. Even as the industry matured in the mid-1980s, it maintained growth in terms of dollar volume, though not in units. Interest in windsurfing had grown from a small pool of enthusiasts to a large and growing population, an estimated 2 to 3 million people internationally.

Established in 1976 in Bassersdorf near Zurich (Switzerland), Mistral rapidly won an international reputation among windsurfers. Its success was enhanced by two promotional strategies. First, from the start, Mistral had signed up Robby Naish, a young Californian who had won all the major distinctions and titles in this sport. Using Mistral equipment, Robby Naish had become the 1977 World Champion at age 12 and had dominated this sport ever since. In 1986, he won the world title for the tenth time in a row. Second, Mistral had promoted its brand by supplying several hundred windsurfs free of charge to such leisure organizations as Club Méditerranée that gave the brand visibility around the world.

Mistral also enjoyed an advantage over other windsurf manufacturers by concentrating on the upper price and quality range of the market. Worldwide, Mistral's equipment was considered the best. Robby Naish's name and the high quality and reliability of Mistral's products had helped build an extensive network of distributors in 30 countries. In 1980, the company had its own subsidiary in the United States, where it generated about one-third of its global sales and market share. Mistral was also directly represented in a number of European countries such as France, Germany and the Benelux. For the rest of the world, Mistral used exclusive agents who were responsible for selling Mistral products in specific regions.

Recent Market Developments in Windsurfing

Recently, a number of factors had combined to dampen the sales of windsurfs in the U.S. market. Patent infringement fights had led to the forced withdrawal of Bic and Tiga, both French manufacturers, from the market. With a total sales of 16,000 units, the two companies were among the major brands in the United States. Meanwhile, a number of European manufacturers had gone bankrupt, thus reducing even further the supply of and marketing expenditures on windsurfing equipment. Market saturation had also contributed to the decline of sales from 73,000 units in 1985 to 62,000 in 1986.

In Europe, where windsurfing had grown at spectacular rates over the years, the market was showing signs of a slowdown. According to the French market research group ENERGY, windsurfing equipment sales in France had risen from less than 600 units in 1974 to more than 115,000 units in early 1980s. However, cool weather conditions as well as general market saturation had reduced French sales to 65,000 units in 1986. In Germany, the second largest market after France, sales had also declined to below 60,000 units from the high levels of the early 1980s. Sales had leveled off in Italy at around 35,000 units, in Holland at 45,000 units, and in Switzerland at 15,000 units.

European sales were dominated by European brands. In France, for example, Bic and Tiga together accounted for 45,000 sales. Mistral was the top imported brand. In Germany,

Klepper was the leading local brand; Mistral was a distant fourth in market share. In 1986, the distribution of Mistral's global sales of 45,620 units was the United States, 25%; Europe, 30%; and the rest of the world, 45%. Windsurfing equipment accounted for 60% of the company's $52 million sales, while the rest was divided between sportswear (20%) and spare parts and accessories (20%).

The Skisailer and Mistral's Diversification Policy

Mistral Windsurfing AG had contacted David Varilek at the beginning of 1984 after ADIA management learned about the Skisailer from a four-page article in a major Swiss magazine. David Varilek was interested in establishing a relationship with Mistral because the company was the world leader in windsurfing equipment.

The Skisailer seemed an appropriate product diversification for Mistral. The Skisailer could also fit in with the new line of winter sportswear and other ski-related products that Mistral's management was planning to develop. Mistral had full support from ADIA to launch the project.

In the spring of 1984, a contract for development, manufacturing, and distribution of the Skisailer was formally signed between David Varilek and Mistral. For the duration of the agreement, all Skisailer patent and trademark rights would be transferred to Mistral, but David would serve as technical adviser to the company and would receive in return a 2% royalty on sales. It was also agreed that David would demonstrate the Skisailer in competitions and exhibitions where Mistral was participating. Should total sales fall short of 5,000 units by the end of 1986, either party could terminate the agreement, with trademarks and patents reverting back to David Varilek. Mistral could also counter any competitive offer made to David, a "first right of refusal."

Introducing the Skisailer

During the summer of 1984, two prototypes of the Skisailer were developed at Mistral for presentation in November at ISPO, the largest European sports exhibition held annually in Munich, Germany. Between May and November 1984, the engineers developed several innovations that were added to the Skisailer. For example, the connecting bar and mounting blocks were strengthened to resist shocks and low temperatures. The equipment was also modified to accommodate the Mistral windsurf sailing rig.

In Munich at ISPO the Skisailer was widely acclaimed as a truly innovative product that would certainly win public enthusiasm. However, at this early stage of development, the product still lacked promotional support. No pamphlet, video, or pictures had been developed to present the product and educate potential users. David thought that the pictures used to introduce the product to Mistral's distributors were not attractive enough to trigger interest and buying. Nevertheless, some distributors liked the product and placed immediate orders.

The formal launch of Skisailer got underway in 1986. Mistral produced 2,000 Skisailers, consisting of a mast foot, sail (available from its standard windsurf line), and the connecting bar. They were to be distributed worldwide through the company's network of wholesalers and independent sports shops in large and medium-sized cities. For example, in Lausanne, Switzerland, a city of 250,000 inhabitants with 30 skishops and three windsurf equipment stores, Skisailer was sold in three locations. Of the three stores, two specialized in ski equipment and the third sold windsurfing products.

Skisailer was priced at $410 retail; the price included the bar connection and its mounting blocks, but excluded the sail and mast, which cost an additional $590. Retail margins on the Skisailer and its rig were set at 35%. The wholesale margins were also 35%. Skisailer cost Mistral $85 per unit to produce and ship to distributors; the cost for the sailing rig was around $200.

It seemed to David that the 1986 promotional budget of $15,000 set for Skisailer was too low. Mistral management had already turned down a $35,000 proposal from David to produce a promotional video showing Skisailer in action. Nevertheless, David decided to arrange for the shooting of such a video on his own at Mammoth Lake, California. Mistral later refunded David the $10,000 that the video had cost him.

As of early 1987, Mistral had invested more than half a million dollars in Skisailer:

Engineering and tooling	$214,000
Other costs	74,000
Development costs	**288,000**
Inventory: Assembled and spares	
At central warehouse	180,000
At distributors	68,000
Total	**$536,000**

MARKET RESEARCH FINDINGS

Because of his concern about the future of the Skisailer, David had commissioned the group of MBA students to study the global market for Skisailer and report on their findings. By early fall, the students had completed the first phase of their study, which dealt with estimating the market potential for Skisailer, competing products, ski market developments, and a survey of buyers, retailers, and wholesalers. A summary of the findings follows.

Potential Market

Based on interviews with buyers of the Skisailer, the team had learned that the potential customers were likely to be those who did both skiing and windsurfing. Building on industry reports suggesting a total worldwide population of 2 million windsurfers and 30 million skiers, the team estimated that a maximum of 60% of windsurfers, or a total of 1.2 million individuals, were also skiers. The "realizable market" for the Skisailer, according to the MBA students, was far below this maximum, however. They identified at least four "filters," which together reduced the realizable market potential to a fraction of the maximum:

Filter 1: Customer type. As a relatively new sport, Skisailer appealed to a group of enthusiasts whom the MBA students referred to as "innovators." Their study suggested that these buyers were in the 15 to 25 age bracket, liked sports but, for the most part, could not afford the price tag of the Skisailer. The next most likely group of buyers, called "early adopters," were older, less sporty, and more image conscious. For this segment, price was not a major factor. The team believed that sufficient penetration of the first segment was necessary before the second group showed any interest in the new product.

Filter 2: Location. Users of the Skisailer reported that ideal skisailing conditions, such as flat ice- or snow-covered fields, were not always accessible. This location factor, the team believed, tended to reduce the potential for the product.

Filter 3: Climate. Climate, according to the MBA students, was another inhibiting factor. The Skisailer required not only suitable snow or ice, but also a good wind. The minimum required wind speed was around 20 kilometers/hour. The study identified a number of regions as meeting both the needed snow and wind conditions: Scandinavia and central Europe, certain parts of North America, and parts of Southern Australia.

Filter 4: Competing products. Four similar products were identified but, according to the student report, all lacked brand image, wide distribution, and product sophistication. Although information on competing products was scanty, the students had assembled the following information from different sources:

Brand (origin)	Retail Price	Total Units Sold	Main Sales Area
Winterboard (Finland)	$395	4,000	Finland, United States
Ski Sailer (Australia)	$ 90	3,500	Australia, United States
ArticSail (Canada)	$285	3,000	Canada, United States
Ski Sailer (United States)	$220	300	United States

Based on their initial estimate of the maximum size of the potential market, as well as the limiting effects of the four filters, the students arrived at an estimate of 20,000 units as the total realizable market for Skisailer. This volume, they believed, could grow by as much as 10% per year. (Refer to Exhibit 2 for an estimate of the market potential and Exhibit 3 for the levels of sales the students believed Skisailer could achieve over the next 5 years.)

EXHIBIT 2   Skisailer Market Potential

Market	Size	%	Filters
Potential market	1.2 million	100	Customer type
Available market	800,000	66	Location, Climate
Qualified market	80,000	7	Indirect competition (monoski, skates, etc.)
Served market	40,000	3.5	Direct competition (Winterboard, Articsail, etc.)
Realizable market	20,000	1.7	Customer type

EXHIBIT 3   Skisailer Achievable Sales Estimate
Source: MBA Student Report

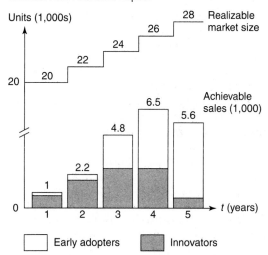

Early adopters   Innovators

Competing Products

Winterboard

Winterboard, a light windsurfing board with skis, had been invented in Finland. It could be used on both ice and snow, and its performance was said to be impressive. Some rated the Winterboard as the best performing windski after the Skisailer. In terms of sales, Winterboard had been the most successful windski product. Over the last five years, 4,000 units had been sold, mainly in Scandinavia and the United States, in regular sports shops. Winterboard was being sold at a retail price of $395, excluding the sailing rig. Retail margins were at 40%. The skis were already integrated into the board and did not need to be purchased as an extra.

According to the research team, Winterboard's management believed that prices, retail margins, and advertising expenditures were relatively unimportant in their marketing strategy. The key to success was organizing events, because people wanted sportive social gathering on weekends in the winter. When they had to go out snowsailing in the cold by themselves, they quickly lost interest.

Australian-made Ski Sailer

This product was essentially a simple bar with a mastfoot on it that could be attached to normal ski boots and used with either conventional skis or roller skates. The Ski Sailer had an equalizing slide and joint mechanism, so maneuvers such as parallel turns, jump turns, and snowplowing were possible. Any sailing rig could be fitted to the Ski Sailer's mast post.

The U.S. distributor for this product reported cumulative sales of about 3,000 units (30% through ski shops, 70% through surf shops) at a retail price of $90 each. But he admitted that he had lost interest in the product when he realized that only customers who were tough and resistant to the cold enjoyed windsurfing in the wintertime. This meant a much smaller customer base than for his other leisure and sportswear products.

ArticSail Board

This product was essentially a W-shaped surfboard for use on snow, ice, or water. It was distributed by Plastiques L.P.A. Ltd. in Mansonville, Quebec, Canada, approximately 50 miles from the U.S.–Canadian border.

The ArticSail was especially designed for snow and ice, but it could also be used on water, in which case the rear filler plates would be replaced by two ailerons, also supplied with the board. Adjustable footstraps, included with the board, also had to be repositioned for

use on water. The product was made of a special plastic, usable at both normal and very low temperatures. The producer warned users to watch for objects that could damage the underside of the sled.

The company reported a cumulative sales of approximately 3,000 units (600 estimated for the winter of 1987–1988), mostly in Canada, at a retail price of $285 (including a 38% retail margin). Promotion expenses were about 15% on Canadian and U.S. sales, mainly spent on a two-man team demonstrating at skisailing resorts.

American-made Ski Sailer

Yet another Ski Sailer had been invented by a young Californian, Carl Meinberg. The American Ski Sailer also used a small board mounted on skis and was similar to the product developed by David Varilek. On his own, the inventor had sold about 50 Ski Sailers retailing at $220 each. During the winter season, Carl Meinberg toured a number of ski resorts, demonstrating the Ski Sailer; he spent the rest of the year selling his invention.

Recent Developments in the World Ski Market

As background to their study, the research team also obtained information on the ski market. The 1986 sales of downhill (also called alpine) and cross-country skis are given in Exhibit 4.

The total world alpine skiing population was estimated at 30 million people in 1987. Competition in the ski market was intensive, and production capacity exceeded demand by an estimated 25% to 30% in 1987. Prices for skis were under pressure and retailers used discounts to build traffic. Retail profits were mostly made on sales of accessories and skiwear.

In distribution, specialty shops were losing market share to the large chains. Production was concentrated, with seven manufacturers controlling 80% of the market. The falling exchange rate for the U.S. dollar had put the large European producers such as Fischer and Kneissel at a disadvantage in the U.S. market.

Ski Sales	Pairs Sold
Alpine	
Austria, Switzerland, Germany	1,450,000
Rest of Europe	1,550,000
United States and Canada	1,600,000
Japan	1,100,000
Other countries	300,000
Total	6,000,000
Cross-country	
Austria, Switzerland, Germany	700,000
Scandinavia	800,000
Rest of Europe	400,000
United States and Canada	750,000
Other countries	150,000
Total	2,800,000

Marketing skis depended heavily on successes in world championships and the image associated with the winning skis. In the mid-1980s, customers in the United States appeared to be losing interest in skiing, but these signs had not been observed in Europe and Japan, where the sport remained popular at a stable level.

A new innovation in skiing was the snowboard, a product with increasing popularity among younger customers. A snowboard was essentially a single large ski with two ski bindings positioned in a similar way as the footstraps on a windsurf.

The board had been available in the United States for many years, but had only recently been introduced in Europe. Snowboard's worldwide sales had doubled every year, reaching an estimated 40,000 in the 1986 season. One U.S. manufacturer, Burton, accounted for 50% of the market. Many manufacturers of winter products had taken advantage of the opportunity and had started producing their own versions of the snowboard. The product was very popular in the European distribution channels, and expectations for further growth were high.

Buyers' Survey

The research team had interviewed a small number of Skisailer customers in Germany, Austria, the Benelux countries, the United States and Canada. Highlights of their comments on the advantages and disadvantages of the Skisailer follow:

Advantages of the Product

- Sure, skisurfing in winter is great; it's a lot of fun.
- You can do quick maneuvers, nice turns, beautiful power turns, and fast changes of the grips. It (the Skisailer) gives a good opportunity to train for windsurfing, as you have to drive the way you surf—with the pressure on the inner ski.
- I did not have any problem with turns.
- It is not difficult to learn if you have some feeling for sailing.
- It simulates surfing in your backyard.
- It is the right device if you want to do something on Sunday afternoon (with no time to drive somewhere in your car).
- Fun, different, new, good.
- It is the only thing with a mountain touch that you can use on the plain.
- It turns. That makes it much more fun than the other products on the market. You can do jives, curve jives, jumps . . . it is close to sailing a shore boat . . . it's a lot of fun.
- If the conditions are ideal, it's a lot of fun.

Disadvantages of the Product

- The feet get twisted; sailing on the wind requires exceptional twisting of the legs and knees.
- Both of the white caps at the end of the bar came off and it was virtually impossible to get spare parts.
- Difficult in heavy snow.
- Difficult to find the perfect conditions.
- You use it three or four times a season. For this, the price is too high.
- It is uncomfortable to use. You have to loosen up your boots; otherwise, the rim of the shoe cuts into your twisted leg.
- If the snow is too deep, you cannot use it. What you want is strong wind.
- The price is too high.
- My problem is that there is hardly any wind in winter.
- In the beginning, I was getting stiff in the unnatural position and my knees hurt, but later I got more relaxed and with time you have a lot of fun.
- In mid-winter, it is too cold to use it; spring is ideal.

Retailers' Opinions of the Mistral Skisailer

A dozen retailers of the Skisailer—in Germany, Canada, Austria, and France—were also surveyed. Highlights of their comments follow:

Advantages of the Product

- You could sell a lot of them in the first year, but I do not see it as the absolute "barnstormer."
- It is a first-year novelty.
- It is a lot of fun in the snow . . . and for people with a lot of money. It is a new gimmick.
- It combines two favorite sports . . . skiing and windsurfing.
- It is better than all self-built products . . . you have full movability.
- Easy to use. It is an original idea.
- You can use your ski, it is flexible and easy to store.
- Very thoroughly constructed, very stable.

Disadvantages of the Product

- Unhappy product. Usable only under specific weather conditions.
- It is only a fad.
- You just don't drive with your ski to a lake and try it on the ice.
- Maybe it sells better in a winter shop.
- Your position on the skis is abnormal—the snowboard is a better alternative.
- We do not think that it will be a fast-turning product. . . .
- Impossible to sell—nobody tried it.
- In my environment, there is no space to do it, no lakes, no fields.
- For a backyard product, the price is too high. Even Mistral's good image doesn't help. Maybe this will change if the product is better known.
- Customers watched the video with enthusiasm, but when they learned the price, enthusiasm was nil. We are offering our last piece now at a discount of 40%.
- If you ski and windsurf, your hobbies cost you a lot of money. Often the early user is the sportive freak with a low income. How will you convince him about the product?

Distributors' Comments

The research team interviewed Mistral distributors in 10 different countries in Europe and North America. Highlights of comments from five distributors follow:

Europe

- We first learned about the Skisailer at ISPO in Munich and ordered some.
- From Mistral we got some folders and the video. If you see it on the video, you want to use the Skisailer right away.
- We did not support the retailers very much because we felt that the Skisailer's marketing was not done professionally from the beginning. For instance, Skisailer deliveries were late.
- The product would have potential if the price were lower and the promotion were done professionally all the way through.
- We bought the Skisailer, which is good for use in our winter climate, after Mistral contacted us in 1985.
- The product is expensive and not really functional.
- Promotion was not good at all, only a few folders and a video, which was not free of charge. When there were product breakdowns, spare parts were not available.
- A Finnish competitor now has captured the market with a product that looks like a surfboard with two skis fitted into it. We have the right places for skisailing here!
- We used all our contacts and spent approximately $7,500 in mid-1987 to promote this product on television.
- The retail price is too high for a product to be used only a few weekends in the winter.
- The snowboard, especially made for surfing on ski slopes, is much more fashionable.
- Surf and ski shops make higher margins on clothing and accessories that are sold in larger quantities.
- You don't create a product first and then look for the market; this is the wrong way around. The Skisailer is more a product for Scandinavia and similar regions in America or Canada.
- We didn't know the product but found the demonstration film to be convincing. Therefore, we organized ski resort demonstrations in the French Alps at racing events where there are many spectators. We also pushed about 40 Skisailers in several retail shops.
- For this product, finding suitable locations where you can have a training session with wind and snow is necessary.

- We estimate that the retailers have sold about half their inventory, but we do not want to get more involved and have the rest sent back to us. Retailers are looking for customer demand, which is lacking.

North America

- I cannot see further sales of the Skisailer without more product support. At low temperatures the rubber joints failed, but when we asked for replacements, there was no reply from Mistral. In the end, we had to strip other Skisailers to get the spare parts.
- We have good skisailing conditions (in South Ontario/Quebec) and a group of interested enthusiasts here. The product has been promoted to thousands of people! The folder and video are very good.
- On a trade show in Toronto, the product was well received except for the price, which is a problem.

CONCLUSION

In reviewing the research team's report, David was searching for clues that could explain the Skisailer's poor performance in its first selling season. Was it the product design that needed further refinement? Or the Skisailer's price, which was perceived by some as being high? Was the absence of high promotional support, which he always suspected to be a problem, a key factor? Or maybe Mistral's selective distribution was the core issue? What else could explain why his invention had failed to match everybody's expectations?

An additional piece of information had heightened the need for immediate action. David had just received the final sales and inventory figures for the Skisailer from Mistral; while 708 units had been sold to the trade, only 80 units had been bought at retail.

| Country | Unit Sales | | |
	To Distributors	To Retailers	To End Users
United States and Canada	233	98	45
Germany	250	50	10
Switzerland	42	30	1
France	56	40	20
Benelux	60	0	0
Others	67	12	4
Total shipped	**708**	**230**	**80**

David knew that Mistral management was about to review the future of the Skisailer. He feared that without a convincing analysis and action plan from him, the Skisailer would be dropped from Mistral's line. He was therefore impatiently waiting for the MBA research team's recommendations based on the data already collected.

Porsche AG (A)

During the second half of 1985, members of the *Vorstand* (managing board) of Porsche AG were conducting a major review of the company's competitive position and future prospects. The previous 5 years had been a period of unprecedented growth and profitability for Porsche. Sales for the fiscal year ending July 31, 1985, were 173% above those of 1981, while net income was up 1,104% (Exhibit 1). Management's concern stemmed from rapid appreciation of the deutsche mark against the U.S. dollar during 1985. The DM had moved from a low of 3.40/$U.S. in March to 2.46 on December 31, and further appreciation was expected in 1986. Exports to the United States had accounted for slightly more than 50% of Porsche's unit volume in fiscal 1985 (Exhibit 2).

Immediate decisions were required on a U.S. pricing strategy. To what extent should management seek to maintain revenues by instituting price increases? What impact would price increases have on demand for the company's various automobile models? What profit impact could be expected? Longer term, management recognized that it would have to develop a strategy for competing in the United States during a period of deutsche mark strength of unforeseeable duration.

COMPANY HISTORY

Professor Dr. Ferdinand Porsche (1875–1952) was one of the founding fathers of the German automotive industry. His career as a designer and engineer extended over 50 years, encompassing development of racing and sports cars, aircraft engines, farm tractors, tanks, and conventional automobiles. During 1899–1929, Professor Porsche held senior technical and management positions in the Austrian and German Daimler companies and in Austrian automakers Lohner and Steyr. In 1930 he started his own design firm in Stuttgart. Much of this firm's early work centered on contract design of advanced automotive engines and transmissions, many for racing cars. In 1934, the firm was commissioned to design and produce prototypes for the Volkswagen, an automobile that never went into full production until after World War II. During the war, the Porsche organization was responsible for design of the Leopard and Tiger tanks, other military vehicles, and rocket engines. In 1945, Allied occupation forces seized Porsche's German operations, and Professor Porsche was imprisoned for 2 years.

Remnants of the Porsche organization reformed at a temporary facility in the small Austrian village of Gmünd (Carinthia). It was here that the first Porsche sports car, the 356, was developed and built during 1947–1949. In 1950 the firm returned to Stuttgart, working first out of rented facilities and later recovering its original factory. Porsche's growth into a sports car manufacturer with a worldwide reputation was directed by Dr. Ferry Porsche, son of the founder. The younger Porsche had

This case was prepared from public sources by Professor Stephen A. Allen, Babson College as a basis for classroom discussion. Copyright © 1990 by Stephen A. Allen.

EXHIBIT 1 Operating and Financial Information FY Ending July 31 (DM millions, except where indicated)

	1981	1982	1983	1984	1985
Net sales	1,165.2	1,488.2	2,133.7	2,494.3	3,175.7
Net income	10.0	37.6	69.6	92.4	120.4
Total assets[a]	517.6	671.5	866.6	1,192.2	1,444.2
Shareholders' equity[b]	118.3	145.6	183.0	335.0	413.5
Capital expenditures	80.5	125.7	131.1	254.5	290.8
Depreciation	51.1	46.3	71.1	101.7	143.6
Dividends paid	6.0	14.0	15.0	18.4	25.2
Employees at year end (000)	4.9	5.3	5.9	6.5	7.9
Return on sales (%)	0.9	2.5	3.3	3.7	3.8
Return on assets (%)	1.9	5.6	8.0	7.8	8.3
Asset turnover (X)	2.3	2.2	2.5	2.1	2.2
Return on shareholders' equity (%)	8.5	25.8	38.0	27.6	29.1

[a] Differs slightly from Exhibit 11 due to treatment of certain unconsolidated units.

[b] Differs from Exhibit 11 due to exclusion of certain reserves and treatment of certain unconsolidated subsidiaries.

joined his father's firm in the early 1930s and was managing director during 1951–1971. During this period, three sons of the younger Dr. Porsche and two nephews joined the firm. In 1971 the decision was made that members of the owning Porsche and Piëch families should remove themselves from day-to-day management of the company.[1] Dr. Ferry Porsche retained the role of chairman of the supervisory board (*Aufsichtsrat*) and still occupied that position in 1985 (Exhibit 3).

In 1984, Porsche AG had its first public offering, consisting of 700,000 voting shares and 700,000 preference shares. All voting shares and 450,000 of the preference shares remained in the hands of members of the Porsche and Piëch families. Preference shares traded on the Frankfurt Exchange.

MODEL RANGE AND MARKETS

The Porsche marque carried a distinctive image: speed; power; precision transmissions;

responsive handling; quality craftsmanship; and a classic, aerodynamic body style. Durability was another feature. All models had zinc-plated steel bodies and carried 10-year rust-free warranties. By the same token, there were certain features a Porsche did not provide: quiet engine operation; cushioned, high-comfort ride; and low fuel consumption.[2] In perceptual mapping studies by market researchers, the Porsche was typically described as high-priced, personal/expressive (versus family/conservative), having spirited performance, appealing to young people, fun to drive, and sporty looking (Exhibit 4).

Prime sales prospects were typically in the top 4% of disposable income in developed economies. In the United States the typical Porsche customer was a college-educated professional, 34 to 55 years old, with 1985 household income exceeding $65,000. While many Porsche customers were automobile enthusiasts, a significant number were not. A study of Porsche owners conducted by Arthur D. Little in 1983 found that a majority were not impulse buyers. Rather, they compared several automobiles before settling on a Porsche and regarded the purchase as an investment. Estimated U.S. resale value (in constant dol-

[1] Dr. Anton Piëch, son-in-law of Ferdinand Porsche, had worked for the Porsche organization from its founding until his death in 1952. After 1957 the company was equally owned by the two Porsche children and eight grandchildren. After the 1971 decision, family members sought alternative careers. Ferdinand Piëch went on to become technical director and later chairman of the management board of Audi AG. In 1985, Dr. Piëch and Dr. Wolfgang Porsche were members of Porsche AG's supervisory board.

[2] Estimated fuel consumption was 21 to 26 miles per gallon (highway) and 14 to 19 (city), depending on the model.

EXHIBIT 2   Unit Automobile Sales by Model Family and Geographic Area FY Ending July 31

		1981	*1982*	*1983*	*1984*	*1985*
911	Domestic	3,586	3,746	4,437	4,746	4,800
	U.S.	2,889	4,416	5,437	4,748	5,293
	Other export markets	2,261	2,411	3,115	2,803	3,498
	Total	8,736	10,573	12,989	12,297	13,591
928	Domestic	1,043	893	808	966	1,150
	U.S.	1,595	2,186	2,302	2,437	2,662
	Other export markets	1,153	1,223	1,099	1,067	1,277
	Total	3,791	4,302	4,209	4,470	5,089
924	Domestic	5,039	3,652	2,426	1,697	1,321
	U.S.	3,312	2,541	—	—	—
	Other export markets	7,105	4,785	3,457	2,556	1,904
	Total	15,456	10,978	5,883	4,253	3,225
944	Domestic	—	2,156	4,493	4,793	4,953
	U.S.	—	2,339	12,496	13,462	16,925
	Other export markets	—	1,865	4,755	4,695	5,582
	Total	—	6,360	21,744	22,950	27,460
Total sales	Domestic	9,668	10,447	12,164	12,202	12,224
	U.S.	7,796	11,482	20,235	20,647	24,880
	Other export markets	10,519	10,284	12,426	11,121	12,261
	Total	27,983	32,213	44,825	43,970[a]	49,365

[a] Reflects loss of 5,500 units of planned output due to industrywide strike by IG Metall.

lars) for a Porsche 5 years after purchase ranged from 65% to 85% of initial list price, depending on the model.

In 1985 Porsche offered four model fami-lies, each with variations in engine design and coupe versus convertible options. The 911 series was the classic Porsche, a two-door, rear-wheel-drive sports car with a 6-cylinder, rear-

EXHIBIT 3   Members of Supervisory and Management Boards

Aufsichtsrat (supervisory)

Ferdinand (Ferry) Porsche (Prof. Dr. Ing. h.c.)	Chairman
Franz Blank[a]	Vice-chairman
Wolfgang Berger[a]	General division manager
Dr. Konrad Eisenmann	Member, board of management, Robert Bosch GmbH
Ernest Eisenmann[a]	District manager, Metal Workers' Union (IG Metall)
Hans Epple[a]	Safety engineer
Klaus Luft	Chairman, board of management, Nixdorf Computer AG
Ferdinand Piëch (Dr. techn. h.c.)	Chairman, board of management, AUDI AG
Wolfgang Porsche (Dr., Dipl.-Kfm.)	Member
Heinz Schilling[a]	Trade union secretary
Franz Steinbeck[a]	Chairman of labor council, Zuffenhausen/Ludwigsburg
Walther Zügel (Dr.)	Chairman, board of management, Landesgirokasse offentliche Bank und Landessparkasse

Vorstand (management)

Peter W. Schutz	Chairman
Heinz Branitzki (Dipl.-Kfm.)	Finance
Helmuth Bott (Prof. Dr.-Ing. E.h.)	Research and Development
Heiko Lange (Dr.)	Employment
Rudi Noppen (Dr.)	Production

[a] Employees' representatives.

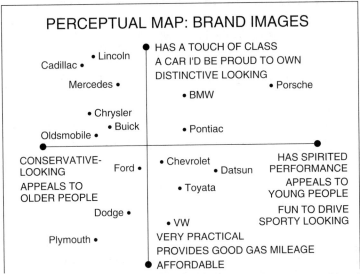

PERCEPTUAL MAP: BRAND IMAGES

[a] Based on market research conducted by Chrysler Corp. Data are for overall brand images. Individual models could locate differently.

EXHIBIT 4   Brand Images in U.S. Market—1984[a]   *Source: Wall Street Journal,* March 22, 1984.

mounted, air-cooled engine. Introduced in 1964 to replace the 356, the 911 was offered in the following configurations and U.S. list prices:[3]

Carrera coupe, 3.2-liter engine	$32,528
Targa coupe, 3.2 liter	$34,028
Cabriolet (convertible), 3.2 liter	$37,028

A 3.3-liter 911 Turbo Cabriolet was to be introduced in 1986 at $48,000. Also planned for 1986 was production of 200 units of a new, limited-edition model 959 aimed at racers and collectors.

Introduction of the 924 series in 1976 represented a major departure for Porsche. This was a two-door, hatchback body design with a 4-cylinder, 2-liter, front-mounted, water-cooled

Audi engine and rear-wheel drive. This model had been discontinued in the United States in 1983 in favor of the 944. However, a 924S with a detuned 944 engine continued to be sold in Germany and in other export markets. The 1982 U.S. list price for the 924 had been $16,900 ($21,500 with turbo engine).

The 928, which was introduced in 1978, was another hatchback with front-mounted, water-cooled engine. However, it carried a 5.0-liter, V-8 engine and a U.S. list price of $50,000.

In 1982, Porsche introduced the 944, another 4-cylinder, hatchback with front-mounted, water-cooled engine. In 1985, offerings and U.S. list prices were as follows:

| Coupe, 2.5-liter engine | $22,108 |
| Turbo coupe, 2.5 liter | $29,500 |

A small two-seat mid-engine sports car, code named 984, was under design with a targeted introduction date of 1989.

---

[3] Excluding destination charges and consumption taxes.

United States market researchers, such as J.D. Powers Associates and Ward's Automotive, classified Porsche as competing within the luxury specialty segment of the market (Exhibits 5 and 6). *Vorstand* Chairman Peter Schutz stated,

Our competition really comes from two totally different places. We compete with such things as sailboats, summer homes, and airplanes—discretionary purchases. Then we compete with other automobile manufacturers. Here our three product lines compete very differently. The 944/924 has the most competition. It competes with everything from Corvettes to Japanese entries, such as the Mazda RX-7 and Nissan 300ZX, to Pontiac Fieros. That's a very tough, competitive business. The 911, on the other hand, is unique. It drives like no other car and sounds like no other car. The 928, in turn, competes with Jaguars, Ferraris, the big Mercedes coupes, the new Cadillac two-seater. So that's a bit different segment.

EXHIBIT 5 U.S. Luxury Specialty Car Segment: Calendar Years (units sold)[a]

	1984	1985
Import models		
Porsche	19,611	25,306
Mercedes 560 SL/SEL	10,939	12,235
Volvo 260 GT	4,794	8,504
Audi 5000 Turbo	6,380	7,843
BMW 6-Series	2,697	3,825
Jaguar XJ-S	3,480	3,784
Alfa Romeo GTV-6	919	1,052
Ferrari	568	624
Mercedes 190E-16	—	299
Audi 5000 Turbo Quattro	—	223
Audi Turbo Quattro Coupe	64	71
Lancia	21	—
	49,473	64,126
U.S. models		
Corvette	30,424	37,956
Toronado	41,605	32,093
Riviera	53,398	48,834
Cimarron	18,014	23,754
Seville	36,249	29,034
Eldorado	70,577	58,310
Continental	31,110	27,679
Mark	29,496	19,853
	310,873	277,513
Total luxury specialty	360,346	341,639

[a] From *Ward's Automotive Yearbooks.* Segmentation based on overall car size, marketing intent, and price.

In one sense, we have a relatively homogeneous market. Fifty thousand cars—that's one week's production for Chevrolet. We wouldn't know where to start segmenting. Now a lot of people drive a 944 because that's the least expensive Porsche, and it's the only one they can really afford. But once you get into the 911 and 928 range, you're dealing with folks who can buy any car they want. They don't drive a 911 because they can't afford a 928. And they don't settle for a coupe instead of a convertible because the convertible costs 10% more.[4]

Company-sponsored market research in the United States provided additional insights. Median ages of Porsche buyers, like those of other buyers of European luxury cars, were, respectively, 10 and 20 years younger than the median ages of Cadillac and Lincoln buyers, who were in their upper fifties. Compared to all U.S. car buyers, Porsche buyers were more sensitive to the rise and fall of stock market averages and would postpone purchases. Results of a 1985 study were reported as follows:

Through various focus groups the company discovered it had a blurred image among non-owners. It also became apparent that the 928 and 944 models were not seen as members of the Porsche family. The research showed that, among Porsche owners, the 911 was regarded as the true Porsche while the 928 was still considered a "dentist's car" and the 944 was held as the "entry-level" model.

Porsche wants to change that concept by making sure the public realizes that the 928 is the "most sophisticated" model it offers in the U.S. and that the 944, far from being an entry-level car, is an all-around Porsche that is fun.[5]

On a geographic basis, sales were relatively concentrated. In 1985, 86% of unit sales came from the United States, Germany, the United Kingdom, Switzerland, France, and Italy. Three national markets—the United States,

---

[4] "Porsche on Nichemanship (Interview with Peter Schutz and Jack Cook)," *Harvard Business Review*, March–April 1986.

[5] "Porsche Seeking a New Image," *Automotive News*, February 18, 1985. The 928 had been voted International Car of the Year for 1978.

EXHIBIT 6 U.S. Automobile Volume Trends: Luxury Segments versus Total Market, Calendar Years (000 units, %)

	1978	1979	1980	1981	1982	1983	1984	1985
All segments								
U.S. models	9,000.0	8,005.6	6,291.7	6,012.2	5,485.7	6,466.8	7,951.5	8,204.5
Imports	1,946.1	2,351.1	2,469.2	2,431.7	2,268.6	2,457.4	2,438.8	2,837.6
Total	10,946.1	10,356.7	8,760.9	8,443.9	7,754.3	8,924.2	10,390.3	11,042.1
Luxury regular segment								
U.S. models	331.3	262.8	157.4	163.5	188.3	277.8	470.9	526.9
Imports	N.A.	N.A.	N.A.	N.A.	144.0	134.8	205.8	241.6
Total					332.3	412.6	676.7	768.5
% Total market					4.3%	4.6%	6.5%	7.0%
Luxury specialty segment								
U.S. models	208.5	200.0	161.3	241.4	239.2	278.5	310.8	277.6
Imports	41.3	36.5	30.6	38.0	33.6	43.4	49.6	63.5
Total	249.8	236.5	191.9	279.4	272.8	321.9	360.4	341.1
% Total market	2.3%	2.3%	2.2%	3.3%	3.5%	3.6%	3.5%	3.1%
Selected luxury specialty brands								
Corvette	40.4	40.2	36.4	29.6	21.4	26.0	30.4	38.0
Porsche	17.5	14.1	10.6	11.4	14.4	21.8	19.6	25.3
Mercedes SL/SEL	6.9	6.6	7.0	7.7	11.0	11.2	10.9	12.2
BMW 6 Series	1.0	0.8	1.2	1.1	1.5	2.6	2.7	3.8
Jaguar XJ-S	1.1	0.7	0.4	0.2	1.4	2.7	3.5	3.8
Alfa Romeo	—	—	0.5	0.6	0.7	1.1	0.9	1.1
Ferrari	—	0.7	0.8	0.9	0.7	0.5	0.6	0.6

Source: Ward's Automotive Yearbooks.

Germany, and the United Kingdom—accounted for 79% (Exhibit 7).

COMPANY STRATEGY

Recent performance notwithstanding, Porsche management did not view growth as a primary goal. Rather, its intent was to maintain stable volume and employment levels and to have a revenue base sufficiently large to fund ongoing development activities from internal sources. Mr. Schutz explained,

The priorities of the Porsche family are very clear. Growth is simply not a prime objective of this business. It is far more important to our controlling shareholders to build the image and reputation of this company than it is to build sales and profits. When the Porsche family hired me in 1981, they set no goal for growth or any objectives like that. They want this company to be independent and to continue to be what it is and become more of what it is.

We plan to increase production only modestly. If we build too many cars, we will lose our exclusivity and cease being what we are. We can only increase production if we add more models. We can't

build more of what we already have. If you get too many of them around, all of a sudden it's nothing special.[6]

Decisions to launch the 924 and 928 during the 1970s reflected, in part, management's belief that the 911 would not represent a base wide enough and stable enough to guarantee the long-term viability of the company. Porsche's first move outside its classic model family had been the 1969 introduction of the 914, a small sports car developed in partnership with Audi/Volkswagen. The 924 began as another collaboration with Volkswagen; however, VW withdrew from the project in 1971 due to heavy funding requirements it was encountering in its own new-car programs. Porsche acquired VW's share of the project for DM 120 million and contracted out assembly of the 924 to VW's Neckarsulm factory.[7] Dur-

---

[6] Ibid. "Porsche on Nichemanship."

[7] VW agreed to finance the acquisition with a DM 120 million loan. Porsche's production contract avoided the expected closure of Neckarsulm.

EXHIBIT 7 Porsche New Vehicle Sales by National Market and Total Annual Production (units, calendar years)[a]

	1978	1979	1980	1981	1982	1983	1984	1985
United States	17,488	14,073	10,597	11,421	14,407	21,831	19,611	25,306
Germany	11,368	12,001	10,525	9,602	10,327	12,176	11,133	11,394
Switzerland	1,093	1,316	1,260	1,205	1,625	1,420	1,416	1,394
France	863	1,036	1,060	1,283	1,538	1,612	1,370	1,432
Italy	304	839	1,210	1,186	1,161	1,054	909	867
Japan	1,083	1,219	855	611	560	535	518	619
Netherlands	242	276	265	182	160	213	166	225
Sweden	N.A.	N.A.	N.A.	110	163	209	293	455
Belgium	N.A.	N.A.	N.A.	478	521	516	488	460
Austria	N.A.	N.A.	N.A.	N.A.	N.A.	N.A.	N.A.	451
Spain	N.A.	N.A.	N.A.	N.A.	N.A.	N.A.	190	330
Portugal	12	27	39	135	147	151	6	62
Luxembourg	N.A.	N.A.	N.A.	N.A.	N.A.	93	80	84
Ireland	N.A.	N.A.	N.A.	N.A.	N.A.	11	7	5
	32,453	30,787	25,811	26,213	30,609	39,821	36,187	43,084
Annual production	36,879	36,011	28,622	31,734	36,329	48,288	44,017	50,985
Unaccounted for[b]	4,426	5,224	2,811	5,521	5,720	8,467	7,830	7,901

Source: Motor Vehicle Manufacturers' *World Vehicle Data* and *Ward's Automotive Yearbook.*

[a] Based on national statistics for new car registrations or retail sales. The United Kingdom, Porsche's third largest market, did not provide breakdowns by manufacturer for limited-volume imported sports cars. United Kingdom sales were 1,850 in 1979 and 3,438 in 1985.

[b] Represents retail sales to other markets plus increases in dealer and manufacturer inventories.

ing this same period, Porsche spent some DM 100 million on development of the 928. These investments represented significant risks in the face of the OPEC oil price increases of 1973–1974 and 1979. Both models ultimately proved successful, and Porsche's unit sales more than doubled by 1978 (Exhibit 8).

Engineering

In fiscal 1985, Porsche spent DM 300 million (equal to 9.2% of revenues) on research and development. Most of these activities took place at a modern development center at Weissach, in the countryside outside Stuttgart. Facilities included a foundry and plastics shop, testing chambers, and three test tracks. More than 40% of Weissach work was for research contracts for outside clients. In recent years, these contracts had included design of engines, transmissions, and entire automobiles; product and project evaluation studies; work on the European Leopard tank project; and styling of the European A310 Airbus cockpit.

Work was also underway on an aircraft engine to be manufactured by Porsche, based on design principles used in the 911 automobile engine.

In a 1978 interview Professor Ernst Fuhrman, *Vorstand* chairman during 1971–1980, described Porsche's approach to model development:

A basic principle is to design models which are capable of plenty of development. There are two possibilities for handling model development. One is to invest a big amount in a model and produce it for four to six years with a very limited further investment; this is the way most big companies do it. The other way is to develop a car to a reasonable limit. Then you build it for 15 years, having a further stab at development every two years or so. This is the way we do it, and for a small company like us the investment is actually lower. There is no point in changing tooling every five years—at the rate we build, tools last 25 years.

The 911 is a classic example of this policy. The same bodyshell—and therefore the same tools—is being used today as when it was launched in 1964. But it now performs very differently, and has had va-

EXHIBIT 8   Business Activity, 1931–1981

	Units Produced	Employees	Revenues (DM millions)	Models
1931	—	13	N.A.	
1944	—	588	5.9	
1949	50	12	0.6	356 introduced
1950	298	108	4.4	
1955	2,952	616	38.0	
1960	7,598	1,100	N.A.	
1965	11,243	N.A.	N.A.	911 introduced in 1964
1970	16,757	N.A.	N.A.	914 introduced in 1969
1971	10,905	N.A.	N.A.	
1972	14,503	N.A.	N.A.	
1973	15,415	N.A.	N.A.	
1974	9,915	N.A.	N.A.	914 discontinued
1975	9,424	N.A.	353.0	
1976	32,554	N.A.	604.0	924 introduced
1977	36,130	2,826	1,000.0	
1978	36,879	N.A.	1,123.0	928 introduced
1979	36,011	N.A.	1,350.0	
1980	28,622	N.A.	1,235.0	
1981	31,734	4,900	1,165.0	

riety added with the introduction of the turbo-charged vehicle into the range.[8]

Mr. Schutz outlined the role of engineering as follows:

We stay competitive technically through outside engineering, which is the company's heritage. It serves several purposes. One of them, of course, is that it makes money.[9] It gives us a little more balance, something to lean on in the cyclicality of the automobile business.

The second thing is that we are a small company and yet do extremely progressive engineering. That requires the committed support of a lot of suppliers. And it is questionable whether—without outside engineering—we would get the support we need on the basis of the small quantities that we subsequently purchase from them. With the outside engineering—we do work for a lot of big companies like Ford, General Motors, Volkswagen, Volvo and many others—we get support of suppliers who want to be a part of that development in order to have the inside track for subsequent opportunities. When we get a request from Ford to take an engine and convert it from carburetor to fuel injection, Bosch works on the project with us so that it can later develop fuel injection equipment for millions of cars. Bosch is the biggest supplier of ignitions, motors, and batteries, and it's just three kilometers from here. Outside engineering is the only way we get folks like that to help us develop pistons and other components for race cars.

The third thing is that we have the best and most innovative engineers because the heart of this business is its technology. We attract and hold them with a very broad range of technical projects to work on, like styling the interior of the Airbus cockpit or designing, building, and supporting a Formula 1 racing engine.

We do a whole lot of work for other companies on improving performance of engines, or brakes, or transmissions—we design whole automobiles. We had a long project with Russia to design a small economy car like a Volkswagen Rabbit.[10]

Marketing and Service

Retail sales and service activities were conducted through networks of independent dealers in each national market. Porsche dealers numbered 207 in Germany and 324 in the United States (Exhibit 9). Wholesale prices of autos to U.S. dealers were set at 83 to 85% of list price, depending on the model.

Wholesale marketing subsidiaries in each major export market were responsible for de-

[8] "Gambling in Pursuit of Power," *Financial Times*, January 3, 1978.

[9] Revenues from license fees and third-party development services were DM 100 million in fiscal 1985.

[10] Ibid.

EXHIBIT 9   U.S. Dealer Locations in 1985

By region	
New England	28
Atlantic Coast	94
North Central	65
South Central	43
Mountain	25
Pacific Coast	69
	324

Ten states with largest dealer coverage	
California	50
New York	22
Texas	17
New Jersey	14
Ohio	14
Florida	13
Massachusetts	12
Pennsylvania	12
Illinois	11
North Carolina	10
	175

veloping national marketing and advertising strategies; order processing and importing; and warehousing, predelivery inspection, and delivery to dealers. Porsche marketing subsidiaries in the United States, United Kingdom, Germany, and Italy were fully or majority owned by the company. French and Spanish subsidiaries were minority owned (31% and 40%, respectively).

Factory pickup and tourist delivery programs played an important role in distribution. In Germany, 60% of Porsches sold were picked up in Stuttgart by their owners. For U.S. buyers the figure was roughly 10%. Mr. Schutz noted,

The more high profile Americans who see how a Porsche is built, see the research facilities, and come home and talk to their friends about all of it at cocktail parties, the better it is for us. Word-of-mouth advertising is much more credible than advertising we pay for.[11]

Although the basic Porsche image was the same throughout the world, advertising differed among national markets with respect to media emphasis and message. Mr. Schutz explained,

In America you do a lot more television. Here in Germany there is no advertising on television or ra-

dio. In Germany it's mostly newspapers and magazines. A lot of our advertising is really PR rather than ads—e.g., reports about racing in magazines such as *Road and Track, Motor Trend,* and *Car and Driver.*[12]

In fiscal 1985, Porsche spent an estimated $9 million on U.S. advertising. In 1984 its advertising account had been moved from Doyle Dane Bernbach to Chiat/Day. The advertising message had also changed from one that emphasized facts and figures about model performance to a focus on the people who engineered Porsches and experiences of people who bought them. Porsche had also hired its own U.S. customer representatives to work with high-profile buyers and sales prospects, such as celebrities, athletes, and senior executives of Fortune 500 companies.

United States distribution arrangements had undergone major change during 1984–1985. From 1969–1984, Porsche's sole U.S. distributor had been the Audi Division of Volkswagen of North America. This arrangement was terminated in August 1984 in favor or direct distribution by Porsche. John A. Cook, formerly head of BMW of North America, was hired to set up Porsche Cars of North America, Inc., headquartered in Reno, Nevada. Porsche's initial plan was to set up 40 company distribution centers around the United States using former dealers as agents (working on an 8% commission basis). This plan was terminated in the face of some $3 billion of dealer lawsuits. Contracts with most former Porsche–Audi dealers were renewed. Porsche invested $22 million to set up two warehousing and delivery centers—in Reno and Charleston, South Carolina—for serving this dealer network.

The company's motivations for establishing its own distribution in the United States included achieving more direct customer contact, better coordination of dealer selling and service activities, improved customer service, and increased service content to counteract growing competition from European and Japanese specialty cars. Another motivation

---

[11] Ibid.

[12] Ibid.

seemed to be to eliminate Audi's middleman profit. *Fortune* noted,

Schutz had no say over selection of dealers, who also sold Audis and sometimes Volkswagens as well. He felt a big mass retailer was the wrong outlet for his low volume, high priced cars. He also feared the Japanese would soon invade the high performance sports car market in the U.S., and he wanted to set up his own American organization before that happened.[13]

Porsche's sales were typically supported by minimal finished goods inventories. For example, in early 1984, U.S. inventories were equivalent to 17 days of sales, and most of this figure represented in-transit, sold orders. Buyers of a significant proportion of 911 and 928 models ordered special features, such as paint colors and special dashboards or upholstery. Production involving standard options was limited by the company, both for financial and market image reasons. Mr. Schutz explained,

We would like to build one less Porsche than the demand. The last thing we would want to see is a dealer shouting from the rooftops that he has 500 Porsches sitting there and they've all got to go by next month. If a dealer has cars it can't move, we'll take them and find a dealer that can move them.[14]

Manufacturing

Porsche's home factory at Zuffenhausen (Stuttgart) produced 911 and 928 models and racing cars. The 944 and 924S were assembled on a contract basis by Audi/VW's factory at Neckarsulm (some 50 kilometers north of Stuttgart).

Purchased materials and supplies accounted for approximately 70% of Porsche's total operating expenses (including parent selling and administrative expenses). Most suppliers were located in the state of Baden–Württemburg. Porsche's manufacturing value-added consisted mainly of engine production, welding and assembly of bodies, painting and trim, and final assembly and testing. Operations at Zuffenhausen, except for engine production, were characterized by low volume and high variety. Somewhat higher volumes and greater standardization were found at Neckarsulm. The business press described these manufacturing environments as follows:

Exceptional skill, care, and patience go into assembly. The most expensive Porsches are put together at work stations. The less costly ones are assembled on a stop-and-start conveyor which allows ample time to add each section and component. All the craftsmen are highly skilled (many were trained in Porsche's own apprentice school, which has a waiting list), and 15% of the production work force are assigned to inspection and quality control. Each engine is individually tested, and every completed car is given a road test over 30 kilometers.[15]

The assembly line, when it moves at all, creeps along at a barely discernible pace. Elsewhere in the factory, workers fashion seat coverings out of the elephant hide shot by one customer; and they paint a car in the same red shade as the lipstick worn by another customer's wife.[16]

Most of Porsche's production workers were members of the large automotive industry union, IG Metall, which in 1984 had successfully negotiated an industry-wide 38½-hour workweek. The annual vacation allowance for workers in the German automotive industry was 6 weeks. Approximately 30% of factory workers were foreign nationals. As required by German law, workers were represented by elected members on a factory works council, which had powers of advice and consent regarding conditions of work, and by labor representatives making up half of the *Aufsichtsrat*.

Production levels had increased by 53% during fiscal 1982–1985 (26% at Zuffenhausen and 77% at Neckarsulm). By the end of fiscal 1985, daily production rates were 100 at Zuffenhausen and 150 at Neckarsulm. Most of the

---

[13] "Porsche's Civil War with Its Dealers," *Fortune*, April 16, 1984.

[14] Ibid.

[15] "The Power at Porsche," *Management Today*, February 1979.

[16] "Porsche Succeeds in Revving up U.S. Sales," *Wall Street Journal*, July 3, 1989.

increase at Zuffenhausen was accomplished by running various operations on a two- or three-shift basis. In 1985 the company had completed more than half of a 3-year, DM 900 million facilities modernization program. These capital expenditures, which were primarily aimed at reducing bottlenecks and increasing manufacturing flexibility, included construction of new painting facilities and a new body assembly plant. The company had no plans for major facilities expansions.

Financial Policies

Porsche's financial statements reflected the revenue–cost–asset relationships resulting from the operating policies and practices described previously (Exhibits 10, 11, and 12). Its financial policies centered around maintaining a strong balance sheet and remaining an independent company. *Euromoney* outlined these policies as follows:

The company does not go to outside sources for any loan—not even for export credits. Its self-sufficiency has come about partly through family shareholders taking very modest dividends.

Porsche runs a payments system of cash against documents [letters of credit]. "The cars aren't unloaded if the cash isn't there," says finance chief Heinz Branitzki, "and there are only minor exceptions to this rule, in faraway countries." Importers in America, the company's biggest export market, are invoiced in dollars. The rest have to pay in deutsche marks.

The company's house bank, Landesgirokasse, a small public company based in Baden–Württemburg, is in the unusual position, in German terms, of neither owning shares of its client nor lending to it. It is used for Porsche's payments, and for management of part of the company's cash. Together with two or three other banks it also handles the company's foreign exchange business. "We're not interested in making money on exchange," Branitzki said, "but we want to make sure that we get what we calculated we would."

He added, "We believe in working with a small local bank. One has to make up one's mind between many big banks, where a small company like Porsche is a minor part of their business, and a well-known but smaller bank where one is one of the bigger clients. In Baden–Württemburg, Porsche is viewed as one of the province's own companies. You find people here working over generations with particular companies—Daimler–Benz, Porsche, Bosch. A local bank has an interest in the welfare of this area and it sees us as an important partner in its

EXHIBIT 10 Consolidated Profit and Loss Accounts FY Ending July 31 (DM millions)

	1983	*1984*	*1985*
Revenues:			
Net sales[a]	2,133.7	2,494.3	3,175.7
Change in work in process, finished goods inventories, and unfilled contracts, plus company-produced additions to plant and equipment	55.9	(14.7)	32.3
Total output	2,189.6	2,479.6	3,208.0
Other income[b]	43.0	56.5	70.1
	2,232.6	2,536.1	3,278.1
Cost of materials and supplies	1,430.9	1,559.0	2,001.3
Personnel expenditures[c]	366.5	396.4	538.0
Depreciation	71.1	101.7	143.6
Other expenses	166.0	198.8	254.1
Interest expenses	3.6	3.4	4.3
Taxes[d]	124.9	184.4	216.4
Net income	69.6	92.4	120.4

[a] Includes revenues from third-party engineering contracts and sales of parts.

[b] Includes income from investments in foreign subsidiaries and associated companies, interest income, gain on sales of fixed assets, and income from elimination of provisions and special reserves.

[c] Wages and salaries, social security levies, and cost of pension and related benefits.

[d] Taxes on income and property and other taxes.

EXHIBIT 11   Consolidated Balance Sheets (DM millions)

	July 31	
	1984	*1985*
Assets		
Cash and securities	323.6	354.7
Accounts receivable: trade	44.7	57.4
subsidiaries	23.9	44.2
Inventories[a]	262.9	314.9
Other current assets	36.2	37.4
	691.3	808.6
Prepaid expenses	2.3	2.9
Investments in subsidiaries and associated companies	71.5	76.8
Property, plant, equipment: net	412.8	542.8
Intangible assets	2.6	1.3
Adjustments from consolidation	7.6	7.6
Total assets	1,188.1	1,440.0
Liabilities and Shareholders' Equity		
Accounts payable: trade	171.7	212.2
Other current liabilities	157.2	105.2
	328.9	317.4
Liabilities payable after 4 years	1.2	1.6
Lump-sum allowance on receivables	11.2	10.7
Deferred income	2.7	3.4
Provisions[b]	462.6	632.9
Special reserves[c]	7.0	6.2
Minority interests	0.3	0.3
Shareholders' equity:		
Capital stock: common	35.0	35.0
preferred[d]	35.0	35.0
General reserves	258.0	337.3
Unappropriated surplus	46.2	60.2
	374.2	467.5
	1,188.1	1,440.0

[a] Inventories plus cost of unfilled contracts.

[b] For pensions, defined repairs, warranty coverages, early retirement obligations, and deferred taxes.

[c] According to German Income Tax Act and Foreign Investment Act.

[d] Nonvoting.

work. We see Landesgirokasse as our partner in the sense that we talk about our plans with it, and maybe in the future we will need capital from it. And once, 20 years ago, I should have mentioned, we borrowed from it." [17]

Porsche's 1984 public offering of preference shares was prompted by one family mem-

[17] "Porsche Owes Only to Porsche," *Euromoney*, February 1984.

ber's desire to sell his shares. It also permitted other family members future flexibility in raising cash. However, family members had reputedly agreed that none would sell preference shares without prior agreement by all others.

U.S. MARKET STRATEGY

Historically, the United States had been a large and occasionally volatile market for Porsche. During the 1950s, roughly 65% of output had gone to the United States. In the 1960–1978 period, the figure was typically 50%. However, during fiscal 1978–1981, U.S. unit sales fell from 17,300 to 7,800, reflecting, in part, a strong deutsche mark, rising U.S. interest rates, and the beginning of a deep U.S. recession. When Mr. Schutz joined Porsche in 1981, he identified rebuilding the company's U.S. presence as a major priority.

Appointment of Mr. Schutz as *Vorstand* chairman represented a significant departure in that he had not come from within the Porsche organization and had spent much of his career in marketing. A German-born American, he had worked as an engineer for the engine division of Caterpillar Tractor, as a marketing executive at Cummins Engine, and as *Vorstand* chairman of Kloeckner–Humboldt–Deutz AG, a German truck and farm equipment producer.

Mr. Schutz's stated objective was to achieve a U.S. sales level that ranged between 30,000 and 35,000 units yearly, depending on economic conditions. He planned to accomplish this by increasing sales of lower-priced models, broadening the range of 911 and 928 models offered, expanding dealer coverage in certain sunbelt regions, and significantly improving customer service.

U.S fiscal and monetary policies created a positive economic environment for Porsche's new U.S. strategy. During 1983–1985 inflation rates were considerably reduced; interest rates, though historically high in real terms, dropped; and GNP grew at a 4.3% annual rate (Exhibit 13). At the same time, the deutsche mark continued to depreciate against the dol-

EXHIBIT 12   Percent of Year-to-Year Increases (Decreases) in Net Sales and Operating Expenses, FY Ending July 31

	1982	1983	1984	1985
Net sales				
Due to physical volume	16.6	40.3	(2.2)	13.9
Due to price realization	11.1	3.0	19.1	13.4
	27.7	43.3	16.9	27.3
Price realization: domestic sales	8.5	7.6	16.4	5.6
export sales	12.7	2.0	20.3	17.0
Operating expenses				
Materials and supplies	28.1	41.9	28.4	16.5
Personnel expenditures	17.1	19.1	8.2	35.9
Depreciation	(9.4)	53.6	43.0	41.2
Other expenses	28.7	42.8	19.8	27.9
Total operating expenses	24.1	37.6	12.8	27.9

lar. Tax law changes introduced in 1982 increased disposable income and made it possible to develop more favorable automobile leasing packages (for example, a 10% investment tax credit and more favorable depreciation schedules). Porsche's U.S. unit sales grew from 7,796 in fiscal 1981 to 24,880 in 1985 (Exhibit 2).

SITUATION IN 1985

During fiscal 1981–1985 total export sales had grown from 62% to 75% of consolidated sales, despite a near doubling of domestic sales (Exhibit 14). The rapid growth of export sales resulted to a considerable extent from a combination of higher unit sales and price realization in the U.S. market. Higher U.S. price realization, in turn, had resulted from a combination of modest price increases and an appreciating dollar (Exhibit 15). Local currency appreciation had not been a factor in other export markets during this period (Exhibit 16).

By late 1985, several factors pointed toward a more difficult U.S. market environment. During March–August 1985, the deutsche mark had appreciated from 3.40 to 2.79. In September 1985, finance ministers of the Group of Five industrial nations (the United States, Germany, France, the United Kingdom, and Japan) announced an agreement aimed at forcing further depreciation of the dollar.[18] By December 31, the deutsche mark

[18] During 1980–1985, the Reagan administration had taken the position that the value of the dollar should be determined by market forces and had avoided significant intervention in foreign exchange markets. Rapid appreciation of the dollar combined with a robust U.S. economic recovery created large trade deficits and declining market shares for many U.S. companies. This led, in turn, to growing pressure within the U.S. Congress for restrictive trade legislation. The Plaza agreement of September 1985 was aimed in part at diffusing these pressures. The G-5 countries made a commitment to joint and, if necessary, heavy intervention in currency and financial markets to drive down the dollar. Japanese and European ministers also agreed to consider (no firm commitments were made) fiscal and monetary measures that would stimulate their

EXHIBIT 13   U.S. Economic Indicators, Calendar Years

	1980	1981	1982	1983	1984	1985
Gross national product in 1980 dollars (1980 = 100)	100	102	99	104	109	112
Consumer price index	100	110	117	121	126	131
Prime rate (%)	15.3	18.9	14.9	10.8	12.0	9.9
Dow-Jones industrial average[a]	891	932	884	1,190	1,179	1,328
DM/$U.S. exchange rate[b]	1.82	2.26	2.43	2.55	2.85	2.94

[a] Annual average of monthly figures.

[b] Average annual.

EXHIBIT 14   Export versus Domestic Sales, FY Ending July 31

	1981	1982	1983	1984	1985
Net sales (DM millions)					
Domestic	442.5	519.7	651.1	759.7	804.1
Export	722.7	968.5	1,482.6	1,734.6	2,371.6
Total	1,165.2	1,488.2	2,133.7	2,494.3	3,175.7
Export %	62.0	65.1	69.5	69.5	74.7
Units					
Domestic	9,668	10,447	12,164	12.202	12,224
Export	18,315	21,766	32,661	31,768	37,141
Total	27,983	32,213	44,825	43,970	49,365
Export %	65.4	67.6	72.9	72.2	75.2
Price realization (DM 000)[a]					
Domestic	45.8	49.7	53.5	62.3	65.8
Export	39.5	44.5	45.4	54.6	63.9

[a] Net sales ÷ units. Domestic figures reflect changes in price and product mix and include revenues from third-party engineering contracts. Export figures reflect changes in price, product mix, and exchange rates.

traded at 2.46/$U.S. Many economic forecasters were predicting a rate of 1.60 to 1.80 within 2 years.

United States market prospects were further clouded by possible changes in tax laws. While the Reagan administration remained opposed to any tax increases, many congressmen viewed higher tax receipts as essential in reducing federal budget deficits. Several proposals under debate could negatively affect demand for consumer durables and luxury goods. These included removal of preferential tax treatment

economies and reduce international differences among real interest rates. The Reagan administration agreed to continue efforts to reduce the growing U.S. federal budget deficit, reduce U.S. interest rates, and resist protectionist pressures from the U.S. Congress.

of capital gains, elimination of deductions for interest paid on consumer debt, less favorable depreciation schedules, elimination of the investment tax credit, and introduction of a value-added tax. Washington analysts were divided in their opinions of whether any major changes would ultimately be enacted into law.

As *Vorstand* members reviewed the situation, a number of questions were raised. Should Porsche raise U.S. list prices to compensate for depreciation of the dollar? What impact could be expected on unit sales? When the company had encountered a more gradual appreciation of the deutsche mark from 3.66 to 1.83 during 1970–1980, it had increased U.S. prices to maintain DM price realization from each car sold. Where possible, major

EXHIBIT 15   Price Increases, Exchange Rate Changes, and Unit Sales in the U.S. Market, Calendar Years

	Average U.S. List Price Increase (%)				Change in DM/$U.S. Exchange Rate[a]	Total Unit Sales
	911	928	924	944		
1977						19,883
1978	20.6	—	20.5	—	−13.4%	17,488[b]
1979	13.2	14.5	23.1	—	−9.0%	14,073
1980	N.A.	19.1	10.1	—	−0.5%	10,597
1981	N.A.	9.6	7.1	—	+24.1%	11,421
1982	1.9	1.7	1.9	—	+7.5%	14,407
1983	3.6	8.9	—	2.9	+4.9%	21,831
1984	6.5	2.3	—	13.0	+11.8%	19,611[b]
1985	1.7	1.5	—	3.1	+3.2%	25,306

[a] Based on average annual rates. (+) indicates $U.S. appreciation.

[b] Output was reduced in 1978 and 1984 by strikes in the German automotive industry.

EXHIBIT 16 Exchange Rates for Porsche's Six Largest Export Markets, Calendar Years (DM/local currency, average annual rates)

	1980	1981	1982	1983	1984	1985
United States	1.82	2.26	2.43	2.55	2.85	2.94
United Kingdom	4.24	4.58	4.26	3.88	3.82	3.79
Switzerland	1.08	1.15	1.20	1.21	1.21	1.20
France	0.43	0.42	0.37	0.33	0.33	0.33
Italy	0.0021	0.0020	0.0018	0.0017	0.0016	0.0015
Japan	0.008	0.010	0.010	0.011	0.012	0.012

price increases had been coupled with introduction of improved models and/or additions to standard options. United States unit sales had remained stable at historically high levels during 1970–1973. They then fell by 33% during the 1973–1975 OPEC-induced recession. Unit sales recovered somewhat in 1977–1978 and then fell during 1979–1981, a period that witnessed a second round of OPEC price increases and a U.S. recession (Exhibit 15). Drawing precise inferences from 1970s' experiences regarding the impact of price increases on unit demand seemed nearly impossible due to the confounding effects of oil shocks, recessions, and introduction of the 924 and 928 models. Furthermore, Porsche's U.S. product mix had changed significantly by 1985.

Issues of pricing versus unit volume extended beyond direct impacts on revenues and earnings. Porsche viewed itself as having a social contract with both its own employees and those at Neckarsulm to provide employment security. Porsche's own employment levels had grown from 4,900 to 7,900 during 1981–1985. A sustained shortfall in unit sales could force a reduction in employees, voiding the social contract and requiring substantial severance payments. Some *Vorstand* members recalled with sadness the difficult period 1974–1975 when the company had been forced to reduce its work force by 25%.

The current situation also raised issues for longer-term financial planning. Porsche's technological momentum depended on internal funding. Some DM 400 million would be required to complete the current modernization program. Funding would also be required for new models. The 911 chassis had been in existence since 1964. Increasingly stringent minimum fuel economy standards in the United States would require new engine development programs. Development and tooling of a replacement for the 911 in the 1990s could easily require DM 1 billion.

Porsche AG (B)

During much of 1985–1987 members of the *Vorstand* of Porsche AG were reexamining and adapting the company's strategy in light of significant appreciation of the deutsche mark against currencies of its two largest export markets, the United States and United Kingdom (Exhibit 1). Background information on this situation is provided in Case 2A.

U.S. STRATEGY

In March 1985, Porsche began buying DM/$U.S. forward currency contracts with maturities extending as far as 1 year, based on planned U.S. deliveries. This had the effect of locking in realized DM revenues from $U.S. invoiced deliveries at exchange rates of 3.32 to 3.22 during March, 1985, to February, 1986. Revenue realization during calendar 1984 had been at an average rate of 2.85. Revenue realization rates began to fall after March 1986, as forward contracts became progressively expensive. For example, forward rates on 6-month contracts entered into on March 1, 1985–1987, were 3.30, 2.18, and 1.82, respectively.

United States list prices saw little change in 1986. This was followed by increases of 18% to 22% in 1987 and announced 1988 increases of 10% to 35% (Exhibit 2). During this period the company sought to widen its revenue base by introducing additional models: a 911 Turbo, an upgraded 928, a 3.0-liter engine

944, and a 924 with a Porsche engine. United States television advertising expenditures were increased from some $7 million in 1985 to $10.5 million and $12.0 million in 1986 and 1987, respectively. The 1988 advertising budget was $15 million.

Efforts were also undertaken to further strengthen the U.S. dealer network. Porsche Financial Services was established in late 1986 to provide dealers with inventory and retail financing programs. Porsche Cars of North America was conducting a study of the feasibility of leveraging its wholesale operations and dealer network by distributing upscale models of at least one other foreign automobile manufacturer.

On a calendar year basis, Porsche U.S. retail sales grew from 25,306 units in 1985 to 30,471 in 1986. These results were helped in part by customer buying in anticipation of price increases and U.S. tax law changes that were to take effect in 1987. Tax law changes included phased elimination of deductions for interest on consumer debt and passive activity losses, elimination of deductions for sales taxes paid, taxation of capital gains at regular rates, elimination of the investment tax credit, and less attractive depreciation schedules.

In February 1987, *Vorstand* Chairman Peter Schutz forecasted U.S. sales of 34,000 to 35,000 units by 1990 and indicated that growth could be even greater if the company decided to introduce major new products. Retail sales for calendar 1987 came in at 23,632 units, down

This case was prepared from public sources by Professor Stephen A. Allen, Babson College as a basis of classroom discussion. Copyright © 1990 by Stephen A. Allen.

EXHIBIT 1   Exchange Rates for Porsche's Six Largest Export Markets, Calendar Years (DM/local currency, average annual rates)

	1985	1986	1987	1988	1989
United States	2.94	2.17	1.80	1.76	1.88
United Kingdom	3.79	3.19	2.95	3.14	3.08
Switzerland	1.20	1.21	1.21	1.21	1.14
France	0.33	0.31	0.30	0.30	0.29
Italy	0.0015	0.0015	0.0014	0.0014	0.0014
Japan	0.012	0.013	0.012	0.012	0.014

22.4% from 1986. Monthly sales fell from 2,300 in September to 1,280 in December 1987, reflecting, in part, buyer cautiousness in the wake of the October 19 stock market crash. Particularly hard hit were sales of 944/924S models, which were also encountering increased competition from Japanese sports models. Despite an appreciating yen, Japanese producers had been able to price these new entries well below the 924 because they incorporated mass-produced components and frames.

U.K. SITUATION

Despite pound-based retail price increases averaging 21% in 1986, U.K. unit sales grew from 3,438 to 3,705 for calendar year 1985–1986. Sales were aided by rising stock prices and deregulation of U.K. financial markets (the "Big Bang"). Sales fell to 2,793 units in 1987,

reflecting customer resistance to further price increases and the October stock market decline.

FINANCIAL RESULTS

Porsche's fiscal July 31 year revenues and earnings reflected the market situation (Exhibits 3 and 4). While revenues for 1985–1987 were DM 3.2, 3.6, and 3.4 billion, respectively, net income fell from DM 120 to 52 million. Spending on capital programs and development activities was maintained. However, dividends were reduced (Exhibit 5).

PRODUCTION PLANS

By the end of 1987, worldwide inventories of unsold Porsches reached 15,000 units, of

EXHIBIT 2   U.S. List Prices and Unit Sales, Calendar Years (units)

	1985	1986	1987	1988[a]
List prices ($U.S.)				
911: Carrera coupe, 3.2 liter	32,528	31,950	38,500	45,895
Cabriolet, 3.2 liter	37,028	36,450	44,500	52,895
Targa convertible, 3.2 liter	34,028	33,450	40,500	48,230
Turbo coupe, 3.3 liter	—	48,000	58,750	68,670
928-S4, 5.0 liter	—	50,000	58,900	69,380
944: Coupe, 2.7 liter	22,108	22,950	22,950	30,995
S 2 coupe, 3.0 liter	—	—	28,250	36,830
Turbo coupe, 2.5 liter	29,500	33,250	39,765	47,600
924S	—	19,900	21,900	26,560
Retail unit sales				
911	5,890	8,084	7,890	
928	2,582	2,780	1,968	
944	16,834	16,511	10,179	
924S	—	3,096	2,975	
	25,306	30,471	23,632	

[a] As announced in 1987.

EXHIBIT 3   Unit Sales and Revenues, FY Ending July 31

	1985	1986	1987
Units			
911	13,591	16,854	17,033
928	5,089	4,518	4,843
944/924	30,685	31,882	28,100
	49,365	53,254	49,976
Domestic	12,224	11,340	7,844
U.S.	24,880	28,671	30,718
Other export markets	12,261	13,243	11,414
	49,365	53,254	49,976
Revenues (DM millions)			
Domestic	804.1	779.6	659.7
Export	2,371.6	2,788.3	2,748.9
	3,175.7	3,567.9	3,408.6
Price realization (DM 000)[a]			
Domestic	65.8	68.7	84.1
Export	63.9	66.5	65.2

[a] Net sales ÷ units. Domestic also reflects revenues from contract engineering.

which 8,000 were in the United States. In November 1987, the company announced plans to cut 1988 production by 7,300 units. Production was to be halted for 47 days during the first half of 1988, including extension of workers' Christmas holidays through January 22. At the same time, Porsche announced that it would scale back planned 1988 price increases by 2.4%, depending on the model.

In a December 1987 interview, Mr. Schutz said,

You can't fight currency movements, you have to learn to live with them. Eventually we may have little alternative but to produce cars in the U.S. At the current exchange rate of 1.70, we aren't at a level where we would do that. But if it got much below 1.5, we'd have a real problem. While we aren't considering U.S. production at this time—how would you split such low volume production between the home market and the U.S.?—we don't exclude anything that would make for financial success.[1]

MANAGEMENT CHANGES

On December 17, 1987, Mr. Schutz resigned from his position as *Vorstand* chairman. The business press speculated that Schutz's departure reflected deteriorating relations with *Vor-*

---

[1] "Porsche Still Says Maybe to U.S Plant," *Ward's AutoWorld*, December 1987.

EXHIBIT 4   Consolidated Profit and Loss Accounts, FY Ending July 31 (DM millions)

	1985	1986	1987
Revenue:			
Net sales[a]	3,175.7	3,567.9	3,408.6
Changes in inventories and company-produced additions to plant and equipment	32.3	25.5	17.9
Total output	3,208.0	3,593.4	3,426.5
Other income[b]	70.1	73.6	122.9
	3,278.1	3,667.0	3,549.4
Cost of materials, supplies, merchandise	2,001.3	2,331.2	2,262.4
Personnel expenditures[c]	538.0	556.9	586.5
Depreciation	143.6	179.8	182.2
Other expenses	254.1	375.2	366.6
Interest expenses	4.3	1.5	1.8
Taxes[d]	216.4	146.3	98.0
Net income	120.4	76.1	51.9

[a] Includes revenues from third-party engineering contracts and sales of parts.

[b] Includes income from investments in foreign subsidiaries and associated companies, interest income, gain on sale of fixed assets, and income from elimination of provisions and special reserves.

[c] Wages and salaries, social security levies, and cost of pension and related benefits.

[d] Taxes on income and property and other taxes.

EXHIBIT 5 Operating and Financial Information, FY Ending July 31 (DM millions, except where indicated)

	1985	1986	1987
Net sales	3,175.7	3,567.9	3,408.6
Net income	120.4	75.3	51.9
Total assets	1,444.2	1,528.1	1,591.8
Shareholders' equity[a]	407.8	469.0	505.9
Research and development expenses	300.0	360.0	380.0
Capital expenditures	290.8	272.2	272.3
Depreciation	143.6	179.8	182.2
Dividends paid	25.2	21.7	14.7
Employees at year end (000)	7.9	8.5	8.3
Return on sales (%)	3.8	2.1	1.5
Return on assets (%)	8.3	4.9	3.3
Asset turnover (X)	2.2	2.3	2.1
Return on shareholders' equity (%)	29.5	16.1	10.3

[a] Excluding income available for distribution.

stand colleagues and members of the Porsche and Piëch families as concerns grew regarding the viability of his marketing-driven, U.S.-focused strategy. Retrospective commentary on Schutz's strategy included the following:

Porsche has always lived dangerously in its tiny market wedge by making the rich few pay a high price for the exalted thrill of driving a hard, high tech sports car. Now that things have backfired, Schutz has become the scapegoat and is widely criticized for risking too much in a heavily market oriented strategy that neglected model development and virtually ignored other sales in favour of rich pickings in the U.S. Several industry observers agree that's mainly due to the quick-buck marketing fixation of the German-born, U.S.-trained Schutz that major new models weren't waiting in the wings when the market began to weaken. "Typical American three-month management," sneers PA Technology consultant Georg von Römer.

One rival's in-house analysis concludes that Porsche's four ranges are such a stylistic jumble that only the classic 911 makes customers feel they're joining an elite adventurers' club. The frequently reworked 911 still has loyal followers after 25 years but lacks modern standard technology like anti-lock brakes and badly needs a convincing successor, most critics say.

Three years of stiff U.S. price increases for a largely unimproved product range allowed Japan's far cheaper Mazda, Toyota, and Nissan imitations to overtake Porsche's smaller 924 and 944 models in sales. In its domestic market, the Japanese clones teamed up with a new breed of Mercedes–Benz and BMW sport-tuned luxury compacts to give the 924/944 range an even worse drubbing.[2]

Stephen Reitman, auto analyst for Phillips & Drew, contends that the root of Porsche's trouble is neither the dollar nor concentration on the U.S. but the decision to grow the 924/944 models. Both represented an attempt to increase sales by going downscale, producing an "affordable" Porsche. Instead, what the company really created were "tarted-up Volkswagens." And by 1988 these were listing in the U.S. for $15,000 more than a Corvette.[3]

Mr. Schutz was succeeded by Mr. Heinz Branitzki, formerly *Vorstand* member responsible for finance. The 58-year-old Mr. Branitzki had joined Porsche in 1962. The U.S. business press described him as a "soft-spoken man with an unassuming manner, who spends his leisure time playing chess, reading history books, and hiking in the mountains."[4] *International Management* noted that he was highly regarded within the Porsche organization for sound management of the company's balance sheet and as architect of a skillful hedging program which had helped cushion results from a declining dollar.[5]

---

[2]"Porsche's U.S. Backfire," *International Management*, April 1988.

[3]"Stalled Porsche," *Barrons*, June 27, 1988.

[4]*Wall Street Journal*, July 3, 1989.

[5]Ibid.

Porsche AG (C)

During 1988–1990, Porsche's *Vorstand* and its recently appointed Chairman, Mr. Heinz Branitzki, took a number of steps aimed at repositioning its model ranges and reducing the scale of operations. Developments leading to these decisions are described in Cases 2A and 2B.

In late 1989, Mr. Branitzki described the company's future objectives as (1) selling no more than 40,000 units yearly; (2) concentrating on the high end of the specialty luxury market; and (3) deriving roughly equal revenues from Germany, the United States, and other export markets.

MODEL RANGES AND PRICING

A revamped 911 family featured a wider model range, more powerful 3.6-liter engines in all models, and all-wheel-drive options. In 1990 Porsche offered seven basic 911 models at the following U.S. list prices:

Carrera coupe, rwd	$61,400
Carrera Targa convertible, rwd	62,900
Carrera Cabriolet convertible, rwd	70,000
Carrera coupe, awd	72,700
Carrera Targa convertible, awd	74,200
Carrera Cabriolet convertible, awd	81,300
Turbo, rwd	95,700

Two upgraded 928 models (S4 and GT) each listed at $78,200 in 1990.

The 924S had been discontinued in 1989. Remaining 4-cylinder models were fitted with more powerful 3.0-liter engines, resulting in the following 1990 offerings:

944 S2 coupe	$44,050
944 S2 Cabriolet convertible	51,050

Exhibit 1 shows average U.S. list price increases and unit sales by model family for calendar years 1987–1990. Exhibit 2 shows trends in unit demand for the overall U.S. luxury auto market. United States sales for all Porsche models had fallen from 30,471 in 1986 to 9,140 in 1990. These results reflected direct consumer reactions to price increases, plus increasing low-end competition from Japanese luxury models, a U.S. recession, and rising white-collar unemployment. Beginning in 1991, autos would be subject to a U.S. luxury tax of 10% on the portion of their price exceeding $30,000.

OTHER MARKETS

Exhibit 3 shows Porsche's unit sales and revenues by geographic area on a July 31 fiscal year basis. For fiscal 1990, unit sales in Germany exceeded those in the United States, although, at 8,729, they remained well below a 1985 peak of 12,224. Sales to export markets

---

This case was prepared for public sources by Professor Stephen A. Allen as a basis for classroom discussion. Copyright © 1990 by Stephen A. Allen.

EXHIBIT 1 Price Increases, Exchange Rates, and Unit Sales in the U.S. Market, Calendar Years

	1987	1988	1989	1990
Average U.S. list price increase (%)				
911	21.5	18.5	9.2	6.0
928	17.8	17.8	7.4	4.6
944	9.8	25.1	18.7	4.9
924S	10.1	21.2	—	—
Unit sales				
911	7,890	5,843	5,714	5,465
928	1,968	1,427	835	620
944	10,179	6,145	2,794	3,055
924S	2,975	2,321	136	—
	23,012	15,736	9,479	9,140
DM/$U.S. exchange rate[a]	1.80	1.76	1.88	1.62

[a] Average annual rate.

other than the United States were a record 14,654, reflecting improved sales in Japan, France, Spain, and Italy.

PRODUCTION AND DISTRIBUTION

During fiscal 1988, production rates were cut by more than 60% in order to match output and dealer inventories to reduced demand. Employment was reduced by 500, or 6%, during 1988–1989 through a combination of hiring freezes, early retirements, and a liberal voluntary severance program. The production

contract with Audi's Neckarsulm plant was to be terminated in December 1990; and work was underway to transfer the remaining 944 production to Zuffenhausen. Management also sought to increase production efficiencies. However, one commentary noted,

Branitzki says a luxury sports car maker cannot take the volume producer's cost cutting modular approach too far. Intensive efforts to standardize machining procedures for various engine types brought few results, he admits. He concedes that there is costly duplication of design in many components, ranging down to different door lock mechanisms on every model. "Perhaps we've been an

EXHIBIT 2 U.S. Luxury Car Retail Sales, Calendar Year (000 units, %)

	1986	1987	1988	1989	1990
Luxury regular segment					
U.S. models	585.8	484.2	483.4	498.1	511.1
Imports	306.6	302.3	293.5	273.2	293.5
Total	892.4	786.5	776.9	771.3	804.6
% Total U.S. market	7.8	7.7	7.3	7.9	8.7
Luxury specialty segment					
U.S. models	186.3	156.1	187.0	198.8	206.4
Imports	73.8	90.3	79.6	81.6	68.1
Total	260.1	246.4	266.6	280.4	274.5
% Total U.S. market	2.3	2.4	2.5	2.9	3.0
Selected luxury specialty brands					
Corvette	33.0	25.4	23.3	23.9	22.7
Porsche	30.5	23.6	15.7	9.5	9.1
Mercedes SL/SEL	16.0	14.6	13.7	9.2	9.6
BMW (sports)	3.0	6.2	22.8	19.5	n.a.
Jaguar XJ-S	4.9	5.4	4.8	4.3	4.5

Source: Ward's Automotive Yearbooks.

EXHIBIT 3   Unit Sales and Revenues, FY Ending July 31

		1987	1988	1989	1990
Units	911	17,033	13,463	15,557	19,540
	928	4,843	4,069	3,465	3,067
	944/924	28,100	13,830	9,995	8,628
		49,976	31,362	29,017	31,235
	Domestic	7,844	6,710	7,515	8,729
	U.S.	30,718	14,984	10,186	7,852
	Other export markets	11,414	9,668	11,316	14,654
		49,976	31,362	29,017	31,235
Revenues (DM millions)					
	Domestic	659.7	640.1	747.0	968.4
	Export	2,748.9	1,842.3	1,779.3	2,171.3
		3,408.6	2,482.4	2,526.3	3,139.7
Revenue realization (DM 000)[a]					
	Domestic	84.1	95.4	99.4	110.9
	Export	65.2	74.7	82.8	96.5

[a] Net sales ÷ units. Domestic also reflects revenues from contract engineering.

extreme case in feeling that we have to re-invent the wheel."[1]

Distribution networks were scaled back to reflect lower sales prospects. The domestic dealer network was reduced from 207 to 105. United States dealerships were reduced from 324 in 1985 to 270 in 1990, mainly through mergers and dealer decisions not to renew expiring franchises. Porsche Cars of North America initiated personnel reductions and a reorganization under which its Charleston, South Carolina, unit took over all vehicle preparation and delivery activities, while Reno, Nevada, operations assumed duties for parts distribution. PCNA President John Cook resigned and was replaced by Mr. Brian Bowler, formerly president of the Detroit office of the advertising agency DDB Needham.

FINANCIAL RESULTS

Exhibits 4 and 5 show consolidated financial results for fiscal 1988–1990. Sales fell from a record DM 3.6 billion in 1986 to DM 2.5 billion in 1988, recovering to DM 3.1 billion in 1990. Net income fell from a record DM 120 million in 1985 to DM 25 million in 1988, re-

covering to DM 57 million in 1990. Research and development expenses remained above DM 400 million per annum, reflecting repositioning of current model ranges, design work on potential new model families, and expansion of outside engineering projects.[2] Porsche's balance sheet remained strong, with liquid assets of some DM 500 million and no debt.

MANAGEMENT CHANGES

In 1989, Porsche had recruited Dr. Ulrich Bez, formerly of BMW, as its chief engineer and *Vorstand* member for research and development. Bez was charged with the development of successors for the current 911, 928, and 944 families, which would likely be launched during 1992–1996.

Mr. Branitzki retired in March 1990 and was succeeded by Mr. Arno Bohn, 42, formerly marketing member of the *Vorstand* of computer maker Nixdorf AG. Mr. Branitzki stated,

The reason for the change now is that we had given our engineers a lot of exciting projects for the future, and I think it is the fair thing that the guy who

---

[1] "Porsche's U.S. Backfire," *International Management*, April 1988.

[2] Billings from outside engineering contracts had grown to DM 200 million by 1990.

EXHIBIT 4 Consolidated Profit and Loss Accounts, FY Ending July 31, (DM millions)

	1988	1989	1990
Revenues:			
Net sales	2,482.4	2,526.3	3,139.7
Changes in inventories and company-produced plant and equipment additions	75.7	89.5	132.2
Total output	2,558.1	2,615.8	3,271.9
Other income	116.6	105.3	75.7
	2,674.7	2,721.1	3,347.6
Cost of materials, supplies, merchandise	1,630.8	1,589.1	1,973.7
Personnel expenditures	570.1	576.3	700.0
Depreciation	170.7	181.8	173.0
Other expenses	266.0	275.6	354.1
Taxes	11.8	44.1	89.8
Net income	25.3	54.2	57.0

decides which direction we will go will be responsible for the result. . . . What we need is a manager who can see all aspects and bring them together. The key decision is not whether a future car has 330 or 340 horsepower. We have so many experts in every field. The question is what is the vision for the future and how to make a team from all the talent we have.[3]

A few weeks later Dr. Ferry Porsche, 80, was succeeded as chairman of the *Aufsichstrat* by his eldest son, Ferdinand Alexander Porsche, 55. The younger Dr. Porsche had joined Porsche AG in 1958, took over responsibilities for design in 1962, and had been deputy man-

[3] Quoted in "New Porsche Boss Faces Host of Product Decisions," *Automotive News*, January 29, 1990.

aging director during 1968–1972. In 1972 he had left to form Porsche Design, a successful creator of cameras, watches, sunglasses, leather goods, and motorcycles.

In 1990, Porsche remained the last independent, limited-line specialty car maker. Faced with a combination of volatile revenues and rising financial requirements for model development and facilities modernization, companies such as Rolls Royce, Lotus, Maserati, Alfa Romeo, and Ferrari had merged with broad-line U.S. or European producers. In 1989, Ford had acquired a reluctant Jaguar PLC for some $2.5 billion after a protracted bidding contest with General Motors. GM subsequently acquired a 50% stake in the troubled automobile unit of SAAB–Scania.

EXHIBIT 5 Operating and Financial Information, FY Ending July 31 (DM millions, except where indicated)

	1987	1988	1989	1990
Net sales	3,408.6	2,482.4	2,526.3	3,139.7
Net income	51.9	25.3	54.2	57.0
Total assets	1,591.8	1,596.8	1,791.2	2,052.7
Shareholders' equity	505.9	576.8	603.9	732.0
Cash and securities	367.4	310.5	459.4	502.0
Research and development expense	380.0	425.0	405.0	431.0
Capital expenditures	272.3	236.2	181.7	208.5
Depreciation	182.2	170.7	181.8	185.5
Dividends paid	14.7	14.7	16.1	17.5
Employees at year end (000)	8.3	8.0	7.8	8.8
Return on sales (%)	1.5	1.0	2.2	1.8
Return on assets (%)	3.3	1.6	3.0	2.8
Asset turnover (X)	2.1	1.6	1.4	1.5
Return on shareholders' equity (%)	10.3	4.4	9.0	7.8

Porsche AG (D)

In late 1990, the management of Porsche AG announced plans to introduce two new model ranges and a major redesign of the 911 over the coming 5 years. Evolution of the company's strategy in the 1980s is detailed in Porsche AG (A), (B), and (C).

Net income for fiscal 1991 had fallen 70% on a 1% decline in sales (Exhibits 1 and 2). In September 1992, the company reported that unit sales for fiscal 1992 had fallen to 22,481 (versus 26,541 for the previous year). Revenues were estimated at DM 2.7 billion, a 13% decline from 1991. Results had been somewhat cushioned by continued growth of outside engineering contracts and by contract manufacturing of the Mercedes model 300CE at Porsche's Zuffenhausen plant.

Employment had been reduced to 8,062 by the end of fiscal 1992, and plans called for cutting another 1,850 jobs during fiscal 1993. Management indicated that these moves would permit the company to break even at annual unit sales of 20,000. During this period, seven senior executives had left the company, including *Vorstand* Chairman Arno Bohn.

NEW MODEL PROGRAMS

Porsche's development efforts were focused on three new or substantially redesigned model families:

1. The 968, which replaced the 944 in early 1992, featured more powerful 4-cylinder engines and

EXHIBIT 1   Consolidated Profit and Loss Accounts, FY Ending July 31 (DM millions)

	1990	1991[a]
Revenues:		
Net sales	3,139.7	3,102.2
Changes in inventories and company-produced plant and equipment additions	132.2	(2.4)
Total output	3,271.9	3,099.8
Other income	75.7	86.8
	3,347.6	3,186.6
Cost of materials, supplies, merchandise	1,973.7	1,787.2
Personnel expenditures	700.0	795.2
Depreciation	173.0	170.7
Other expenses	354.1	373.2
Taxes	89.8	43.2
Net income	57.0	17.1

[a] Costs include a DM 60 million charge for restructuring and severance payments for 550 nonproduction employees.

major body and interior redesigns. Targeted price for the lowest-priced model had been $44,500. However, the entry-level model was actually introduced at a U.S. list price of $39,850.

2. The 989, which was to replace the 928 by 1996, featured a 4.2-liter, V-8 engine, four-wheel steering, double-wishbone suspensions, and Tiptronic automatic transmission. The 989 shared few features with prior models, and its development and tooling costs were estimated at DM 1.1 billion. It was targeted at a retail price range of $88,000 to $124,000 and annual sales of 15,000 units.

3. A radically redesigned 911 was targeted for introduction by 1996. Plans called for substantial

This case was prepared from public sources by Professor Stephen A. Allen as a basis for classroom discussion. Copyright © 1992 by Stephen A. Allen.

EXHIBIT 2 Operating and Financial Information, FY Ending July 31 (DM millions, except where indicated)

	1990	1991
Net sales	3,139.7	3,102.2
Net income	57.0	17.1
Total assets	2,052.7	2,155.1
Shareholders' equity	732.0	725.7
Capital expenditures	208.5	254.0
Depreciation	185.5	170.7
Dividends paid	17.5	13.3
Employees at year end (000)	8.8	9.0
Return on sales (%)	1.8	0.6
Return on assets (%)	2.8	0.8
Asset turnover (X)	1.5	1.4
Return on shareholders' equity (%)	7.8	2.4

changes in exterior and interior styling and replacement of the boxer engine with a rear-mounted 4.2-liter V-8.

CAR magazine reported that these product decisions had emerged from a heated, year-long debate within the company:

The decision-making process had started in the mid-80s under former chief engineer Dr. Helmuth Bott. When his replacement, Dr. Ulrich Bez, arrived from BMW, he started with a clean sheet of paper.

First, the long-running proposal of an affordable, entry-level sports car was dismissed as financially not feasible. Bez and chief designer Harm Lagaay (formerly also at BMW) also pushed aside other pending projects, including variations of the 944, a common components concept based around the indestructible boxer engine, a four-door version of the 928, a 928 Cabriolet, and a high-tech mid-engined sports car positioned halfway between the 944 and 928.

The team at Porsche's Weissach R&D center took a long time to get used to the allegedly very authoritarian new chief engineer. Bez is by no means an undisputed leader. But he enjoys the support of the new chairman, Arno Bohn. While Bohn is a corporate strategist, he readily admits that he did not understand a lot about cars when he accepted his new position. Bez and Lagaay took the opportunity to push through their ideas.

The only person who could have overruled the decisions is Ferdinand Alexander Porsche, the new supervisory board chairman. But he didn't interfere, partly because he got involved a little too late, and the 989 had already advanced beyond the point of no return. Also, the 989, which is a 4-door saloon

rather than a coupe, was a favorite concept of former chairman Ferry Porsche. It's said that this helped clear all the hurdles, including F. A. Porsche, who did not want to vote against his father.[1]

Dr. Ulrich Bez resigned in September 1991, reportedly because of disagreements over 989 styling and the future of Porsche's racing program. In January 1992, management announced that plans for introduction of the 989 would be shelved until market conditions improved. At the same time, management indicated plans to introduce 968 and 911 models during the second half of 1992 at lower price points. One example was the 911 Carrera, RS America priced at $63,900 (versus $72,700 for the most comparable current model). *Fortune* reported,

Buyers of the RS America will have to tolerate some privations. You get corduroy seat covers, instead of leather, and a nylon strap to open the door from the inside, instead of a handle. And sorry, no radio. Other sacrifices: The car comes stripped of most of its sound-deadening material and has stiffer springs and shock absorbers, along with manual rather than electronic controls to adjust the seats. Porsche reports "substantial" orders for the new hot rod.[2]

MARKET CONDITIONS

Exhibit 3 shows unit sales and revenues by model and geographic region. While sales in Germany remained relatively strong, U.S. sales had fallen to 4,000 units in fiscal 1992. Sales to other export markets had also fallen significantly, due in part to continuing recession in the UK and soft demand in Japan and Italy.

Management denials notwithstanding, several industry analysts speculated that Porsche could be forced to withdraw from the U.S. market. The *Wall Street Journal* stated,

Porsche's U.S. sales target is 10,000 to 12,000 cars annually—a mark it hasn't reached since 1988. The

---

[1] George Kacker, "Oracle" column, *CAR*, November 1990.

[2] "Rolls and Porsche: Blimey, Mate und Gott im Himmel," *Fortune*, April 20, 1992.

EXHIBIT 3   Unit Sales and Revenues, FY July 31

		1990	*1991[a]*	*1992[a]*
Units	911	19,540	19,530	
	928	3,067	1,951	
	944	8,628	4,360	
		31,235	25,841	
	Domestic	8,729	10,444	11,404
	U.S.	7,852	6,112	4,000
	Other export markets	14,654	9,985	7,077
		31,235	26,541	22,481
Revenues (DM millions)				
	Domestic	968.4	1,347.1	
	Export	2,171.3	1,755.1	
		3,139.7	3,102.2	2,700.0(E)
Revenue realization (DM 000)[b]				
	Domestic	110.9	129.0	
	Export	96.5	109.0	
	DM/$U.S. exchange rate[c]	1.78	1.59	1.65

[a] 1991 and 1992 domestic units and revenues include contract manufacturing for Mercedes–Benz. Industry analysts estimated 1992 output sold to Mercedes–Benz at approximately 3,200 units.

[b] Net sales ÷ units. Domestic also reflects revenues from contract engineering.

[c] Average annual rate for fiscal years.

company's dealer base has shrunk to 270, and it was forced to dismiss 77 of its 339 U.S. employees in September, 1991.

The U.S. is crucial to Porsche, which heightens the company's anxiety over any thought of being forced out. No fewer than 260,000 of the 560,000 Porsche cars currently in existence are in the U.S. "If the U.S. falls away, then you've lost a third of your market—and that's hard to swallow," says Joachim Bernsdorff, an analyst for Bank Julius Baer in Frankfurt.

Porsche has a far stronger image in America than recent European exits, such as Peugeot S.A. and Rover's Sterling Motor Cars unit. But now that image may be a liability. Luxury sports cars may be too flashy and frivolous for the simple-things life style of the 1990s.[3]

MANAGEMENT TURMOIL

By early 1992, six senior executives had left the company, including Dr. Bez and Mr. Brian Bowler, president of Porsche North America. In February 1992, the business press reported rumors that Porsche's *Aufsichtsrat* would not renew the management contract of *Vorstand* Chairman Arno Bohn and had offered the position to Dr. Wolfgang Reitzle, research director of BMW. Dr. Reitzle had reportedly been offered a high salary and a 5% shareholding in the company. In any event, Dr. Reitzle did not join Porsche, and Mr. Bohn announced that he would resign if the *Aufsichtsrat* did not vote unanimously to renew his contract within one week. On February 26, 1992, Mr. Bohn's contract was extended for an additional 3 years.

On September 24, 1992, Mr. Bohn resigned as *Vorstand* chairman, citing differences of opinion over business policy with members of the *Aufsichtsrat*. He was replaced by Mr. Wendelin Wiedeking, the 40-year-old *Vorstand* member for production. Mr. Wiedeking's title was "spokesman" for the *Vorstand*, rather than chairman. The business press speculated that this might indicate a caretaker role and/or that the *Aufsichtsrat* no longer wanted a strong *Vorstand* chairman.

FUTURE PROSPECTS

Management indicated that it expected further declines in sales and profits in fiscal 1993.

---

[3] "Porsche, a Favorite in Times of Plenty, Struggles to Survive," *Wall Street Journal*, January 27, 1992.

In June 1992, Mr. Bohn had noted, "At present there are no signs of improvement in international markets. The desire to buy luxury cars is not there. And there are problems with the social acceptability of cars costing DM 100,000 or more."[4]

Industry observors speculated that the company would be sold or seek a joint venture partner. In September 1991, Daimler Benz AG had publicly indicated that it would be prepared to take a position in any new equity offering by Porsche. Other companies rumored to be interested in Porsche were BMW, Toyota, and Volkswagen AG.[5] Management pointed out that Porsche had more than DM 600 million in liquid funds and stated that it was determined to maintain the company's independence.

---

[4] Quoted in "Porsche to Shed Another 850 Jobs," *Financial Times,* June 3, 1992.

[5] Porsche *Aufsichtsrat* member and shareholder, Dr. Ferdinand Piëch, had been nominated as VW *Vorstand* chairman in 1992.

DowBrands Ziploc™
The Case for Going International

CHESTER COLLEGE LIBRARY

In October 1990, Stewart James, vice-president of international for DowBrands, Inc., was reviewing the success of Ziploc™ brand zippered bags outside the United States:

The jury is still out. In Canada, we're at about break even. In Latin America, we've built a plant—we've put a stake in the ground for Ziploc™—but have yet to show operating profits. We're in the process of buying back a joint venture in Japan, after which we should make some money. We sell some product in Europe through our own organization, but none of our European subsidiaries is convinced that there is much of a future for Ziploc™; and some recent market research seems to support the conclusion that it will never be more than a niche product in those countries. Sometimes in these cases, the only way to find out for sure is to make a commitment and go for it.

In my view, DowBrands should grow Ziploc™ at all costs, and this means taking it to the rest of the world. It is our number 1 product in sales and profitability, and my experience has shown that estimating volume potential where behavioral changes are required is a very difficult question to research anyway. We are the low-cost producer in this category, and for a product that is as much a production art as it is a science, we are still far ahead on the learning curve. We are facing increased competition and margin erosion in the U.S. market, and now is the time to go forth in the international arena. The only problem is: how do we get the rest of the organization fired up about this opportunity?

DowBrands, Inc.

As a separate corporate entity, the DowBrands subsidiary of the Dow Chemical Company was only 5 years old, although its genesis was with the marketing of Saran Wrap™ in 1953. Saran Wrap™, a thin plastic film, was originally conceived to protect military arsenal stored at the end of World War II, but someone discovered it made an excellent wrap for the preservation of fresh and/or leftover foods. In time, Dow added other food-care products and such cleaning products as Dow Bathroom Cleaner™ to the line.

The parent company was a successful, $18 billion, multinational chemical company, but the consumer-products portion had never reached what many executives believed was its full potential. Dow spent $1 billion for research and development, and its inventors—dubbed "the molecule movers"—had an excellent track record for inventing new chemical compounds, but the company had been less successful in realizing the full market potential from those inventions. A notable example was a moisture-absorbing technology that Dow developed but sold to Procter & Gamble. It became one of P&G's most profitable products ever. Dow believed that the rewards of such inventions were reaped more by the successful marketer than by the successful inventor. Based on the idea that a dollar in

This case was made possible by the cooperation of DowBrands and is intended for classroom discussion rather than as an illustration of effective or ineffective handling of an administrative situation. Some names and data are disguised. Copyright© 1990 by the University of Virginia Darden School Foundation, Charlottesville, VA. All rights reserved. **Ziploc**™ and **Dow Bathroom Cleaner**™ are trademarks of DowBrands. **Saran Wrap**™ and **Handi-Wrap**™ are trademarks of the Dow Chemical Company.

sales of a specialty product would deliver more profit than a dollar of basic commodity sales, an ongoing discussion at DowBrands was how to exploit markets for its inventions.

The mission for the consumer-products division was to become a *technology-driven* packaged-goods concern, with the basis for excellence coming from highly protected technical advantages. The importance of good marketing skills could not be ignored, however, so in 1985 Dow bought the Texize Division of Morton Thiokol, who not only made and manufactured a line of complementary cleaning products, but also employed personnel skilled in the design and marketing of consumer packaged goods. Texize was combined with the consumer-products division to form the new DowBrands business unit. In 1989, DowBrands acquired the European operations of the First Brands Company, which marketed the well-known Glad brand of plastic bags and wraps in the United States. Its Glad and Albal brands of household wrappers were well established in Europe. (See Exhibit 1 for

EXHIBIT 1 Selected DowBrands International Division Products[a]

Canada:	Dow bathroom cleaner; Glass Plus; Fantastik spray cleaner, bathroom cleaner, and upholstery cleaner; K2r, Spray'N Wash, Spray'N Starch; Ziploc™, Saran Wrap™, Handi-Wrap™, Stretch'N Seal
Italy:	Domopak brand aluminum foils, aluminum containers, plastic wraps, food and garbage bags
Brazil:	Zipy (Ziploc™), Mr. Magic (Fantastik lemon), Thunder (Dow bathroom cleaner)
Argentina:	Radiante brand cleaners
Japan:	Reed/Ziploc™ food bags and microwave cooking bags
Hong Kong:	Ziploc™
Singapore:	Ziploc™
Europe:	Albal aluminum foils and containers, Albal food and garbage bags; Glad aluminum products, plastic film, food and garbage bags

Source: Company records, dated 3/24/90.

[a] Ziploc™ is a trademark of DowBrands. Saran Wrap™ and Handi-Wrap™ are trademarks of the Dow Chemical Company. "Glad" is used under license to DowBrands.

a listing of major DowBrands products sold internationally.)

Division sales for 1990 were forecast at $1 billion, with food care representing about a third of this amount and international sales about 20% Ziploc™ sales at retail were about $300 million and represented about 70% of the division's food-care business. The president and chief executive officer of DowBrands reported to the chairman of the board of DowBrands.

Ziploc™ Storage Bags

With the rise of private automobiles, home refrigerators and freezers, and large supermarkets in the United States after World War II, shopping trips for groceries became less frequent than daily, and the need arose for a way to protect fresh food (and leftovers) from becoming stale and hard. The need was met by aluminum foil, wax paper, and plastic wraps, augmented in 1962 by small plastic bags. The plastic bag (using a thin polyethylene film) was first introduced as a wrap for sandwiches, and it grew in sales at over 15% a year. Dow tried to protect its own plastic-wrap business with the Handi-Wrap™ sandwich bag, but was unsuccessful in coming up with a form and packaging that were competitive. At the same time, the use of plastic bags for large storage (garbage, leaves, and the like) was introduced; this market grew at 10% a year.

In 1966, Dow R&D personnel saw a custom bag with a plastic "zipper" at a trade show; the zipper used a unique technology that allowed the open end of a plastic bag to be closed by gently pressing a plastic ridge on one edge into a plastic track on the opposing edge. Not only did the zipper offer a convenient, reusable closure, but consumers believed it also served to seal out hostile air more thoroughly than traditional twist-tie closures then in use. Dow obtained exclusive rights to the manufacture of zippered bags for grocery-store distribution, but lack of consistent quality led to high consumer returns, and the project was dropped.

Dow continued to work on perfecting the manufacture of zippered bags while looking for untapped applications for nonzippered bags, especially at the premium end of the price spectrum. By 1970, Dow had determined that "unique, leak-proof seal" was a more important benefit to stress to consumers than "convenient/easy-to-use"; in fact, the zipper seal was perceived as *not* easy to use, because beginning the zippering process was not always easy, and determining whether the zipper had "caught" or closed fully enough to make a perfect seal was not always clear. Dow changed the name of the product to Ziploc™ and introduced it nationally in 1972 with heavy advertising to educate consumers about the benefits and use of the zipper system.

A number of favorable elements in the climate helped Ziploc™ sales take off in 1973—increased U.S. disposable income, which reduced the importance of the premium price and a shortage of glass products for food storage and freezing. New positioning for the storage bag included nonfood uses, and in 1975 Ziploc™ storage bags led the market with a 33% share. A Ziploc™ sandwich bag was also introduced in 1975. A premium pricing strategy was effected by (1) offering fewer bags at the same price as competitors' packages while (2) continuing to advertise heavily and consistently to demonstrate zipper-seal benefits. While competitors tended to offer consumer and trade discounts, Dow did neither; it used its advertising to build strong consumer loyalty.

When consumer research revealed that a third of Ziploc™ bags were used in freezers, a bag especially designed for this harsh environment was offered in 1980. A period of high inflation in 1981–1983 led to an advertising theme of cutting high food costs through the use of high-quality storage protection. Consumers still complained about the difficulty of using the zipper, however, and in 1983 a new, wide-track seal was developed. Nevertheless, market research showed that, given products of equal "ease of use," to claim "ultimate in food protection" would still capture more business.

In 1984, continued consumer-behavior research confirmed three distinct uses for Ziploc™: storage (refrigerator and cupboard), lunch bag/box sandwiches, and freezer. In addition, the Ziploc™ positioning was changed to focus on an end benefit of fresh, good-tasting food. The zipper feature was no longer the chief focus, but was used to support the "fresh" promise. Advertisements differentiated the three product types (storage, sandwich, and freezer), and Dom DeLuise was selected as the Ziploc™ spokesperson.[1]

Dow continued to make product improvements and line extensions, including pint-sized freezer bags for single servings, jumbo bags for nonfood use, wide-track zippers on freezer bags, "grip strips" for easier opening on all products, "pleated" bags for easier use, "write-on labels" for freezer bags, and "Microfreez" bags for storing, reheating, and cooking in the microwave oven (which were not successful).

Dow management believed that a consumer "information overload" was forming by the late 1980s (because of the proliferation of new products) that would lead to a "big brand" era. Because consumers had less time or desire to experiment than in the past, this trend would benefit major brands that had established good recall based on dependability and value. Hence, in 1989 Dow advertising began to emphasize Ziploc™'s quality heritage. A new advertisement campaign focused on "put your trust in a Ziploc™ bag," and new package graphics were aimed at improving the product's positioning of high quality.

By 1990, zippered bags had obtained a 70% share of the $600 million U.S. retail storage/freezer/sandwich bag market (60% of 365 million cases). Ziploc™ accounted for about half of the total dollar market (about 40% of the total unit market); it was the seventeenth largest-selling nonfood item in U S. food stores.

---

[1] DeLuise is a well-known television comedian whose ample frame was augmented by his notorious love of good food. Advertisements showing DeLuise peering into a refrigerator, cooing over "my precious little [. . . sausage. . . , . . . coq-au-vin. . . , and the like]" protected by Ziploc were designed to create viewer involvement in a low-salience product.

Competitors were First Brands' Glad bags (about 25% of the total dollar market, split between zippered and regular products), private-label bags (about 20% of the dollar market, roughly split between zippered and regular), and Reynolds Metals' Sure-Seal Zippered Bags and Mobil Oil's twist-tie Baggies, which together accounted for the remainder. First Brands had bought the Glad business from Union Carbide in 1986 and, soon after, introduced a bag with a unique seal that changed colors when the bags had been properly sealed. Despite Reynolds' small share, Dow was watching its Sure-Seal brand carefully, because whereas Ziploc™'s strategy had consistently been to use consumer advertising and promotions with few trade incentives, Reynolds' strategy was apparently to round out its protective-packaging line, rather than make early profits, by offering a parity product with heavy trade and consumer promotion. This strategy yielded Reynolds a price advantage versus Ziploc™ of 30 to 40 cents for a package of 20 quart storage bags. Glad had responded with heavy trade promotions, while Ziploc™ maintained its strategy of heavy advertising, reminding consumers of its premium protection.

By summer 1990, Glad seemed to be maintaining its share, while Sure-Seal had gained 5 share points, mostly from Ziploc™. The group brand manager for Ziploc™ bags, Dawn Miller, responded to this threat by a consumer deal offering "get three for the price of two." Response was great, but Miller was concerned by eventual price erosion of Ziploc™. The possibility of introducing a lower-priced "fighter brand" was rejected, since the slotting allowances of almost $500,000 would reduce the return to an unacceptable level. As Miller said,

Our main task will be to continue improving the product through performance features. However, this is tricky, since the production process is so complex: one small change might affect many other parts of the production process. It is far from a trivial act to tinker with any part of it! Gone is the time when we were the only product on the market, able to establish and hold our premium positioning through advertising alone. Consumers understand our concept well: Ziploc™ is a high-quality, low-volume storage product, almost like a disposable Tupperware, only better, because it seals better while taking up less room.

The challenge is whether we can continue to add value to command a premium price. While we may be the low-cost producer because we can make the bags faster, I wonder whether the large investments required to support our automated factories offsets this advantage. If a price war starts, we will learn fast how far our cost advantage extends! I know that there is a segment for whom quality or price/value is no issue, but I am concerned that this segment is a shrinking one. This is an interesting time to be in this job!

First Brands/Europe Acquisition, 1989

The acquisition of the First Brands/Europe wholly owned subsidiary (FBE) in early 1989 was consistent with DowBrands' strategic plan to increase international sales to $230 million by 1995. The strategic objective was to become a leader in the food-care/disposables (fcd)[2] category in Japan, Latin America, and Europe, with Europe targeted as a priority area.

In assessing world opportunities, the DowBrands strategic planners noted that, because no large plastics or hydrocarbon firms were selling fcds outside the United States, given Ziploc™'s U.S. position, it could be considered the strongest premium fcd brand in the world. Unlike other DowBrands categories, the worldwide fcd market was serviced mostly by small regional manufacturers whose strengths seemed to be more in manufacturing than in marketing; only First Brands/Europe appeared to have built any meaningful multinational business. The planners also based Dow's strong future potential in this category on its superior and protectable technology.

Europe seemed to be especially attractive. Although household expenditures for fcds were just half ($10.62 per household) those of the United States ($20.43), the number of 1987 households in the five countries of France, Italy, Germany, Spain, and the United Kingdom exceeded that of the United States (100 million in Europe versus the United States' 91

---

[2] The term, fcd, as used here covers all nondurable products used to transport, store, freeze, and dispose of food, including foils, wraps, papers, and bags.

million). Moreover, annual fcd growth rate in Europe was attractive (10% compared to 3% in the United States). The leading four competitors held only 30% of the business (versus 70% in the United States).

The premium category was of special interest. It consisted of products that offered the extra benefits of convenience or product strength, such as Ziploc™, drawstring garbage bags, and pleated food bags. Industry experts estimated that these products had high gross margins (50% or better), but that selling expenses were also high (typically 35%). The premium fcd business was estimated to be 36% of all fcd sales dollars in the United States (annual growth was 10%), but it was only a "few millions dollars" in Europe (less than 1% of the fcd market). The gross margin potential differed substantially by country, as did trade margins, as the following table indicated:

	Average Price/ Nielsen Unit ($)	Estimated Average Trade Margin (%)
Germany	1.06	36
United Kingdom	.98	40
France	2.20	27
Italy	1.22	33

Source: Company records.

The DowBrands planners expected such factors as increasing numbers of European homemakers in the work force and the growing penetration of large refrigerators and freezers to push this segment's growth. Appendix A gives selected data on major European markets.

FBE had sales of $96 million in 1988 with pretax profits of $3 million. It marketed a full line of fcds with strong shares in France and Spain (the Albal brand) and in Scandinavia and Belgium (the Glad brand). The Glad brand was sold in all the European countries except Ireland. Over 40% of FBE's business was in France, 30% in Spain and Portugal, and the rest in Germany (private label only), Scandinavia, and the Benelux countries. Of its 312 employees, 200 were in manufacturing and the rest in sales and administration. FBE had a plastic bag and wrap factory in Germany and

an aluminum-rewinding plant in France. Some 54% of its dollar sales were in aluminum foil (the most important fcd in Europe), 14% in garbage bags, 13% in food bags, 8% in plastic wraps, and 11% in other products. Branded sales represented 75% of FBE's total sales.

DowBrands planners summed up their arguments for acquiring First Brands/Europe this way:

The acquisition appeal is due to First Brands' strength in France and Spain, two of DowBrands target markets where we currently have no position. It also has a leading position in food bags and wraps in Scandinavia and Belgium. It is unique in Europe because it has pioneered the premium product segment by introducing both state-of-the-art zippered food bags and drawstring trash bags into France. Together with Domopak [DowBrands' existing operation in Italy] this acquisition would form a potent food care/disposables company, competing for the strongest position in the category in Europe.

(See Appendix B for the planners' detailed comments on FBE's strengths.)

Upon the acquisition of FBE in March 1989, DowBrands created a new position of managing director for Europe, which reported to the vice-president of international. Under the managing director were regional managers for four country subsidiaries, each with a full-functioned organization (Italy, France, Spain, and Germany); the German subsidiary was also responsible for sales organizations in Scandinavia, the Benelux countries, and the United Kingdom. In the managing director's headquarters were the European managers for manufacturing, marketing research and business development, human resources, and so on.

Stewart James

As vice-president and Global Product director, James had responsibility for all DowBrands' businesses abroad. Reporting to him were the general managers of the company's operations in Canada, South America (headquarters in Sao Paulo and a plant in Rio de Janeiro, Brazil), the Pacific Rim (headquarters in Tokyo), and Europe (the former First Brands/Europe companies; headquarters in Germany).

James, 40, came to his job in October 1989 from previous positions in marketing and sales at DowBrands and at a southeastern food manufacturer; his most recent assignment had been vice-president of sales for DowBrands. While he had had no prior experience in international sales, he was perceived by his colleagues as accomplished, aggressive, and well suited to lead DowBrands into the international arena because of his energy and all-consuming desire to succeed.

He made these comments in the most recent DowBrands newsletter:

We're going to do about $235 million this year—that's in excess of 20% of DowBrands overall sales. But I'm not so concerned about that increasing in terms of percentage as I am in terms of the quality of our business. My vision for the future is that we should, given our size, be considered a multinational company and not a global package good company at this time.

My vision is to build critical mass in the top strategic countries. Strategic countries are those countries that have a large concentrated urban population and gross domestic product and have the type of homemakers that can afford to buy our products. . . . For example, Japan, with half the population of the States and more gross per capita income than the United States, is a tremendous opportunity. We must stop thinking of Japan as a $20 million market and then go to Taiwan, Korea and Hong Kong, etc., etc. Instead, we ought to think of Japan as a potential $100 million market 5 years from now and therefore use these other satellite countries to feed that investment. The top strategic countries are the ones that count and the ones that in the long term will enable us to do other things.

FINDINGS FROM CONSUMER RESEARCH ON THE FCD MARKET IN EUROPE

In the fall of 1987, the U.K. office of DowBrands had conducted a set of comparison "awareness and usage" surveys for fcd products in Great Britain, France, and Germany in or-

der to set priorities for the Ziploc™ opportunities in those three countries. (Spain had been eliminated as a possible candidate in an earlier study.) Data were collected regarding the types of uses for fcds, perceptions regarding strengths and weaknesses of the existing

EXHIBIT 2 Extrapolated Number of Monthly Occasions for Total Populations in Each Country[a]

	D	F	GB
Percentage of households represented by survey:	85	92	84
Household universe (millions) represented:	21.9	19.4	17.8
Average number of occasions per month, per household:	**80.9**	48.3	65.6
Extrapolated numbers (millions) of:			
Monthly foodcare occasions for the total household population:	**1,771**	937	1,167
Monthly fcd usage occasions (aluminum, wraps, or bags):	**1,332**	834	1,063
Monthly fcd usage occasions using rigid containers or other materials:	(439)	(103)	(104)

Source: Company records, dated May 1988.

[a] "D" was the international symbol for West Germany, "F" was France, and "GB" was Great Britain.

EXHIBIT 3 FCD Usage Occasions, Weighted Incidence: Shares of the Grand Total Number of Usage Occasions/Month

	Germany %	France %	Great Britain %
Base 100% =	*36,919*	*21,436*	*30,816*
Materials			
Aluminum	23	**56**	30
Wraps	**33**	14	**35**
Bags	17	15	21
Containers	25	11	13
Other	2	4	1
	100	100	100
Destination			
Freezer	19	21	15
Refrigerator	**64**	**62**	33
Kitchen	9	2	6
Oven	1	4	10
MWO	—	1	9
Out of home	7	9	**27**
	100	100	100

Source: Company records, dated May 1988.

Kitchen = out in the open in the kitchen; MWO = microwave oven.

brands of wrappings, and those brands' respective images. About 425 in-depth home interviews conducted in each country asked what had been wrapped (fish, meat, and so on), for where (refrigerator, freezer, and so on), what material was used (aluminum foil, plastic, and so on), and how frequently respondents usually performed such an action (for example, "wrapped fish for the freezer with aluminum foil less than three times a month"). A summary report was issued in May 1988; following are selected findings from that report.

Overall, the extrapolated monthly "fcd occasions" ranged from 1.3 billion in Germany to 1.1 billion in the United Kingdom to 0.8 billion in France. Exhibit 2 gives the extrapolation calculations for this study, Exhibit 3 presents a breakdown by materials and destinations, and Exhibit 4 is a summary graph of destination and materials combined. (The second part of Exhibit 4 compares the usage of bags in these countries with earlier data from the United States.) As shown in Exhibit 5, the 10 most frequently specific uses varied considerably by country.

The researchers clustered respondents psychographically based on their answers to a number of life-style questions. The relative size

EXHIBIT 4   FCD Usage Occasions Summary

Source: Opportunity study, 1987.

Comparison of Destination of Bags in Four Countries[a]

	France	West Germany	Great Britain	United States[b]
Base (usage occasions):	(3,119)	(5,914)	(6,294)	(45,647)
	%	%	%	%
Refrigerator	24	27	18	22
Freezer	**76**	**61**	37	14
Microwave	—	—	1	—
Oven	—	1	1	—
Out of home	—	11	43	63
	100	100	100	100

Source: Company records, dated May 1988.

[a] Europe, 1987; United States, 1984.

[b] U.S. data from diary panel, 1984.

	Germany	France	Great Britain
Base 100% =	36,919	21,436	30,816
Occasions within 10 most frequent in at least two countries	%	%	%
Cheese/refrigerator	**12.7**	**14.7**	7.9
Veg–fruit/refrigerator	**10.4**	6.8	3.2
Raw meat/freezer	4.8	7.7	3.1
Bread–cakes/out house	3.6	2.5	3.1
Veg–fruit/freezer	4.1	4.3	3.6
Raw meat/refrigerator	2.3	8.6	—
Sandwiches/out house	—	4.3	**21.6**
Cooked meat/refrigerator	—	**10.9**	6.3
Leftovers/refrigerator	—	**10.7**	6.0
Other frequent occasions specific to one country			
Deli meat/refrigerator	**18.4**		
Bread–cakes/kitchen	6.1		
Bread–cakes/refrigerator	5.3		
Bread–cakes/freezer	4.5		
Fish/refrigerator		2.6	
Veg–fruit/microwave			3.1
Raw meat/oven			6.9
Total top 10	**72.2**	**73.1**	64.8

Source: Company records, dated May 1988.

of the six clusters for each country and their use of major fcd materials are shown in Exhibit 6.

Respondents were asked to name what material they would have used as an alternative if the material actually used had not been available (the materials were aluminum, plastic wraps, plastic bags, and rigid containers). In France, the biggest "winner" was rigid containers; in Germany, aluminum; and in Great Britain, aluminum. Plastic bags did not show a material "win" in any country. Exhibit 7 details the substitution data within each country.

A test of "satisfaction with each wrap" compared with use revealed that, in France, aluminum foil was highest in use and in satisfaction; in Germany, plastic wrap was highest in use but rigid containers were highest in satisfaction; and in Great Britain, plastic wrap had the highest use but plastic bags had the highest satisfaction, higher than in the other two countries.

In general, homemakers in all three countries displayed average-to-high levels of satisfaction with all materials across the majority of destinations and use occasions. German homemakers tended to be less satisfied with substitutes than those in France and Great Britain. A summary of the three most important material attributes is given in Exhibit 8. A perceptual map of users of each of the fcds in each country is reproduced in Exhibit 9.

Respondents were shown a number of "photoprompts" of the major fcd brands and asked, for a number of image items (for example, "high quality," "good value for money," and so on), which brands were best or worst for that image or feature. In Germany, the Melitta and Frapan brands were positioned closely together at the quality end of the high/low quality spectrum for all fcds; in France, again for all fcds, the Propsac, Handy Bag, Sopalin, and Albal (foil and bags only) brands were perceived as "national brands with high availability"; not surprisingly, the major brands in all countries were associated with "high availability," and retailers' (private) brands were associated with "not available everywhere." In all countries, respondents perceived most positively those brands that they "currently use" and/or the one they designated as the "leading brand." In Great Britain, however, retailers' brands often had a good image, especially with respect to "good value for the money."

In general, the researchers concluded that the greatest opportunity for Ziploc™ in Great Britain was for the sandwich-bag market, but in France and Germany, it was for Ziploc™ freezer bags. They were encouraged that one of the most important fcd attributes discovered for all countries was "airtight closure," a major Ziploc™ selling feature; they also noted the importance given to "keeping food fresh and tasty" and "isolating odors well."

The Decision

James was familiar with the marketing research results, but he felt that they might not provide enough support for launching an aggressive Ziploc™ program in Europe:

As detailed and well executed as it is, the research only shows that there is promise in Europe, espe-

EXHIBIT 6 Usage of Material Types by Cluster Groups

Cluster sizes	NF	EG	HO	OP	EXP	RE
Germany (D)	13	16	16	20	12	23
France (F)	18	15	23	14	16	14
Great Britain (GB)	12	18	38	14	9	9
Aluminum						
D index:	99	47	**118**	91	**128**	**118**
Share:	13	8	19	18	15	**27**
F index:	**123**	**109**	82	77	**130**	80
Share:	**22**	16	19	11	**21**	11
GB index:	76	93	**106**	**104**	**134**	84
Share:	9	17	**40**	15	12	8
Wraps						
D index:	84	84	89	**138**	113	87
Share:	11	13	14	**28**	14	**20**
F index:	83	**103**	113	48	**142**	100
Share:	15	15	**26**	7	**23**	14
GB index:	73	98	84	**125**	113	**159**
Share:	9	18	**32**	18	10	14
Bags						
D index:	46	58	99	**121**	108	**137**
Share:	6	9	16	**24**	13	**32**
F index:	61	69	97	101	**131**	**156**
Share:	11	10	**22**	14	**21**	**22**
GB index:	96	82	96	**113**	60	**178**
Share:	12	15	**36**	16	5	16

Source: Company records, dated May 1988.

An earlier awareness and usage study uncovered six cluster groups based on an analysis of the pattern of respondents' answers. The groups were described as follows:

RE = *Role enhancer:* High positive association with all items relating to home cooking, make own foods, home care, and so on, but negative with "spend most of the day away from home." High awareness and usage of fcd brands. (Not found in Spain.)

EXP = *Experimentalist:* High purchase of recently launched products. Tend to be "away from home most of day." High microwave ownership.

OP = *Own produce preserver:* High scores for freezing produce grown by self or bought directly from producer. Not experimental. High deep freezer ownership.

HO = *Home oriented:* High scores for "home" and "cooking" items. Not necessarily high for "freezing." Tend to be non-working.

EG = *Easy going:* Lowest scores for home-oriented items. Tendency to score low on freezing items. Often spend day away from home. Youngest group.

NF = *Nonfreezing:* Lowest scores on freezing times. May have high home-oriented scores. Low freezer ownership. Older group, lower social class.

The entries following "cluster sizes" show the percentages of each cluster by country (for example, the NF cluster represents 13% of the German sample but 18% of the French sample). An *index* is the ratio of a cluster's share of usage compared to its size (for example, the NF cluster in France uses 22% of aluminum, which, compared with its 18% of the sample, yields an index of 123.)

cially in the large markets of France, Germany, and the United Kingdom. It has the usual defect in that it shows more about what *is* with respect to current products and segments than what *might be* the prospects for an emerging premium segment. The detailed study was not carried out in Spain, since refrigerators tend to be small and freezers nonexistent, and everyday shoppers apparently don't perceive the need for the superior protection of Ziploc™. And, frankly, this is the attitude that some of our people still have about food-shopping habits even in France and Germany. So, you can picture the resistance I am getting from my management in Europe against making the kind of investment spends we will need to do to build the premium segment of zippered bags.

We have to use imagination: we might have done more research in Spain, and we should do it in the rest of Europe, all with an open mind for spotting opportunities. When you ask customers to relate current usage to new ideas, they have great difficulty in doing that. I wonder if the typical A&U [attitude and usage] studies are up to the task. What they do do is to give my European management the wrong kind of ammunition. And these people remind me that we can't expect the same high profit margins abroad that we have here in the States and that start-up expenses will be high. But even with a lower margin in Europe, I still see Ziploc™ improving the overall margin mix after the expenses of the sell-in are absorbed. . . .

How would I go? I need to hammer, hammer, hammer my vision. Perhaps I should set up a "President of Ziploc™" in Europe. The Glad people there are not convinced; with $130 million in sales, they don't need it. They say, "Look how long it took to develop the Ziploc™ business in Canada." I must show them success stories in Europe. That's why we bought Europe, and now it's time to act.

• Exchange of switchings

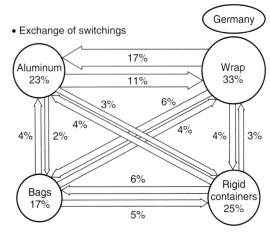

• Result of net gains/losses

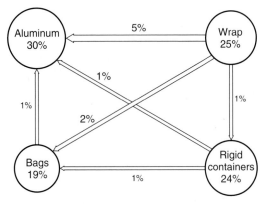

EXHIBIT 7   Substitution between Materials

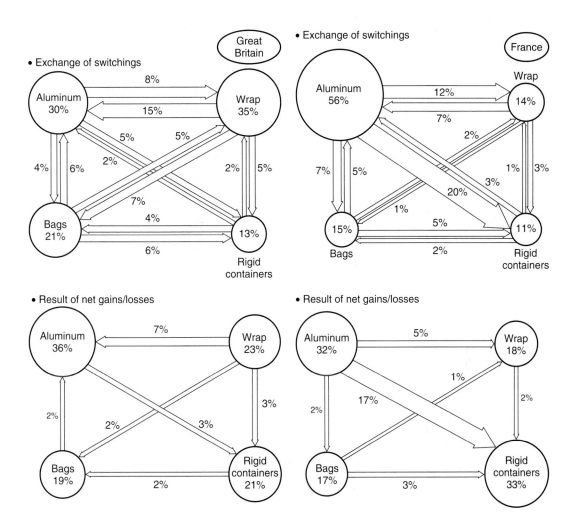

The question was: "If the material you used had not been available when you did that occasion, what would you have used instead?"

EXHIBIT 7 *(Continued)* *Source:* Company records, dated May 1988.

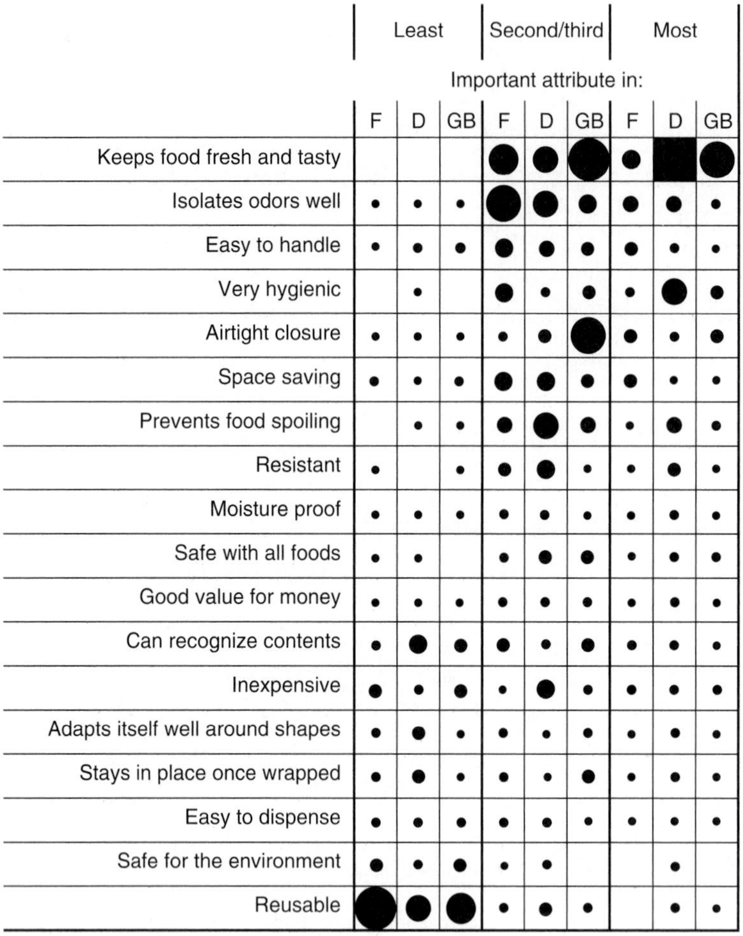

	Least			Second/third			Most		
Important attribute in:	F	D	GB	F	D	GB	F	D	GB
Keeps food fresh and tasty				●	●	●	•	■	●
Isolates odors well	•	•	•	●	●	•	•	•	•
Easy to handle	•	•	•	●	●	•	•	•	•
Very hygienic		•		●	•	•	•	●	•
Airtight closure	•	•	•	•	•	●	•	•	•
Space saving	•	•	•	●	●	•	●	•	•
Prevents food spoiling		•	•	●	●	•	•	●	•
Resistant	•		•	●	●	•	•	●	•
Moisture proof	•	•	•	•	•	•	•	•	•
Safe with all foods	•	•		•	●	•	•	•	•
Good value for money	•	•	•	•	•	•	•	•	•
Can recognize contents	•	●	•	●	•	●	•	•	•
Inexpensive	●	•	•	•	●	•	•	•	•
Adapts itself well around shapes	•	●	•	•	•	•	•	●	•
Stays in place once wrapped	•	●	•	•	•	●	•	•	•
Easy to dispense	•	•	•	•	•	•	•	•	•
Safe for the environment	●	•	●	•	•			●	
Reusable	●	●	●	•	●	•		•	•

The sizes of the circles are relative to "keeps food fresh and tasty" in Germany, which received the greatest percentage response across all questions and countries.

EXHIBIT 8 Importance of FCD Material Attributes in Three European Countries (% for Least, Second/Third, Most Important)[a] *Source:* Company records, dated May 1988.

Images of FCD materials
Analysis of correspondence based on users of aluminum foil (A), plastic wrap (W), plastic food bags (B),
permanent (PC), and disposable (DC) rigid containers in each country
axis 1 (vertical) and 2 (horizontal) variance explained = 86%

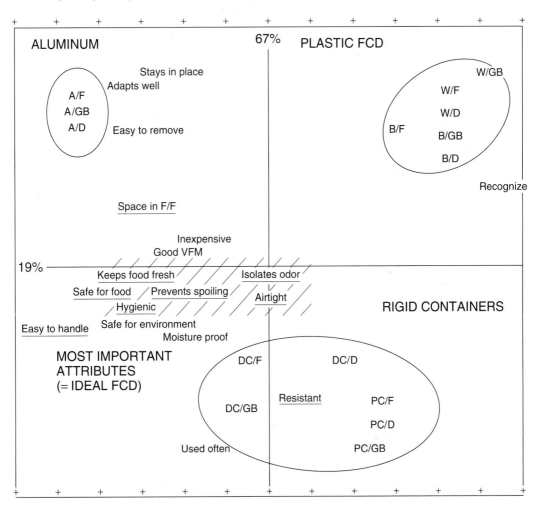

EXHIBIT 9　Images of FCD Materials　*Source:* Company records, dated May 1988.

Selected Data on Major European Markets[a]

Demographic Profiles of the 5 Major European Countries

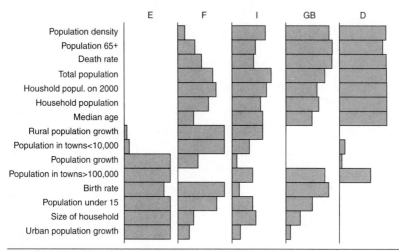

NOTES: – See Definition of Each Indicator in Data Table Below.
– The Graph Above Highlights Differences Among Countries by Using, for Each Indicator, the Minimum and Maximum Values as the Edge of Constant Scale

	E	F	I	GB	D	USA
Population density pers./Km2, 1988	78	102	191	233	246	26
Population 65+ %, 1988	12.6	13.6	14.0	15.5	15.3	12.3
Death rate Deaths per 1,000, 1988	8.3	10.1	9.9	11.8	11.7	8.8
Total population millions	39.2	55.8	57.5	56.9	61.0	248.0
Household popul. in 2000 extimated millions	15.2	23.8	23.1	22.1	25.8	106.0
Household population millions, 1987	11.7	21.1	20.4	21.2	25.8	90.5
Median age 1988	32.5	34.3	36.2	35.5	38.2	32.4
Rural population growth av. anual 1980-85	−1.7	.2	−.5	−1.8	−1.8	.7
Population in towns<10,000 %	26	50	33	23	26	NA
Population growth Total % change 1986/60	33	19	10	8	9	33
Population in towns>100,000 %	42	16	27	36	33	NA
Birth rate Births per 1,000. 1988, 1988	13.1	13.6	11.0	13.4	10.6	15.3
Population under 15 %, 1988	21.7	20.4	17.7	18.7	14.7	21.5
Size of household av. number of persons	3.76	2.77	3.4	2.72	2.31	2.67
Urban population growth av. annual 1980-85	1.4	.4	.3	.2	.1	.9

SOURCES: – Trends & Opportunities Aboard, 1988 AmericanDemographics Inc. – 'EBM '87', European Basic Data, G.F.K.

[a]"E" is the international symbol for Spain and "I" for Italy.

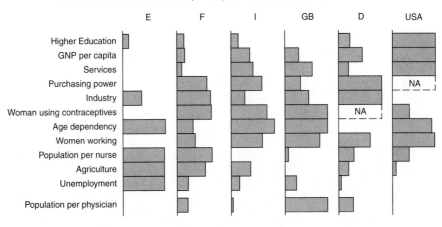

Socioeconomic Profiles of the 5 Major European Countries and the USA

NOTES: –See Definition of Each Indicator in Data Table Below.
  –The Graph Above Highlights Differences Among Countries by Using, for Each Indicator, the Minimum
   and Maximum Values as the Edge of Constant Scale
  –The Indicator Population per Physician is isolated because of the Peculiarity Shown

	E	I	F	GB	D	USA
Higher education enrollment in	26	26	27	20	29	57
GNP per capita $	4,290	6,520	9,540	8,460	10,940	16,690
Services % labor force in	46	48	56	59	50	66
Purchasing power Index, 1986 (100–AV.16 European countries)	57	109	112	86	133	NA
Industry % labor force in	37	41	35	38	44	31
Women using contraceptives Married 15-49	59	76	79	83	NA	68
Age dependency Ratio (# of 0-14 & 65+ & aged 15-64	52	46	52	52	43	51
Women working % women 15-64 working	27	41	53	56	52	62
Population per nurse	280	250	110	120	170	180
Agriculture % labor force in	17	12	9	3	6	4
Unemployment rate, 1985	22.0	10.6	9.9	11.5	7.3	7.1
Population per physician	390	750	460	1,991	420	500

Foodcare Appliances Ownership – 1987
• In the five major European countries • By multiownership groups

Source: Europanel, January '87

Country (Household millions)	D (25.8)	GB (21.2)	F (21.1)	I (20.4)	E (11.7)

% Housewives owning

None of the three appliances	3	2	3		3
Refrigerator only	20	21	26	20	52
Combined refrigerator-freezer only	18	33	30	59	
Separate refrigerator only	49	36	29	9	41
Both types of freezers	10	8	12	12	3 / 1

	D	I	GB	F	E
Separate deep freezer	(59)	(44)	(41)	21	4
Combined refrigerator-freezer	28	(41)	(42)	(71)	(42)
Any freezer	(77)	(77)	(72)	(80)	46

Source: Company records dated April 1988.

France:	First Brands/Europe has a solid No. 2 position in the $300 million French market, the largest food care/disposables market in Europe. And at just under 12% growth over the last 4 years, France is Europe's second fastest growing market. FBE's sales force has done a good job in getting its products onto French supermarket shelves and the consumer awareness of the Albal brand is the best among all fcd brands in France. FBE's French business originated with the acquisition of the Albal trademark from the French national aluminum company in 1985. Following this, FBE added plastic wraps and bags into what was previously an aluminum-based business. FBE's plastics business and its overall share of the French market have grown steadily ever since.
Spain:	Spain's fcd market is $60 million and is the fastest growing European market at over 12% a year. FBE has become increasingly enthusiastic about the growing Spanish market and purchased the operating business from its distributor in October 1988. They are the market leader with Albal in aluminum and with Glad in wraps and bags.
Premium Bags:	FBE launched a zipper-closure food bag in France in late 1987, under the brand name AlbaZip. This product is identical to the colored-zipper Glad Lock product that competes with Ziploc™ in America. This market is still very small, but after only months on the market, AlbaZip has already captured more than half of the premium food bag market. The key competitors, by the way, are utilizing bags with the outdated Mini-Grip-style zipper. Both the Ziploc™ and the Glad Lock closures (used on AlbaZip) are overwhelmingly preferred by the consumer. FBE has also recently launched a premium drawstring trash bag into France called Lock-Up. Premium trash bags represent a promising growth area for us throughout Europe.
Competitors:	There are no dominant leaders across the continent [see table attached]. Only FBE has a major position in more than one country. The significant role played by private labels is evident, especially in the United Kingdom and, to a lesser extent, in France. FBE is a major private label supplier in Germany (and also in France and Spain). Melitta's dominant share in Germany gives it the overall lead in these five markets. When combined with our strong position in Italy, the marriage of FBE and Domopak not only puts us in a solid position in three of the five key Western European markets, but it also positions DowBrands well to compete effectively in Europe 1992.

Source: Company records, dated 11/23/88.

Western Europe Competitive Environment, 1987

France ($306M)	Share (%)	United Kingdom ($281M)	Share (%)	Germany ($245M)	Share (%)	Italy ($163M)	Share (%)	Spain($60M)	Share (%)
Leaders		Leaders		Leaders		Leaders		Leaders	
ELF/Aquitaine (Handy Bag)	22	Polylina	17	Melitta	45	Cuki	22	FBE	37
FBE	12	Br. Alcan	11	Pely	6	Domopak	21	Reynolds	21
Akzo (Propsac)	11	HD. Plastics	3	Kraft	5	Comiset	2		
Private label	36		65		22		N/A		N/A

Share of Total, Five Countries	
Melitta	10.8%
ELF/Aquitaine	6.3
FBE	8.6
Domopak	8.2
Private label	32.7
Total	66.6%

Source: Company records, dated 11/23/88.

M = millions.

2

Challenges in Emerging Markets

Background Terminology

The term *emerging market* is relatively new for international marketers. Historically, we have referred to countries that have not yet reached the economic development of the industrial world as less developed countries (LDCs). Then, in the 1980s the term *developing countries* became increasingly used to signal that, while these countries were not yet of a high level of economic development, they were developing nevertheless and improving their economic status. Those who were more rapidly developing, the economies of the Pacific Basin (Taiwan, Korea, Thailand, and others) were referred to as newly industrialized countries (NICs) to be added to the list of OECD countries, which traditionally consisted of the leading 20 industrial countries in Europe and the United States, and Canada and Japan. *Emerging markets* then increasingly applied to countries who were emerging from the state of lesser development and often making rapid progress toward the status of an industrialized nation.

Definition of Countries

Emerging countries included such countries as India, China, Indonesia, Thailand, Malaysia, Brazil, and Mexico, among others. They typically had per capita incomes of less than US$2,000, but experienced high growth rates that sometimes reached in excess of 10% during the late 1980s and early 1990s. In many statistics, the countries of the former Soviet Union and other Eastern European countries transitioning from command to market economies are also considered part of the emerging market group. However, since the challenges faced in these countries are very different from those faced in countries that operate traditionally with a market and/or mixed economy, we have separated these situations into a different section, which follows this section.

TABLE 1   Emerging Markets

Country	Population (million)	GDP (billion US$)	GDP per capita (US$)
Brazil	153.3	406	2,647
Chile	13.4	37	2,780
China	1,175.0	373	324
India	890	239	289
Indonesia	186.4	123	664
Malaysia	18.6	55	2,946
Mexico	84.1	332	3,957
Pakistan	117.3	46	390
South Korea	43.6	296	6,773
Thailand	59.4	94	1,582

Source: Emerging Market Economies Report 1993; IMD, Lausanne; and World Economic Forum, Geneva *Economist Intelligence Unit* (1993).

MARKETING CHALLENGES IN EMERGING MARKETS

Characteristics of Emerging Markets

Emerging markets are characterized by a high, above-average economic growth rate. This rate of growth for many countries is above 5%, compared to the major industrialized nations with rates of 2% to 3%. For the period 1987–1991, real GDP growth amounted to 11.75% in Thailand, 9.15% in Malaysia, 6.74% in Indonesia, and 5.61% in India.[1] In some areas of China, particularly in the southern provinces located toward Hong Kong, growth rates in excess of 10% have been registered during the early 1990s. Such substantial growth has attracted many international firms. India, a market with a population of almost 1 billion, has become an important market since the combination of population and growth combines to provide formidable long-term potential.

Although these countries still have a per capita GNP of well below $2,000 and therefore have small economies in real terms, even a small gain on a per capita basis translates into substantial economic growth. In 1991, India's GNP of $265 billion was surpassed by Australia ($282 billion) and the Netherlands ($286 billion) and barely exceeded that of Switzerland ($242 billion) and Sweden ($230 billion).[2] While small as overall economies, the real potential of these countries comes from their large population. Emerging countries include some of the most populous countries of the world (see Table 1).

Opportunities

Why then would international marketers be interested in these emerging markets? Clearly, such markets have been hard to enter. Balance of payments restrictions have led many of them to institute programs of import substitution favoring local suppliers. When international firms could not remit profits, many of them shied away from investing. It was therefore not unusual to use licensing as entry strategies for emerging markets. A low level of demand on a per capita basis relegated these countries to second-class status. With the recent global marketing strate-

---

[1] *The World Competitiveness Report 1993*, 13th ed., IMD (Lausanne) and World Economic Forum (Geneva), p. 317
[2] Ibid., p. 310.

gies of many companies, these markets suddenly took on a different role. For many consumer goods firms in basic consumer items such as food, household products, and cosmetics, the large potential volumes could eventually result in a change of the global market priorities. For Gillette, China and India might become two of the most important markets in the next century. This leads such firms to accept a higher level of risk for establishing themselves early in these markets and using this base for future development. International marketers have therefore a strong incentive to learn how to deal with the specific differences and challenges of such emerging markets. One key feature of these markets is the low per capita income levels of their populations. With per capita incomes of typically less than $2,000, marketers from developed economies have to learn how to market to consumers who have only a fraction of the income of consumers in a developed country. Typically, such markets are characterized by a much higher level of price elasticity. What is a necessity in a developed country might be viewed as an elective item in a low-income country. For the populations in emerging markets, more alternatives exist to source products and services outside the regular money economy. As a result, customers make price and value choices not seen in developing countries.

In addition, the trade-offs are frequently made across product categories. A consumer in the United States might be looking for a TV and search for the best buy in several stores. A week later that same consumer might look for a vacuum, and the search process starts all over again. Consumers in emerging markets may treat both TV sets and vacuums as luxury products signaling status. They may therefore make trade-offs across several categories and select from a different set of products. This will affect positioning strategies as consumers compare a product or service with others, as opposed to just within a category.

Just as we have now become sensitive to the differences in price elasticity due to lower income levels, international markets must be constantly reminded that the income distribution in emerging markets is often more skewed than in the developed countries of Europe or North America. Although the average per capita income might signal few opportunities, there are always income segments that can afford even the best and resemble top income groups of the developed markets. Although these segments tend to be small for each country, applied to a large population base they may turn out to be significant enough to explore. Likewise, the burgeoning middle class in countries such as Brazil or India has turned out to be the main beneficiaries of economic growth. Although in many emerging economies no more than some 20% to 30% of total population, as an economic power they equal the purchasing power of smaller developed countries such as Belgium, Sweden, or Denmark.

Comparisons of regular income levels by translating economic data at current exchange rates do not always tell the entire story, however. Many economists prefer to look at the issue in terms of purchasing power parity. While the Indian per capital income is translated from local currency (rupees) into US$, it must be clear to marketers that whatever you can buy with a rupee in India (goods, services, and the like) is more than its exchange rate equivalent spent in the United States. This is due to the fact that emerging economies with low income levels have low wage rates and generally low costs for many business activities. As a result, while the few rupees translated into US$ may not seem to amount to much, they may present a considerable amount of income in India. India has become a center for software development, and engineers might be paid a salary of $5,000 to $7,000. In California, the same engineer might earn 10 times that amount. However, with an annual income of $5,000 in India, an engineer can afford to live comfortably (by Indian standards), have a family, a house, employ servants, and purchase many products and services in India at local prices. If we translated the income data of emerging markets at purchasing power parity, the ranking among the G7 countries (the leading economies making up the seven largest economies and meeting annually as the Group of 7 for their economic summit) would undergo substantial change. Currently made up of the United States, United Kingdom, Japan, Germany, France, Italy, and Canada, the G7 countries would then have to include both China as the third largest economy in the world and India as well.

Marketing Infrastructure

Moving from a developed economy mind-set to an emerging market requires considerable adjustment in terms of expectations for the marketing infrastructure. The infrastructure might include such areas as trade and retail structure, logistics, telecommunications, and support services such as advertising and media structure. Executives dealing with developed markets have become accustomed to a high level of infrastructure, both in terms of what is available and its standard. Engaging in marketing in emerging markets frequently requires substantial differences in what is available. We are not addressing here differences due to culture. Rather, we concentrate on the infrastructure differences that result from different levels of economic development.

The retail structure of the United States and many parts of Western Europe, with its emphasis on large retail chains, discounting, and super stores, is totally absent in such countries as India or China. Here, the small shop dominates, and self-service as we know it in the developed world is largely absent. This requires adaptation in terms of distribution and sales strategy, with generally greater reliance on independent wholesalers. In many markets, the many choices of advertising media ranging from electronic to print are largely nonexistent. Print media is of less importance due to lower literacy rates and the relatively high cost of purchasing print media. Consequently, international marketers will be challenged to adjust their media mix to the specific requirements of such markets. Although the choices and technical sophistication of the marketing support industry (research, advertising, and so on) may not be as developed as elsewhere, we should note that emerging markets have many talented marketing professionals who have achieved considerable experience in the use of marketing concepts. Emerging markets that have had a long tradition of market-driven economies, such as Brazil, Mexico, and India, tend therefore to be more advanced in these fields than a country such as China, where marketing is still a relatively new concept.

Local Competition

In most emerging markets, local companies may offer products competitive with those of international firms. However, because local products are sometimes of a lower level of complexity, international firms tend to disregard these players. Particularly where the local firm has been established and successful for some time, such companies can offer fierce competition to new international entrants. Both India and Brazil are good examples where local firms, with their own special affinity for local consumer requirements, have beaten back the attack of more sophisticated and larger foreign competitors. Established players, both local and foreign owned, also tend to have better connections to government agencies, which are often needed to obtain important requests, licenses, and other permissions. Such contacts with key government officials are sometimes used to prevent foreign entrants from gaining a foothold in a market. All this leads to the conclusion that, although apparently less important or powerful, established local competition needs to be carefully analyzed before a company makes a move.

Political Challenges

Government policies, on both the political and economic front, have a significant impact on the growth path of emerging countries. In many cases, economic growth spurts are the direct result of changed economic policies. One special feature of emerging economies is their more frequent and more radical change in political and economic direction than is the case for the industrialized world.

Growth in China has been a product of liberalization and opening toward market forces that started in the 1980s. Chinese economic power was significantly shaped by the import policies of its government and by the extent to which foreign firms were allowed to open their own operations. These economic policies and the direction of the country were suddenly questioned following the Tiannamen Square protests. To this day, there is considerable debate among observers as to what the Chinese government would do if caught between an overheated economy and the need for political change. Whether or not China will eventually reach the status of one of the largest economies in the world in the early part of the next century depends largely on such political decisions.

Other countries, too, have seen changes in government policies that affected growth. India's economy started to take off following rapid liberalization of imports in the late 1980s. Brazil turned itself around and moved from almost complete import control to free trade, thus changing the dynamics of its economy. Similarly, Mexico completely changed its approach to its economic policies in the late 1980s and, together with Chile and Argentina, began to improve rapidly economically. However, the risk of sudden political changes remains, and may suddenly turn an "emerging" country into the opposite. Likewise, some presently languishing countries might become the sudden growth market of the next decade as a result of changes in economic policies.

Summary

The following cases in this section are meant to challenge students to deal with the particular difficulties of emerging markets. They take us to India, where at issue is the launch of a Wilkinson razor blade on license and the competition from locally made blades. Wiltech India, the Wilkinson licensee, is challenged with finding a successful marketing formula for the introduction of its new line of blades. The case on P.T. Food Specialties takes us to Indonesia, where this subsidiary of a large MNC is confronted with the sudden prohibition of TV advertising. Since this was the company's most powerful selling tool, the entire marketing strategy needs to be changed to reflect sudden new circumstances. Finally, in the case of Ericsson do Brasil, we are in the situation of the Brazilian subsidiary of a Swedish firm considering the re-launch of a new paging technology and the selection of the appropriate target segment.

Wiltech India Limited

In August 1983, Malay Chadha and Suresh Metha,[1] general manager and marketing manager of Wiltech shaving products, were reviewing the preceding year's sales. Wiltech had introduced a complete line of five products in July 1982 and had succeeded in associating the Wiltech name with the quality image and reputation of Wilkinson Sword. However, actual sales had been far below target figures, and the low sales volume contrasted poorly to industry-wide sales of Rs1,850 million versus Wiltech's Rs27 million.[2] Therefore, Chadha and Metha had to consider what changes in Wiltech's marketing program could increase sales to the desired level. Such changes would require a complete review of Wiltech's pricing, advertising, and distribution strategies. Wiltech needed to improve the near-term situation, while also considering its long-term goal to become India's market leader in shaving products. In addition, an established multinational competitor was planning new plant construction.

Suresh Metha felt that prices could be maintained if Wiltech introduced one new blade and positioned its existing five brands more effectively. Malay Chadha, on the other hand, believed that Wiltech had focused too much on India's wealthier segments and that prices should be adjusted. Chadha also saw that ex-port opportunities existed and strongly favored trading with the Soviet Union. A detailed plan had to be ready in 1 week for presentation to the board. Despite this deadline, Chadha and Metha were unable after 2 days to agree on what Wiltech's problems were and how to correct them. High humidity and record temperatures did not help spirits as the two resumed their discussion.

WILTECH BACKGROUND

In 1979, Wilkinson Sword, the U.K. shaving systems company, entered into a licensing agreement to expand its international presence into India. Wiltech, for Wilkinson technology, was funded by Asian Cables Corporation Limited and the government-owned Karnataka State Industrial Investment Development Corporation. Equity participation was shared among Asian Cables 25%, the state government 26%, and the public 49%. The licensing agreement required Wilkinson to construct a manufacturing facility in Belagola, 100 miles from the central Wiltech office in Bangalore, Karnataka (see Exhibit 1). Wiltech's licensing terms included the following payments to Wilkinson:

1. £130,000[3] for design, drawings, and documentation

---

[1] Pseudonyms.

[2] 10 Rupees (Rs) = $1 in 1983.

[3] £0.66 = $1.

This case was prepared by Robert Howard under the direction of Jean-Pierre Jeannet, Visiting Professor at IMEDE and Professor of Marketing and International Business at Babson College, Wellesley, MA, USA. This case was prepared for class discussion rather than to illustrate either effective or ineffective handling of an administrative situation. This case was based upon earlier work by Sameer Kaji, MBA candidate at Babson College. Copyright © 1988 by IMEDE, Lausanne, Switzerland. The International Institute for Management Development (IMD), resulting from the merger between IMEDE, Lausanne, and IMI, Geneva, acquires and retains all rights. Not to be used or reproduced without permission from IMD, Lausanne, Switzerland.

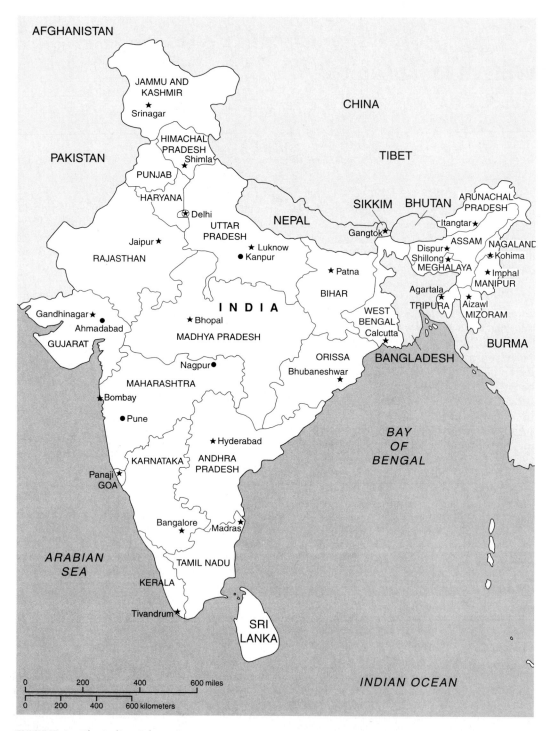

EXHIBIT 1 The Indian Subcontinent

2. £260,000 for plant installation and commissioning

3. From the start of commercial production, a 2% royalty on all products sold up to 5 years or £175,000, whichever came first

Wilkinson paid a tax of 20% to the Indian government on items 1 and 2 in three installments. A gratis time commitment of 7,840 worker-hours by Wilkinson engineers was also included in this payment plan. Moreover, to ensure continued interest in the project, Wilkinson's chief executive and technical director were appointed to Wiltech's board of directors.

Wilkinson's Role in Shaving History

Wilkinson Sword was founded by Henry Nock in 1772 to manufacture personal and military defense weapons. Nock and his partner, James Wilkinson, emphasized close tolerances, quality control, and innovation in the design of their products. This attention to detail led to being appointed gun and sword-makers for British royalty, an honor that has continued to the present day. Henry Wilkinson, son of James, took full control of the business in 1825 and, in 1898, the company extended Wilkinson's image as a maker of quality steel cutting edges from swords to razor blades. Starting with the Pall Mall safety razor, Wilkinson maintained its position as a leader in shaving comfort and technology and pioneered several shaving breakthroughs.

One of Wilkinson's more recent innovations was the use of stainless steel. Double-edged carbon steel blades had been the industry norm until Wilkinson introduced its double-edged stainless steel blades in 1956. Wilkinson developed their stainless steel blades further by coating them with Teflon and introduced these to the marketplace in 1961. A combination of product quality and a 2-year lead time allowed Wilkinson to increase its U.K. market share from 7% to 45%, with similar gains in other countries. In 1970, Wilkinson championed another first in shaving technology when it launched its bonded shaving system. The bonded shaving system, which contained a single blade permanently fixed inside a cartridge, was available throughout the world by the end of 1974. And, in 1976, Wilkinson introduced its adjustable twin-blade cartridge system, similar to the Gillette Trac II.

THE INDIAN MARKET

India in Transition

After gaining political independence from Britain in 1947, India attempted a series of centrally planned economic programs. From 1950 onward, however, the rate of economic expansion continued to remain only 1.5% ahead of the rate of population growth. Attempts to speed up India's growth rate began in the 1970s when forces emerged calling for reforms to move the country away from the planning process by freeing the private sector, reducing the dominance of the public sector, and liberalizing import policy insofar as it restricted the importation of new technologies.

Indira Gandhi accelerated these efforts to attract foreign investment and raise the standard of living. Attempts to attract foreign business did not, however, include relaxing the laws on foreign ownership. India's leaders were concerned about foreign exchange shortages and, as a result, preferred to encourage the production of import substitutes and licensing arrangements with foreign firms. Although Wilkinson Sword was the first to negotiate such a licensing arrangement in the shaving industry, it was inevitable that other multinational competitors would soon follow.

Such firms were attracted to the Indian shaving market for a number of reasons, one of which was its potential size. In 1981, India's population was estimated at 685 million and was expected to reach 844 million by 1990 and 994 million by 2000. This population was slow to urbanize by western standards, and only 23% of the country resided in urban areas. Within this group of 156 million urban dwellers, 42 million (27%) lived in India's 12 metropolitan cities (see Exhibit 2). India's youth represented a disproportionate amount of the total population, with 40% of the coun-

EXHIBIT 2   Distribution and Growth of India's Population[a]

	1981	1971	1961	1951	1901
Number of towns	3,245	2,636	2,421	2,890	1,851
Urban population (millions)	156.2	109.1	78.9	62.4	25.9
Urban as % of total population	23.3	19.9	18.0	17.3	10.8
Percent of Towns					
Class I (Includes metro. cities[b])	6.7	5.6	4.3	2.6	1.4
Class II	8.3	6.9	5.4	3.3	2.3
Class III	22.8	22.1	19.0	11.6	7.4
Class IV	32.3	33.1	30.8	21.8	21.4
Class V	22.9	25.7	31.5	40.0	40.9
Class VI	7.1	6.5	9.1	20.6	26.7
Total	100.0	100.0	100.0	100.0	100.0
Percent of Urban Population in:					
Class I	60.4	55.8	50.2	43.4	25.8
Class II	11.7	11.3	11.1	10.4	10.8
Class III	14.4	16.3	17.5	16.0	16.0
Class IV	9.5	11.3	13.0	14.0	20.9
Class V	3.6	4.7	7.3	13.1	20.2
Class VI	0.5	0.5	0.9	3.2	6.3
Total	100.0	100.0	100.0	100.0	100.0

Source: Statistical Outline of India 1986–1987, pp 32, 46. Tata Services Limited, Department of Economics and Statistics, Bombay House, Bombay, India, 400 001.

[a] The definition of *urban* adopted in the 1981 census, as in the previous two censuses, was as follows:

  (a) All statutory towns with a Municipal Corporation, Municipal Board, Cantonment Board or Notified Town Area, or the like.

  (b) All other places with (i) a minimum population of 5,000, (ii) at least 75% of male working population engaged in nonagricultural and allied activity, and (iii) a density of population of at least 400 per square kilometer (1,000 per square mile).

An urban agglomeration is defined as one consisting of one or more towns, including in some cases villages or parts of a village that can be considered as urbanized and contiguous to the town or towns concerned. Urban agglomeration has been treated as a single unit. Class I towns (called cities) are those with a population of 100,000 and above; class II: 50,000 to 99,999; class III: 20,000 to 49,999; class IV: 10,000 to 19,999; class V: 5,000 to 9,999; and class VI: less than 5,000.

All figures for 1981, except the all-India urban ratio (23.3%) excludes Assam and Jammu and Kashmir.

[b] Metropolitan cities have populations of 1,000,000 or more and include Calcutta, Bombay, Delhi, Madras, Bangalore, Hyderabad, Ahmedabad, Kanpur, Pune, Nagpur, Lucknow, and Jaipur.

try under the age of 15 and only 9% of the country 55 or older (see Exhibit 3).

Exacting descriptions of Indian society by income level were not available. Instead, the Center for Monitoring the Indian Economy classified Indian society into approximate income groups according to five-member families (see Exhibit 4). Beyond an urban versus rural reference, information in Exhibit 4 did not indicate how India's consumer wealth was distributed countrywide. These data were available on a per capita income basis for each of India's states (see Exhibit 5).

In addition to a tremendous diversity in population and income distribution, there were 15 major languages, 1,650 dialects, and several religions spread throughout India's 25 states and union territories. This diversity made it difficult to come up with any one best description of an "average" consumer in the shaving market. There was sufficient evidence, however, to indicate that the majority of Indian males shaved each day and that it was considered a prerequisite prior to beginning the day's activities. Those who did not shave were considered unclean and were un-

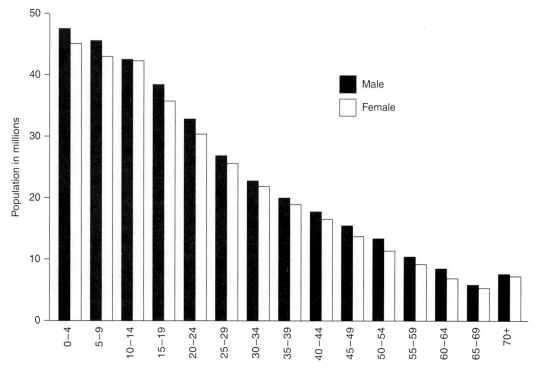

EXHIBIT 3 Age Distribution of India's Population

able to participate in religious practices or other daily activities. The research also revealed that consumers were dissatisfied with India's current shaving products, yet were unaware of alternatives.

The government expansion of agricultural and social programs as well as the more liberal industrial policies created enthusiasm for investment as India entered the mid-1980s. Hence, with the indications that consumers were ready for alternative shaving products, Wiltech saw an excellent chance to secure a place in the Indian market.

The Indian Shaving Market

Worldwide, shaving markets were classified into wet and dry segments; the dry segment corresponded to electric and cordless razors, the wet segment, to a variety of razors and blades. In India, the dry shaving market was insignificant and most males used wet shaving products. Razors and blades in India

could be further classified by the type of steel used: carbon or stainless. Wiltech had two types of stainless steel products: (1) double-edged blades with a cutting edge on each side, and (2) twin blades where two blades were carefully positioned above each other in a cartridge. The term *shaving system* referred to blades packaged and purchased in conjunction with a razor.

Segmentation

In the shaving industry, market size, sales volume, and market share were typically described in terms of blades sold. After 1961, stainless steel blades became the industry standard worldwide. In India, however, the market transition from carbon steel to stainless steel did not begin until the mid-1970s and by 1983 was still not complete.

In 1983, the value of the entire Indian razor blade market was Rs439 million, three-quarters from stainless steel and the balance from

EXHIBIT 4   Structure of Indian Society

Position	Group	Annual Income per Five-member Family	Education	Standard of Living
Top 1%: Ruling elites living in larger cities	(a) Big owners of all types of business and property (land, factories, trading, transport, contracting, and broking) (b) Leaders of central, state, and local governments, cooperatives, and ruling parties; most members of central and state legislatures (c) Top leaders of large national or metropolitan trade unions	>Rs500,000	Varies	Opulent; conspicuous consumers
Next 4%: Supporting power elite living in cities	(a) Medium owners of business and property and very rich farmers (b) Second-rank political leaders of ruling parties and first-rank leaders of opposition parties (c) Top bureaucrats and technocrats at all levels of government (d) Top executives in large public- and private-sector business units (e) More affluent self-employed professionals (doctors, lawyers, etc.)	Rs100,000–500,000	Generally well educated (tertiary level)	Fairly affluent; good apartments, furnishings, cars, TVs, telephones, sound systems, other durables
Next 5%: Relatively prosperous by Indian standards; living in urban areas	(a) Small property owners and rich farmers (b) Petty bureaucrats, junior and medium business executives, and other supervisory cadre (c) Workers and employees organized in unions (d) Second-rank leaders of large trade unions (e) Less affluent self-employed (f) Others in "middle class"	Rs15,000–100,000	Generally well educated	Generally good housing, moderately furnished, some durables
Next 10%: Above average by Indian standards; living in urban areas	(a) Upper-middle farmers (b) Owners of very small business and property (c) Supervisory and lower staff in unorganized business (d) Others regarded as lower middle class	Rs10,000–15,000	Poorly educated but literate	Barely tolerable housing and furnishing; some durables
Next 30%: Barely above poverty line; living in towns and large villages	(a) Middle farmers (b) Lowest layers of employees in unorganized sector (c) Lowest layer of self-employed (d) Urban people in low-paid jobs	Rs6,000–10,000	Half literate; other half illiterate	Level of poverty visible to visitors
Last 50%: Below poverty line; living in villages	(a) Poor farmers (b) Irregularly employed, underemployed, and unemployed (c) Tribals and scheduled castes (d) Landless agricultural laborers	<Rs6,000	Illiterate	Abject poverty, bare subsistence

Source: INDIA: Limited Avenues to an Unlimited Market, pp 14, 15. Business International, 1985.

Note: Indications and figures are approximate and indicate only broad magnitudes. Incomes include fringe benefits, open and hidden perquisites, and black-market income. Farmers generally live in villages, but some have been grouped with the urban population for simplification of presentation.

EXHIBIT 5   1983–1984 Per Capita Income by State (rupees)

State	Per Capita Income
Andhra Pradesh	1,955
Assam	1,762
Bihar	1,174
Gujarat	2,795
Haryana	3,147
Himachal Pradesh	2,230
Jammu and Kashmir	1,820
Karnataka	1,957
Kerala	1,761
Madhya Pradesh	1,636
Maharashtra	3,032
Manipur	1,673
Orissa	1,339[a]
Punjab	3,691
Rajasthan	1,881
Tamil Nadu	1,827
Tripura	1,206[b]
Uttar Pradesh	1,567
West Bengal	2,231
Delhi	3,928
Goa, Daman, and Diu	3,479
Pondicherry	3,693

Source: Statistical Outline of India 1986–1987, p. 22. Tata Services Limited, Department of Economics and Statistics, Bombay House, Bombay, India, 400 001.

Note: Owing to differences in source material used, the figures for different states are not strictly comparable.

[a] 1982–1983.

[b] 1980–1981.

carbon steel blades. Of a total 1,434 million blades sold, stainless steel blades accounted for 67% and carbon steel 33%. These two blade segments were also classified demographically, urban versus rural (see Exhibit 6), with urban consumers classified further according to town class (see Exhibit 7).

EXHIBIT 6   Urban versus Rural Blade Consumption in India (millions of blades)

Area	Blade Type		
	Stainless Steel	Carbon Steel	Total
Urban	672.7	130.3	803
Rural	288.3	342.7	631
Total	961.0	473.0	1434

Source: Company records.

COMPETITION IN THE INDIAN RAZOR BLADE MARKET

Malhotra Group

The Harbanslal Malhotra Group of companies was formed in the late 1940s after India achieved its independence. In 1954 the government of India banned imports of several consumer goods to preserve scarce foreign exchange reserves. Razor blades were thus prohibited from legally entering the country, which gave the Malhotra Group a near monopoly. In the subsequent three decades, the Malhotra Group enjoyed substantial gains in market share and was virtually unchallenged until Wiltech entered the scene.

Malhotra's product lines consisted of four different double-edged blades and three shaving system products. Malhotra's biggest seller was the Topaz brand. Although the Topaz was made of local steel, it was Malhotra's popular blade. Aimed at users in cities and smaller towns, Topaz was priced at 45 paise[4] per blade and sold in packs of five. Malhotra also had slightly less expensive blades, each of which sold in packs of five. Their respective names and prices were Silver Prince at 35 paise, Ashok at 30 paise, and Panama at 30 paise. Malhotra had a near-perfect monopoly with its three shaving systems, Ashok, Gallant, and SuperMax, all priced in the Rs7 to 12 category.

Malhotra's product line was able to meet the diverse needs of the entire Indian shaving market, urban and rural, as well as the carbon and stainless steel segments. This diverse market was reached by the Malhotra Group's 300 salesmen and 1,000 stockists (distributors). Malhotra maintained strong market awareness with a unique promotion strategy, sponsoring a variety of sporting events and musical concerts aimed at Indians in the 25 to 40 age group. The combination of a broad product line, an aggressive pricing policy, a promotion level three to four times that of Wiltech, and a long time presence in the Indian shaving market contributed to Malhotra's 82% market share and its image as a leader in the Indian market.

---

[4] 1 rupee = 100 paise.

EXHIBIT 7 Urban Blade Consumption by Town Class
Distribution (millions of blades)

	Blade Type		
Town Class	Stainless Steel	Carbon Steel	Total
Metropolitan	193.3	23.4	216.7
Class I	229.8	35.2	265.0
Class II	90.2	16.9	107.1
Class III	82.3	24.8	107.1
Class IV	77.1	30.0	107.1
Total	672.7	130.3	803.0

Source: Company records.

Centron and Erasmic

Aside from Malhotra, the only other significant participants in India's razor market were Centron and Erasmic. Both firms made only blades and, hence, depended on Malhotra and black-market shaving systems for the sale of their blades. Centron was a small manufacturer who concentrated sales in India's eastern region. Centron offered two blades in the 60 to 65 paise category: the Super Swish and the Centwin, both in packs of five. In the 1970s, Centron was acquired by Brooke Bond, a large multinational that marketed tea all over the country. Although Centron's operations concentrated on a limited region, Brooke Bond had an extensive, national distribution network that Wiltech management expected would be used countrywide to attack the razor market. Erasmic was another domestic manufacturer, but marketed its blades primarily in Northern India. Erasmic's blades were priced at 45 paise for packs of five.

Black-market Blades

Blades sold on the black market were either Wilkinson or Gillette and typically cost 70 paise to Rs1 each. Gillette International marketed the majority of Gillette's products abroad and was Wilkinson's most serious competitor in the worldwide shaving market. Gillette knew that Indian consumers were willing to buy its shaving products on the black market and therefore welcomed an opportunity to enter the Indian marketplace legally. India's improved political and economic climate motivated Gillette management to establish a joint venture with Poddar of Calcutta. Gillette planned to manufacture its products by 1986 and, despite being a few years behind Wiltech, would use its full resources to secure a share of India's market.

Each competitor sought to differentiate itself from the others to protect their respective markets. One result of this differentiation was a wide range in razor blade prices. (The range of prices and product segments are summarized in a brand positioning chart in Exhibit 8.)

MARKETING PRACTICES IN INDIA

India's Distribution Channels

After leaving a factory, blades in India were shipped to and temporarily stored at company-owned depots. Depots were usually located in one or more states in such a way as to minimize interstate sales. Intrastate sales were preferred because of differing tax rates among India's states.

India's vast size affected physical distribution. Unlike North America or Europe, India did not have retail distribution chains organized at the national level; instead, outlets would receive merchandise from the nearest depot. Because it was difficult to handle many towns from a single point, each town would have a stockist to supply the town's retailers. Stockists, of which there were an estimated 25,000 in India, received their shipments from a nearby depot after conversing with a salesman. Stockists' stores typically averaged only 500 square feet, but they played an important

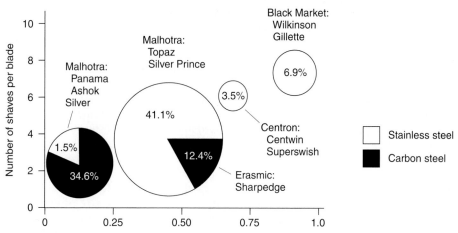

Shaving Systems		Price (Rs)
Malhotra:	Ashok (razor + 2 twin blades)	7.00
	Gallant (razor + 2 twin blades)	10.00
	Gallant (razor + 2 twin blades)	12.00
	SuperMax (5 twin blades)	5.00

EXHIBIT 8 Pre Wiltech Brand Positioning of Razor Blades in India
Source: Company records.

role in the distribution process. These distributors served as wholesalers in India, granting credit and stocking the consumer products their retail customers requested.

Retail outlets also played a major role in India's distribution system. Large retail outlets (such as grocery stores, general stores, and pharmacists) averaged 175 square feet and sold items consumed on a daily basis. Each large retail outlet usually had two to three salesmen in addition to the owner.

Small retail outlets were so limited in space that they had virtually no shelf space for razor blade display, nor could they carry any inventory. Because of these space limitations, a retailer never purchased case lots, only individual units of usually less than Rs100 in value. Small retail outlets were far more numerous than their larger competitors and could be found on almost every street corner, even in residential areas. These small retail outlets also sold items consumed on a daily basis, but their limited space often required re-

peated same-day sales calls in areas with heavy sales, furthering the need for local stockists. Because of limited display space, the consumer could not usually see any blades and would simply ask for a package of blades, allowing the retailer to make the brand decision. To guarantee brand sales, it was customary in India to provide retailers with incentives such as cash or gifts (for example, imported Scotch) at festival times or as an end-of-year bonus. (For a distribution flow chart and 1983 data on blades sold through urban outlets, see Exhibits 9 and 10.)

Advertising in the Subcontinent

Media options for advertising in India consisted of TV, radio, cinema, print, and outdoor. Traditionally, TV advertising had not been used as heavily as in the West. However, this practice began to change over the last decade as incoming multinationals and other large companies responded to the rising num-

EXHIBIT 9 Flow Chart of Wiltech Distribution Channels
Source: Company records

ber of TV viewers. The advent of TV advertising in India had, in fact, redefined the rules of consumer marketing. The success of products like Maggi, Vicco, Rasna, and Niki Tasha were attributed to TV promotion. For most consumer products, TV, cinema, and magazine advertising was preferred because it could project creative and colorful messages.

Statistics for TV ownership were not available for smaller towns, but it was estimated that one TV per 30 individuals was available in larger cities such as Bombay, Delhi, Calcutta, Bangalore, and Madras. Although the single, government-owned TV channel broadcasted only in the late evening and at night, it reached 70% of India's population. Broadcasting began at 6 P.M. with the regional telecast via regional stations and was followed by a national broadcast from 8 to 11 P.M., which usually included advertiser-sponsored programs.

Advertising was only permitted before and after the news or program. Advertisements during the local broadcast were normally in the local language, whereas those aired on the national broadcast were in Hindi or English. The Sunday feature film at 6 P.M. and televised sporting events were the most popular advertising spots. For satisfactory exposure, most firms purchased 30-second TV spots at Rs7,000 to 10,000, which they ran for a 3-month period.

EXHIBIT 10 Volume of Razor Blades Sold through Urban Outlets (millions of blades)

| Outlet | Blade Type | | |
	Stainless Steel	Carbon Steel	Total
Groceries	262.4	58.8	321.2
General stores	228.7	36.3	265.0
Other	174.9	33.9	208.8
Drugstores	6.7	1.3	8.0
Total	672.7	130.3	803.0

Source: Company records.

Television advertisements could also be used in cinemas. Advertisements were aired before the film and during the 10-minute intermission. Cinema is India's most popular form of entertainment, with approximately 11,000 theaters and an industry producing around 800 films a year. The cost of cinema advertising varied from town to town and within towns from locality to locality. Countrywide, costs could be as low as Rs25 per week or as high as Rs1,000 per week, with Rs300 per week considered average in urban markets. The shaving industry considered TV and cinema to be the most effective media for advertising because the entire shaving process could be visualized with audio reinforcement of the message.

Unlike TV, access to radio was more evenly dispersed throughout the country, reaching 87% of the population. In 1983, there was one radio for every eight individuals in India. The one national and several regional radio stations were all government owned. Advertisements from the national station were given in Hindi, the national language, whereas the local stations advertised in the local language. On average, radio spots lasted 30 seconds and cost Rs1,000 to 1,500 per slot, depending on the time of day. Although radio reached a larger population than TV, it was not widely used by the shaving industry as it lacked a visual message.

Print media in India, various newspapers as well as 20 to 25 magazines, reached a total of 54 million people countrywide. These media were considered important in a campaign's introductory phase, but were not frequently continued, due to limited audiovisual capacity, after consumers had reached a certain level of awareness. A full-page advertisement in a daily with a circulation of 200,000 copies per day would cost between Rs10,000 and 15,000 per day. Magazines were read frequently and had a circulation of 20,000 to 100,000 copies per month. The cost of a single full-page advertisement varied between Rs25,000 and 50,000, depending on the magazine and the advertisement's placement.

Outdoor advertising in India included billboards and posters at bus stops, on the outside of buses, on overhead foot bridges, on the doors and sides of retail shops, and on the external walls of buildings and compounds. Like newspapers, outdoor advertising tended to be used for special promotion campaigns or during the introductory phase of a new product. The cost of an average outdoor advertising campaign was Rs30,000 per month.

WILTECH'S COMPETITIVE POSITION

The Wiltech Product Line

All Wiltech blades had the traditional Wilkinson "gothic arch" shape, which enhanced blade strength and extended blade life by about 40% over normal blades. After the rough "gothic arch" production step, Wiltech blades were sharpened, smoothed, and coated with Teflon. To ensure product continuity between the United Kingdom and India, Wiltech maintained strict quality control (QC) checks at each of its operations. Random samples from every lot were sent to Wilkinson in the United Kingdom for inspection. Each QC report through the middle of 1983 confirmed that Wiltech's products were meeting international standards. And, typical of many shaving products, Wiltech blades fit any brand of handle, both Indian and foreign.

Savage was Wiltech's premium blade, with the same quality as imported Wilkinson blades due to a triple coating of chromium nitride, ceramic, and Teflon applied in the last stage of manufacturing. This coating gave each blade a 100% greater life than the regular Teflon-coated blades. Savage's packaging was also superior to Wiltech's other blades. Savage blades were wrapped in specially treated rustproof paper that had a dab of petroleum jelly on each corner to hold the blades firmly in place.

Each pack contained five blades plus a top card that served both as a label and to give instructions on blade use. A purchase reminder card was placed between the fourth and fifth blades, and each pack was wrapped in polystyrene and then cellophane before being shipped. A package of five Savage blades cost Rs4.90.

Wiltedge, with the same specifications as all Wilkinson blades, was marketed as Wiltech's most popular brand. Wiltedge had only Teflon coating and its packaging was less elaborate than Savage's. Wiltedge blades had both an inner and outer wrapper and were packed in a cardboard tuck. A package of five Wiltedge blades cost Rs3.00.

Wilzor was India's only scientifically designed two-piece razor and came with separable handle and shaving head. The shaving head contained double-edged blades adjusted to the optimum shaving angle. Alone, the Wilzor razor cost Rs13.10.

Wilman II represented Wilkinson's fixed twin-blade shaving system. The Wilman was the only twin-blade shaving product manufactured in India and had coatings of chromium, ceramic and Teflon. Designed with a lightweight, heat-resistant holder and two blades adjusted at a precise angle, the Wilman II was the newest shaving concept. Wilman II was offered as a system or a gift pack, both with two twin cartridges, and sold for Rs13.60 and Rs28.40, respectively. Wilman II refill packs of five twin blades were also available for Rs14.50.

Wiltessa was another first in the Indian shaving market, the only ladies' shaving system. The Wiltessa received the same process treatment as Wilman II and was specially designed for women's shaving needs. The Wiltessa was made of pink plastic and sold with two twin cartridges for Rs15.20.

Positioning the Wiltech Product Line

In 1982, Wiltech management felt that the superior quality of its products justified charging premium prices. As a result, Malay Chadha and Suresh Metha agreed to price Wiltech's line higher than the competition. Given India's market characteristics and the level of

Wiltech's manufacturing technology, management decided to focus on stainless steel blades in the urban market. Within the urban market, management selected a target audience of males over 16 years old earning more than Rs1,000 per month. To win this audience, Chadha and Metha selected Savage and Wiltedge, the two brands felt to offer the greatest potential. Savage was promoted as Wiltech's premium blade and aimed at those using black-market blades and dissatisfied users of India's own premium blades. Wiltedge promotion was aimed at consumers of India's popular blades, offering higher satisfaction as well as a chance to upgrade to a higher-quality product.

Wiltech's managers believed that a low awareness level of blade alternatives meant heavy promotion. Consequently, from May 1982 to March 1983 Wiltech spent Rs7,653,000 on advertising and promotion, scaling back in April 1983 when they felt initial brand awareness had been achieved. Press expenditures included six English magazines with nationwide coverage at a cost of Rs50,000 per magazine. Four regional magazines with local language were also used at a cost of Rs25,000 per magazine. The English magazines had a circulation of up to 100,000 versus the regional magazines with a circulation of about 60,000 each.

Advertising Expenditures (Rs in 000s)

	May 1982– March 1983	Proposed April 1983 –March 1984
Cinema screening	773	1,546
TV screening	238	987
Press	5,224	1,110
Others	416	285
Hoarding	436	616
Film production costs	171	—
TV production costs	37	—
Radio production costs	—	155
POP costs (leaflets, posters)	358	828
Total	7,653	5,527

The Wiltech Distribution Network

To minimize the risk of product introduction, Wiltech test marketed its line with apparent success in Bangalore, Bombay, and New Delhi. Because these cities were considered representative of countrywide market behavior, Wiltech felt encouraged and decided to pursue countrywide distribution. Wiltech's 15 depots throughout India housed stock on a transitory basis; the eight primary depots received stock directly from the plant, whereas the seven secondary depots received their stock from the nearest regional office or from a primary depot.

In addition to Wiltech's central office in Bangalore, the company had regional offices in New Delhi, Bombay, and Calcutta. Each office had a regional manager with 3 area sales managers, 6 sales supervisors, and 27 salesmen. Each Wiltech salesman was responsible for a particular territory and was paid a fixed salary of Rs800 to 1,200 per month. Additional incentives existed for meeting monthly target volume, market trends, competitive activities, and stock availability. For successfully meeting targets, salesmen received a Rs350 monthly bonus and for meeting quarterly targets, a bonus of Rs500.

Salesmen had to ensure that the orders of Wiltech's 600 stockists and all retailers were met and that posters portraying the company's products were distributed to retail outlets. In metropolitan areas, a salesman handled one stockist and 600 to 700 retail outlets. Stockists were visited daily and retailers twice a month. Salesmen covering smaller towns handled an average of 10 to 12 stockists and 800 to 1,000 retail outlets. These stockists were visited once or twice a month. With stockists earning 7% and retailers 15%, Wiltech faithfully provided its distribution channels with standard operating margins. Classifying stockists and retailers as outlets, Wiltech's 81 salesmen reached 70,000 of India's 500,000 outlets by August 1983. Sales staff salaries, allowances, and touring expenses accounted for 50 to 60% of Wiltech's marketing expenditures, excluding advertising and promotion.

OPTIONS FOR WILTECH INDIA

Price Reduction with New Advertising

Wiltech had anticipated a volume of 3 to 4 million blades per month for Savage and 4 to

5 million for Wiltedge, but actual sales were only 1 million and 700,000 blades per month, respectively. Since each of Wiltech's brands was priced above the competition, Chadha felt that the pricing policy had caused the lower than expected sales volume. He therefore proposed reducing prices along with a new communication policy.

If the Savage and Wiltedge, priced at Rs 1 and 60 paise per blade, respectively, were each lowered by 10 paise, they should be more competitive with black-market blades at Rs0.7 to 1 and the 45-paise Topaz blade from Malhotra. Furthermore, if Wiltech did choose the price reduction strategy, Chadha felt that the company should reposition Wiltedge as a mass blade, which would require a new communication strategy. Having established Wiltech as a blade manufacturer of international standards, Chadha believed that a new advertising campaign should concentrate on product awareness rather than product quality.

Entry into the Rural Sector

Suresh Metha, on the other hand, felt that Wiltech needed more sales in India's rural sector, with consumers far from cities and modern telecommunications. Metha was aware that this segment, comprised primarily of farmers, provided half of India's market share and used mostly carbon steel blades in the 20- to 35-paise range. Unless Wiltech introduced a blade in the same price range, it could only sell brands priced about twice as high as rural customers were paying. To succeed with existing brands in this segment would require an educational campaign that demonstrated that (1) stainless steel blades were more comfortable than carbon steel, and (2) Wiltech's blades, which were twice as expensive, could give at least twice as many shaves as Malhotra's Ashok, Panama, or Silver Prince blades.

India as an Export Base

In addition to taking corrective action for Wiltech's domestic strategy, Chadha wanted to review the advantages of using India as an export base to the USSR and the Middle East. India's diplomatic relations with these countries had led to several successful commercial opportunities over the years; in 1981–1982, access to the Soviet market accounted for 19.3% of all Indian exports. Consumer goods were particularly important, because the USSR purchased 83% of India's cosmetics and detergent exports and 45% of India's coffee exports. Their bilateral trade agreement provided India with Soviet crude oil and capital equipment. The biggest advantage was that neither had to pay with scarce hard currency; trade was conducted in Indian rupees, with rupee surpluses or deficits carried into the following year.

As an incentive to preserve scarce foreign exchange earnings, the Indian government granted tax breaks to firms committing production to exports. In 1982–1983, Wiltech's exports were only 2% to 3% of total sales, but yielded a tax break of Rs47,000. The size of this tax break would be substantially larger if export volume were increased. Chadha did not foresee a problem in capacity utilization if domestic demand continued to be lower than originally expected.

Capacity Utilization

Actual Production (millions of units)	Installed Capacity (millions of units)	
Double-edged blades	28.2	100
Shaving systems and twin-blade units	5.4	20
Razor handles	0.8	5
Two-piece systems	0.2	0.25

Wiltech could continue to use the market channels originally developed by Asian Cables Corporation, which had provided its 2% to 3% export base. However, if Chadha decided to boost exports, he would have to increase contacts with foreign trade organizations in the USSR and attend exhibitions where contact with the right officials could be made. The Soviet reputation on negotiating was the only drawback to this option that Chadha could see. The Soviets could offer margins of 5% to 6%, but had been known to offer as little as 1% to 2% on certain products. On the other hand, Soviet central planners always placed bulk orders for an entire year. Success in the USSR and the Middle East would certainly be noted at Wilkinson headquarters in England. Market achievements in these regions would fit in with Wilkinson's worldwide perspective and could lead to a substantial career move for Chadha.

After two days, Chadha and Metha had little time left to work out Wiltech's strategy for fiscal 1984, but were still unable to identify the key issues and how they should be handled. They had to consider Gillette's anticipated 1986 market entry and how to respond if Malhotra used its standard tactic of flooding the marketplace with shaving products via product-line expansion. Another concern was Centron's acquisition by Brooke Bond, a large multinational, clearly indicating that yet another international competitor with vast resources was targeting the Indian shaving market. All these factors reinforced the need for Wiltech to make the right moves and to do so in a timely manner.

P.T. Food Specialties, Indonesia (FSI)

On Tuesday morning, January 21, 1981, Ian Souter, marketing manager of FSI, was congratulating himself on having gotten an early start, as the Jakarta traffic seemed even worse than normal. He had allowed himself some extra time in order to prepare the agenda for a 10 o'clock meeting with his staff. On the way to the office he asked the driver to turn on the radio in order to catch the beginning of the English language news. One block from the office he was reeling with shock as he learned that the Indonesian government was banning all TV advertising as of April 1, 1981. As the car pulled into his parking space, it occurred to him that his entire organization, his marketing strategies and campaigns, and his own job structure had become obsolete in one single day.

P.T. FOOD SPECIALTIES (FSI)

FSI was owned jointly by Nestle S.A., a large multinational food products company, and a group of Indonesian investors. Nestle S.A. had been founded in Vevey, Switzerland, in 1867 by Henri Nestle as a small producer of milk products. In 1905, it merged with the Anglo-Swiss Condensed Milk Co. Between 1905 and 1980, this merged unit expanded rapidly, becoming Switzerland's largest multinational company and the largest company in the food industry in the world. In 1905, Nestle already had 80 factories, 300 sales offices, and 12 subsidiaries worldwide. By 1980, the Nestle group produced revenues of almost Sfr. 24.5 billion through its sales offices and factories in more than 100 countries worldwide. Prior to 1972, Nestle operated under the name Indonepro Distributors, Inc., as the importer and distributor of Nestle's products to Indonesia. In 1972, it began operating as a manufacturer and marketer of food products. It had discontinued its distribution operations after the introduction of an Indonesian law that restricted distribution activities to companies that were wholly owned by Indonesians. Since 1972, FSI had lost the right to sell its products directly to retailers or consumers.

In 1981, FSI produced and marketed six products in Indonesia. The most important of these was Milkmaid Sweetened Condensed Milk. Introduced in 1972 after a long history of importation, Milk Maid accounted for roughly 40% of FSI's annual turnover. It was perhaps the least profitable of its six products. The Indonesian sweetened condensed milk market was both very large and competitive. It was dominated by three large organizations, Frisian Flag (with 50% of the market), Indo Milk, in conjunction with the Australian Dairy Board (with 34% of the market), and FSI (with 15% of the market. A 14-ounce can of Milkmaid had a selling price of approximately 400 rupiah in 1981.[1]

---

[1] In 1981, 300 rupiah = Sfr. 1.00; 625 rupiah = $1.00.

This case was prepared by Barbara Priovolos, research associate, under the direction of Visiting Professor Jean-Pierre Jeannet for purposes of class discussion only. Copyright © 1982 by IMEDE, Lausanne, Switzerland. The International Institute for Management Development (IMD), resulting from the merger between IMEDE, Lausanne, and IMI, Geneva, acquires and retains all rights. Not to be used or reproduced without written permission from IMD, Lausanne, Switzerland.

Dancow powdered milk had also been introduced in 1972. It was sold in two forms, regular and instant. In 1981, Dancow accounted for approximately 30% of FSI's total revenue. It was also one of FSI's most profitable products. The Indonesian powdered milk market was dominated by two large organizations. FSI had a 45% market share, and Frisian Flag had a 52% market share. The balance of the market was held by several imported brands. A 454-gram package (about 1 pound) of Dancow regular carried a suggested retail price of 1,200 rupiah in 1981.

In 1978, FSI had introduced two infant cereals into Indonesia. Neither of these products was to be used as breast milk substitutes. Cerelac contained powdered milk, whereas Nestum did not. These had become two of FSI's most profitable products and accounted for approximately 10% of FSI's annual revenue. The infant cereal market was fairly small, but FSI controlled almost 63% of it. The balance of the branded cereals were supplied largely by one local producer, P. T. Sari Husada, whose brand SNM had a 31% share of the market. All other brands, most of them imported, shared the remaining 6% of the market. Homemade cereals were very popular, and although few firm data were available on the subject, FSI executives believed that the vast majority of the children's cereal consumed in Indonesia was homemade. A 400-gram box of Cerelac and a 250-gram box of Nestum had 1981 retail prices of 1,000 and 750 rupiah, respectively.

Milo, a chocolate-malted powder that was mixed with milk to produce a high-energy drink, accounted for 8% of FSI's revenue. It was a moderately profitable product that had been introduced in 1974. The market for Milo was thought to be fairly small. It consisted primarily of children who used Milo as a "growing up" high-nutrition drink and sports-conscious adults who used it as a high-energy drink. FSI had approximately 45% of this market segment. It shared the market with the Ovaltine brand, which had a 47% market share and the Malcoa brand, which had an 8% market share. In 1981, the retail price for Milo was 100 rupiah for a 350-gram box.

PRODUCT DISTRIBUTION

Products found their way from the factory to the consumer's cupboard through a rather intricate series of distributors and wholesalers. SFI itself had only two customers. It sold all its output to one of two main distributors, a Chinese–Indonesian company, and a Pribumi, or native Indonesian, company. These two main distributors sold FSI's products to subdistributors or to agents for subdistributors. The approximately 45 subdistributors then sold the products to wholesalers or directly to small shops. As a result, FSI's products changed hands a minimum of four times and often as many as six times on their way from the factory to the consumer. See Exhibit 1 for a diagram of this distribution network.

FSI suggested price levels for both the retail and the wholesale outlets and paid for, although did not arrange, product transportation from the factory to the retailer. It also employed marketing personnel who served as advisors to the subdistributors and the retailers. Twenty area supervisors advised the subdistributors with regard to stock hygiene, merchandising, and promotional activities. They also trained subdistributor sales personnel to set up in-store displays, point-of-sale selling materials, and on-the-shelf product arrangement for maximum consumer impact. This type of support was considered by FSI executives as crucial. Many Indonesian retailers saw little difference between having a product in the store and making a product available to, or even attractive to, the customer. Many retailers ordered products that were left in cartons behind desks, in storage rooms, or in similar areas well out of reach of the consumer. This marketing support was also consistent with the marketing advice of businessmen based in Indonesia who believed that personalized attention was an effective marketing tool in Indonesia.

In most cases, the subdistributors were grateful for the help provided by the area supervisors. Some conflicts of interest did occasionally occur. The subdistributors had a short-term view of business. They were generally most interested in products that were currently selling in large volumes. The area supervisor was inter-

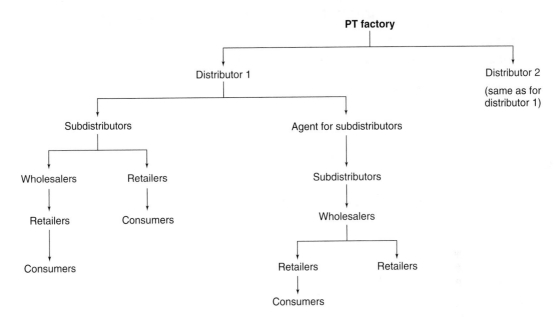

EXHIBIT 1 Product Distribution

ested in marketing every product and in building the market for new products, thus ensuring that the FSI brand was associated with goodwill and confidence in the mind of the extremely brand loyal Indonesian consumer. See Exhibit 2 for retail distribution data for FSI's products and its competitors' products.

The FSI marketing office also included one national sales coordinator to whom all the area supervisors reported and one product executive for each FSI product group. The product executives were responsible for developing and implementing supplemental promotional activities for their products, both trade oriented and consumer oriented, and for monitoring their products in the Indonesian market. See Exhibit 3 for the FSI marketing department organization chart.

THE INDONESIAN BUSINESS CLIMATE

In 1981 Indonesia was the fifth largest country in the world in terms of population, behind China, India, the USSR, and the United States. Its 150 million people lived on approximately 6,000 of the roughly 13,000 islands that, straddling 5,000 km (3,000 miles) of the equator, made up Indonesia. It was a country of uncharted jungles and densely populated cities. Twenty percent of all Indonesians were city dwellers and two-thirds of them lived on the islands of Java, Madura, and Bali. These islands contained only 7% of Indonesia's land mass and were among the most densely populated areas on earth. Indonesia's capital city of Jakarta was home to 7 million people. See Exhibit 4 for a map of Indonesia.

The Indonesian people were of more than 300 different ethnic groups, most of them of Malaysian origin. More than 90% of the population were followers of Islam, giving Indonesia the world's largest Moslem population. Although more than 300 languages and dialects were in regional use, the national language of Bahasa Indonesia was believed to be understood by all but the most remote village dwellers.

Indonesia had been under Dutch colonial rule for almost 300 years prior to its occupation by the Japanese between 1942 and 1945. In 1945, two days after the surrender of the Japanese, Indonesia made a unilateral declaration of independence. In 1949, the Netherlands un-

EXHIBIT 2   Retail Distribution for P.T.

Milkmaid:	Distribution largely urban
	80% of supermarkets, 16% of independent shops, 20% of bazaar shops stock product
	Sweetened condensed milk as a product category sells:
	0.5% Volume through supermarkets
	30% Volume through independent shops
	70.5% Volume through bazaar shops

Dancow: Distribution largely urban

	Standard	Instant	
Supermarkets	97%	90%	} stock product
Independent shops	15%	10%	
Bazaar shops	30%	20%	

Full-cream powdered milk as a product category sells:
2% Volume through supermarkets
35% Volume through independent shops
63% Volume through bazaar shops

Cerelac/Nestum: Exclusively urban distribution

	Cerelac	Nestum	
Supermarkets	95%	94%	} stock product
Independent shops	10%	10%	
Bazaar shops	20%	27%	

Milo: Exclusively urban distribution with concentration
in five or six main towns
98% of supermarkets
12% of independent shops
37% of bazaar shops stock product
Tonic food beverages sell:
5% Volume through supermarkets
32% Volume through independent shops
64% Volume through bazaar shops

Competition to Milkmaid

Frisian Flag: 91% of supermarkets
60% of independent shops   } stock product
60% of bazaar shops

Indomilk: 91% of supermarkets
31% of independent shops   } stock product
39% of bazaar shops

Respective market shares:

Frisian Flag	50%
Indomilk	34%
Milkmaid	16%

Competition to Dancow

Frisian Flag Standard: 97% of supermarkets
27% of independent shops   } stock product
46% of bazaar shops

Frisian Flag Instant: 98% of supermarkets
14% of independent shops   } stock product
22% of bazaar shops

Respective market shares:

Dancow Standard	27%
Dancow Instant	18.3%
Frisian Flag Standard	43.2%
Frisian Flag Instant	8.6%

EXHIBIT 2 *(Continued)*

Competition to Nestum/Cerelac

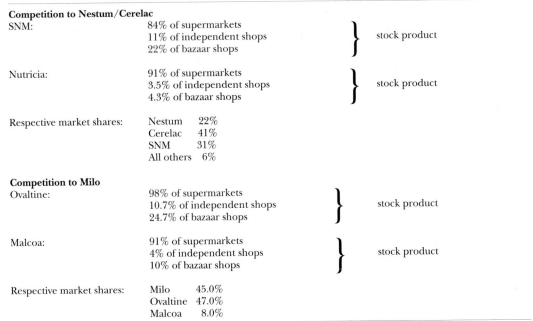

SNM:	84% of supermarkets 11% of independent shops 22% of bazaar shops	} stock product
Nutricia:	91% of supermarkets 3.5% of independent shops 4.3% of bazaar shops	} stock product
Respective market shares:	Nestum 22% Cerelac 41% SNM 31% All others 6%	

Competition to Milo

Ovaltine:	98% of supermarkets 10.7% of independent shops 24.7% of bazaar shops	} stock product
Malcoa:	91% of supermarkets 4% of independent shops 10% of bazaar shops	} stock product
Respective market shares:	Milo 45.0% Ovaltine 47.0% Malcoa 8.0%	

conditionally recognized the sovereignty of Indonesia. The political climate of Indonesia was stable. Its president, Suharto, had been in power since 1965. Although he was considered by many to be slow in initiating reforms that would stimulate economic growth, his leadership had been credited with reducing inflation from over 200% in the mid 1960s to under 10% in 1981, opening up Indonesia to some private and foreign investment, reducing the rate of its population growth, and bringing the country to the brink of self-sufficiency in rice production, after having been the world's largest rice importer for many years. Indonesia was a

EXHIBIT 3 Marketing Department

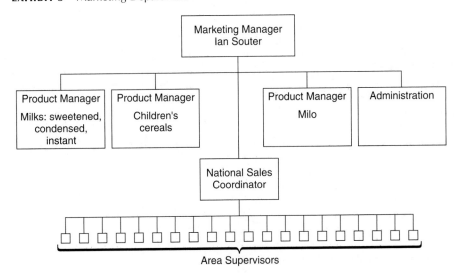

Area Supervisors

EXHIBIT 4 Map of Indonesia

country very rich in natural resources, but with a very poor population. It was a country that was deeply preindustrial, but one with a pocket of high-technology industries.

Indonesia was a member of OPEC and the largest oil producer in Southeast Asia. It had proven reserves of 14 billion barrels and an estimated 50 billion barrels of reserves yet to be officially confirmed. Oil export earnings accounted for 75% of its foreign income in 1981. Oil was not the only important natural resource in Indonesia. Indonesia was the world's second largest producer of liquified natural gas and the largest producer of tin. It also produced significant quantities of bauxite, nickel, coal, iron, manganese, gold, silver, copper, phosphates, and sulfur. Nevertheless, the Indonesian economy was primarily agricultural. Agriculture, forestry, and fishing employed two-thirds of the Indonesian labor force and accounted for almost one-third of GNP. Small farms produced food for domestic consumption, as well as natural rubber, coffee, pepper, and tobacco for export. Large plantations, holdovers from its colonial days, produced Indonesia's most important agricultural exports: timber, rubber, coffee, tea, palm oil, and sugar.

The Indonesian manufacturing sector was very small, accounting for less than 5% of exports and only 7% of GNP. The trading sector of the economy, wholesale and retail, accounted

for approximately 16% of the GNP and was dominated by Indonesia's Chinese minority. Until 1965, Indonesia's 5 million Chinese had had a virtual monopoly of business and manufacturing activities within the country, and their influence in 1981 was still considerable.

In 1981, Indonesia had at least US$ 10 billion in hard currency reserves that did not benefit the economy due to an underdeveloped banking and financial services sector. Poverty was acute in Indonesia, and many of its income statistics were misleading. Although the per capita income was about $370 per year, the concentration of wealth was such that certain economists estimated that 40% of the population existed on less than $90 per year.

The Indonesian population could be classified into five separate economic classes in terms of disposable household income,[2] as follows:

Economic Segment	Percentage of Population (%)	Monthly Disposable Income (in rupiah)
A	3–5	100,000
B	13–18	75,000–100,000
C	25–30	50,000–75,000
D	29–30	30,000–50,000
E	34	30,000

[2] Each household contained approximately seven people. This classification was based on the best estimates of foreign businesspeople operating in Indonesia during 1981.

FSI'S MARKETING MIX

As marketing manager, Ian Souter had generally emphasized developing customized campaigns for each of FSI's six products. The campaign budgets were divided between "above the line" mass media activities and "below the line" consumer promotion and trade promotion activities. In line with Nestle and FSI company policy, which called for mass media promotion in order to build long-term brand loyalty and confidence in their products, 60% to 90% of a campaign's budget was spent on mass media advertising. FSI executives felt that price promotions produced customers who only used the product while it was selling for the reduced price. These customers were likely to change brands again as soon as other manufacturers lowered their own prices. See Exhibit 5 for media spending data, Exhibit 6 for media cost data, and Exhibit 7 for some magazine advertisement samples.

Mr. Souter felt that the 1980 Milkmaid campaign had been especially important. Mr. Souter had, in an effort to increase market share, attempted to reposition Milkmaid from a "growing up" childrens' drink to an "energy" drink for all ages. In 1980, FSI had for the first time created its own TV campaign for Milkmaid, rather than adopting a campaign that had been developed by the Nestle subsidiaries in Malaysia or the Philippines. This change in direction was seen by Mr. Souter as very important. Developing his own campaign had been both a lengthy and at times frustrating process. However, it had given him the ability to adapt his campaign to the Indonesian market by using Indonesian actors, actresses, and locations.

All FSI's advertisements required approval by the Nestle home office staff in Switzerland. In addition, working with the relatively inexperienced Indonesian film and creative personnel was frustrating even at the best of times. Thus the process of creating an Indonesian campaign required almost 6 months versus the 2 to 3 months that were required when already approved Malaysian or Philippine ads were adapted for use in Indonesia.

Dancow powdered milk was promoted in two versions. The instant version received 90% of the promotional funds. Dancow instant, or "the 4-second milk," had been the first locally produced instant milk in Indonesia. It had been a huge success. The instant form had, since its introduction, been advertised on TV and in women's magazines. Because the brand name was the same for both the instant and standard varieties, it was believed that the standard form also benefited from the advertisements for the instant form. The ad budget for the standard form was used for newspaper and cinema slide advertisements.

FSI's two infant cereals were both mass marketed and promoted to the medical profession with the help of samples and literature. Cerelac, the milk-based cereal, had been introduced using TV ads that had been developed in Malaysia. This reliance on Malaysian TV advertisements had continued, as had the product's success in the marketplace. Nestum, a nonmilk cereal, had been introduced with magazine advertisements and had experienced very moderate initial sales. In mid-1979, a TV campaign for Nestum was introduced, and sales increased dramatically. The TV campaign and the impressive sales results had both continued throughout 1980.

Milo was advertised primarily on television, with some backup advertisements in women's magazines and children's comic books. It was also the only FSI product advertised in outdoor media. At selected sports events, Milo had been advertised using A-boards (wooden signs placed back to back to form an A shape) around the entrance area to the event. Occasionally, these A-boards had also been used along parade routes.

TELEVISION ADVERTISING IN INDONESIA

Mr. Souter believed that

There is no substitute for television. Without television my job, the job of marketing these products, would be nearly impossible, and the job of introducing a new product would be entirely impossible. There is no other marketing tool in Indonesia that can ever come close to reaching exactly my market with exactly my message, the message that FSI prod-

EXHIBIT 5   Media Spending per Product, 1979 to 1981 (planned)

Media: Product	TV	Radio	Newspaper	Magazine	Cinema	Outdoor (form and amount)	Trade promotion (form and amount)	Consumer promotion (form and amount)	Total
				1979 *in million rupiah*					
Sweetened condensed milk	40.55	7.73	—	7.66	0.01	—	0.60	—	56.55
Dancow instant	37.43	—	0.83	17.04	—	—	0.85	—	56.15
Dancow standard	22.46	—	8.69	—	11.90	—	0.52	—	43.57
Nestam	29.82	—	—	—	—	—	—	3.87	33.69
Cerelac	42.97	—	—	—	—	—	—	3.59	46.56
Milo	33.07	—	—	—	—	2.00	0.07	0.45	35.59
Total	206.30	7.73	9.52	24.70	11.91	2.00	2.04	7.91	272.11
				1980 *in million rupiah*					
Sweetened condensed milk	65.14	12.91	—	12.23	0.03	—	0.50	0.07	90.88
Dancow instant	65.71	—	—	26.82	—	—	0.77	—	93.30
Dancow standard	36.97	—	13.19	—	11.40	—	0.65	—	62.21
Nestam	72.90	—	—	—	—	—	0.11	2.40	75.41
Cerelac	51.73	—	—	—	—	—	0.11	2.24	54.08
Milo	90.82	—	6.29	21.21	—	0.24	2.79	2.04	123.39
Total	383.27	12.91	19.48	60.26	11.43	0.24	4.93	6.75	499.27
				1981 (planned as of January 20, 1981) *in million rupiah*					
Sweetened condensed milk	120.0	20.1	—	17.6	2.3	—	18.0	3.0	181.0
Dancow instant	124.0	—	—	66.0	—	—	13.0	30.0	233.0
Dancow standard	50.0	—	—	38.8	11.2	—	18.0	4.0	122.0
Nestam	91.0	—	—	29.0	—	—	5.5	5.5	131.0
Cerelac	90.0	—	—	—	—	—	5.5	6.0	101.5
Milo	120.0	—	—	30.0	—	—	20.0	28.0	198.0
Total	595.0	20.1	—	181.4	13.5	—	80.0	76.5	966.5

ucts are consistently high quality products, products that one ought to use.

There were approximately 2 million television sets in Indonesia in 1981. They could tune into one government-owned network, Televisi Republik, Indonesia (TVRI). Television advertisements were carried during two blocks per day, as well as before, during, and at the end of programs or sports events that the advertiser himself had sponsored. The early evening advertising block, from 5:30 to 6:00, was for regionally based commercials. The late evening block, from 9:00 to 9:30, was immediately before the late evening news break and carried national advertisements.

Some Western businesspeople operating in Indonesia believed that television advertising in Indonesia, thanks to a happy and rare coincidence of business need and cultural forces

EXHIBIT 6 January 20, 1981 Media Costs: Development and Production, In Thousand Rupiah

Media	Cost to Develop One Spot	Cost to Broadcast One Spot
TV		476.7[a] / 75.7[b]
Radio	287.0	2.0 / 0.05
Newspaper	102.0	217.3 / 52.1
Magazine	2,300.0	1,358.9

[a] Prime time or urban.

[b] Not prime time or regional

Outdoor Media	Fixed Investment/Unit[a]
A-Boards	20,000[b] / 15,000
Billboards	25,000[c] / 15,000
Footbridges	140,000

[a] All quotes include taxes and annual maintenance

[b] In stadium/outside.

[c] Strategic location/ordinary.

working together, pleased just about everyone. Indonesia's television audience seemed to eagerly await the televised signals that one of the twice daily commercial breaks was about to begin. Cartoon-type drawings of consumer product packages bearing generic names such as coffee, soap, or milk lined up on the screen and a butterfly flew into view to alight briefly on several packages, as if to select them for its own use. Many marketing executives felt that the television appearance of a commercial product was as appealing to the Indonesian consumer as those packages were to that butterfly. To the Indonesian consumer it was the sign that the product was of high quality, dependable, "real," and deserving of their confidence and trust.

Although firm statistics on television viewership did not exist, FSI executives believed that Indonesia's 2 million television sets were located almost entirely in urban areas. Beginning in the late 1970s, the Indonesian government supported a program to put a television set in every village for educational purposes.

The number of sets involved in this program was never made clear. FSI executives also estimated that 11% of the televisions were in use during the early evening advertising break and that 24% were in use during the late evening advertising break. They were not sure who was watching. They felt that during the early break it was primarily children and domestic household help. Mr. Souter continued:

I can control television advertising. I know, roughly, who sees it, and when they see it, I know what they see and I can judge how they interpret it because the visuals are so powerful. I can produce a TV campaign 1,000 times more efficiently than any other mass media campaign. Or, for that matter, any other marketing or promotion effort whatsoever. That is not to say that producing a TV campaign is easy. It's not! But other campaigns are much more difficult to create—and much, much, much more difficult to implement.

When a television campaign was employed for a FSI product, it was used to create the themes that were repeated and reflected by advertisements in other media. Mr. Souter believed that every product's ad campaign needed to be cohesive and self-reinforcing. To ensure this, he always developed TV campaigns first and then designed the radio, magazine, cinema, outdoor, and point of sale advertisements to reinforce and support the initially designed television message.

Not only FSI, but all its competitors as well, felt that television advertising was the most important factor in a product's marketing success. Competition for the 40- to 60-second advertising spots was breathtaking. Advertising spots were distributed by the government bureaucracy specifically charged with this mission. Simply filing a request for a spot entailed making one's way around an obstacle course of problems that governmental bureaucrats throughout the world seemed so skilled in designing. At this point, simple arithmetic brought the real scope of this situation into focus. FSI's experience, which they believed to be similar to that of most other advertisers as well, was that roughly one in every ten requests was granted. On average, FSI was granted three national and five regional spots per month. To in-

EXHIBIT 7   Ad Sample for Milkmaid for Growth

crease their television presence, FSI sponsored each year 8 to 10 nationally televised series, 12 to 15 nationally televised sports events, and several regionally televised programs.

Television campaigns were also costly. One hundred million rupiah per year per product was required for an effective television campaign. Each regional spot cost about 300,000 rupiah to broadcast, and each national spot cost about 750,000 rupiah to broadcast. In addition, the production costs for one spot, in both a 60- and 40-second version, were about 10 million rupiah.

Two phrases highlighted both the advantages television advertising provided for a mar-keting manager operating in Indonesia in 1981 and the relative disadvantages of other media forms and promotional efforts: "ability to control" and "not labor intensive."

The production and broadcast of a television ad required the management and cooperation of a small team of professionals. Production required more people than might have been required in a country with a more experienced television establishment. However, one could identify fairly easily who was needed and what they needed to do. Similarly, to broadcast an advertisement was not a difficult task. Once permission had been granted, the result was available for all to see and to

EXHIBIT 7 (*Continued*)   Ad Sample for Cerelac, a Nutritious Product for Your Baby

monitor. In addition to the ability to self-monitor a TV campaign, both TVRI and the advertising agencies provided certificates of broadcast for each broadcasted spot.

INDONESIA'S OTHER MASS MEDIA

Radio networks, in contrast to television, were operated only regionally. One government-owned station serviced major cities, and many private stations served both cities and rural areas. The radio networks were characterized by their variety in format, location, and language. A radio campaign with national coverage cost 40 to 50 million rupiah and required the participation of 70 to 80 different radio stations. Local radio spots were arranged through local advertising agents. Neither the station nor the agents provided certificates to confirm that the ad had actually been broadcast. It was extremely difficult for FSI head office person-

EXHIBIT 7 (*Continued*)   Ad Sample for Nestum

nel to ensure or confirm that the radio ads that they had paid for had been aired.

Obtaining the translations for the regional stations posed another problem when using radio advertisements. According to Mr. Souter, "no two Indonesians will ever agree on an exact translation." The translation of only three advertisements into three dialects had recently required "months and months" to complete.

The Indonesian radio population was believed to be many times that of its TV population, so, theoretically at least, radio could have had as much, if not more, penetration value as TV.

Radio advertising could be booked throughout the day. The times most in demand, though, were early morning (workdays began around 7:00) and early evening before the TV was tuned in. During the Moslem fasting month in

The best milk for growth. Every child wants to grow healthy and strong. DANCOW Instant is the best milk for growth. DANCOW Instant is enriched with vitamins, is easy to prepare and is delicious.

EXHIBIT 7 (*Continued*)   Ad Sample for Dancow

June or July, advertisements for food and drink could be carried only after sunset.

Advertising in cinemas was fairly common in Indonesia. Most cinema advertising was in the form of slides that were shown before the start of the film. FSI had advertised Milkmaid in cinemas in smaller towns, but had not been very satisfied with the effectiveness of this media. Indonesian cinemas were of two classes. Class A cinemas were in major cities and were very expensive to attend, especially when good or well-known films were being shown. Class B cinemas were in smaller towns. They were less expensive to attend and were often rather shabby in appearance. Operational problems plagued both classes of cinema. In FSI's experience the slides, when they were shown at all, were often presented out of sequence or upside down.

FSI used some of Indonesia's magazines having national circulations for full-page color advertisements that reflected their television advertisements. In magazine advertising, their strategy was to cluster together several ads in several magazines in order to create an impact.

MILO. : Padat gizi, kaya energi.

MILO, PADAT GIZI, KAYA ENERGI karena MILO mengandung bahan-bahan alami yang bermanfaat, yaitu malt yang berenergi tinggi, susu yang menyehatkan, gula, coklat yang lezat serta vitamin dan mineral utama.

ANDA SEKELUARGA MEMBUTUHKAN ENERGI MILO
Setiap orang menggunakan energi pada hari-hari penuh kegiatan, terutama bagi anak-anak aktif yang sehat dan energi ini harus diganti.
MILO dengan rasa coklat yang lezat menyediakan energi ini setiap saat sepanjang hari baik dirumah, di sekolah dan bahkan pada saat berolah raga, untuk membantu pertumbuhan yang sehat dan kuat.

AYO! DAPATKAN ENERGI MILO.   **Nestlé**

MILO is full of nutrition and rich in energy because it is full of nutrients like malt, sugar, milk, the main vitamins and the main minerals. Your family needs MILO energy. Everyone uses energy every day, especially healthy, active children. This energy needs to be replaced. Chocolate flavored MILO gives this energy every day—at school, at home, and while exercising—to help one grow healthy and strong.

EXHIBIT 7 (*Continued*)   Ad Sample for Milo

They would then use these advertisements in cycles. For two months the clustered ads would appear in several different magazines and then, for one month, no magazine advertisements would be employed. When magazine advertising was the only mass medium used for a product, as had been initially the case for Nestum, a yearly ad budget of 56 million rupiah was required to obtain what they felt was effective penetration.

High-caliber magazines were costly to the consumer. They had newsstand prices of between 800 and 1000 rupiah per issue and were generally issued bimonthly. This high cost led to very high readership figures per issue. Advertising agency personnel multiplied circulation estimates by eight to compute actual readership. For its market, FSI executives felt that a multiple of five was more realistic. It was, however, very difficult, if not impossible, to estimate readership at all due to the very poor circulation figures that were available. Audited circulation figures were virtually unavailable, and some FSI executives believed that the only way to really know who read which magazines was to survey the market by themselves.

Indonesia had six general-interest magazines. Three of these were women's magazines that reported on fashion, decorating, and cooking. These had very impressive European formats. *Femina* and *Kartini* were aimed at the upper-class housewife, and *Gadis* was designed for younger women. Research figures seemed to indicate that readership duplication was approximately 60% within this category. *Intisari*, a *Reader's Digest*-style monthly, *Tempo*, a Time-style magazine, and *Executif*, for high-level business executives, had not been used often by FSI. However, these magazines were very popular among Indonesia's elite.

FSI used newspaper advertising primarily for special promotions and as a signal to the trade that FSI was very interested in supporting a given product. Mr. Souter felt that newspaper advertising was of strategic importance in dealing with the trade. Newspaper market penetration seemed to be fairly low. It was also a medium that was more effective in reaching a male audience than a female audience. Agency figures indicated that total readership was five times circulation figures although, again, circulation figures were considered to be very unreliable. FSI executives accepted a multiple of three in terms of their own market. New ads needed to be created for all newspaper campaigns because magazine artwork did not reproduce effectively in black and white. Mr. Souter estimated that 40 million rupiah were required, over a 3-month period, for an effective newspaper campaign.

The range of newspapers was very wide. Probably the most important were the two Jakarta based nationals *Kompas* and *Sinar Harapan*. Their primary circulation was in Jakarta. In other important regional markets they were very often second in circulation after the local newspaper. There were two rather low circulation English language newspapers, the *Observer* and the *Indonesian Times;* these were not cited by FSI. In addition, a Chinese newspaper with a small but very influential readership was available. The advertising rates for the national and Chinese newspapers were much higher than those of the other newspapers.

Outdoor advertising was very popular in Indonesia, although FSI had rarely employed it. Billboards in shimmering or plain versions, footbridges, bus-stop shelters, and A-boards were all used for advertising purposes. Mr. Souter believed that few of the outdoor advertising opportunities were appropriate for FSI because of the nature of their products. Outdoor locations soon became dirty, especially those in crowded cities. He did not feel that a dirty environment was appropriate for food products. Nonetheless, many of FSI's competitors did make use of outdoor advertisements. A second problem with outdoor advertisements were the negotiations involved in arranging them. Various fees and taxes were often imposed on the advertisers for which no receipt was ever given.

Outdoor advertisements were not inexpensive, and each form had its own particular drawbacks. Billboards needed to be leased for 3 to 5 years at a time, payable in advance. Bus-stop shelters advertising different brands of the same products tended to line up one after the other. A similar problem arose with A-boards. These were often used temporarily at the entrance to sports events or along parade routes. They would often be massed so close together that the impact of each board was substantially reduced.

Pedestrian footbridges were an expensive, but popular, advertising medium. A company could build, for approximately 15 million rupiah, a pedestrian footbridge over a crowded street. The company would become liable for all maintenance charges and the ever popular annually negotiated tax. In return, advertisements could be painted on the bridge for 5 years. At one time, FSI executives had considered building such a bridge but had decided against it on the basis of cost and their reluctance to negotiate the "taxes."

TRADE-BASED PROMOTION

Indonesia's wholesalers and retailers always welcomed trade-based promotions that involved distributing premiums such as drinking glasses, which were a particular favorite, or product samples. These were promotions that they could easily participate in. To them, the immediate nature of the reward was a tremendous allure. They disliked coupon-type promotions that required them to give up something first by accepting less money for a product or accepting only a coupon for a product in anticipation of later reimbursement by the company sponsoring the promotion. The concept of a monetary society was new to some retailers, who were far more comfortable being barter traders.

TUESDAY AFTERNOON

It was late in the afternoon of Tuesday, January 21, 1981, and Ian Souter had spent the day reviewing the marketing campaigns for each of the six products FSI manufactured and marketed in Indonesia. He now had less than 10 weeks to redesign and implement a non-TV campaign for each of these products. The campaigns needed to be finalized by mid-March for their April introductions. He needed to meet those deadlines despite the delays and interruptions that he had come to expect during his 3 years in Indonesia. He felt that his list of campaign and promotion ideas would serve as the basis of a very intensive review meeting the next day with the staff of the Fortune Advertising Agency, who had served FSI for 22 years, and his own superiors.

Ericsson do Brasil

After several months of careful investigation, Jose Castanheira, director of Ericsson do Brasil's general sales division, was approaching a point where he had to make a decision on how to relaunch ERICALL in the Brazilian market. ERICALL was an electronic paging system that had been on the Brazilian market for several years. The last 2 years had shown the first significant sales growth, and Castanheira was considering a major effort in this area. The general sales division (GSD) was to lead Ericsson do Brasil away from its traditional overdependence on the government sector. Both the Brazilian company and its Swedish parent, L. M. Ericsson, believed strongly that ERICALL could make a major contribution for a company reorientation toward the private sector. With the product launch date of August 1982 only 3 months away, it was now up to Castanheira to approve the marketing plan for ERICALL's introduction.

THE ERICALL SYSTEM

ERICALL was a personal paging system. A person, if equipped with a pocket receiver, could receive various types of signals via a radio transmitter operated from a central system. Depending on the configuration of central transmitter and receivers, the system could simultaneously handle several thousand different receivers.

Four types of battery-powered receivers were available. The basic model, EC 401, was able to emit a sound signal, or "beep," plus a light-coded signal. The EC 401 was equipped with two small lights and could receive up to four flashes on any one of them. Consequently, a maximum of eight types of combinations could be received. The model EC 400V was also equipped with the double-light feature. It differed from the more basic version because of its vibration mechanism. When active, the person carrying the EC 400V would feel a single vibration once, twice, three, or four times. The combination of light, color, and pulsations indicated the type of message. As a result, eight different signals could be transmitted, but the signals were only noticeable to the intended receiver due to the absence of sound.

The Model EC 405 receivers were substantially more sophisticated since both came equipped with a display for alphanumeric characters. The EC 405 had a sound activator and could transmit voice. The EC 405V had a vibrator instead of sound/voice. The four-digit alphanumeric display unit could be used to transmit codes of up to eight alphanumeric characters. The second set of four was activated by simply pressing a button. The message remained activated, or available, until erased by the next message. The display unit was sufficient to accommodate Brazil's seven-digit telephone numbers. For a sketch of the four types of receivers, see Exhibits 1a, 1b, and 2.

This case was prepared by Professor Jean-Pierre Jeannet of Babson College. Copyright © 1983 by IMEDE, Lausanne, Switzerland. The International Institute for Management Development (IMD), resulting from the merger between IMEDE, Lausanne, and IMI, Geneva, acquires and retains all rights. Not to be used or reproduced without written permission from IMD, Lausanne, Switzerland.

ERICSSON

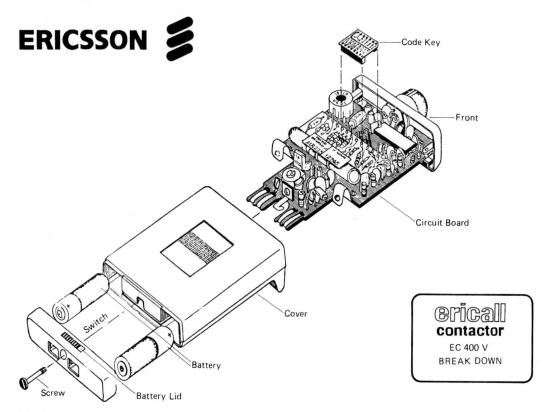

EXHIBIT 1(a) ERICALL Contactor

The central switching unit was an important element in the ERICALL system. Two types existed: a compact version and a modular system. The simpler compact version required that the operator activate manually any type of receiver. The receiver capacity in the simpler compact version was 3375, independent of the mix of receivers. The EC 405 or 405V types permitted the user to send more than 30 million different alphanumerically coded messages to each receiver in any combination of one to eight characters consisting of digits between zero and nine and letters from A to E. The compact system allowed for the direct connection of up to three alarm points without operator interference. See Exhibit 3 for additional details.

The modular system was a more powerful paging system. It could be connected into a PABX system that allowed calls to be routed directly to the intended person without operator interference. Furthermore, up to 256 different alarm points could be connected automatically. The modular system could be expanded by the possible simultaneous use of more than one transmitter or codifier. Its key advantage, however, was automatic operation compared to the manual compact system. For more details, see Exhibit 4.

For both systems, the keyboard allowed the selection of three-digit receiver codes, that is, 000 through 999, or letters A, B, C, D, and E, or an alphanumeric combination such as AA3, C23, D14, and so on. This allowed for a combination of up to 4096 different codes, or the maximum number of receivers that could be handled on one system. The ERICALL system also included a transmitter with an output in watts that depended on distances to receivers. Ericsson do Brasil manufactured the small transmitters in its own factory. The company helped customers in the purchase of the re-

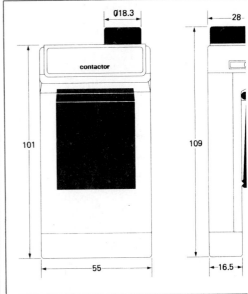

Receivers EC 400 and EC 401   Receiver EC 405

EXHIBIT 1(*b*)   Technical Data Recall Receivers

quired transmitter from a supplier in Brazil if a stronger signal was needed. If necessary, several transmitters could be combined into a single system to ensure that all intended receivers could be contacted.

POTENTIAL APPLICATIONS FOR ERICALL

The ERICALL system was adaptable to a very wide range of applications. Its principal advantage was automatic activation without operator interference. Consequently, through Ericsson's advanced centrals, any receiver could be activated individually through its internal code. The system was adaptable to interface with any alarm system. For example, a company could connect smoke detectors through the central system. If one of the detectors was activated, the alarm would be transmitted automatically to the intended receivers.

The respective codes indicated the location of the activated smoke detector, allowing for immediate action. Similar alarm systems could be coupled with burglar alarms.

Receivers with alphanumeric displays provided transmission of various messages. Alerted either through sound or vibration, the person carrying the receiver could check for the coded message on the display unit. It might contain a telephone number to call or any prearranged coded message. For units with voice, a verbal message could be transmitted from the central unit. The range of possible applications appeared limitless.

In terms of pager systems technology, the ERICALL was considered advanced, although pager systems technology in general was fairly stable. ERICALL was the only pager system in Brazil to offer a choice of contact by sound, vibration, voice, or alphanumeric code. Competitors in the Brazilian market offered systems with sound contact only. The feature of either

EXHIBIT 1(*b*)   (*Continued*)

Technical Data

Order no.	EC 400 EC 400 vibrator EC 401 high audio level EC 405 display EC 405 display and vibrator	Power supply	2 Alkaline cells, 1.5 V/700 mAh[a] e.g., Mallory MN 9100 or 2 Mercury cells, 1.4 V/800 mAh[a] e.g., Mallory RM 401 or 2 NiCd cells, 1.25 V/150 mAh[a] e.g., DEAC 151 D
Order key	SRA 1316-R3-167080		
Radio frequency	25–42 MHz	Approximate operating time	300 h/100 mAh with 5 calls per day including lamp indication, display, or vibrator.
Frequency stability	±0.2%		
Selectivity		Current consumption	Standby	<270 µA
At > 6 dB	±120 kHz		Tone signal	< 30 mA
At > 40 dB	±300 kHz		Tone and lamp signal	< 90 mA
At > 60 dB	±400 kHz		Tone and LED signal	< 50 mA
Sensitivity			Speech	< 15 mA
Code	< 30 µV/m		Vibration	< 100 mA
Speech	< 100 µV/m at 12 dB S/N		Vibration and LED signal	< 130 mA
Alerting signal frequency	3.2 kHz		Tone and display	< 90 mA
			Vibration and display	< 160 mA
Sound level at 30-cm distance (not applicable on vibrating receiver)	EC 400 68 dB(A) EC 401 87 dB(A) EC 405 87 dB(A)	Battery test	Press reception button (sound or vibration)
		Ambient temperature (max 6-dB sensitivity decrease)	−10°C to +55°C
Dimensions			
Standard receiver	93 × 55 × 16.5 (28) mm	Options	Light indication using lamps (EC 400/401)
Display receiver	101 × 55 × 16.5 (28) mm		Light indication using LEDs (EC 400/401)
Weight excluding batteries	93–105 g		Vibrator
Weight of 1 battery set	20–27 g		Display

We reserve the right to change technical data or modify the equipment without previous notice.

[a] Reservation for variations in battery quality.

voice and/or alphanumeric code eliminated the need of finding a telephone and calling a central switching office to receive the message. Voice data or code data could instantly convey the action required by the recipient provided the action was based on prearranged signals, as in the case of alphanumeric codes. Castanheira and his colleagues at Ericsson do Brasil believed that this direct contact capability would create an entirely new range of applications for this pager system. They were particularly excited about its use in the medical and security fields.

COMPANY BACKGROUND

Ericsson do Brasil Comercio e Industria S/A (EDB) was an associated company of L. M. Ericsson (LME). LME, a Swedish-based multinational company, had annual sales of about $2.5 billion in 1981. With its more than 160 subsidiaries, associated companies, or technical offices, LME had installed some of the world's most advanced telephone switching equipment. More recently, LME had started a major effort to enter the high-technology market for

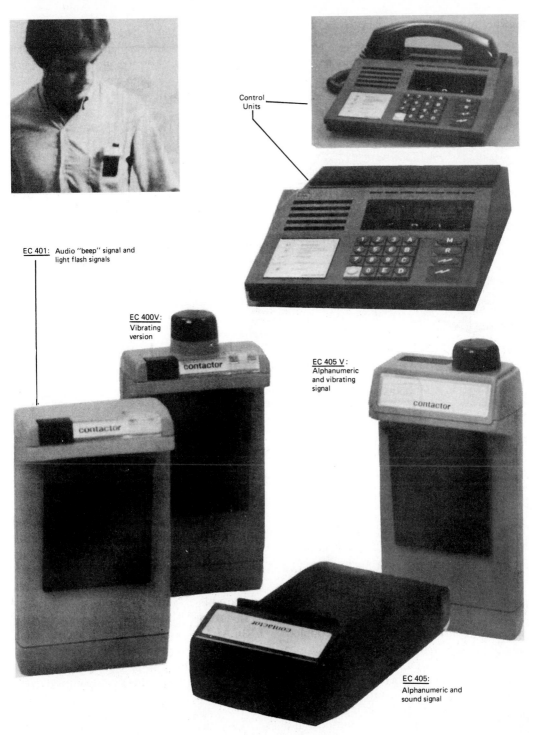

Control Units

EC 401: Audio "beep" signal and light flash signals

EC 400V: Vibrating version

EC 405 V: Alphanumeric and vibrating signal

EC 405: Alphanumeric and sound signal

EXHIBIT 2   Receivers and Control Units

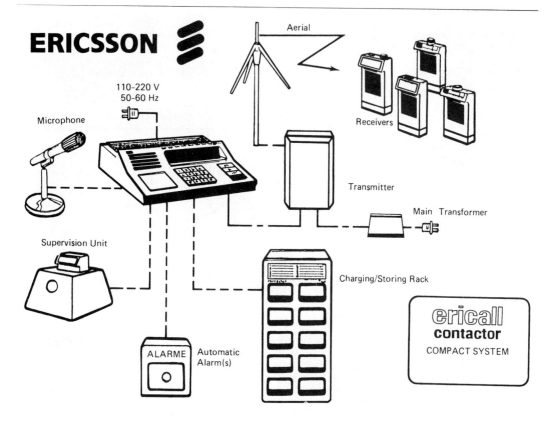

ERICSSON

Aerial

110-220 V
50-60 Hz

Microphone

Receivers

Transmitter

Main Transformer

Supervision Unit

Charging/Storing Rack

ericall
contactor
COMPACT SYSTEM

ALARME Automatic
Alarm(s)

EXHIBIT 3 The Compact System

office systems and radio communication devices.

LME owned 64% of EDB's outstanding capital but controlled only 26% of its voting shares. The remainder of the voting shares were in the hands of Brazilian investors. Despite the de jure independence of EDB, the operational relationship between LME in Sweden and EDB was similar to that of any other parent–subsidiary relationship. LME tended to appoint the chief operating executive, who at that time happened to be from Sweden, and the Brazilian partner appointed the majority of the directors.

EDB was organized along functional lines. Reporting to top management were six directors, one each for administration, commercial, finance, production, public relations, and research and development. The commercial director, Lois Falcao, had responsibility for both

the general sales division headed by Castanheira, and the telephone exchange division. Castanheira's GSD employed about 900 people. For an organization chart, see Exhibit 5. Marketing at GSD was divided into two regions: south and north. The Southern Department included the two large branches in Rio de Janeiro and São Paulo (Exhibit 6). "There is a basic difference in business between the more industrialized south and the more rural north," said Castanheira. In the south of Brazil, where about 70% of the population was concentrated, economic activity was dominated by large manufacturing companies. In the north, small companies engaged in trade and commerce were relatively important.

This difference between north and south was also reflected in GSD's sales mix. In the

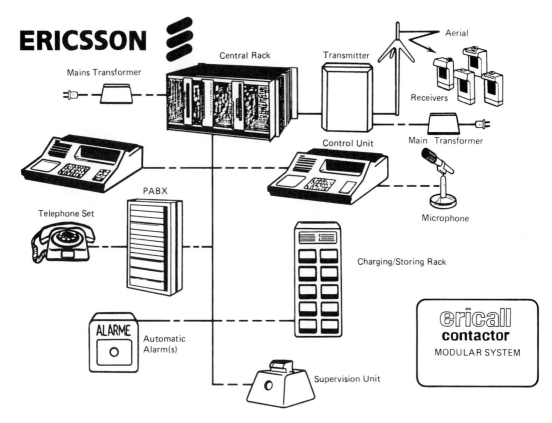

ERICSSON

Mains Transformer

Central Rack

Transmitter

Aerial

Receivers

Main Transformer

Control Unit

PABX

Telephone Set

Microphone

Charging/Storing Rack

ALARME

Automatic Alarm(s)

Supervision Unit

ericall
contactor
MODULAR SYSTEM

EXHIBIT 4   The Modular System

south, sales of larger PABX systems dominated and the average system had about 200 lines. In the north, systems had up to 50 lines with an average of about 30. Furthermore, the sales approach was reflective of the cultural differences. Business in the north was more informal. Ericsson salespeople frequently had direct access to the company's top person. Many businesspeople did not wear ties to work. In the south, business was more formal, and sales contracts at larger firms were usually at a lower level than in the north.

Each of the 10 branches had a sales group and service and administrative personnel. In the larger branches of the south, sales were specialized according to PABX or key systems.[1]

In the north, where sales of smaller key systems were common, the same sales force tended to sell both systems.

In the market for PABX systems, EDB had a dominant market share of about 45%. The company sold about 1,000 systems annually and had a separate maintenance and service organization for its approximately 10,000 clients in Brazil. It competed against Siemens, Philips, ITT, NEC, and GTE, as well as two local companies, Daruma and Telequip.

Responsibility for the ERICALL system had

---

[1] PABX was a commonly used abbreviation for private access business exchange with a capacity of up to several

hundred lines. Installed by businesses and government agencies, they required skilled personnel to operate. Key system was a PABX with a small capacity for internal and external communications. For this system, companies did not use specialized operators, and the user received and started his or her own telephone calls. In the United States, the abbreviation PBX is preferred.

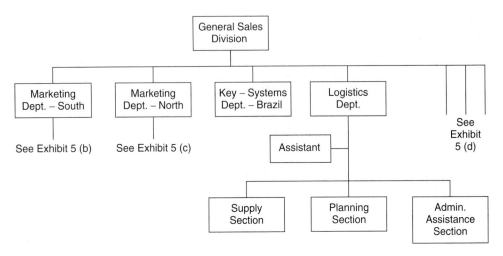

EXHIBIT 5(*a*)   Organizational Chart

been assigned to Arnaldo Curvello, who headed the special systems section. This section was created shortly after Castanheira had taken over responsibility for GSD to give more emphasis to the new and special products. The signal systems and fire alarm systems were under Curvello as well.

With a total employment of more than 7,000 persons, EDB was LME's largest unit in its worldwide network of subsidiaries, affiliates, and companies. EDB's factory on the outskirts of São Paulo, with its 4,000 employees, was the largest single LME factory in the world. EDB enjoyed a leading position in its markets and had been operating profitably for several years.

ERICSSON DO BRASIL'S PAST EXPERIENCE WITH ERICALL

ERICALL had been imported by EDB since the early 1970s. Sales had been sporadic to the on-site market for which the system was intended. EDB depended entirely on direct imports of ERICALL elements from Sweden. Although it was marketed successfully, SRA, an Ericsson subsidiary that manufactured the ERICALL system in Sweden, tried in vain to get EDB to push for more volume. An older executive was responsible for the system at EDB, and he told SRA executives on several occasions that he "just couldn't get the support he needed to push up the volume."

EXHIBIT 5(*b*)   Organizational Chart

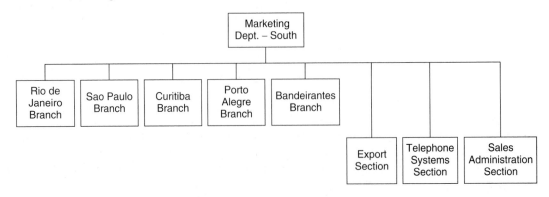

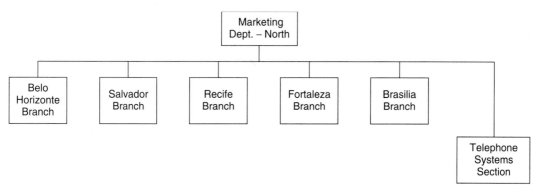

EXHIBIT 5(c)   Organizational Chart

Following Castanheira's appointment as director of the general sales division in 1979, GSD was entirely reorganized. "I wanted everybody to be responsible for their own budget and to concentrate on a particular product," recalled Castanheira. It was at that time that he appointed Arnaldo Curvello as chief of special systems, a department consisting of all specialized products sold through GSD. Curvello at first found considerable resistance to ERICALL, as the sales force was accustomed to selling PABX systems only. The salespeople viewed ERICALL as a system that could not be sold and that had an image of lesser importance.

To change the negative attitude of the sales force, Curvello convinced the sales supervisors that, if presented properly, the ERICALL system could be sold to the same client who bought Ericsson's PABX system. His insistence paid off, and, suddenly, EDB's volume in ERICALL systems took off. "Two years later, in 1981, the SRA people came back, but this time they wanted to know what we did to suddenly increase the volume," remembered Castanheira. With volume up, it was becoming increasingly difficult for EDB to rely on imports alone. At this point EDB suggested that SRA arrange for a license to produce ERICALL locally.

Although sales had barely totaled 50 systems, each averaging about 20 receivers, most of these sales had come during the last 2 years. SRA would have preferred to export finished products to Brazil, but realized that the strict import licensing practices of the Brazilian government did not support a continuation of the export business.

A major breakthrough came in the second half of 1981. The Ericsson salespeople who visited the IBM head office, a part of the territory, picked up a hint that IBM was in need of a paging system to manage its service representatives in the major Brazilian cities. However, the need was for a company-owned citywide system and not the on-site system for which ERICALL had been designed. IBM, which liked the various features of ERICALL, subjected the system to intensive testing. After several months of negotiations, IBM ordered ERICALL for several of its branch offices. The total contract amounted to about U.S. $1 million. "We suddenly found ourselves reconsidering the 4% salespersons' commission we allowed on our equipment. We just hadn't thought that such large-scale applications would be in the cards," said Castanheira.

The IBM contract, having come through at the time when EDB was ready to gear up for a larger effort for ERICALL, made everybody at EDB question the more traditional on-site strategy. With a successful application for citywide use, Castanheira found himself in a situation where two alternatives became available, where before there was only on-site usage. "The IBM contract changed our view of things."

Castanheira knew, however, that there were two basic reasons why LME and SRA would have preferred a concentration on the on-site market. First, in Sweden, for some time a competitive company had made available a city-

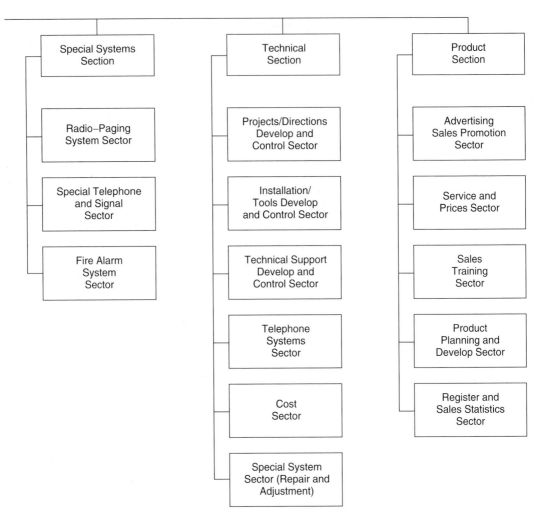

EXHIBIT 5(d) Organizational Chart

wide paging system based on FM band radio. That system had functioned well and allowed for a direct call via radio to a specific telephone set. With this market in Sweden firmly in the hands of the competition, a broadcasting company, there had been little interest at LME to enter the public paging market with ERICALL. Second, Castanheira believed that SRA and LME wanted to go into the public or citywide market with a new and more sophisticated system, currently in the developing stage. However, Castanheira was of the opinion that Brazil did not need a system more sophisticated than ERICALL.

EDB'S PRODUCTION LICENSE

The resurgence of ERICALL sales brought about some inquiries by SRA in Sweden, the L. M. Ericsson unit that was responsible for the ERICALL system. SRA suggested a willingness to extend a production license to EDB as it became increasingly difficult to obtain import licenses for the growing volume. Arnaldo Curvello, as section chief of special systems, made several trips to Sweden to negotiate an agreement with SRA. The major difficulty was not in coming to terms with SRA but striking a deal that was also acceptable to the various

EXHIBIT 6 Map of Brazil

Brazilian authorities: the Carteira de Comercio Exterior (CACEX), or Brazilian Foreign Trade Authority; the Conselho de Desenvolvimento Industrial (CDI), or Industrial Development Council; and the Instituto Nacional de Propriedade Industrial (INPI), the National Institute of Industrial Property.

To arrange for the introduction of ERICALL, all three of these Brazilian authorities had to be consulted, each playing a special role. Curvello started with CDI, where he first gave a general presentation of the ERICALL project. CDI was responsible for deciding on the important index of nationalization. The in-dex represented the percentage of local content required for the production of a product. For its decision, CDI looked at each component of ERICALL. Whatever could be sourced in Brazil had to be part of the local content. Furthermore, CDI would check if a local producer already manufactured such a product. If that were so, CDI might not grant permission for local production at all. CDI certification was needed to compete for official tenders. Since both government and semigovernment agencies accounted for a substantial part of the Brazilian economy, the nationalization indexes certified by CDI were important to many companies. In the case of ERICALL, Curvello negotiated for 64% nationalization in year 1, rising to 68% in year 2, and to 70% in year 3. "At that point we will have to negotiate with CDI for another 3 years," explained Curvello.

In the next step, Curvello took his plan to INPI. "The Brazilian government does not allow for the royalty payment from affiliated and associated companies," said Curvello. Since the licensing agreement with SRA had to be negotiated through LME, ERICALL did not qualify for royalty payments. INPI's role was to look at all contracts that entailed payments for technology to assure a fair deal and to prevent excessive payments. INPI allowed a lump-sum payment of U.S. \$700,000.[2] This amount was made up of payments for documentation (40%), training and technical visits (40%), and technical assistance (20%).

With both CDI and INPI approval, Curvello could now approach CACEX. This agency controlled both the nature and volume of imports into Brazil through a system of import licenses. CACEX followed its own rules, and, occasionally, earlier agreements with CDI and INPI had to be renegotiated because CACEX might not approve a certain component for importing. For the approved components, EDB would have to pay import duties averaging 118% of C.I.F. value. CACEX could be a strong ally for companies producing locally as it had the power, and often used it, to outlaw the import of finished products once production existed.

The negotiations with CACEX could not be successfully completed without submitting a production schedule on ERICALL. "Each year," Curvello went on, "we negotiate our production levels for the coming year with CACEX. As a net importer of components, Ericsson do Brasil has to get CACEX approval for import levels that are tied to our production or sales forecasts. If we are over our goals, it might be difficult to get additional foreign exchange. If we are consistently under our own estimates, we might not get as much as we want the next year. Therefore, we have to be quite accurate in our forecasts."

---

[2] U.S. \$1.00 = Cruzeiros Cr 93.125.

The production level was finally set at 100 ERICALL systems for 1982, increasing by 10% each of the following years. It was estimated that 26 receivers would be sold with each system. Sufficient capacity existed to produce the necessary components. EDB's flexibility was such that a volume of 20% in excess of target could still be handled. Anything above would have to be accommodated only after a renegotiation with CACEX.

PRODUCTION PLANNING

ERICALL systems and receivers would be manufactured at EDB's factory near São Paulo where about 4,000 people were employed. For the ERICALL systems, about 50 new semi-skilled assembly jobs would be created. The only skilled labor needed were four testers for the equipment after final assembly. Production was planned in batch form, with assembly concentrating on one individual product at a time. Focus would thus shift from centrals to receivers on to other components, and so on. The additional investment needed for production equipment was minimal since most of the components could be produced by EDB's existing machinery or sourced from local suppliers.

Total investment for the ERICALL system was estimated at Cr \$12.5 million. This cost was relatively low since the plastic case for the keyboards and receivers could be imported. EDB thus saved the investment in plastic molding equipment.

Unit production costs for the modular system consisting of centrals connected to PABX and transmitters amounted to Cr \$1.1 million. The compact system including transmitter had a unit cost of Cr \$1 million. The receivers' unit costs amounted to Cr \$25,000 for the simple 401 model and Cr \$35,000 for the 405. Total unit costs were further subdivided into variable costs of 85% and a fixed costs contribution of 15%. The variable costs consisted of 80% material and 20% direct labor. Imported components made up almost two-thirds of direct material costs.

THE MARKET FOR PAGER SYSTEMS IN BRAZIL

Two major market segments existed in the Brazilian pager market. The industry differentiated between citywide and on-site systems. Citywide systems were equipped with stronger radio transmitters and thus had a wider reach. They were operated by independent companies that sold or rented their services to a wide range of companies and individuals. On-site systems were installed for a company's or institution's use and were typically restricted to the client's premises. Although technically the systems only differed in the power of their radio transmitters, substantial differences existed between the two segments in terms of applications, buyer behavior, competition, volume, and future growth possibilities. One of Castanheira's principal strategic decisions with respect to the relaunch of ERICALL was in connection with the appropriate weighing of the importance of each of these two segments. Any decision had to be founded on a complete understanding of the dynamics involved with each segment.

The Market for Citywide Paging Systems

Citywide paging systems had existed in Brazil for about 15 years. According to information collected by EDB, about 130 systems had been licensed throughout the country. Licenses were granted by Dentel, an agency at the Brazilian Ministry of Communications, which controlled radio communications. Since paging systems required the use of radio transmitters, it was Dentel that opened areas for bidding. The company receiving the award for a license in a given city would install a central system, a radio transmitter equipped with the stipulated power, or watts, and the licensed frequency, and make its services available to private subscribers. EDB executives estimated that by 1981 a total of 45,000 individual receivers were in operation throughout Brazil. In São Paulo alone, some 25,000 receivers were estimated to be in use. Presently, EDB research had estimated the annual volume of new receivers in this segment to be 4,000 to

4,800 receivers for 1982. Annual growth for the next 4 years was estimated at anywhere from 10% to 20%.

The currently operating citywide paging systems were limited, however, by their existing technology. All systems used sound-activated receivers only, signaling via a high-pitched sound, or "beep." The person receiving the signal was then obliged to go to a telephone and call a central operator who would transmit the message. Furthermore, the receiver had to be manually activated by a central operator for the system.

The paging service companies promoted their services through a variety of channels to the general public. EDB executives believed that professionals, such as lawyers, doctors, and architects, accounted for about 80% of the subscribers. Other users were people employed as service technicians, in transport, in construction, and in the news media.

Two companies dominated the market for supplying equipment for citywide paging systems. The largest one, Intelco Radio Communicacao S/A, was located in São Paulo and accounted for about 80% of the market. Established in 1968, Intelco had used a double strategy. In the largest cities of Brazil, Intelco was the licensee for the operation of its own paging systems. For smaller cities, Intelco made the entire package available to independent companies, which then bid for the license. Typically, Intelco sold the equipment outright to the independent paging service operators. Service subscribers, however, rented receivers for the duration of their subscription period.

Intelco's receivers were equipped for sound only. Their design was based on an early model of Motorola, a U.S. company. Motorola was the original supplier of components that were then assembled in Brazil by Intelco. This agreement was discontinued when import restrictions made it impossible for Intelco to continue importing components. Intelco then began manufacturing receivers similar to Motorola's using Brazilian components only. All official licensing or royalty relationships between Intelco and Motorola have been severed.

Intelco employed about 270 persons and depended entirely on paging systems for its revenues. The company was believed to be very profitable and had an estimated annual output of about 2,000 receivers. Throughout Brazil, Intelco employed 28 salespeople. Of these, 8 were concentrated in São Paulo and 6 in Rio de Janeiro. Intelco was actively advertising its service in high-volume newspapers and magazines. Castanheira personally estimated Intelco's advertising expenditures at about Cr $50 million. Some full-page ads in the popular VEJA magazine were priced at about Cr $500,000 alone. Intelco was known to have had service and maintenance problems with their receivers. Earlier this year, the company had started to replace older receivers with smaller, but still only sound-activated, models.

Telefones em Automoveis Sitam S/A was the second competitor in the market for city-wide paging systems. Believed to produce about 600 receivers annually, Sitam also operated its own service "Ondafone" in larger cities and supplied entire packages to operators elsewhere. The company employed about 85 people and maintained a relatively large sales force. Ten of its 17 salespeople were concentrated in the São Paulo area. Its advertising budget was estimated by Castanheira at about Cr $5 million to 10 million. Sitam was known to be price competitive, offering lower rental fees than Intelco. Castanheira, however, suspected that a pricing agreement existed between the two companies because Intelco could easily lower prices to drive Sitam out of the market. Sitam operated in fewer cities than Intelco. Actually, Castanheira believed that Sitam's large sales force stimulated business for Intelco as well. Typically, potential customers contacted by Sitam would check with Intelco before signing up. This allowed Intelco to strike back and try to sign the customer up before Sitam finalized the sale.

Sitam's receivers employed a technology similar to Intelco's. Its receivers' designs were based on a mix of Motorola-like components and elements from other U.S. firms. No official licensing agreement had ever existed between Sitam and the foreign firms. Sitam produced its receivers from Brazilian-sourced components only. Sitam receivers were sound activated only.

Brazil's local telephone companies offered a message system that could be considered an alternative to the paging systems. Incoming telephone calls could be routed to a central message office where all messages were recorded. At any time during the day, the subscriber could call the center and ask for messages, usually telephone numbers, which had been left. The service's major disadvantage was the delay as the message recipient could not be contacted immediately. However, the local telephone companies offered this service because it generated additional traffic. In Brazil, all calls, even local, were metered. With switching equipment underutilized during the off-peak hours of 11 to 12 A.M. and 4 to 5 P.M., the telephone companies looked for any opportunity to get additional usage and increase "traffic."

In the opinion of Castanheira, EDB's ERICALL system offered major advantages to present operators and users of existing paging systems. First, the modular system allowed direct connection into a PABX system. Incoming calls could be routed directly to the intended receiver via radio communications without the manual operation of an operator. Second, the ERICALL receivers, even the most basic ones, allowed for the transmission of signals, and the more sophisticated models for the direct transmission of a telephone number. Thus, the time-consuming first call to the central switchboard was avoided, and the message recipient could get in touch with the person looking for him or her without delay. Consequently, the ERICALL system promised substantial improvements in both service and efficiency.

But Castanheira was looking even further ahead. He became intrigued by the possibility of connecting ERICALL receivers directly to the telephone companies' central switching equipment. If such a connection were feasible, then the market for receivers would literally explode. When he inquired about the technical feasibility of such an installation, Castanheira found out that LME technical staff in Sweden did not have test results available at that time. Instead, LME engineers had been involved heavily with the development of a mobil telephone for Sweden. "That's O.K. for Sweden," Castanheira replied, "but such an installation would cost about U.S. $35,000 in Brazil. And then it still only works as long as you are in the car. What about when you are away from the car?"

Despite the attractiveness of the citywide paging systems market, Castanheira felt there were several unresolved questions. First, he was not at all sure how Intelco and Sitam might react to Ericsson's entry into that market. He was concerned that they might be able to secure new technology to compete with receivers that could also display alphanumeric characters. He was certain, however, that they would not get any import licenses easily. Somehow, they would have to source their components in Brazil.

Still unresolved was how Ericsson could compete in the citywide market. Castanheira had little interest in getting involved with the operations of the competing paging services. Licenses for top markets had already been granted. There existed, however, a possibility of acquiring either Intelco or Sitam. He had no idea if either of the companies would be for sale or even what the acquisition price might be. At the present time, both companies were profitable. An acquisition would certainly accomplish the elimination of competitive suppliers of paging equipment. Since EDB was primarily unconcerned with the sale of paging equipment, Castanheira was wondering how an acquisition might fit in with his long- to medium-term strategy. And yet there was no doubt that the citywide segment offered the largest potential growth opportunities.

The Market for On-site Paging Systems

The market for on-site paging systems appeared to be much less developed than the citywide market. Typically, on-site installations were limited to the use of a single company or organization. The radio transmitters were less powerful and usually did not exceed a range of more than 3 miles. Technically, the equipment for on-site paging systems was identical to that used for citywide systems with the exception of the transmitter. A major difference

was the preponderance of outright sales to users instead of rentals. The company also obtained a license for its radio transmitter from Dentel that determined the allowable signal strength and frequency.

Only one company was active in the on-site field. Embracom Electronica S/A, located in São Paulo, was a company formed in 1972 and active in a range of electronic applications. The company employed about 350 persons and was active in the manufacture of transmission equipment. Embracom, a Brazilian-owned company, actively cooperated with the government in the development of various electronic products. The company distributed its on-site systems through independent distributors located in major Brazilian cities. Embracom was believed to install about 50 systems annually and to produce about 1,000 receivers in an average year. Last year, however, it was believed to have built 2,800 receivers.

Based on market research data, EDB executives believed that about 15,700 companies existed in Brazil for whom it was worthwhile to own a system. EDB estimated that annual receiver sales would grow from about 2,500 annually in 1981 to 3,800 in 1985. Primary users were hospitals, with 23% of the market, industrial companies with 30%, banks with 7%, hotels with 10%, and the rest scattered over a wide range of applications. EDB research identified top executives as the primary decision makers in about 80% of all cases. Purchasing departments were influencing the decisions in about 12% of situations, and the actual user played a role in only about 8% of all situations.

"We know that Embracom has a poor reputation for quality of equipment and service," explained Castanheira. Embracom was believed to be slow in responding to service calls. Its systems were based on outdated Motorola technology and allowed for sound signaling only. The equipment, though closely resembling Motorola designs, was not based on any formal licensing agreement. Embracom paging systems required manual operation on the part of a company's central switchboard operator. Its equipment was not compatible with central telephone equipment, and only one transmitter could be handled by the same system. A maximum of 100 receivers could be accommodated by the Embracom system.

"You have to know the special government regulations concerning telephone operators to understand our situation in Brazil," explained Castanheira. The regulations stipulated that central switchboard operators could work no longer than 6 hours. To cover a full working day at its corporate offices, EDB employed two shifts of two operators each. But smaller companies could not afford this. "In our Rio de Janeiro branch office, we just have the operator arrive 2 hours later in the day," said Castanheira. "During the first 2 hours, our phone traffic is traditionally light, and we equipped executive phones with direct lines." In general, companies were concerned with overloading operators. In the opinion of Castanheira, the Embracom system required an unnecessary additional call for the company operator and was thus likely to create a bottleneck if too many receivers were part of the system.

The Marketing Plan for ERICALL

Castanheira had been assigned the responsibility of proposing a marketing plan to Curvello, who, as section chief, had been in charge of the product's sales for almost 3 years. His preliminary proposal, which was based on his successful negotiations with SRA, LME, and the Brazilian government, addressed the major decisions Castanheira would face. Basically, ERICALL could be targeted both to citywide and on-site use. The sales responsibility was to be delegated to a specialized sales force of about a dozen people divided into two groups, one for each segment. Both groups would be based in São Paulo, the head office of EDB. In terms of pricing, the proposal suggested setting prices for the basic, sound-only systems, equal to those of EDB's competitors, and asking for a 15% to 20% premium for the systems with alphanumeric receivers. This proposal, combined with a detailed budget, was now in Castanheira's hands. The preliminary budget was based on sales of 100 systems in year 1, 120 systems in year 2, increasing to 160 systems by

year 5. Similarly, receivers were to increase from 2,100 to 3,360 in 5 years. The total market in receivers was forecast to grow from 7,100 units to 11,000 units over the same time period, giving EDB a market share of about 30%.

As Castanheira looked at the proposal, three key areas stuck out in his mind. First, the target group selection was likely to cause considerable discussion with LME in Sweden. Second, the sales force decision had to be reviewed in light of past experiences he had in GSD. And, finally, the pricing strategy would have to be looked at carefully in view of the various competitors' responses. If he could come to a conclusion in these areas, the final budget could be drawn up, he thought.

Target Market Selection

As the proposal stood, LME and SRA executives who would eventually review the plan preferred a concentration on the on-site segment. Castanheira remembered the discussions when IBM wanted to acquire ERICALL for what amounted to a citywide system operated by IBM in key Brazilian cities.

Although designed as an on-site system with a maximum reach of about 3 miles, EDB executives and its technical staff were convinced that ERICALL could function well in citywide systems. The only difference was the need for a stronger transmitter depending on the reach required. IBM had subjected ERICALL to intensive testing before it accepted the system. "Somehow, back at LME they find it difficult to believe that it really works."

ERICALL's successful performance in several European markets in the on-site segment had obviously had its impact at LME head office and at SRA as well. Even Castanheira had to admit that the system was extremely well suited for on-site use. On the other hand, the citywide segment, or public use of paging systems, was a larger market than on-site uses only. He did not want to miss out in what he believed to be the much larger market. Castanheira did not believe that LME would actually stop him from entering the citywide market. He also wanted to take such a step only after careful consideration. After all, targeting both segments meant competing with different companies. It might also influence his sales force decision.

The Sales Force Decision

Castanheira was well aware of the reasons why Curvello had asked for a small but specialized sales force. When he had assumed his present position as director of GSD, he had moved toward a strategy concentrating on one product that eventually led to a reorganization of the entire division. "To understand fully the difficulties with our sales organization, you have to understand the situation I found when I took over the division," said Castanheira. The division's principal products were telephone equipment sold to the private market as opposed to the switching division that sold primarily to telephone companies. The product line consisted of PABX systems, or in-house telephone central switching equipment for companies. Ericsson's PABX could accommodate up to 200 external trunk lines and up to 10,000 internal lines. In this market, Ericsson was the leader in Brazil.

Also marketed by GSD were key systems, or telephone central systems with a small capacity of up to 25 incoming lines and a maximum of 50 internal lines or connections. Of much smaller importance, but also within the responsibility of GSD, were ERICALL, railroad signaling equipment, and signaling systems for traffic lights. The major challenge for Castanheira, however, was to redress the balance between PABX and key systems sales. PABX, key systems, and ERICALL had been sold through the same geographically organized sales force. Originally, each salesperson was responsible for selling all three product lines. In reality, however, all the attention went into PABXs. As Castanheira remembered: "I found our sales force made offers for a PABX system to a client who did not really need one. Then our competitors moved in with an offer for a key system. By the time our salesperson realized what was going on, it was too late. Our sales force would rather sell a PABX than a key system. However, I would rather sell a key system than no system at all."

The market for key systems was much larger than the market for PABXs. Most firms in Brazil were too small to warrant a PABX. While Ericsson enjoyed a market share of almost 40% in PABXs, it trailed in key systems with a market share of only 10% to 15%. The leaders in the key systems segment were GTE, a U.S. firm, and NEC of Japan. To obtain better coverage for the key systems market, Castanheira decided to split his sales force with each regional office assigning salespeople to only one of the two markets. Later, the specialization for the smaller branch offices in the North was discontinued.

The EDB sales force of about 100 was paid a fixed salary of Cr $37,250 per month and a commission of about 4% of sales. A good salesperson could thus earn about Cr $185,000 per month. Special government regulations required that each salesperson be assigned an exclusive selling territory. If a salesperson was reassigned, the company was liable to maintain his or her income for another 12 months. Consequently, a change in sales territories was something that had to be thought through carefully.

Castanheira remembered the long discussions they had after their salesperson brought in the IBM contract. The 4% commission amounted to almost 2 years of income for the salesperson. There were many executives who believed that the commission in such a case need not be paid. In the end, the salesperson was granted the commission, and the rate remained unchanged at 4%.

Past experience indicated strongly that an organization that focused responsibility more directly did show positive results. This was also borne out with ERICALL under Curvello. However, a new sales force would represent additional fixed costs that would not arise if ERICALL was sold through the existing organization. If the existing organization was given ERICALL, then sales territories would have to be assigned carefully. At this point, Castanheira had little indication as to which salespeople were the best for ERICALL. Moreover, if a salesperson's territory included a very large company, he wanted to make sure that the potential was actually realized. Later reassignment might turn out to be a problem.

The Pricing Decision

EDB research had attempted to determine the possible price premium for ERICALL. Since none of EDB's potential competitors offered systems with comparable sophistication and capabilities, the research department had asked potential users how much more they would be willing to pay for the ERICALL system. The consensus was that users would be willing to pay a 25% to 40% premium for ERICALL's most advanced systems equipped with modular central and the alphanumeric display receivers. Currently, Embracom offered its system for about Cr $1,115,000. If the user wanted to have the Embracom paging system connected to the PABX, an additional connection charge would arise. "Marketers of PABX systems had little interest in such modifications," explained Castanheira. "If we were approached by one of our PABX clients to connect an Embracom paging system, we would probably try to convince them to buy our system. And other PABX suppliers would most likely price the same way."

Currently, receivers were priced at Cr $31,500 by all competitors. This price applied to the basic sound-activated receivers only since no others were on the market. For citywide subscribers, a one-time fee of Cr $1,500 was charged, and the receiver rental was about Cr $2,600 per month. Castanheira was concerned about how local competitors might react to any kind of pricing decision he might take. If possible, he wanted to come close to the gross margin EDB earned in its PABX business of about 40%. His general administrative overhead for launching the ERICALL system would amount to about Cr $30 million annually.

BRAZIL'S ECONOMIC OUTLOOK

Jose Castanheira was very concerned about one aspect of the ERICALL introduction that he could do very little to change—the ERICALL was to be introduced at a time when Brazil's economy continued with its decline, or was further decline inevitable?

Economic growth in Brazil had been strong, but erratic, since 1972. The oil price increases of 1974 and 1976 had a strong negative impact on the economy and led to sharp increases in Brazil's external debt and a deteriorating trade balance as Brazil struggled to pay its increased oil bill. To reduce its dependence on imported oil and to increase export earnings, the Brazilian government had launched a range of investment projects during the mid-1970s that had been financed with foreign debt. By 1979, debt-service requirements were absorbing most of Brazil's export earnings and inflation was soaring. Under these circumstances the government decided to cool down economic activity. Interest rates were allowed to increase dramatically to restrict the money supply. Consequently, industrial output increased slightly in 1980 before it nosedived in 1981. Similarly, exports, which had grown an average of 17% every year between 1974 and 1981, were actually decreasing by 9% in the first months of 1982.

Inflation had peaked at 120% annualized in April 1981 and declined to 91% per year in early 1982, only to show signs of increasing again in May 1982. Inflation was not an insurmountable problem to wage-index-linked Brazilian wage earners, but the number of unemployed who received no form of government assistance was increasing at an alarming rate. In 1981, Brazil's GNP declined by 3.5%. It was Brazil's worst recession in many years. High debt charges and worldwide recession were compounded by falling prices for Brazil's most important commodity exports. Sugar prices were less than 40% of their 1975 level. Soybean prices were below 1979 and 1980 levels, and coffee prices had plunged from an index-linked 410.6 in 1977 to 168.2 in 1981 (1975 = 100).

These economic difficulties were aggravating problems that had already begun to plague the government's efforts to reduce the considerable disparities between Brazil's industrialized south and rural north. In São Paulo, for example, the per capita GNP in 1980 was U.S. $3,300 while for the rest of the country it was

U.S. $1,432, which was barely higher than that of other Latin American countries. The government's projects in the northwest region had been expected to greatly increase employment opportunities in that area. An oil substitution project involving substantial sugar cane production for an alcohol-based fuel had run into problems. It was discovered that the ethanol engine fuel created ecological problems if expensive automobile engine alterations were not made. This led to a slowdown of sales volume for alcohol-powered cars. The second project, named Carajas, was aimed at increasing Brazil's mineral exports. The project was being implemented, but world demand and prices for iron ore, copper, bauxite, nickel, and manganese were falling owing to the persistent worldwide recession.

EXPORT POSSIBILITIES FOR ERICALL

Jose Castanheira had also discussed with LME the possibility of producing and exporting ERICALL systems to other Latin American countries. As Brazil was strategically placed on the Latin American continent, it would be easy for EDB to give the necessary support to other LME subsidiaries and to sell and offer technical assistance on ERICALL. LME currently sold very few ERICALL systems in other Latin American countries.

The Brazilian market combined with export sales would permit EDB to reach a volume of production that would result in economies of scale. Labor costs in Brazil would be another contributing factor that would lead to a lower-cost product. Possible opportunities for LME included selecting EDB to produce and sell ERICALL to the world market, providing the same level of quality at a lower price.

Export volume would substantially strengthen Castanheira's hand in negotiations with Brazilian authorities to obtain the necessary import license for key components. Also, exporting would be profitable since the Brazilian government granted considerable subsidies on export sales amounting to about 20% of sales and access to subsidized low-interest loans. On the other hand, Castanheira believed that his division's performance in marketing ERICALL in Brazil might have considerable bearing on whether he might be granted export rights by LME.

Reviewing all the data his staff had collected over the past few months, Jose Castanheira felt that he had about as much information as he could hope to get on the relaunch of ERICALL. It was now up to him to make the required decisions on the target market, as well as the related decisions on sales force organization and pricing. The final budget could be completed once these key decisions had been made.

3

Marketing in Eastern European Markets

Probably no other region has seen such wholesale change over the past 5 years as the countries in Eastern Europe. With the liberalization of the formerly communist countries in 1989 and the dissolution of the Soviet Union into its individual republics in 1991, a market comprising some 400 million people has suddenly opened to international marketers. For decades, these countries had been characterized as state trading nations where all economic activity had been controlled by the government. If an international firm wanted to market its products or services there, the company had to navigate numerous government agencies and did not have much chance of establishing its own outlets. As a result, Eastern Europe, or the Comecon area as it was called for its economic pact involving the Soviet Union and the other Eastern European countries, tended to be a market primarily for industrial products, with fewer opportunities for consumer goods.

The immense transition is partly political and partly economic. On the political side, the former structure of the Soviet Union and the other seven Eastern European countries has been swept away. Emerging in its place are 27 independent territories. The majority of these consist of the former Soviet Republics, but other countries such as Czechoslovakia and Yugoslavia have been dissolved into a number of independent territories (see Table 1).

The marketing environment of these countries is very diverse and dynamic and subject to major changes. All these countries are moving by varying degrees from state control of their economies to market economies using privatization as a major tool. The leaders are Hungary, the Czech Republic, and Poland. In those countries, Western firms have substantial freedom of movement in terms of opening and establishing companies and using whatever marketing infrastructure is present. These countries are also moving as quickly as possible to reach the position of free convertibility of their local currencies. This rapid progress toward free and open market economies, however, did not come without a price. As a result of the shift to private production, the economies of all Eastern European countries entered a serious recession. Many state-owned companies were closed down and total output fell. Only now are these countries showing signs of improvement. The road to recovery is anticipated to take several years. But it is believed that Poland, Hungary, and the Czech Republic will take many years before they can expect to reach the income levels of the average Western European country.

For all other Eastern European countries, the road to recovery and economic stability is

TABLE 1 Political Transformation of Eastern Europe, 1989–1993

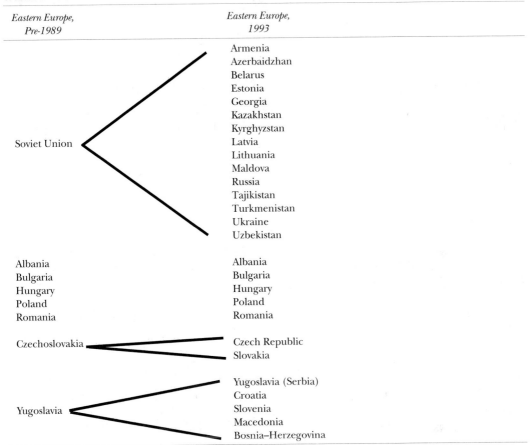

Eastern Europe, *Pre-1989*	*Eastern Europe,* *1993*
Soviet Union	Armenia Azerbaidzhan Belarus Estonia Georgia Kazakhstan Kyrghyzstan Latvia Lithuania Maldova Russia Tajikistan Turkmenistan Ukraine Uzbekistan
Albania Bulgaria Hungary Poland Romania	Albania Bulgaria Hungary Poland Romania
Czechoslovakia	Czech Republic Slovakia
Yugoslavia	Yugoslavia (Serbia) Croatia Slovenia Macedonia Bosnia–Herzegovina

expected to take much longer. This is particularly true for areas where political stability has not yet been achieved. Since the progress of the economic reform movement depends on the political direction of these countries, uncertainties and changes in political direction will have negative impact on growth prospects. Large public-sector deficits have brought about high inflation. These rates reached 196% for Russia in 1991 alone, with many of the other former Soviet republics in triple-digit inflation also. Coupled with extremely low foreign exchange rates, the translated income statistics for many of these countries are among the lowest anywhere in the world. We need therefore to consider the purchasing parity for these countries and, as is the case for emerging markets in Asia and Latin America, the comparison with other countries' changes. (See Table 2.)

Why then are many international companies from all parts of the world concentrating on Eastern Europe despite its political uncertainty, negative economic growth, and hyperinflation? For most firms, Eastern Europe represents one of the last economic frontiers. With its huge population, this region may someday become the battleground for many firms who are looking for growth beyond the industrialized Western countries. In the past, this area was not freely accessible and therefore for many MNCs did not "exist." The prospects to invest freely and to repa-

TABLE 2 Economic Statistics of Countries in Eastern Europe, 1991

Country	Population (millions)	GDP (US$ millions)	GDP per Capita (US$)
Albania	3.3	N.A.	N.A.
Armenia	3.4	475	130
Belarus	10.3	2,176	212
Bulgaria	9.1	7,646	898
Croatia	4.8	15,146	3,223
Czech Republic	10.3	23,330	2,265 (est.)
Estonia	1.6	523	334
Hungary	10.5	32,900	3,121
Kazakhstan	16.8	4,768	286
Kyrghyzstan	4.5	514	115
Latvia	2.7	N.A.	N.A.
Lithuania	3.8	1,185	315
Macedonia	2.0	2,324	1,140
Moldova	4.4	760	174
Poland	38.2	77,896	2,033
Romania	23.3	27,600	1,191
Russia	150.3	36,213	244
Slovenia	2.0	8,998	4,495
Ukraine	52.5	7,940	153
Uzbekistan	21.3	1,865	88
Slovakia	5.3	9,090	1,715 (est.)
Azerbaidzhan	7.3	N.A.	N.A.
Georgia	5.5	N.A.	N.A.
Yugoslavia (Serbia)	10.3	N.A.	N.A.
Bosnia–Herzegovina	4.3	N.A.	N.A.
Tajikistan	5.5	N.A.	N.A.
Turkmenistan	3.7	N.A.	N.A.

Source: Emerging Market Economics Report 1993, IMD (Lausanne); and World Economic Forum (Geneva) *The Economist Intelligence Unit* (1993).

triate profits have led many firms to disregard present difficulties. Interest so far has focused on the most advanced countries (Poland, the Czech Republic, and Hungary) and the large countries of Russia and Ukraine.

MARKETING CHALLENGES IN EASTERN EUROPEAN COUNTRIES

Consumers in Eastern European countries have had contacts with Western products over the years. Contacts have come much less through purchasing such items, since they were largely unavailable before 1989, but through advertising exposure. Sports programs of major events such as the Olympics or world championships have been televised widely and always carried stadium-type advertising of company or product names. Through such exposure, many Eastern Europeans know of leading Western and Japanese brands and products, and companies had achieved substantial brand equity in such markets. Once the barriers of importing disappeared, companies moved in to take advantage of this already existing demand. Some companies found out, however, that, while consumers knew of a certain brand or product, they often had no clear view of its use in mind and needed to be provided more details on its use than did Western consumers. This tended to affect the advertising and positioning strategies for consumer products.

Presently, the lack of purchasing power depresses existing latent demand for most products. Prior to 1989, most consumers had savings that accumulated in banks due to a lack of items to be purchased. If a consumer wanted to buy a car, payments often had to be made in advance and the waiting period might be several years. Today, the opposite is the case. Scarcity of products has disappeared, and the availability of most items has substantially improved. What consumers are lacking is the ability to pay for the new, mostly imported products. Actual sales are therefore low in comparison with potential, but growth can be far greater than in established markets. The lack of demand is particularly strong for many imported products, whose prices when paid for by devalued local currencies are beyond the reach of most consumers. Only in countries such as Poland, Hungary, and the Czech Republic do enough consumers have access to foreign exchange to start creating stronger consumer pull.

The challenges for industrial products are different. Volume for international firms has declined substantially, even for long-term exporters to the regions. This has been the result of two factors. First, privatization and economic liberalization have eliminated the international trading firms who had a monopoly for the international trade for a given country and a given product range. With these agencies rapidly disappearing, many international firms have lost their key contacts and need to build them up with the newly independent firms, who can now deal directly with Western partners. But even where contacts have been reestablished, demand has been declining substantially due to economic disruptions throughout the region. Many large industrial firms used to export a substantial amount of their sales to the former Soviet Union. With the old Comecon trade group abolished, all trade has to be concluded in convertible currency, such as US$. The inability to get sufficient access to convertible currency has eliminated a large part of the trade in the region. Some Eastern European firms have tried to export to Western Europe as one way to escape the decline. This has caused problems for many Western European firms, particularly for basic industrial products such as chemicals, who are confronting low-priced Eastern European surplus production in Europe as Western Europe is in the grips of a major slowdown.

MARKETING STRATEGIES FOR EASTERN EUROPE

International firms confront numerous issues when entering Eastern Europe today. Entry strategies are characterized by a rapid need to build a market presence for fear of losing out to quicker competitors. Companies have a choice of either building up a presence from scratch, usually starting with a sales office and eventually adding their own production, or developing partnerships with existing firms. The privatization process has made it possible for international firms to buy equity in larger local companies. These local firms become the production base for the companies' international brands. This requires that the production base be revamped and modernized. Joint ventures with established firms are another possibility. Lack of access to foreign exchange makes the import strategy possible for only the most advanced Eastern European nations.

The distribution presence is another challenge faced by international firms. Throughout

Eastern Europe, the retail and distribution structure is not up to Western standards, and mass retailing or merchandising knowledge is largely absent. With the old international trade structure abolished, international companies need to build up their own distributor networks, often by recruiting and encouraging new talent into the business.

Since the concepts of advertising and promotion are new to most managers in Eastern Europe, there is still only a small group of experts. However, international advertising agencies have set up shop in most larger Eastern European countries, following their international clients who needed local support. Commercial media are available in most markets, but the details made available in other countries on media usage and media research are absent. The same can be said for marketing research.

Overall, the infrastructure needed for business in most Eastern European countries is below international standards. As in many emerging economies, telecommunications connections, travel, and hotels are not yet upgraded to Western standards. Large investments, however, are being undertaken to remedy the situation. One important positive feature is the large number of well educated, literate, people living in these countries. Observers therefore assume that these required changes will come about, although at a slower speed than originally anticipated, and that Eastern Europe will present a substantial economic opportunity to most international companies.

The following cases are intended to provide the reader with an idea of the marketing challenges encountered in this region. First, the Sony in Poland case deals with the entry strategy of a well-known international company into Poland and shows how to deal with the various distribution alternatives. Iskra Power Tool shows the reverse processes, dealing with a local firm from Slovenia (part of former Yugoslavia) that needs to reorient itself toward the Western European market. Finally, Bloshevicha Apparel Company gives the reader a first glimpse of what it means to run a business in Russia.

Iskra Power Tools

As he walked through his factory one frigid winter morning in January 1991, Miro Krek, general manager of Iskra Industrija za Elektricna, Orodja in Kranj, Yugoslavia, commented to his visitors,

There are certain things we need to do in aligning our marketing and manufacturing. As you walk through here, you can see that our efficiency could easily be improved by 10% to 15%. For example, we could put in longer lines and plan larger volume runs to get better efficiency. At the same time, we are considering concentrating our manufacturing on certain parts such as motors.

Placing his hand on his chest, he said with considerable emotion, "Motors are at the heart of any power tool—we need to manufacture them!"

For Iskra's management, the situation in Yugoslavia was tumultuous. Krek explained:

Over the last 3 months, Yugoslavia has undergone incredible political change toward adopting a Western style market economy. As this change has touched all aspects of our society, so it has forced us to rethink our entire power tool business. The question for me is, "Should we try to become a major player in the West and East European power tool markets or should we only focus on a few select markets or customers? Then, too, what would be the consequences for the Iskra organization?"

Soon after the government approved several free-enterprise laws in Yugoslavia in January 1989, revolutions occurred in many of the neighboring countries in Eastern Europe. Prior to those events, Iskra had concentrated its sales primarily on Western power tool markets, where the management believed their competitive advantages were low labor costs and, to a lesser extent, a few niche products. In fact, until January 1991, these two dimensions had formed the basis of Krek's plans for leading the Iskra Power Tool Division into the 1990s. Now, however, with Europe's political landscape in upheaval, new markets were emerging and old advantages were threatened. Consequently, it was necessary to review the interrelated issues of manufacturing and marketing power tools.

As Krek saw it, there were at least three options available for Iskra Power Tools. First, continue to capitalize on Yugoslavia's low labor costs and compete on price in Western markets. Alternatively, Iskra could build on the two major successes that it had enjoyed and manufacture and market a select few power tools in Western niche markets. Third, the management of Iskra Power Tools could try to build on Yugoslavia's tradition as a commercial link between East and West and develop the power tool markets of Eastern Europe.

Along with these options, Miro also had the continuing worry of how to preserve Iskra's do-

This case was prepared by Research Associate Robert C. Howard, under the direction of Professors William A. Fischer and Per V. Jenster as a basis for class discussion rather than to illustrate either effective or ineffective handling of a business situation. This case is part of IMD's institutional research program on Managing Internationalization. Copyright © 1991 by IMEDE, Lausanne, Switzerland. The International Institute for Management Development (IMD), resulting from the merger between IMEDE, Lausanne, and IMI, Geneva, acquires and retains all rights. Not to be used or reproduced without written permission from IMD, Lausanne, Switzerland.

mestic position at a time when the firm was under direct attack from a Black & Decker assembly operation in Yugoslavia. With less than 2 weeks to prepare for his final presentation to senior management of the Iskra Group, Krek knew a full review of the options for the 1990s was necessary.

THE ISKRA GROUP OF COMPANIES

The Iskra Group of Companies was founded in Ljubjana in 1961 through the merger of four major electrical companies in Slovenia, Yugoslavia's northernmost republic. The group based its name on the oldest of these companies, *Iskra*, which means *spark* in Slovenian and thus symbolizes the electronic nature of the group's products. By 1991, Iskra had become the leading electronic and electrical manufacturer in Yugoslavia, manufacturing and marketing a broad range of products through 14 domestic subsidiaries and 18 foreign offices. Moreover, in Slovenia, Iskra was home to roughly 25,000 employees, making the Iskra Group of Companies the largest Slovenian employer.

Iskra Power Tools

Although the Iskra Group was founded in 1961, the origins of some of its companies could be traced to the end of World War II or earlier. What became Iskra Power Tools, for example, had begun as a textile company in Kranj during the 1930s when Czechoslovakian textile manufacturers moved their operations to Northern Yugoslavia to take advantage of the low-cost labor force. During World War II, the Nazis gained control of Yugoslavia and transformed the textile facility into a military factory for aircraft engine parts; in the process, they transferred substantial metal working and engineering skills into the Iskra factories.

Throughout the postwar era, the mechanical expertise brought to Iskra by the Germans grew increasingly intertwined with electronics, supported by the expertise in Iskra's elec-

tronics companies. Until the early 1950s, Iskra's employees had channeled that expertise into industrial and consumer products for rebuilding the Yugoslavian infrastructure and meeting the needs of the domestic market, respectively. Included among the group's industrial products were electric power meters, transformers, capacitors, and electric motors. In the consumer area, typical products included automotive electronics, such as starters, alternators, and voltage regulators, and household appliances, such as vacuum cleaners, toasters, and power tools.

In time, the Kranj production facility became too constrained to continue manufacturing the entire Iskra product offering, and several products were transferred to other sites in the area. Power tool production, however, along with kilowatt meters and telecommunications switching equipment remained in Kranj. (See Exhibit 1 for the Iskra Power Tools organization chart.)

Iskra Commerce

As was typical in many centrally planned economies, the production and distribution of Iskra Group's products were partitioned into separate responsibilities. While the factories concentrated on production, a separate sales organization, Iskra Commerce, was founded in 1961 to handle the marketing and distribution responsibilities of the organization. Originally, Iskra Commerce had served as a central commercial organization, conducting all purchasing and selling for the Iskra Group of Companies both inside and outside Yugoslavia. In the early 1970s, following marked growth in size and responsibility, Iskra's domestic companies began to purchase and sell directly in Yugoslavia. However, Iskra Commerce retained responsibility for foreign commercial intercourse.

In foreign markets, Iskra Commerce continued purchasing and selling for all companies within the Iskra Group until the late 1980s. Thereafter, Iskra's foreign companies, like the ones in Yugoslavia, began to establish direct commercial links with suppliers and buyers. Mitja Taucher, former senior advisor

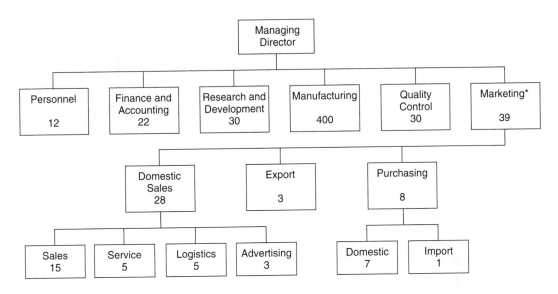

EXHIBIT 1   Iskra Power Tool Organization Chart   *Source:* Company records.

of Iskra Commerce, recalled the organization's mission:

When Yugoslavia had strong regulations regarding imports, it made a lot of sense to channel all the group's purchases and sales through one organization; the group was stronger as a whole than as individual companies. Now, however, with the changes in Yugoslavia concerning imports and the strength of our individual companies, it makes sense for Iskra Commerce to serve in a different capacity.

THE POWER TOOL INDUSTRY

Generally, power tools included any tool containing a motor that was capable of being guided and supported manually by an operator. Thus, power tools played an intermediary role between traditional hand tools and sophisticated machine tools. Typical products in the power tool family included the household drill, circular saw, jigsaw, router, angle grinder, hedge trimmer, chain saw, and less familiar and more specialized products such as nut runners and impact wrenches used in assembly line manufacture. The wide availability of electrical energy and the relatively low cost of electric tools facilitated their use in small workshops, the building and construction industries, and households.

Analysts and participants classified the industry into two broad segments according to end usage: professional and hobby. In the professional category, users worked in industries such as assembly-line manufacture, foundries, shipbuilding, and woodworking. The building and construction trade, on the other hand, covered both user segments, that is, tools dedicated to the professional builder as well as tools designed for the home enthusiast or do-it-yourself (DIY) market. Worldwide, power tool purchase behavior varied as a function of labor costs and disposable income. Generally, the professional power tool sector was most developed in high-labor-cost countries; the DIY market tended to be more pronounced in countries with higher personal disposable incomes.

In 1989, the worldwide electric power tool industry was valued at just over DM 10 billion,[1]

---

[1] In 1989, average exchange rates were 1 ECU = DM2.02 and US$1 = DM1.88.

with sales concentrated in three major markets: North America, 28%; Europe, 47%; and the Far East, 18%. Although the industry had grown an average of 3% per annum on a worldwide basis since 1980, market growth rates varied considerably among individual countries (*as indicated in Table 1*). Within Europe, where the industrial segment had traditionally dominated, Germany, France, Great Britain, and Italy represented 75% of the region's sales (*as summarized in Table 2*).

TABLE 1 Percent of Growth of European Power Tool Markets in 1989 and 1990

Country	% Growth 1989	Country	% Growth 1990
Portugal	20	Greece	35
Spain	18	Germany	18
Italy	15	Portugal	18
Greece	15	Italy	12
Finland	12	Netherlands	10
Austria	12	Sweden	10
Sweden	10	Ireland	8
Great Britain	8	Belgium	6
Germany	8	Spain	6
France	8	Austria	4
Belgium	8	Denmark	3
Switzerland	8	Switzerland	3
Netherlands	5	France	0
Ireland	5	Great Britain	0
Denmark	-5	Norway	0
Norway	-5	Finland	-3

1989 Source: Databank.

1990 Source: Bosch.

TABLE 2 1989 Unit Sales in Europe's Four Largest Markets

Country	Thousands of Pieces	% European Sales
Germany	7,000	28
France	5,000	20
Great Britain	4,300	17
Italy	2,500	10
Other countries	6,200	25
Total	25,000	100

Source: Bosch.

Segments and Channels

Professional tools were traditionally bought in hardware stores, from wholesalers, from large tool specialists, or from a manufacturer's or distributor's direct sales force. Quality products suited to specific tasks, durability, and after-sales service were viewed as important buying criteria. In addition, some manufacturers of high-end tools viewed education and problem solving as part of the sales effort, with trained salespeople needed to meet the technical requirements of the user.

In the hobby segment, customers bought from wholesalers, hardware stores, department stores, home centers, mail-order houses, and supermarkets. In this segment, manufacturers considered image, product quality, and price as important purchase factors. Also in this segment, competition was becoming increasingly like that of other consumer products; that is, brand name and packaging were gaining in importance relative to other product features. At the low end of the market, products were designed to meet an expected lifetime use of 25 hours. At the high end, on the other hand, which tended to enlarge as the market matured, there was more emphasis on durability and ergonomic characteristics, similar to professional products.

In Europe, a shift in purchasing patterns had led to a shift in the distribution of power tools. In the professional sector, direct sales had begun to play a more significant role in the distribution process, particularly in the more mature and structured markets. And, in the consumer segment, the volume of tools sold through mass merchandisers was growing at the expense of conventional tool sellers. In short, increased specialization in power tool usage, combined with a proliferation of applications, was leading manufacturers to establish more direct links to professional users and more visible links to the DIY segment. The volume of power tools sold through any one of these channels varied as a function of country. Generally, the markets in Northern Europe were more mature and more structured than those in the Mediterranean countries. Likewise, mass merchandisers and direct sales played a more significant role in the North than in the South. (*Table 3 contains comparative data on power tools sold through different channels in Germany versus Italy.*)

TABLE 3 Percent of Country Sales by Distribution Channel, 1990

Channel	DIY Segment	
	Germany	Italy
Wholesalers	5	25
Hardware stores	55	45
Department stores (mass merchandisers)	15	11
Home centers	21	—
Others (cash and carry, mail order)	4	19
	Professional Segment	
Direct	10	—
Hardware	50	55
Wholesalers	40	25
Large Tool Specialists (mass merchandisers)	—	20

Source: Black & Decker, Iskra company records.

Manufacturing

Power tools embodied a range of technologies including a motor shaft around which copper wire was wound to form an armature, gears, plastic or metal housing, switches, and cables. In conjunction with a trend in production specialization in the postwar era, power tool manufacturers relied heavily on subcontractors to produce many of these components. Generally, the major competitors only made components that were central to the performance of the final product, such as the motor. (*The outline below summarizes the key elements in a typical power tool.*)

Typically, power tools were mass produced, although the extent of mechanization varied with the volume of production, nature of the product, and efficiency of the individual manufacturer. According to one industry analyst, purchased materials accounted for 50% of a power tool firm's manufacturing costs; machining, 15%; diecasting and molding, 9%;

motor winding and assembly, 12%; and final assembly, 14%.

Trends

By the late 1980s, a number of trends began to influence the level and nature of competition in the worldwide power tool industry. Among these were a growing preference for battery-powered tools, globalization of the industry, and the opening up of Eastern Europe.

Battery-powered Tools

During the 1980s, battery-powered (also known as cordless) tools benefited significantly from advances in technology. Because of their low energy storage, initial battery-driven products were limited to the smaller jobs of the DIY market. However, the combination of superior power storage and lighter materials that was developed during the 1980s permitted battery-operated tools to be used in more demanding applications, thus facilitating their penetration of the professional market. At the end of the 1980s, cordless tools represented 20% of all power tool production worldwide and, like many products using electronics, the Japanese were particularly adept at developing cordless power tools. During the 1990s, advances in materials science and battery technology were expected to increase both the usage life between recharges and the number of applications cordless tools could handle.

Globalization

Throughout the 1980s, the electric power tool industry became increasingly globalized, enabling larger players to have an operational flexibility unavailable to smaller companies. By decreasing a firm's reliance on a single market,

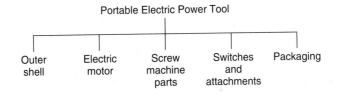

multinational power tool companies were able to leverage their positions worldwide. That is, firms with manufacturing as well as sales in many markets were able to exploit uncertainties in exchange rates, competitive moves, or government policies far better than their smaller rivals.

Eastern Europe and the USSR

During 1989, communist dictatorships across Eastern Europe were replaced by a variety of governments that, in general, expressed their commitment to develop market economies. Analysts believed that these developments would influence the power tool business in two ways. First, these newly opened markets and their power tool manufacturers were expected to be the targets of firms already established in the West. Second, once the legal issues surrounding privatization became clear, the surviving power tool manufacturers in Eastern Europe could begin to restructure their own operations and market their products at home and abroad.

Competition

In 1989, there were approximately 75 power tool manufacturers worldwide. Generally, these competitors could be grouped into two categories: large multinationals and primarily domestic manufacturers. Typically, the large players offered a full range of power tools to both the professional and the DIY segments, as well as a complete line of accessories such as drill bits, saw blades, battery packs, and after-sales service. Smaller power tool manufacturers, on the other hand, tended to concentrate production on a limited line of tools, augmented by OEM products to one or a few segments of the market. Although these small firms lacked the product offering of their larger rivals, they were well known and respected for their expertise in their chosen fields.

Black & Decker

Black & Decker was the largest power tool maker in the world. With manufacturing plants in 10 countries and sales in nearly 100, the company reported 1989 power tool sales of $1,077 million. With approximately 25% of the total market, Black & Decker commanded a worldwide share more than twice that of its next biggest rival. Like most of its competitors, the company segmented the industry into professional and DIY sectors; between the two, Black & Decker derived two-thirds of its revenue from consumers and one-third from professional users.

In addition to its sheer size, Black & Decker enjoyed a number of competitive advantages. New product introduction, for example, was a high priority; the company launched 77 products in 1989 alone and, in the same year, new and redesigned products accounted for 25% of revenues. By 1991, the company expected new entries to represent more than half its sales.

In Europe, where Black & Decker pioneered the introduction of products to the DIY segment, its name was virtually synonymous with power tools. In Britain, for example, it was not uncommon for DIY remodelers to "Black & Decker" their homes. And, in France, individuals "plugged in" to the social scene were said to be "*très Black & Decker.*"

One company spokesman attributed his company's success to proper market segmentation and a restructuring that had begun in the mid-1980s. Thus, when the market for power tools as a whole was growing at a rate of only 5% to 6%, Black & Decker achieved 11% growth in 1989, twice the rate of the markets served, due in part to its concentrated focus on accessories and cordless products. Although the latter grew 30% in 1989, Black & Decker's successful identification of the trend toward cordless products allowed its sales in this segment to grow by 70%, reaching $100 million in 1989.

From the mid-1980s onward, the management of Black & Decker devoted significant attention to "globalizing" its worldwide operations and, by the beginning of the 1990s, design centers, manufacturing plants, and marketing programs were adept at making and selling products to a worldwide market. As early as 1978, Black & Decker had undertaken the standardization of its motors and armature shafts, and it had, over the years, consistently pursued manufacturing approaches that combined product variety with volume output, such as dedicated lines and facilities for specific items (focused factories and group technology), flexible manufacturing systems (FMS),[2] just-in-time manufacturing (JIT),[3] and significant vertical integration of the fabrication and assembly process. In addition, Black & Decker achieved substantial cost savings through global purchasing programs and saved millions of dollars by restructuring its manufacturing facilities. In one facility, for example, the company standardized production around a limited number of motors. In another case, the company consolidated production of drills from five different plants to two.

To strengthen its presence in Eastern Europe, Black & Decker had recently established an assembly operation via a joint venture in Kranj. Although the company owned only 49%, its proximity to Iskra was seen as a serious challenge to the latter's position in Yugoslavia. And in May 1989 in Czechoslovakia, Black & Decker entered into a joint venture to produce DIY tools and lawnmowers for the Czechoslovakian and West European markets. Once the joint venture reached full capacity, planned for the start of 1990, Black & Decker intended to cease production at its French and Italian facilities and rely on its new Eastern European manufacturing platform.

Makita

Based in Japan, the Makita Electric Works had entered the power tool market in the 1950s. In the mid-1970s and the 1980s, Makita established itself in a number of foreign markets by emphasizing its price competitiveness.

---

[2] Flexible manufacturing systems consisted of sophisticated computer-driven lines, with relatively independent routing and intelligent machining centers.

[3] JIT referred to the Japanese-inspired approach to manufacturing, which originated with the philosophy of continuous improvement, superior quality, low changeover costs, and greatly reduced work-in-process inventories.

At one point in the mid-1970s, for example, Makita products were selling at price levels that were 20% to 30% lower than the industry average. Nonetheless, by the beginning of the 1990s, Makita had established a solid reputation for quality and after-sales service, supported by a 3-day repair policy. And, through engaging a large number of distribution outlets in target markets to promote and service its products, Makita had climbed to number 2 in the industry by 1991.

In contrast to Black & Decker, Makita concentrated only on the professional segment of the market, with a broad range of tools for professionals. The company attributed its success in overseas markets to superior after-sales service and a close working relationship with well-informed retailers who kept in touch with consumers regarding the latest in product development. Beginning with two factories in Japan in the mid-1970s, Makita had decided to globalize its operations during the 1980s, establishing factory operations in the United States, Canada, and Brazil.

In Europe, Makita's 1989 sales increased by 15% and, in the same year, a company spokesman stated that Makita intended to become the largest power tool supplier in the region. In a step toward fulfilling this vision and meeting the company's expressed goal of supplying 25% of European sales with locally manufactured products, Makita began constructing a new power tool plant in the United Kingdom in March 1990. Scheduled to begin operating in early 1991, the plant would initially make cordless and percussion drills, angle grinders, and circular saws for the professional sector. Ultimately, however, the plant was to produce only electric motors. As of January 1991, Makita had not begun to compete in any of Iskra's markets.

Robert Bosch

Robert Bosch was the third largest power tool producer in the world and had manufacturing plants in Germany, the United States, Brazil, and Switzerland. Like Black & Decker, Bosch produced a variety of power tools for both the professional and the DIY segments, buying the portable tool division of Stanley

Tools in the United States in 1979. The company was particularly strong in Europe, where it distributed through all channels. In 1990, despite an unfavorable trend in the $/DM exchange rate, Bosch's sales increased 14% to over DM 2.2 billion.

Following the unification of East Germany and West Germany, Bosch management announced plans for a joint venture with VEB Elektrowerkzeuge Sebnitz to assemble power tools in Dresden (formerly East Germany) to be distributed through the latter's network of 1,400 hardware outlets. By the end of 1990, the Sebnitz facility was a fully owned subsidiary and earmarked for DM 50 million in investment, initially for producing one-handed angle grinders and small drills. In the longer term, the management of Bosch planned to concentrate all export production in Sebnitz.

Skil

Skil was a major manufacturer of power tools based in the United States, where the company was originally known as a professional tool supplier. More recently, however, Skil had concentrated on developing tools that fulfilled needs somewhere between the professional and consumer levels. In Europe, Skil had positioned itself in the Nordic markets as a professional tool company. It approached the rest of Europe, on the other hand, in the DIY market with a strong price emphasis and was particularly strong in Germany and France.

Niche Players

Aside from the larger multinational power tool companies, numerous successful, albeit smaller, players in Europe pursued niche strategies. In Germany, for example, Festo and ELU were well known for their fine-crafted woodworking tools, especially circular saws. Likewise, Kango, a British company, was renowned for its percussion drills. Generally, niche players in the European power tool business charged premium prices and earned the majority of their sales in their home markets. (*See Exhibits 2 and 3, respectively, for a summary of Iskra's competition according to category and a competitor positioning diagram prepared by a team of Iskra management.*)

ISKRA POWER TOOLS' COMPETITIVE POSITION

Market Development

From its beginning in the early 1950s, the Iskra Power Tool division concentrated its sales in the Yugoslavian market. Ventures into Western Europe did not begin until the 1960s when the management sought to expand its product offering, consisting primarily of electric drills, based on the company's expertise in small electric motors. The cornerstone of this expansion strategy was exchange programs with other power tool manufacturers.

In 1966, Iskra entered into a cooperation agreement with Perles, a small power tool manufacturer in Switzerland. In exchange for Perles' angle grinders sold under the Iskra name in Yugoslavia, Perles received Iskra's drills, which it distributed through its own network under the Perles label. In 1971, Iskra management sought to build on the Perles name and distribution network by acquiring the Swiss-based manufacturer. Mitja Taucher commented that, in the early 1970s, Iskra management realized they would have difficulties with an unknown name in Europe and thus decided to acquire Perles. "Perles is still in existence mostly for its name, not its manufacturing capacity, which is small," recalled Mitja. He added, "It was a good name across Europe for large angle grinders and some drills."

Bolstered by its first co-marketing arrangement with Perles, in 1972 the management of Iskra entered into an agreement with Skil Europe. In exchange for Iskra's small drills, sold under Skil's name through its European distribution network, Skil supplied Iskra with percussion drills, belt sanders, and circular saws, sold in Yugoslavia under the Iskra name.

EXHIBIT 2   Iskra's Main Competitors in Europe

Competitor	Location of Corporate Headquarters	Specialist (S) or Generalist (G)	Perceived Successful by Iskra
AEG	D	G	
Black & Decker	US	G	+
Bosch	D	G	+
Casals	E	G	
ELU	D	S, woodworking tools, esp. circular saws	
Fein	D	S, metal-working tools, esp. drills and angle grinders	
Festo	D	S, same as ELU	+
Hilti	D	S, drills	+
Hitachi	J	G	
Impex	D	S, drills	
Kango	UK	S, percussion drills	
Kress	D	G	
Makita	J	G	
Metabo	D	G	
Peugeot	F	G	
Rockwell	US	G	
Rupes	I	S, table saws	
Ryobi	J	G	+
Skil	US, NL	G	
Stayer	I	G	+
Wegoma	D	S, same as ELU	

Source: Company records.

D = Germany USA = United States

E = Spain J = Japan

UK = United Kingdom F = France

I = Italy NL = Netherlands

Eastern European Ventures

Following the first of a series of oil crises that began in 1973, it was difficult for Iskra to continue its expansion plans into Western markets. As an alternative, the management of Iskra Power Tools began to strengthen business ties with its socialist neighbors in Eastern Europe.

Czechoslovakia

Iskra's Eastern European experience began in 1978 with Naradi, a power tool manufacturer, and with Merkuria, a trading company, both based in Czechoslovakia. Due to a lack of convertible currency in Czechoslovakia, Iskra devised a three-way trading agreement: Perles shipped drills from Switzerland to Naradi, which marketed the products under the Naradi name, and to Merkuria, which sold products under the Iskra name. In turn, both Czech firms delivered products to Iskra; the process was completed when Iskra sent its power tools to Perles in Switzerland. Although Iskra achieved nearly a 10% market share through these two agreements in Czechoslovakia, its success was not without problems.

One executive stated that the weak point in the process was the power tools from Czechoslovakia; tools made by Naradi did not measure up to the quality standards demanded by Yugoslavian consumers. Moreover, after a few years, Naradi's products were out of date in comparison to competitors' offerings. Finally, because of the difficulties posed by the lack of real distribution channels or a service network in Czechoslovakia, Iskra management terminated the agreement in 1988.

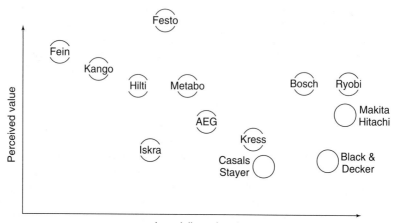

EXHIBIT 3 Competitor Positioning Diagram

Poland

Iskra had also participated in a cooperative arrangement to exchange power tools with Celma, a Polish power tool manufacturer. Like the agreement with Naradi in Czechoslovakia, Iskra marketed Celma's products under the Iskra name in Yugoslavia. However, Celma's products were of such low quality that Iskra soon found itself inundated with repair requests. Consequently, the management of Iskra devised a new agreement for close cooperation on specialty tools such as shears, steel cutters, and die grinders.

USSR

More recently, Iskra Power Tools had tried manufacturing in the USSR. After 5 years of negotiating with the Institute for Power Tools in Moscow, in 1984, the first 100 power tools were brought to Yugoslavia. Unfortunately, due to the length of the negotiating period, the products were out of date on arrival. Like the previous efforts in Czechoslovakia and Poland, Iskra brought its Russian efforts to a halt.

Refocus on Western Europe

Like many firms that manufactured in and exported from Yugoslavia, Iskra earned a certain level of income from the domestic market. Although that income was not guaranteed,

limited competition in the Yugoslavian power tool market had almost always provided Iskra with a source of funding to manufacture tools sold outside the country. By the beginning of the 1980s, however, the management of Iskra Power Tools grew concerned about becoming too dependent on the domestic market. Moreover, when it combined the uncertainties of the domestic market with its unsuccessful ventures in Eastern Europe, the management concluded it was time to resume strengthening ties with Western power tool producers.

Iskra as OEM Supplier

ELU

In 1980, Iskra signed a cooperation agreement with ELU, a German manufacturer of woodworking tools. Despite Iskra's successful development and initial manufacture of a small circular saw for sale under the ELU label, the management of ELU canceled the agreement after 2 years. According to Branko Suhadolnik, export manager for Iskra Power Tools, Iskra was simply unable to supply the quantity of saws specified in the contract because of delays in starting production.

Kango

Iskra also began manufacturing for Kango, a U.K. company specializing in drills. In exchange for Kango's rotary hammer, sold under the Iskra name in Yugoslavia, Iskra provided Kango with circular saws sold under the Kango name in the United Kingdom.

Iskra as Volume EOM

Skil

In the mid-1980s, Iskra management expanded its cooperation with Skil. In addition to supplying Skil with a small drill, Iskra provided a small angle grinder, circular saw, and orbital sander. These items were sold under the Skil name in support of Skil's low-price strategy. In November 1990, the management of Iskra approached Skil to discuss strengthening their partnership still further. However, as of January 1991, no additional cooperation had been agreed to.

Ryobi

In 1990, Miro Krek and Branko Suhadolnik began negotiating a joint venture agreement with Ryobi from Japan. Suhadolnik explained the Ryobi was considering Yugoslavia as an entry point into the European Economic Community and wanted to capitalize on Yugoslavia's comparative advantage in labor costs. In return for supplying angle grinders to Ryobi, Iskra was to market Ryobi's battery-operated power tools in Yugoslavia. Although the management of Ryobi was impressed with Iskra's products, they said that the manufacturing costs were too high; to meet Ryobi's terms, Iskra had to invest in more equipment. Shortly thereafter, the management of Ryobi decided to postpone further dealings in Eastern Europe until the political environment stabilized.

Bosch

In its most recent effort to supply a foreign manufacturer, Iskra approached Bosch concerning a router that complemented Bosch's offering. This deal, too, nearly succeeded, but was contingent on Iskra's dissolving its independent sales network in Germany and elsewhere. Because Bosch was not willing to purchase what Iskra management believed was the required volume necessary to compensate for the loss of its sales network, Iskra declined the offer.

In summary, the management of Iskra had made several attempts over the years to increase its attractiveness to foreign firms. With Skil, a generalist in the power tool industry, Iskra's competitive advantage was being a low-cost supplier; with ELU, Kango, and Bosch, on the other hand, Iskra's success was based on the high perceived value of a niche product. With Ryobi, price competitiveness and market presence in Eastern Europe were important.

Iskra's Products and Channels

At the beginning of 1991, Iskra marketed a range of 200 products; 10 of these were obtained from other manufacturers via exchange agreements, while the balance were designed and produced by Iskra alone. Roughly speaking, accessories accounted for 20% of Iskra Power Tools' turnover, while drills and angle grinders accounted for approximately 50% and 30%, respectively, of tool sales. (*See Exhibit 4 for an overview of Iskra's product offering.*) Outside Yugoslavia, Iskra distributed its own products under the Perles name, almost exclusively through specialist hardware outlets in both the DIY and professional segments. In addition, Iskra Commerce marketed Iskra's power tools through its own offices. Although the influence of the latter was declining, Suhadolnik commented that, until the late 1980s, Iskra Commerce's foreign companies often made policies to survive for the short term, with little attention to the long term. For example, in those markets where the two organizations overlapped, prices sometimes differed between Iskra Power Tools and Iskra Commerce for the same products. More recently, he added, Iskra management had succeeded in changing this policy but, Suhadolnik commented, "To change something with a life of its own is not so easy."

In Yugoslavia, where Iskra had a market

Iskra

orodje za vsake roke

EXHIBIT 4 Overview of Iskra's Power Tool Offerings

EXHIBIT 4 (*Continued*)

share of 50% in 1989, the company sold its power tools through Iskra Commerce with its own network of shops in each republic. However, the company had a significantly larger market share in Serbia than in Slovenia or Croatia. According to Branko, natives of the latter two provinces, because of their proximity to Italy and Austria, were not only better informed as to Western power tool alternatives, but could more easily access these alternative products. Power tools were also sold through the Iskra Power Tools sales organization and directly from the factory in Kranj.

Design

In 1990, the design group at Iskra consisted of six people, all working primarily with pencil and paper. By contrast, their Western counterparts worked with computer-aided design (CAD) systems. Despite the lack of modern design equipment, the Iskra design team possessed strong artistic talents and lacked the engineering bias of Western designers. In describing the evolution of the relationship between design and manufacturing at Iskra, one manager commented that, until the early 1980s, there was a "We draw, you make" attitude. A few years thereafter, employees in the two functions began taking a more interdisciplinary approach to designing and making Iskra's power tools. Designers, for example, began asking those in manufacturing about the costs associated with individual parts; those in manufacturing, on the other hand, asked designers for new technological solutions. "Yet," recalled one designer, "new solutions were not possible because they required too much investment in new technology."

As of January 1991, there were two ways of concentrating on new product development at Iskra Power Tools. One was via direct cooperation with manufacturing on existing product lines, a process that tended to focus on minor changes and had been practiced for at least 15 years. The second pertained to new products and was primarily concerned with shortening product development time, through interdis-

ciplinary teams, to a level comparable to Iskra's competition.

Not unlike the design–manufacturing relationship, the interaction between design and marketing was based on a philosophy of "We design, you sell." Beginning in the mid-1980s, however, this relationship also began to change as collaboration with Iskra's partners, Skil and Perles, on new designs began to increase, and greater and earlier cooperation between the two functions began to evolve.

Iskra was receptive to ideas from the marketplace communicated to the design team via Iskra's customers and foreign distributors. In 1988, for example, Iskra formed a multidisciplinary team to determine which products had to be produced in the subsequent 5 years, at what price, and in what quantity. In the export market, ideas were solicited from Iskra's agents and distributors via an annual conference. As for feedback from end users, Iskra conducted market research for both its professional and its DIY customers, albeit only in Yugoslavia. (*See Table 4 for design information at Iskra Power Tools.*)

Manufacturing

Despite Iskra's product offering of 200 power tools, most were variations of a common manufacturing mix of 10 to 15 models, all made in one factory using traditional batch production. Depending on the model, the array of products was manufactured on a monthly, quarterly, or annual basis. For example, Iskra had 70 variations of its drill, which was produced throughout the year in the same way as its angle grinders and circular saws. On the other hand, smaller-volume products such as sanders and routers were made only on a quarterly basis.

Planning

At Iskra, batch sizes and sequencing were developed by a central planning department located in the Kranj factory. Typically, the planning department estimated the year's production and adjusted their forecast quarterly. In addition, three planners prioritized

TABLE 4 Information on Iskra Power Tools' Design Function

Year	1982	1983	1984	1985	1986	1987	1988	1989	1990
No. of designers	5	5	5	5	5	3	6	6	5
Average age	40	41	42	42	43	35	37	40	41
Years of experience (absolute)	38	43	48	49	54	20	26	28	33
Reconstructed products	6				7				3
Modifications	148				208				190
Commercial variants	717				1,802				827
New products	0	1	3	1	2	1	0	1	0

Source: Company records.

Note: A reconstructed product was one that had been developed and produced, but corrected for flaws. A modification, on the other hand, corresponded to a product with an incremental innovation such as a new spindle, a different type of handle, or an additional speed. As the name implied, commercial variants were simply the number of variations possible for Iskra's products needed to meet the different demands of Iskra's many markets and customers.

the work at each factory workstation based on the assembly plan, which, in turn, was based on delivery promises. Prior to final assembly, the manufacturing department received figures for specific markets and attached the correct lables to the final package.

Differences between the batches produced and the amounts needed for assembly at any point in time (due to lead time variations) were stored in inventories until needed. In other words, purchasing of components and product fabrication at Iskra were always begun before the ultimate destination of a power tool was known, thereby limiting the ability to use dedicated machining in the first and last stages of the production process. From 1987 to 1989, Iskra Power Tools' inventory turnovers averaged 4.4, with the biggest inventories occurring at the beginning of the assembly process. By comparison, one manager estimated that Bosch's inventory turnover was in the range of 5 to 10 per year.

Milan Bavec, manufacturing manager, believed that parts inventories were too high because of difficulties in linking purchasing more closely to assembly. As an example, he explained that, on August 1, he might begin a series of 3,000 sanders, for which he ordered parts 3 months in advance. However, he said, when some parts took 6 months to arrive, one simply had to maintain the necessary inventory. All parts, he continued, were moved in and out of inventory. That is, whether Iskra produced or purchased its parts, all parts were stored in a warehouse until the full range was available to make a particular product. As an aside, Igor Poljsak, financial and accounting department manager, mentioned that the constant shifting of parts between Iskra's many buildings added 10% to 15% to production costs. Then, too, at 40% to 50% per year to borrow money, he estimated that the interest on working capital was 10% to 12%. Within manufacturing, some believed that if the individual market demands could be better coordinated with the manufacturing function, inventories could be reduced and more dedicated assembly implemented, thereby raising productivity.

Productivity

In terms of performance, productivity at Iskra Power Tools was somewhere between that of Eastern and Western power tool makers, with direct labor estimated at 10% to 12% of the cost of goods sold. (*See Table 5 for productivity figures, Table 6 for a breakdown of the manufacturing costs associated with a typical product, and Exhibits 5 and 6 for the Iskra income statement and balance sheets, respectively.*)

In discussing productivity, the management of Iskra acknowledged that labor costs were a serious burden and that the company probably had three times as many people as necessary. Commented one executive, indirect costs are always too high, and we think that we have extremely high indirect costs for our production volume. For example, we have data indicating that Skil, with approximately the same number of people as Iskra, produces nearly 1 million pieces. Kress employs 400 to 500 people and produces around 1 million pieces. We have around 550 people, recently reduced from 760 without any strikes; however, I don't believe that will hold if we try to reduce further.

In addition to too many employees, Iskra's productivity was influenced by significant differences in production. Specifically, work was performed both in batch and in sequence, and, because all parts (except motors) were continually moved in and out of physical inventory, the flow of goods through the factory was complicated. (*See Exhibit 7 for the flow path of a typical item.*) On the third floor of the factory, where a dedicated motor assembly line was located, the situation was even more chaotic; there was little apparent continuity among workstations and, although the production machinery was only about 10 years old, the manufacturing process appeared much older. Finally, the area for final assembly of tools was like a rabbit warren, with lots of discontinuities. As an example, newly finished goods often sat for several days waiting for complementary parts, such as chuck keys, which had become stocked out.

Quality

The management of Iskra Power Tools was well aware that it needed to establish, improve, and maintain quality in products and processes. In fact, the manager responsible for quality had organized statistical process control (SPC) procedures within the factory but, to date, had

TABLE 5 Productivity Figures for Selected Power Tool Firms

Company or Location	No. of Workers	Output (units/year)
Iskra	550	600,000
Bulgarian	5,000	40,000
Czechoslovakian	2,000	150,000
Western firm	250	600,000

Source: Company records.

TABLE 6 Breakdown of Manufacturing Costs for Angle Grinders (%)

Purchased materials	65.1
Machining, diecasting, and molding	15.9
Motor assembly	9.1
Final assembly	9.9
Total	100.0

Source: Company records.

had only mixed success. Specifically, the level of quality was nowhere near that required to move to a production process like JIT, which could significantly reduce work-in-process inventories.

As of early 1991, incoming goods continued to be checked on arrival, according to prearranged contractual standards, using a standard acceptance sampling (acceptable quality level or AQL) system. In fact, acceptance sampling was done at final production and final assembly, as well as with incoming items. In all cases, quality control (QC) was based on the first five pieces in a batch, followed by statistical sampling.

For the future, the quality manager hoped to integrate a quality attitude throughout the company. As part of the process, management had prepared a book containing quality standards based on the International Standards Organization (ISO) 9000 series set of standards.[4] As of January 1991, management had not had much success implementing quality improvement. To do so, management believed, would require reshaping the attitudes of Iskra's workers.

The Production Workers

Iskra Power Tools' production process was characterized by low employee involvement, poor changeover performance between different models, and relatively poor maintenance performance. The assembly line workers were analyzed using modern time and methods analysis (work factor), and the analysis was used to allocate labor staffing. However, since as-

---

[4] ISO 9000 was a technical standard that required the establishment of a complete system for monitoring quality standards.

EXHIBIT 5 Income Statement for Iskra Power Tools

Fiscal Year Ending December 31 ($US'000)	*1986*	*1987*	*1988*	*1989*	*1990*
Sales Revenue					
Domestic	25,362.9	4,842.5	18,196.4	20,658.6	24,886.9
Exports	7,559.2	12,311.6	11,882.3	10,204.6	12,815.1
Others	1,932.5	1,852.7	486.0	406.2	548.5
Total sales	**34,854.6**	**39,006.8**	**30,564.7**	**31,269.4**	**38,250.5**
Cost of sales	18,753.8	27,596.4	22,948.2	23,676.4	27,425.9
Gross income	16,100.8	11,410.4	7,616.5	7,593.0	10,824.6
Selling and administrative expenses	10,065.4	8,226.5	5,032.3	5,191.8	6,020.4
Operating income	**6035.4**	**3,183.9**	**2,584.2**	**2,401.2**	**4,804.2**
Other income:					
Interest	58.3	3.3	36.6	14,928.1	797.5
Sundry income	1,049.6	269.3	152.8	406.2	2,320.8
Total other income	**1,107.9**	**272.6**	**189.4**	**15,334.3**	**3,118.3**
Other expenses:					
Interest	3,611.4	907.9	1,753.9	12,201.8	4,558.6
Sundry expenses	1,380.5	583.0	482.5	13,664.8	4,781.7
Total other expenses	**4,991.9**	**1,490.9**	**2,236.4**	**25,866.6**	**9,340.3**
Obligatory contributions to community funds	1,090.7	1521.9	507.6		
Net income (loss)	**1,060.7**	**443.7**	**29.6**	**(8,131.1)**	**(1,417.8)**
Allocation of net income (loss):					
Business fund	140.6				
Reserve fund	269.7	292.8	26.6		
Collective consumption fund	557.2	128.6			
Joint venture partners	93.2	22.3	3.0		
Depreciation	1,109.7	1,402.7	1,269.9	1470.2	2,591.5
Net income	1,060.7	443.7	29.6	(8,131.1)	(1,417.8)
Cash generation	2,170.4	1,846.4	1,299.5	(6,660.9)	(1,173.7)

Source: Company records.

sembly was performed on a paced line, it was not possible for the employees to work faster. Thus, no pay incentives existed for higher output and workers were paid as a group. On occasion, quality bonuses were paid within the factory, despite the fact that some of the production being "rewarded" was not actually perfect.

Jakob Sink, quality assurance manager, commented on the difficulties met in transforming the mind-set of Iskra employees. "It is a new idea to send back a QC approval form within a few weeks. 'Why not do it in a couple of months?' is still very much the attitude of those working in production." Then, too, Sink added, the worker was concerned that identifying poor quality could cause either himself or a co-worker to be fired. Also, he mentioned that some employees might resist altering manufacturing processes discussed by manage-

ment in an attempt to deal with high variety manufacturing in a more efficient format. In defense of the work force, Sink said that incoming materials played a key role in the quality problem and that, although Iskra controlled what it bought, it sometimes cost as much to control incoming materials as to produce a finished product.

The Supply Situation

Given that all major players in the power tool industry relied on suppliers for major components, it was not surprising that Iskra was also involved in such relationships. However, in Iskra's case, there was widespread agreement among the management team that the supply relationships were a competitive disadvantage. In fact, some thought that Iskra's manufacturing costs

EXHIBIT 6   Iskra Balance Sheets

Fiscal Year Ending December 31 ($US '000)	1986	1987	1988	1989	1990
Current Assets:					
Bank balances and cash	68.2	71.9	13.7	29.0	24.3
Bills and trade receivables	6,068.1	6,815.3	4,954.3	5,791.2	10,257.3
Prepayments and other receivables	1,734.9	1,497.4	4,931.1	520.8	137.3
Current portion of long-term receivables	29.1	1.8	0.5	408.6	184.1
Inventories:					
Raw materials	4,104.0	3,506.8	2,289.7	856.8	3,367.0
Work-in process	1,538.8	1,367.4	957.8	245.9	1,148.0
Finished products	1,367.9	1,211.4	640.9	802.2	1,750.0
Subtotal	7,010.7	6,085.6	3,888.4	1,904.9	6,265.0
Total Current Assets	**14,911.0**	**14,472.0**	**13,788.0**	**8,654.5**	**16,868.0**
Long-term receivables	106.3	67.8	56.6	2,503.3	3,500.0
Investments	1,187.9	1,324.7	1,289.1	34.1	
Deposits for capital expenditure	147.4	16.9	201.8	28.9	998.4
Fixed Assets:					
Land and building	1,635.0	1,343.1	1,199.8	1,453.9	2,611.6
Equipment	12,571.4	12,804.9	11,697.2	17,554.8	32,520.9
Deferred expenditure	0.2	15.8	14.0	188.0	
Construction in progress	241.3	24.9	70.5	107.5	191.9
Total Gross Fixed Assets	**14,447.9**	**14,188.7**	**12,981.5**	**19,304.2**	**35,324.5**
Less: Accumulated depreciation	7,238.1	7,495.2	7,542.2	12,363.5	25,093.6
Net fixed assets	7,209.8	6,693.5	5,439.3	6,940.7	10,230.9
Intangible assets			125.9		
Net assets allocated to funds					
Reserve fund	501.7	338.6	94.1	69.6	137.4
Collective consumption fund	1328.1	847.3	466.1	169.6	380.6
Other funds	43.9	21.4	9.6	21.3	168.5
Subtotal	1,873.7	1,207.3	569.8	260.5	686.5
TOTAL ASSETS	**25,436.1**	**23,782.2**	**21,470.5**	**21,089.8**	**35,987.9**
Liabilities and Funds					
Current Liabilities:					
Bills and trade payables	2,859.0	2,945.6	2,581.5	7,656.1	4,282.7
Payables for fixed assets	2.6	6.5	1.3		
Customers deposits and other					
current liabilities	4,231.5	2,648.2	2,689.5	0.9	3,836.9
Short-term loans	3,224.9	5,381.4	5,981.1	4,325.3	7,188.4
Current portion of long-term loans	1,503.3	889.5	511.1	502.7	263.2
Amounts due to reserve and collective					
consumption funds	91.2	309.3	17.3		
Deferred sales	2,158.8	1,355.9	1,111.5	172.1	4,207.3
Total Current Liabilities	**14,071.3**	**13,536.4**	**12,893.3**	**12,657.1**	**19,778.5**
Long-term loans	3,024.2	3,362.5	3,345.4	2,788.3	5,001.0
Joint venture partner investments:					
Domestic partners	107.9	17.8	22.1	0.7	
Foreign JV partners					
Business funds	6,476.4	5,668.0	4,659.5	5,368.9	10,541.4
Other funds:					
Reserve fund	501.7	338.6	94.1	160.2	137.4
Collective consumption fund	1,236.9	847.2	448.8	69.6	380.6
Other funds	17.7	11.7	7.3	35.2	149.0
Subtotal	1,756.3	1,197.5	550.2	265.0	667.0
TOTAL LIABILITIES AND FUNDS	**25,436.1**	**23,782.2**	**21,470.5**	**21,080.0**	**35,987.9**

Source: Company records.

were 20% to 25% more expensive than for Bosch, for example, because of the supply situation. Then, too, the company faced the added complication that one of its major suppliers was based in Serbia, a republic with which political tensions had been growing.

Within Yugoslavia, the manufacturing director distinguished suppliers according to raw materials or finished components such as gears and cables. He commented that, aside from having a lower quality, raw materials were also more expensive in Yugoslavia than in Western Europe. Furthermore, there were few finished component suppliers to choose from in Yugoslavia, and those that did exist did not possess a high quality standard. To use domestic components, Iskra would have to take what was available from several firms and remachine those components before assembling its power tools. In other words, the absence of quality suppliers and subcontractors added yet another step to Iskra's manufacturing.

As one remedy, Iskra forged close working relationships with its local suppliers. Generally, these suppliers were able to respond to major design changes without any real problem, but efforts to upgrade the quality of the finished components had been unsuccessful. Despite the close relationships, it was highly unlikely that Iskra could put SPC into a supplier facility. According to Milan Bavec, "SPC is still too new,

and even though we've held seminars, run films and the like, our results are still poor. At present, the real problem is getting the suppliers to comply with Iskra's own quality checklists. And that will take at least another 2 to 3 years."

Foreign Suppliers

Another manager pointed out that an obvious remedy to the problems encountered with domestic suppliers was to source from foreign firms. In general, sourcing at Iskra began after Iskra Power Tools had identified a potential supplier and negotiated the contract. Iskra Commerce then handled the commercial issues, such as invoicing and foreign exchange, for which it charged a fee of 4% to 6%. In addition, Iskra Power Tools paid an import duty of 4% to 5% on all items that it re-exported. For items sold on the domestic market, however, the import tax was 45%.

Another sourcing disadvantage for Iskra was customs delays. Typically, it took the company up to 1 month to obtain import clearance. To counter such delays, Iskra was obliged to order large stocks in advance. Additional factors that complicated Iskra's sourcing arrangements were premium prices because of small order volumes, payment problems due to foreign exchange availability, and the problem of Yugoslavia's external political image.

EXHIBIT 7   Flow Path for Power Tool Gear Manufacturing *Source:* Company records.

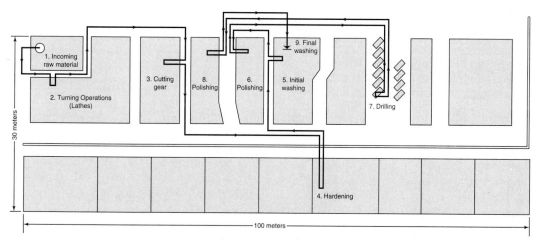

To summarize, one Iskra executive prepared a business system chart depicting the company's contribution to added value. For a customer paying a price of 100 (without VAT), distribution accounted for 50%, while parts, fabrication, and assembly represented the balance as follows:

The Iskra Business System

Parts	Fabrication	Assembly	Distribution	Customer
32.5	8.0	9.5	50.0	100.0
	→ Value added →			

Source: Company records.

FORMULATING A STRATEGY

In formulating Iskra's future strategy, Branko Suhadolnik believed the company should concentrate on less mature and less structured markets such as France and Italy. He reinforced his point by stating that the only way to succeed in these markets was to establish the Perles brand name and structure the distribution. Revamped manufacturing facilities, Branko added, would play a primary role in associating the company's image with quality products. Although he also supported the idea of serving as an OEM, he favored serving the niche players, provided Iskra could overcome what he believed was the company's inability to supply a requested volume of product at a competitive price.

On the other hand, Miro Krek believed the company's future lay in concentrating on becoming an OEM supplier to high-volume producers, not trading under the Perles brand or worrying about distribution. As an OEM supplier, Krek felt that Iskra's inability to attract outside cooperation was due to a lack of price competitiveness, quality, and supply reliability. Consequently, special attention should be devoted to developing its price competitiveness and strengthening its ties with volume players such as Skil.

Then, too, a third group of Iskra executives believed that now was the time to attack Eastern Europe and the USSR. Specifically, these executives believed that Western suitors saw Iskra as a possible entryway into the Soviet Union.

Western Markets with Perles Branding

Based on the company's experiences through January 1991, Branko Suhadolnik felt that any activity in Western Europe required a concentrated focus on France, the second biggest market in Europe. Branko emphasized that with more than 8% growth in 1989 and 5 million power tools sold, France represented 20% of the total European market and warranted further attention.

He went on to say that in France, there was no strong national producer of power tools. Second, the market was not nearly as developed as in Germany or the Netherlands and, therefore, customers bought more on price, less on quality and tradition. Third, the distribution channels in France were not well defined. "Then too," he added, "we believe the Latin way of life in France is closer to our way of life than the Germans, who are more formal and direct."

Like France, Suhadolnik also stressed the need for Iskra to target the Italian market.

Italy has a small power tool producer, but most of its production is exported; almost 60%. In value, almost 70% of the Italian market is imported. Bosch is number 1 and Black & Decker number 2 with its own production through Star, a local company. Moreover, all the Japanese and other companies are minor, the market is close to Yugoslavia and, therefore, transport costs are low. Finally, Yugoslavia and Italy have a clearing agreement that allows unlimited import and export.

One of Suhadolnik's colleagues added that the clearing agreement was one reason why Iskra entered the Italian market in the first place; Italy was the cheapest source of raw materials for cables, switches, plastic, and blades—almost half of Iskra Power Tools' raw materials.

In developing a strategy for the Italian market, Suhadolnik proposed to concentrate on the half of the professional segment that catered to specialty repair shops. "In Italy," one manager commented, "where the first thing for an Italian man is his car, there are an abundance of repair shops to service those cars." The manager then referred to a market research survey stating that Italy had about 100,000 known repair shops of all kinds; the unknown number was anyone's guess. The study also mentioned a trend in these shops toward building maintenance. "That's why," the manager concluded, "we believe Iskra can reach a 3% market share in Italy within 2 years, up from our present 1.3% to 1.5% share of market."

Western Markets as Volume OEM

It was no secret that one of Iskra's competitive advantages in foreign markets was low price. In Germany, for example, Metabo sold one of its drills for DM 299, AEG sold a comparable drill for DM 199, and Iskra, under the Perles name, sold its drill for DM 139. A number of Iskra managers believed that a low price should be vigorously pursued. In their opinion, bolstered by favorable comments from foreign power tool manufacturers, Iskra's products possessed good value for money. Therefore, one executive added, he saw no reason why Iskra could not continue to use its low-labor-cost advantage and underprice the competition.

Western Markets as Niche OEM

During one meeting, Suhadolnik emphasized that Iskra was simply too small and had too few resources to offer a full range of products the way Bosch did. On the contrary, he added, Iskra should concentrate on angle grinders and drills, beginning with a new focus on R&D and production. In other words, focus on those products that represent Iskra's distinctive competence, beginning with design, followed by component sourcing and new manufacturing technology.

Taucher added,

Our output is 600,000 pieces per year. All our large European competitors are in the order of 1.5 to 2 million pieces per year. That is probably the threshold; we are much too small to compete on their terms. We are too small and we don't have a name like Bosch or AEG. That's the problem and, to be a niche manufacturer, you still need the name. We are not a Formula 1, but a Yugo on which we have put a Maserati label.

Eastern Europe

In Eastern Europe, Iskra management knew of power tool manufacturers in Poland, East Germany, Bulgaria, Czechoslovakia, and the Soviet Union. In three of these countries—Poland, Czechoslovakia, and the Soviet Union—Iskra had had some experience. In general, Suhadolnik explained that all these markets were virtually untapped and thus presented a tremendous opportunity for Iskra. Nonetheless, with the exception of East Germany, which was now part of Germany and where the one power tool manufacturer had been purchased by Bosch, none of the remaining countries could pay hard currency for Iskra's products. Therefore, Iskra was required to sell its products via counterpurchase agreements as it had done with Naradi in Czechoslovakia. Despite these countries' hard currency shortages, an executive pointed out that some of Iskra's competitors had not been discouraged from taking a further look at these markets. In particular, both Bosch and Black & Decker had planned to start manufacturing in the Soviet Union and were actively looking for personnel to run these facilities and market their products.

Sony in Poland

In June 1991, Jack Schmuckli, chairman European operations at Sony Europa GmbH in Germany, recalled the evening of November 9, 1989, when the Berlin wall was opened.

Suddenly, one of the most potent symbols of Europe's political and economic division was breached. As I watched television and saw the crowds streaming from East into West Berlin, it was evident that we were confronted with a significant business opportunity and needed to rethink our strategy regarding the COMECON countries.[1] Imagine, a region comprising some 400 million consumers, 20% more than Western Europe, was at last opening up. In 1989, the COMECON markets accounted for roughly 1% of our DM 7.7 billion in sales for all of Europe, This region, which we once considered low priority and best served by intermediaries, was at last joining the world of free markets. Sales of consumer electronics in these markets, estimated to be worth nearly $40 billion by the turn of the century, had to be looked at in a new perspective. How was Sony to enter this world and serve these countries?

I immediately called Kazuo Matsuzaki, General Manager of Sony's European Operations Office,

and urged him to accelerate Sony's development in Eastern Europe. At the time, he reminded me that we were in the midst of a major expansion with Mitte, an Austrian trading company that acted as the distributor of our products to Poland, Hungary and Czechoslovakia, through those countries' foreign trade organizations (FTOs). He was quick to point out, however, that with the collapse of the wall, Mitte's value as a distributor became questionable. For that matter, we had to reconsider our trading arrangements throughout the region, and ask whether they would hold up or whether we should begin to build national subsidiaries immediately. Our initial focus concentrated on Poland which accounted for almost 35% of our 1989 East European sales. Moreover, Poland, with over 40 million inhabitants was the first country in the former East bloc to attain a non-Communist government and to implement market reforms.

For Sony, the most important of these reforms was the move toward a free market, enabling the country's retailing entrepreneurs to begin legitimate operations. A part of this move was currency convertibility. Prior to 1989, only those citizens who had worked abroad or with relatives in foreign countries were allowed to possess hard currency. Thus, for companies such as Sony, retail distribution was limited to hard currency outlets and sales were restricted to tourists and the few Poles with access to hard currency. In mid-1989, the government had relaxed its currency restric-

---

[1] The Council of Mutual Economic Assistance (CMEA or COMECON) was formed in 1949 by the Soviet Union and the then communist states in Eastern and Central Europe to divert trade away from Western nations and achieve a greater degree of self-sufficiency among communist nations. At that time, COMECON included the USSR, Bulgaria, Czechoslovakia, East Germany, Hungary, Poland, and Romania.

This case was prepared by Research Associate Robert C. Howard, under the direction of Professor Robert S. Collins, as a basis for class discussion rather than to illustrate either effective or ineffective handling of a business situation. The support of Sony Europa GmbH executives in the development of this material is gratefully acknowledged. Copyright © 1992 by IMEDE, Lausanne, Switzerland. The International Institute for Management Development (IMD), resulting from the merger between IMEDE, Lausanne, and IMI, Geneva, acquires and retains all rights. Not to be used or reproduced without written permission from IMD, Lausanne, Switzerland. Selected data in this case have been disguised to maintain confidentiality.

tions, making it legal for all Poles to possess hard currency. Sony's 1988 sales of DM 7.9 million subsequently climbed to DM 25 million for 1989.[2] On January 1, 1990, in a first step toward having a convertible currency,[3] Poland devalued the zloty by nearly 60%. Even though the devaluation made Western goods more expensive for those paying in zlotys, by the end of the year, Sony's sales had reached DM 33.5 million.

Despite increased supply. demand for consumer electronics exceeded the official supply available through Photex, the FTO used by Mitte in Poland. To meet this demand, Polish entrepreneurs, or private dealers, began selling Sony products on the gray market,[4] independently of Photex. Matthew Lang, assistant manager in Sony's Corporate Strategy Department, felt that the mere existence of a gray market implied something was wrong with the current channel arrangement. "Was Sony supplying enough product to the market? Were its products priced too high? Were existing channels ineffective?" he asked.

In devising a future strategy for Poland, Matsuzaki and Lang had two major objectives: increasing sales through legitimate sales channels and establishing an authorized sales and service network in an intermediate step toward a national company. Because a national subsidiary implied terminating agreements with Mitte and Photex, some managers were reluctant to invest any more time and energy into upgrading the existing Mitte–Photex distribution channel and wanted to establish a Sony-owned network as soon as possible. In part, the desire to establish a fully owned distribution network stemmed from Sony's 30+

years of experience in Western Europe. On more than one occasion, local distributors had become so powerful that they were able to influence the distribution policy to a greater extent than Sony preferred. Not surprisingly, deciding when and how to alter distribution agreements was of paramount concern to Sony management. In Poland, where Photex, a representative of the old system, already accounted for nearly 100% of Sony's sales, some managers believed that it was in the company's best interest to build a counterbalance to Photex's market presence by developing business with Poland's emerging private dealers.

By contrast, some other managers believed it was too soon for Sony to invest independently in Poland and that extricating itself from Mitte and Photex could not be accomplished quickly, due to Photex's dominant position. Moreover, this same group of managers cited Photex's extensive retail chain in Poland as another reason to stick with, or modify, the existing distribution agreement. Ideally, Matsuzaki and Lang sought a solution that would satisfy Poland's demand for consumer electronics and preserve the company's goodwill with each stakeholder. As the two resumed their discussions, they were keenly aware that any decisions and actions in Poland would be viewed as an indication of how, or how not, Sony might approach other markets in Eastern Europe and the USSR.

SONY IN EUROPE

One of Sony's stated objectives was to achieve share leadership in all major product categories in each national market. To achieve its goal, the company nurtured each market segment with strong competitive products and an excellent sales and service network.

Sony had begun marketing its products in Europe during the 1960s through Sony Overseas SA (SOSA), a subsidiary based in Switzerland. From the 1960s on, SOSA expanded the company's sales and service activities throughout Europe by appointing national distributors. By 1970, these distributor organizations were taken over or changed to Sony's own sub-

---

[2] In 1989, $1 = DM 1.88; in 1990, $1 = DM 1.62.

[3] Convertibility referred to the right of an enterprise to obtain foreign exchange to pay for imports, with no restrictions from a government or central bank. Under internal convertibility, on the other hand, any legal import could be paid for by bringing zlotys to a bank with the invoice for import. Thereafter, the bank paid the invoice in foreign exchange, converted at the official rate.

[4] The gray market, also known as "parallel imports," referred to trade in legal goods and services that took place outside the channels normally controlled by distributors or company-owned sales subsidiaries.

sidiaries so that, by 1990, Sony had 10 national organizations in Europe, plus two regional organizations—Sony Scandinavia and Sony Europe International (SEI); the latter served Eastern Europe and the USSR. Each organization reported to the European headquarters and normally consisted of three main marketing divisions: consumer products, professional products, and magnetic products.

In this evolution, SOSA typically identified a country distributor, which, at a later date, might become a joint venture partner. Some years after that, these same entities might become wholly owned Sony subsidiaries. Sony devoted significant energy to managing the relationships with its distributors, especially during the transition period to joint venture partner and/or wholly owned subsidiary. Matsuzaki emphasized that how and when Sony made these transitions was key and represented a part of the company's corporate ethic. He added, "Sony's image works both for and against us. If we cut links to a distributor abruptly, we may find it difficult to recruit distributors in other parts of the world thereafter. With long-standing distributorships, Sony typically does not simply terminate agreements, but offers phaseout periods with generous compensation."

In planning the company's approach to Eastern Europe, and Poland in particular, Matsuzaki and Lang had to keep these points in mind. At the same time, however the two also had to consider the challenge of managing distributor relationships in Europe. As an example, Lang cited Nissan's problems in the United Kingdom. When Nissan had first entered the U.K. market, it had sold its cars through Nissan UK, an independent privately owned distributor. In 1990, executives from Nissan and Nissan UK began arguing over the pricing policy for the Nissan Primera. According to Octav Botnar, chairman and managing director of Nissan UK, Nissan's pricing was unfair to British consumers because U.K.-built Nissan cars sold more cheaply in Germany, the Netherlands, and Belgium where the distributors were owned by Nissan Motor Company itself. Eventually, the relationship between Botnar and Nissan management became so strained that Nissan chose to establish a wholly

owned distributorship with a view to disenfranchising Botnar. Throughout the process, both parties became involved in highly publicized legal proceedings. At Sony, management was loath to become involved in such disputes.

Sales and Service in Europe

Within Sony Corporation, management was proud of its after-sales service. According to Lang, Sony's products had one of the lowest failure rates in the industry but, nonetheless, service was considered an integral part of the marketing mix and the company's "customer satisfaction" philosophy. He added that the key elements for providing service were reliability and speed and that together the two maintained Sony's image and brand reputation. Therefore, training for Sony personnel, from the telephone operator at a service center through to the service technician, emphasized a customer orientation.

Apart from training, each national sales organization decided the best way to handle service in its particular market. As a result, no standard Sony service concept existed Europewide. Generally, though, Sony sold its products through authorized dealers who, typically, also sold competing brands. Sony service, on the other hand, fell into one of three categories: fully owned service departments, authorized service stations, or a combination of both.

Fully Owned Service Departments

As noted, Sony established sales and service organizations in Europe from 1968 on. Initially, national subsidiaries identified and authorized dealers to sell, but not repair, Sony products. Customers faced with a repair problem in these markets could return the product to the dealer who, in turn, sent the product to the service department at the country subsidiary. A customer could, of course, take the product directly to the service department himself.

Authorized Service Stations

With the growth of sales in larger markets, some subsidiaries authorized dealers to service, as well as sell, Sony products. Typically, an authorized service station repaired Sony as well as other brands of consumer electronics. Customers seeking repair in these markets could take their products to an authorized Sony service station.

Mixed Service Organizations

More recently, some markets had established mixed service organizations. In these markets, a customer could go to a fully owned service department directly or to a dealer who sold, but did not repair, Sony products. Alternatively, a customer could go to an independent authorized dealer who sold as well as repaired Sony and other brands of consumer electronics.

In addition to repairing locally purchased products, Sony's West European subsidiaries were obliged to service Sony products purchased in other markets. Aside from these service options, customers in any market could take a chance with an unauthorized service station. Those willing to do so ran the risk of having non-Sony components installed in their products or, worse, untrained personnel damaging their products. It was this scenario that Matsuzaki and Lang wanted to avoid in Poland, lest Sony's brand image be damaged. Nonetheless, the two remained uncertain whether to adopt a fully owned service department, authorized service stations, or a mixed service organization in Poland.

Eastern Europe

In the near future, Sony management believed that the opening of Eastern Europe would be one of the most important events to influence their business. Indeed, with most of the consumer electronics markets in the developed world at or near saturation, Sony's competitors had already begun to focus on Eastern Europe's emerging markets. According to one market research firm,[5] the market for consumer electronics in Eastern Europe

was forecast to reach $38 billion by the year 2000 based on the 50% penetration of electronic consumer goods achieved in Western countries.

In addition to the companies active in Poland (described later), other companies in Eastern Europe included Philips, the large Dutch electronic and electrical goods company. In mid-1990, Philips announced plans to establish offices in Poland, Czechoslovakia, and Hungary in order to identify opportunities for cooperation and to serve as the nucleus for future sales organizations in those countries. In Czechoslovakia, with 1991 sales of its consumer electronic products expected to reach Sch 150 million,[6] the company announced plans for a network of 75 retail shops. In the USSR, Philips had established a sales and service organization and had announced joint manufacturing plans for videocassette recorders (VCRs).

Additional companies building an East European presence included Nokia Consumer Electronics, Europe's third largest consumer electronics manufacturer. Specifically, Nokia announced plans to supply and assemble kits, in former East Germany, for distribution throughout Eastern Europe. Following the reunification of East and West Germany, Grundig, the German consumer electronics firm based in Fuerth, concentrated its East European sales efforts on the former DDR. In mid-1991, a Grundig spokesman said the company had targeted a turnover in excess of DM 100 million in the former East Germany. To achieve its goal, the company established a marketing outlet in Boehlitz–Ehrenberg, in what was previously East Germany, to supply retail dealers with its consumer goods.

Other companies involved in manufacturing deals were Akai with videocassette recorders in Bulgaria, Samsung with color television in Hungary, and Thomson with color television and VCRs in Hungary and the USSR. Regardless of the company, each of

---

[5] BIS Mackintosh Ltd. in *Electronic-World-News*, July 23, 1990, p. 6.

[6] In Czechoslovakia, the koruna or crown was devalued several times in 1990 and 1991. For this reason, sales forecasts were often denominated in hard currencies. In 1990, $1 = Austrian Sch 11.4.

these joint venture activities was building a local manufacturing presence in Eastern Europe. For the management of Sony, who saw Eastern Europe as a natural extension of their presence in Western Europe, success in Poland played a key role in securing its place in an increasingly volatile global battle.

DOING BUSINESS IN POLAND

In 1991, Poland celebrated the 200th anniversary of a constitution proclaimed on May 3, 1791, by Stanislaus Augustus, King of Poland. During those 200 years, Poland had been subjected to a number of wars and territorial revisions that had positioned the country substantially west of its traditional boundaries. Because of these geographical changes, significant Polish minorities still lived in Lithuania, Byelorussia, and the Ukraine. For example, in Lithuania, roughly 8% of the population in the Vilnius area was Polish. Likewise. in Byelorussia, approximately 12% of the population was of Polish extraction. One analyst commented that, because of this distribution of minorities, there was a certain "artificiality" to Poland's borders. Moreover, Polish, Lithuanian, Byelorussian, Ukrainian, and Russian belonged to the same subgroup of languages and thus shared many common words and expressions. In brief, because of its historical, economic, and cultural place in Europe, Poland was seen by many as a springboard for future investment into the neighboring republics of the USSR. (Refer to Exhibit 1 for maps depicting the changes in Poland's borders from the 18th century through World War II.)

Excluding the USSR, Poland was the single biggest market in Eastern Europe, with a population of 37.9 million. With a growth rate of 5.7% between 1980 and 1988, Poland had one of the fastest growing populations on the continent, most of which was concentrated in urban communities. And, unlike other countries in Central and Eastern Europe, such as Czechoslovakia or Yugoslavia with their many ethnic groups, Poland had a more homogeneous population, a factor many analysts believed would contribute to future political as well as economic stability. Indeed, in 1990, the Polish government's statistical office estimated that the output of private industry grew by 50% and accounted for 18% of national income, up from 11% in 1989. Moreover, the number of people employed in private enterprise grew by more than 500,000 in 1989, bringing the total to between 1.8 and 2 million people.[7]

One journalist, commenting on Polish behavior, went so far as to say that no other group in Eastern Europe rivaled the Poles for being the most business minded and that Polish merchants were favored for their bold and widespread commercial activities.[8] Typically, he added, merchants bought low-priced commodities in Poland and earned a substantial gain in foreign currency by selling these commodities in the West. Profits were easily doubled by using the gain to purchase Western merchandise for resale back in Poland. Normally, these goods were sold through private enterprises, instead of Poland's FTOs.

For Sony, product demand was driven by the company's outstanding brand image and by the unexpected volume of zlotys and dollars circulating in Poland. To clarify, a survey in five European countries rated Sony number 3 after IBM and Mercedes Benz in terms of popularity, dynamism, and corporate image.[9] In another survey, Sony was considered number 1 in Poland and the USSR in "image power."[10] With respect to currency, one spokeswoman commented that Poles had been saving their money for years and were a lot more Western in their thinking than others in the former East bloc. Then, too, hard currency remittances to Poles from relatives living abroad were estimated at over $3 billion in 1990.

Despite the growth of private industry, other factors, such as the lack of effective communications, hindered business conduct in Poland. According to one businessman, Poland had one of the worst telecommunications infra-

---

[7] *The Economist,* January 26, 1991.

[8] *Living in Europe,* May 18, 1990.

[9] *Le Point,* June 1990.

[10] Landor Associates.

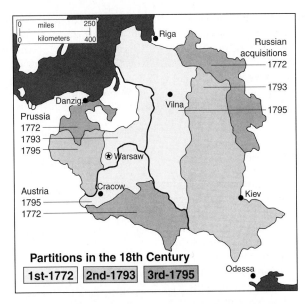

Poland divided between Austria, Prussia and Russia

Poland as divided by the Molotov-Ribbentrop Pact

Postwar Poland shifted westward on both borders

EXHIBIT 1 Poland: Historical Maps *Source: Financial Times,* May 3, 1991.

structures in Central and Eastern Europe. With only seven phones per 100 people, it was extremely difficult to perform tasks taken for granted in the West. Fax machines, mobile phones, data transmission, and other advanced services were equally, if not more, scarce than telephones. Yet another burden was the lack of local managers with experience in accounting, finance, and other Western business practices. In summary, the poor infrastructure and shortage of managerial talent in Poland could prolong the country's transition from a centrally planned to a market economy.

Foreign Trade Organizations

As of mid-1991, most foreign trade in Poland was still carried out by specialized foreign trade organizations (FTOs) with monopoly positions. Typically, an FTO acted as the main authority for foreign trade transactions dealing with any one product or related group of products. FTOs were responsible for all commercial activity with foreign partners in that product area, including negotiating and signing contracts, preparing and implementing cooperation agreements, conducting market research, organizing sales and purchases, advertising, and participating in international trade fairs. After-sales service, however, was strictly limited to products purchased within the country and from a particular FTO.

Of the 86 FTOs in Poland, Photex[11] and Baltona were the two largest that specialized in consumer electronics. With roughly 350 outlets throughout Poland, Baltona was the second largest of the two consumer electronics FTOs and sourced its products primarily from Hitachi and other smaller, less well known Japanese companies.

From 1990 onward, there was increasing talk of privatization of state-owned enterprises in Poland. Retailing was at the forefront of the government's privatization program and, according to one ministry official, roughly 90% of the 120,000 state stores were expected to be transferred to private owners by 1996. It was hoped that the largest of these, including Photex and Baltona, would be privatized before the end of 1991. In an interview on the eventual privatization of Photex, Managing Direc-

tor Marian Zacharski proposed allocating 49% of Photex's shares to Western companies, 20% to employees, and the rest to domestic investors. Despite this insight about Photex's possible future owners, Photex was still 100% state owned as of mid-1991.

COMPETITION IN POLAND

Matsushita Electric Industrial Co. Ltd

With 1990 sales of nearly $38 billion, Matsushita was by far the world's largest consumer electronics company. Within the industry, Matsushita was considered to be less innovative than its competitors, although it was renowned for its manufacturing skills. With the help of 25,000 company-owned shops in Japan, Matsushita usually flooded the domestic market and crushed the competition before repeating the exercise in overseas markets. In contrast to Sony, whose goods tended to appeal to more affluent consumers, Matsushita's products were geared for the mass market, for families of modest means with little technical interest.[12]

Additional brands owned by Matsushita included Panasonic, Quasar, Technics, and National. Also, JVC was 51% owned by Matsushita. The Panasonic brand was distributed exclusively by the Mitsubishi Trading Company (MTC) in Poland. MTC worked through Photex; however, Panasonic was unofficially reputed to be looking for private dealers, independent of MTC.

To reinforce Panasonic's brand awareness in Poland, second to Sony in 1990, Panasonic began a massive promotion campaign using posters on buses and trams. In this way, the company hoped to strengthen its image position and, at the same time, maintain its 2:1 lead, in unit terms, against Sony. To service Panasonic's products, the MTC had established two service stations in Poland and planned to open ten more in the near future. Although the service network was fully owned by MTC, Panasonic provided technical assis-

---

[11] Additional information on Photex is given in the next section.

[12] *The Economist*, April 13, 1991, "A Survey of Electronics", pp. 10–11.

tance. As part of their ongoing cooperation, Panasonic and Mitsubishi announced plans in early 1991 to form a joint manufacturing venture in Poland. They had not disclosed, however, which products would be made.

Hitachi

Hitachi had conducted its business in Poland for 9 years through International Trade & Investment (ITI), a trading company founded by two Poles, which sold Hitachi products through Baltona. In contrast to Sony or Matsushita, however, which had approached private dealers directly, Hitachi had allowed ITI to manage such contacts in Poland. Then, so as not to miss out on the growing opportunity with entrepreneurs, in the spring of 1991, ITI started offering Hitachi products to private dealers, supported by an office building ITI was constructing for Hitachi in Warsaw. According to one industry participant, ITI's competitive advantage in consumer electronics was its having the best service network in Poland.

Philips

One analyst commented that, with the exception of Philips, which sold its products through Brabok, a private dealer with only two shops, non-Japanese brands were not nearly as popular in Poland as Japanese products. He added that Philips had jointly produced video-cassette recorders in Poland since 1986 and, more recently, had concluded a deal with a local company, Pratork, to assemble televisions in Poland bearing the Philips brand name.

Others

Aside from Sony, Matsushita's Panasonic brand, and, to a lesser extent, Hitachi, Sanyo, and Sharp were the only other significant Japanese brands sold in Poland. Although Sanyo and Sharp were sold through Photex, both had also been offered to private dealers, independently of Photex.

DISTRIBUTION AND SERVICE OF CONSUMER ELECTRONICS IN POLAND

The political and economic changes in Poland since 1989 gave birth to a significant gray market in consumer electronics. Sony management, eager to preserve and expand its share of the Polish market, felt an arrangement was needed to balance the interests of Mitte, Photex, and Poland's private dealers, to shift distribution away from the gray channels.

Mitte

Mitte was an affiliate of an Austrian holding company based in Vienna and, from the 1960s on, played an important role in supplying Sony products to the Polish as well as the Hungarian and Czechoslovakian markets, through the monopolies of the countries' state-owned foreign trade organizations. One part of the holding company, Mitte Technische GmbH, looked exclusively after Sony and had established representative offices in Warsaw, Prague, and Budapest, as well as service stations in Budapest and Warsaw.

Prior to the collapse of the Berlin wall, Sony considered Eastern Europe to be a minor part of its business, best handled by an intermediary, that is, Mitte. One manager pointed out, however, that Mitte was not a typical distributor. Unlike other Sony distributors, with operations in the country they served, Mitte was based in Austria. As a result, once the wall fell, Mitte offered little to Sony as a joint venture partner or acquisition candidate. On the other hand, some executives believed Mitte's role was still valuable. In particular, this group of executives emphasized that Mitte carried the risk of nonpayment from Photex, not an insignificant point given the volume of Sony's sales and the pace of change in Poland.

Photex

Photex, based in Warsaw, was Poland's largest and best run retail operation with approximately 1,010 outlets across the country.

In 1990, Photex reported sales of $936 million, up 68% over 1989 with profits averaging 7% to 9% of sales when expressed in Western accounting terms. According to Marian Zacharski, managing director of Photex, sales in 1991 were forecast to reach nearly $2 billion. Traditionally, Photex had been known for luxury goods but, with Poland's move toward a market economy, it added thousands of items to its product offering, including toys, clothing, drugs, and foodstuffs. At the same time, Zacharski expanded Western-style displays and self-service. In addition, contrary to Polish shopping customs of the past, customers were no longer required to stand in separate lines for each purchase category. One Photex customer commented, "In my local store, if I want bread, beer, meat and candy, I must queue four times. Photex is undoubtedly worth the extra money."

Like Photex customers, Photex employees were highly motivated. On December 31, 1990, Photex employees stayed after hours to convert pricing to the Polish zloty so that the stores could open on time January 2, 1991. By contrast, Baltona was closed on January 2 to reprice. To maintain and improve its position in Poland, Photex spent $30 million on a fully computerized accounting and inventory control system.

In Poland, all after-sales service requests for Sony products sold through Photex were handled by Mitte's Warsaw-based service organization, Mittropol, which received all spare parts and training from Mitte Technische GmbH in Vienna. Despite the proliferation of goods sold at Photex, the retail chain was slow in building its service network. Specifically, customers seeking after-sales service for consumer electronics in Poland had to go to Photex's one service station in Warsaw. Alternatively, customers could deposit their products at one of eight Photex outlets in Poland. Once a week, all products in need of repair were sent to the central service station in Warsaw. For Sony products bought outside Poland or for products bought inside Poland but outside the Photex chain, Polish customers had no alternative but to take their chances with an unauthorized service station.

After visiting Mittropol, Lang commented that the Photex staff members were familiar with technology on traditional products such as stereos, but were not well qualified to service products such as compact disc players or camcorders based on more sophisticated digital and optical technologies. In a move to upgrade the repair skills of Photex's staff and, at the same time, minimize any damage unauthorized service stations might do to Sony products and the company's image, he and Matsuzaki proposed organizing a training program in Warsaw. Although seen as a first step, both knew full well that the training initiative would eventually have to be followed by a more comprehensive service organization.

Poland's Retailing Entrepreneurs

Matsuzaki described those in control of the gray market as typical entrepreneurs—dynamic individuals quick to identify and capitalize on an opportunity. He went on to say that one group of three university colleagues owned their own trading company, Digital, based in Gdansk. It had a staff of over 300. The group was clever and hard working and had franchised businesses across Poland. Moreover, the group was well versed in Western business methods and approaches, using Western-style advertising to sell imported personal computers and satellite antennas, as well as Sony products (purchased from Sony Deutschland GmbH). For all these products, Digital paid hard currency and resold in zlotys.

By comparison, a newspaper journalist described an individual who sold Polish commodities in Germany and then used the DM proceeds to buy videocassette recorders for resale in Poland. After purchasing 20 VCRs, the individual would reenter Poland at an obscure border crossing where a small bribe to the border guards secured his passage with the goods at a customs fee below the goods' true value. Under this system, the private dealer earned a profit of roughly $1,000 per month, approximately 15 times the monthly salary of an average worker in Poland.

Last, Matsuzaki mentioned a Polish company called Selko, whose owner bought personal computers in Berlin and resold them in Poland, the Ukraine, and Lithuania. According to Matsuzaki, this entrepreneur had become so successful that he had purchased a near bankrupt bookshop in Warsaw, transformed it into a profitable business, and was planning to convert the same building to a personal computer outlet. To top it all off, this same individual, unable to source sufficient product from Sony Deutschland, obtained container loads of Sony products from Singapore, shipped directly to his warehouse in Poland. Like other entrepreneurs, Selko paid for its purchases in hard currency, which it resold for zlotys in Poland.

Unauthorized Service Stations

Aside from selling products on the gray market, several entrepreneurs in Poland had started service stations for consumer electronics. On one visit to Warsaw, a Sony representative identified five unauthorized Sony service stations in the telephone directory. Although each station claimed they could repair Sony products, none had in fact received training nor did they use Sony parts. For Sony, the possibility of faulty product repair by unauthorized stations posed a serious threat to its brand image.

Sony Europe International

Within the Sony European operations, Sony Europe International (SEI) was responsible for trading with Poland. Strictly speaking, Photex placed its orders through Mitte, which, in turn, passed the orders on to SEI. Once received, SEI instructed its warehouse in Holland to ship the products directly to Photex's main office in Warsaw, where they were then distributed to Photex's 1,010 outlets across the country for sale to the Polish consumer. Payment occurred in two steps: (1) Photex converted zlotys into hard currency, and (2) it paid Mitte, which in turn paid SEI.

As Poland moved toward a market economy, SEI proceeded to establish contact with 15 private dealers in Poland. Normally, these dealers contacted the SEI sales manager with

product requests. Unlike its arrangement with Mitte, however, SEI would not ship from its warehouse to these dealers until it was paid in full in hard currency. (Refer to Exhibit 2 for a summary of the flow of orders, products, and capital between Poland and the Sony organization.)

OPTIONS

To establish a direct presence in Poland meant renegotiating Sony's distribution agreement with Mitte. Based on past experience, any renegotiation would prove lengthy and, according to one manager, could cost up to DM 10 million. All the same, some managers favored making the transition from distributor to local subsidiary sooner rather than later, based on experiences in both North America and Europe. As Matsuzaki and Lang continued their discussions, they concentrated on four options, all focused on Poland. In a larger context, however, the two were also aware that their decision and the results that followed would be scrutinized as an indication of how, or how not, to approach Sony's other markets in Central and Eastern Europe.

Continue Present Arrangements

Until the end of 1992, Sony was obliged to honor its exclusive agreement with Mitte as the distributor to all state-owned organizations in Poland. Sony was permitted, however, under the terms of the agreement, to develop its own network with private companies. Thus, Sony could wait until its agreement with Mitte expired at the end of 1992 and, simultaneously, allow the parallel imports to continue.

On the plus side, Lang mentioned that maintaining the status quo was the easiest option as it obviated any immediate renegotiation and/or compensation to Mitte. Also, under the present agreement, Mitte would continue to bear the risk of Photex's nonpayment. On the other hand, taking a *laissez-faire* stance would increase Sony's reliance on Mitte to expand the sales and service network in

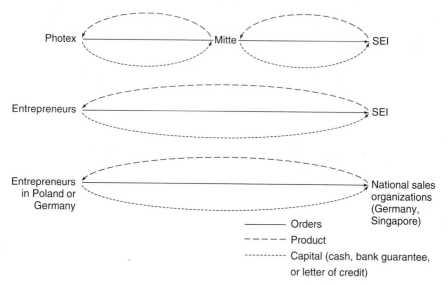

EXHIBIT 2 Order, Product, and Capital Flow for Sony Products Sold in Poland
Source: Company records.

Poland and thus did little to enhance Sony's control over sales and marketing policy.

Allowing the parallel imports to continue did not mean taking no action. On the contrary, if Sony chose to continue its arrangement with Mitte, it was also intent on furthering its cooperation with some of Poland's private dealers in preparation for the post-1992 era. By waiting until its agreement with Mitte expired, Sony would have 18 months to select some of Poland's entrepreneurs and develop them as local sales and service representatives. Because many of these entrepreneurs had already demonstrated their ability to market Sony's products via the gray market, Matsuzaki believed that with the proper incentive these same individuals could be persuaded to join a future Sony Poland organization. In so doing, Sony might be able to unify its parallel markets in Poland and, at the same time, nurture a pool of talent for an eventual Polish subsidiary.

Supply Directly with Photex

As one alternative to maintaining the status quo, Sony could terminate its agreement with Mitte and deal directly with Photex, an idea proposed by Marian Zacharski. As Poland's largest retailer, Photex clearly had an established sales network and possessed formidable buying power. With one-third of Photex's nearly $1 billion 1990 sales attributed to consumer electronics, direct cooperation entailed serious consideration. Specifically, direct cooperation with Photex would allow Sony to exercise more control over the sales and marketing of its products. As an example, Lang mentioned that Photex, with Mitte acting as an intermediary, was unwilling to cut its margins by lowering prices, a factor that may have contributed to the gray market. Photex's intransigence, he added, was in part due to Mitte, which lacked the clout of a Sony or other manufacturer, to persuade Photex to reduce prices. Some managers believed that, in a direct relationship, Photex would be more cooperative.

On the other hand, direct cooperation with Photex implied that Sony would have to renegotiate its agreement with Mitte. Aside from any settlement costs, direct cooperation with Photex meant that Sony would also be fully exposed to the nonpayment risk now borne by Mitte. Then, too, with the growth of private dealers in Poland, there was no guarantee that Photex could maintain or increase its impressive $1 billion in sales revenue. Furthermore, Matsuzaki pointed out, cutting the supply line to Poland's FTOs via Mitte might jeopardize Sony's access to the Hungarian and Czechoslovakian markets, one-quarter and one-third the size of the Polish market, respectively.

While keeping the preceding in mind, Sony management was also keeping a close eye on privatization in Poland. If Photex were privatized before the end of 1992, Sony would be free to supply Photex directly and cut Mitte out of the picture, without violating its agreement. Short of negating any settlement costs with Mitte, the advantages of a privatized Photex were the same as with the existing state-owned FTO.

Supply Directly to Private Dealers from SEI

In a third option, Sony could sever its current channels, through Mitte and Photex, and supply Poland's private dealers directly via SEI. As advantages, dealing with Poland's private dealers would enable Sony to control its sales and service network directly. As disadvantages, however, Sony would have to carry the risk of nonpayment and disentangle itself from Mitte, with the aforementioned cost problem and distribution risks to Hungary and Czechoslovakia. Furthermore, there was no guarantee that private dealers could maintain the country's current sales volume. Finally, despite the existence to date of private dealers in Poland, Sony management was uncertain about the total number of such private dealers or their capacity to perform after-sales service.

Establish Sony Poland

As a fourth option, the management of Sony could initiate its ultimate, longer-term, objective and establish a Sony Poland subsidiary. Aside from providing immediate control over its sales and service network, a local subsidiary would also be able to closely monitor any risk of nonpayment. Most importantly, a Polish subsidiary could well enhance Sony's local image and would coincide with the company's philosophy of global localization.

To implement this option, Sony would have to renegotiate its agreement with Mitte with the same disadvantages cited previously. Moreover, Matsuzaki and Lang did not believe a Sony Poland could support itself below a sales volume of DM 150 million per year. Below that level, a subsidiary would be certain to incur losses for an indefinite period. Then, too, although the management of Sony believed they could select a few future employees from among Poland's private dealers, the same possibility did not apply to someone capable of heading up a subsidiary. In Matsuzaki's opinion, the managing director of a Sony Poland would, in addition to speaking Polish, need to speak English to communicate within Sony and be comfortable with Lithuanian, Byelorussian, and Ukranian to cultivate the neighboring markets in the USSR.

The Bolshevichka Apparel Company: Managing in Perestroika

In early August 1991, Mr. Vladimir Gurov, general director of Bolshevichka, Moscow's best-known men's apparel manufacturer, was pondering the variety of strategic options available to him. At a time of great uncertainty, with the Soviet Union[1] experiencing political and economic upheaval, Gurov's problems were immense, yet the possibilities appeared to be unlimited. Privatization of the currently state owned enterprise seemed imminent. Joint ventures—to gain foreign know-how, capital, technology and supplies—were being fashioned. Other options included expansion or contraction of the existing productive assets and the possibility of vertical integration into a greater retailing presence. Also, a decision needed to be made about brand names. Should the company continue to use its well-known Bolshevichka trademark, select a new name, or perhaps even totally abandon brand names and serve instead as a low-cost manufacturing platform for Western brand names? In many ways, the new managerial autonomy associated with perestroika was offering Russian managers both the best of times and the worst of times.

Bolshevichka produced what were arguably the best men's suits in the country, providing suits for a number of top Soviet leaders. In an economy where demand far outstripped supply, Bolshevichka regularly sold its entire production stock daily, leaving it with almost no finished goods inventory either in the factory or its retail outlets. This situation, however, was not uncommon. Many consumers hastened to buy whatever products were available in a market characterized by chronic and acute product scarcity. In mid-1991, people used consumer items as a hedge against inflation, reasoning that such investments allowed them to be sure that their money kept pace with inflation—something that one could not trust a Russian bank account to do.

Yet, despite such apparent success, there was much uncertainty to be dealt with in the enterprise's operating environment. New laws, new realities (even the distinct possibility of new national boundaries), new competitors, new suppliers, new markets, all coincided to create both opportunities and problems. Vladimir Gurov, as general director of a Russian enterprise, had to carefully pick and choose which directions he wanted his enterprise to take and those he needed to avoid.

---

[1] For convenience, the case setting will be referred to as Russia and occasionally the Soviet Union. At the time of the actual decision making of the case issues, in the late summer of 1991, Russia's full name was the Russian Soviet Federated Socialist Republic (RSFSR).

Managing in an Economy of Scarcity: Planning and Reforms of Planning

Since its beginnings in 1917, the Soviet Union had been essentially a poor country,

This case was prepared by Research Associate Vivian Watt, under the supervision of Professors William A. Fischer and George Taucher, as a basis for class discussion rather than to illustrate either effective or ineffective handling of a business situation. Copyright © 1992 by IMEDE, Lausanne, Switzerland. The International Institute for Management Development (IMD), resulting from the merger between IMEDE, Lausanne, and IMI, Geneva, acquires and retains all rights. Not to be used or reproduced without written permission from IMD, Lausanne, Switzerland.

with little attention paid to consumer markets or the development of market infrastructure. As was typical in such economies of scarcity, the Soviet state market had led the nation's productive resources into a hierarchical economic system, with centralized planning being imposed throughout in an effort to avoid redundancies and reduce the misallocation of society's scarce resources. Productive resources became the property of the state, with enterprises and managers responsible to the state plan. Unique to the Stalinist economic logic of the Soviet Union, heavy industry (the manufacture of steel, machinery, and the like) took precedence over light industry (the manufacture of textiles, apparel, and other consumer goods). Consequently, throughout its history, demand in the Soviet Union consistently surpassed the ability of Soviet industry to supply the desired goods and services to meet consumers' needs. In the early 1960s, however, a major problem of Soviet light industry was having excessive, rather than nonexistent, finished-goods inventories—a result of factories producing goods that nobody wanted. Despite the great scarcity of products, the modest prices of suits, and increased personal savings, Soviet people at the time preferred to refrain from purchasing goods that were deemed unacceptable due to poor quality of fabrication and outmoded design. By the end of 1963, the total soft goods inventory being held in warehouses and retail outlets throughout the country was valued at Rb 12 billion,[2] about half the amount of retail sales in soft goods that year.

Responding to this situation, in June 1964, Premier Nikita Khruschev allowed a small number of companies across the nation, including Bolshevichka, to participate in an experiment: the intent was to seek ways of modifying production and distribution systems so that there would be greater market influence in managerial decision making. This experiment became known as the Liberman reforms, after Evsei Liberman, the university professor who suggested them.

The Liberman reforms were designed to decentralize economic decision-making by:

1. Emphasizing greater managerial autonomy, so that the enterprise could be more responsive to market demands
2. Establishing direct links between the enterprise and the retail outlets that sold its goods
3. Creating more effective managerial incentives by tying enterprise performance evaluation and managerial bonuses directly to market performance

The results of the Liberman reforms were mixed. Although the reforms did provide some benefits to industry, these advantages were outweighed by numerous drawbacks in the administration of the reforms. Bolshevichka started experiencing stockouts and faster inventory turnover, but did not flourish as much as had been expected for several reasons. The company had difficulty adjusting to the new demand trends of an uncontrolled market; for example, there was an unexpected consumer preference for Dacron suits, which carried a smaller profit margin than traditional suits. The management was also unable to adjust sourcing relationships to meet the demand conditions, as suppliers were still under the controls of Gosplan (the central planning system of the USSR). Even under the premiership of Alexei Kosygin, who insisted on broadening the experiment, the reforms ultimately fell victim to Soviet bureaucracy and were recentralized during the 1970s.

After nearly 70 years of planned production and controlled prices, the late 1980s saw another series of incomplete and often haphazard reforms to free prices and stimulate market influences in a variety of industry sectors. Prior to 1989, Bolshevichka had been directly led by the Moscow Regional Association of the Sewing Industry, which provided the enterprise with its production quotas and customer orders, secured its supplies, provided its working and investment capital, and, in general, served as an agent of corporate governance and direction.

The Ministry of Light Industry

Under the old system (pre-1989), the Russian Ministry of Light Industry and the Moscow Association of the Sewing Industry were responsi-

[2] Equal to $13.2 billion at the official exchange rate.

ble for nearly all aspects of planning, pricing, product development, marketing, distribution, and production policies. The enterprise was merely a manufacturer of product requirements generated by higher authorities and distributed by others. Having grown up under the umbrella of central planning, many Russian managers lacked essential general management skills. CEOs were merely production supervisors whose main goal was to produce a few more than the necessary number of product units with the designated budget. They were not responsible for such decisions as product line, pricing, inventories, distribution, marketing, and finance.

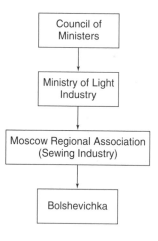

The Pre-1989 Four-tier Structure under Gosplan

THE 1991 BUSINESS ENVIRONMENT IN THE SOVIET UNION

The Restructuring of Soviet Industry in April 1991

In 1989 the Moscow Regional Association was annulled and the Ministry of Light Industry was reorganized. Then, between July and October 1990, the ministry itself was liquidated. It formerly had provided orders and pricing, funds for investment, hard currency, financing and support in raw materials purchasing. At this point, individual enterprises such as Bolshevichka were, for all intents and purposes, completely on their own.

In men's apparel, prices that had been previously fixed became totally free for (self-defined) fashionable goods on April 1, 1991. Furthermore, Bolshevichka was suddenly independent of all planning, after years of being guided by the Russian Republic's planning mechanism for apportioning its production schedule, managing its supplies, and otherwise arranging the procurement and assignment of all productive assets. By mid-1991, Bolshevichka consisted of 3,000 workers (80% of whom were women) and was 100% owned by the Russian Republic. Also in 1991, Bolshevichka was making its own production plan and securing its own raw material supplies, hard currency, managers, employees, equipment and spare parts. The company had to forge direct links to its suppliers and retailers and was solely responsible for negotiating its contracts with both groups.

In the absence of a ministry, however, the managers of Bolshevichka did not know exactly to whom they were responsible because there was no explicit system of accountability or discipline. Given the political uncertainty and the legacy of fear and reprisal in the Soviet Union, many managers inevitably tended to feel unsure about exercising this newfound autonomy. Someday in the future, if the 1991 situation reversed, they might be questioned and prosecuted for controversial decisions they had made. Owners were not represented because no one knew who the owners were Mr. Gurov determined his salary simply by suggesting a sum to his council, and all agreed he would earn Rb 3,000 monthly. For his vacation, Mr. Gurov wrote a note giving himself permission to leave on holiday. In the new environment, the enterprise cell of the Communist Party of the Soviet Union no longer appeared to be a viable agent of discipline or motivation. In fact, all Communist Party cells were abolished from Russian factories as of August 4, 1991. (Refer to Exhibit 1 for the former role of the party cell in factories.)

Along with the virtues of free enterprise, however, came chaos caused by the confusion of changing from one type of economy and

EXHIBIT 1   Former Role of Communist Party Cell in Factories

The party had a leading four-way role in Soviet institutions:
1. To determine policy directives
2. To check on policy fulfillment
3. To list the people (through the nomenclature) who have been singled out for leading posts
4. To ensure the support of the masses

It was the fourth task that usually kept the party secretary in the factory most active.

As of August 4, 1991, all party cells in companies and factories in Russia were abolished.

mind-set to another. Crime, formerly a foreign concept to Muscovites, was on an uncontrolled upward spiral. It was no longer possible for Bolshevichka to have a second shift because of the danger workers risked returning home at night. No worker was willing to take the second shift for any amount of payment. Mr. Gurov had a relative who confided, "I'm working in the cooperative. I'm earning Rb 1,000 a month, and I don't know where to spend it, how to spend it. I'm afraid of going out on the streets at night. Five years ago I earned Rb 300 a month and I could buy everything in the stores . . . not everything, but a lot of things. I wasn't afraid; I felt safe."

By November, the former ministry officials declared themselves the Association of Light Industry; they intended to smooth the process to free enterprise. The former minister became secretary of the association. Under central planning, the minister had been an autocrat: as secretary of the association, however, he described himself as a "servant of the members." Members were allocated state orders and were promised purchasing and management development services. Assistance was to be supplied to the weakest members. The privatization process was delegated by the members to the secretary of the association. The association, by serving as the agent of the enterprise, could—as in "the old days"—arrange both sales and supply sourcing, leaving enterprise managers in almost the same position of limited responsibility that had characterized their positions in the prereform economy. The idea was sufficiently attractive for nearly 1,100 of the enterprises formerly led by the ministry to join the trade association. Bolshevichka, however, did not. According to Gurov, "This arrangement makes no sense to us. It is going to be temporary, and we do not see how we could get any help from them."

The new structure became, in theory, simpler:

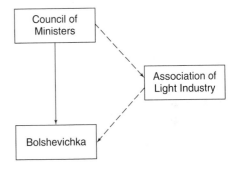

(Dotted lines suggest indirect relationships. Interaction with the Association of Light Industry was on a voluntary basis.)

Privatization Law

One of the great sources of uncertainty in Russian industry in mid-1991 was the prospect of enterprise ownership. A privatization law was proposed in 1991 in the Russian Republic. It dealt with the sale of state and municipal commercial property in order to establish an effective free market economy. Under this proposal, individuals or public companies would be able to purchase state-owned enterprises from the state by using private savings. The state proposed to make a 3-year detailed plan that included the enterprises to be privatized, preferable modes of privatization, conditions and terms of credit, and distribution of eventual income resulting from the process. Expenditure of the income generated from privatization would be under the control of the supreme soviet of the RSFSR (Russian Soviet Federated Socialist Republic), supreme soviets of areas and districts in the RSFSR territory, and local trade unions.

In addition, there would be institutions supporting the very complicated privatization procedures: the state committee, local property management committees, the supreme soviet, the Russia Fund of Federal Property, property funds, and the Investment Fund. The state committee, financed by the RSFSR budget, was to have ultimate responsibility for the privatization program. The actual process would be carried out by local property management committees financed by the funds accumulated in the privatization process. The committees were to report annually to the supreme soviet of the RSFSR, who in turn would discuss and adopt annual reports of the status of these funds. The Russia Fund of Federal Property would act as underwriter for privatizing firms by selling and exchanging share certificates and allocating dividends without interfering with business activities or share prices. The Russia Fund was to have the exclusive right to sell state property. The Investment Fund would possess only 10% of voting shares in a company. Buyers could not be organizations of which the state or a local trade union had more than 25% ownership. Workers of an enterprise could be buyers and could start public companies.

Bolshevichka's Mid-1991 Situation

Bolshevichka, which was 100% state-owned by the Russian Federation, consisted of six factories and two stores. The three factories in Moscow made high-quality men's suits (the highest quality was made in the main Moscow factory), and the three in Kaluga made very low quality (that is, poor material, poor assembly, and totally unfashionable design) "sports apparel" for both men and women.

One of the Moscow factories had received permission by the council of ministers of the RSFSR to leave the group as of September 1991 and become an independent plant. It had been forced to join Bolshevichka during the 1960s and, from the beginning, employees at that plant had wanted to separate. "Finally, their dream had come true!"

In 1991, Bolshevichka was making just over 1,200 suits per day and the finished goods inventory averaged Rb 4.5 million on any given day (according to the production director). Mr. Gurov, however, did not consider that there was any finished goods inventory, as the daily stock was delivered to the stores and sold each day.

Bolshevichka produced more than 100 models of men's suits (counting the different sizes produced, as well as designs and fabrics), based mostly on quarterly orders. Although the company distributed to more than 50 customers, 95% of its product was sold in Moscow and the remaining 5% elsewhere in the Soviet Union. Some small percentage of output was traded by Bolshevichka for consumer products that its workers otherwise had difficulty obtaining. In 1990, Bolshevichka produced 618,000 suits. By mid-1991, that figure had declined to roughly 500,000 per year, or 2,000 suits per day. Among the reasons for the decline was the repatriation of 140 Vietnamese guest workers, in accord with a decision by the council of ministers to dispatch Vietnamese guest workers from the city. Managers within Bolshevichka noted that these workers "did not work hard, and the quality of their work was very poor." This allowed a return to a one-shift operation, drastically increased wages for the remaining Russian workers (comparable with the price rise), and covered the process with a sufficient number of machine operators, a luxury that Bolshevichka did not have with the two shifts. The second shift had become a problem anyway due to the difficulty of attracting night-shift workers in Moscow, and second-shift work at Bolshevichka had been characterized as being of lower quality than that produced during the first shift. Furthermore, the labor force on the later shift exhibited high turnover (25%).

The company did not export any of its products; according to Gurov,

It makes no sense, given the taxes involved. We do sell our suits, however, within the Soviet Union to owners of hard currency. Last year (1990), we earned $500,000 that way. We have used that money to import equipment and supplies. Our strategy is to produce only high-quality goods and prepare ourselves to integrate into the Western markets. I am confident that we can produce medium quality men's suits for Western markets!

Manufacturing and Logistics

Under the old "marketing" system, which was still prevailing in July 1991, "order meetings" were held twice a year in the Soviet Union, where producers and customers met to settle the production and delivery agendas for the following 6 months. At Bolshevichka, all suits were produced to order. The factory insisted that orders be made for at least 2,500 pieces, using the choice of fabrics that were currently on hand. Within these agreements, Soviet law allowed some changes to take place up to 45 calendar days before the item was to be shipped, although the normal throughput time for an item was typically 12 to 15 days. The factory thus built in 5% to 10% allowances at the beginning of the planning process for size and fabric changes.

Work within the factory was scheduled to meet the objective of establishing "smooth production, all year long." Sizing and sequencing of the work were based on the existing capacity of the cutting work and the quantity of the fabric required by any specific order. Bolshevichka's productive assets were largely composed of new, mostly Western, equipment including a modern CAD/CAM (computer-aided design and computer-aided manufacturing) system. Each day, the foremen received the day's work plan from the planning office. Although there was no significant setup cost for changing fabrics or styles, everything was regulated by a special schedule to make the process run smoothly. Despite such close control and planning throughout the entire ordering and manufacturing process, the factory experienced chronic shipment errors. As one manager put it, "The trick is that the customers never get what they order." There were usually deviations in sizes and fabrics. Bolshevichka based its production scheduling on the capability of the cutting section (stripes, for example, were extra work and took longer), the number of people engaged in the operation, the quantity of fabric needed, and how much was in stock. However, the extremely tight amount of space available for finished goods inventory within the factory (4 days of capacity) left the factory with no buffer for correcting production mistakes that occurred prior to shipping. Because of the major capacity problems—the cutting room being at the front end and the inventory stock room at the back end—a need for fewer clients and larger orders was called for.

Occasionally, there were rush orders to be filled. Suits for the Olympic teams and for mass events in Red Square were often produced at Bolshevichka. Being special orders, they would be done accurately, but these standards were not applied to everybody, and "regular" customers suffered as a result.

The delivery schedule was negotiated on the basis of shipping considerations, such as the economies of scale achievable by shipping full truckloads rather than partial loads. According to Soviet law, if Bolshevichka did not honor the due date, the customer could refuse the merchandise, and Bolshevichka would receive a fine of up to 5% of the total cost of goods not delivered on time. Written into most contracts, however, was a clause that forbade any penalty to Bolshevichka. Furthermore, conditions within an economy of scarcity meant that customers never returned an order for fear of losing it or risking future retribution by the factory.

Marketing and Distribution through the Company-owned Retail Outlets

Bolshevichka owned two retail stores in Moscow, both of which were separate legal entities. The stores were virtually empty and nothing was done esthetically to market the goods: no window displays, no mannequins displaying merchandise. Advertising was not an issue. According to Gurov, "We are not interested in advertising as we don't need it." A visitor to the Gorky Street outlet noted that there were only a handful of suits available for sale and that many of the racks were bare. (Refer to Exhibit 2 for photographs of the store.)

EXHIBIT 2   Store Display

INDUSTRY

Raw Material Supply

The raw materials required for suit making were subjected to persistent quality problems and, in 1991, spiraling price rises. The price of wool in the Soviet Union tripled in April 1991, due to free pricing and no competition. Soviet fabric, although less expensive than imported fabric ($1 to $2/meter in Russia versus $6 to $12/meter abroad), could not compare in quality. In addition to fabric, suit producers also required interlinings and glue. Interlining was the material used in suits to give them shape and to help them hang well. Soviet interlining tended to be thick and stiff, resulting in a starchy, heavy-looking suit. The glue was used to attach the interlining to the exterior fabric. Glue was unavailable in Russia. Without the constant supply of the hard currency needed to import interlining and glue, suit production would come to a halt. Access to hard currency for the purchase of raw materials was vital to the success of Bolshevichka's operation. Foreigners supplying such raw materials were rarely willing to accept rubles or bartering; they often demanded hard currency. There were three legal but very expensive ways in which to acquire hard currency.[3] It was quite likely that additional, although not entirely legal, methods were also available for currency conversion. It was believed that the further devaluation of the ruble in July 1991[4] brought the RSFSR's economy closer to convertibility. A likely result of convertibility would have been an increase in foreign competition, but also easier supply conditions.

Bolshevichka relied heavily on both foreign and domestic producers of woolen fibers for its raw fabric. After free pricing began in 1991, however, the ministry was no longer available to guarantee either the raw materials or the items needed to maintain the imported equipment from abroad (spare parts, special threads, oils, and so on). Bolshevichka financed such purchases with short-term loans (the enterprise had a Rb 17 to 20 million line of credit). Gurov worried about the future of sourcing relationships. He recognized that increased competition, both domestically and internationally, would increase Bolshevichka's need to obtain high-quality raw materials, spare parts, and equipment. Yet his limited holdings of foreign exchange offered him little leverage in dealing with the suppliers of such items.

Pricing and Taxation

During the days of central planning in the USSR, prices of all goods and services were set by a pricing committee. Gurov explained, "There were state prices for everything—all were fixed in books, volumes of books. Prices depended on the cost and quantity of material."

Following the 1991 reforms, beginning on April 1, 1991, it was possible for Bolshevichka to charge any price it wished for a "fashionable" product[5]—the factory defined what was and was not fashionable. In 1990, when the price was still determined by the state (fixed by product, material, and size of the pattern), the average price of a Bolshevichka suit was Rb 187; by early 1991, that average price had risen to somewhere in the range of Rb 400 to 500, and by mid-year the price of most suits had increased tenfold to the Rb 2,000 range. The norm was that all suits were paid for in advance. Inflation reached a rate of 90% per annum during the second quarter of 1991 and continued to accelerate.

---

[3] The three legal but expensive methods were the following: (1) A number of banks sometimes have tax auctions where they sell dollars and one can buy dollars for rubles. (2) The association is a partner of a number of banks that are permitted to convert and, on behalf of the association, they make the conversion. (3) A bank makes a closed conversion. For example, rubles are converted to dollars and then to rupees, and vice versa, without any cash transaction.

[4] Rb 32 = US$1.

[5] In the past, an enterprise could raise its state-assigned price by 20% for fashionable items. Now, while it was free to charge whatever price it desired, a product priced so as to yield 50% profitability had a 32% surtax, plus the customer's additional 5% "presidential" tax. Above 50% profitability, there was a progressive tax of up to 100% on each marginal ruble of sales.

When profit on sales was 50% or less, a 32% income tax was due. As profitability increased, so did the tax due. As a result, there was very little incentive to sell merchandise above 50% profitability.

Competition

"There is no competition in this country!" commented Mr. Gurov. His statement was indeed true in the past because it had been a centrally planned economy. It was also true today. Despite a number of companies producing and selling the same goods, with the chronic shortage of everything, no company had a problem selling its goods; competition became irrelevant in a sellers' market. Gurov was still worried, though, about the company's ability to defend itself against the impending entry of foreign rivals:

Today I'm nervous, because I haven't created a viable, competitive structure. I haven't got a partner to help me. If I had a structure, it would be OK. On the one hand, we are interested in opening up the borders because I want to be able to choose between a domestic producer and an import [raw materials]. There should be competition, then the prices would go down. It's the only thing that could make the suppliers reduce the cost and reduce the price. On the other hand, if you open the borders and the domestic companies are not ready to compete, they'll be just ruined.

Take Chilean imports, for example. They cost $60 a suit, that's Rb 2,000—the same price we charge for our suits; but they have a foreign label, they have a brand name, they have the idea of an imported suit. It's very different. The companies that are bringing them into the Soviet Union, in a JV for example, are willing to accept both rubles and hard currency.

STRATEGIC OPTIONS

In the summer of 1991, Mr. Gurov faced a number of major decisions, any one of which could result in a major strategic change for Bolshevichka. These decisions were identified as follows.

Brand Name

Gurov, and other managers within the company, had some serious concerns about the product's name, Bolshevichka—a powerfully Communist name recalling all the trauma of recent Soviet history—and especially its impact for exporting. Gurov had considered changing the name or disregarding brand names altogether to serve instead as a low-cost manufacturer for Western companies.

Design

Vladimir Obergan was the chief designer for Bolshevichka. Because of Obergan's growing frustration at not having his own name on the suits he designed, Mr. Gurov provided equity capital and let him form his own company at the end of July 1991 so that he could act as a subcontractor for Bolshevichka. Mr. Gurov had his doubts about Mr. Obergan's success, but nevertheless gave him the chance.

Mr. Obergan, who had been with the company since 1974, had noted three types of customers for fashion items: (1) conservative; (2) fashionable but not "ridiculous" (that is, fancy, avant-garde); and (3) "ridiculous." In particular, Mr. Obergan wanted to design, produce, and sell expensive (Rb 2,500 to 3,000) avant-garde suits for individuals (the second category). First, however, he needed money, especially hard currency, to buy the special fabric he wanted from abroad. Without the required money, he would have to start out by making "regular" custom-made suits. These suits would carry his name—Obergan written in Latin script—and would sell for about Rb 2,000. He would obtain fabric from Mr. Gurov—mostly wool and semiwool, the same as that used by Bolshevichka—and assumed that he would continue to get fabric from the same supplier as Mr. Gurov. His suits would be produced by Bolshevichka's workers, and so, without the imported fabric, there would be little difference between his suits and those of Bolshevichka.

Accordingly, he stressed his keen interest in having a foreign joint venture partner, but purely for tax breaks. He was looking for a foreigner who was simply a legal entity; know-how and experience from the partner were unimportant to him. Mr. Obergan had had some experience with a French textile company, but did not contribute his designs to this company because all its suits were designed in France.

Organization and Divestiture of Kaluga

Gurov was also wrestling with the idea of significantly downsizing Bolshevichka by divesting it of the Kaluga factories.

All the company's goods carried the Bolshevichka label, even though Kaluga merchandise was of significantly poorer quality than that produced in the other Bolshevichka factories. The three Kaluga plants wanted to stay in the group but, because of the image issue of the Bolshevichka name, Mr. Gurov was undecided about keeping these factories. Despite the Kaluga plants' outstanding profitability and the fact that they represented much needed manufacturing capacity (in a seller's market), Gurov considered divesting the company of these plants to separate their low-quality image and culture from the rest of Bolshevichka. He also wanted to reduce the managerial problems associated with having to span two very different corporate cultures; it was felt that the Kaluga plants were not skillfully managed.

For the second quarter of 1991, profits from the Moscow factories were Rb 24,480/worker (1,760 workers), as opposed to Rb 25,540/worker (670 workers) for the Kaluga factories. (Refer to Exhibit 3 for financial information.)

Joint Venture Propositions

Because of constantly changing laws, the business situation in the Soviet Union was highly fluid. Yet, regardless of political volatility, Mr. Gurov thought that "the situation has been completely stable with regard to profit making in this country." There were opportunities to create offshore business abroad for state-owned companies, cooperatives, private companies, and Soviet citizens. In addition, any new joint venture with a foreign firm had rights to a 2-year tax holiday.

Bolshevichka had discussed alliances over a period of 2 years with the French company Chargeur. By autumn of 1990, all discussion between the two firms had ended, with no agreement reached. Chargeur was one of the world's largest producers of high-quality fabrics, as well as men's suits and designs. Mr. Gurov hoped that a company such as Chargeur would be interested in a relationship with Bolshevichka, possibly even an equity position.

Regarding such a possibility, one of Chargeur's directors gave the following response:

1. In 1990, we did $50 million of business with the USSR alone. We are one of the largest producers of high-quality fabrics in the world.
2. Bolshevichka is a very small fish. I'm not even sure I remember exactly what sort of business we did together. I doubt very much that the company would have any place in our strategy. If we were interested in the USSR, we would probably want to look at a much larger enterprise.
3. It is true that the main reason for being interested in the Soviet Union is its large market size. It is doubtful whether low-cost production can be developed in the foreseeable future. Asia has both the skills and the know-how in addition to the lowest costs in the world. Of course, we might have to produce locally to enter the market, but we would tread very carefully, given the political and social environment.
4. But, in fact, only a madman would want to jump into that market today. The commercial risks are too great and, with the political climate so uncertain, making any investment in management time, not to mention money, is undesirable at this time. Of course, things could change, but we do not have a pioneer mentality.

The "Saturday Special"

Bolshevichka had operations on Saturdays with a Swiss company managed by a Russian émigré. Bolshevichka simply subcontracted its manufacturing capacity to a joint venture, of which it was not an equity partner. The agreement was executed in October 1990 and brought the company Rb 2 to 3 million in net profit. Production took place only on Saturdays because, being a state-owned firm, from Monday to Friday Bolshevichka had to fulfill its

EXHIBIT 3   TABLE 1: First Quarter, 1991 (in Rb 000s)

Factory	Material Cost	Wages	Social Cost	Indirect Cost	Production Cost	Transport	COGS
Main Moscow factory (Golov factory)	9,004.0	313.6	113.2	662.3	1,089.1	1.7	10,094.8
Perov section (jackets)	226.6	27.3	9.8	57.9	95.0	0.1	321.7
Zavor section (jackets)	89.1	1.2	0.4	2.8	4.4	—	93.5
Nadom section (jeans, jackets)	156.6	52.4	18.8	6.9	78.1	—	234.7
Others[a]	60.6	22.6	8.0	37.9	68.5	—	129.1
Lyublin factory (suits, trousers, jackets)	6,569.7	278.6	99.9	591.6	970.1	0.5	7,540.3
Kazem factory/Kaluga 3 (trousers, jackets, shirts)	2,445.2	138.7	49.7	291.8	480.2	0.2	2,925.6
Suhinish factory/Kaluga 4 (suits, trousers, shirts)	5,042.5	195.3	80.2	105.6	381.1	23.4	5,447.0
Baryatin factory/Kaluga 5 (trousers)	243.6	11.7	4.3	26.0	42.0	—	285.6
Total	23,837.9	1,041.4	384.3	1,782.8	3,208.5	25.9	27,072.3

[a] Production of the training center, the shop that processes waste, and the design center.

Production cost = wages + social cost + indirect cost.

COGS = material cost + production cost + transport.

TABLE 1:   Second Quarter, 1991 (in Rb 000s)

Factory	Material Cost	Wages	Social Cost	Indirect Cost	Production Cost	Transport	COGS
Main Moscow factory (Golov factory)	12,157.1	619.1	247.1	1,098.4	1,964.6	10.6	14,132.3
Perov section (jackets)	529.5	50.2	20.4	88.7	159.3	0.4	689.2
Zavor section (jackets)	127.3	3.7	1.6	6.7	12.0	0.1	139.4
Nadom section (jeans, jackets)	274.7	90.9	37.0	24.9	152.8	0.3	427.8
Others	139.4	35.6	13.7	58.5	107.8	0.6	247.8
Lyublin factory (suits, trousers, jackets)	7,453.5	427.4	167.7	767.8	1,362.9	6.6	8,823.0
Kazem factory/Kaluga 3 (trousers, jackets, shirts)	2,827.0	175.1	68.0	301.3	544.4	2.6	3,374.0
Suhinish factory/Kaluga 4 (suits, trousers, skirts)	7,712.5	360.9	143.4	190.0	694.3	23.6	8,430.4
Baryatin factory/Kaluga 5 (trousers)	397.1	18.8	7.5	33.2	59.5	0.3	456.9
Total	31,618.1	1,781.7	706.4	2,569.5	5,057.6	45.1	36,720.8

TABLE 2:   Profit per Worker in Moscow and Kaluga Factories, (Not Including Factory 2) (in Rb 000s)

Moscow (1,260 workers)		Kaluga (673 workers)	
First quarter 1991			
Main factory	16,899.0	Kazem	4,382.2
Cooperative	4,002.4		
		Suhinish	7,559.0
		Baryatin	413.1
	20,901.4		12,354.3
Profit/worker	Rb 15/worker/year		Rb 16.6/worker/year
Second quarter 1991			
Main	21,479.5	Kazem	4,690.7
Cooperative	4,679.1		
		Suhinish	11,745.0
		Baryatin	752.6
	26,158.6		17,188.3
Profit/worker	Rb 20.8/worker/year		Rb 22.5/worker/year

EXHIBIT 3 (*Continued*)   **TABLE 3**

| | Sales Volume | | Profit | | Capital Investment | |
| | In Rb 000s | Index (1985=100) | In Rb 000s | Index (1985 = 100) | New Equipment | Construction |
					(Rb 000s)	
1985	120,866	100	16,928	100	584	0
1986	130,143	107.7	19,282	113.9	236	2,479
1987	122,477[a]	101.3	20,463	120.9	770	0
1988	128,092	106.0	22,802	134.7	992	0
1989	133,055	110.1	21,878[b]	129.2	1,692	838
1990	135,937	112.5	21,255	125.6	1,082	1,005

[a] Change in amount of imported material (very high demand for denim and corduroy).

[b] Decrease because too expensive to import. Before 1989, Gosplan allocated hard currency to each company. When perestroïka started, however, no more hard currency was allocated from above, and due to the very high cost of exchanging rubles for hard currency, it became too expensive to import.

TABLE 4:   Inventory (in Rb 000s)

Raw materials	30,565	41,705
Work in process	6,599	6,818
Finished goods	4,473	4,647
Total inventory	41,637	53,170

state commitments. The suits were sold mostly in Russia. On Saturday, both the factory and the workers were available, but it was their choice whether to work or not. The pay offered was up to 10 times greater on a Saturday than during the week; thus a worker could double his monthly salary simply by working one or two Saturdays. Mr. Gurov, however, thought that his decision to run the factory for nonstate operations might be looked at adversely if it were discovered. Consequently, although audit checks did not take place in the Soviet Union, he was aware that this practice could start one day and that auditors might question his actions. He felt sure that he was not breaking any law, but he knew that the laws changed weekly, making his decision somewhat risky. Morally, he justified his actions by paying a fee to the state for the use of the factory.

The Hungarian Deal

Mr. Gurov was also considering a contract deal with a Hungarian textile company in which the Hungarian company would virtually take all responsibility for the risk involved. It would enable Bolshevichka to make high profits and have a source of supply diversification and would be a tax-free arrangement for 2 years. Bolshevichka would make a profit of Rb 300 per suit, a fixed price for Bolshevichka's labor and profit, while the Hungarian firm would be responsible for selling the goods in the Soviet Union. The Hungarian company wanted to sell the suits for Rb 1,500 to 2,000, but Mr. Gurov was dubious. He felt that the amount was too high, since the fabric would be imported from Hungary and was thus of very poor quality. Production would take place on Mondays and Fridays, but as that was state time, the plant would actually be leased on a temporary basis from the state. An important advantage that the deal offered Bolshevichka was protection against inevitable raw material price rises in the Soviet Union.

MR. GUROV

Mr. Gurov was 38 years old in 1991. He was a member of the Communist Party. His education had been at the Moscow Institute of Light Industry, specializing in the technology of sewn goods. In 1975, he became a foreman in the cutting section at Bolshevichka. A year and a half later, he advanced to the position of chief of the sewing production section, and after that he became chief administrator of the design section. Mr. Gurov spent a year as chief of the technical department in the Ministry of Light Industry, but disliked the bureaucratic life intensely. After a year in the ministry, he returned to Bolshevichka and spent 4 years as technical director. Mr. Gurov was appointed general director in 1987 at age 34. "Nobody wanted to take this job. The company was in a very bad position. The former general manager, the sales manager, the chief accountant, and his two deputies had all left. The fiscal situation was very poor, plans very demanding, responsibility very high, and wages very low." Mr. Gurov had attended a management training course for Soviet managers at Duke University in the United States and was also considering attending MBA and executive programs in late 1991. He was not a bureaucrat, but a manager sincerely interested in developing his professional managerial training. A man of action, he disliked his bureaucratic year in the ministry, and he welcomed the challenge that awaited him as general director of Bolshevichka.

On the wall of his office was a photograph of a seriously deformed infant—a victim of Chernobyl:

That boy was born a year after the Chernobyl accident. He lived one year with his family and then they rejected him, so now he is in the orphan house. Despite his average intelligence, he lives with severely handicapped children. It is a tragedy. We (Bolshevichka) donate RB 100,000 just to provide his staying in a special house. And I personally give another Rb 1,500. This is my personal interest, but it also is a remembrance not to be very greedy. There are a lot of such children in Byelorussia now.

Despite the excitement of increased managerial freedom that had suddenly resulted from the cataclysmic changes, Mr. Gurov was concerned about what he saw as the erosion of social values. Mr. Gurov had thoroughly enjoyed his childhood days in a small community house that his family shared with 12 other families.

I was brought up in a community environment. You see, the relationships we have here in the Soviet Union are quite different from those you have in the West. There, the basic ideology is individualism, and here we have a basic ideology of collectivism. We got used to living in big communities, to deal and to speak and to laugh, and we didn't care about the future and the day after tomorrow; we were always sure about the next day. Now we have to transform into individualists, and that's what I feel sorry about.

4

The Challenge to Market in Japan

During the last 20 years, the success of Japanese enterprises in fields as diverse as machine tools, electronics, automobiles, and, more recently, new materials and mechatronics (the combining of mechanical engineering with electronics to increase automation) has brought about an abundant stream of literature on different aspects of Japanese management. Quality management, human resources management, manufacturing technology, negotiating know-how, and financial management are among the fields of Japanese management that have been thoroughly covered by specialists. But what about marketing?

Peter Drucker has written that *"marketing was invented in Japan around 1650."*[1] Indeed, in the 17th century, firms like Mitsukoshi (today one of Japan's leading department stores) already had systems in place to deliver products tailor-made to their customers. Back in 1685, Mitsukoshi provided employees with manuals on customer care that could very much be used today in customer satisfaction training sessions. Yet, despite the marketing success of Japanese firms over time, very little so far as been said or written on the way Japanese firms approach marketing.[2] As one Japanese executive from the world's leading consumer electronics firm explains; *"this is probably due to the fact that we Japanese use our good common sense and apply the basic marketing principles developed in the West very well."*

GOLDEN RULES FOR MARKETING IN JAPAN

Marketing products and services in Japan is often considered by foreign firms as a very difficult if not impossible mission, reinforcing the perception (and/or the reality) that the Japanese market is closed. Today, only a few sectors remain closed to foreign competition. Traditional protected sectors such as tobacco have recently been opened up, causing losses of significant market shares to domestic companies. Yet the great success in Japan of companies like IBM, Benetton,

---

[1] Peter Drucker, *Management*, Heinemann, London, 1974, p. 62.

[2] Philip Kotler, Liam Fahey, and Somkid Jatusripitak, *The New Competition*, Prentice Hall, Englewood Cliffs, N.J., 1985.

Club Med, or General Electric demonstrates that foreign-market-led companies can win large market shares in Japan provided that they follow five golden rules:

Rule 1: "The Client is god"

"In Europe, one often says that the client is king; in Japan, the client is god," explains Dieter Schneidewind, a German who has been the director of the Japanese subsidiary of Wella (the German leader in hair cosmetics) for many years. He has had a great deal of experience with the difficulties of the Japanese market. *"When we deliver to a client, each bottle of hair lotion is removed from its batch to be carefully checked one by one. If there is the slightest defect in our packaging, the product is immediately sent back."*[3]

Many western companies have thus learned that the Japanese client is one of the most demanding in the world. Any product, whether manufactured by a local or a foreign company, must be absolutely irreproachable in quality, which includes the product itself, its packaging—even if it has nothing to do with the intrinsic value of the product—the delivery time, and after-sales service. The Japanese have even made up an expression for this standard: *miryokutekina hinshitsu* (literally, "quality that appeals"). The experience of providing excellence to Japanese consumers can sometimes be very frustrating. Take the case of Lestra Design, a company that specialized in feather and down-filled products. This French enterprise, uncontested leader in its domestic market for more than 50 years, experienced many unexpected challenges. However, as its director general explained, *"We had to compete with the Japanese on their own ground to understand the market demands. Indeed, it is not easy to change, especially after all these years of success in the European market. Therefore, without the Japanese market experience, we would certainly not have reached the level of service quality which we have today."*[4]

Rule 2: Take the Long-term View

Tabasco was introduced in Japan at the end of World War II by U.S. occupation forces. By 1993, Japan was McIlhenny's largest international market. What contributed to the success of **Tabasco** in Japan was the unicity of its products, the astute marketing of the McIlhenny's management together with a strong sense of persistence. Obviously, the success of this very American product did not come overnight. Japanese firms are reknowned for taking a long-term view of their business. Foreign companies who strongly wish to succeed in Japan must therefore develop long-term plans to conquer this market. As Vernon R. Alden emphasized, *"no one is going to hand you market share on a platter—you have to earn it."*[5]

Rule 3: Innovate or Die

As Akio Morita, the CEO of Sony, often likes to repeat, *"In Japan, if you don't make your own product obsolete, the competition will do it for you."* Every day, an incredible mass of new products appears in the Japanese market, many of which are inevitably doomed to disappear within the following weeks or months, while a few will be able to survive. In Japan, the *shinhatsubai* (literally,

---

[3] Interview with the author.

[4] Interview with the author.

[5] Vernon R. Alden, "Who Says You Can't Crack Japanese Markets?" *Harvard Business Review,* January–February 1987.

new product) fever is particularly strong in the public sector—food, cosmetics, and electronics. More than 700 new nonalcoholic drinks are introduced every year in Japan and less than 3% survive 2 years. This poses the challenge to many firms (both Japanese and non-Japanese) to make a quick appraisal of the long-term success of a particular new product.

Even Coca-Cola has had to get in tune with this major Japanese trend. Today, the American multinational provides in Japan a range of products twice as large as the one in the United States. Of course, *shinhatsubai* does not necessarily refer to a revolutionary new product; more often, it is a more or less important innovation such as a new design, a new function, or new packaging. Therefore, particularly in this context, foreign companies find themselves rapidly out of the competition if they are not ready to keep up with innovation.

Rule 4: Redefine Market Segmentation

The perpetual search for innovation accounts for the fact that Japanese enterprises are continuously segmenting and resegmenting their markets. By combining technical innovation with consumer analysis, most Japanese manufacturers have demonstrated that they are able to create desire before need. Although the Japanese have not created the concept of the market niche, they have proved that they can make the most of it. From the Subaru 4 × 4 to the Mazda MX5 roadster, or from the Nissan Figaro (memories of the 1960s) to the Toyota Lexus, the car manufacturers' policy to segment has been fully tested.

Likewise, Kirin, the beer leader in Japan, and its competitors, Sapporo and Suntory, also had to review their whole market segmentation in order to counter the drive by Super Dry, a slightly more alcoholic beer launched by Asahi, a fourth competitor. As a result, more than 60 new beers and different kinds of packaging have appeared annually in the Japanese market during recent years.

Rule 5: Use the Japanese Market to Become Truly Global

No company is truly global if it does not compete in Japan. Many international firms have learned that Japan can be a major battlefield for international brand competition. It forces western firms to develop new competencies in serving the most demanding customers in the world. Many first-rank companies see it as the market for reference. As the general manager of a European company emphasized, *"If we can compete in Japan, we can compete anywhere else in the world."*

SUMMARY

The cases in this section serve two purposes. The Kirin Brewery case will introduce students to the marketing environment in Japan and its very intensive competition. The "battle of the beers" is truly one of Japan's most celebrated marketing battles from which many foreign marketing executives can learn. The next three cases, Philip Morris K.K., Lestra Design, and Delissa, will introduce students to the particular challenges of entering the Japanese market as a foreign importer.

Kirin Brewery Co. Ltd.: The Dry Beer War

On February 22, 1988, Kirin Brewery decided to launch its own dry beer to compete with Asahi's Super Dry in the Japanese beer market. Kirin's decision to launch Kirin Dry was backed by strong consumer pressure. In liquor stores, more and more regular Kirin consumers were asking for Kirin's dry beer, and disappointed customers were switching to Asahi's Super Dry. Kirin's executives had anticipated that both Suntory and Sapporo would jump at the new opportunities created by Asahi to attack Kirin and gain a larger share of the beer market by developing the dry niche. In fact, a few days after the introduction of Kirin Dry, both Sapporo and Suntory launched their own dry beers. By early autumn, the market for dry beer had expanded enormously, and Asahi was currently selling half of the dry beer produced in Japan.

In late September 1988, Kazuhisa Tani, who headed Kirin's Beer Division, organized a meeting with several managers from the marketing and corporate planning departments. After reviewing Kirin's performance, Tani remarked:

Kirin may have lost this summer's battle, but we are still fighting the war. Kirin must swallow its pride and commit itself to the dry beer competition, because the market is truly different now. It's all part of the game—even if dry beer triumphs enough to dislodge the old standbys, lager and draft. Campaigning for the 1989 sales year starts now. We have to be ready for the next round of the fight.

THE JAPANESE BEER INDUSTRY

The beer industry in Japan was born in 1853 when a doctor "test-brewed" some beer at home using the description in a Dutch book. Although Shozaburo Shibuya was said to have been the first Japanese to brew and sell beer as a business in 1872, it was not until the Sino-Japanese War (1937–1941) and then World War II, that millions of Japanese people, mostly soldiers, enjoyed their first taste of beer.

By 1987, beer was a popular beverage throughout Japan, representing 67% of all alcoholic beverages consumed. It was followed by Japanese sake, 17.7%; Shochu (a white spirit), 7%; and whisky and brandy, 4%. Per capita consumption of beer had doubled from 20.2 liters in 1965 to 43.8 liters, while total consumption of all alcoholic beverages had grown from 36.3 liters to 65.3 liters. Japan was the fourth largest beer market in the world, with an annual per capita consumption of just under 500 million kiloliters (kl). However, international comparative data ranked the Japanese as the 28th greatest consumers of beer in the world on a per capita basis, with a

This case was prepared by Professor Dominique Turpin and revised with Professor Christopher Lovelock and Research Associate Joyce Miller as a basis for class discussion rather than to illustrate either effective or ineffective handling of an administrative situation. Some names have been disguised to respect confidentiality. Copyright © 1990 by the International Institute for Management Development (IMD), Lausanne, Switzerland. IMD retains all rights. Not to be used or reproduced without written permission from IMD, Lausanne, Switzerland.

consumption less than half the American figure and under one-third that of Germany, Czechoslovakia, Denmark, and New Zealand.

Production

The production and sale of beer were heavily influenced by seasonality, with 36% of sales made during the three months of June to August. Kirin's production manager estimated that the process of brewing beer was similar among competitors. But economies of scale could be significant.

The production of beer was controlled by the state through a licensing system, which made it difficult for newcomers to enter the market. According to Kenji Yamamoto, deputy manager in Kirin's Beer Division, "Investment in production is still dictated by market share, and today, one point market share is worth ¥5 billion in terms of marginal profits."[1] In 1987, Kirin had 14 brewing plants, while Sapporo, Asahi, and Suntory had 10, 6, and 3 plants, respectively. Yamamoto believed that its extensive network of production facilities gave Kirin a logistical cost advantage. Also, most of Kirin's breweries were built close to Japan's largest cities to ensure freshness, an element that had become a major selling point for many Japanese consumers. Yamamoto noted, "For beer lovers, the fresher, the better."

Each brewery had an average production capacity of 250,000 kl. Kirin executives estimated that in 1987 building a new brewery would represent a ¥50 billion investment (including the price of land). However, around Tokyo, such a construction could require an investment of up to ¥80 to 90 billion.

Product Categories and Market Segmentation

The Japanese beer market was divided into two major categories: lager and draft. By international standards, lager was a beer with a long brewing process. However, in Japan, consumers regarded lager as a beer pasteurized by heat, while draft beer (also called *nama* in Japan) was unpasteurized under strict microbiological control, a technique called microfiltration. While draft beer represented 9% of the total beer market in 1974 (versus 91% for lager), its share had grown to 20% in 1980. By 1987, draft accounted for 42%, lager for 51%, with the balance going to malts, dry, light, and foreign beers. Kirin held over 90% of the lager category, while sales of draft were split among the four brewers (*refer to Exhibit 1*). Kirin's Lager was by far the best-selling beer in Japan, and the firm's dominant position over the past 40 years had been built almost exclusively on this single product.

Foreign beer accounted for 3% of the total beer market. All the major Japanese brewers had tied up with large foreign brewers to distribute and brew their brands in Japan. Budweiser (from the United States), brewed and distributed in Japan by Suntory, was the most popular foreign brand with the equivalent of 3.1 million cases[2] sold in 1987. Heineken (from the Netherlands) had a similar agreement with Kirin and was the second best-selling brand. Beer imports, primarily from the United States, West Germany, France, and Denmark, had doubled in volume between 1984 and 1987, reaching 22.4 million liters.

The total adult population (aged 20 years old and over) in Japan was increasing at an average annual rate of 1.2%. The population of males aged 40 and over (regarded by Japanese brewers as the heavy-user segment) had been growing more rapidly, at an average annual rate of 1.4%. Heavy users, Asahi's key target for Super Dry, were defined as consumers drinking more than the equivalent of 8 regular (633 ml) bottles of beer each week. They represented 15% of the beer drinking population and accounted for 50% of beer consumption. Middle users (15% of beer drinkers) consumed the equivalent of 3 to 8 bottles of beer weekly. Finally light users (70% of beer drinkers) consumed fewer than 3 bottles each week. Middle and light users each represented about 25% of the volume of beer consumed.

---

[1] In 1988, ¥ 1,000 = US $7.25 = SF 10.44 = £4.30.

[2] One case contained 20 bottles of 633 ml each.

EXHIBIT 1 Beer Sales by Japanese Brewers by Segment, 1986–1988 (in kiloliters)

	Lager	Draft	Dry	All Malts	Total[a]
1986					
Kirin	2,352,900	388,800	0	22,100	2,763,800
Asahi	71,400	436,100	0	2,500	510,000
Sapporo	207,800	783,200	0	33,500	1,024,500
Suntory	0	408,200	0	41,500	449,700
	2,632,100	2,016,300	—	99,600	4,748,000
1987					
Kirin	2,491,800	479,000	0	42,000	3,012,800
Asahi	60,200	441,900	165,000	19,200	686,300
Sapporo	170,400	886,500	0	33,900	1,090,800
Suntory	0	394,800	0	110,000	504,800
	2,722,400	2,202,200	165,000	205,100	5,294,700
1988[b]					
Kirin	2,001,600	245,500	501,800	37,900	2,786,800
Asahi	12,500	210,800	943,100	14,000	1,180,400
Sapporo	105,800	712,300	275,200	38,700	1,132,000
Suntory	0	234,000	182,000	89,000	505,000
	2,119,900	1,402,600	1,902,100	179,600	5,604,200

[a] Totals exclude sales of light beer (15,000 kl) and imported foreign beers (32,000 kl).

[b] Projections for 12 months as of late September 1988.

Source: Kirin Brewery Co. Ltd.

In Japan, less than 10% of the total population never drank beer.

One notable trend was the growing number of female beer drinkers. Japanese women tended to be more health and weight conscious than men. To meet the needs of this segment, as well as to increase daytime consumption, Kirin had introduced Kirin Beer Light in 1980 and Kirin Palm Can in 1985. Kirin Beer Light had a lower alcohol content and attractive packaging that differentiated it from Kirin's other beer products. During the 1987 season, sales of light beer represented 0.3% of Kirin total beer revenues versus 83% for lager.

In Japan, 70% of the beer volume sold was consumed at home versus 30% in bars and restaurants. The Japanese associated no class connotation with beer, and it was quaffed with equal enthusiasm everywhere from four-stool diners to elite restaurants. However, consumption patterns were somewhat different from many Western countries. Most beer was consumed after 6:00 P.M., before dinner, after the traditional *ofuro* (Japanese bath), or after sports. A Kirin executive explained:

Drinking together after working hours is as much a part of Japanese business as coming to work on time.

However, most Japanese feel guilty drinking beer during the day on workdays. Because we Japanese have a different enzymology (enzymes in the human body), we tend to blush very quickly after a drink or two. If employees have a beer during the day, their working colleagues would notice immediately, and this could be quite an embarrassing situation.

Japanese consumers considered beer to be a light casual drink, while wine was perceived as light but more formal. Kirin's consumer research showed that beer was seen as a healthy and natural drink because it was brewed with no artificial additives. Shochu, another popular drink, was also considered casual, but it was a strong drink and was losing its popularity. The consumption of shochu, a distilled spirit, had experienced a major boom from 1982 to 1987. However, shochu was now seen by industry analysts as a fashion fad, and some predicted that the Super Dry boom could be the same.

COMPETITION AND MARKETING ACTIVITIES

The Japanese beer market was an oligopoly with four companies (Kirin, Asahi, Suntory, and Sapporo) representing over 99% of the total sales volume. Two small brewers, Hokkaido Asahi and Orion, operated on a local basis only—on the northern island of Hokkaido and in Okinawa in the most southern part of Japan, respectively.

Kirin Brewery

Kirin was the top brewer in Japan and the fourth largest in the world after Anheuser-Busch and Miller of the United States and Heineken of the Netherlands. Kirin's 1987 sales amounted to ¥1,300 billion with profits of ¥31,000 million. Kirin traced its origins back to 1870 when an American entreprenuer, W. Copeland, established Spring Valley, 40 kilometers south of Tokyo. The brewery was active until 1884. The organization was subsequently revamped, and operations resumed under the management of Japan Brewery Company Ltd., which was taken over by Kirin Brewery Company Ltd. in 1907. Building on its predecessor's philosophy, Kirin established the management tenets that still guided the company 80 years later: "quality first" and "sound management."

In 1954, Kirin captured top share in the beer industry from Sapporo Breweries. However, Asahi, Kirin, and Sapporo remained close competitors with roughly one-third of the market each (*refer to Exhibit 2*). Since the 1950s, as far as the public was concerned, "Beer meant Kirin." In 1966, Kirin's market share passed 50%. But Kirin pushed its advantage even further, seizing a 63% share of the Japanese beer market in 1979. At this point, under the provision of the Japanese Antimonopoly Law, the Fair Trade Commission threatened legislation to break Kirin Brewery into two separate companies. In the end, the Kirin organization remained intact.

In 1971, Kirin began to diversify its operations. Through an agreement with the Canadian firm J. E. Seagrams & Sons, Kirin began to import liquor produced overseas, including Chivas Regal. Five years later, a joint venture in Australia was established, and through a domestic venture, Kirin began to market Koiwai food products. In 1977, Kirin established KW,

Inc., to bottle and market Coca-Cola in the United States, and later created Kirin USA, Inc. Kirin also planned to expand its presence in the U.S. market using beer brewed in Canada by Molson Ltd. In addition, Kirin had tied up with Heineken N.V., Europe's largest beer brewer, and the company had set up several joint ventures in the United States in the field of biotechnology. In 1987, Kirin arranged to exchange information and technology with several organizations in Czechoslovakia.

Despite its diversification into soft drinks, dairy products, whisky, and biotechnology, Kirin was still heavily dependent on beer. Kirin's president elaborated, "In 1987, beer represented 93% of our sales volume. This makes us vulnerable to Asahi's recent attack. We need to review the market situation and also to react adequately to Asahi's challenge."

Sapporo Breweries Ltd.

Sapporo had once been the dominant player in the market. However, it had gradually lost share to its three competitors. In 1987, it was the second largest brewer in Japan with a 20% share of the domestic market. Sapporo had a dominant position in the draft segment, holding a 40% share (*refer to Exhibit 1*). Although Sapporo had diversified into soft drinks, wine, and imported liquors such as J&B whiskies, beer still accounted for 94% of the company's total revenues.

Suntory Ltd.

Established in 1899 by Shinjiro Torii, the father of the firm's current president, Suntory was the major producer of whisky in Japan, as well as a leading importer of Scotch whiskies, bourbons, whiskies, cognacs, wines, liqueurs, beers, and the like. In 1986, Suntory had total sales of ¥625,843 million and was credited with a 63% share of the Japanese whisky market. In comparison, Kirin-Seagram (the third largest whisky company) held a 7.6% share and Nikka Whisky (the second largest local whisky producer) had a 21% share.

Suntory was a privately held company headed by Keizo Saji, who had a reputation for

EXHIBIT 2   Comparative Market Shares in the Japanese Beer Industry, 1949–1987 (%)

Brewers:	Asahi	Kirin	Sapporo	Suntory	Takara
1949	36.1	25.3	38.6	—	—
1950	33.5	29.5	37.0	—	—
1951	34.5	29.5	36.0	—	—
1952	32.5	33.0	34.5	—	—
1953	33.3	33.2	33.5	—	—
1954	31.5	37.1	31.4	—	—
1955	31.7	36.9	31.4	—	—
1956	31.1	41.7	27.2	—	—
1957	30.7	42.1	26.2	—	1.0
1958	30.9	39.9	27.5	—	1.7
1959	29.3	42.4	26.5	—	1.8
1960	27.2	44.7	26.0	—	2.1
1961	28.0	41.6	27.8	—	2.6
1962	26.4	45.0	26.4	—	2.2
1963	24.3	46.5	26.3	0.9	2.0
1964	25.5	46.2	25.2	1.2	1.9
1965	23.2	47.7	25.3	1.9	1.9
1966	22.2	50.8	23.8	1.7	1.5
1967	22.0	49.4	25.0	3.2	0.4
1968	20.2	51.2	24.4	4.2	—
1969	19.0	53.3	23.2	4.5	—
1970	17.3	55.4	23.0	4.3	—
1971	14.9	58.9	22.0	4.2	—
1972	14.1	60.1	21.3	4.5	—
1973	13.6	61.4	20.3	4.7	—
1974	13.1	62.6	19.5	4.8	—
1975	13.5	60.8	20.2	5.5	—
1976	11.8	63.8	18.4	6.0	—
1977	12.1	61.9	19.5	6.5	—
1978	11.6	62.1	19.6	6.7	—
1979	11.1	62.9	19.2	6.8	—
1980	11.0	62.2	19.7	7.1	—
1981	10.3	62.6	20.1	7.0	—
1982	10.0	62.3	19.9	7.8	—
1983	10.1	61.3	20.0	8.6	—
1984	9.9	61.7	19.5	8.9	—
1985	9.6	61.4	19.8	9.2	—
1986	10.4	59.6	20.4	9.4	—
1987	12.9	57.0	20.5	9.6	—

Source: Figures up to 1981: estimated by the Brewers Association of Japan. 1982–1987: Case writer's estimates.

an aggressive management style. In 1960, Saji had turned his attention to beer making, since Suntory had reached a virtual monopoly position in whisky. Most beers available in Japan at that time were German-style lager beers, so Suntory began searching for alternatives. After considerable research, Saji concluded that beer produced under strict microbiological control—similar to Danish-style beer—would have a "cleaner and milder" flavor and be a better match for Japanese cuisine. Suntory's first beer went on the market in 1963. Four years later, the company began producing only un-

pasteurized bottled and canned draft beer. Suntory had gradually caught up to Asahi in terms of market share. By the end of the 1987 season, Suntory had captured 9.6% of the total beer market. The company focused on the draft segment and was the leading brand in the "all malts" draft subsegment (*refer to Exhibit 1*).

In addition to brewing its own beers, Suntory produced and marketed several foreign beers in Japan through licensing agreements with Anheuser-Busch Co., Inc., of the United States and Carlsberg, a Danish brewer. Since 1984, Suntory had also brewed beer in China.

In fiscal year 1986, beer represented 27% of Suntory's total revenues.

Asahi Breweries Ltd.

Asahi was the third largest brewer in Japan in 1987. The company had gradually lost ground to Kirin, Sapporo, and Suntory, falling below 10% market share in 1985. While sales had grown substantially between 1976 and 1986, net profits declined from ¥2,130 million in 1976 to ¥1,510 million in 1986, but climbed up again in 1987. An Asahi manager explained:

In the 1970s, our company was the prisoner of a vicious circle. Sales were gradually slowing down, resulting in slower inventory turnovers and changing tastes, which affected our sales and our image. Also, since consumers did not have a high opinion of our products, retailers did not push our products, no matter how much effort our salesmen put in the trade. The salesmen blamed the engineers for not turning out good products, and the engineers blamed the salesmen for not being able to sell a product that they thought was as good as the competition.

To overcome Asahi's declining market share, management pushed to reduce the dependence on beer by expanding sales of soft drinks, foods, and pharmaceuticals. Asahi had, in fact, become less dependent on beer than both Kirin and Sapporo. In 1987, soft drinks represented 25% of Asahi's total sales. On the basis of field research indicating that consumer preference was shifting from the bitter and richer taste of Kirin's Lager to a sharper draft taste, Asahi's marketing department proposed changing the taste of the company's draft beer. Launched in early 1986, the new Asahi Draft, *koku to kire* (rich and sharp), got off to a smooth start. However, Asahi's share of the total beer market continued to drop, and the number of retailers carrying the Asahi brand was also declining.

Marketing Activities

Marketing expenditures by the four brewers had almost doubled from ¥65 billion in 1984 to ¥117 billion in 1987, partly as a result of Asahi's launch of Super Dry (*refer to Exhibit 3*). Typically, 80% of all marketing expenditures were made between January and May.

Advertising and Promotion

For Koichi Matsui, the general manager of Asahi's marketing department, advertising was crucial in Japan's highly competitive marketplace "where neon is king and gimmickry is commonplace." Matsui was referring to a packaging war that occurred between 1984 and 1986 when various "gadget products," such as the Suntory Penguins and the Kirin Beer Shuttle, had been used to attract consumer attention. By 1987, Matsui felt that consumers had become bored with such sales tactics.

Pricing

The National Tax Agency advised Japanese brewers on the appropriate prices for alcoholic beverages. In Japan, beer was the most heavily taxed alcoholic beverage, at a rate of 46.9% (versus 36.3% for whiskies and brandies and 17% to 20% for sakes and shochus). This meant that when a consumer paid ¥300 for a regular 633-ml bottle of beer, ¥140.7 was collected by the state. Kirin executives estimated that profits increased by ¥4 billion for each yen in price increase.

Distribution

The brewers sold beer to the consumer through a group of primary wholesalers. In turn, some of these sold to subwholesalers, who distributed products through a large number of retail outlets. Wholesalers and retailers were both licensed by the state, which strictly limited the issue of new licenses. Most distributors in the Kanto (Greater Tokyo) dealt with all four brewers, while exclusive distributors had a stronger position in the Kansai region (western Japan). The number of subwholesalers was declining; developing personal relationships with the wholesalers was still a key success factor for the brewers. In 1987, more than 1,800 wholesalers distributed beer and other alcoholic beverages. Kirin

	Advertising Expenses	Promotion Expenses	Total Marketing Expenses	As Percent of Beer Sales
Kirin				
1983	11.4	18.1	29.5	2.7
1984	15.9	21.7	37.6	3.2
1985	13.9	21.4	35.3	2.9
1986	15.9	28.1	44.0	3.5
1987[b]	18.4	35.2	53.6	4.2
Asahi				
1983	7.9	7.5	15.4	7.1
1984	8.9	10.0	18.9	8.4
1985	7.9	10.9	18.8	7.9
1986	11.7	13.8	25.5	9.8
1987[b]	18.9	19.2	38.1	11.0
Sapporo				
1983	8.6	4.9	13.5	3.7
1984	11.0	5.5	16.5	4.3
1985	12.1	6.0	18.1	4.5
1986	13.3	7.8	21.1	4.8
1987[b]	15.1	8.7	23.8	5.1
Suntory				
1983	27.9	39.6	67.5	7.9
1984	26.7	39.8	66.5	8.7
1985	22.8	39.6	62.4	8.1
1986	22.9	46.6	69.5	9.2
1987[b]	27.1	53.6	80.7	10.3

Source: Dentsu Inc., 1987.

[a] Expenditures are for all products, including beer.

[b] Estimated.

Note: Beer as a percentage of total sales (1983–1987): Kirin, 93%; Asahi, 79%; Sapporo, 94%; Suntory, 28%

worked with 800 of these and had exclusive agreements with 70% of them.

Distribution was said to be a major barrier of entry for new entrants. As the executive of a Danish brewery explained:

It's pretty difficult to distribute beer in a country with more than one million bars, pubs, and restaurants, and hundreds of thousands of stores in huge cities with virtually no street names. Tying up with a local player is almost a prerequisite. To establish our own distribution network through primary wholesalers, secondary wholesalers, and sometimes tertiary wholesalers would probably take us at least 10 years.

Retailers were liquor store owners who sold to consumers as well as to neighborhood bars and restaurants. Typically, retailers independently selected which beer to sell according to the popularity of each brand. However, each major brewer had a merchandising sales force to ensure that their company's products were effectively displayed in the stores.

Junichi Nakamura, a 54-year-old retailer in Shinagawa and one of the 130,000 liquor store owners in Japan, wondered how successful Asahi's Super Dry would be in the long run. He was used to seeing some 40 kinds of new beer packaging arrive on his shelves every year and then disappear after a few months because the brewers launched new products one after another and gave up quickly when a new product did not sell well. Nakamura also wondered if many consumers could really tell the difference between Asahi Dry and other regular beers.

ASAHI SUPER DRY

In the spring of 1986, Hirotaro Higuchi took over the presidency of Asahi Breweries, replacing Tsutomu Murai, who was appointed as the company's chairman. Higuchi intended to pursue the objective set earlier by Murai, to turn Asahi into a truly customer oriented company. His ultimate objective was to restore Asahi's market share to the level the company had enjoyed right after World War II, when Asahi competed neck and neck with Sapporo and Kirin.

Higuchi felt that over the past 30 years Asahi had developed a corporate culture where everyone blamed someone else for the annual loss of market share. His first step was to change the perception of Asahi Beer within the company. Higuchi's new corporate philosophy emphasized quality first, followed by customer orientation, respect for each other, labor–management conciliation, cooperation with the trade, and social responsibility. A corporate booklet with 10 commandments was distributed to all employees as a guide to daily behavior. These commandments were also read aloud at work each morning so that every employee would understand Asahi's new direction.

To change Asahi's image, Higuchi decided to develop new packaging. All beers carrying the old-fashioned imperial flag were recalled from the retailers' shelves. Higuchi aimed to send the trade, the public, and the competition a strong message that Asahi had changed significantly. As well, he implemented a quality-first policy and instructed the purchasing department to use only the best raw materials, even if this meant higher costs. Finally, Higuchi decided that the company would increase its advertising and promotional expenditures, even at the risk of eating up all net profits.

When Higuchi discussed the "dry" concept for the first time with 12 Asahi executives in the fall of 1986, no one really supported the idea. Higuchi recalled that his production director went so far as to say, "We can't produce a dry beer, this is nonsense to me." The marketing people explained that the meaning of the word "dry" was important, "Dry suggests something new, decisive, and bold. We found out that a 'wet' person is very strongly attached to family, the company, and friends, while a 'dry' type is more individualistic."

Higuchi felt that he should postpone the launch of Super Dry until the new Asahi draft had established a stronger position in the market. Yet young managers in the marketing, R&D, and production departments were quite comfortable with the concept of Super Dry. As well, the production engineers indicated that "dry beer" would not require a major breakthrough in production technology. A young marketing executive had told Higuchi, "I think that the 'dry' concept is viable, but can't tell you how much we can expect to sell."

The Launch of Super Dry

By early 1987, the R&D department had managed to develop a "dry" beer. Meanwhile, the marketing department had gathered more data using hands-on test markets to determine favorable consumer attitudes. They had developed a comprehensive marketing plan and set a first year sales target of 800,000 cases. On March 17, 1987, Asahi's Super Dry beer was officially launched.

Super Dry was designed as a draft beer targeted at heavy drinkers. Made with less residual sugar, the beer was less sweet. It contained 0.5% more alcohol than the 4.5% regular draft beers and had been defined as much sharper and softer than traditional draft beers (*refer to Exhibit 4*). Super Dry was made using the best hops from Czechoslovakia and Germany and malts from the United States, Canada, and Australia. Asahi's production engineers had shortened the time from production to consumption to an average of 20 days, while other brewers operated on a 23- to 25-day cycle. The Super Dry silver label with Asahi's new logo and modern lettering reinforced the image of a truly different product.

Asahi's marketing budget had been increased from ¥25.5 billion in 1986 to ¥38.1 billion (*refer to Exhibit 3*), and ¥4.2 billion was spent on advertising to promote Super Dry in 1987. Hakuhodo, Japan's second largest advertising company, designed a campaign featuring Nobuhiko Ochiai, a former U.S. oilman who had become a respected, international journalist. To launch Super Dry, Asahi ran full-page advertisements in all five major dailies. The ads

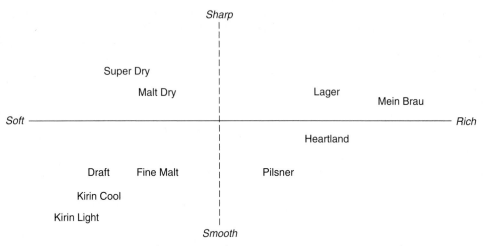

EXHIBIT 4 Positioning Map for Kirin's Products *Source:* Kirin Brewery Co. Ltd.

were spread across three weeks: a "coming soon" preview, a "debuts today" announcement, and a "have you tried it yet?" follow-up ad. Television commercials were double the normal volume for a new product campaign. Asahi also distributed free samples to a million people throughout Japan. In addition to its 500 salespeople (versus 520 for Kirin), Asahi had set up sales teams with 1,000 "field ladies" to promote and merchandise the new product at the retail level and collect additional marketing data from consumers regarding preference, purchase habits, and so on.

In the fall of 1987, while the beer market in Japan had grown by 7%, Asahi's total sales had soared by 34%, mainly thanks to Super Dry.

KIRIN'S RESPONSE TO ASAHI

Asahi's performance had had the effect of a small earthquake within the Kirin organization, and various teams were put to work to generate alternatives to meet the Asahi challenge. In late October 1987, Kirin's president, Hideo Motoyama, called a special meeting of the Beer Division's executives to decide Kirin's strategy for the 1988 beer season. The outcome of this meeting included decisions to launch three new products—Kirin Dry, Kirin Fine Malt, and Kirin Fine Draft—to re-

launch Kirin Beer as Kirin Lager beer, and to make a price cut.

The objective in launching Kirin Dry was to respond to consumers' needs, fill the niche created by Asahi, and beat Asahi on its own turf with a superior product. The Kirin Dry concept was similar to Asahi's Super Dry. The new product had 5% more alcohol than regular beer, the same number of calories, and a drier, less sweet taste. Kirin's Dry (like the dry beers launched by Suntory and Sapporo) used the same silver packaging that Asahi had used for its Super Dry and contained the following message in English:

Our superior fermentation technology and carefully selected hops have produced a beer with an exceptionally delicate taste, well-balanced with a dry finish. The connoisseur's beer, "KIRIN DRY," will add a new taste of pleasure to your day.

Kirin Dry was offered in 633- and 500-ml bottles and in 500- and 350-ml cans. Asahi's Super Dry was sold in 633-, 500-, and 334-ml bottles, in 350-, 250-, and 135-ml cans as well as in 2-, 3-, and 10-liter barrels for on-premises outlets.

On April 20, 1988, Kirin announced that it would cut the price on one of its mainline products, 500-ml cans, citing an increase in foreign exchange gains due to the appreciation of the yen as the reason. Kirin had indeed saved ¥3.4 billion over the past 2 years on imported hops and malt used in the brewing process. The result for the consumer was a reduction in the retail price of a 500-ml can of beer from ¥280 to ¥270. A Goldman, Sachs & Co. analyst commented:

The major reason for Kirin's action was to restore its market share under the impact of increased competition from Asahi's Super Dry. Kirin's price cut was immediately followed by Asahi and Sapporo. These cuts (all ¥10 per can) were the first changes in 26 years. The Kirin people believed that the impact of such a price cut would be minimal, while Sapporo and Asahi would each suffer damage in the range of ¥300 million by following Kirin down in price.

Real competition in dry beer is starting now. We believe that distribution capability and financial resources to back strong advertising campaigns will dictate that Kirin wins in view of its larger size.

Kirin's management decided to change the name as well as the packaging of Kirin's regular beer from Kirin Beer to Kirin LAGER Beer, with a large red LAGER printed on all labels. In mid-June 1988, just before the summer season, Kirin launched Kirin Fine Malt and Kirin Fine Draft, both positioned as "after-dry" products to reinforce Kirin's presence in the draft segment and to signal an end to the dry beer boom. Kirin Fine Malt was first introduced in some local areas and launched nationally a few months later.

Reorganization at Kirin

In early 1988, Kirin's president appointed Kazuhisa Tani to head a task force to recommend and implement a new corporate strategy for Kirin's Beer Division. Tani had broad responsibilities for marketing and corporate planning, and he reported directly to Motoyama.

Tani had joined Kirin Brewery in 1962 right after graduating from university. He had first worked as a controller in the Amagasaki brewery before joining headquarters in 1971 to work on Kirin's joint venture with Seagrams. From 1982 until early 1988, Tani had headed Kirin–Seagram, apart for 1 year at the M.I.T. Sloan School of Management in the United States to earn an MBA degree. Kirin–Seagram was considered to be much more market oriented than the conservative Kirin organization, and Motoyama expected that Tani would be able to transfer some of the entrepreneurial spirit of the joint venture.

Tani recommended the development and the introduction of two new management control systems: MRS (management reporting system) and ME (marketing engineering). MRS was a system to evaluate each salesperson's performance in relation to sales volumes and expenses. The ME system involved developing a marketing database for the brand managers. Under the new organization of the Beer Division, headquarters and the breweries were cost centers, and the only profit centers were the sales branches, with brand managers responsible for the profitability of their own operations.

In the spring of 1988, Tani recommended accelerating the plan to expand the sales network from 17 branches to 40 additional sales offices and to increase the sales force from 550 to 800 by 1990. Tani also pressed to speed up the development of the KIC network (Kirin intelligence and communication), which would enable Kirin to monitor the market more closely. Information technology had been a central theme of Kirin's 1981 diversification plan. In May 1985, Kirin became the first Japanese brewer to offer a line of computers (the KN line) to wholesalers and retailers throughout Japan. The KIC project aimed to install on-line computers in an additional 350 liquor wholesalers and 1,000 retail stores by 1990, providing them with a variety of speedy services, such as cash register, inventory control, sales data, and invoicing. The computer network would also provide Kirin's management with immediate feedback on the rotation of stocks and daily sales trends for all Kirin products, as well as those of the competitors.

THE DRY WAR

The simultaneous introduction of dry products by Kirin, Sapporo, and Suntory triggered an immediate marketing war. None of these dry beers was clearly differentiated from Asahi's Super Dry in concept, taste, or packaging, which led Asahi to request that its competitors modify both the packaging and the concept of their dry beers.

Asahi's rising voice against unfair competition attracted the attention of the press, and the dry war suddenly became a national affair. While Asahi and its competitors were fighting through the intermediary of the press, an advertising war was also taking place. Asahi was massively advertising Super Dry using journalist Nobuhiko Ochiai as the central character of its campaign. Meanwhile, Kirin had signed up the Hollywood actor Gene Hackman for its Kirin Dry campaign around the theme "I'm so happy I could cry Dry, Dry!" Suntory had developed an advertising campaign featuring Mike Tyson, the world boxing superchampion: "Hi, I'm Mike Tyson. I like Suntory DRY." A Suntory manager explained that Tyson had been chosen "to communicate the power and the punch of dry beer." Finally, Sapporo had signed up Japanese sports celebrities for its Sapporo Dry campaign.

Suntory and Sapporo had followed Kirin's strategy, advertising and aggressively pushing their traditional products: 100% Malt for Suntory and Black Label for Sapporo. The four brewers had increased their advertising budgets by an average of 20% over the previous year, exposing consumers to more beer advertising than they had probably seen in their entire lives. Although consumers had been somewhat confused at first by the dry war, they did realize that Asahi was the original inventor of the dry beer concept. A liquor store owner in Tokyo commented:

Japanese consumers are fascinated by this all-out marketing war. They enjoy reading about the battle for market share in their newspapers. They also like watching hired hands (Mike Tyson vs. Gene Hackman, for example) fight it out in a deluge of TV and print ads. Keeping up-to-date dominates the chats in my store. Employees also discuss the beer war with their colleagues. When I deliver beer to the neighboring bars and restaurants, I can hear people expressing opinions on possible upcoming trends. People wonder what will happen next. It's a social phenomenon.

The Situation in Autumn 1988

By summer's end, when beer consumption typically began to decline, Asahi had clearly won the dry beer sweepstakes. In the beer industry, where a hit product reached sales of 1 million cases in its first year, the 13.5 million cases achieved by Super Dry was an amazing success. Asahi had reached three major milestones that would have been unthinkable a scant 16 months earlier. For the first time in two decades, Asahi's share of total beer sales in Japan had broken the 20% market share barrier. In August 1988, Asahi confirmed that after 23 years it had overtaken Sapporo as Japan's second largest brewery. Asahi was now selling half of the dry beer produced in Japan.

In July 1988, Kirin was actually producing more dry beer than Asahi, although Asahi's sales of the new product remained larger by a slim margin. At this time, total beer sales were 1% lower than the year before. The summer's relatively cool, rainy weather had been bad for beer sales, but ironically good for Asahi. A month later, dry beer accounted for a heady 34% of total beer sales, while lager had 38% and draft, 25%. Yoshio Matsuda from the Brewers Association of Japan remarked:

This is an amazing phenomenon. Just think—in the US it took 18 years for light beers to obtain a 25% share of the total beer market, and it took Asahi only 16 months to achieve a similar result in Japan. Only a year earlier, 51% of all beer sold in Japan was lager and 42% was draft. The good weather in August and September put a new kick in the beer industry and by early October 1988, the market had grown by 7.6%. Meanwhile, Asahi sales had shot up by 72%. I think that the rapid growth of the dry beer market was due to three factors. First, Super Dry was a unique concept and a well-accepted taste, based on extensive marketing research. Second, having the total participation of the four major breweries involved in an advertising war with massive budgets developed awareness and interest in the dry segment. Third, Japanese consumers are inclined to quickly follow fashion trends.

However, other factors had played an important part in Asahi's success. Sales activities had aimed at promoting fresh product rotation. Over the past year, Asahi increased its capital investment in plant and equipment by 50%. By 1988, its production capacity was 2.5 times the level it was in 1986.

The dry war had social consequences as well. Since August, many liquor store owners had placed apologetic signs on their doors saying they were out of Super Dry beer. The press had also reported that Asahi's president had asked his employees not to buy Super Dry because every precious drop had to be reserved for its customers. An Asahi manager acknowledged that the company's success was also an issue:

This summer, we had a major problem with capacity. We were planning to sell 13.5 million cases in 1988, but we are only at the end of September and we have already sold more than 83 million! Right now, we have 3 plants producing beer only and 5 plants producing both beer and juice. To meet the demand during the summer, we had to stop producing juice and turn all these plants into breweries. Asahi is now devoting nearly all of its brewing capacity to Super Dry. Despite these efforts, we could cope with only 70% of the demand for dry beer. Moreover, we don't have enough capacity to brew Coors locally, as originally agreed under Asahi's 5-year 1987 licensing pact with Adolph Coors. Last June, our capacity crunch was so severe that we arranged to import the Coors we couldn't brew in Japan. To meet the bare minimum of our licensing agreement, Asahi—at a cost of $2.3 million—chartered 15 Boeing 747 jumbo jet freighters to transport 141,450 cases of Coors and Coors Light in 12-oz. cans and bottles from Golden, Colorado, over a period of three months. We now have to decide whether to invest in building one or two new breweries, since we expect industry sales to grow at around 7% annually over the next three years.

The dry war that had been taking place in Japan had also attracted the attention of the large foreign brewers. The Miller Brewing Company, for instance, had recently begun conducting market research on dry products in the United States.

New Competitive Moves in Japan

In the fall of 1988, the future of the dry boom remained uncertain. Asahi had recently pub-lished the results of a marketing survey called "The Asahi Super Dry Era," concluding that Super Dry was here to stay. However, Asahi's competitors were more divided about the future of the dry segment. In 1988, each major brewer was strong in a different type of beer. Kirin's best-seller was lager, Asahi had dry, and Sapporo had draft. Looking at Asahi's success, Kazuo Arakawa, Sapporo's executive vice-president, said, "Asahi helped Sapporo by jolting Kirin. Dry beer has gotten people talking about beer, has widened the range of products available, and generally invigorated the market."

Taking advantage of the turbulent environment created by the dry war, all brewers were launching new products to prepare for what Sapporo executives called the "after-dry era." Japanese consumers now had a wide choice of beers available, varying from 4.5% to 9% in alcohol content. Sapporo had recently launched its On-the-Rocks Beer, a high alcohol (9%) beer that was meant to be sipped over ice like whisky. Sapporo had also announced its Winter's Tale beer to be sold only from November to February. Suntory had launched 5.5, a dry beer with a higher alcohol content (5.5% versus 5% for regular dry beers).

Ken Takanashi, a Suntory manager believed that Suntory's malts could be a particular threat to Asahi Super Dry. He explained, "Malts were a hit last year until being eclipsed by the dry war along with lager and draft, but as of August they seem to be bubbling again." To counter an expansion of the malt subsegment, Kirin had introduced Kirin Fine Malt (a 100% malt beer) in June 1988, initially on a regional basis, then nationally in the fall of 1988. Kirin Fine Malt was positioned as a new draft beer.

Defining Kirin's New Product Line Strategy

In late September 1988, Kazuhisa Tani met with several managers from the marketing and corporate planning departments. After reviewing Kirin's performance relative to the competition in each of the major categories of beer (*refer to Exhibits 1 and 5*), he asked his product managers to put forward their proposals for new products.

Messrs. Fukuyama and Makita, respectively in charge of R&D and marketing for the Beer Division, presented two new products. **Malt Dry** was a 100% malt draft beer with a 5% alcohol content, which would occupy a unique position on the market. In Makita's opinion, Malt Dry was a new concept serving the two fastest growing segments of the market: dry and all malt. **Kirin Cool** was an extra smooth beer with a 4.5% alcohol content and a softer taste, targeted at men and women aged 20 to 25. It was positioned in the "soft and smooth segment" of the market (refer to Exhibit 4). Kirin Cool's unique selling proposition was "a taste never before experienced."

Makita also indicated that **Kirin Fine Pilsner** was ready to be launched. Positioned in the "rich and smooth" segment, Kirin Fine Pilsner would be targeted at people in their 20s and 30s. Its unique selling proposition was "A new standard beer with creamy froth like a velvet touch." The corporate planning department favored launching all three products in the next year, reasoning that a full-line strategy would give Kirin complete coverage of the market. Makita was not convinced:

"With so many new products on the market, we run the risk of confusing the consumer. Moreover, the launch of each new product will cost us at least ¥1 billion. For next year, I would personally favor launching "Malt Dry" and *only* "Malt Dry."

Ryosuke Murata, also from the marketing department, disagreed: "I don't think that we should launch a new dry beer. We should get away from this segment and prepare for the after-dry era. I am in favor of pushing Kirin Lager more aggressively. After all, it's still our best-selling product, and it has a rich thick taste with a fine aroma."

Makita presented a final proposal concerning **Kirin Fine Draft**, which aimed to reposition Kirin in the draft segment by "re-creating the taste in beer halls."

Tani also had in front of him some new marketing data collected by the Mitsubishi Research Institute (*refer to Exhibit 6*), as well as some data on dry beer blind tests in which consumers had been asked to compare competitive products according to different attributes (*refer to Exhibit 7*). It was now time to make a decision on Kirin's product strategy and develop a marketing plan for 1989.

EXHIBIT 5   Comparative Performance of Japanese Brewers, 1987–1988

Comparative Market Shares by Segment (%):

	Lager		Draft		Dry		All Malts	
	1987	1988[a]	1987	1988[a]	1987	1988[a]	1987	1988[a]
Kirin	91.5	94.4	21.8	21.5	0	26.4	20.5	29.6
Asahi	2.2	0.6	20.1	14.3	100	49.6	9.4	7.0
Sapporo	6.3	5.0	40.2	48.3	0	14.5	16.5	19.2
Suntory	0	0	17.9	15.9	0	9.5	53.6	44.2
Total	100	100	100	100	100	100	100	100

Comparative Product Mix by Brewer (%):

	Lager		Draft		Dry		All Malts		Total	
	1987	1988[a]	1987	1988[a]	1987	1988[a]	1987	1988[a]	1987	1988[a]
Kirin	82.7	69.6	15.9	11.0	0	17.4	1.4	2.1	100	100
Asahi	8.8	1.1	64.4	17.9	24	79.9	2.8	1.2	100	100
Sapporo	15.6	9.3	81.3	62.9	0	24.3	3.1	3.4	100	100
Suntory	0	0	78.2	46.3	0	36.0	21.8	17.6	100	100

Source: Kirin Brewery Co. Ltd., 1988.

[a] As of September 1988.

Survey Design

Area: Tokyo
Timing: September 1988
Sample: 504 people (all beer drinkers)

Question 1: What is your favorite type of beer?

Responses by sex (%):

	Men	Women	Total
Lager	15.8	6.0	12.1
Draft	20.9	20.2	20.6
Dry	55.6	65.6	59.3
All malts	4.9	4.9	4.9
Light	1.3	2.2	1.6

Responses by age bracket (%)

	20s	30s	40s	50s
Lager	6.2	9.2	17.0	27.3
Draft	21.2	20.9	20.6	18.2
Dry	61.6	63.8	54.6	50.0
All malts	7.5	3.7	4.3	2.3
Light	2.7	1.2	0.7	2.3

Question 2: What made you drink dry beer?

	%
I saw some commercials on TV	64.0
I read an article about it	37.7
I saw it in a store	14.3
I read some comparative studies	36.2
It's available at home	34.2
People around me drink it	36.2

Question 3: What made you drink . . .

	%			
	Asahi Super Dry?	Kirin Dry?	Sapporo Dry?	Suntory Dry?
I saw some commercials on TV	63.4	62.8	72.0	76.2
I read an article about it	38.8	35.9	38.0	33.3
I saw it in a store	14.6	12.8	12.0	28.6
I read some comparative studies	34.8	37.2	38.0	42.9
It's available at home	35.1	30.8	32.0	38.4
People around me drink it	34.8	37.2	38.0	42.9

Question 4: Why do you think beer drinking attitudes changed?

Preferences have changed	12.7%
New products have been introduced	68.8%
People make comparisons	18.5%
Newspapers and magazines reported on it	30.2%
Life-styles have changed	16.0%

Question 5: What were your impressions when you first tasted a dry beer?

It tastes different	28.0%
It has good body	30.8%
It has a sharp taste	38.1%
It has a smooth taste	35.6%
It has more alcohol	20.3%
It tastes like other beers	17.8%
It is trendy	15.1%
It has a good label and a good name	15.3%
Others	2.9%

EXHIBIT 6 (continued)

Question 6: What do you mean by "beer with good body"?

A sharp beer	22.9%
A thick beer	52.2%
A bitter beer	30.4%
A sweet beer	18.8%
A good feeling in the throat	19.0%
It smells good	17.0%
A stronger beer	14.4%
The real beer	57.5%
Others	2.4%

Question 7: What type of beer do you associate most with this concept of good body?

Lager	14.0%
Draft	17.8%
Dry	28.5%
All malts	20.6%
Light	0.2%
Black	11.7%
Others	1.6%

Question 8: What do you mean by "a sharp beer"?

A good feeling in the throat	60.1%
A pure taste	38.5%
Bitterness disappears rapidly	51.6%
No bitterness	20.0%
A beer with a higher degree of fermentation	24.3%
A stronger beer	14.6%

Question 9: With what kind of beer do you associate most with this concept of sharpness?

Lager	5.5%
Draft	21.9%
Dry	55.1%
All malts	4.7%
Light	3.8%
Black	0.2%
Others	1.6%

Question 10: Do you think that your consumption of dry beer will increase or decrease?

Will decrease	23.2%
Will remain stable	48.7%
Will increase	25.2%

Question 11: Why will your consumption of dry beer decrease?

It is not my taste	44.6%
I don't see any difference from other beers	8.0%
I don't drink it because it is a fad	4.5%
People around me don't drink it	8.9%
It does not taste good	28.6%
I'm getting tired of it	28.6%
That's the way it is	25.0%
Other reasons	10.7%

Question 12: "Why will your consumption of dry beer increase?

I like the taste	52.2%
People around me drink it	17.6%
It's trendy	21.3%
I'd like to try other beers	19.1%
It tastes good	63.2%
It's available at home	25.7%
I'm tired of other beers	5.1%
Other reasons:	8.1%

Source: Mitsubishi Research Institute, September 1988.

EXHIBIT 7 Blind Tests for Different Beers

Survey Design
Area: Tokyo
Timing: September 1988
Sample: 450 people

Products:	Kirin Lager[a]	Asahi Dry	Sapporo Draft
Attributes			
Flavor	100	99.4	98.8
Bitterness	100	92.6	94.9
Softness	100	113.3	113.0
Lightness	100	116.0	114.5
Richness	100	88.1	91.7
Carbonization	100	99.3	97.0

Source: Kirin Brewery Co. Ltd.

[a] Index: a higher figure indicates rated better than Kirin; a lower figure indicates rated worse.

Philip Morris K.K.

On January 7, 1988, Leonard D. Spelt, marketing manager of Philip Morris K.K. (PMKK), had gathered his marketing team at the PMKK headquarters in Tokyo to discuss the recent decision of competitor R. J. Reynolds to introduce a ¥200[1] cigarette brand in the Japanese market. After having reviewed and discussed all the options available, Leo Spelt had returned to his office to ponder the various alternatives that had surfaced during one of the most exhausting meetings he had had in Tokyo.

PHILIP MORRIS COMPANIES, INC.

Based in New York City, Philip Morris Companies, Inc., was the largest and most diversified tobacco, food, and beverage company in the United States and one of the three largest in the world. With an operating income of $4.2 billion out of operating revenues of $27.6 billion for fiscal year 1987 (refer to Exhibit 1), Philip Morris Companies, Inc., was also ranked tenth in size among the U.S. Fortune 500 industrials.

Since its early days in 1847, when Philip Morris, Esq., first opened a tobacco shop on Bond Street in London (England), Philip Morris's core business had focused on the tobacco industry. In 1902, Philip Morris & Co. Ltd. was incorporated in the United States (in New York)

by Gustav Eckmeyer, Philip Morris's sole agent in the United States for importing and selling the English-made cigarettes since 1872. In 1919, a new firm owned by American shareholders acquired the U.S. Philip Morris Company and incorporated it in Virginia under the name Philip Morris & Co. Ltd., Inc., which in turn became Philip Morris, Incorporated, in 1955.

The present organization had been set up in 1985 when the corporate framework of Philip Morris, Incorporated, was restructured to form Philip Morris Companies, Inc., a holding company located in New York City. In 1988, Philip Morris Companies, Inc., was still concentrating mainly on the tobacco industry. The two core companies, Philip Morris USA and Philip Morris International, were accounting for 27% and 25%, respectively, of Philip Morris Companies, Inc.'s, total operating revenues in 1987. In the 1980s, Philip Morris Companies, Inc., also made major diversification moves into the food industry by acquiring Oscar Mayer in 1981 and then General Foods Corporation in November 1985. In 1970, Philip Morris Companies, Inc., had also acquired the world's second largest brewer, the Miller Brewing Company, which currently accounted for 10% of total operating revenues. Financial services and real estate were the fourth major business activity of Philip Morris Companies, Inc., representing 2% of total operating revenues.

Several of Philip Morris's cigarette brands,

---

[1] Average exchange rate in 1987: ¥145 = $1.00

This case was prepared by Professor Dominique Turpin as a basis for class discussion rather than to illustrate either effective or ineffective handling of a business situation. Copyright © 1989 by IMEDE, Lausanne, Switzerland. The International Institute for Management Development (IMD), resulting from the merger between IMEDE, Lausanne, and IMI, Geneva, acquires and retains all rights. Not to be used or reproduced without written permission from IMD, Lausanne, Switzerland.

EXHIBIT 1   Financial Data (in $millions except per share amounts)

	1987	1986	1985
Operating revenues	$27,695	$25,409	$15,694
Net earnings	1,842	1,478	1,255
Earnings per share	7.75	6.20	5.24
Dividends per share	3.15	2.475	2.00
Funds from operations per share	11.73	9.28	7.41
Percent Increase over Prior Year			
Operating revenues	9.0%	59.2%	15.6%
Net earnings	24.7%	17.7%	41.3%
Earnings per share	25.0%	18.3%	44.6%
Dividends declared per share	27.3%	23.8%	17.6%
Operating Revenues			
Philip Morris U.S.A.	$7,576	$7,053	$6,611
Philip Morris International, Inc.	7,068	5,638	3,991
General Foods Corporation	9,946	9,664	1,632
Miller Brewing Company	3,105	3,054	2,914
Other[a]	—	—	816
Total operating revenues	$27,695	$25,409	$15,964
Income from Operations			
Philip Morris U.S.A.	$2,683	$2,366	$2,047
Philip Morris International	631	492	413
General Foods Corporation	722	741	120
Miller Brewing Company	170	154	132
Philip Morris Credit Corporation[b]	51	55	23
Mission Viejo Realty Group, Inc.[b]	21	18	12
Other[a]	19	(8)	45
	$4,297	$3,818	$2,792
Amortization of goodwill	104	111	32
Total income from operating companies[c]	$4,193	$3,707	$2,760

Compounded Average Annual Growth Rate	1987–1982	1987–1977
Operating Revenues	19.0%	18.2%
New earnings	18.7%	18.6%
Earnings per share	20.0%	18.7%

Source: Philip Morris Companies, Inc., Annual Report, 1987.

[a] Composed of the Seven-Up Company, of which substantially all the operations were sold in 1985.

General Foods Corporation was acquired in November 1985. Accordingly, consolidated results shown above include the operating results of General Foods Corporation after October 1985.

[b] Represents equity in net earnings of these unconsolidated subsidiaries.

[c] Income from operating companies is income before corporate expense and interest and other debt expense, net

such as Marlboro, were among the most popular in the world. Originally introduced in 1924 as an unfiltered cigarette, Marlboro had rapidly become Philip Morris's flagship cigarette brand after being repositioned in 1955 as a full-flavored cigarette for men. Supported by the first Marlboro cowboy advertising campaign, its red and white package soon became familiar. In 1987, despite a decline in the total consumption of cigarettes in the American market, Marlboro had gained market share in the United States for the 23rd consecutive year to approach a 25% share of the U.S. cigarette market. Worldwide, Marlboro also continued to be the best-selling cigarette brand since 1971.

The success of leading full-priced brands, for example, Benson & Hedges, Merit, Virginia Slims, Parliament, Lark, Chesterfield, and Philip Morris (*refer to Exhibit 2*) also reinforced Philip Morris's leading position in the world tobacco industry. Philip Morris International's products were sold in more than 160 countries around the world. In free-

EXHIBIT 1 *(Continued)* Selected Financial Data: 15-Year Review

Summary of Operations	*1987*	*1986*	*1985*
Operating revenues	$27,695	$25,409	$15,964
United States export sales	1,592	1,193	923
Cost of sales:			
Cost of products sold	11,264	11,039	6,318
Federal excise taxes	2,085	2,075	2,049
Foreign excise taxes	3,331	2,653	1,766
Income from operating companies	4,193	3,707	2,760
Interest and other debt expense, net	685	770	308
Earnings before income taxes	3,348	2,811	2,329
Pretax profit margin	12.1%	11.1%	14.6%
Provision for income taxes	$ 1,506	$ 1,333	$ 1,074
Net earnings	1,842	1,478	1,255
Earnings per share	7.75	6.20	5.24
Dividends declared per share	3.15	2.475	2.00
Weighted average shares	238	239	240
Capital expenditures	$ 718	$ 678	$ 347
Annual depreciation	564	514	367
Property, plant, and equipment (net)	6,582	6,237	5,684
Inventories	4,154	3,836	3,827
Working capital	1,396	1,432	1,926
Total assets	19,145	17,642	17,429
Long-term debt	5,222	5,945	7,331
Total debt	6,378	6,912	8,009
Deferred income taxes	1,288	994	872
Stockholders' equity	6,823	5,655	4,737
Funds from operations	2,789	2,214	1,775
Net earnings reinvested	1,093	888	776
Common dividends declared as % of net earnings	40.6%	39.9%	38.1%
Book value per common share	$ 28.83	$ 23.77	$ 19.85
Market price of common share (high–low)	124 ½–72⅝	78–43⅞	47⅝–31
Closing price, year end	85⅜	71⅞	44⅛
Price/earnings ratio, year end	11	11	8
Number of common shares outstanding, year end	237	238	239
Number of employees	113,000	111,000	114,000

Source: Philip Morris Companies, Inc., Annual Report, 1987.

Note: Certain amounts appearing in the prior years' consolidated statements of earnings have been reclassified to conform with the current year's presentation.

competition[2] markets, Philip Morris International enjoyed leading market share. For example, in the European Economic Community, Philip Morris's aggregate market share for tobacco exceeded 20%.

Developing established brands and introducing new ones had traditionally been Philip Morris Companies, Inc.'s, strategy for increasing volume and market share worldwide. In particular, Philip Morris International had seen great potential in Asia, where lowered trade barriers in several markets had recently allowed Philip Morris brands to compete more effectively with products marketed by local government monopolies. Since Philip Morris's share in most international cigarette markets was far below its U.S. level, Philip Morris executives felt that there was considerable room for future growth in this part of the world.

PHILIP MORRIS K.K.

Philip Morris had been present in Japan since the early 1950s, using Mitsui & Co., the trading company of the giant Mitsui Group, as the agent for importing its cigarettes into Japan. Its competitor, R. J. Reynolds, had designated

[2] Markets without state monopolies.

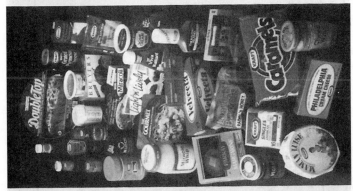

EXHIBIT 2 Philip Morris International Product Line

Mitsubishi Corporation, the trading company of the Mitsubishi Group, as its import agent. In Japan, the products of Philip Morris's diversified businesses, like General Foods and Miller, were managed separately from PMKK through joint ventures with local companies.

Because tobacco in Japan was a government monopoly until 1985, Mitsui & Co. was basically handling Philip Morris cigarettes on behalf of the monopoly corporation. In the late 1970s, Philip Morris entered into an association with Nissho Iwai, another large Japanese trading company, when Nissho Iwai acquired the distributor for Liggett & Myers Tobacco Co. in Japan. Liggett & Myers was an independent American tobacco company, producing the cigarette brands Lark, L&M, and Eve. In the early 1970s, Philip Morris had acquired the rights to produce and distribute Liggett & Myers' products outside the United States. Following Nissho Iwai's acquisition of Liggett & Myers's distributor in Japan, Philip Morris K.K. (PMKK) renegotiated the distribution of all its tobacco products with Mitsui & Co. and Nissho Iwai. As a result of the new agreement, Mitsui & Co. became the exclusive distributor of all PMKK's brands in eastern Japan, while Nissho Iwai became PMKK's sole distributor in the western part of Japan. With the liberalization of the Japanese tobacco industry in 1985, Philip Morris K.K. was established as a wholly owned subsidiary of Philip Morris Companies, Inc.

PMKK developed all Philip Morris's marketing activities in Japan. PMKK's tasks also included initiating and coordinating product development and production of cigarettes with the United States. Jack Howard, vice-president of PMKK, expected to continue importing Philip Morris products as long as the parameters for the cigarette industry in Japan remained as they were at present. More than ever in 1988, production costs for the tobacco industry in Japan were higher than in the United States. Moreover, since the manufacture of cigarettes in Japan was still the monopoly of Japan Tobacco, Inc. (JTI), PMKK did not plan to consider manufacturing locally in the near future.

At this stage in its development, PMKK's objective was to grow as fast as possible by offering consumer products of the highest quality and by maintaining a good balance between market share and profitability. A major objective for PMKK was also to retain and expand its dominant share in the fast growing imported segment. In terms of product diversification, Jack Howard believed that

this had to be put into context gradually. We want to build a good durable image for franchises which we can then expand over time. Therefore, we want to concentrate on a few good franchises that can be developed. Obviously, there will be new franchises coming on the market, and each of the existing franchises can also be expanded. Lark is a good example of franchise diversification. We now have this brand in various formats and sizes, which were introduced into the market over time.

THE TOBACCO INDUSTRY

In 1988, the world tobacco industry (90% cigarettes) included free markets, such as West Germany, the Netherlands, England and, some developing countries; state monopolies, such as Austria, Spain, and most socialist countries; and officially free markets, where customs or administrative regulations limited access to foreign products, such as the United States, Canada, France, and South Africa. The majority of cigarette consumption (60%) occurred in the free world, with the Communist countries accounting for the other 40%. The world's leading four tobacco producers were China (960 billion units), the United States (682 billion units), the USSR (380 billion units), and Japan (320 billion units). During the last 20 years, the world tobacco industry had doubled; the 1988 volume was estimated at 5.2 trillion units.

The international market had gradually become an oligopoly. Five major companies—Philip Morris, Brown & Williamson (an affiliate of British American Tobacco Co.), R. J. Reynolds, American Tobacco Co., and Rothmans International (also known as Tobacco Exporters International or TEI)—represented 80% of total free market sales volume (*refer to Exhibit 3*). With more than a decade of external pressure from antismoking campaigns and internal pressure for growth, the six largest multinational companies had become increasingly

EXHIBIT 3 Worldwide Cigarette Industry: Unit Volume Estimates (millions)

	1980	1981	1982	1983	1984	1985	1986	1987
Total world industry	4,474,400	4,571,000	4,583,800	4,563,700	4,700,000	4,850,000	4,975,000	5,118,000
USA industry	620,500	638,100	614,000	597,000	599,700	594,700	583,500	571,000
World minus USA	3,853,900	3,932,900	3,969,800	3,966,700	4,100,300	4,255,300	4,393,060	4,547,000
Philip Morris total	429,550	448,742	447,107	449,458	469,805	488,468	506,835	540,780
USA	191,191	199,436	204,429	204,677	211,575	213,590	214,573	215,559
International	238,359	249,306	242,678	244,781	258,230	274,878	292,262	325,221
BAT total	548,900	563,200	550,000	522,500	522,000	543,000	554,000	542,500
USA	84,490	87,750	83,180	68,520	67,990	70,700	67,970	62,740
International	464,410	475,450	466,820	453,980	454,010	472,300	486,030	479,760
R. J. Reynolds total	283,710	295,280	289,390	271,620	274,440	274,900	278,020	284,290
USA	201,710	207,180	208,790	187,520	189,740	188,100	188,320	185,390
International	82,000	88,100	80,600	84,100	84,700	86,800	89,700	98,900
American Tobacco total	106,005	95,515	87,265	85,455	81,295	79,500	77,000	79,500
USA	66,630	59,770	55,350	51,500	47,250	44,800	41,810	39,440
International	39,375	35,745	31,915	33,955	34,045	34,700	35,190	40,060
Rothmans total	162,011	158,866	154,183	151,400	145,700	138,500	133,000	134,400
USA	500	500	500	500	500	400	500	400
International	161,511	158,366	158,683	150,900	145,200	138,100	132,500	134,000
JTS total	304,500	308,208	310,100	307,400	307,100	304,500	296,500	280,000
Liggett & Myers USA	14,350	15,450	17,900	28,600	34,000	29,200	22,730	20,280
Lorillard USA	60,200	57,560	54,360	55,000	48,900	48,100	47,440	46,970

diversified, moving into paper, food and beverages, cosmetics, packaging, financial services, real estate, and other areas.

THE JAPANESE TOBACCO MARKET

Japan was the second largest tobacco market in the non-Communist world; in 1987, 308 billion cigarettes at a total retail value of ¥3 trillion were sold (a decline of 6% in volume and a 20.5% in value over the previous fiscal year). Although smoking was declining among Japanese adult males,[3] the 62.5% rate of smokers was among the highest in the developed world. As S. Katayama, a PMKK Group Brand Manager, explained, "Japan offers great opportunities for international tobacco companies. Not only will no one tell you to put out your cigarette at a bar or restaurant, but the practice of keeping a cigarette box and matching table lighter in the meeting rooms of many Japanese companies is a tradition still being maintained." Among females, only 12.5% claimed to be smokers. However, experts believed the figure was much higher, because many women smokers were reluctant to admit this fact to public researchers.

The Japanese cigarette market, just as in Europe or the United States, was experiencing growth in flue-cured tobacco products and a decline in the dark tobacco sector. Flue-cured tobacco was a bright yellow tobacco to which flavoring ingredients were added to create distinctive aromas. Flue-cured tobaccos could be divided into several types; American blended and straight Virginia of the blond tobacco variety were the most common. Most cigarettes sold in the United States and Europe were the American blended variety. However, in the United Kingdom and most Commonwealth countries, the straight Virginia tobacco products were overwhelmingly the most popular. The Japanese consumer's taste was somewhere between these two varieties. The really distinctive feature of the cigarettes in Japan, however, was the traditional charcoal filter imposed over time by the Japan Tobacco, Inc., monopoly.

These charcoal filters were made of tiny porous charcoal spheres that reduced the tar and nicotine while giving a smoother taste and aroma.

Until recently, international tobacco firms had traditionally commanded only a marginal share of the Japanese market. Despite a 1972 license agreement with Japan Tobacco and Salt Public Corporation (JTS) to manufacture Marlboro cigarettes, Philip Morris had never achieved the significant size in Japan that it had typically enjoyed in free markets. High import duties (up to 350% in 1978) and the government monopoly had meant that Japan was practically a closed market for foreign tobacco manufacturers.

Before the market was liberalized in the early 1980s, PMKK had been confronted by a number of tariff and nontariff barriers. Jack Howard had found that restricting the distribution of cigarette products to a given number of retailers had seriously limited the potential of PMKK's business. He also believed that the high duties imposed on imported cigarettes had forced PMKK to increase its prices to the point of being priced out of most of the market, because the Japanese consumer was not willing to buy a given product at any price.

Under pressure from the United States since 1978 to accelerate the opening of its market, Japan had started in the early 1980s to progressively liberalize its tobacco industry. In April 1985, JTS's monopoly was removed and, as a private company, became the Japan Tobacco, Inc. (JTI). As part of the Japanese program to liberalize the tobacco market, retailers were then allowed to handle tobacco imports and to receive the same 10% margin on imported as on domestically made cigarettes. Moreover, import duties had been eliminated by April 1987, and promotional activities including advertising were being permitted up to a limit of 6,300 GRPs[4] per brand family for TV advertising. As a result, international tobacco firms saw their sales jump two and a half times

---

[3] Over 20 years old.

[4] GRP (gross rating point) equaled the sum of all airings of a program or spot announcement during a given time period. For example, a once-a-week program constantly recording a 15% rating (15% of TV homes) received 60 GRPs for a 4-week period.

to 32 billion cigarettes in 1987 and their market share grow from 2.0% in 1984 to as high as 8.4% in a mere 3 years (*refer to Exhibit 4*).

The rapid success of international tobacco companies in Japan could be explained by their careful consideration of the Japanese market. Most salespeople used by the trading companies to distribute foreign tobacco products in Japan were being paid by the international tobacco companies. By listening to advice from their sales force, foreign producers were able to develop products especially tailored for the Japanese market. For example, Winston and Camel brands did not have a charcoal filter in the United States, but they did in Japan. The nicotine and tar contents of Kent Mild and Philip Morris Lights were kept at the same level as in Mild Seven Lights, the competing domestic brand. Another part of the foreign companies' strategy had been to keep the retail margin on foreign cigarettes higher than on Japanese cigarettes. Although retail margins were set at 10% of the retail price, the higher price of foreign cigarettes enabled retailers to receive a higher contribution. In S. Katayama's opinion, this was one reason that foreign cigarettes had become more competitive at the distribution stage. Moreover, S. Katayama believed that foreign cigarettes had a "high-class" image among Japanese consumers. He felt that this image, good marketing, and large advertising expenditures were the key success factors that had helped foreign tobacco firms gain a quick share of the Japanese market.

JAPAN TOBACCO, INC.

After its privatization in April 1985, the presidency of JTI was assumed by Minoru Nagaoka,

EXHIBIT 4   Japan Market

1. Total Market	1983	1984	1985	1986	1987
Sales volume (billions sticks)					
Industry	311.7	312.5	310.5	309.2	307.6
Domestic	306.4	306.1	303.3	298.6	281.7
Import	5.4	6.4	7.3	10.6	25.9
Share of market (%)					
Domestic	98.3	98.0	97.7	96.6	91.6
Import	1.7	2.0	2.3	3.4	8.4
2. Import Segment					
Sales volume for non-Japanese companies (millions sticks)					
PMKK	4,241	4,766	5,391	7,945	16,077
B&W	316	335	430	829	6,203
RJR	584	827	951	1,171	2,364
Rothsman (TEI)	101	160	282	330	369
AT	62	77	97	264	663
Share of market in the imported segment (%)					
PMKK	79.0	74.8	74.4	74.7	62.0
B&W	5.9	5.3	5.9	7.8	23.9
RJR	10.9	13.0	13.1	11.0	9.1
Rothsman (TEI)	1.9	2.5	3.9	3.1	1.4
AT	1.1	1.2	1.3	2.5	2.6

Source: Philip Morris K.K., 1987.

PMKK   Philip Morris K. K.

B&W   Brown & Williamson (British American Tobacco/BAT)

RJR   R. J. Reynolds

TEI   Tobacco Exporters International (Rothman International)

AT   American Tobacco

a former vice-minister in the Ministry of Finance (the most powerful position in Japan's public administration). In December 1987, JTI's sales were predicted to drop 2.3% for the previous term (ending March 31, 1987) to ¥2,875 trillion, while current profits were expected to dip sharply by 20% to Y85 billion. "Japan Tobacco is following a rocky path," President Nagaoka stated.

In response to this situation, JTI had mobilized its 2,700 sales personnel in a desperate attempt to fight back. Japan Tobacco, Inc., spent only 0.13% of sales on advertising compared to the 3% average outlayed by U.S. companies. In 1986–1987, JTI had also come out with 30 new products, compared to 27 during the preceding 5-year period. As a result, Japanese consumers were able to watch TV commercials that showed a female revue at the Crazy Horse in Paris where the dancers used their legs to spell out the letters LIBERA, one of the company's newest brands. Another commercial depicted happy American college students on campus, smoking JTI's Mild Seven FK cigarettes. JTI had also changed its marketing strategy by focusing less on traditional "mom and pop" shops and more on large national retailers.

JTI's major handicap in competing with foreign brands was that it had to use a domestic tobacco leaf that cost three to five times more than an imported leaf. Japan Tobacco, Inc., was required by law to purchase the entire domestic production of tobacco (¥200 billion in fiscal year 1986). Since the same amount of imported tobacco would cost only ¥70 billion, JTI was spending an extra ¥130 billion a year to abide by a political decision made by the Japanese government to protect domestic farmers. As a result, JTI was permitted to import only around one-third of its needs from abroad. This tobacco was subsequently blended with domestic tobacco.

Ever since the tobacco industry monopoly had been eliminated in Japan, JTI's share of market had steadily declined. However, Kazuo Obata, special adviser in the marketing and planning section of Japan Tobacco, Inc., had predicted in a recent press interview that Japan would not experience a serious penetration of foreign tobacco as had happened in France or Italy, where international tobacco firms had gained shares of 40% and 30%, respectively. Obata argued that Japanese employees were striving for higher sales and were not like the Italians and French who "had no loyalty." He also maintained that JTI's experience with Philip Morris's Marlboro brand had taught the company much about American blend tobacco. "We know the market intimately," he said.

In the meantime, Philip Morris had been able to maintain its share at around 60% of the total foreign tobacco market. At the end of 1987, JTI still commanded 91% of the cigarette market; PMKK was a distant second with a 5.2% share of market (*refer to Exhibit 5*). Although JTI's market share was still comfortably large, some industry analysts believed that JTI would be under pressure to close one of its 32 factories whenever it lost two points of market share to the competition. However, Leo Spelt felt that the relationship between the loss of market share and factories closing was much more complex than that.

OTHER COMPETITORS

With JTI as the dominant manufacturer and distributor of cigarettes in Japan, competition in the imported markets clearly came from the other major international tobacco manufacturers: Brown & Williamson (B&W), R. J. Reynolds (RJR), American Tobacco Co., and Tobacco Exporters International (TEI). At the end of 1987, these four groups together with Philip Morris commanded 99% of the imported cigarette segment in Japan. In the imported brands market, PMKK commanded a 62% market share of this segment by the end of 1987, followed by B&W and RJR with a 25% and 9% market share, respectively (*refer to Exhibit 4*).

The three largest international competitors (Philip Morris, B&W, and R. J. Reynolds) were competing mainly in the ¥220 or ¥250 segments with some of their traditional international brands: Kent, Lucky Strike, and John Player Special (JPS) for B&W; Salem, Camel, Winston, and More for R. J. Reynolds. JTI, on the other hand, had a broader product line with one brand in the ¥200 segment (Hi-Lite)

EXHIBIT 5   Japan Pricing: 1987 Share of Market (SOM) by Price Category and Manufacturer, %

¥/Pack	JTI	PMKK	B&W	RJR	AT	TEI	Others	Total Market
70	0.36	—	—	—	—	—	—	0.36
90	0.14	—	—	—	—	—	—	0.14
110	3.41	—	—	—	—	—	—	3.41
120	0.40	—	—	—	—	—	—	0.40
130	3.10	—	—	—	—	—	—	3.10
140	1.31	—	—	—	—	—	*	1.31
150	0.15	—	—	—	—	—	—	0.15
180	—	—	—	—	—	—	—	—
200	5.00	—	—	—	—	—	*	5.00
220	64.65	1.26	1.49	0.19	0.10	—	*	67.69
230	—	—	—	—	—	—	*	*
240	12.13	—	0.08	—	*	—	*	12.22
250	0.37	2.84	0.42	0.45	*	*	*	4.10
260	0.46	—	*	—	0.05	—	—	0.51
270	—	—	0.01	—	—	—	*	0.01
280	0.01	1.07	*	0.05	*	0.08	*	1.22
290	—	—	—	—	—	—	*	*
300	0.02	—	—	0.06	—	—	*	0.08
320	—	—	—	—	—	*	*	*
350	—	0.03	—	—	—	0.01	*	0.04
380	—	—	—	—	—	*	—	*
400	—	—	—	*	—	—	—	*
550	—	—	—	—	—	—	*	*
600	—	—	—	—	—	—	*	*
650	0.06	—	—	—	—	—	—	0.06
Total	91.52	5.21	2.00	0.75	0.21	0.11	0.09	99.89

Source: Philip Morris K.K., 1987.

1. Sum of SOM by manufacturer in this table does not add up to 100% due to unknown volume by brands that are sold independently.

2. Sum of SOM by price category and by manufacturer is not necessarily equal to total figure due to rounding.

3. ¥110 and ¥120 brands for JTI are sold in 10s, while ¥650 is sold in 50s by JTI. Also, ¥70 brands are promotion packs.

4. * Denotes numbers that are too small to record.

5. — Denotes no participation.

and one in the ¥130 segment (Echo). (*Refer to Exhibits 6 through 8.*)

DISTRIBUTION OF CIGARETTES IN JAPAN

The distribution of cigarettes in Japan remained almost unchanged after the monopoly was lifted from the Japanese market. Unlike in the United States, distributors were not easily chosen, and all shops selling tobacco had to be licensed. Moreover, supermarkets could not use tobacco as a specialty product for big sales, offering a lower price than usual. Haiso, the company associated with JTI for distribution of tobacco in Japan, continued to distribute PMKK's products to the retailers through five regional operating companies. These wholesaling companies were in turn serving a total of 260,755 licensed retailers. Stores selling only tobacco, as well as liquor and grocery stores, each represented roughly 14% of total cigarette retail sales in Japan.

A major characteristic of the Japanese tobacco market was the importance of vending machines in distributing cigarettes. In 1987, there were more than 1.6 million vending machines installed along Japanese streets (more than one machine for every 100 inhabitants) distributing almost everything from canned coffee, beer, and whisky to batteries, newspapers and magazines, telephone cards, and even Bibles. The 428,000 vending machines installed in

EXHIBIT 6 Competitive Profile in Japan, 1987

Philip Morris Main Brands	Price/(¥)	Sales Volume (bn)	Est. Sales[a] Revenues (¥ bn)	Share of Volume (%)
Lark Milds KS	250	5.55	19.81	34.51
PM Super Lights[b]	220	1.63	4.72	10.14
Lark KS	250	2.11	7.53	13.12
Parliament 100's	280	1.81	7.67	11.26
PM Lights[b]	220	2.24	6.49	13.93
Lark Super Lights	250	0.86	3.07	5.35
VSL Menthol[c]	250	0.46	1.95	2.86
Lark Milds 100's	280	0.56	2.37	3.48
Others		0.86	3.07	5.35
Total		16.08	56.68	100.00

Source: Philip Morris K.K., 1987.

[a] Sales revenues = retail price − taxes − distribution fee − retailer's margin.

[b] PM: Philip Morris Super Lights

[c] VSL: Virginia Slims Lights

restaurants, bars, and the like, as well as the ones along the streets, were used exclusively to distribute cigarettes. They accounted for 40% of all cigarettes sold in Japan. Typically, vending machines were owned by retailers (tobacco and/or liquor stores, restaurants, hotels, newsstands, and others), although manufacturers would also lease or give away some machines. Each cigarette vending machine had 6 to 25 columns. Typically, retailers would arrange the cigarettes in the columns according to brand popularity. Generally, a retailer with a 12-column machine would place the 12 best-selling brands in the 12 columns. Since JTI dominated the cigarette

EXHIBIT 7 PMKK Brand Mix Development in Japan

Philip Morris Main Brands	1982	1983	1984	1985	1986	1987
Lark Milds KS[a]	33.3	33.3	35.4	37.0	31.6	34.5
Lark KS	38.9	33.3	25.0	22.2	16.4	13.1
Lark Superlight KS	—	—	—	1.8	5.1	5.3
Lark Milds 100's	—	—	10.4	9.3	6.4	3.5
Lark Deluxe Mild 100's	—	—	—	1.8	1.3	0.6
Other Lark	8.3	9.5	8.3	5.7	3.8	2.5
Total Lark	80.5	76.1	79.1	77.8	64.6	59.5
PM Superlights[b]	—	—	—	—	—	10.1
PM Lights	—	—	—	—	12.6	13.9
Total Philip Morris	—	—	—	—	12.6	24.0
Parliament 100's (soft)	8.3	11.9	16.7	18.6	16.4	11.3
Parliament KS	—	2.4	2.1	1.8	1.3	1.2
Total Parliament	8.3	14.3	18.8	20.4	17.7	12.5
VSL Menthol[c]	—	—	—	1.8	3.8	2.9
VSL Regular 20's	—	—	—	—	—	0.5
Total VSL	—	—	—	1.8	3.8	3.4
Other	11.2	9.6	2.1	—	1.3	0.6
Total PMKK (%)	100.0	100.0	100.0	100.0	100.0	100.0

Source: Philip Morris K.K., 1987.

[a] KS: King size

[b] PM: Philip Morris

[c] VSL: Virginia Slims Lights

EXHIBIT 8   Competitors in Japan, 1987

R.J. Reynolds Main Brands	Price/¥	Sales Volume (bn)	Est. Sales[a] Revenues (¥ bn)	Share of Volume (%)
Salem Lights	250	0.91	3.20	38.56
Camel KS	250	0.13	0.45	5.51
Winston KS	220	0.18	0.51	7.63
More	250	0.14	0.49	5.93
Others		1.00	2.22	42.37
Total		2.36	6.87	100.00

JTI Main Brands	Price/¥	Sales Volume (bn)	Est. Sales[a] Revenues (¥ bn)	Share of Volume (%)
Mild Seven	220	80.51	259.89	28.59
Mild Seven Lights	220	41.41	133.67	14.70
Seven Stars	220	30.52	98.52	10.84
Caster	220	22.29	71.95	7.91
Cabin Milds	240	18.29	67.20	6.49
Hi-Lite	200	15.38	42.79	5.46
Hope 10's (10 sticks)	110	10.28	33.18	3.65
Echo	130	8.34	21.81	2.96
Libera Milds	220	2.71	8.75	0.96
Peace Lights	240	3.98	14.62	1.41
Marlboro Family	240	1.45	5.33	0.51
Others		46.49	150.07	16.52
Total	Total	281.65	907.78	100.00

Brown & Williamson Main Brands	Price/¥	Sales Volume (bn)	Est. Sales[a] Revenues (¥ bn)	Share of Volume (%)
Kent Milds	220	3.80	10.93	61.29
Lucky Strike	250	1.29	4.58	20.81
JPS Charcoal	220	0.26	0.75	4.19
Kent 100's	250	0.11	0.46	1.77
Others		0.74	2.62	11.94
Total		6.20	19.34	100.00

[a] Sales revenues = retail price − taxes − distribution fee − retailer's margins.

market, distributors for foreign manufacturers had to convince retailers to allocate enough columns to them for their respective brands. Given the frequent difficulties in gaining adequate space, some distributors would buy columns by offering free products or financial incentives to major tobacco retailers.

In addition to importing, Mitsui & Co. and Nissho Iwai employed a sales merchandising force of slightly over 500 people whose function was to merchandise PMKK's products at the retail level. In other words, Haiso only acted as a distributor, while Nissho Iwai, Mitsui & Co., and PMKK acted as partners in marketing, advertising, and merchandising. Competitors had a similar sales force, ranging from 2,700 sales representatives for JTI to 200 salespeople each for B&W and R. J. Reynolds.

PMKK'S PRODUCT LINE

The Japanese cigarette market could be segmented in many different ways (sex, brands, imported versus domestic, cigarette lengths, and the like). However, PMKK relied primarily on two major dimensions: price and flavor (that is, tar and nicotine content). (*Refer to Exhibits 9 through 11 for marketing information.*)

In January 1988, Philip Morris K.K. was distributing three major brands. For many years, Lark had been PMKK's best-selling brand (*refer to Exhibit 12*). To meet smokers' changing tastes, PMKK had progressively extended the Lark line, adding Lark Milds KS (King Size), Lark Milds 100's, and Lark Super Lights. Lark Milds KS was now the best-selling imported brand In Japan. At the end of 1987, the Lark

EXHIBIT 9 Japan Market: Segmentation by Price, 1987

Units in Millions

¥ Price/Pack[a]	Jan '87	Feb '87	Mar '87	Apr '87	May '87	Jun '87	Jul '87
Premium (¥280 + above)	264.29	203.12	384.62	388.37	370.64	351.64	394.63
High (¥221–¥279)	3,519.31	3,568.15	4,416.16	4,641.09	4,549.77	4,347.39	4,639.58
Medium (¥220)	14,813.43	16,087.65	18,701.70	18,209.16	18,716.02	18,265.79	19,332.16
Low (below ¥220)	2,214.13	2,308.74	2,622.77	2,613.76	2,700.83	2,610.38	2,734.45
Unknown	0.00	0.00	0.00	0.00	0.00	0.00	0.00
Total	20,811.16	22,167.65	26,125.25	25,852.39	26,337.26	25,575.19	27,100.82

Share of Market

¥Price/Pack[a]	Jan '87	Feb '87	Mar '87	Apr '87	May '87	Jun '87	Jul '87
Premium (¥280 + above)	1.27	0.92	1.47	1.50	1.41	1.37	1.46
High (¥221–¥279)	16.91	16.10	16.90	17.95	17.28	17.00	17.12
Medium (¥220)	71.18	72.57	71.58	70.44	71.06	71.42	71.33
Low (below ¥220)	10.64	10.41	10.04	10.11	10.25	10.21	10.09
Unknown	0.00	0.00	0.00	0.00	0.00	0.00	0.00
Total	100.00	100.00	100.00	100.00	100.00	100.00	100.00

Source: Philip Morris K.K. 1988.[a]
All pack sizes other than 20s are treated as equivalent to 20s.

EXHIBIT 10 Japan Market: Imported Segment by Price, 1987

Units in Millions

¥ Price/Pack[a]	Jan '87	Feb '87	Mar '87	Apr '87	May '87	Jun '87	Jul '87
Premium (¥280 + above)	260.03	198.33	379.39	383.17	359.43	335.77	376.73
High (¥221–¥279)	505.07	417.54	773.15	1,058.41	1,156.77	1,103.76	1,219.39
Medium (¥220)	122.78	114.71	312.91	656.71	912.15	919.82	1,057.80
Low (below ¥220)	0.00	0.00	0.00	0.00	0.00	0.00	1.73
Unknown	0.00	0.00	0.00	0.00	0.00	0.00	0.00
Total	887.88	730.58	1,465.45	2,098.29	2,430.48	2,359.35	2,655.64

% Share of Import Market

¥ Price/Pack[a]	Jan '87	Feb '87	Mar '87	Apr '87	May '87	Jun '87	Jul '87
Premium (¥280 + above)	29.29	27.15	25.89	18.26	14.79	14.23	14.19
High (¥221–¥279)	56.89	57.15	52.76	50.44	47.59	46.78	45.92
Medium (¥220)	13.83	15.70	21.35	31.30	37.53	38.99	39.83
Low (below ¥220)	0.00	0.00	0.00	0.00	0.09	0.00	0.06
Unknown	0.00	0.00	0.00	0.00	0.00	0.00	0.00
Total	100.00	100.00	100.00	100.00	100.00	100.00	100.00

Source: Philip Morris K.K., 1988.

[a] All pack sizes other than 20s are treated as equivalent to 20s.

EXHIBIT 9 (*Continued*)

				Units in Millions				
Aug '87	Sep '87	Oct '87	Nov '87	Dec '87	YTD '87	YTD '86	% VAR
384.71	373.08	387.75	357.35	467.87	4,328.06	3,338.04	29.66
4,649.80	4,460.34	4,235.65	4,052.54	5,419.59	52,499.38	50,080.79	4.83
19,122.07	19,624.55	17,767.73	16,964.25	22,247.71	219,852.21	221,314.02	−0.66
2,749.51	2,608.20	2,474.06	2,353.26	2,932.41	30,922.51	34,471.85	−10.30
0.00	0.43	0.37	0.17	0.24	1.22	0.00	100.00
26,906.09	27,066.60	24,865.57	23,727.57	31,067.83	307,603.37	309,204.70	−0.52%

				Share of Market				
Aug '87	Sep '87	Oct '87	Nov '87	Dec '87	YTD '87	YTD '86	% VAR
1.43	1.38	1.56	1.51	1.51	1.41	1.08	0.33
17.28	16.48	17.03	17.08	17.44	17.07	16.20	0.87
71.07	72.50	71.46	71.50	71.61	71.47	71.58	−0.10
10.22	9.64	9.95	9.92	9.44	10.05	11.15	−1.10
0.00	0.00	0.00	0.00	0.00	0.00	0.00	0.00
100.00	100.00	100.00	100.00	100.00	100.00	100.00	

EXHIBIT 10 (*Continued*)

				Units in Millions				
Aug '87	Sep '87	Oct '87	Nov '87	Dec '87	YTD '87	YTD '86	% VAR
360.23	353.23	371.88	337.73	439.32	4,155.23	3,305.97	25.69
1,195.12	1,191.90	1,202.98	1,098.74	1,421.95	12,344.78	6,143.09	100.00
1,058.76	1,101.78	1,076.83	922.51	1,167.32	9,424.09	1,185.85	100.00
1.54	2.49	2.49	6.29	7.33	24.00	0.00	NA
0.00	0.43	0.37	0.17	0.24	1.22	0.00	100.00
2.615.66	2,649.83	2,654.56	2,365.44	3,036.17	25,949.32	10,634.91	100.00

				% Share of Import Market				
Aug '87	Sep '87	Oct '87	Nov '87	Dec '87	YTD '87	YTD '86	% VAR
13.77	13.33	14.01	14.28	14.47	16.01	31.09	−15.07
45.69	44.98	45.32	46.45	46.83	47.57	57.76	−10.19
40.48	41.58	40.57	39.00	38.45	36.32	11.15	25.17
0.06	0.09	0.09	0.27	0.24	0.09	0.00	NA
0.00	0.02	0.01	0.01	0.01	0.00	0.00	0.00
100.00	100.00	100.00	100.00	100.00	100.00	100.00	

EXHIBIT 11   Japan Market: Flavor Segmentation, 1987

			Units in Millions				
Flavor	*Jan '87*	*Feb '87*	*Mar '87*	*Apr '87*	*May '87*	*Jun '87*	*Jul '87*
Full flavor (16 MG+)	3,232.08	3,338.52	3,879.62	3,908.45	3,978.57	3,826.84	4,048.67
Medium (11.1–16)	11,084.96	11,771.90	13,821.82	13,567.31	13,828.22	13,281.11	13,935.83
Low (6–11)	6,462.58	7,032.87	8,376.85	8,329.25	8,485.31	8,424.68	9,068.54
Ultra low (below 6)	20.80	16.48	36.31	34.41	30.03	28.32	31.31
Unknown	10.74	7.87	10.65	12.97	15.13	14.23	16.48
Total	20,811.16	22,167.65	26,125.25	25,852.39	26,337.26	25,575.19	27,100.82

			Share of Market				
Flavor	*Jan '87*	*Feb '87*	*Mar '87*	*Apr '87*	*May '87*	*Jun '87*	*Jul '87*
Full flavor (16 MG+)	15.53	15.06	14.85	15.12	15.11	14.96	14.94
Medium (11.1–16)	53.26	53.10	52.91	52.48	52.50	51.93	51.42
Low (6–11)	31.05	31.73	32.06	32.22	32.22	32.94	33.46
Ultra low (below 6)	0.10	0.07	0.14	0.13	0.11	0.11	0.12
Unknown	0.05	0.04	0.04	0.05	0.06	0.06	0.06
Total	100.00	100.00	100.00	100.00	100.00	100.00	100.00

Source: Philip Morris K.K., 1988.

EXHIBIT 12   Top 20, Brand Family Evolution

1981		1982		1983		1984	
Brand	*SOM $*	*Brand*	*SOM $*	*Brand*	*SOM $*	*Brand*	*SOM $*
1. M. Seven	37.54	M. Seven	41.47	M. Seven	43.99	M. Seven	44.20
2. S. Stars	17.07	S. Stars	15.64	S. Stars	13.83	S. Stars	12.93
3. Hi-Lite	10.96	Hi-Lite	9.52	Hi-Lite	8.04	Cabin	6.98
4. Hope	5.71	Hope	5.18	Cabin	5.04	Hi-Lite	6.95
5. Echo	5.17	Cabin	5.09	Hope	4.81	Caster	6.87
6. Cabin	4.08	Echo	4.71	Caster	4.42	Hope	4.45
7. Peace	3.34	Peace	3.15	Echo	4.22	Echo	3.75
8. Cherry	3.28	Cherry	2.62	Peace	3.06	Peace	3.06
9. Partner	2.89	Partner	2.56	Wakaba	2.03	Wakaba	1.78
10. Wakaba	2.42	Wakaba	2.23	Cherry	2.02	Cherry	1.58
11. **Lark**	0.95	**Lark**	1.01	Partner	1.72	**Lark**	1.24
12. Mine	0.91	Tender	0.97	**Lark**	1.15	Partner	1.09
13. Shinsei	0.84	Mine	0.89	Tender	0.79	Mine	0.60
14. Tender	0.67	Shinsei	0.72	Mine	0.73	Tender	0.56
15. Just	0.63	Ministar	0.54	Shinsei	0.64	Shinsei	0.54
16. Ministar	0.57	Just	0.46	Ministar	0.50	Sometime	0.52
17. Current	0.48	Champagne	0.44	Sometime	0.46	Ministar	0.45
18. Mr. Slim	0.38	Sometime	0.40	Just	0.33	Mr. Slim	0.30
19. Sometime	0.33	Current	0.37	Mr. Slim	0.32	**Parliament**	0.27
20. Hitone	0.32	Mr. Slim	0.36	Hitone	0.26	Just	0.27

Source: PMKK Segmentation Analysis.

Boldface: Philip Morris brands; Marlboro family (produced by JTI under license from Philip Morris).

SOM: Share of market.

EXHIBIT 11 (*Continued*)

			Units in Millions				
Aug '87	*Sep '87*	*Oct '87*	*Nov '87*	*Dec '87*	*YTD '87*	*YTD '86*	*% VAR*
4,033.21	3,873.11	3,660.54	3,465.94	4,401.48	45,647.03	49,035.83	−6.91
13,698.58	13,293.79	12,204.17	11,593.03	15,208.47	157,289.19	172,683.48	−8.91
9,130.12	9,853.71	8,951.70	8,621.56	11,398.18	104,135.36	87,183.95	19.44
29.44	30.08	29.29	25.32	32.73	344.52	239.94	43.59
14.74	15.91	19.87	21.72	26.97	187.27	61.51	100.00
26,906.09	27,066.60	24,865.57	23,727.57	31,067.83	307,603.37	309,204.70	−0.52%

			Share of Market				
Aug '87	*Sep '87*	*Oct '87*	*Nov '87*	*Dec '87*	*YTD '87*	*YTD '86*	*% VAR*
14.99	14.31	14.72	14.61	14.17	14.84	15.86	−1.02
50.91	49.12	49.08	48.86	48.95	51.13	55.85	−4.71
33.93	36.41	36.00	36.34	36.69	33.85	28.20	5.66
0.11	0.11	0.12	0.11	0.11	0.11	0.08	0.03
0.05	0.06	0.08	0.09	0.09	0.06	0.02	0.04
100.00	100.00	100.00	100.00	100.00	100.00	100.00	100.00

EXHIBIT 12 (*Continued*)

1985		*1986*		*1987*	
Brand	*SOM $*	*Brand*	*SOM $*	*Brand*	*SOM $*
M. Seven	44.41	M. Seven	45.92	M. Seven[a]	43.21
S. Stars	12.06	S. Stars	11.53	S. Stars[a]	10.58
Caster	8.41	Caster	7.72	Caster[a]	7.73
Cabin	7.31	Cabin	7.33	Cabin[a]	6.85
Hi-Lite	6.07	Hi-Lite	5.56	Hi-Lite[a]	5.00
Hope	3.94	Peace	4.27	Peace[a]	3.87
Echo	3.36	Hope	3.75	Hope[a]	3.44
Peace	3.08	Echo	3.01	**Lark**	3.10
Wakaba	1.58	**Lark**	1.67	Echo[a]	2.71
Lark	1.31	Wakaba	1.42	Kent[b]	1.43
Cosmos	1.30	Cherry	0.97	Wakaba[a]	1.30
Cherry	1.24	Cosmos	0.83	**P. Morris**	1.26
Partner	0.81	Sometime	0.65	Sometime	0.90
Sometime	0.58	Partner	0.54	Libera[a]	0.88
Mine	0.54	Mine	0.47	Cherry[a]	0.78
Tender	0.49	**Parliament**	0.45	**Parliament**	0.67
Shinsei	0.43	Tender	0.42	Cosmos[a]	0.66
Ministar	0.42	Shinsei	0.42	**Marlboro**	0.49
Parliament	0.35	Ministar	0.38	L. Strike[b]	0.43
Mr. Slim	0.28	**P. Morris**	0.34	Tender	0.42

Boldface: Philip Morris brands; Marlboro family (produced by JTI under license from Philip Morris).

[a] JTI brands.

[b] B&W brands.

SOM: Share of market.

family represented 56% of PMKK's cigarettes sales in Japan, while PM, PMKK's second best-selling brand, accounted for another 24%. Parliament represented 11% of PMKK's share of sales volume. The Marlboro family was produced under license by JTI, but it did not account for a significant share of the Japanese market (*refer to Exhibit 13*).

Despite PMKK's success with light and mild cigarettes in Japan, Philip Morris had never introduced any new product in the ¥200 segment. Moreover, the 5% share of the Japanese market gained by Hi-Lite, the only brand in this price segment (launched by JTI), was declining (*refer to Exhibit 13*). In addition, given the time constraints with New Year approaching, there had been little time for the PMKK marketing team to investigate the overall implications of the new ¥200 segment.

THE RJR CHALLENGE

Through retailers, Philip Morris K.K. first heard rumors in the middle of November 1987 about a new brand introduction by R. J. Reynolds, but it was not until December 15, 1987, that Leo Spelt received confirmation of RJR's decision to introduce Islands Lights in Japan at ¥200 as of February 1, 1988. Immediately, PMKK's marketing department decided to evaluate the possible alternatives to counter the RJR initiative. That same day, a project time schedule was made for potential development of a new product, including packaging, research, and commercial production. PMKK executives were not familiar with RJR's Islands Lights brand, since this brand had never been introduced in the United States or in any other market before. It seemed, therefore, that Islands Lights was either a code name

EXHIBIT 13 Japan Market Facts: Top 20 Brands

Family SOM (%)	*1981*	*1982*	*1983*	*1984*	*1985*	*1986*	*1987*
1. Mild Seven	37.54	41.17	43.99	44.20	44.41	45.92	43.21
2. Seven Stars	17.07	15.64	13.83	12.93	12.06	11.53	10.58
3. Caster	—	0.10	4.42	6.87	8.41	7.72	7.73
4. Cabin	4.08	5.09	5.04	6.98	7.31	7.33	6.85
5. Hi-Lite	10.96	9.52	8.04	6.95	6.07	5.56	5.00
6. Peace	3.34	3.15	3.06	3.06	3.08	4.27	3.87
7. Hope	5.71	5.18	4.81	4.45	4.07	3.75	3.44
8. **Lark**	0.95	1.01	1.15	1.24	1.31	1.67	3.10
9. Echo	5.17	4.71	4.22	3.75	3.36	3.01	2.71
10. Kent[a]	0.07	0.05	0.04	0.04	0.04	0.05	1.43
11. Wakaba	2.43	2.23	2.03	1.78	1.58	1.42	1.30
12. **Philip Morris**	—	—	—	—	0.01	0.34	1.26
13. Sometime	0.33	0.40	0.46	0.52	0.58	0.65	0.90
14. Libera	—	—	—	—	—	—	0.88
15. Cherry	3.28	2.62	2.02	1.58	1.24	0.97	0.78
16. **Parliament**	0.08	0.11	0.19	0.26	0.35	0.45	0.67
17. Cosmos	—	—	—	0.30	1.30	0.83	0.66
18. **Marlboro**[b]	0.12	0.15	0.14	0.09	0.09	0.21	0.49
19. Lucky Strike[a]	a	a	a	a	0.04	0.12	0.43
20. Tender	0.67	0.97	0.79	0.56	0.49	0.42	0.42

Source: Philip Morris K.K., 1987.

Top 20 brand family ranking list is based on 1987 performance; Boldface are PMKK's brand families.

[a] Kent and Lucky Strike belong to B&W's brand families.

[b] Marlboro belongs to Philip Morris, but is being produced and distributed in Japan by JTI under license from Philip Morris.

    All other names belong to JTI's brand families.

SOM: Share of market.

for an existing RJR brand or a completely new brand tailored for the Japanese market.

Because of the adjective "Lights," L. D. Spelt and PMKK brand managers assumed that Islands Lights would be positioned in Japan in the low-tar segment to compete with other light and mild cigarette brands. (Tobacco manufacturers were using either the adjective "light" or "mild" to label low-tar cigarettes, but no particular definition had been attached to either word.) In Japan, as in other industrialized markets, the low-tar segment had been growing more rapidly than other segments as smokers increasingly considered high-tar cigarettes less healthy.

In 1987, the low-tar segment accounted for 34% of the total cigarette market in Japan. By comparison, the full flavor (16 mg+) and the medium tar (11.1 to 16 mg) segments, representing respectively 15% and 51% of the market, were slowly declining to 1% to 2% a year. The ultra low-tar segment (below 6 mg) was quite stable with 0.10% of the cigarette market in Japan (*refer to Exhibit 11*).

After the confirmation of RJR's decision to introduce Islands Lights in Japan, Leo Spelt and other marketing executives had tried to determine RJR's motivations and the objectives of its strategic move into the ¥200 segment. In Leo Spelt's view, R. J. Reynolds had been less successful than other international tobacco firms in the Japanese market. Its Camel brand, launched in 1983 by RJR Japan, had never achieved a significant market share in Japan. Moreover, in 1987, its Winston Lights brand had been ruined overnight by a report from Japanese authorities that Winston Lights cigarettes contained traces of a herbicide. This instant blow to R. J. Reynolds meant that Salem, a menthol cigarette, was that company's only successful brand in Japan.

Leo Spelt had almost no information on how much R. J. Reynolds would spend on advertising and promotion to launch Islands Lights, but judging from his own experience in Japan, he estimated that the launch would require around $20 million, with a potential payback period of 2 to 3 years (quite short by industry standards; over 5 years was typical).

THE ALTERNATIVES

During the meeting with L. D. Spelt, the marketing team had outlined the various alternatives for PMKK:

1. *Joining forces with JTI:* Since RJR's launch of Islands Lights on February 1, 1988, had been confirmed, various options had been reviewed. George R. Austin, president of PMKK, had considered meeting with K. Katsukawa from JTI to discuss the ¥200 issue as well as a possible import licensing agreement for Philip Morris's L&M Milds brand. This idea had been triggered by PMKK's reluctance to compete directly with R. J. Reynolds in a price segment that meant smaller margins. Moreover, to distribute a new ¥200 segment in vending machines would mean convincing the owners either to grant Philip Morris one additional column in their machines or have Philip Morris lose a column containing a more expensive, higher-contribution brand.

2. *L&M Milds,* which belonged to Philip Morris through its agreement with Liggett & Myers (an independent American tobacco manufacturer), was one brand being considered for licensing to JTI as part of PMKK's countermove against the RJR initiative. Philip Morris International had introduced L&M in West Germany, where it had achieved a market share of 1.3% in 1987. In the United States, L&M's share under Liggett & Myers in this same year was 0.3%.

George R. Austin was not sure how JTI would respond to his proposal, since two obstacles had to be overcome. First, producing L&M Milds under license would force JTI to import more American tobacco leaves, which would mean having to renegotiate its import policy with the Japanese authorities. Second, JTI management would also have to negotiate for the support of JTI labor union leaders, who had a strong voice in JTI. Austin had proposed that JTI equally share the costs of launching this new brand by having PMKK handle all advertising and promotional costs. Austin believed that this licensing agreement could benefit both JTI and PMKK, providing an estimated additional $1 million per month to JTI and a break-even position for PMKK.

If JTI were to decline Austin's offer, PMKK could possibly launch L&M Mild or another new brand alone. However, this new product had to be imported from the United States with the technical modifications necessary to meet the tastes of Japanese consumers.

3. *L&M Milds in West Germany:* Philip Morris had launched L&M in West Germany In 1982 following a competitive move in 1980 from Reemtsma, a local tobacco manufacturer. Until the end of the 1970s and early 1980s, Reemtsma had been the leader in the German cigarette industry. Then the company steadily began losing market share. One of its brands, Ernte, was seriously affected by competition from Marlboro. German discount chains, locked into heavy competition among themselves, had added generic brands of cigarettes to their product lines. These generics were being marketed about 25% below the prevailing price level for nationally advertised brands which were retailing at DM 3.80 to 4.00.[5] To counter this market trend, Reemtsma launched a new brand named West in 1980. The advertising packaging, and the like, were clearly aimed at the market for Marlboro cigarettes. However, despite an expenditure of DM 150 million, the West brand had captured only 0.4% share of the market by the end of 1982. After losing that battle, Reemtsma decided to cut the price of its West brand further, from DM 3.80 to 3.30. This time, West's market share grew rapidly, reaching 5% within a 3-month period.

Philip Morris Germany followed West's dramatic increase with concern, since it definitely affected Philip Morris's leading brands. The company chose L&M because all the other brands in the German market were either too small or too narrow in appeal. At only DM 3.00 for a pack of 19 cigarettes, L&M was the lowest-priced national brand on the market. It was advertised as an international brand and supported with readily available media. To enhance the brand's image, only box packs were used. L&M was first introduced in the southern part of Germany where it rapidly achieved a 15% market share, thus becoming the second best-selling brand after Marlboro. L&M was later launched in the northern part of Germany.

By mid-1983, other major cigarette marketers had also reacted. L&M was no longer the only low-priced brand on the market. All major brands had lost market share to new low-priced competitors that had appeared everywhere. When one major competitor rolled back its prices from DM 3.80 to 3.50 for its leading brand, others including Philip Morris followed. L&M and other low-priced brands lost appeal and consumers switched back to national brands. In 1987, L&M had 1.3% of the German market, a 0.2% loss over the previous year. In 1987, leading brands, including Philip Morris's Marlboro, regained their dominant positions and price levels stabilized. At the end of the German cigarette war, Philip Morris had regained its former competitive position, albeit at a somewhat lower price level than before. The overall cost of launching L&M was $10 million.

While reflecting again on the German episode, Leo Spelt believed that the German price war and its successive price cuts had had major financial repercussions for Philip Morris in Germany. In Tokyo, Leo Spelt wanted to minimize the financial risk linked to a potential price war in Japan. Leo Spelt wondered whether the L&M advertising concept currently being used in Germany could work in Japan as well, if PMKK decided to introduce L&M in the Japanese market. However, in any case, PMKK could not use any TV commercials from Germany since tobacco advertising on television had been banned there. Moreover, Leo Spelt felt that L&M as a brand had two major weaknesses. First, L&M was difficult for Japanese consumers to pronounce, and the name would not mean anything in Japan.

4. *Cambridge:* Because of these considerations, Cambridge, a Philip Morris brand of cigarettes made with a flue-cured tobacco, was also being considered as a launch possibility in the ¥200 segment. Cambridge could easily be pronounced by Japanese consumers, and the

[5] US$1 = DM 1.8 in 1982.

EXHIBIT 14   Sales Revenue per 1,000 Sticks, 1987 (PMKK estimates)

Philip Morris			
	¥220	¥250	¥280
	× 50	× 50	× 50
	11,000	12,500	14,000
Retail margin	1,100	1,250	1,400
Excise tax	6,572	7,253	7,934
Distribution	430	430	430
	¥2,898	¥3,576	¥4,236

B&W			
	¥220	¥250	¥280
	× 50	× 50	× 50
	11,000	12,500	14,000
Retail margin	1,100	1,250	1,400
Excise tax	6,572	7,253	7,934
Distribution	450	450	450
	¥2,878	¥3,547	¥4,216

RJR			
	¥220	¥250	¥280
	× 50	× 50	× 50
	11,000	12,500	14,000
Retail margin	1,100	1,250	1,400
Excise tax	6,572	7,253	7,934
Distribution	480	480	480
	¥2,848	¥3,517	¥4,186

JTI				
	¥130	¥200	¥220	¥240
	× 50	× 50	× 50	× 50
	6,500	10,000	11,000	12,000
Retail margin	650	1,000	1,100	1,200
Excise tax	3,135	6,118	6,572	7,026
Distribution	100	100	100	100
	¥2,615	¥2,782	¥3,228	¥3,674

Source: Philip Morris K.K., 1987.

name had more potential for identification. However, Cambridge had not been successful in the U.S. market. Sold as a generically priced product, Cambridge had been positioned in the low-price segment with the help of discount coupons. In the United States the product was advertised in newspapers and magazines, but was not supported by image advertising. As a result, no advertising concept could be imported for use on Japanese television. Although Leo Burnett Kyodo Co. Ltd., one of the international advertising agencies under contract with PMKK, had its office in the same building as Philip Morris K.K., Akio Kobayashi, a PMKK brand manager, described getting approval for a new advertising campaign as "a nightmare" and "too risky." Kobayashi said, "Any new advertising concept must be approved by Philip Morris's Asian headquarters in Hong Kong and then by the head office in New York City. Developing an effective advertising and promotional campaign in just 3 weeks is a big risk that PMKK should avoid. By rushing too fast, we could easily blow up the whole thing."

5. *Philip Morris Superlights:* During the meeting, A. Kobayashi suggested that PMKK reduce the price of either Philip Morris Lights or Philip Morris Superlights from ¥220 to ¥200. In Mr. Kobayashi's view, repositioning one of these two brands was the quickest and safest way to respond to the Islands challenge. However, pricing issues on tobacco products had to

be cleared first with the Japanese government, and it typically took 30 to 60 days to obtain government approval.

6. *Other Alternatives:* Other options discussed during the meeting were the following: PMKK could choose to undercut R. J. Reynolds by launching L&M or Cambridge at ¥180 for a pack of 20 cigarettes. The exchange rate between the dollar and the yen during fiscal year 1987 had been favorable to imports into Japan, and a ¥180 price would still leave PMKK with a positive profit margin.

Another alternative was either to offer L&M or Cambridge at Y200 for a pack of 22 cigarettes or Y220 for 25. Although some retooling in the U.S. manufacturing facilities would be required, Philip Morris had ready production capacity to implement this option. Players was the only brand sold in the United States with 25 cigarettes in a pack, and its success had been limited. Larger packs would not be a problem for distribution in Japan, however, since Japanese vending machines could handle both the 22- and 25-pack sizes.

Leo Spelt's task now was to review all the alternatives discussed during one of the most animated meetings he had ever witnessed during his career at PMKK. It was also important that decisions regarding the marketing program be resolved quickly. How should the company allocate the sales force, what advertising methods would be adequate, should soft or hard packs be used, and so on? The one point on which everyone had agreed was that it was essential that any new product launched by PMKK in Japan be a winner.

Lestra Design

In May 1985, Claude Léopold, president of Lestra Design, was wondering what action he should take regarding the Japanese market. For several years, Lestra Design had been trying to enter the Japanese market for comforters and eiderdowns. The Japanese market for these products was certainly the largest in the world, but Lestra Design had faced a number of obstacles that had cooled Claude Léopold's enthusiasm. Then, recently, he had met again with Daniel Legrand, a French consultant in Tokyo who had been supervising Lestra Design activities in Japan for the last 2 years. Daniel Legrand had explained that despite the earlier difficulties experienced by Lestra Design, the company had several alternatives that could enable it to be successful in Japan.

LESTRA DESIGN

Lestra Design was a subsidiary of Léopold & Fils, a family business established in Amboise, a medium-sized town about 250 kilometers southwest of Paris (France). Claude Léopold's father had established the parent company in the early 1930s as a feather and down company. At first the company was mainly trading in down and feathers, but Léopold & Fils soon became a major French manufacturer of feather- and down-filled cushions, pillows, bolsters, and eiderdowns. In 1971, when Claude

Léopold took over the business from his father, he decided to establish two new companies: Lestra Design to produce and distribute feather and down comforters; and Lestra Sport to manufacture and distribute feather and down sleeping bags (see Exhibits 1 and 2). By using more aggressive sales management and the talents of his wife Josette, a renowned French fashion designer, Lestra Design rapidly became the leading comforter company in France. Josette Léopold's creative ideas for using innovative fabric designs with attractive prints helped Lestra Design and Lestra Sports quickly establish an international reputation for high-class, fashionable products. Although in 1985 Léopold & Fils, together with its two subsidiaries (Lestra Sports and Lestra Design), had only 128 employees for revenues of FF72 million,[1] Claude Léopold believed that the prospect of growth in international markets was extremely promising.

Sales over the past 5 years had experienced double-digit growth, and exports to England, West Germany, and other European countries had recently started to boom, representing 20% of Lestra Design sales. A few years earlier, Lestra Design had also placed an order in Japan through Kanematsu–Gosho Ltd., a *sogo shosha* (large trading company) affiliated with the Bank of Tokyo and traditionally strong in textiles. However, the Japanese trading com-

[1] FF7.10 = US$1 in 1985.

This case was written by Professor Dominique Turpin as a basis for class discussion rather than to illustrate either effective or ineffective handling of an administrative situation. Copyright © 1989, IMEDE, Lausanne, Switzerland. The International Institute for Management Development (IMD), resulting from the merger between IMEDE, Lausanne, and IMI, Geneva, acquires and retains all rights. Not to be used or reproduced without written permission from IMD, Lausanne, Switzerland.

EXHIBIT 1 Lestra Product Line

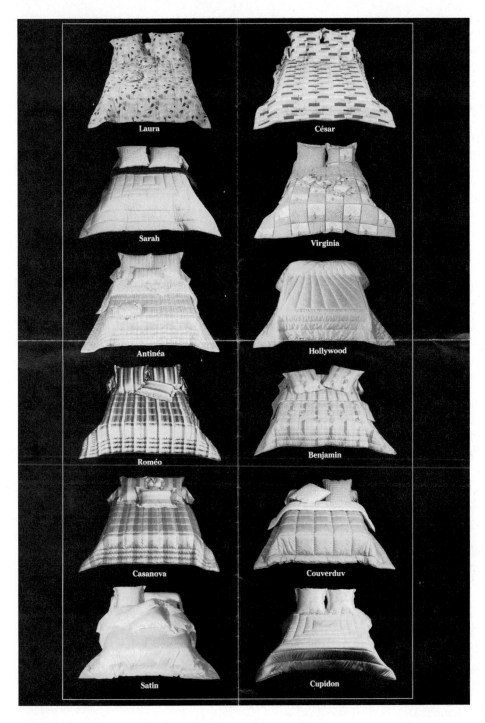

EXHIBIT 2   Lestra Sport Product Line

pany had not reordered any product from Lestra Design since 1979.

LESTRA DESIGN IN JAPAN

In 1978, Georges Mekiès, general manager, and Claude Léopold, president of Lestra Design, had met with Daniel Legrand, a French consultant established in Tokyo. That same year, Legrand had conducted a market survey for C. Léopold that clearly indicated that a major opportunity for growth existed in Japan. With close to 120 million inhabitants and half of the population using comforters, Japan was clearly the largest market for comforters in the world.

In 1978 and 1979, Claude Léopold had been preoccupied with developing Lestra Design sales in Europe. As a result, he had not taken any immediate action to investigate further the potential of the Japanese market for Lestra Design products. Léopold first wanted to provide the French and other European markets with good service before addressing any other market in either the United States or Japan. In autumn 1979, during the ISPO exhibition in Frankfurt (West Germany), Claude Léopold and Georges Mékiès were approached by a manager from Ogitani Corporation, a Japanese trading company based in Nagoya. Hiroshi Nakayama, the representative of Ogitani Corporation, wanted to import and distribute Lestra Design products in Japan. He especially liked the unique designs of Lestra Design's comforters and eiderdowns. He told Léopold and Mekiès that the innovative designs as well as the French image with the "Made in France" label would be the two strongest selling points in Japan.

THE TRADEMARK ISSUE

In December 1979, Ogitani ordered 200 comforters to be delivered to Nagoya. However, after the goods were shipped, Georges Mekiès did not hear anything from his Japanese distributor. By chance, Mekiès discovered on a trip to Japan in April 1980 that Ogitani had registered the two trademarks, Lestra Sport and Lestra Design, under the Ogitani name. Mekiès decided to call Nakayama and request a meeting in Nagoya to discuss the trademark issue. Nakayama responded that he was too busy. Mekiès then insisted that another executive from the trading company talk with him, but he received only a rebuff.

That same day, a furious Georges Mekiès called Yves Gasquères, the representative of the French Textile Manufacturers Association in Tokyo, for advice. Yves Gasquères, who also represented the well-known Lacoste shirts in Japan, explained that Lestra Design was not the only such case. The best advice he could give Mekiès was to contact Koichi Sato, a Japanese lawyer specializing in trademark disputes.

Georges Mekiès also saw Daniel Legrand, who confirmed Gasquères' advice. Legrand said that, although trademark disputes were rapidly disappearing in Japan, there were still some recent disputes between Western and Japanese firms, especially with several big French fashion houses like Cartier, Chanel, and Dior. Legrand also mentioned the recent example of Yoplait, a major French yoghurt producer. A few years ago, Yoplait had signed a licensing agreement with a major Japanese food company to manufacture and distribute yoghurt in Japan. While negotiating the contract, executives at Yoplait discovered that the Yoplait name had been registered by another Japanese food company under various Japanese writing transcriptions.[2] Although the French company decided to fight the case in court, Yoplait finally decided to use another name (Yopuleito, using the *Katagana* transcription) for its products in Japan.

Before going back to France, Georges Mekiès arranged for Daniel Legrand to supervise the trademark dispute with Ogitani. A few weeks later, Legrand learned from Nakayama at Ogitani that the Japanese firm had registered the Lestra Design and Lestra Sport brands under its own name only to prevent

-----

[2] The Japanese use 3 different types of transcription, together with the occasional use of the Roman alphabet. In addition to Chinese ideograms (*Kanji*), *Katagana* is used for the exclusive transcription of foreign words and names. *Hiragana* is used for all other words not written in *Kanji*.

other Japanese competitors from doing so. Mekiès was not fully convinced, however, about the sincerity of this answer. One month later, he learned from Legrand that the legal department of the French Embassy in Tokyo was going to intervene in Lestra Design's favor. Finally, at the end of 1982, Legrand informed Léopold & Fils that Ogitani had agreed to give up the two trademarks in exchange for full reimbursement of the registration fees paid by Ogitani to the Tokyo Patent Office.

LOOKING FOR A NEW DISTRIBUTOR

During his short stay in Japan, Georges Mekiès was able to size up the many business possibilities offered by the Japanese market. Despite the bad experience with Ogitani, Claude Léopold and Georges Mekiès felt that Lestra Design had a major opportunity for business development in Japan. The Lestra Design trademark was now fully protected by Japanese law. In April 1983, Claude Léopold commissioned Legrand to search for and select a new Japanese partner. To shorten the traditional distribution chain and reduce costs (see Exhibits 3 and 4), Daniel Legrand decided to use his personal contacts at some of the major Japanese department stores. Department stores such as Mitsukoshi, Takashimaya, and Seibu, which sold luxurious products, enjoyed a reputation of considerable prestige in Japan. Moreover, department stores had branches all over Japan, which would enable Lestra Design to cover the whole Japanese market. Most of these department stores were already carrying competitive comforters from West Germany and France, including prestigious brands like Yves Saint Laurent and Pierre Cardin. Legrand thought that department stores would be the right outlet for Lestra Design to position its products in the upper segment of the Japanese comforter and eiderdown market. Legrand also went to various Japanese companies in the bed and furniture industry, as well as to several large trading companies such as Mitsui & Co., Mitsubishi Corporation, and C. Itoh. He also visited Mr. Inagawa, in charge of the Home and Interior Section of Kanematsu–Gosho, which used to import from Léopold & Fils. But Inagawa said that his company did not intend to import any more comforters from Lestra Design because its products were too highly priced.

The general reaction from potential Japanese buyers was that Lestra Design's colors (red, green, white) were not appropriate for the Japanese market. However, most of these buyers agreed that, with some modifications to accommodate the Japanese market, the "Made in France" image was a great asset for selling Lestra Design products in Japan. Comforters and eiderdowns under names like Yves Saint Laurent, Courrèges, or Pierre Cardin were being manufactured in Japan under license. They were being sold successfully because Japanese distributors and potential customers tended to view French interior textiles as another fashion product for which France was so famous.

To attract distributors, Legrand had advised Léopold & Fils to participate in the yearly Home Fashion Show held in Tokyo. However, Léopold and Mekiès had not responded to this suggestion. By June 1983, some potential distributors had already been identified, but most of them wanted to license the design and then manufacture in Japan rather than import the final products from France. However, Léopold clearly preferred to export directly from France and thus create more jobs for his own employees.

AKIRA ARAI

In July 1983, Legrand met with Akira Arai, president of Trans-Ec Co. Ltd., Japan, a firm specializing in importing and exporting down and feathers. Arai, 41 years old, had started his own company 6 years earlier after working for a large trading company since his graduation from Keio University.

Akira Arai was enthusiastic about French comforters and quilts and the Lestra Design products mainly because of the "Made in France" label and the prestige attached to French textiles. Like most of the potential distributors Legrand had talked to, Arai also perceived Lestra Design products as French

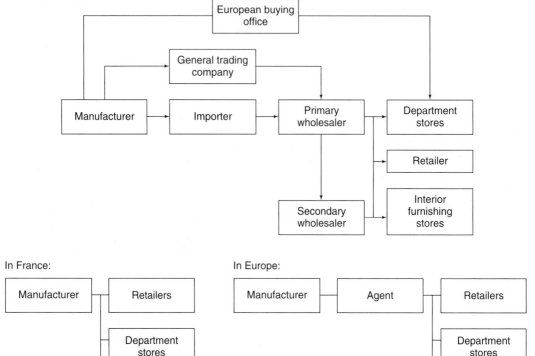

EXHIBIT 3   Comparative Distribution Channels for Comforters and Interior Textiles

fashion products similar to the comforters and quilts sold in Japan under prestigious names like Yves Saint Laurent, Cardin, or Courrèges. Some French fashion designers almost unknown in France had built a very strong reputation in Japan. Both Arai and Legrand felt that there was room in Japan for Lestra Design to achieve a strong brand recognition. Akira Arai had had some experience working with other French firms. In the past, he had imported down and feathers from Topiol, a French company that was an indirect competitor of Léopold & Fils. Legrand thought that Arai, who had already heard about Lestra Design, could be a potential partner for the French company. Arai knew the down and

feather industry thoroughly, and he had good connections in the complex distribution system of the Japanese comforter industry. Arai had also been highly recommended by Eiko Gunjima, in charge of fashion items at the Commercial Section of the French Embassy in Tokyo.

MEETING JAPANESE TASTES

In July 1983, Legrand and Arai met again in Roppongi, a fashionable district of Tokyo where Arai's office was located. Akira Arai explained that it would be difficult to sell Lestra Design comforters in Japan as they appeared

EXHIBIT 4   Short Note on Distribution in Japan

In the early 1980s, many foreign businesspeople were commenting that Japan's distribution system was lengthy and complex. Common criticism were that:
- Distribution channels are long and complex.
- Some distribution channels are controlled by large manufacturers.
- Some import agents prefer high margins and low volume, leading to high prices for imported goods.
- Costs of setting up one's own distribution are high and time consuming.

The Japanese Retail Market
The Japanese retail market was extremely fragmented. In 1984, independent stores accounted for 57% of retail sales in Japan compared to 3% in the United States and 5% in the United Kingdom. Japan had 1,350 shops for every 100,000 persons, twice as many as in most European countries.
According to a publication by the Japan External Trade Organization (JETRO),[5] the reasons for the fragmentation of retailing were closely related to Japan's social, cultural and economic environment:

- *Shopping patterns:* The typical Japanese housewife usually shops once a day. This custom is directly related to the size of the average home in Japan, which cannot accommodate large quantities of food.
- *Economics:* The price of land in Japan precludes establishing Western-style supermarkets. Most retail sales in Japan are still handled by small independent retailers who own the land on which the store is located. These family stores do not have to consider return on investment, as would a supermarket setting up a large-scale operation on the same site.
- *Regulation:* Opening a supermarket requires that a company make 73 applications for 26 separate approvals under 12 different laws.
- *Service:* Smaller stores are located near one's home and give housewives a place to socialize. Small retail stores also have longer business hours, which make it easier to shop at night. Independent retailers will also deliver orders for their customers and extend credit. The neighborhood shopping center near a subway or train station is a firmly established institution in Japan.

In the same publication, the JETRO also predicted that the number of small retail stores would continue to rise. In conclusion, the report stated that, given the Japanese preference for more convenience and service, the retailing sector in Japan was not necessarily a backward and underdeveloped system.

Implications
The implications of greater fragmentation in retailing were that either the manufacturer or the wholesaler must provide the services for small stores that they cannot provide for themselves. Some of the most important examples were finance, collection of bills, inventory, risk absorption, marketing and merchandising, and marketing feedback.

Trade Practices
- *Margins:* For comforters, the margin for the primary wholesaler (as a percentage of retail price) is approximately 15% and that of the secondary wholesaler about 10%.
- *Rebates:* Payments from the manufacturer to the wholesaler and from the wholesaler to the retailer on such factors as sales performance are a common practice in Japan.
- *Physical distribution:* Construction of delivery centers has been encouraged to modernize physical distribution. When a distribution center has been constructed, typically the merchandise flows directly from the manufacturer to the center and then to retail outlets, even though orders and other information may pass through wholesaler intermediaries.
- *Payment terms:* Payment periods run from 60 to 180 days after delivery of goods.
- *Consignment sales:* Sales on consignment are the rule in most Japanese industries. Retailers and wholesalers can reserve the right to return unsold goods to the manufacturer.
- *In-channel sales promotion:* Wholesalers engage in sales promotion activities similar to those of manufacturers.

[5] "Planning for Distribution in Japan," Jetro Marketing Series, Tokyo, 1983.

in the current Lestra Design catalogue. In his opinion, Lestra Design would have to adapt its products for the Japanese market. Arai proposed that Lestra Design send him a sample that would meet the market requirements (sizes, colors, fillings, and the like). In particular, he felt that the choice of colors was very important. Although Arai liked the innovative motifs and the colors of Lestra Design products, he told Legrand that Japanese customers would rarely buy a red, pink, or black comforter. Most comforters sold in Japan were in soft colors with many flowers in the design. Legrand emphasized that Lestra Design was introducing something really new to the Japanese market, but Arai insisted that most Japanese customers would prefer floral motifs on their comforters. Indeed, Legrand had noticed that almost all the Japanese comforters displayed in Tokyo stores had designs with floral motifs.

Second, Arai recommended that Lestra Design comforters be smaller than French comforters and should be paving blocked (quilted) to prevent the down from moving too freely inside the comforter. Arai noted all these requirements, including all the technical details needed to manufacture the comforter, so that Lestra Design could meet the Japanese trade expectations. Arai's product was quite different from those manufactured by Lestra Design, but Legrand was confident that the French company had the flexibility to adapt its products to the Japanese market. Arai also requested that Lestra Design deliver the sample within a month. Legrand had trouble explaining that Lestra Design, like most French firms, would be closed during the whole month of August for its summer holidays. Arai joked about the French taking so much holiday in the summer, but he agreed to wait until the beginning of September.

THE DUST PROBLEM

At the beginning of October 1983, Legrand went to Arai's office with the sample that he had just received from France. With almost no hesitation, Georges Mekiès had agreed to completely redesign a comforter to meet the Japanese customer's expectations. The fabric was printed with floral motifs, paving blocked and, exactly the requested size. Arai seemed pleased when he first saw the product. Then, as Legrand watched, Arai picked up the sample, carried it to the window, folded it under his arm, and slapped it vigorously with his hands. Both men were surprised to see a small cloud of white dust come from the comforter. Arai placed the sample on his desk, shook his head in disappointment and stated, "This is not a good product. If Lestra Design wants to compete against the big Japanese, German, and other French brands, the product must be perfect."

Legrand immediately telexed Arai's reaction to Georges Mekiès. In Arai's opinion, the problem had to do with washing the comforter. Although Mekiès was surprised by the result of Arai's test, he agreed to send a new sample very soon.

Just after New Year's Day, Legrand arrived at Arai's office with a new sample. Naoto Morimoto, in charge of the bedding and interior section of Katakura Kogyo,[3] a major textile trading company, had also been invited by Arai to examine the new sample. Naoto Morimoto was an old friend of Arai as well as a potential customer for Lestra Design products. After the ritual exchange of business cards between Legrand and Morimoto, Arai proceeded with the same test. Again, some dust came out although less than last time. Arai and Morimoto decided to open the comforter and look inside for an explanation to the problem. In their opinion, the feathers had not been washed in the same way as in Japan. Morimoto suspected that the chemicals used to wash the comforter were very different from those traditionally used in Japan. Moreover, Arai found that the comforter was filled with both gray and white down. He asked Legrand to recommend that Lestra Design use only new white down and no feathers at all, even very small ones. In front of Legrand, Akira Arai also demonstrated the same test with several Japanese and German comforters. No dust came out. As a result, Legrand and Arai decided to send Mekiès samples of both a Japanese and a German comforter so that he could test the dust problem himself. With the two samples, Arai attached a note emphasizing that "to compete successfully in Japan, Lestra Design products must be perfect, especially since the Japanese customer generally believes that textiles and fashion products from France are of high quality."

---

[3] In 1983, Katakura Kogyo had profits of US$5.5 million on sales of US$2.8 billion and employed 1,852 people.

At the end of March 1984, a third sample arrived in Tokyo. Mekiès had phoned Legrand beforehand, emphasizing that the utmost care had been given to this sample. But again the sample failed Arai's test. Legrand immediately phoned Mekiès to inform him of the situation. Arai was frustrated and, as he listened to Mekiès's voice on the telephone, it sounded as if Léopold & Fils were about to give up on the Japanese market. Georges Mekiès could not fully understand Arai's problem, because in his whole career at Lestra Design he had never heard any complaint about dust coming out Lestra Design comforters.

Legrand thought that the only way to save the Japanese business would be for Georges Mekiès to visit Tokyo. Legrand emphasized again the considerable opportunities offered by the Japanese market and thus convinced Mekiès and Jacques Papillault, Lestra Design's technical director, to board the next flight for Tokyo. Mekiès said they would only be able to stay 48 hours in order to meet with Arai.

GEORGE MEKIÈS'S TRIP TO TOKYO

A few days later, Mekiès and Papillault were in Tokyo. Arai claimed that he was genuinely interested in selling Lestra Design products in Japan, but he explained that to compete with existing Japanese comforters Lestra Design products had to meet the local standards of quality. Arai and Morimoto insisted that, since French textile products carried such a high image in Japan, they should be of the finest quality. Arai also stressed that only new white goose down should be used to fill the comforter. In an aside conversation with Daniel Legrand, Georges Mekiès asked if this requirement came directly from the final customer. Legrand replied that it did not seem to be the case. He himself had interviewed Japanese customers in down and comforter shops and had found that the average customer did not know about different qualities of down nor did customers seem to care whether the down was gray or white. Mekiès was therefore a bit surprised by Arai's requirement. In France, as in most European countries, the customer was usually only concerned about price and design. Legrand explained that Arai meant to use "new white goose down only" as a major selling point to market Lestra Design comforters as a high-quality product to the distributors and the retailers. From previous conversations with both wholesalers and retailers, Legrand explained that "new white goose down only" was indeed a reasonable expectation, consistent with the upper positioning of European products in Japan as well as with the high quality associated with French fashion items.

According to the trade, the "new white goose down only" argument would also justify the premium price charged by the retailers for Lestra Design products. Retail prices for Lestra Design products in Japan were expected to range from ¥60,000 to ¥110,000[4] and to be comparable to competitive high-quality products imported from West Germany. However, prices varied greatly, from a retail price index of 100 to 300, depending on the quality of the down and feathers and their mixture inside the comforter. In fact, some stores, both in Japan and Europe, allowed customers to choose the filling for their comforters and eiderdowns, a policy that gave the customer a lot of pricing flexibility.

Retail prices for Lestra Design in Japan were more than two times higher than in France. Such a difference could be explained by the typically lengthy distribution system in Japan, which contributed to inflating the price of imported goods (see Exhibit 4). For an ex-factory price index of 100, cost, insurance, and freight would add 4% and duties an additional 6%. Then Arai would price the goods so that he could gain a 12% markup on his selling price to Morimoto, who would receive a 10% commission from the smaller wholesalers. In turn, the small wholesalers would put a 20% markup on their selling price to the retailers, who would finally sell Lestra Design products at a price that would allow them a 40% to 60% markup. On a retail price basis, Lestra Design products in Japan would be about 30% to 50% more expensive than most local products of similar quality. Cheap models (either made lo-

---

[4] ¥240 = US$1 in 1985.

cally or imported from China) would sell for ¥40,000. On the other hand, Nishikawa, the market leader, offered many models in Lestra Design's price range, as well as a few prestigious models over ¥1,000,000. In selling competitive products from West Germany in Japan, the German tradition in making comforters was strongly emphasized. Advertising for these products would often carry the German flag, feature the "Made in Germany" label, and include a commercial slogan in German.

THE WASHING FORMULA

The conversation between Arai and Mekiès then moved to the dust problem. Arai explained that, in his view, the problem lay with the composition of the chemical formula used to wash the down. Arai had already made arrangements to visit a Japanese comforter and eiderdown manufacturer in the afternoon. To get this Japanese company to open their doors, he had simply told the plant manager that a group of French importers was interested in buying the company's products. As a result, the Japanese manufacturer was quite willing to let the French group visit the factory. Georges Mekiès and Daniel Legrand were impressed by the state-of-the-art equipment used by the Japanese firm. Jacques Papillault noticed that the Japanese were using microscopes and some very expensive machines that he had never seen in Europe to determine, for example, the greasiness of the down. Georges Mekiès was also amazed to observe three Japanese employees in white smocks separating down from small feathers with medical tweezers. According to Jacques Papillault, not a single Western manufacturer was as meticulous as this Japanese company. During the visit, Georges Mekiès also picked up some useful information about the chemical formula used by the Japanese manufacturer to wash the down and feathers.

The next day George Mekiès and Jacques Papillault flew back to France fully aware that much remained to be done to crack the Japan-ese market. Before leaving, Mekiès told Arai that this trip had been extremely useful and that Léopold & Fils would work hard to make a new sample that would meet the Japanese quality standards. Arai also promised Mekiès that he would try to get more information about the chemical formula used by the Japanese company they had visited.

NEW CHALLENGES

Two weeks later Arai sent Léopold & Fils some additional information on the chemical formula. Georges Mekiès then contacted a large French chemical company that immediately produced an identical formulation for Lestra Design. At the end of April, Arai told Legrand that Lestra Design should hurry with its new samples. Most wholesalers would be placing orders in May for late October delivery to the retail shops. Arai also indicated that Morimoto from Katakura Kogyo had already selected some designs and had basically agreed to order 200 comforters at the FOB price of FF1,200 each, provided that Lestra Design solved the dust problem.

In late May 1984, three new comforter samples arrived in Japan. Arai found them much better than the previous ones. However, he still felt that the dust problem was not completely solved. Arai and Morimoto decided to have the fabric inspected in the laboratories of the Japanese Textile Association in Osaka. They both explained to Daniel Legrand that the fabric used by Lestra Design did not have the same density of threads per square inch as most Japanese comforter fabrics had. Legrand reported this latest development to Georges Mekiès, who was obviously upset by this new complaint from the Japanese. Legrand was also worried that the time required to have the fabric inspected would further delay the manufacturing of the 200 comforters that Morimoto was planning to order. In the meantime, Lestra Design had been obliged to order the fabric with the printed design selected by Morimoto in order to get exclusivity from its French supplier.

GOKAI (Misunderstandings)

At the end of June 1984, Takeshi Kuroda, an executive from Katakura Kogyo who was on a business trip in the southern part of France, visited Mekiès and Léopold in Amboise. Mekiès had trouble communicating with the Japanese executive because of Kuroda's limited ability in English. However, Mekiès understood from Kuroda that Lestra Design had the green light to manufacture 200 comforters using the fabric selected by Morimoto. Mekiès communicated the good news to Legrand, who phoned Morimoto to thank him for the order. Morimoto was surprised by Legrand's call because he personally had not taken any steps to confirm the order. Morimoto had first wanted to have the results of the test being conducted in Osaka. Finally, in early July, the report from the Japanese Textile Association brought bad news for Lestra Design. The Japanese laboratories found that the density of Lestra Design's fabric was far below that of most Japanese comforter fabrics.

The test results confirmed the fears of Arai and Morimoto that the fabric problem created a major obstacle for selling Lestra Design comforters in Japan. Although the test could not legally prevent Lestra Design from selling on the Japanese market, Arai and Morimoto insisted that the French products had to be perfect to be sold in Japan. Thus, Naoto Morimoto told Daniel Legrand that he would not be able to proceed with importing the 200 comforters into Japan. Daniel Legrand tried to counter with the argument that the test was merely a nontariff barrier for Lestra Design products in Japan. However, Morimoto answered that Lestra Design had to meet the market requirements to succeed in Japan.

When Daniel Legrand phoned the Lestra Design office in Amboise, Georges Mekiès was very upset. As far as he knew, the Japanese were the only ones in the world to conduct this kind of investigation, which he believed was a nontariff barrier to prevent non-Japanese products from entering the Japanese market. Georges Mekiès's exasperation was increased because, following Kuroda's visit, the 200 comforters

for Katakura Kogyo had already been manufactured. Because the comforters had been made to fit Japanese specifications, they could only be sold in Japan. Legrand replied that he would explain the situation to Morimoto and that he would try to convince him to do something about it. During the following days, Legrand tried hard to persuade Naoto Morimoto to accept the order. It seemed to him that Kuroda was directly responsible for the misunderstanding. But Morimoto remained inflexible and said that he could not buy products inferior in quality to those sold by Japanese competitors.

During the latter half of 1984, little communication took place between the French and the Japanese. Claude Léopold and Georges Mekiès were upset by the attitude of the Japanese. On the Japanese side, Arai and Morimoto said that it was too late to meet with the distributors as most of their orders had already being placed in late July for the winter season. However, Daniel Legrand and Akira Arai had remained loosely in touch. At the end of February 1985, Arai said that he was still interested in importing Lestra Design products. Both Legrand and Arai were also convinced that, despite all the setbacks, there was still hope for Lestra Design to grasp a share of the huge Japanese market for comforters. Daniel Legrand had learned that Lestra Design's major French competitor had faced similar problems in Japan and had decided to give up the Japanese market. On the other hand, he knew that several German competitors were operating successfully in Japan.

In April 1985, Legrand took advantage of a business trip to France to visit Léopold and Mekiès in Amboise. He was aware that Lestra Design was making a successful start in the United States. In fact, Léopold was just back from an exhibition in New York where a major order had been placed. Legrand emphasized again the great potential of the Japanese market and the need to take a long-term view of this market. Legrand recognized that, although Japan was a tough market to crack, persistence would eventually pay off. Léopold said that he had already tried hard and confessed that he was still quite disappointed by the Japanese market. However, at the end of the meeting, Léopold said that he would consider one last try.

THE ALTERNATIVES

In early May 1985, Daniel Legrand again met with Akira Arai and Naoto Morimoto. Morimoto also mentioned that he would be interested in buying the original designs from Josette Léopold and then have the comforters manufactured in Japan under license. Claude Léopold was not keen about this idea. He knew that Yves Saint Laurent, Lanvin, and Courrèges comforters were manufactured this way in Japan. Léopold also knew that Lacoste shirts, although considered a universal product, had been completely adapted to suit the Japanese market. The colors, shape, and even the cotton material of Lacoste shirts sold in Japan were different from the Lacoste products sold in the rest of the world. Bernard Lacoste, the son of the famous tennis player and a personal friend of Claude Léopold, ran the Lacoste business around the world. A few months earlier, Léopold had heard from Lacoste himself that in the previous year the Lacoste company had had trouble with its Japanese licensee. Yves Gasquères, the French consultant in Tokyo who was monitoring Lacoste's operations in Japan, had discovered that the licensee had at one point in time "forgotten" to pay the full amount of royalties due to Lacoste in France. Léopold was therefore wondering if licensing would be the best solution.

Arai had also proposed that Lestra Design buy some Japanese fabric and manufacture the comforters in France. He argued that this would definitely solve the dust problem. Moreover, then Lestra Design products could still carry the "Made in France," label which was so appealing to Japanese customers.

Another alternative recommended to Mekiès was buying fabric for the comforters from West Germany, where textile standards were similar to the ones in Japan. Lestra Design could then print Josette Léopold's designs on the German cloth and still manufacture the comforters in France. Because the Japanese insisted on floral motives, Lestra Design could even buy fabric with floral prints in West Germany. Arai had found that many Japanese companies like Nishikawa (the leading comforter manufacturer in Japan) were already buying a lot of German fabric for comforters. However, to be granted the design exclusivity, Mekiès needed to buy a minimum amount of fabric, the equivalent of 300 comforters.

As he was reviewing these different alternatives for Lestra Design, Claude Léopold wondered if he should continue trying to gain a foothold in the Japanese market, or should he simply forget about Japan and focus more on Europe and the United States?

Delissa in Japan

"We can maintain our presence in Japan or we can pull out. . . ."

In the autumn of 1991, Bjorn Robertson, who had recently been named managing director of Agria, Sweden's leading dairy products cooperative, met with his team to review the international side of the business. The four men sat around a table piled high with thick reports, Nielsen audits, film storyboards, yogurt cups, and a mass of promotional material in Japanese. Agria's Delissa line of fresh dairy products was sold all over the world through franchise agreements. Several of these agreements were up for review, but the most urgent one was the agreement with Nikko of Japan.

"In the light of these results, there are several things we can do in Japan. We can maintain our presence and stay with our present franchisee, we can change our franchisee, or we can pull out. But, let's look first at how badly we are really doing in Japan." Bjorn Robertson, looked across the conference table at Peter Borg, Stefan Gustafsson, and Lars Karlsson, each of whom had been involved with Agria's Japanese business over the past few years.

Bjorn Robertson read out loud to the others a list of Agria's major foreign ventures featuring the Delissa yogurt brand: *"USA launch date 1977, market share = 12.5%; Germany launch 1980, market share = 14%; UK launch 1982, market share = 13.8%; France launch 1983, market share = 9.5%; Japan launch 1982, market share to-*
day = 2% to 3%." Robertson circled the figure with his marker and turned to look around at his team. "Under 3% after 10 years in the market! What happened?" he asked.

HISTORY

Agria was founded in 1967 when a group of Swedish dairy cooperatives decided to create a united organization that would develop and sell a line of fresh dairy products. The principal engineers of the organization were Rolf Andersen and Bo Ekman who had established the group's headquarters in Uppsala, near Stockholm. In 1970, after the individual cooperatives had been persuaded to drop their own trademarks, the Delissa line was launched. This was one of the few national lines of dairy products in Sweden. It comprised yogurts, desserts, fresh cheese, and fresh cream. In the two decades that followed, Agria's share rose from 3% to 25% of the Swedish fresh milk products market. Rolf Andersen's vision and the concerted efforts of 20,000 dairy farmer members of the cooperative had helped build Agria into a powerful national and international organization.

By 1991, more than 1.1 billion Delissa yogurts and desserts were being consumed per year worldwide. In fiscal year 1990, Delissa had sales of $1.6 billion and employed 4,400 people in and outside Sweden.

This case was prepared by Research Assistant Juliet Burdet-Taylor and Professor Dominique Turpin as a basis for class discussion rather than to illustrate either effective or ineffective handling of an administrative situation. All names and figures have been disguised. Copyright © 1992 by the International Management Development Institute (IMD), Lausanne, Switzerland. IMD retains all rights. Not to be used or reproduced without written permission from IMD, Lausanne, Switzerland.

Industrial franchising was rare in the 1970s, and Swedish dairy products firms did not usually invest money abroad. However, Ekman's idea of know-how transfer ventures, whereby a local licensee would manufacture yogurt using Swedish technology and then market and distribute the product using its own distribution network, had enabled Delissa to penetrate over 13 foreign markets with considerable success and with a minimal capital outlay. In contrast, Delissa's biggest competitor worldwide, BSN, a French food conglomerate marketing a yogurt line under the Danone brand name, had gone into foreign markets mainly by buying into or creating local companies or by forming regular joint ventures.

By the time Bjorn Robertson took over as European marketing director in 1985, the Delissa trademark—with the white cow symbol so familiar in Sweden—was known in many different countries worldwide. Delissa was very active in sponsoring sports events, and Bjorn Robertson, himself a keen cross-country skier and sailor, offered his personal support to Delissa's teams around the world.

When he reviewed the international business, Robertson had been surprised by the results of Agria's Japanese joint venture, which did not compare to those achieved in most foreign markets. Before calling together the international marketing team for a discussion, Robertson requested the files on Japan and spent some time studying the history of the alliance. He read:

Proposal for entry into the Japanese market

In early 1979, the decision was made to enter the Japanese market. Market feasibility research and a search for a suitable franchisee is underway, with an Agria team currently in Japan.

Objectives

The total yogurt market in Japan for 1980 is estimated at approximately 600 million cups (l00mn ml). The market for yogurt is expected to grow at an average of at least 8% p.a. in volume for the next 5 years. Our launch strategy would be based on an expected growth rate of 10% or 15% for the total market. We have set ourselves the goal of developing a high quality range of yogurts in Japan, of becoming well known with the Japanese consumer. We aim to reach a 5% market share in the first year and 10% share of market within three years of launch. We plan to cover the three main metropolitan areas, Tokyo, Osaka and Nagoya, within a two-year period, and the rest of the country within the next three years.

Robertson circled the 10% with a red pen. He understood that management would have hesitated to set too high a goal for market share compared to other countries since some executives felt that Japan was a difficult market to enter. But, in 1987, 6 years after the launch, the Japanese operation had not reached its 3-year target. In 1991, Delissa's share of the total yogurt market had fallen to 2%, without ever reaching 3%. Bjorn Robertson wrote a note to the Uppsala-based manager responsible for Far Eastern business stating that he felt Agria's record in Japan in no way reflected the type of success it had had elsewhere with Delissa. He began to wonder why Japan was so different.

The report continued with a brief overview of the Japanese yogurt market:

Consumption

Per capita consumption of yogurt in Japan is low compared to Scandinavian countries. It is estimated at around 5.3 cups per person per year in Japan, versus 110 in Sweden and 120 in Finland. Sales of yogurt in Japan are seasonal, with a peak period from March to July. The highest sales have been recorded in June, so the most ideal launch date would be at the end of February.

Types of yogurt available in Japan—1980

In Japan, yogurt sales may be loosely broken down into three major categories:

- Plain (39% of the market in volume): Called "plain" in Japan because the color is white, but it is really flavored with vanilla. Generally sold in 500 ml pure pack cups. Sugared or sometimes with a sugar bag attached.

- Flavored (45% of the market in volume): Differentiated from the above category by the presence of coloring and gelifiers. Not a wide range of varieties, mainly vanilla, strawberry, almond and citrus.

- Fruit (16% of the market in volume): Similar to the typical Swedish fruit yogurt but with more pulp than real fruit. Contains some coloring and flavoring.

Western-type yogurts also compete directly in the same price bracket with local desserts—like puddings and jellies—produced by Japanese competitors.

Competition

Three major Japanese manufacturers account for about half of the total real yogurt market:

Snow Brand Milk Products is the largest manufacturer of dairy products in Japan and produces drinking milk, cheeses, frozen foods, biochemicals and pharmaceuticals. Turnover in 1980 was ¥293.322 million *($1 = ¥254 in 1980)*.

Meiji Milk Products, Japan's second largest producer of dairy foods, particularly dried milk for babies, ice cream, cheese. Its alliance with the Bulgarian government helped start the yogurt boom in Japan. Turnover in 1980 was ¥410,674 million.

Morinaga Milk Industry, Japan's third largest milk products producer processes drinking milk, ice cream, instant coffee. It has a joint venture with Kraft US for cheeses. Turnover in 1980 was ¥250,783 million.

The share of these three producers has remained stable for years and is approximately: Yukijirushi (Snow Brand) 25%; Meiji 19%; Morinaga 10%.

The Japanese also consume a yogurt drink called "Yakult Honsha" which is often included in statistics on total yogurt consumption as it competes with normal yogurt. On a total market base for yogurts and yogurt drink, Yakult has 31%. Yakult drink is based on milk reconstituted from powder or fresh milk acidified with lactic acid and glucose. Yakult is not sold in shops, but through door-to-door sales and by groups of women who visit offices during the afternoon and sell the product directly to employees.

Along with some notes written in 1979 by Ole Bobek, Agria's director of international operations, Bjorn Robertson found a report on meetings held in Uppsala at which two members of Agria's negotiating team presented their findings to management.

Selecting a franchisee

We have just returned from our third visit to Japan where we once again held discussions with the agricultural cooperative, Nikko. Nikko is the country's second largest association of agricultural cooperatives; it is the Japanese equivalent of Agria. Nikko is a significant political force in Japan but not as strong as Zennoh, the National Federation of Agricultural Cooperatives which is negotiating with Sodima, one of our French competitors. Nikko is the price leader for various food products in Japan (milk, fruit juice, rice) and is active in lobbying on behalf of agricultural producers. Nikko is divided into two parts: manufacturing and distribution. It processes and distributes milk and dairy products, and it also distributes raw rice and vegetables.

We have seen several other candidates, but Nikko is the first one that seems prepared to join us. We believe that Nikko is the most appropriate distributor for Agria in Japan. Nikko is big and its credentials seem perfect for Agria, particularly since its strong supermarket distribution system for milk in the three main metropolitan areas is also ideally suited for yogurt. In Japan, 80% of yogurt is sold through supermarkets. We are, however, frustrated that, after prolonged discussions and several trips to Japan, Nikko has not yet signed an agreement with Agria. We sense that the management does want to go ahead but that they want to be absolutely sure before signing. We are anxious to get this project underway before Danone, Sodima or Chambourcy[1] enter Japan.

The same report also contained some general information on the Japanese consumer, which Bjorn Robertson found of interest:

Some background information on the Japanese consumer

Traditionally, Japan is not a dairy products consumer, although locally produced brands of yogurt are sold along with other milk-based items such as puddings and coffee cream.

Many aspects of life in Japan are miniaturized due to lack of space: 60% of the total population of about 120 million is concentrated on 3% of the surface of the islands. The rest of the land mass is mountainous. In Japan, 85% of the population live in towns of which over one third have more than half a million people. This urban density naturally affects lifestyle, tastes and habits. Restricted living space and lack of storage areas mean that most Japanese housewives must shop daily and consequently expect fresh milk products in the stores every day as they rarely purchase long-life foods or drinks. The country is fairly homogeneous as far as culture and the distribution of wealth [are] con-

---

[1] Chambourcy was a brand name for yogurt produced and distributed by Nestlé in various countries. Nestlé, with sales of $27 billion in 1990, was the world's largest food company; its headquarters were in Vevey (Switzerland).

cerned. Disposable income is high. The Japanese spend over 30% of their total household budget on food, making it by far the greatest single item, with clothing in second place (10%).

The market is not comparable to Scandinavia or to the US as far as the consumption of dairy products is concerned. There are young housewives purchasing yogurt today whose mothers barely knew of its existence and whose grandmothers would not even have kept milk in the house. At one time it was believed that the Japanese do not have the enzymes to digest milk and, only a generation ago, when children were given milk, it was more likely to be goat's milk than cow's milk. However, with the market evolving rapidly towards "Westernization," there is a general interest in American and European products, including yogurt.

Although consumption of yogurt per capita is still low in Japan at the moment, research shows that there is a high potential for growth. When we launch, correct positioning will be the key to Delissa's success as a new foreign brand. We will need to differentiate it from existing Japanese brands and go beyond the rather standardised "freshness" advertising theme.

Distribution

Traditionally, Japanese distribution methods have been complex; the chain tends to be many layered, making distribution costs high. Distribution of refrigerated products is slightly simpler than the distribution of dry goods because it is more direct.

The Japanese daily-purchase habit means that the delivery system adopted for Delissa must be fast and efficient. Our basic distribution goal would be to secure mass sales retailer distribution. Initially, items would be sold through existing sales outlets that sell Nikko's drinking milk, "Nikkodo." The milk-related products and dessert foods would be sold based on distribution to mass sales retailers. The objective would be to make efficient use of existing channels of distribution with daily delivery schedules and enjoy lower distribution costs for new products.

The Japanese retail market

The retail market is extremely fragmented with independent outlets accounting for 57% of sales (vs. 3% in the US). With 1,350 shops for every 100,000 people, Japan has twice as many outlets per capita as most European countries. Tradition, economics, government regulations and service demands affect the retail system in Japan. Housewives shop once a day on average and most select the smaller local stores, which keep longer hours, deliver orders, offer credit and provide a meeting place for shoppers. Opening a Western-style supermarket is expensive

and complicated, so most retailing remains in the hands of the small, independent, or family business.

Japan has three major metropolitan areas: Tokyo, Osaka and Nogaya, with a respective population of 11, 3, and 2 million inhabitants. Nikko's Nikkodo, with a 15% share of total, is the market leader ahead of the many other suppliers. Nikko feels the distribution chain used for Nokkodo milk would be ideal for yogurt. Each metropolitan area has a separate distribution system, each one with several depots and branches. For instance, Kanto (Great Tokyo)—the largest area with over 40 million people—has five Nikko depots and five Nikko branches.

Most of the physical distribution (drivers and delivery vans) is carried out by a subsidiary of Nikko with support from the wholesalers. The refrigerated milk vans have to be fairly small (less than 2 tons) so that they can drive down the narrow streets. The same routes are used for milk delivery, puddings and juices. Our initial strategy would be to accept Nikko's current milk distribution system as the basic system and, at the same time, adopt shifting distribution routes. Japan's complicated street identification system, whereby only numbers and no names are shown, makes great demands on the distribution system and the drivers.

The Franchise Contract

Bjorn Robertson opened another report written by Ole Bobek, who had headed up the Japan project right from the start and had been responsible for the early years of the joint venture and who left the company in 1985. This report contained all the details concerning the contract between Agria and Nikko. In November 1979, Nikko and Agria had signed an industrial franchise agreement permitting Nikko to manufacture and distribute Delissa products under license from Agria. The contract was Agria's standard Delissa franchisee agreement covering technology transfer associated with trademark exploitation. Agria was to provide manufacturing and product know-how, as well as marketing, technical, commercial and sales support. Agria would receive a royalty for every pot of yogurt sold. The Nikko cooperative would form a separate company for the distribution, marketing, and promotion of Delissa products. During the prelaunch phase, Per Bergman, senior area brand manager, would train the sales and marketing team, and Agria's technicians would supply know-how to the Japanese.

By 1980, a factory to produce Delissa yogurt, milk and dairy products had been constructed in Mijima, 60 miles northwest of Tokyo. Agria provided Nikko with advice on technology, machinery, tanks, fermentation processes, and the like. Equipment from the United States, Sweden, Germany and Japan was selected. A European-style Erka filling machine was installed that would fill two, four, or six cups at a time and was considered economical and fast.

Robertson opened another report by Bobek entitled "Delissa Japan—Prelaunch data." The report covered the market, positioning, advertising and media plan, minutes of the meetings with Nikko executives and the SRT International Advertising Agency, which would handle the launch, analysis of market research findings, and competitive analysis. Robertson closed the file and thought about the Japanese market. During the planning phase before the launch, everything had looked so promising. In its usual methodical fashion, Agria had prepared its traditional launch campaign to ensure that the new Agria/Nikko venture ensured a successful entry into Japan for Delissa. "Why then," wondered Bjorn Robertson, "were sales so low after 9 years of business?" Robertson picked up the telephone and called Rolf Andersen, one of Agria's founders and former chairman of the company. Although retired, Andersen still took an active interest in the business he had created. The next day, Bjorn Robertson and Rolf Andersen had lunch together.

The older man listened to the new managing director talking about his responsibilities, the Swedish headquarters, foreign licensees, new products in the pipeline, and so on. Over coffee, Robertson broached the subject of the Japanese joint venture, expressing some surprise that Delissa was so slow in taking off. Rolf Andersen nodded his understanding and lit his pipe:

Yes, it has been disappointing. I remember those early meetings before we signed up with Nikko. Our team was very frustrated with the negotiations. Bobek made several trips. and had endless meetings with the Japanese, but things still dragged on. We had so much good foreign business by the time we decided to enter Japan, I guess we thought we could just walk in wherever we wanted. Our Taiwanese franchise business had really taken off, and I think we assumed that Japan would do likewise. Then, despite the fact that we knew the Japanese were different, Wisenborn—our international marketing manager—and Bobek still believed that they were doing something wrong. They had done a very conscientious job, yet they blamed themselves for the delays. I told them to be patient . . . to remember that Asians have different customs and are likely to need some time before making up their minds. Our guys went to enormous pains to collect data. I remember when they returned from a second or third trip to Japan with a mass of information, media costs, distribution data, socioeconomic breakdowns, a detailed assessment of the competitive situation, positioning statements, etc., . . . but no signed contract. [*Rolf Andersen chuckled as he spoke.*] Of course, Nikko finally signed, but we never were sure what they really thought about us . . . or what they really expected from the deal.

Bjorn Robertson was listening intently, so Rolf Andersen continued:

The whole story was interesting. When you enter a market like Japan, you are on your own. If you don't speak the language, you can't find your way around. So you become totally dependent on the locals and your partner. I must say that, in this respect, the Japanese are extremely helpful. But let's face it, the cultural gap is wide. Another fascinating aspect was the rite of passage. In Japan, as in most Asian countries, you feel you are observing a kind of ritual, their ritual. This can destabilize the solid Viking manager. Of course, they were probably thinking that we have our rituals, too. On top of that, the Nikko people were particularly reserved and, of course, few of them spoke anything but Japanese.

There was a lot of tension during those first months, partly because France's two major brands of yogurt, Yoplait and Danone, were actually in the process of entering the Japanese market, confirming a fear that had been on Bobek's mind during most of the negotiation period.

Rolf Andersen tapped his pipe on the ashtray and smiled at Robertson, "If its any consolation to you, Bjorn, the other two international brands are not doing any better than we are in Japan today."

What about These Other European Competitors?

The discussion with Rolf Andersen had been stimulating and Robertson, anxious to get to the bottom of the story, decided to speak to Peter Borg, a young Danish manager who had replaced Bergman and had been supervising Agria's business in Japan for several years. Robertson asked Borg for his opinion on why Danone and Yoplait were apparently not doing any better than Delissa in Japan. Borg said:

I can explain how these two brands were handled in Japan, but I don't know whether this will throw any light on the matter as far as their performance is concerned. First, Sodima, the French dairy firm, whose Yoplait line is sold through franchise agreements all over the world, took a similar approach to ours. In 1981, Yoplait tied up with Zennoh, the National Federation of Agricultural Cooperative Association, the equivalent of Sodima in Japan. Zennoh is huge and politically very powerful. Its total sales are double those of Nikko. Yoplait probably has about 3% of the total Japanese yogurt market, which is of course a lot less than their usual 15% to 20% share in foreign markets. However, Zennoh had no previous experience in marketing yogurt.

Danone took a different approach. The company signed an agreement with a Japanese partner, Ajinomoto. Their joint venture, Ajinomoto–Danone Co. Ltd, is run by a French expatriate together with several Japanese directors. A prominent French banker based in Tokyo is also on the board. As you know, Ajinomoto is the largest integrated food processor in Japan, with sales of about $3 billion. About 45% of the company's business is in amino acids, 20% in fats, and 15% in oil. Ajinomoto has a very successful joint venture with General Foods for Maxwell House, the instant coffee. However, Ajinomoto had had no experience at all in dealing with fresh dairy products before entering this joint venture with Danone. So, for both of the Japanese partners—Ajinomoto and Zennoh—this business was completely new and was probably part of a diversification move. I heard that the Danone joint venture had a tough time at the beginning. They had to build their dairy products distribution network from scratch. By the way, I also heard from several sources that it was distribution problems that

discouraged Nestlé from pursuing a plan to reintroduce its Chambourcy yogurt line in Japan. Japanese distribution costs are very high compared to those in Western countries. I suspect that the Danone–Ajinomoto joint venture probably only just managed to break even last year.

"Thanks, Peter," Robertson said. "It's a fascinating story. By the way, I hear that you just got married . . . to a Japanese girl. Congratulations, lucky chap!"

After his discussion with Peter Borg, Bjorn Robertson returned to his Delissa–Nikko files. Delissa's early Japanese history intrigued him.

Entry Strategy

The SRT International Advertising Agency helped develop Delissa's entry into what was called the "new milk-related products" market. Agria and Nikko had approved a substantial advertising and sales promotion budget. The agency confirmed that, as Nikko was already big in the "drinking milk" market, it was a good idea to move into the processed milk or "eating milk" field, a rapidly growing segment where added value was high.

Bjorn Robertson studied the advertising agency's prelaunch rationale, which emphasized the strategy proposed for Delissa. The campaign, which had been translated from Japanese into English, proposed:

Agria will saturate the market with the Delissa brand and establish it as distinct from competitive products. The concept "natural dairy food is good to taste" is proposed as the basic message for product planning, distribution, and advertising. Nikko needs to distinguish its products from those of early-entry dairy producers and other competitors by stressing that its yoghurt is "new and natural and quite different from any other yogurts."

The core target group has been defined as families with babies. Housewives have been identified as the principal purchasers. However, the product will be consumed by a wider age bracket from young children to high school students.

The advertising and point-of-sale message will address housewives, particularly younger ones. In Japan, the tendency is for younger housewives to shop in convenience stores (small supermarkets), while the older women prefer traditional supermarkets. Housewives are becoming more and more insistent that all types of food be absolutely fresh, which means that Delissa should be perceived as coming directly from the manufacturer that very day. We feel that the "freshness" concept, which has been the main selling point of the whole Nikko line, will capture the consumers' interest as well as clearly differentiate Delissa from other brands. It is essential that the ads be attractive and stand out strikingly from the others, because Nikko is a newcomer in this competitive market. Delissa should be positioned as a luxurious mass communication product.

The SRT also proposed that, as Japanese housewives were becoming more diet conscious, it might be advisable to mention the dietary value of Delissa in the launch rationale. Agria preferred to stress the idea that Delissa was a Swedish product being made in Japan under license from Agria Co, Uppsala. They felt that this idea would appeal to Japanese housewives, who associated Sweden with healthy food and sophisticated taste. The primary messages to be conveyed would, therefore, be "healthy products direct from the farm" and "sophisticated taste from Sweden." Although, it was agreed that being good for health and beauty could be another argument in Delissa's favor, this approach would not help differentiate Delissa from other brands, all of which project a similar image.

To reinforce the product's image and increase brand awareness, the SRT proposed that specific visual and verbal messages be used throughout the promotional campaign. A Swedish girl in typical folk costume would be shown with a dairy farm in the background. In the words of the agency, "We feel that using this scene as an eyecatcher will successfully create a warm-hearted image of naturalness, simplicity, friendliness, and fanciful taste for the product coming from Sweden." This image would be accompanied by the text: *"Refreshing nature of Delissa Swedish yogurt; it's so fresh when it's made at the farm."*
Also included in the SRT proposal:

Advertising
To maximize the advertising effort with the budget available, the campaign should be run intensively over a short period of time rather than

successively throughout the year. TV ads will be used [because] they have an immediate impact and make a strong impression through frequent repetition. The TV message will then be reinforced in the press. The budget will be comparable to the one used for launching Delissa in the US.

Pricing
Pricing should follow the top brands, (Yukijirushi, Meiji, and Morinaga) so as to reflect a high-class image, yet the price should be affordable to the housewife. The price sensitivity analysis conducted last month showed that the Delissa could be priced at 15% above competitive products.

Launch

In January 1982, Delissa's product line was presented to distributors prior to launch in Tokyo, Osaka, and Nagoya. Three different types of yogurt were selected for simultaneous launch:

- Plain (packs of two and four)
- Plain with sugar (packs of two and four)
- flavored with vanilla, strawberry, and pineapple (packs of two). (Fruit yogurt, Delissa's most successful offering at home and in other foreign markets, would be launched a year or two afterward.)

All three types were to be sold in 120-ml cups. A major prelaunch promotional campaign was scheduled for the month before launch with strong TV, newspaper, and magazine support, as well as street shows, in-store promotions, and test trials in and outside retail stores. On March 1, 1982, Delissa was launched in Tokyo, and on May 1, in Osaka and Nagoya.

1985: DELISSA AFTER THREE YEARS IN JAPAN

Three years after its launch, Delissa, with 2% of the Japanese yogurt market, was at a fraction of target. Concerned by the product's slow progress in Japan, Agria formed a special task force to investigate Delissa's situation and to continue monitoring the Japanese market on a regular basis. The results of the team's research now lay on Robertson's desk. The task force from Uppsala included Stefan Gustafsson (responsible for marketing questions), Per Bergman (sales and distribution), and Peter Borg (who was studying the whole operation as well as training the Nikko sales force). The team spent long periods in Tokyo carrying out regular audits of the Delissa–Nikko operations, analyzing and monitoring the Japanese market, and generating lengthy reports as they did so, most of which Robertson was in the process of studying.

Borg, eager to excel on his new assignment, sent back his first report to headquarters:

Distribution/Ordering system

I feel that the distribution of Delissa is not satisfactory and should be improved. The ordering system seems overcomplicated and slow, and may very well be the cause of serious delivery bottlenecks. Whereas stores order milk and juice by telephone, Delissa products are ordered on forms using [the] following procedure:

Day 1 a.m.: Each salesman sent an order to his depot.

Day 1 p.m.: Each depot's orders went to the Yokohama depot.

Day 2 a.m.: The Yokohama depot transmitted the order to the factory.

Day 2 p.m.: Yogurt was produced at Nikko Milk Processing.

Day 3: Delivery to each depot.

Day 4: Delivery to stores.

Gustafsson agrees with me that the delivery procedure is too long for fresh food products, particularly as the date on the yogurt cup is so important to the Japanese customer. The way we operate now, the yogurt arrives in the sales outlet two or three days after production. Ideally, the time should be shortened to only one day. We realize that, traditionally, Japanese distribution is much more complex and multilayered than in the West. In addition, Tokyo and Osaka, which are among the largest cities in the world, have no street names. So, a whole system of primary, secondary and sometimes tertiary wholesalers is used to serve supermarkets and retailers. And, since the smaller outlets have very little storage space, wholesalers often have to visit them more than once a day.

I wonder if Nikko is seriously behind Delissa. At present, there are 80 Nikko salesmen selling Delissa, but they only seem to devote about 5% of their time to the brand, preferring to push other products. Although this is apparently not an uncommon situation in many countries, in Japan it is typical—as the high costs there prohibit having a separate sales force for each line.

Borg's report continued:

Advertising

Since we launched Delissa in 1982, the advertising has not been successful. I'm wondering how well we pretested our launch campaign and follow-up. The agency seems very keen on Delissa as a product, but I wonder if our advertising messages are not too cluttered. Results of recent consumer research surveys showed only 4% unaided awareness and only 16% of interviewees had any recall at all; 55% of respondents did not know what our TV commercials were trying to say.

A survey by the Oka Market Research Bureau on advertising effectiveness indicated that we should stress the fact that Delissa tastes good . . . delicious. Agria's position maintains that according to the Oka survey, the consumer believes that all brands taste good, which means the message will not differentiate Delissa. Research findings pointed out that Delissa has a strong "fashionable" image. Perhaps this advantage could be stressed to differentiate Delissa from other yogurts in the next TV commercial.

DELISSA IN JAPAN: SITUATION IN AND LEADING UP TO 1991

In spite of all the careful prelaunch preparation, 10 years after its launch in Japan, Delissa had only 3% of the total yogurt market in 1991. Although Agria executives knew the importance of taking a long-term view of their business in Japan, Agria's management in Sweden agreed that these results had been far below expectations.

A serious setback for Agria had been the discovery of Nikko's limited distribution network outside the major metropolitan areas. When Agria proposed to start selling Delissa in small cities, towns, and rural areas, as had been agreed to in the launch plan, it turned out that Nikko's coverage was very thin in many of these regions. In the heat of the planning for the regional launch, had there been a misunderstanding on Nikko's range?

Robertson continued to leaf through Agria's survey of Japanese business, reading extracts as he turned the pages. A despondent Borg had written:

1988: The Japanese market is very tough and competition very strong. Consumers' brand loyalty seems low. But the market is large with high potential—particularly amongst the younger population—if only we could reach it. Nikko has the size and manpower to meet the challenge and to increase its penetration substantially by 1990. However, Nikko's Delissa organization needs strengthening quickly. Lack of a real marketing function in Nikko is a great handicap in a market as competitive as Japan.

Distribution is one of our most serious problems. Distribution costs are extremely high in Japan, and Delissa's are excessive (27% of sales in 1988 vs. 19% for the competition). Comparing distribution costs to production costs and to the average unit selling price to distributors of ¥54.86 ($1 = ¥145 in 1988), it is obvious that we cannot make money on the whole Delissa range in Japan. Clearly, these costs in Japan must be reduced while improving coverage of existing stores.

Distribution levels of about 40% are still too low, which is certainly one of the major contributing factors for Delissa's poor performance. Nikko's weak distribution network outside the metropolitan areas is causing us serious problems.

1989: Delissa's strategy in Japan is being redefined (once more). The Swedish image will be dropped from the advertising since a consumer survey has shown that some consumers believed that "fresh from the farm" meant that the yogurt was directly imported from Sweden—which certainly put its freshness into question! Ads will now show happy blond children eating yogurt. . . .

Over time, the product line has grown significantly and a line of puddings has recently been added. Nikko asks us for new products every 3 months and blames their unsatisfactory results on our limited line.

By 1991, plain yogurt should represent almost half of Delissa's Japanese sales and account for about 43% of the total Japanese market. The plain segment has grown by almost 50% in the past 3 years. However, we feel that our real strength should be in the fruit yogurt segment, which has increased by about 25% since 1988 and should have about 23% of the market by next year. So far, Delissa's results in fruit yogurt have been disap-

pointing. On the other hand, a new segment—yogurt with jelly—has been selling well: 1.2 million cups 3 months after introduction. Custard and chocolate pudding sales have been disappointing, while plain yogurt drink sales have been very good.

Bjorn Robertson came across a more recent memo written by Stefan Gustafsson:

Mid-year results

Sales as of mid-year 1991 are below forecast, and we are unlikely to meet our objective of 55 million 120-ml cups for 1992. At the present rate of sales, we should reach just over 42 million cups by year end.

Stores covered

In 1991, Delissa yogurt was sold mainly in what Nielsen defined as large and super large stores. Delissa products were sold in about 71% of the total stores selling Nikko dairy products. We think that about 7,000 stores are covered in the Greater Tokyo area, but we have found that Nikko has been somewhat unreliable on retailer information.

Product returns

The number of Delissa products returned to us is very high compared to other countries. The average return rate from April '90 to March '91 was 5.06% vs. almost 0% in Scandinavia and the international standard of 2% to 3%. The average shelf life of yogurt in Japan is 14 days. Does the high level of returns stem from the Japanese consumer's perception of when a product is too old to buy (i.e., 5 to 6 days)? The level of return varies greatly with the type of product: "healthy mix" and fruit yogurt have the highest rate, while plain and yogurt with jelly have the lowest return rate.

Media planning

Oka's latest results suggest that Delissa's primary target should be young people between 13 and 24 and its secondary target, children. Budget limitations demand that money be spent on advertising addressed to actual consumers (children), rather than in trying to reach the purchasers (mothers) as well.

However, during our recent visit to Japan, we found that Nikko and the agency were running TV spots that were intended for young people and children *from 11:15 to 12:15 at night*. We pointed out that far more consumers would be reached by showing the spots earlier in the evening. With our limited budget, careful media planning is essential. Nikko probably was trying to reach both the consumer and distributor with these late night spots. Why else would they run spots at midnight when the real target group is children? Another question is whether TV spots are really what we need.

Looking at some figures on TV advertising rates in Japan, Bjorn Robertson found that the price of a 15-second spot in the Tokyo area was between ¥750,000 and ¥1,500,000 in 1990 depending on the time it was run, which seemed expensive compared to European rates (*$1 = ¥144 in 1991*).

Robertson continued to peruse the report prepared by Stefan Gustafsson:

Positioning

I'm seriously wondering whom we are trying to reach in Japan and with what product. The Nielsen and Oka research findings show that plain yogurt makes up the largest segment in Japan, with flavored and fruit in second and third positions. It is therefore recommended that regular advertising should concentrate on plain yogurt, with periodic spots for the second two categories. However, according to Nikko, the company makes only a marginal profit on plain yogurt; thus they feel it would be preferable to advertise fruit yogurt.

In light of this particular situation and the results of the Oka studies, we suggest that plain yogurt be advertised using the existing "brand image" commercial (building up the cow on the screen) and to develop a new commercial for fruit yogurt based on the "fashion concept." We also believe that, if plain yogurt is clearly differentiated through its advertising, sales will improve, production costs will drop, and Nikko will start making money on the product.

Last year, to help us understand where we may have gone wrong with our positioning and promotional activities, which have certainly changed rather often, we requested the Oka agency to conduct a survey using in-home personal interviews with a structured questionnaire; 394 respondents in the Keihin (Tokyo–Yokohama) metropolitan area were interviewed between April 11 and April 27, 1990. Some of the key findings are as follows:

Brand awareness

In terms of unaided brand awareness, Meiji Bulgaria yogurt had the highest level with 27% of all respondents recalling Bulgaria first and 47% mentioning the brand without any aid. Morinaga Bifidus was in second place. These two leading brands were followed by Yoplait and Danone with 4% unaided awareness and 14% and 16% recall at any time. For Delissa, the unaided awareness was 3% and 16% for recall. In a photo-aided test, Delissa plain yogurt was

recognized by 71% of all respondents with a score closer to Bulgaria. In the case of fruit yogurt, 78% recognized Delissa, which had the same level as Bulgaria. Awareness of Delissa was higher than Bifidus and Danone but lower than Yoplait. In the case of yogurt drink, 99% of all respondents were aware of Yakult Joy and 44% recognized Delissa (close to Bulgaria).

Interestingly, the brand image of Meiji Bulgaria was the highest of the plain yogurt brands in terms of all attributes except for "fashionability." At the lower end of the scale (after Bulgaria, Bifidus, and Natulait), Delissa was close to Danone and Yoplait in brand image. Delissa was considered less desirable than the top three, especially as far as the following characteristics were concerned: taste, availability in stores for daily shoppers, frequency of price discounting, reliability of manufacturer, good for health. Delissa's image was "fashionable." [*"Is this good or bad?" Gustafsson had scribbled on the report. "Should this be our new platform??? We've tried everything else!"*]

Advertising awareness

In the advertising awareness test, half of all respondents reported that they had not noticed advertising for any brand of yogurt during the past 6 months. Of those who had, top ranking went to Bifidus with 43%, Bulgaria 41%, and Delissa in third place with 36%. Danone was fifth with 28% and Yoplait sixth with 26%. Respondents noticed ads for Delissa mainly on TV (94%), followed by in-store promotion (6%), newspapers (4%), and magazines (4%); 65% of the people who noticed Delissa ads could recall something about the contents of the current ads, and 9% recalled previous ads. However, when asked to describe the message of the Delissa ads, 55% of the respondents replied that they did not know what the company was trying to say.

Consumption

Seventy-seven percent of all respondents had consumed plain yogurt within the past month: 28% Bulgaria, 15% Bifidus, 5% Yoplait, 4% Danone, and 3% Delissa. The number of respondents who had at least tried Delissa was low (22%) vs. 66% for Bulgaria, the best scoring brand. In the plain category, Delissa was third of the brands mainly consumed by respondents. Bulgaria was number 1 and Bifidus number 2. In the fruit segment (under yogurt consumed within the past month), Delissa was in third place (5%) after Yoplait (10%) and Bulgaria (8%). Danone was in fourth place with 3%. [*"So where do we go from here?" Gustafsson had scrawled across the bottom of the page.*]

Robertson closed the file on Gustafson's question.

Where Do We Go from Here?

Bjorn Robertson looked around the table at the other members of his team and asked, "What happened? We still haven't reached 3% after 10 years in Japan!" Bjorn knew that Borg, Gustafsson, and Karlsson all had different opinions as to why Delissa had performed badly, and each manager had his own ideas on what kind of action should be taken.

Stefan Gustafsson had spent months at Nikko, visiting retailers with members of the sales force, instigating new market research surveys, and supervising the whole Nikko–Delissa team. Language problems had made this experience a frustrating one for Gustafsson, who had felt cut off from the rest of the Nikko staff in the office. He had been given a small desk in a huge room along with over 100 people with whom he could barely communicate. The Japanese politeness grated on him after a while and, because no one spoke more than a few words of anything but Japanese, Gustafsson had felt lonely and isolated. He had come to believe that Nikko was not committed to the development of the Delissa brand in Japan. He also felt that the joint venture's market share expectations had been absurd and was convinced the franchisee misrepresented the situation to Agria. He felt that Nikko was using the Delissa brand name as a public relations gimmick to build itself an international image. When he spoke, Stefan's tone was almost aggressive:

I don't know what to think, Bjorn. I know I don't understand our Japanese friends and I was never quite sure that I trusted them, either. They had a disconcerting way of taking control right from the start. It's that extreme politeness. . . . You can't argue with them, and then suddenly they're in command. I remember when the Nikko managers visited us here in Sweden . . . a busload of them smiling and bowing their way around the plant, and we were bowing and smiling back. This is how they get their way and this is why we had such mediocre results in Japan. Agria never controlled the business. Our distribution setup is a perfect example. We could never really know what was going on out there because language problems forced us to count on them. The same with our positioning and our advertising. . . . "We're selling taste; no, we're selling health; no, we're selling fashion . . . to babies, to grandmas, to mothers." We thought we were in control but we weren't, and half the time we were doing the opposite of what we really wanted.

Bjorn, the Japanese will kill Delissa once they've mastered the Swedish technology. Then, they'll develop their own brand. Get out of the joint venture agreement with Nikko, Bjorn. I'd say, get of Japan altogether.

Robertson next turned his attention toward Peter Borg, who had a different view of the problem. He felt that the Nikko people, trained to sell the drinking milk line, lacked specific knowledge about the eating milk or yogurt business. Borg, who had also taken over sales training in Japan after replacing Bergman, had made several trips a year to train the Nikko people both in marketing the Delissa brand and in improving distribution and sales. He had also trained a marketing manager. Borg had worked closely with the Japanese at the Tokyo headquarters.

Borg said, "I understand how Stefan feels . . . frustrated and let down, but have we given these people enough time?"

"Enough time!" said Gustafsson, laughing. "We've been there for over 10 years and, if you look at our target, we have failed miserably. My question is "have they given *us* enough support?" Turning to Stefan, Borg continued:

I know how you feel, Stefan, but is 10 years *that* long? When the Japanese go into business abroad, they stay there until they get a hold on the market, however long it takes. They persevere. They seem to do things at their own speed and so much more calmly than we do. I agree on the question of autonomy. It's their very lack of Western aggressiveness that enables them to get the upper hand. Their apparent humility is disarming. But, Bjorn, should we really leave the joint venture now? When I first went to Japan and found fault with everything we were doing, I blamed the whole thing on Nikko. After nearly 6 years of visits, I think I have learned something. We cannot approach these people on our terms or judge them as we would judge ourselves. We cannot understand them . . . any more than they can understand us. To me, the whole point is not to even *try* and understand them. We have to accept them and then to trust. If we can't, then perhaps we should leave. But, Bjorn, I don't think we should give up the Japanese market so easily. As Stefan says, they can be excruciatingly polite. In fact, I wonder—beneath that politeness—what they think of us.

Lars Karlsson, the product manager, had been looking after the Japanese market only a short time, having been recruited by Agria from Procter & Gamble 18 months earlier.

Bjorn, for me, perhaps the most serious defect in our Japanese operation has been the poor communication between the partners and a mass of conflicting data. I came into the project late and was amazed at the quantity of research and reporting that had taken place over the last 10 years by everyone concerned. Many of the reports I saw were contradictory and confusing. As well, the frequent turnover of managers responsible for Japan has interrupted the continuity of the project. And, after all the research we did, has anyone really used the findings constructively? How much is our fault? And another thing, have we been putting enough resources into Japan?

There are so many paradoxes. The Japanese seem to be so keen on the idea of having things Western, yet the successful yogurts in Japan have been the ones with that distinctive Japanese flavor. Have we disregarded what this means? Agria people believe that we have a superior product and that the type of yogurt made by our Japanese competitors does not really taste so good. How can this be true when we look at the market shares of the top Japanese producers? It obviously tastes good to the Japanese. Can we really change their preferences? Or should we perhaps look at our flavor?

It's interesting. Yoplait/Zennoh and Ajinomoto/Danone's joint ventures could be encountering similar problems to ours. Neither has more than 3% of the Japanese yogurt market and they have the same flavor that we do.

Bjorn Robertson listened to the views and arguments of his team with interest. Soon, he would have to make a decision. Almost 10 years after launching Delissa with Nikko, should Agria cancel its contract and find another distributor? Or should the company renew the arrangement with Nikko and continue trying to gain market share? Or should Agria admit defeat and withdraw from Japan completely? Or was it, in fact, defeat at all? Robertson was glad that he had gathered his team together to discuss Delissa's future. Their thoughts had given him new insights on the Japanese venture.

5

The Pan-European Challenge

THE EUROPEAN COMMUNITY

The economic and political integration of Western Europe has been a process that began more than 30 years ago with the formation of the European Economic Community (EEC). From its original six member states (France, Germany, Belgium, Netherlands, Luxembourg, and Italy) the EEC expanded in the 1970s to include the United Kingdom, Denmark, Ireland, and more recently Greece, Portugal, and Spain (see Table 1). The EEC expanded from what was largely a free trade association, where products could move from one country to another without any duties, to a much more inclusive community of 12 nations. A major move toward integration was made in 1985 with the adoption of the Single European Market Act. This act is better known as the 1992 Initiative. To signal the passing from a primarily economic association to economic and political integration, the name was changed to the European Community (EC); it is headqaurtered in Brussels, Belgium.

The Single European Market Act of 1985 envisioned that by January 1, 1993, all internal barriers to free trade, both for products and services, would be removed. The implementation of the Single European Market Act was envisioned sector by sector, or industry by industry, and triggered the enactment of close to 300 directives. These directives attacked both general barriers to trade, as well as those that were primarily present in one industry. Among others, local governments would in the future be prohibited from favoring local suppliers. Purchases of a certain amount would be registered so that firms from all European countries could compete on equal terms. Standards in many industries would be harmonized to a common European level. Regulation in certain industries was to reach a common level, in some industries leading to considerable deregulation. This was particularly the case in such areas as telecommunications, air transport, banking, and insurance.

The overall impact of the Single European Market Act led to a substantial change in business practices among European firms and created the drive toward pan-European strategies. For manufacturing companies, important changes were the abolition of visible custom barriers between EC countries, and the long truck lines awaiting custom clearance disappeared for traffic among EC countries. The resulting improvement in transport efficiency through the gain of speed in delivery made many manufacturers rethink their supply concepts. More and more companies were able to deliver over larger distances without any reduction in service levels. The result was fewer plants with pan-European charters, for example, the responsibility to supply a limited part of the entire product line across Europe.

For service firms, the Single European Market Act brought added freedom. In sectors such as banking and insurance, the licensing practices were changed. In the future, it would be sufficient to be licensed once in a company's home market and then to be able to enter all other markets in the EC. As a result, a bank licensed to do business in Italy would automatically gain the right to open branches throughout the EC. This prospective freedom of movement caused a flurry of mergers in service industries and several cross-border mergers in banking and insurance. Pan-European strategies suddenly became common in many sectors where previously companies managed on a country-by-country basis.

TABLE 1 Western European Markets (EEA)

Country	Population (millions)	GDP (US$ billions)	GDP per capita (US$)
EC Members			
Germany	80.4	1,331.4	16,700
France	57.3	1,033.7	18,300
Italy	57.9	965.0	16,700
United Kingdom	57.8	915.5	15,900
Belgium	10.0	171.8	17,300
Netherlands	15.1	249.6	16,600
Luxembourg	0.4	7.8	20,200
Denmark	5.2	91.1	17,700
Ireland	3.5	39.2	11,200
Portugal	10.4	87.3	8,400
Greece	10.0	77.6	7,730
Spain	39.1	487.5	12,400
EFTA Members			
Austria	7.9	164.1	20,985
Finland	5.0	80.6	16,200
Norway	4.3	72.9	17,100
Sweden	8.6	147.6	17,200

Source: Central Intelligence Agency, *World Factbook 1992.*

The free movement of people was another aspect of the Single European Market Act. Although citizens of EC member states had long had the automatic right to work permits throughout the EC, such movements were restricted through the licensing procedures for professionals. Under the Single European Market Act, members of such professions as law, medicine, and accounting would obtain the right to exercise their professions through the EC as long as they were licensed once in one member country. This would allow law firms, accounting firms, and medical doctors to reside and compete anywhere in the EC.

THE EFTA COUNTRIES

In the 1950s, several European nations formed the European Free Trade Association, or EFTA, as a response to the foundation of the EEC (see Table 1). EFTA members were not prepared to go as far as the EEC with respect to political coordination. Today consisting of largely smaller European countries (Finland, Sweden, Austria, Switzerland, and Norway), the EFTA nations' 40 million people represent some of the highest per capita income in the world. In the 1970s, several original members of EFTA joined the EEC/EC, the United Kingdom, Portugal, and Denmark among them. The EFTA nations have also achieved largely duty free trade among themselves. Due to a long-term arrangement with EC countries, there is also largely duty free trade between EFTA and EC countries. It is also expected that several of the EFTA countries will apply for EC membership in the future, thus leaving the status of this associations in doubt.

CREATION OF THE EUROPEAN ECONOMIC AREA

To extend the free trade practices of both the EC and EFTA to all Western European nations, members of both associations created the European Economic Area (EEA). This act, accepted by all EFTA nations except Switzerland, will essentially extend the key features of the Single European Market Act to a combined EC and EFTA territory and create a virtually free market with 400 million people. Originally expected to be in force by mid-1993, the adoption of this act was delayed due to the decision of the Swiss voters not to join. The EEA will become effective sometime in 1994, however, and will, as an economic act, be of equal importance than some of the other, later EC initiatives. In the long term, the EEA might include other European countries not previously members of either EC or EFTA, such as Hungary, Poland, and the Czech Republic, bringing the total population covered to close to 500 million.

THE MAASTRICHT TREATY

Concluded in December of 1991 in the Dutch city of Maastricht, this treaty was to take the EC beyond the Single European Market Act (1992) initiative and its largely economic impact into the reality of a true political union (European Political Union, EPU). EC member states aimed at passing increasing decision-making power from the member nations to the EC. The Maastricht Treaty consisted of several related parts. Among the most widely known ones is the European Monetary Union (EMU) that aims at using the *ecu* as the common currency and the establishment of a European-type central bank.

The actual implications of the Maastricht Treaty can only be adopted if all 12 member states ratify it. Ratification ran into serious difficulties following a first refusal by the Danish voters, followed by close votes in France and other countries. With the difficulties experienced in 1993 by the European Monetary System (EMS), which was created to limit the fluctuations of European currencies within a narrow band, many observers doubt whether any of the goals of the Maastricht Treaty, and in particular the EMU, will be achieved in the foreseeable future. Although the news on the EC tends to be dominated by the difficulties incurred with implementing the Maastricht Treaty and its subsidiary provisions, businesses in Europe have benefited from the progress on the Single European Market Act (Europe 1992 Initiative). Coupled with the implementation of the EEA, which combines the free movement of goods and services across all Europe, substantial forward momentum along an economic integration path remains. While many political leaders remain committed to the Maastricht Treaty goals, most executives are happy to implement changes and pursue opportunities created through the other initiatives that are largely of an economic type. Whether Europe needs further political integration (Maastricht) to fully realize its potential along with economic integration (EEA, Single European Market Act) is a question currently debated across Europe. The Maastricht Treaty has been accepted late in 1993 and the name of the EC has been changed to European Union (EU).

EUROPEAN INTEGRATION AND THE IMPACT ON MARKETING STRATEGIES

As we can see from the preceding description of the European environment, the various moves toward integration have created a vast economic area where individual firms will find it much easier to enter various markets. This opportunity is not limited to European companies alone. U.S. and Japanese companies, by locating somewhere in the EC or EEA, can gain substantially the same benefits. Originals fears, often voiced in the United States and Japan under the label of "Fortress Europe," have proved to be overrated and in fact are much less frequently mentioned now.

What is of interest to us here, however, is the impact of all these trends on the marketing strategies of firms who want to be active in Europe or, better, across Europe. In line with this concern, we will examine the merits of pan-European marketing strategies and the key issues faced by companies who want to compete in Europe.

The Euro Consumer

The entire focus of the European integration movement was to create a single, large market that would not have any barriers to the freedom of marketing products or services. While this assures, among other things, that a Dutch physician may practice medicine freely in Spain, it does not and is not intended to force Spanish citizens to avail themselves of the services of a Dutch physician in Spain. Customers remain free to choose to buy from whom they want as long as this is done in a free and open market. As a result, the playing field has been evened out, but preferences among customers will persist. First, language barriers remain across Europe, and income levels are still substantially different comparing, for example, Greece and Germany. Preferences of European customers, both for business products and consumer products, have not been brought to the same level through the Single European Market Act. As many firms have found out, the Euro consumer, or Euro customer, is still an elusive concept in many industries. This does not mean that differences have not narrowed. Similarities among consumers in Europe have in fact grown over the decades, but the narrowing of differences is not equal to their elimination. It still needs to be established industry by industry to what extent pan-European customers exist and if their presence is sufficient to engage into pan-European marketing strategies.

Pan-European Marketing Strategies

Pan-European marketing strategies are chosen by firms who sense that the pan-European logic in their business or industry is sufficiently strong to warrant a change from the normally practiced country-by-country or multilocal approach. Just when a firm should shift its strategy is hotly debated. It has become clear, however, that an increasing number of firms are moving in this direction.

A firm is using a pan-European strategy if most of the marketing strategy elements, such as target market/segment, positioning, and other parts of the marketing mix, tend to be employed in a coordinated way across Europe. This practice differs substantially from the previously favored approach of designing marketing strategies that fit each individual market or country.

A firm is adopting a pan-European product strategy if substantial similarities exist in the design of a product or service, including such elements as branding. A Euro product is generally referred to when the product features are similar. When this is combined with a common brand name and similar positioning, marketers speak of a Euro brand. Euro branding has been favored in circumstances where customers travel frequently across countries and thus could be exposed to only one brand rather than many. Barriers to Euro products or brands are typically differences in product standards or user practices. Although some of the legal requirements for different standards are slowly being eliminated, different consumption habits may call for different products for years to come.

Pan-European advertising is a concept that has rapidly gained acceptance in the mid-1980s. With the liberalization of the European media, particularly TV and radio, pan-European TV channels have been formed that permit the delivery of pan-European advertising strategies. Companies soon realized, however, that to utilize this new opportunity they needed pan-European brands. Different product histories and different experience levels on the part of European customers often limit the opportunity for pan-European advertising. And the many languages spoken require some adaptation for what are otherwise standardized campaigns.

Pan-European Distribution

Probably in no other area are the differences across countries as substantial as in the area of distribution. For both industrial and consumer products, distribution remains a locally driven parameter. Distribution patterns vary greatly from one European country to another. This is particularly true for the retail distribution, for which the penetration of modern mass distribution is most advanced in the United Kingdom, but much less so in countries such as Greece, Spain, or Italy. With pressure for efficiency rising, some distribution firms have begun to branch out beyond their local markets. However, there are still few truly pan-European distribution operations. The spread of mass distribution similar to that in the United States is advancing, and some very successful U.S. firms such as Toys-R-Us have made great inroads, but many legal obstacles remain in the areas of store opening hours, permits, building sites, and others. The initiative under the umbrella of the Single European Market Act is intended to remove some of these barriers. However, their implementation will take several more years. This will leave the distribution aspect as the most locally driven parameter of a pan-European marketing mix.

For industrial products, the manufacturers themselves have typically built marketing subsidiaries in key markets. These sales subsidiaries function as a pan-European distribution system, but they are not viable to other companies. For firms using independent distributors, it remains difficult to find distributors with an international or even pan-European coverage.

Pricing has been one of the most affected marketing mix elements in the new European context. Pan-European pricing policies have been adopted by firms who could no longer enforce significant price differences. This has been caused by the right of middlemen to source across Europe. A drugstore in the Netherlands, for example, is legally allowed to purchase a certain drug in France if the wholesale price there is lower. These practices have made companies monitor their prices across Europe carefully to avoid large price discrepancies. But pan-European pricing strategies are more likely to be found for standardized Euro products, whereas companies marketing differentiated products have maintained a greater amount of pricing freedom.

Conclusions

As we have seen, significant changes have moved the European marketing setting into a direction where the use of pan-European marketing strategies is more and more common. International firms would do well to capitalize on this European transformation and to develop integrated programs where appropriate. The following cases will allow the reader to develop some practice in applying pan-European marketing concepts. Nokia Data, a case on a Finnish computer company, raises the issue of when, or for whom, pan-European marketing strategies might be more appropriate. Pharma Swede Gastirup takes us into the pharmaceutical industry and forces the adaptation of the marketing strategy, particularly pricing, to the new Single European Market Act. Finally, Alto Chemicals is a case series in which the challenge of implementing new marketing strategies across independent local sales organizations is demonstrated.

Nokia Data

Early in 1989, the top management of Nokia Data was mapping the key elements of the firm's strategy for growth and international expansion through the mid-1990s. In the previous year, the Finnish computer company had acquired the Data Systems Division of Sweden's LM Ericsson as a first step toward becoming a major player in the European market for information technology. However, despite the acquisition, less than a quarter of Nokia Data's $1.2 billion sales was generated outside the Nordic market,[1] where it now held the leading position. Management intended to improve the company's spotty international presence by aggressively expanding into the large but also highly competitive markets in the rest of Europe.

A cornerstone of Nokia Data's European growth strategy was what management referred to as a "multidomestic" approach. Management believed that in the fast maturing European market for computers, the key to competitive advantage lay in customer orientation achieved through a strong local identity and domestically tailored marketing programs in each European country. Thus, local hardware and software customization, local branding, local marketing, and local sales and support services constituted the main ele-

ments of Nokia Data's multidomestic approach.

Top executives were keenly aware that their planned approach went counter to industry practices, which were increasingly emphasizing pan-European integration and marketing. In fact, some Nokia managers had expressed doubts regarding the wisdom of the multidomestic approach.

According to Kalle Isokallio, president of Nokia Data:

We have a different view of the industry than what one reads in the papers. Our industry is no longer high growth or high tech. Both sales and technology are maturing. In this competitive market, we can't compete with majors like IBM or Siemens in volume or new technology. We don't have the resources. Where we can outperform them is by being closer to the computer buyer who prefers to buy from a domestic supplier. In every country where we compete, therefore, we want to be considered as one of the top domestic vendors. Pan-European identity and integration don't make sense for us. We are too small for that.

THE NOKIA GROUP

Nokia was founded in 1865 in the village of Nokia, Finland, as a timber and paper company. In the subsequent 100 years, Nokia grew and diversified into tires, power transmission, radio, telecommunications, electronics, and

---

[1] The Nordic market consisted of the three Scandinavian countries (Sweden, Norway, and Denmark) plus Finland.

This case was prepared by Research Associate Robert C. Howard, under the supervision of Professor Kamran Kashani, as a basis for class discussion rather than to illustrate either effective or ineffective handling of a business situation. Copyright © 1989 by IMEDE, Lausanne, Switzerland. The International Institute for Managment Development (IMD), resulting from the merger between IMEDE, Lausanne, and IMI, Geneva, acquires and retains all rights. Not to be used or reproduced without written permission from IMD, Lausanne, Switzerland.

computer technology. In 1988, the Nokia Group of companies had sales of $5,500 million, earned a net profit of $215 million, and spent 5% of net sales on research and development. With its 44,000 employees, Nokia conducted operations in 32 countries, 17 of which had manufacturing facilities. By 1988, the Nokia Group of companies was Finland's largest publicly traded industrial enterprise. In addition to Helsinki, Nokia shares were listed on the stock exchanges in Stockholm, London, Paris, and Frankfurt. (Refer to Exhibit 1 for information on the Nokia Group of companies.)

Nokia Information Systems (NIS)

Nokia's experience with computers dated from 1962, the year when Nokia Electronics was formed to capitalize on the company's recent purchase of its first mainframe. At this time, Nokia implemented a time-sharing system with outside companies to handle bookkeeping and other data-processing activities. In the late 1960s, Nokia began serving as a sales agent for Honeywell, marketing its complete product line of mainframes, terminals, and printers to the Finnish market. During this period, Nokia management combined their increasing knowledge of hardware with their data-processing know-how from time-sharing. In the early 1970s, Nokia developed, manufactured, and sold its own minicomputer.

Throughout the 1970s, the Honeywell product line represented a main source of revenue at Nokia Electronics. However, in 1977, prompted by the growth of its customer base in the banking and retailing sectors, Nokia formed a separate department for its own products. In 1981, Nokia expanded its product offering further with its first personal computer, the Mikro Mikko 1. In 1985, Nokia Electronics was split into four divisions: Information Systems, Telecommunications, Mobile Telephones, and Consumer Electronics.

As of 1987, the Honeywell line accounted for 40% of Nokia Information System's revenues in Finland. Honeywell's role was limited to manufacturing, performed in the United States, Italy, or Scotland, and to providing operating system software. Aside from adding its own terminals to Honeywell's computers, Nokia was responsible for all applications software and postsales services. In 1987, Nokia Information Systems enjoyed the leading market share in Finland, where it generated 75% of its total sales.

Nokia Data

With limited growth opportunities in the small Finnish market, Nokia management began searching for an acquisition candidate within the Nordic countries. In 1988, Nokia Information Systems purchased the Data Systems unit of the Ericsson Group in Stockholm and merged the two operations to form Nokia Data. Data Systems produced and marketed a range of minicomputers, personal computers, telephone exchanges, and printers throughout Europe in addition to Hong Kong and Australia. Aside from keeping sales offices in North America and other overseas markets, the Ericsson Group retained a 20% share ownership in Nokia Data. Nokia, on the other hand, was able to strengthen its share of the Nordic countries market and gained the opportunity to expand into Germany, France,

EXHIBIT 1   The Nokia Group OF Companies: Group Sales ($ millions)

Industry Segment	1988	1987	1986
Electronics			
Information systems	1,170[a]	459	336
Telecommunications	359	364	197
Mobile telephone	271	214	178
Consumer electronics	1,432	678	441
Cables and Machinery			
Cables	557	529	438
Machinery	255	188	163
Electrical wholesaling	245	180	75
Paper, Power, and Chemicals			
Paper	628	589	447
Chemicals	130	110	81
Rubber and Floorings			
Rubber products	342	337	271
Floorings	75	64	51
Group total[a]	5,237	3,500	2,519

Source: Company records.

[a] Less interdivision sales and sales between industry segments.

Britain, and a number of other European markets. Management believed that increased geographic coverage translated into greater credibility among Nokia's customers and helped ensure the company's survival in the Nordic countries at a time of industry consolidation. By the end of 1988, with sales of $1.2 billion, Nokia Data was the largest computer company in the Nordic countries. The firm employed 8,500 employees and had subsidiaries in 10 European countries and a European installed base of over 700,000 terminals and personal computers. (*Refer to Exhibit 2 for the Nokia Data reporting structure.*)

THE INFORMATION TECHNOLOGY INDUSTRY

In its broadest sense, information technology (IT) was defined as the industry that combined the data processing and storage power of computers with the distance-transmission capabilities of telecommunications. The industry included all types of computers, word processors, printers, plotters, disk drives, telephones, telephone networks, public databases, and related software. Virtually all organizations used these products. In Western Europe, the manufacturing, finance, retail, and public sectors accounted for the largest expenditures. In 1987, the worldwide market for IT was valued at $407 billion, with volume distributed heavily among three geographic markets: North America, 38%; Europe, 26%; and Japan, 30%. For 1989, total industry sales were forecast to reach $505 billion.

Nokia's Data Business

In the vast information technology field, Nokia Data management defined its core

EXHIBIT 2 Nokia Data: Partial Organization Chart *Source:* Company records.

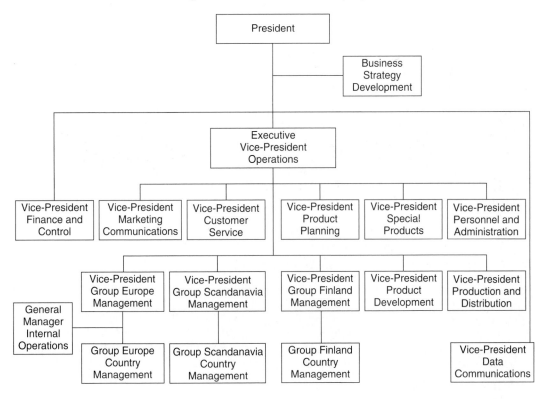

business as the sector of the computer industry that focused on terminals, personal computers, and related networks. While the total European computer industry in 1987 was valued at $86 billion, management estimated its industry sector accounted for $20 to $22 billion.

Nokia Data's product offering included terminals, personal computers, minicomputers, local area networks (hardware connected to share and exchange information among a group of users), and the related communication links for connecting different brands and classes of computers. In addition to hardware, Nokia Data provided application software and services tailored to meet the needs of its five primary customer segments: retailing, banking and insurance, manufacturing, government, and general business. Typical examples of general business applications included materials administration, purchasing, order handling, invoicing, database management, word processing, graphics, and spreadsheets. Across Europe, the five segments in which Nokia Data competed were forecast to grow between 7% and 10% per year through the early 1990s.

Markets and Competition

In Europe, Nokia Data competed directly and indirectly with a large number of firms. (*Exhibit 3 shows the top 25 manufacturers in the European data-processing market, ranked by their total volume of business in the region.*) Nokia Data's management believed that such rankings were misleading because not all firms competed in the market sector defined as terminals, personal computers, networks, and related products and services. Instead, to delineate the competition, management used the diagram *shown in Exhibit 4*, which clustered industry participants around four product/system zones: terminals, personal computers, local area networks, and systems. The four zones differed in their volume potential and product/system configuration. (*Refer to Exhibit 5 for a summary of Nokia Data's key competitors and their product offerings along the four zones.*)

Terminals

The European terminal market, consisting of keyboards and screens, represented approximately 6% of the European sector in which Nokia Data competed and was valued at $2.2 billion. Terminals had no data-processing power of their own and, hence, had to be connected to a host computer. Sales were divided between add-on terminals (90% to 95%), where customers expanded an existing system by adding new terminals, and upgrades (5% to 10%), where customers substituted new terminals for old. The terminal market was contested for by mainframe and minicomputer suppliers, such as IBM and DEC, which were able to sell their own terminals on the strength of their computers, and by a large number of component suppliers. Among these were Memorex Telex, of U.S. origin and SEL of Germany, which made terminals compatible with existing computers, as well as disk drives, cassettes, and other computer accessories. Across Europe, Nokia Data management considered IBM, Memorex Telex and Olivetti as their primary competitors in the terminal market.

Typical customers for terminals included large organizations, such as banks and insurance agencies, that processed data with a large central computer and a score of dispersed terminals. Customers purchasing terminals from component suppliers, instead of the large computer companies, cited price as an important factor. More recently, ergonomics had become a criterion because it was believed to contribute to improved employee comfort and productivity. Since the terminal market was primarily an add-on market, functions performed for the customer were installation and, when necessary, after-sales repair.

According to Nokia Data management, keys to success in the terminal market were compatibility with hardware from the major computer companies, competitive pricing, and credibility as a terminal supplier. Credibility, a sales manager clarified, meant a supplier was known for dependable products and was large enough to survive any industry shakeout.

In unit sales, the terminal market was pro-

EXHIBIT 3 The 25 Largest Computer Companies Competing in Europe

1987 Rank	Company	Origin	Total Revenue ($ million, 1987)	European Revenue ($ million, 1987)	Europe as % of Total	Estimated Revenues from Nokia Data's Industry Sector[a]	Major European Markets
1	IBM	USA	50,485.7	18,332.5	36	3,520	F, G, I, UK
2	Siemens	Germany	5,703.0	4,961.6	87	357	G
3	Olivetti	Italy	4,637.2	3,802.5	82	1,041	I, G, F
4	Digital (DEC)	USA	10,391.3	3,533.0	34	73	F, G, I, UK
5	Nixdorf	Germany	2,821.5	2,652.2	94	266	G, F, UK
6	Groupe Bull	France	3,007.5	2,345.8	78	30	F, SP, UK
7	Unisys	USA	8,742.0	2,272.9	26	28	F, SW
8	Philips	Netherlands	2,601.6	2,055.2	79	271	NL, G, B, L
9	Hewlett–Packard	USA	5,000.0	1,800.0	36	0	F, G, I, UK
10	STC	UK	2,123.9	1,720.4	81	40	UK
11	NCR Corp.	USA	5,075.7	1,583.6	31	144	G, F, UK, NL
12	IM Ericsson[b]	Sweden	1,511.6	1,284.9	85	—	S, G, DK
13	Alcatel NV	France	2,052.1	1,272.3	62	229	F
14	Inspectorate	Switzerland	1,225.0	1,033.0	84	0	SW
15	Société Générale	France	970.1	970.1	100	0	F
16	Atlantic Computers	UK	959.7	892.7	93	0	UK
17	Honeywell Bull	USA	2,059.0	885.4	43	21	F, SP, I, UK
18	Memorex Intl.	Netherlands	1,041.1	832.9	80	54	G, NL
19	Wang Laboratories	USA	3,045.7	822.3	27	49	F, G, I, UK
20	Mannesmann AG	Germany	686.0	617.0	90	90	G
21	Apple Computer	USA	3,041.2	547.4	18	204	F, S
22	Cap Gemini Sogeti	France	682.3	545.8	80	0	F
23	Econocon Intl.	Netherlands	674.3	525.9	78	0	NL
24	Amstrad plc	UK	533.0	501.0	94	250	UK, F, SP
25	Amdahl Corp.	USA	1,505.2	493.1	33	0	F, G, I, UK

Source: Datamation, company records.

[a] Nokia Data's industry sector is defined as terminals, personal computers, LANs, and vertical systems installed in the company's five end-user segments.

[b] Figures are for year-end 1987, prior to Nokia Information System's acquisition of the Ericsson Data Systems Division. Following the acquisition by Nokia Data in 1988, parts of the company were sold off.

Country codes: F, France; G, Germany; I, Italy; UK, United Kingdom; SP, Spain; NL, Netherlands; S, Sweden; SW, Switzerland; B, Belgium; L, Luxembourg; DK, Denmark.

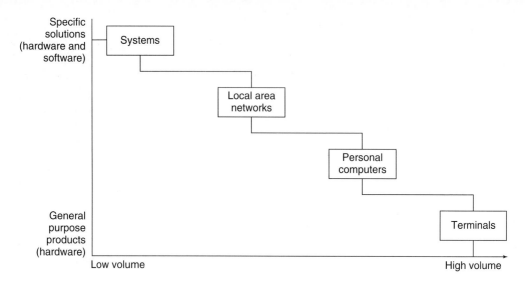

Notes:

All terminals and personal computers contained a keyboard plus a video screen.

Terminals had no data-processing ability of their own, were connected to a host computer, either a minicomputer or a mainframe, and were used primarily for entering, retrieving, or manipulating data.

Personal computers had their own data-processing capabilities, were used primarily on a stand-alone basis, but could also be connected to other computers.

A loca area network or LAN was a connection of terminals and/or personal computers that allowed communication among users in the same network.

A system was a set of hardware to which tailor-made software had been added.

EXHIBIT 4 Nokia Data's Industry Sector: Product/Service Zones *Source:* Company records.

jected to remain stagnant through the early 1990s and decline thereafter. In 1989, the market was becoming increasingly competitive. The average terminal price in Europe had declined by about 8% in recent months.

Personal Computers

In 1988, the European personal computer market was valued at $11 billion and expected to reach $18 billion by 1993. Competitors in this zone were well-known personal computer manufacturers such as IBM, Olivetti, Siemens, Amstrad, Apple, and Compaq. These firms were further classified by Nokia Data management according to their origin and historic customer base. More specifically, IBM, Siemens, and Olivetti, for example, had begun with and enjoyed established reputations in the business community and were described by

Nokia Data management as having an "institutional" market background. On the other hand, Amstrad, Apple, and Compaq, a few among a large number of companies, were originally associated with the mass market and said by management to have a "consumer" background.

From 1984 to 1987, the share of all personal computers sold by the institutional group in Europe had declined from 45% to 35%, with the balance of sales accounted for by the consumer group. Nokia Data considered that it had a more institutional than consumer background.

Regardless of their original customer base, by the late 1980s, competitors from both groups offered stand-alone personal computers direct to large accounts and, via retail outlets, to the medium-sized and small business and consumer markets. Typically, larger ac-

EXHIBIT 5 Nokia Data's Main Competitors

Company/Product	Systems[a]	LANs	Personal Computers	Terminals
IBM	All	×	×	×
Siemens	M, G, GB, I	×	×	×
Olivetti	B, R, BG,	×	×	×
Digital (DEC)		×		×
Nixdorf	All	×		×
Bull	GB, M	×	×	×
Unisys	GB, M	×	×	×
Philips	B, I, M, GB	×	×	×
STC	GB, M	×		×
NCR	B, R	×	×	×
Alcatel				×
Memorex				×
Wang	GB	×	×	×
Mannesmann	All	×	×	
Apple	GB	×	×	
Amstrad				
Compaq		×	×	
Commodore			×	

Source: Company management.

[a] Nokia Data management defined systems competitors as those offering solutions in the company's five end-user segments. Yet, because the management viewed the competition in terms of industry standards, proprietary systems, and horizontal product offering, a number of the companies listed in Exhibit 3 were not seen as direct competitors.

Systems code: B, banking; I, insurance; R, retail; M, manufacturing; G, government; GB, general business.

counts relied on the manufacturer for installation and after-sales services. Smaller accounts as well as individual buyers relied on the manufacturer's dealer or repair network for help, a process that was considered less reliable.

According to Goran Hermannson, a marketing manager in Sweden, to succeed in marketing personal computers to large accounts, a hardware supplier had to be known for reliable products and perceived by the customer as large enough to survive the computer industry's eventual consolidation. Companies from the institutional group had an advantage because they already enjoyed a reputation as suppliers of mainframes and minicomputers. More recently, compatibility with hardware from multiple vendors had become an important factor for supplying personal computers to large accounts. Major institutional companies such as IBM, which had traditionally employed its own proprietary systems, were now facing increasing pressure to abandon these in favor of industry standards and multiple vendor compatibility.

Nokia Data management believed that to succeed in the mass market, on the other hand, a supplier needed low manufacturing cost, extensive retail distribution, and a favorable price/performance image in the eyes of the customer. Examples of such companies included Amstrad, Commodore, and Compaq.

Local Area Networks

Local area networks (LANs) were a collection of computers, printers, cables, and other communications links that allowed a network of users to process data and communicate with one another.

In addition to hardware, LANs were equipped with operating systems software, applications software, and sophisticated LAN management software that allocated data processing among the computers in a network. As a concept in computing, LANs were relatively new to the industry, represented $670 million of the $20 to $22 billion segment in which Nokia Data competed, and were expected to grow 20% to 30% per annum through the middle 1990s. Although LANs could include mainframes and minicomputers, they were built primarily using personal computers. One advantage of LANs was their attractive cost–performance ratio. An independent estimate showed that it cost less than $10,000 per employee to set up a network of personal computers versus $12,000 for a seat at a minicomputer and $14,000 at a mainframe. In addition to lower hardware costs, networks eliminated the inefficiencies of multiple training staffs, multiple software packages, and data transmission costs.

Typical customers in the LAN segment, according to Goran Hermansson, were companies or departments with fewer than 100 personal computer users. He explained that it was technically easier to implement LAN solutions in smaller companies than in ones with hundreds of personal computers. In addition, he believed that the LAN technology was less popular with central data processing management in larger companies because it allowed individual departments to decide on their own systems independently.

Due to the complexity associated with the design, installation, and maintenance of a LAN, services accounted for a large portion of the purchase price. In addition, customers were keenly aware of the importance of vendor support in the early phases of a LAN's installation. In the words of one Nokia Data customer, it was important to have "someone to shoot" if something went wrong.

According to Nokia Data management, to be successful as a LAN supplier, a company had to enjoy the same qualifications as a personal computer vendor, that is, reliable products, hardware compatibility in a multivendor environment, and customer-perceived longevity. In addition, it had to have the technical know-how to act as a systems integrator, connecting products from one or many vendors. Most important, a LAN supplier had to be willing to service a network that contained products from vendors other than itself and guarantee against a network failure.

Because LANs were built primarily with personal computers, competitors came from both the institutional and consumer groups. In the institutional group, Nokia Data's largest competitor in Europe was IBM, although companies such as Olivetti and Philips were strong in their local markets. The largest competitor in the consumer group was Compaq.

Systems

At Nokia Data, a system was defined as a set of hardware and software products tailored to meet a specific need within an industry or industry segment. A system could consist of terminals sold with tailor-made software utilizing a client's existing mainframe or minicomputer. Alternatively, a system could be based on LAN products, complemented by customized software. In 1988, the European systems business was estimated to be $7 billion and projected to grow 10% to 15% annually through the early 1990s.

As with the personal computer market, systems competitors were categorized by Nokia Data management into institutional and consumer groups. The distinguishing feature between these groups, according to a Nokia Data sales executive, was knowledge about their customers' industries. He explained that companies like IBM and Siemens had accumulated a vast base of experience in industries such as insurance, banking, and manufacturing for which centralized data processing, using mainframes and terminals, had been practiced for over two decades. On the other hand, newcomers such as Compaq and Amstrad, with a consumer background, relied more on the industry knowledge of third parties, including value-added resellers (VARs), to compete in the systems market (VARs are discussed later).

Systems customers were typically large organizations that sought to decentralize their data-processing activities to a department or work group level. Decentralized data processing was attractive because it eliminated the users' dependence on a single computer, particularly important in organizations such as banks, for which a computer breakdown might force shutdown of operations.

Leif Lindfors, a sales manager for Sweden, believed that, as in the LAN market, success in systems required reliable hardware and software. However, he explained, the most important requirement for success in systems was to have a sales force with industry-specific knowledge, assisted by a technical support staff capable of developing customized software. Nokia Data management identified its primary systems competitor as IBM, followed by other institutional companies such as Unisys, Siemens, Olivetti, Nixdorf, and Philips.

Industry Trends

Industry observers, as well as Nokia Data executives, believed several trends were influencing the level and nature of competition in the European data-processing market. Among these trends were slowing growth, improved price–performance ratio of hardware, growth of decentralized computing, emergence of industry standards, proliferation of VARs, and the anticipated European integration toward a single market after 1992.

Slowing Growth

In the late 1980s, the overall growth in the European computer industry was slowing down to single digits. As of 1988, annual growth had declined for the first time below 10%, and some analysts were predicting only 6% yearly growth through 1992. Mainframes and minicomputers had experienced the biggest decline in growth rates as customers shifted to lower-cost computing alternatives such as personal computers and LANs. In fact, analysts expected mainframe and minicomputer sales to grow at only 8% and 3%, respectively, into the early 1990s. Demand for personal computers, however, was expected to remain strong, with 10% growth forecast through 1992.

Price–Performance Ratio

Advances in computer chip technology had substantially reduced the cost of computing power during the 1980s, a trend that was expected to continue into the 1990s. For example, in 1981, a mainframe capable of processing 1 million instructions per second cost over $400,000; by the early 1990s, hardware with similar performance was expected to be priced around $50,000. More importantly, the computing power associated with some earlier mainframes was, by 1988, available in a desktop computer at a fraction of the cost, a trend referred to in the industry as "downsizing." Furthermore, as more and more processing power was provided to end users, analysts believed that powerful personal computers would replace terminals connected to mainframes and minicomputers.

Decentralized Computing

In the early days of computing, companies needed a mainframe and a multitude of dumb terminals to perform all data processing centrally. The first step toward decentralization occurred with minicomputers, allowing users to process up to 95% of their data within their own departments. The next step in decentralization came with the personal computer, placing data-processing capability directly on the end user's desk. Personal computers were, however, limited in their computing capacity and, as stand-alone hardware, did not allow communication among users.

The recent arrival of LAN technology provided an alternative means to decentralize computing by distributing data processing among a work group's or a department's interconnected computers. The use of personal computers in a network gave LANs a computing capacity similar to minicomputers at a fraction of the cost. In the opinion of many analysts, downsizing and distributed processing together were substantially changing the way companies competed in the computer industry. One analyst believed that decentralization was providing end users with more say in computer purchase decisions, leading to an increasing number of specialized narrow segments. The net result, according to another observer, was that the more expensive minicomputers and mainframes would lose sales to the less costly personal-computer-based LANs.

Industry Standards

Throughout the 1980s, minicomputer and mainframe manufacturers such as IBM, DEC, and Siemens sold their hardware with proprietary software, thus locking customers into a specific data-handling method. Having made a substantial investment in hardware and software, few customers were willing to purchase new systems from other manufacturers, a decision that could entail the difficult and expensive tasks of rewriting old programs.

In contrast to proprietary systems, U.S.-based AT&T developed and licensed UNIX, a nonproprietary operating system that allowed different brands of computers to communicate with each other. Preferred by an increasing number of computer buyers, the use of UNIX-based hardware and software was on the rise worldwide. Industry observers believed that interconnectivity would become an important buying criteria in the 1990s.

Proliferation of VARs

During the 1980s, the focus of competition in the computer industry had shifted away from hardware toward software and services. Staffan Simberg, vice-president of Group Europe, attributed this trend to the "commoditization" of computers, where substantive technological differences in hardware were narrowing among different manufacturers. Another factor was what many in Nokia Data management referred to as the "declining technical sophistication of the average buyer." Increasingly, computer decisions in small- to medium-sized companies were being made by noncomputer people who were more concerned with the quality of solutions than the technicalities of the "black box."

The two trends combined had given rise to value-added resellers (VARs), independent companies who filled a gap between manufacturers and small- to medium-sized clients. VARs bought hardware from a variety of producers, adding customized software and services for narrow vertical user segments such as the legal and medical professions, specialized retailers, plumbing, and farming. VARs competed among themselves and with computer manufacturers in the LANs and systems markets. From modest levels in the 1970s, the number of VARs in Europe had grown in recent years to several hundred. Together, they accounted for an estimated $3 billion in industry sales.

To use a VAR for competitive advantage, explained one Nokia Data sales executive, a company had to provide hardware with an attractive price and encourage the resellers to develop applications in their special end-user segments. In an average installation, 65% of the price paid by a customer was accounted for by the cost of hardware to the reseller, the rest went to cover expenses, including costs associated with application development, and margins.

European Integration

The European Economic Community (EEC) had chosen 1992 as the date to integrate its internal market by liberalizing trade and removing barriers among its 12 member states. Increased competition among manufacturers in an open market implied that government procurement could no longer favor a local vendor over another vendor from the EEC. Hence, 1992 posed a serious challenge to national computer companies for which 50% of sales was to the local government. Increased competition was also expected to lead to concentration in the industry, as companies strove to achieve critical mass and economies of scale. Recent examples of such activities included Alcatel, formed through the merger of ITT's European business and the French CGE group, and Memorex Telex, formed by the merger of Memorex International and the U.S. Telex organization.

Also, in anticipation of 1992, companies such as Apple, IBM, Siemens, and Olivetti were integrating regional operations toward a "European" posture and identity. In the case of Apple, its management had recently created a European research and development center in Paris. "We want to form a strong European identity so that we are able to be part of the European economy."[2] By adopting a regional profile, both European and non-European companies wanted to be better positioned to

---

[2] *Business Marketing*, September 1988.

compete for local government bids after 1992, when procurement policies were no longer biased toward domestic suppliers. In this respect, Olivetti's executive vice-president, Elserino Piol, maintained, "The European companies that remain 'national champions' are going to suffer after 1992." The same article concluded, "Europe's computer makers have all opted for the same survival strategy. Each is scrambling to go pan-European as fast as possible."[3]

NOKIA DATA'S EUROPEAN STRATEGY

Current Position

At the end of 1988, Nokia Data manufactured its products in Sweden and Finland and operated wholly owned sales and service branches in all four Nordic countries (Sweden, Norway, Denmark and Finland) in addition to Germany, the Netherlands, Spain, the United Kingdom, France, and Switzerland. In Germany, Nokia Data's largest non-Nordic countries operation, the company employed a total of 450 in sales and service. Nokia Data also used sales agents, who had previously sold Nokia Information System or Ericsson Data System products, in Finland, Sweden, Belgium, Austria, Italy, Portugal, Hong Kong, and Australia.

The company assembled most of its products in its own facilities; a minor share of total production was subcontracted to third parties in Nordic countries as well as the Far East. Management saw definite advantages to sourcing internationally and using its own facilities for assembly. Currently, components purchased as far away as the United States and the Far East accounted for 70% of the total cost of production; the rest of the cost was divided equally between labor and plant overhead. Efficient sourcing and materials management were considered critical to overall cost performance. A recent estimate indicated that well-run procurement and manufacturing operations, including rationalized purchasing

and investment in modern assembly, could potentially save the company as much as 40% on the production costs of terminals and PCs. One-half of the projected savings would have come from reduced materials cost. Some Nokia Data executives believed that, while potential for savings existed, it probably was less than the estimated 40%.

Nokia Data marketed what management called its "horizontal products"—terminals, personal computers and LAN-based hardware—in all markets. With minor exceptions, these products were based on nonproprietary technologies. "Vertical systems," as management called them, were sales of hardware and software to target segments in banking/insurance, retailing, manufacturing, government, and general business. Nokia Data did not use VARs in a market until management believed the company had a strong local presence. Hence, as of 1988, VARs were only used in Finland and Sweden. Less than 3% of the company's sales were generated through sales agents or VARs.

In Finland, Nokia Data used the Mikko brand for its entire line. In all other markets, Nokia Data used the Alfaskop brand name acquired from Ericsson Data Systems.

Although its products were sold as far away as Hong Kong and Australia, 95% of Nokia Data's sales were concentrated in Europe, with Finland, Sweden, and Germany representing 40%, 25%, and 11% of total sales, respectively. (*Refer to Exhibits 6, 7, and 8 for a summary of Nokia Data's sales by country, segment, and product.*)

Senior managers thought of their company as a sales-driven organization. Although major strategic decisions were made by product groups at headquarters, the regions and country management in larger markets wielded significant influence on short-term policies and sales action. For example, although product design was a headquarters decision, a local sales operation could ask for the development of a special terminal and keyboard for a large order. Local managers in new and strategic markets such as Germany, France, and Spain were measured and rewarded based on sales performance. In the more established markets such as Finland and Sweden, both sales and

[3] *Business Week International*, September 12, 1988.

EXHIBIT 6 Nokia Data Sales Summary by Segment ($ million, 1988)

Country:	SF	S	DK	N	G	NL	SP	UK	Others	Total	% Total
Retail	34.4	12.1	21.1	2.7	3.0	0	8.3	0	0	81.6	7
Banking/ insurance	199.8	144.3	4.5	14.5	23.5	2.7	19.4	0.7	6.0	415.4	35
Manufac- turing	75.4	92.3	9.7	11.0	25.0	15.9	13.6	24.5	9.4	276.8	24
Government	88.1	50.4	23.7	6.8	74.5	17.2	7.7	0.6	1.5	270.5	23
General business	106.0	3.3	4.3	4.1	5.3	1.2	1.5	0	0	125.7	11
Total	503.7	302.4	63.3	39.1	131.3	37.0	50.5	25.8	16.9	1,170.0	100
% Total	43	26	5	3	11	3	4	2	2	100	

Source: Company records.

Country codes: SF, Finland; S, Sweden; DK, Denmark; N, Norway; G, Germany; NL, Netherlands; SP, Spain; UK, United Kingdom; Others, Belgium, Italy, Austria, Portugal, Hong Kong, Australia.

profitability were considered in performance evaluation.

Competitive Standing

Top management at Nokia Data believed that they enjoyed a number of competitive advantages in their sector of the computer industry. In particular, they believed that the large institutional competitors had been slow to respond to the growing customer demand for multivendor connectivity and were, consequently, up to 1 year behind Nokia Data in developing the necessary LAN expertise. Companies from the consumer group, on the other hand, were believed to be even farther behind in developing networking expertise and, in addition, lacked the industry knowledge of the institutional companies, including Nokia Data. One executive commented that the company's two decades of experience in the banking and retail sectors, combined with its ability to design solutions around hardware from other vendors, were important factors in achieving the 35% and 25% market shares in the Nordic countries' banking and retail segments, respectively.

Nokia Data's other competitive strengths were believed to include the financial backing of a large parent, the Nokia Corporation, the company's small size, and its industry reputation as an ergonomic trendsetter. Because of its smaller size, the company was thought to be more able to keep pace with the evolving industry trends than its larger competitors, such as IBM. Furthermore, ergonomics, translated into improved user comfort and productivity, was proving to be a distinct advantage against the smaller manufacturers, as well as larger competitors from the institutional group. As an example, Goran Hermansson, pointed to the fact that Ericsson, although not a technological forerunner, pioneered the separate keyboard and the tilt-and-swivel screen on personal computers. A more recent innovation was Nokia Data's positive display screen with sharp black characters on a paper white background designed to reduce eye strain.

Despite these advantages, Yrjänä Ahto, vice-president of marketing communication, believed Nokia Data was not sufficiently known outside the Nordic countries, a fact that some customers interpreted as "a risky company" to do business with. Furthermore, although top management considered Nokia Data's size to be an asset, some European country managers believed the company was too small, lacking the critical mass and resources necessary to compete with big players like IBM.[4]

Future Strategy

Nokia Data's top management aimed to make their company a leading supplier of ter-

[4] IBM Europe's operations included 15 plants in six countries in addition to nine R&D facilities, seven scientific centers, and sales and service units in all markets. The company claimed a high degree of European content (92%) in its products and integrated manufacturing across the continent.

EXHIBIT 7 Nokia Data Sales Summary by Product and Service Category ($ million, 1988)

Country:	SF	S	DK	N	G	NL	SP	UK	F	SW	Others	Total	% Total
Terminals	56.3	103.6	34.8	10.2	67.0	13.9	24.1	8.6	5.2	10.4	15.5	349.6	29.9
Personal computers	117.2	137.3	14.2	18.8	54.5	18.0	12.1	6.7	9.0	5.3	7.9	401.0	34.3
Peripherals[a]	8.4	10.2	0.2	1.1	0	0.6	4.0	0	0	0	0	24.5	2.1
Minicomputers	56.0	30.2	8.6	7.5	2.1	2.2	5.8	8.6	2.2	0.3	2.9	126.4	10.8
LANs	10.7	13.7	2.9	0.6	3.5	0.9	1.2	0.9	0.2	0	0	34.6	2.9
Service and Miscellaneous[b]	226.2	1.5	1.2	0.3	1.2	0.9	2.4	0.2	16.6	16.0	26.3	233.9	20.0
Total	474.8	296.5	61.9	38.5	128.3	36.5	49.6	25.0	16.6	16.0	26.3	1,170.0	100
% Total	40.6	25.4	5.3	3.3	11.0	3.1	4.2	2.1	1.4	1.4	2.2	100	

Source: Company records.

[b] The Service and Miscellaneous figure for Finland includes sales of a large number of turnkey-system projects estimated at around $200 million in total.

[a] Peripherals include specialized banking printers, plotters, and personal identification number (PIN) keyboards.

Country codes: SF = Finland; S = Sweden; DK = Denmark; N = Norway; G = Germany; NL = Netherlands; SP = Spain; UK = United Kingdom; F = France; SW = Switzerland; Others = Belgium, Italy, Austria, Portugal, Hong Kong, Australia.

EXHIBIT 8 Nokia Data Sales by Products Category, 1988

	$ Million	Units	$ Average Price
Terminals	349.6	161,106	2,170
Personal computers	401.0	125,312	3,200
Peripherals	24.5	21,993	1,114
Minicomputers	126.4	1,973	64,065
LANs	34.6	245	141,224[a]

[a] Includes related terminals, central processing equipment, and connections.

minals, personal computers, LANs, and systems for the European business community. The management wanted to achieve this goal within the next 5 years and without acquisitions. The targeted turnover for 1993 was set at $2.5 billion, equally distributed between the Nordic countries and the rest of Europe. The targeted revenues represented an annual growth rate of 6% in Nordic countries and 35% outside.

For the next 3 years, the company planned to concentrate on non-Nordic markets where it operated wholly owned subsidiaries. With the exception of minicomputers, Nokia Data planned to sell its full line in each market. Management believed that its own minicomputer, based on a proprietary operating system, was not competitive in a market that increasingly demanded multivendor connectivity.

Outside the Nordic countries, management also aimed to increase Nokia Data's presence in its five target segments by following the product pathway *shown in Exhibit 4,* starting with the sale of terminals. Company executives believed that purchases from Nokia Data had to build on a client's existing systems, because customers had already made substantial investments with other companies in hardware, software, and training. Also, because Nokia Data was not well known outside the Nordic countries, management believed that the first step had to be perceived by the customer as having little, if any, risk. "Consequently," explained Yrjänä Ahto, "terminals were the logical entry point with new clients as they were far less complex than a LAN or a system and considered less risky. Thereafter, as the company

becomes better known and as customers upgrade terminals to personal computers and LANs, Nokia Data can move up the product line, growing in size and perceived ability to deliver at the upper end."

Within its five end-user segments, management planned to target the larger organizations with over 500 terminals tied to minicomputers or mainframes, but with few personal computers. According to management, sales to large customers were the fastest way to generate volume and to build Nokia Data's image as a reliable supplier of computer products and services, especially when the client was a public organization, like a local PTT, for example.

Since 1988, the company had undertaken an extensive European advertising campaign in both local and international media to improve its awareness level and consolidate its corporate image. In 1988, $14 million worth of press advertisements promoted the company's products as "built by Europeans for Europeans." Headlined "For the European Generation," the standardized series of color advertisements promoted the company's Alfaskop brand. It appeared in the international edition of such magazines as *The Economist, Time, Newsweek,* and *Fortune.* (*Refer to Exhibit 9 for sample advertisements.*)

Multidomestic Implementation

Nokia Data's senior management believed that a strong local identity and presence in each major European country were crucial to achieving the company's ambitious strategic goals. More specifically, top management aimed to decentralize decision making by adopting what they referred to as a "multidomestic" approach. This approach contrasted with pan-European integration and implied a strong country management voice in local activities.

According to senior managers, a multidomestic implementation of the company's expansion strategy would affect many aspects of its operations. For example, activities such as product development, production, and marketing were to be delegated to the local orga-

Alfaskop 386.
For the European Generation.

You know that 386 in the computer world means the same as a 3.8 litre engine in a 2.0 litre auto world.

You are a European business professional who has outgrown the standard PCs and is looking for the superior processing power and speed that only a 386 workstation can provide.

Alfaskop TT/386 and Alfaskop WS/386 are two new Scandinavian entries in the turbo class. Both of them super-fast PCs and powerful workstations in Local Area Networks.

Alfaskop workstations. Built by Europeans for Europeans.

NOKIA DATA

Nokia Data is a Scandinavian information technology group specializing in business computers, workstations and networks for the European business community. With more than 600,000 workstations already installed we rank among the biggest suppliers in Europe.

Knowing the facts today will determine the direction of European development far into the next century.

The ambitious curiosity of the increasingly well-educated young Europeans will change the world.

For the business professional, it is the opportunity to access and process the facts with a speed that can't be overestimated.

© Nokia Data: Denmark (02) 843166 Finland (0) 5671 France (1) 4746 707 The Netherlands (03480) 73601 Norway (02) 285500 Switzerland (01) 810502 UK (01) 400 2748 West Germany (030) 86190 Sweden (08) 764 2000 Spain (91) 4570 Sweden (08) 764 2000

EXHIBIT 9

Alfaskop Ergonomics.
For the European Generation.

Ergonomics is a friendly smile.

If the box in front of you makes your work easier, faster and more fun, then it has good ergonomics.

But if you see it as just another tool on your desk, one that may even frustrate you, then you've got the wrong one.

Alfaskop workstations have always been pioneers in ergonomics. Simply because they are built by Europeans for Europeans.

There is one for every system environment and for every individual need. There is one for you.

NOKIA DATA

Nokia Data is a Scandinavian information technology group specializing in business computers, workstations and networks for the European business community. With more than 600,000 workstations already installed we rank among the biggest suppliers in Europe.

Exchanging vital information at the touch of a key, this generation will be uniquely in tune with the times...

Oh, yes – superior ergonomics will help eliminate a lot of elder generation mental blocks...

They'll bring their vitality with them right into their jobs.

Call Nokia Data: **Denmark** (02) 84 18 66 **Finland** (0) 56 71 **France** (1) 47 88 750 **The Netherlands** (15480) 770 0 **Norway** (02) 30 65 00 **Spain** (91) 457 11 61 **Sweden** (08) 794 20 00 **Switzerland** (01) 8228 02 18 (01) 828 27 42 **West Germany** (0202) 60 90

EXHIBIT 9 *(Continued)*

Alfaskop Thinking.
For the European Generation.

You are an important individual.

You need a workstation that makes your job simpler, faster and more fun.

Alfaskop ergonomics.

And you need a workstation that can communicate with the other workstations in your company.

Alfaskop networking.

Alfaskop thinking is that ergonomics and networking is the best way to stimulate your individual creativity and ambitions.

The European solution for the European generation.

NOKIA DATA

Nokia Data is a Scandinavian information technology group specializing in business computers, workstations and networks for the European business community. With more than 600,000 workstations already installed we rank among the biggest suppliers in Europe.

Call Nokia Data: Denmark (02) 84 53 66 Finland (0) 5671 France (1) 47 80 727 The Netherlands (03480) 70 93 Norway (02) 386500 Spain (91) 4 57 91 Sweden (08) 764 20 00 Switzerland (01) 829 62 68 UK (01) 992 7 45 West Germany (0211) 58190

Their thoughts about the future are of vital importance. And they will demand more power and influence than ever in the fulfilment of their ambitions.

What is happening is that today's personalities are already outpacing yesterday's professionals.

You'll be making result-oriented teams where individuality provides the motivation force.

EXHIBIT 9 (*Continued*)

253

Alfaskop Workstations.
For the European Generation.

They come in all sizes, shapes and ages. Ambitious, creative, demanding.

Released individuality can be an elevating force in any business organization.

Give them workstations perfectly adapted to their taste, needs and demands. And wonderful things will happen.

Don't accept dull conformity!

The result of your work depends on your competence, fantasy, creativity, individuality and ambition.

Your workstation is your workmate.

It should make everything easier, faster and more fun. Alfaskop workstations are built by Europeans for Europeans.

There is one for every system environment and every individual need.

There is one for you.

NOKIA DATA

Nokia Data is a Scandinavian information technology group specializing in business computers, workstations and networks for the European business community. With more than 600,000 workstations already installed we rank among the biggest suppliers in Europe.

Call Nokia Data: Denmark (02) 84 53 66 Finland (0) 5671 France (78) 47 90 707 The Netherlands (03480) 70911 Norway (02) 286500 Spain (91) 457110 Sweden (08) 7640000 Switzerland (01) 83199-11 UK (01) 40527-45 West Germany (0231) 40700

EXHIBIT 9 *(Continued)*

254

Alfaskop Networking.
For the European Generation.

Your company is changing. The decisionmaking process is decentralized. The pace is mounting. The competition grows.
You must act!
The solution is networking. More and more people in your company will be able to share essential information. And fast information access and interchange may turn into your company's most competitive weapon.
Use it!
Alfaskop networks.
A European solution made for European needs.
Use it!

Something that'll let you in instead of leaving you out? Correct!

Best thing that has happened in the office? Mmmm...

Alfaskop
for the European Generation

A door opener to a world of new efficiency? Sure!

A gift to mankind? Well...

NOKIA DATA

Nokia Data is a Scandinavian information technology group specializing in business computers, workstations and networks for the European business community. With more than 600,000 workstations already installed we rank among the biggest suppliers in Europe.

Call Nokia Data: Denmark (02) 44 55 66 Finland (0) 5671 France (1) 4760 707 The Netherlands (05480) 70911 Norway (02) 356500 Spain (91) 4571 611 Sweden (08) 764 00 00 Switzerland (01) 8215 22 UK (0) 409 2745 West Germany (020) 60 91

EXHIBIT 9 (*Continued*)

255

nizations that had reached a minimum size. Local branding, in particular, was believed essential for a favorable local identity. Management believed that companies that used the same brand in every market did so to their detriment. "A local image," commented Ahto, "is simply not possible without a local brand—even for companies like IBM that manufacture in almost every European country." Similarly, local manufacturing allowed a company to differentiate itself from the competition by reflecting local tastes more closely. As one top executive commented, "Ultimately, I only care about what the customer wants, even if it's only a red terminal or a blue keyboard." (*The main elements of the multidomestic approach are highlighted in the Appendix and summarized in Exhibit 10.*)

Nokia Data's multidomestic approach went counter to strategies adopted by others in the industry. In 1988, for example, Apple Computer began to integrate its European operations under the control of a stronger Paris headquarters. According to the company, Apple's national subsidiaries would continue to take care of their own local markets while Paris looked for pan-European customers and ways to transfer effective strategies regionwide. In the words of an Apple executive, "When one Apple company comes up with an excellent marketing scheme, Paris headquarters will be responsible for trying to introduce it into other EC countries."[5]

Siemens also had recently restructured its operations to improve competitiveness outside its home market, Germany. Aiming to become a "truly global player," one member of top management was quoted as saying, "In 5 years, Siemens will be a completely different company. Among Europeans, we will be one of the most aggressive."[6] In recent advertisements (*shown in Exhibit 11*), the company had billed itself as "the top European computer company in the world market." On another front, IBM was recently capitalizing on the 1992 European integration issue by promoting the concept of integrated operations for a single European market. In a company-sponsored publication called "1992 Now," IBM Europe's president was quoted as saying "in IBM, we manage our European manufacturing activities as if it were 1992."

Nokia Data's outspoken president, Kalle Isokallio, believed that a pan-European approach was "nonsense" as it assumed homogeneous European markets. He thought that the 1992-related harmonization might bring uniform technical standards, but buyer behavior would still be nationally oriented. To illustrate, Isokallio described a typical German customer as someone "who never buys a prototype and signs nothing but a lengthy and detailed contract." In sharp contrast, he pointed to a typical French customer, "who is willing to try new innovative products and sign a contract on the back of a Gauloise cigarette pack." Kalle Isokallio explained that in a nonhomogeneous EEC, characterized by trends toward decentralized computing and narrow market segments, manufacturers had to get close to their customers. Therefore, he emphasized, "local identity" was the key, with a minimum level of local production, some local development, and strong local brands.

As of early 1989, the company's local presence varied among markets. In Finland and

EXHIBIT 10 Areas of Primary Management Responsibility: A Multidomestic Approach[a]

	Central	Local
R&D		
Basic product design	×	
Applications software		×
Production		
Procurement	Coordination	Purchasing
Manufacturing		×
Marketing		
Advertising: General framework	×	
Execution		×
Branding		×
Segmentation		×
Sales force		×
Distribution		×
Pricing (end-user price)		×
Servicing		×

Source: Company records.[a] This chart refers to a future division of responsibilities under a multidomestic approach.

[5] *Business Marketing,* September 1988.
[6] *Business Week International,* February 20, 1989.

SIEMENS

It's official:
Once again Siemens
ranks as Europe's No.1
in Computers

Every year the international computer magazine "Datamation" publishes a table of the world's leading Information Systems companies.
For the fourth year in succession, Siemens is No. 1 in the European league and, as such, the top European computer company in the world market.

This success can be attributed to four major product groups:

- the BS2000 computers, which run under a single operating system – from small departmental computers right through to the largest mainframes.
- the SINIX™ multi-user system, Europe's best-selling UNIX™ computers.
- the Siemens Personal Computers – made in Europe, with a continually increasing share of the market.
- the digital office communications systems, which are at home throughout the world.

Each of these systems is the result of an intensive, ongoing program of research and development.

Moreover, Siemens itself manufactures the key components, being the sole European source, of the Megabit chip – a chip for both the world electronics market and Siemens computers.

If you would like to know more about Siemens Computing, please write to Siemens AG, Infoservice 134/Z560, P.O.Box 23 48, D-8510 Fürth, Federal Republic of Germany.

Leading European-Based IS Companies

	Company	World IS Rev ($ mil)
1	Siemens AG	$5,703.0
2	Ing.C.Olivetti & Co. SpA	4,637.2
3	Groupe Bull	3,007.5
4	Nixdorf Computer AG	2,821.5
5	NV Philips Gloeilampenfabrieken	2,601.6
6	STC plc	2,123.9
7	Alcatel NV	2,052.1
8	LM Ericsson	1,511.6
9	Inspectorate Intl. Ltd.	1,225.0
10	Memorex Intl.	1,041.1

Source: Datamation, August 1988

SINIX is the UNIX System derivative of Siemens
UNIX is a registered trademark of AT&T

There's a Siemens Computer for every business.

EXHIBIT 11   Siemens Sample Advertising

Sweden, for example, management believed they were rightfully a "domestic" company because of local production, local development and, most importantly, local brands. "Yet," explained Ahto, "before we can claim to be domestic in non-Nordic countries, we must reach a minimum size. After that, we can start local production and introduce a local brand. But, before we reach that critical mass, we will try to be 'European'."

Management Discussions

Although Nokia Data management at all levels agreed with the strategic goal of long-term viability through rapid growth, there was less consensus on the specifics of how that might be achieved. For example, concern was expressed at both the headquarters and country organizations about whether the company would be able in the near future to take advantage of the growth in LANs and vertical systems. For one thing, some argued, the company did not enjoy the needed name recognition in most European markets to be considered a credible supplier of highly technical LANs or sophisticated vertical systems. Furthermore, others argued that even where the company had an established reputation, as in most of the Nordic countries, it was for terminals and personal computers, rather than for the more advanced LANs and systems. "We have too much of an ordinary hardware supplier image," complained Nils Wilborg, head of the information department in the Swedish country organization. On a related point, Ingvar Persson, vice-president of product planning, explained that, while competition centered around hardware in the 1970s and around software in the 1980s, the distinguishing feature in the future would be in services. "Yet," he emphasized, "the market views us as a hardware vendor, not a service provider."

Doubts were also expressed regarding the practicality of and the rationale behind the multidomestic approach. Jürgen Olschewski, the German managing director, believed that Nokia Data's small size in his country was a big obstacle to becoming a full-fledged manufacturing, marketing, and service operation. Nevertheless, he agreed with top management that a strong German identity would be an asset in competing against firms such as IBM or Compaq with no local image. A few others wondered, on the other hand, if a multidomestic approach might not fragment the company too much to compete effectively against the larger and more integrated competitors.

Conclusion

Nokia Data's top management knew that some of their colleagues were concerned about the company's future direction. Yet they believed that Nokia Data's fortunes in a maturing industry depended on innovative thinking and quick action close to customers—elements that they thought were inherent in their overall strategy for growth and the multidomestic approach. Explained Ahto, "Our plans for the future are in line with the corporate culture that we want to establish within Nokia Data—a culture that emphasizes profit performance, business orientation, speedy decision making, and fast action. Doing business under tough conditions has always been fun at Nokia. We want to continue having fun in the future."

Elements of Nokia Data's Multidomestic Approach

Research and Development

As Nokia Data implemented its multidomestic approach across Europe, management planned to consolidate basic product development such as video display and keyboards in Sweden. Market-specific development, such as language translation and application software, however, would all be performed locally.

Production

The management believed local manufacturing was one of the conditions needed for a local identity. Hence, Nokia Data planned to set up production facilities in each market, once an economically viable minimum sales volume, estimated at around 50,000 personal computers or terminals annually, was achieved. Sourcing of components was to be centralized in Sweden.

Segmentation

As of 1989, Nokia Data's penetration in each of its five primary segments varied considerably across different national markets. As part of local strategies, country management would decide which of the five segments to concentrate on. Local management could also decide to develop a share of its business in segments not considered primary by Stockholm.

Branding

Management believed that the Mikko name in Finland and the Alfaskop name in Norway, Sweden, and Denmark were viewed by those markets as local brands with local image. Outside Scandinavia, management planned to introduce local brands, but not until Nokia Data's local brands were perceived to offer Nokia Data a decided advantage, especially over nonlocal international brands.

Communication

At the end of 1988, Nokia Data's subsidiaries used the same pictures, advertisements, and brochures, localized only through text translation. In the future, however, each subsidiary would work from a general framework defined in Stockholm, taking responsibility for local execution. Aside from local campaigns designed to promote local brands, Nokia Data headquarters would continue a European-wide English language corporate advertising campaign in international publications.

Distribution

Currently, decisions regarding the use of VARs or sales agents and the extent of their contribution to local marketing were headquarters decisions. In the future, as sales through such channels increased, local organizations would play a primary role in such decisions.

Pricing

As in the past, future pricing decisions at Nokia Data would be the responsibility of country managers. Aside from pricing in accordance with market conditions, local organizations were to pay Stockholm a transfer price set at their market price, less the local margin of 30% to 40%. However, no central control on local pricing was foreseen.

Customer Service

In the past, Nokia had maintained more service points than sales offices in a local market, a factor that management believed helped to reassure customers of speedy availability of help when needed. In the future, that policy would not change. But, under local management, the customer services concept was to be broadened to incorporate "Care-ware," a comprehensive package designed to meet the total needs of most clients.

The Careware Concept, formulated in Stockholm for implementation in local organizations, went beyond normal after-sales service and included presales consulting, planning and testing, installation, and technical and educational services. Careware was divided into six groups of Customer Service Products. The following list represents the content of Careware Services.

Nokia Data's Customer Careware

Operational Services
Education and training
Systems evaluation
Network services
On-site service representative
Total customer service responsibility
System security services
Standby customer service
Safety tests and checkups
Terminal cleaning

Installation Services
Project management and administration
Cabling
Product installation
Customizing
Nokia on-site/remote services
Customer carry-in services
Nokia software services
Nokia time and material service

Pharma Swede: Gastirup

Early in 1990, Bjorn Larsson, advisor to the president and the head of product pricing and government relations for Pharma Swede, in Stockholm, Sweden, was reviewing the expected consequences of "1992" on Gastirup in Italy. Gastirup was a drug for the treatment of ulcers. Since its introduction in Italy in 1984, this innovative product had achieved considerable success in its category of gastrointestinal drugs. However, the success had come as a result of pricing the drug at a significant discount below the prevailing prices for the same product in the rest of Europe. Higher prices would have disqualified Gastirup from the government reimbursement scheme, the system by which the state health insurance agency reimbursed patients for pharmaceutical expenditures. The government-negotiated prices for Gastirup in Italy were 46% below the average European price.

Bjorn Larsson was concerned that, with the anticipated removal of all trade barriers in Europe, Gastirup would fall victim to massive parallel trading from Italy to the higher-priced countries in the region. Furthermore, with the increased coordination among government health insurance agencies, also foreseen in the years following 1992, price differences among EEC countries were expected to narrow. This likely development highlighted the need for a consistent pricing policy throughout Europe.

As head of product pricing and government relations, it was Bjorn Larsson's responsibility to recommend the actions that top corporate and local Italian management should take to avert potential annual losses for Gastirup, projected in the $20 million to $30 million range. Among alternatives being considered, the most extreme was to forego the large and growing Italian market altogether and concentrate the product's sales elsewhere in Europe. The Italian market for Gastirup had grown to $27 million in recent years and accounted for 22% of European sales. Another option was to remove Gastirup from the Italian government reimbursement scheme by raising the prices to levels close to those prevailing in the higher-priced countries. This action would most likely reduce the drug's sales in Italy by as much as 80%. Still another alternative was to take legal action in the European Court of Justice against the Italian government's reimbursement scheme and the related price negotiations as barriers to free trade. Finally, the company could take a "wait and see" attitude, postponing any definitive action to a time when the impact of "1992" was better known.

COMPANY BACKGROUND

Pharma Swede was formed in 1948 in Stockholm, Sweden; it concentrated solely on pharmaceuticals. In 1989, the company employed

This case was prepared by Professor Kamran Kashani, with the assistance of Research Associate Robert C. Howard, as a basis for class discussion rather than to illustrate either effective or ineffective handling of a business situation. This case was developed with the cooperation of a company that wishes to remain anonymous. As a result, certain names, figures, and facts have been modified. Copyright © 1991 by the International Institute for Management Development (IMD), Lausanne, Switzerland. IMD retains all rights. Not to be used or reproduced without written permission from IMD, Lausanne, Switzerland.

over 2,000 people and earned $50 million on sales of $750 million, distributed among its three product lines: hormones (20%), gastrointestinal (50%), and vitamins (30%). Gastirup belonged to the gastrointestinal product category and, as of 1989, accounted for roughly $120 million of Pharma Swede's sales. (*See Exhibit 1 for a breakdown of Pharma Swede's sales.*)

International Activities and Organization

As of December 1989, Pharma Swede had wholly owned subsidiaries in 11 countries in Western Europe, where it generated 90% of its sales. The balance of sales came from small operations in the United States, Australia, and Japan.

Due to high research and development costs as well as stringent quality controls, Pharma Swede centralized all R&D and production of active substances in Stockholm. Partly as a result of these headquarters functions, 60% of the company's expenditures were in Sweden, a country that represented only 15% of sales. However, the politics of national health care often required the company to have some local production. Consequently, a number of Pharma Swede's subsidiaries blended active substances produced in Sweden with additional compounds and packaged the finished product.

Pharma Swede had a product management organization for drugs on the market (*refer to Exhibit 2*). For newly developed drugs, product management did not begin until the second phase of clinical trials, when decisions were made as to where the new products would be introduced and how. (*Refer to Exhibit 3 for the different phases of a new product's development.*) Besides country selection, product management at headquarters examined different position-

ing and price scenarios and determined drug dosages and forms. It had the final say on branding and pricing decisions, as well as basic drug information, including the package leaflet that described a drug's usage and possible side effects. As one product manager explained, the marketing department in Stockholm developed a drug's initial profile and estimated its potential market share worldwide. However, it was up to local management to adapt that profile to their own market.

As an example, in 1982 headquarters management positioned Gastirup against the leading antiulcer remedy, Tomidil, by emphasizing a better quality of life and 24-hour protection from a single tablet. To adapt the product to their market, the Italian management, with the approval of Stockholm, changed the name to Gastiros and developed a local campaign stressing the drug's advantages over Tomidil, an oral tablet that had to be taken two or three times a day.

As a rule, headquarters limited its involvement in local markets. It saw its role as one of providing technical or managerial assistance to country management, who were responsible for profit and loss.

Product Pricing and Government Relations

The product pricing and government relations department, located at the headquarters, was a recently established function within the company. It prepared guidelines for subsidiary management to use in negotiating drug pricing and patient reimbursement policies with local government agencies. The department was divided into government relations and product pricing. Those in government relations followed ongoing political events and prepared negotiating positions on such issues as employment creation through local production.

The role of product pricing, headed by Bjorn Larsson, was to determine the optimum price for new products. An optimum price, Larsson explained, was not necessarily a high price, but a function of price–volume relationships in each market. An optimum price

EXHIBIT 1 Sales in $ millions

Product Line	1987	1988	1989
Hormones	90	130	150
Vitamins	175	205	225
Gastrointestinal	200	290	375
Total	**465**	**625**	**750**

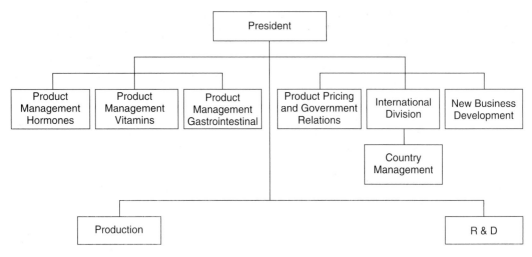

EXHIBIT 2 Partial Organization Chart

also reflected the cost of alternatives, including competitive products and alternative treatments like surgery, and the direct and indirect costs of nontreatment to society and the government. Each of these criteria helped to quantify a product's cost effectiveness or, as government authorities saw it, its treatment value for money.

Using cost-effectiveness data in price negotiations was a recent development in the pharmaceutical industry and corresponded to the increasing cost consciousness among public health authorities. Economic exercises that were initially performed in Stockholm to measure a drug's treatment and socioeconomic benefits were repeated with local authorities during negotiations. In Bjorn Larsson's opinion, the latest measure of "nontreatment cost"

EXHIBIT 3 The Development of a New Drug

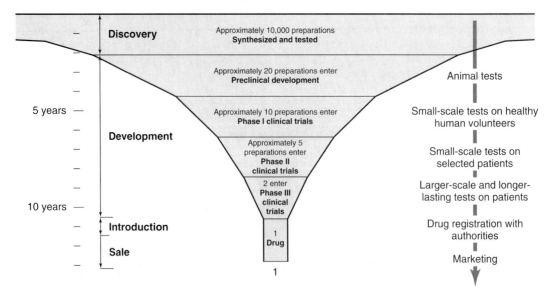

was becoming an important factor. He explained that a thorough understanding of the direct and indirect costs of an illness had come to play a key role in whether or not a government was willing to pay for a product by granting it reimbursement status, as well as the magnitude of that reimbursement. According to industry observers, the task of marketing to governmental agencies had become crucial in recent years as public agencies were scrutinizing drug prices more carefully. (*Refer to Exhibit 4 for an overview and further description of product pricing and government relations.*)

THE PHARMACEUTICAL INDUSTRY

As of 1989, approximately 10,000 companies worldwide competed in the $180 billion pharmaceutical industry. Industry sales were con-

centrated in North America, Western Europe, and Japan, with the 100 largest companies in these areas accounting for nearly 80% of all revenues. Western Europe alone accounted for an estimated 25% of total volume.

The industry classified pharmaceutical products according to how they were sold and their therapeutic status. In the first instance, pharmaceutical sales were classified into two categories, ethical and over the counter (OTC). Ethical drugs, with four-fifths of all pharmaceutical sales worldwide and a 10% annual growth rate, could only be purchased with a doctor's prescription. These drugs were branded or were sold as a generic when original patents had expired. OTC drugs were purchased without a prescription; they included both branded and generic medicines such as aspirin, cough syrups, and antacids. At Pharma

EXHIBIT 4 Product Pricing and Government Relations *Source:* Company records.

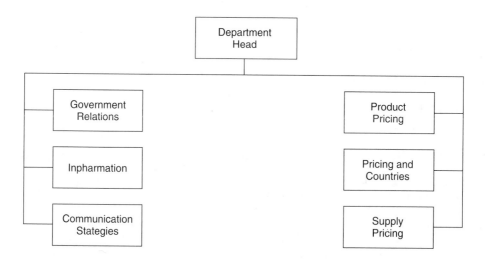

The Government Relations Group observed and recognized potential political problems for the division. When necessary, the group developed counterstrategies and oversaw their implementation.

Inpharmation gathered and managed all pharmopolitical information on both a national and international basis.

The communication strategies group advised the division on product strategies and proposed communications programs.

During drug development, the product pricing group worked to secure drug registration, using economic and social data.

Pricing and countries oversaw and helped build a favorable negotiating environment for pricing decisions.

Supply pricing was responsible for administering prices and managing relationships with Pharma Swede's distributors.

Swede, ethical drugs accounted for more than 90% of total sales.

Ethical drugs were also classified into therapeutic categories, of which gastrointestinal was the second largest, representing 15% of industry sales. Within the gastrointestinal category there were a number of smaller segments, such as antiulcer drugs, used to control and treat digestive tract ulcers, antidiarrhoeas, and laxatives. In 1989, the ethical antiulcer drug segment was valued at $7 billion worldwide and growing at 18% a year, faster than the total prescription market.

Trends in Europe

In parallel with worldwide trends, several factors were expected to play a role in shaping the future of the European pharmaceutical industry. Among these were an aging population, rising R&D and marketing costs, greater competition from generics, and government cost controls.

Aging Population

Europe's stagnating population was gradually aging. The segment of the population over 55 years old was forecast to grow and account for between 33% and 40% of the total by the year 2025, up from below 25% in the mid-1980s. During the same period, the segment below 30 years of age was forecast to drop from about 40% to 30%. The "graying of Europe" was expected to have two lasting effects on drug consumption. First, low growth was projected in the sales of drugs normally used by children or young adults. Second, drug companies marketing products for age-related diseases, such as cancer, hypertension, and heart ailments, could expect growing demand.

Rising R&D and Marketing Costs

Research and development expenses included the cost of identifying a new product and all the tests required for bringing that product to the market. Generally, for every 10,000 products synthesized and tested, only one made it through the clinical trials to appear in the market. Product development costs were estimated to average $120 million per drug, from preclinical research to market introduction. Industry estimates for research and development expenses averaged around 15% of sales in the late 1980s, with some companies spending as much as 20% of sales on new drugs. Research in more complex diseases like cancer, as well as lengthy clinical trials and government registration processes, had raised these costs recently.

Marketing costs had also increased due to a general rise in the level of competition in the industry. In the early-1980s, pharmaceutical firms spent, on average, 31% of sales on marketing and administrative costs. By 1987, the ratio had increased to 35% and was still rising. Some companies were reported to have spent unprecedented sums of $50 million to $60 million on marketing to introduce a new drug.

Growth of Generics

Generic drugs were exact copies of existing branded products for which the original patent had expired. "Generics," as these drugs were known, were priced substantially lower than their originals, and were usually marketed by a firm other than the inventor. Price differences between the branded and generics could be as large as 10 to 1. Depending on the drug categories, generics represented between 5% and 25% of the value of the total prescription drug market in Europe, and their share was expected to grow. For example, in the United Kingdom, sales of generic drugs had grown to represent an estimated 15% of the total National Health Budget and were forecast to reach 25% by 1995. In line with efforts to contain costs, governments in many parts of Europe were putting increased pressure on physicians to prescribe generics instead of the more expensive branded drugs.

Government Role

Governments were one of the strongest forces influencing the pharmaceutical industry in Europe where, in conjunction with public and private insurance agencies, they paid an average of two-thirds of health care costs. In Italy, for example, 64% of all ethical pharmaceutical expenditures were covered by the public health care system. In Germany, France and the United Kingdom, the respective shares were 57%, 65%, and 75%. These ratios had risen considerably throughout the 1960s and 1970s.

European governments were facing two opposing pressures: to maintain high levels of medical care while trying to reduce the heavy burden placed on the budget for such expenditures. Influence on pharmaceutical pricing, according to industry experts, had become an increasingly political as well as economic issue.

Not surprisingly, government agencies seeking to reduce health insurance costs increasingly encouraged the use of generics. In fact, before the advent of generics and official interventions, well-known branded drugs that had lost their patents in the 1970s, such as Librium or Valium, often maintained up to 80% of their sales for several years. In contrast, by the late 1980s, it was more likely that a drug would lose nearly 50% of its sales within 2 years after its patent expired.

GASTIRUP

Ulcers and Their Remedies

Under circumstances not completely understood, gastric juices—consisting of acid, pepsin, and various forms of mucus—could irritate the membrane lining the stomach and small intestine, often producing acute ulcers. In serious cases, known as peptic ulcers, damage extended into the wall of the organ, causing chronic inflammation and bleeding. Middle-aged men leading stressful lives were considered a high-risk group for ulcers.

Ulcers were treated by four types of remedies: antacids, H-2 inhibitors, anticholinergics, and surgery. Antacids, containing sodium bicarbonate or magnesium hydroxide, neutralized gastric acids and their associated discomfort. Some of the more common OTC antacid products were Rennie and Andursil. In contrast, H-2 inhibitors such as ranitidine reduced

acid levels by blocking the action of the stomach's acid-secreting cells. Anticholinergics, on the other hand, functioned by delaying the stomach's emptying, thereby diminishing acid secretion and reducing the frequency and severity of ulcer pain. Finally, surgery was used only in the most severe cases, where ulceration had produced holes in the stomach and when ulcers were unresponsive to drug treatment.

In 1989, the world market for nonsurgical ulcer remedies was estimated at $8 billion, with most sales distributed in North America (30%), Europe (23%), and Japan (5%). Worldwide, H-2 inhibitors and OTC antacids held 61% and 12% of the market, respectively.

The Oral Osmotic Therapeutic System

Gastirup, introduced in 1982 as Pharma Swede's first product in the category of ulcer remedies, used ranitidine as its active ingredient. As of 1982, ranitidine was available as a generic compound, after having lost its patent protection in that year. The U.S.-based Almont Corporation was the original producer of ranitidine and its former patent holder.

What distinguished Gastirup from other H-2 inhibitors, including ranitidine tablets produced by Almont and others, was not its active ingredient, but the method of administration, the Oral Osmotic Therapeutic System (OROS). In contrast to tablets or liquids taken several times a day, OROS was taken once a day. Its tabletlike membrane was specially designed to release a constant level of medicine over time via a fine laser-made opening. By varying the surface, thickness, and pore size of the membrane, the rate of drug release could be modified and adapted to different treatment needs. Furthermore, the release of the drug could be programmed to take place at a certain point in time after swallowing the tablet. Consequently, drug release could be timed to coincide with when the tablet was in the ulcerated region of the upper or lower stomach. (*Refer to Exhibit 5 for a diagram and brief description of the OROS.*)

Drugs supplied via OROS had certain advantages over the others. First, because of a steady release of the medicine, they prevented

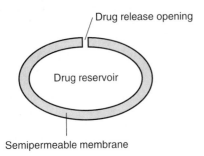

Drug release opening

Drug reservoir

Semipermeable membrane

Although OROS looked like a normal tablet, the system used osmotic pressure as a source of energy for the controlled release of active substance. Water, present throughout the body, passed through the semipermeable membrane as long as the reservoir contained undissolved substance. An increase in reservoir pressure, caused by the influx of water, was relieved by releasing drug solution through the opening. Up to 80% of the drug was released at a constant rate; the remainder at correspondingly declining rate. To guarantee the accuracy of the system, the opening had to comply with strict specifications. Hence, a laser was used to bore a hole through the membrane, in such a way that only membrane was removed, without damaging the reservoir.

EXHIBIT 5   The Oral Osmotic Delivery Syste   *Source:* Company records.

the high and low effects often observed with the usual tablets or liquids. Furthermore, the time-release feature prevented overfunctioning of the liver and kidneys. In addition, because drugs contained in an OROS had to be in the purest form, they were more stable and had a prolonged shelf life. Pharma Swede management believed that drugs administered by OROS could lead to fewer doctor calls, less hospitalization, and reduced health care costs for insurance agencies and governments.

Because OROS was not a drug per se but an alternative method of drug administration, it was sold in conjunction with a particular pharmaceutical substance. By the end of 1989, Pharma Swede was marketing three drugs using OROS. Gastirup was the company's only OROS product in the gastrointestinal category; the other two were in the hormones category. The management of Pharma Swede characterized the use of OROS as an attempt to introduce product improvements that did not necessarily rely on new substances but on new "software," leading to improved ease of use and patient comfort.

Ranitidine, the active ingredient in Gastirup, was not made by Pharma Swede, because of its complex manufacturing process and the fact that since 1982 it was available from a number of suppliers both inside and outside Sweden. Gastirup OROS tablets were manufactured by the company in Sweden; final packaging, including insertion of the drug information sheet, was done in a number of European countries, including Italy.

Patent Protection

OROS was developed and patented by the Anza Corporation, a U.S. company that specialized in drug delivery systems. In Europe, Anza had applied for patents on a country-by-country basis. Patent protection was twofold: OROS as a drug delivery system and its use with specific drugs. The more general patent on OROS was due to expire in all EEC countries by 1991. The second, and more important patent for Gastirup, covered Oral Osmotic Therapeutic Systems containing ranitidine. This latter patent, exclusively licensed to Pharma Swede for Europe, would expire everywhere on the Continent by the year 2000.

Although Pharma Swede sold more than one OROS product, it had an exclusive license from Anza for only the ranitidine–OROS combination. Over the years, a number of companies had tried to develop similar systems without much success. To design a system that did not violate Anza's patents required an expert knowledge of membrane technology, which only a few companies had.

Competition

Broadly speaking, all ulcer remedies competed with one another. But Gastirup's primary competition came from the H-2 inhibitors in general and from ranitidine in particular. Since 1982, when ranitidine joined the ranks of generics, it was produced by a number of companies in Europe and the United States. Despite increased competition, ranitidine's original producer, the U.S.-based Almont Corporation, still held a significant market share worldwide.

Almont had first introduced its Tomidil brand in 1970 in the United States. After only 2 years, the product was being sold in 90 countries, capturing shares ranging between 42% and 90% in every market. Tomidil's fast market acceptance, considered by many as the most successful for a new drug, was due to its high efficacy as an ulcer treatment and its few side effects. The drug had cut the need for surgery in an estimated two-thirds of cases. Pharma Swede attributed Tomidil's success also to centralized marketing planning and coordination worldwide, high marketing budgets, and focused promotion on opinion leaders in each country. Although Almont was not previously known for its products in the ulcer market and the company had little experience internationally, Tomidil's success helped the firm to grow into a major international firm in the field.

In the opinion of Pharma Swede management, Tomidil's pricing followed a "skimming" strategy. It was initially set on a daily treatment cost basis of five times the average prices of antacids on the market. Over time, however, prices were reduced to a level three times those of antacids. After 1982, the prices were cut further to about two times those of antacids. In 1990, competing tablets containing ranitidine were priced, on average, 20% below Tomidil for an equivalent dosage. In that year, Tomidil's European share of drugs containing ranitidine was 43%.

Pharma Swede management did not consider antacids and anticholinergics as direct competitors because the former category gave only temporary relief and the latter had serious potential side effects.

Results

Gastirup's sales in Europe had reached $120 million by the end of 1989, or 7% of the ethical antiulcer market. (*Refer to Exhibit 6 for a breakdown of sales and shares in major European markets.*)

Pricing

Gastirup was premium priced. Its pricing followed the product's positioning as a preferred alternative to Tomidil and other ranitidine-containing tablets by improving the patient's quality of life and providing 24-hour protection in a single dosage. Whereas competitive tablets had to be taken two or three times daily, the patient needed only one Gastirup tablet a day. The risk of forgetting to take the medicine was thus reduced, as was the inconvenience of having to carry the drug around all the time. Because of these unique advantages, substantiated in a number of international clinical trials, management believed that using Gastirup ultimately resulted in faster treatment and reduced the need for surgery. Gastirup was priced to carry a significant premium over Tomidil prices in Europe. The margin over the generics was even higher. (*Refer to Exhibit 7 for current retail prices of Gastirup and Tomidil across Europe.*)

Pharmaceutical Pricing in the EEC

Drug pricing was a negotiated process in most of the EEC. Each of the 12 member states had its own agency to regulate pharmaceutical prices for public insurance reimbursement schemes. From a government perspective, pharmaceuticals were to be priced in accordance with the benefits they provided. Although the pricing criteria most frequently cited were efficacy, product quality, safety, and patient com-

EXHIBIT 6   Sales and Market Shares in Major European Markets (1989 sales in $ millions)[a]

Countries	Total Market (100%)	Gastirup (% share)	Tomidil (% share)	Others[b] (% share)
Belgium	41	2 (5%)	16 (39%)	23 (56%)
France	198	15 (8%)	61 (31%)	122 (61%)
Germany	318	30 (9%)	51 (16%)	237 (75%)
Italy	394	27 (7%)	110 (28%)	257 (65%)
Netherlands	81	8 (10%)	25 (31%)	48 (59%)
Spain	124	5 (4%)	11 (9%)	108 (87%)
Sweden	34	10 (29%)	5 (15%)	19 (56%)
United Kingdom	335	18 (5%)	97 (29%)	220 (66%)
ALL EUROPE	**1,673**	**120 (7%)**	**486 (29%)**	**1,054 (63%)**

[a] All ethical antiulcer remedies.

[b] Includes branded and generic drugs.

fort, European governments were putting increasing emphasis on cost effectiveness, or the relationship between price and therapeutic advantages. Among diverse criteria used by authorities, local production of a product was an important factor. As a result of individual country-specific pricing arrangements,

EXHIBIT 7   Retail Prices in Europe (1989: daily treatment cost)

Countries[a]	Gastirup	Tomidil	Gastirup (%) / Tomidil
Belgium	$3.86	$2.47	+56
Denmark	5.96	3.94	+51
France	3.69	2.12	+74
Germany	5.31	3.54	+50
Greece	3.43	2.36	+45
Italy	2.40	1.35	+78
Netherlands	5.66	3.11	+82
Portugal	3.13	2.24	+40
Spain	4.03	2.82	+43
Sweden	5.91	4.22	+40
United Kingdom	5.40	3.10	+74

* All were members of the EEC except Sweden

there were inevitably widespread discrepancies in prices for the same product across Europe.

For new products, price negotiations with state agencies began after the drug was registered with the national health authorities. Negotiations could last for several years, eventually resulting in one of three outcomes: no price agreement, a partially reimbursed price, or a fully reimbursed price. In the event of no agreement, in most EEC countries the company was free to introduce the drug and set the price, but the patient's cost for the product would not be covered by health insurance. In many EEC countries, a drug that did not receive any reimbursement coverage was at a severe disadvantage. Partial or full reimbursement allowed the doctor to prescribe the drug without imposing the full cost on the patient. Any price adjustment for a product already on the market was subject to the same negotiation process.

Once agreement was reached on full or partial reimbursement, the product was put on a reimbursement scheme, also called a *positive list,* a list from which doctors could prescribe. Germany and the Netherlands were the two exceptions within the EEC employing a *negative list,* a register containing only those drugs that the government would not reimburse. Drugs on the reimbursement list were often viewed by the medical profession as possibly better than nonreimbursed products. (*Refer to Exhibit 8 for a summary of price setting and reimbursement practices within the EEC.*)

Pricing Gastirup in Italy

Pharmaceutical pricing was particularly difficult in Italy. Health care costs represented 8% of the country's gross domestic product and one-third of the state budget for social expenditures. Government efforts to contain health care costs resulted in strict price controls and a tightly managed reimbursement scheme. Italy was considered by Pharma Swede management as a "cost-plus environment," where pricing was closely tied to the production cost of a drug rather than its therapeutic value.

In May 1982, Pharma Swede Italy submitted its first application for reimbursement of Gastirup. The submitted retail price was $33 per pack of ten 400-milligram tablets. On a daily treatment cost basis, Gastirup's proposed price of $3.30 compared with Tomidil's $1.35. Although priced 25% lower than the average EEC price for Gastirup, Italian authorities denied the product admission to the positive list. They argued that Gastirup's therapeutic benefits, including its one-a-day feature, did not justify the large premium over the local price of Tomidil, which was already on the reimbursement scheme. Tomidil and another generic ranitidine-containing brand were produced locally, while Gastirup was to be manufactured in Sweden and only packed in Italy.

Despite the rejection by authorities, Pharma Swede chose to launch Gastirup in Italy without the reimbursement coverage. Management hoped to establish an early foothold in one of Europe's largest markets. Hence, early in 1983,

Gastirup was introduced in Italy at a retail price of $37 for a pack of 10 units and under the brand name Gastiros. This price translated into a daily treatment cost of $3.70, or 16% below the EEC average retail price of Gastirup and nearly three times that of Tomidil in Italy.

The response of the Italian market to Gastiros was better than management had expected. Following an intensive promotional campaign aimed at the general practitioners, sales reached $500,000 a month, or 2% of the market. Meanwhile, the number of requests for reimbursement received by the Italian health care authorities from patients and doctors was growing daily. Management believed that these requests were putting increased pressure on the authorities to admit the product to the positive list.

In a second round of negotiations, undertaken at the initiative of management 9 months after the launch, Pharma Swede Italy reapplied for reimbursement status based on a price of $31 per pack of 10 units. This price represented a daily treatment cost of $3.10 and was 30% below the EEC average. Once again the price was judged too high and the request was rejected. In November 1984, management initiated a third round of negotiations, and in April 1985 Gastiros was granted full reimbursement status at $24 per pack, a price that had not changed since.

Gastirup's Italian sales and market share among H-2 inhibitors grew substantially following its inclusion in the reimbursement scheme. By 1989, factory sales had reached $27 million, representing a dollar share of 7% of the market. Gastirup was Pharma Swede Italy's single most important product, accounting for nearly a quarter of its sales.

In Italy, as in other countries, Pharma Swede distributed its products through drug wholesalers to pharmacies. Typical trade margin on the resale price for pharmacies was 30%. Gastiros' factory price to wholesalers of $15 per pack of 10 tablets had a contribution margin of $3 for the Italian company, which paid its parent $1 for every 400-milligram tablet imported from Sweden. The transfer price was the same across Europe. In turn, the parent

EXHIBIT 8   Price Setting and Reimbursement in the EEC

Countries	Price Setting	Reimbursement

Ireland	No Price control for new introduction.	Positive list (prescription recommended.) Inclusion criteria:
		    Efficacy/safety profile
		    Cost-effectiveness profile

	Prices of prescription drugs are controlled through PPRS (Pharmaceutical Price Regulation Scheme). Control is exercised through regulation of profit levels.	Positive list for NHS prescriptions (National Health Service)
		
		Inclusion criteria:
		    Therapeutic value
		    Medical need

Belgium	Price control by the Ministry of Health on the basis of cost structure.	Positive list (Ministry of Health) Inclusion criteria:
		    Therapeutic and social interest
		    Duration of treatment
		    Daily treatment costs
		    Substitution possibilities
		    Price comparison with similar drugs
		Copayment: 4 categories (100%, 75%, 50%, 40%)

Greece	Price control by the Ministry of Health based on cost structure (support of local industry appears to be of importance).	Positive list (IKA, Social Security Ministry)

Portugal	Price and reimbursement negotiations with the Ministry of Health and Commerce based on:
	    Local prices
	    Lowest European prices
	    Therapeutic value
	    Cost effectiveness
		Positive list
		Inclusion criteria:
		    Therapeutic value
		    International price comparison
		    Cost effectiveness

Spain	Price control based on cost structure	Positive list (Social Security System) Inclusion criteria:
		    Efficacy/safety profile
		    Cost effectiveness

France	No control for nonreimbursable products. Price negotiations with the Ministry of Health for reimbursed products.	Positive list (Transparence Commission and Directorate of Pharmacy and Pharmaceuticals, within the Ministry Health)
		    Price
		    Therapeutic value
		    Potential market in France
		    (Local R&D)
		    Co-payment: 4 categories
		        Non reimbursable, 40%, 70%, 100%

Luxembourg	Price control by the Ministry of Health. Prices must not be higher than in the country of origin.	Positive list
		Inclusion criteria:
		    Therapeutic value
		    Cost effectiveness

Italy	Price control for reimbursed drugs by CIP (Interministerial Price Committee) following guidelines CIPE (Interministerial Committee for Economic Planning) based on cost structure.	Positive list (Prontuario Terapeutico National, or National Health Council) Reimbursement criteria:
		    Therapeutic efficacy and cost effectiveness
		    Innovation, risk–benefit ratio, and local research also considered

EXHIBIT 8 (*Continued*)

Germany	No direct price control by authorities.	Negative list. Reference price system since January 1989.
		Principles:
		  Drugs will only be reimbursed up to
		    a reference price.
		  Patient pays the difference between the
		    reference and retail prices.
		Co payment: DM3 per prescribed product
		(1992: 15% of drug bill)

Netherlands	No price control by authorities.	Negative list. Reference price system since January 1988.

Denmark	Price control based on:
	  Cost structure
	  Reasonable profits
		Positive list
		Inclusion critieria
		  Efficacy/safety profile
		  Cost–effectiveness profile

earned $0.70 in contribution for every tablet exported to its local operations. The variable cost of producing the tablets included raw materials and the licensing fees paid to Anza.

LIFTING THE TRADE BARRIERS

As "1992" drew closer, Pharma Swede management believed that two important issues affecting the European pharmaceutical industry would be manufacturing location and drug pricing. In the past, many of the cost-constraint measures taken by authorities had, by design or coincidence, an element of protectionism and represented national trade barriers. For example, local authorities might refuse a certain price or reimbursement level unless the sponsoring company agreed to manufacture locally. Under current EEC regulations, such actions were considered barriers to trade and were illegal.

As a countermeasure to such barriers, companies could take legal action against local agencies at the European Court of Justice. With the support of the European Federation of Pharmaceutical Industries Associations (EFPIA), drug firms could sue the agencies for violating the EEC regulations. Although the EFPIA had won 12 cases over the preceding

decade, litigation processes lasted sometimes up to 7 years, and the results were often partial and temporary in value. Nonetheless, industry participants were relieved that, after 1992, the element of local production linked to price negotiation would disappear.

Since December 1988, under a new EEC regulation called the Transparency Directive, government pricing decisions were open to review by the pharmaceutical companies. The directive served to eliminate any interference with the free flow of pharmaceutical products within the community caused by price controls or reimbursement schemes. It required state agencies to explain how they set drug prices in general, as well as in each case. If not satisfied, companies that believed they had been discriminated against could appeal a ruling on price, first to local courts, thereafter to the EC Commission, and, ultimately, to the European Court of Justice.

In addition, the new law required that agencies act quickly when a new drug was approved for sale or when a company asked for a price adjustment. On average, it had taken Pharma Swede 1 year to reach agreement on a price for a new product. Price adjustments for old products, on the other hand, had taken as long as 2 years because of delays by local authorities.

Another development related to the creation of a single European market was the expected harmonization in pharmaceutical prices and registration systems among member states. Bjorn Larsson and others in the industry believed that, across Europe, pharmaceutical price differences would narrow in a two-stage process: initially as a result of the transparency directive and thereafter as part of a more comprehensive market harmonization. Larsson thought that harmonization was a gradual process and that the completion of a single European market would occur at the earliest between 1995 and 2000.

Aside from narrowing of the differences in drug prices, possible outcomes for the post-1992 environment included a pan-European registration system and harmonized health insurance. Some observers predicted that a harmonized drug registration system would be put in place sometime between 1992 and 1995, although the exact form it might take remained open. Pharma Swede management believed it was unlikely that such a system would discriminate against non-EEC firms. Harmonization of national health insurance systems, a longer-term consequence of 1992, was not expected before 1995. Industry analysts believed that, in the interim, the states would continue to press for cost containment on a national basis. Private pan-European insurance offerings, on the other hand, were expected to increase with deregulation and the completion of the internal market.

THE PROBLEM

Prior to 1992, Europe's parallel trade in pharmaceutical products had been limited to less than 5% of industry sales. Each country had local-language packaging and registration requirements that tended to restrict or prohibit a product's acceptance and distribution in neighboring markets. Furthermore, according to some Pharma Swede managers, products produced in certain countries, such as Italy or France, suffered a poor quality image in other markets, such as Germany and England. National sentiments aside, distributors

seeking to capitalize on parallel imports had to have approval from local authorities, which often implied repackaging to meet local requirements.

Although parallel imports had been a minor problem in the past, they posed a serious challenge to drug firms, including Pharma Swede, in the post-1992 environment when such trade would be protected by law. Hans Sahlberg, the company's product manager for gastrointestinal drugs, explained that government insurance agencies were already examining price and reimbursement issues on a European-wide basis. For drugs already on the market, it was only a matter of time before authorities reimbursed on the basis of the lowest-priced parallel import. As an example, this implied that Gastirup, priced at $2.40 per tablet in Italy and $5.40 in Germany, would be reimbursed in Germany at the lower price of imports from Italy. If this proved true, West German revenue losses from Gastirup alone could amount to $17 million on current sales. Furthermore, if a system should emerge after 1992 mandating a single EEC price, Pharma Swede would have to revamp its entire price-setting policy.

Management Options

With the upcoming changes in Europe, Gastirup's pricing discrepancies had become a source of major management concern. If not carefully managed, Larsson and his colleagues believed that the company could lose money, reputation, or both. (*Refer to Exhibit 9 for relative prices of Gastirup in Europe.*)

In looking for options to recommend to top management at headquarters and at the Italian operation, Larsson and his staff developed four alternatives. The first, and the most extreme option, was to completely remove Gastirup from the Italian market and concentrate sales elsewhere in Europe. This action would be in defense of prices in the more profitable markets. This alternative was not Larsson's first choice as it implied sales revenue losses of $27 million. It also went counter to Pharma Swede's policy of marketing all its products in every European country. Larsson

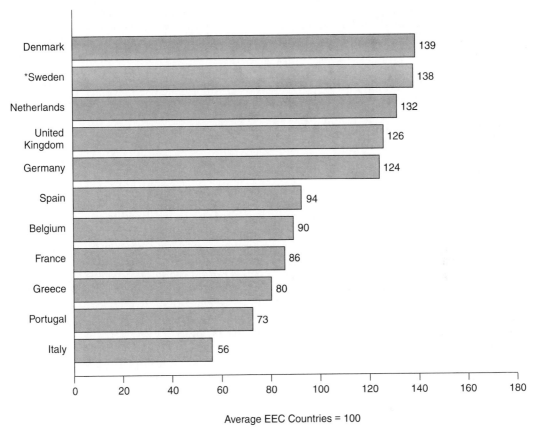

Denmark		139
*Sweden		138
Netherlands		132
United Kingdom		126
Germany		124
Spain		94
Belgium		90
France		86
Greece		80
Portugal		73
Italy		56

0   20   40   60   80   100   120   140   160   180

Average EEC Countries = 100

*Sweden not in EEC

EXHIBIT 9   Relative Retail Prices of Gastirup

feared that such a move would lead to heated discussions between headquarters and local management in Italy. It could even seriously damage the company's public reputation. "How," asked Larsson, "could Pharma Swede, an ethical drug company, deal with public opinion aroused by the apparently unethical practice of denying Gastirup to the Italian market?"

As another alternative, Larsson could suggest removing Gastirup from the reimbursement scheme by raising prices to levels closer to the EEC average. Such action would place Gastirup in the nonreimbursed drug status and lead to an estimated 80% loss in sales. Since the magnitude of this loss was nearly as great as the first option, headquarters did not

believe the Italian management would be any more receptive. Moreover, if Gastirup were removed from the reimbursement scheme, both the product and the company might lose credibility with the medical profession in Italy. According to Larsson, many doctors perceived the drugs on the reimbursement list as "economical" and "really needed."

Nonetheless, shifting the drug to nonreimbursement status would shift the financing burden from the government to the patient, thus coinciding with the Italian government's view that patients should assume a greater financial role in managing their health. With an increased emphasis on cost containment, such a proposal was liable to appeal to Italian authorities. Larsson expected full support for this proposal from managers in high-priced markets whose revenues were jeopardized by low-priced countries such as Italy.

There was, however, a possibility that changing the reimbursement status might backfire. Hans Sahlberg recalled a case in Denmark where, after removing a class of cough and cold drugs from reimbursement, Danish authorities came under pressure from a group of consumer advocates and were forced to reverse their decision. If Pharma Swede requested that Gastirup be removed from the Italian reimbursement scheme and the government were forced to reverse that position, the company's public image and its standing with local authorities might be damaged.

A third option was to appeal to the European Commission and, if necessary, start legal action before the European Court of Justice. As Larsson explained, the artificially regulated low drug prices in Italy placed higher-priced imported drugs at a disadvantage and, hence, acted as a barrier to the free movement of pharmaceutical products. Since the EFPIA had sued and won a similar case against Belgium, Larsson believed that Pharma Swede might have a good case against the Italian government. But as much as Larsson might want to pursue legal action, he recognized the risks inherent in using a legal mechanism with which Pharma Swede had no prior experience.

Headquarters management, on the other hand, looked favorably at this option because it provided the opportunity to settle "once and for all" the conflict with the Italian government over pharmaceutical pricing. Local management, however, feared that any legal action would create resentment and sour the atmosphere of future negotiations. At any rate, legal action could take several years and might even jeopardize Gastiros's status in Italy as a reimbursed drug.

A fourth option entailed taking a "wait and see" attitude until the full effects of "1992" became better known. Larsson explained that for the next 2 to 3 years governments would continue to concentrate on price controls. After 1992, pressure for harmonization would reduce differences in drug prices, although it was impossible to project the direction the prices might take. As an estimate, the product pricing and government relations staff had calculated that uniform pricing translated to an EEC-wide general decrease of 10% in drug prices, although prices in Italy would probably rise by about 15%. Thus, for the next few years, management at Pharma Swede could monitor the changes within the EEC and prepare as carefully as possible to minimize any long-term price erosion. Larsson felt this option argued for vigilance and "having all your ammunition ready." But he was not sure what specific preparatory actions were called for.

CONCLUSION

With the integration of Europe in sight, top management was deeply concerned about the impact that the changing regulatory environment might have on Pharma Swede's operations. Gastirup was the first product to feel the effects of harmonization, but it would not be the last. A decision on Gastirup could set the pattern for the other products. In evaluating the alternative courses of action for Gastirup, Larsson had to consider their likely impact on several stakeholders, including the country management in Italy, the management in high-priced countries and at headquarters, the Italian and EEC authorities, and the medical profession at large. Larsson was not sure if any course of action could possibly satisfy all the parties concerned. He wondered what criteria should guide his proposal to the company president, who was expecting his recommendations soon.

Alto Chemicals Europe (A)

Eberhard Graaff had held the position of headquarters marketing manager for stabilizers at Alto Chemicals Europe (ACE) for only 2 months when problems with subsidiary sales managers began to surface. It was December 1980 and the end of an 8-week period in which Graaff had spent time studying the industry and the company's several European subsidiary sales organizations to familiarize himself with the challenges of his new job. In the preceding week, a number of important decisions had been made by Graaff that would have long-term strategic implications for ACE's stabilizer business. He had informed the subsidiary sales organizations that stabilizers, a chemical used in making plastic products, were no longer to be sold based on low or even competitive prices and that share gaining at the expense of profitability of sales was no longer an acceptable policy. They were also informed that headquarters marketing was to take on a more active role in setting prices and determining target sales volumes for the various subsidiaries.

Reactions from the field to Graaff's decisions were immediate. Subsidiary sales managers were unanimous in their opposition. Expressions used by the managers to describe the new headquarters policies ranged from "unworkable" and "contradictory" to "theoretical" and "dictatorial." What the sales managers appeared to resent most was the notion that their own local judgment on sales matters had to be subordinate to that of headquarters. In the past, they had enjoyed relative autonomy in these areas.

Graaff was not overly perturbed by the negative reaction of the sales organization. He was, however, concerned about the steps needed to assure sound implementation of the revised strategy for stabilizers.

COMPANY BACKGROUND

ACE was the regional headquarters for Alto Chemicals Corporation's operations in Europe. Alto was a major North American-based multinational whose principal activities included production and marketing of commodity and specialty chemicals. With its headquarters and production facilities located in Switzerland and France, ACE accounted for more than a third of Alto's global production and sales volume.

Nine wholly owned subsidiaries, each serving one or more countries in Western Europe, reported to ACE.[1] The products produced and sold by the subsidiaries in the region ranged from finished compounds such as agricultural

---

[1] Alto's subsidiaries operated in the United Kingdom, France, Belgium, West Germany, the Netherlands, Italy, Spain, Portugal, and Sweden.

This case was prepared by Professor Kamran Kashani as a basis for class discussion rather than to illustrate either effective or ineffective handling of a business situation. All names and data have been disguised. Copyright © 1986 by the IMEDE, Lausanne, Switzerland. The International Institute for Management Development (IMD), resulting from the merger between IMEDE, Lausanne, and IMI, Geneva, acquires and retains all rights. Not to be used or reproduced without written permission from IMD, Lausanne, Switzerland.

chemicals to "building blocks" used in the production of other products, such as solvents, elastomers, and stabilizers.

ACE's headquarters organization was by product group. Five directors, each responsible for one or more products, reported to the company's president. Functions such as marketing, manufacturing, and planning were included under each product organization. Every director, in addition to having a region-wide product management responsibility, also supervised one or more of Alto's subsidiaries in Europe. The subsidiary managing directors, who reported to their assigned associate director, were in turn responsible for ACE's operations in their respective national markets. These included sales of all products produced in the region as well as any local production. The subsidiaries were typically organized by function.

The headquarters–subsidiary interaction was best described as a matrix relationship. The "dual boss system" was a common expression used to portray the dual sources of influence on product and subsidiary management.

STABILIZERS

Stabilizers were a category of chemicals used to make plastic products. When mixed with PVC (polyvinyl chloride) resins and dyes, the stabilizers helped prevent the breakdown of polymers in the finished product caused by environmental factors such as temperature, light, and general aging. A plastic product not adequately treated with stabilizers was likely to become brittle and discolored over time. For example, the plastic covering of an electrical cable would lose its flexibility and disintegrate eventually if not protected by stabilizers. Management estimated that close to 40% of all PVC uses in Europe were in applications requiring the addition of a stabilizer.

Product management had identified eight end-use and process segments for the stabilizer market. These segments produced a wide range of goods, from plastic bags and upholstery to wall covering, cables, hoses, and shoes. Although the share of each segment in the total market varied from one country to another, the three largest segments accounted for more than 50% of the market in Europe (refer to Exhibit 1).

In 1980, an estimated 600,000 tons of stabilizers of all types, valued at approximately $600 million, were sold by the industry to approximately 1,100 plastic fabricators in Europe. This was considered as one of the most fragmented markets served by ACE. Stabilizers had experienced an annual growth rate averaging less than 3% in tonnage during the 1970s. The market was expected to remain stagnant, however, for most of the 1980s. As one member of product management explained, "Stabilizers have matured as an industry. All potential applications have been discovered and we do not see any prospect for rapid growth among the existing uses."

The recessionary conditions prevailing in many European user industries during the past year were blamed for the 15% decline in total consumption from the 1979 level. The industry's unutilized plant capacity was estimated at about one-third.

More than 20 companies competed in the European stabilizer market. The four largest producers were Ciba–Geigy (Switzerland), ACE, Berlocher (West Germany), and Lankro (United Kingdom). Together they accounted for approximately one-half of the market in 1980. ACE management pointed out that most competitors had a home base where they were particularly strong. All companies, however, tried to sell their stabilizers regionwide.

The chemical properties of the stabilizers produced by ACE differed from those made by others in Europe. The company's variety was referred to in the trade as "Tin" (Sn)—the generic name representing its chemical structure. The stabilizers most frequently produced by competitors had a different structure and were generically referred to as "Barium" (Ba). Both varieties were general-purpose products with large end-use applications. Differences in properties—such as heat and light resistance, weathering, and oil absorption—were considered by many in management to be minor between the two varieties. Although, in theory, general-purpose stabilizers could substitute

EXHIBIT 1   Stabilizer Market Segments, 1979

End-use Segments	Sample Products	Consumption (% of total)	No. of Fabricators (estimate)
Coated fabrics	Upholstery	17	180
Flooring	Cushion flooring sheets/ tiles	20	160
Wire and cables	Cable jackets and insulation	17	235
Compounds	Shoes	11	55
Process segments			
Platisole	Wall covering, gloves, balls	5	90
Calendering	Very broad: dresses, housing, etc.	13	180
Extrusion	Hoses	11	130
Injection molding	Shoes	6	70
		100	1,100

for one another in most applications, in practice, plastic fabricators could not switch easily from one type to another, as the process technologies required were considerably different. Barium was by far the most commonly used stabilizer in Europe.

Entry Strategy

ACE's decision to enter the European stabilizer market was made in 1970. The original strategy called for a step-by-step penetration of the market toward a long-term market share objective of 20%, projected at 160,000 tons by 1979. The main elements of the entry strategy are described next.

1. *Market exploration:* Because ACE did not have any working knowledge of the European stabilizer industry, the first few years after entry were to be spent exploring "the possibility of becoming a major fully integrated stabilizer supplier by 1980." The long-term choice of stabilizers for ACE was Tin, for which the company's European subsidiaries had ample feedstock or the needed raw material. However, beginning in 1970, ACE entered the market with Barium purchased from European producers.

2. *Third-party production:* Due to the high level of start-up investment in production facilities, ACE's supply of Barium initially, and of Tin later, was to be secured through production agree-

ments with established European producers. A member of the management closely involved with supply negotiations referred to the process as "difficult—something you can do when you have a strong heart and lots of guts." The company foresaw eventual European production once sufficient sales volume was attained.

3. *Conversion:* Barium was to be an entry product in Europe; ACE management intended to gradually convert its customers to Tin. Conversion was to be encouraged through lower initial prices, but also through assuring better product performance. Initial discounts of 2% to 3% below Barium prices were deemed necessary, because conversion required changes in process and machinery that had to be justified economically.

4. *Segmentation:* Product management was keenly aware of the differences among various segments in the stabilizer market. For some, performance was more important than price; for others, the reverse held true. In wire and cables, for example, stabilizer costs were less than 2% of the total cost. As a result, these producers were less sensitive to price than those in flooring, for which the cost ratio was around 10%.

Size also played an important role: large firms purchasing in excess of 500 tons per month paid lower prices than small- and medium-sized firms purchasing one truckload or more at a time. The difference in price could be as large as 5%.

The entry strategy placed its sales emphasis on those segments for which price played a relatively more significant role. As one subsidiary sales manager explained, "We had to get the attention of people when we first started up. We used the tools we had, and price was an important tool."

SELLING STABILIZERS

ACE's Tin stabilizers, branded as Polystab, were sold through a specialized sales force in all the subsidiaries. They were assisted in technical matters by the staff from technical service located in Geneva. The service was thought to be of particular importance for small- and medium-sized clients who did not have one in-house. Management believed that the specialized salespeople and the highly competent technical service, both unique in the industry, had allowed the company to gain and build in-depth knowledge of the various industries and processes using stabilizers.

For selling purposes, the subsidiaries grouped their accounts according to the following classifications:

1. *Base:* Regular Polystab customers mostly converted from Barium.
2. *Strategic:* Important prospects; usually trendsetters in their industry, currently using Barium.
3. *Swing:* "In-and-out" customers; price oriented.

In 1980, the *base* accounts provided the bulk of Polystab sales. The *strategic* accounts, on the other hand, were key targets for conversion and, hence, long-term sources of sales. They required intensive attention from management and often a highly technical type of selling. The *swing* accounts were usually converted, but could not be counted on as regular customers because of their low-price orientation.

The task of converting from Barium to Tin fell on the sales force. The sales management pointed out that selling revolved around establishing tangible advantages for the client to justify the changes in equipment and process that were usually needed. They also mentioned that in certain applications conversion held only small benefits that were hard to demonstrate. In all cases, conversion was a time-consuming process. Product management estimated that it took, on average, 18

months to convert an account. The actual time spent could vary from 6 months to several years. In every case, a minimum of eight to ten visits from the technical service staff in Geneva were required.

For all the subsidiaries, the proportion of selling time spent on conversion had declined since the mid-1970s. In a typical case, in 1980 the sales force spent only a quarter of its time on conversion prospects, whereas in 1975 the ratio was close to 60%.

Since ACE was not the sole supplier of Tin in the market,[2] most converted customers compared prices before placing an order, usually done on a monthly basis. The sales force, therefore, was intimately aware of the importance of price in making sales.

One subsidiary sales manager explained the buying behavior of stabilizer customers: "The larger companies have a professional buying practice. They check with two or three regular suppliers and then place their order. The smaller firms, on the other hand, tend to contact a multitude of producers, trying to negotiate a low price. They often wait till the middle or end of the month hoping for a general deterioration in prices." He added that Barium producers were the price setters in the market and, therefore, a knowledge of their prices, as well as those for Tin, was essential in selling. "Prices do fluctuate during the month, depending on the level of demand and the producers' eagerness to sell their inventory. So timing is critical. When you set your prices high at the beginning of the month and you don't get an order by the tenth, you get pretty nervous. You can easily overreact and then destroy your average price level for the rest of the month." Typically, about two-thirds of each month's sales were made in the first two weeks of the month.

A stabilizer salesperson in the subsidiaries had between 10 and 25 accounts to look after. His days were spent partly in the office, preparing reports and reaching customers by phone,

---

[2] For all other producers, Tin accounted for a minor share of their stabilizer sales because they did not have their own feedstock required for its production.

and partly on the road, visiting companies. Some sales managers insisted on visiting each account a minimum of once a month.

STABILIZER MARKETING ORGANIZATION

The marketing organization for stabilizers is shown in Exhibit 2. Partial job descriptions for key executives in the organization are given in Exhibit 3.

Graaff, who was new to the stabilizer organization, described the matrix structure as one built on "interaction and positive confrontation." Another executive, Peter Hansen, director for stabilizers, referred to the "dual boss system" as working well. "In the old days before the system arrived, the subsidiaries wouldn't even let us into their offices!" A sales manager with many years in the company also commented on the system, "The dual boss relationship can be useful or painful. It depends on the chiefs."

Headquarters marketing had profit responsibility for stabilizers. Graaff described the product line's profitability as a function of production costs, average prices received by the subsidiaries, and the total volume of sales. Management at the subsidiary, on the other hand, was held accountable primarily for the volume of sales generated in their market, in addition to the cost of selling and the level of receivables. Subsidiaries paid a transfer price for stabilizers sold in their market.

The performance of sales managers was evaluated jointly by the subsidiary managing director and headquarters marketing manager Whenever a manager was responsible for the sales of a number of products, a joint performance appraisal would be undertaken for each line. Company executives pointed out that a superior overall performance could mean an increase in annual salary of up to 10% for the sales managers. This merit raise was said to be a "big carrot" and an important incentive.

Before Graaff joined stabilizer marketing, quarterly and annual sales quotas were used as bases for performance evaluation. Quarterly meetings in Geneva between the marketing and sales managers compared the progress in stabilizer sales against quotas.

By company policy, all ACE executives and members of the sales organization were com-

EXHIBIT 2 Stabili`zer Marketing Organization

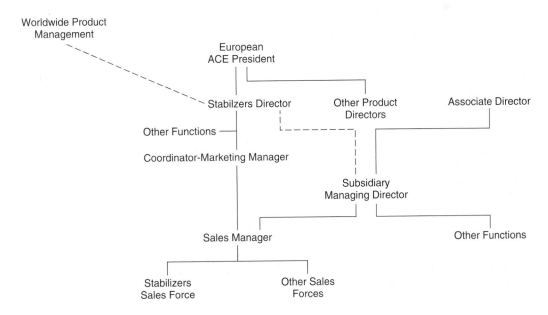

EXHIBIT 3   Partial Job Definitions

Director, Stabilizers	Serves as regional product manager, responsible for all phases of the region's stabilizer business, including technology, manufacturing, marketing and supply, and transportation; establishes regional goals, objectives, plans, and action steps and works with worldwide product manager to assure that these are consistent with the worldwide plan and resources; responsible for proper execution of approved plans; must coordinate his conduct of business with and seek guidance from worldwide product line manager and the regional president.
Stabilizers, Marketing Manager	Responsible for all marketing activities within stabilizers; consults subsidiary marketing and sales personnel to develop the marketing inputs for the stabilizer business plan; responsible for proper execution of approved marketing plan and regionwide results; shares responsibility with subsidiary sales manager for development of sales staff.
Subsidiary Managing Director	Is accountable for all the chemical businesses in the subsidiary; shares responsibility with each regional product line director for planning and conduct of each business within the subsidiary.
Subsidiary Sales Manager	Shares responsibility with each regional product line marketing manager for planning and conduct of the businesses within the subsidiary; must play an important role in high-level contacts with key customers; will advise on overall strategy within the country, including the economic outlook as well as opportunities for new businesses; will encourage a close working relationship between salesforce and the regional product line marketing managers.

pensated by a fixed salary. This policy also applied to the 10-man specialized stabilizer sales force in Europe, whose salaries and performance evaluation procedures were determined at the subsidiary level.

EBERHARD GRAAFF

Eberhard Graaff had been with Alto for 15 years before being assigned to stabilizer marketing. A chemical engineer by training, he had filled various positions in Europe and the Far East as a business analyst, design engineer, plant supervisor, and subsidiary sales manager. This was his first appointment in Geneva; his predecessor had recently retired from the company. In 1980, Graaff was 40 years old and the second youngest member of the stabilizer marketing organization.

"We felt we needed a man with positive leadership," explained Peter Hansen, Graaff's immediate boss. Graaff's outstanding performance as sales manager in France was considered as one factor in his promotion to the marketing position. Graaff himself believed that his "tough name" in the company was also instrumental in his selection.

ACE executives were aware of the difficulties inherent in Graaff's new assignment. Hansen explained, "The job of headquarters marketing is complicated not only by the different market and competitive conditions of each subsidiary, but also by the diversity in personalities and cultures of their management." He felt that the job required, in addition to marketing expertise, skills in establishing a dialogue with the subsidiaries and in building a sales team.

STRATEGY REVISED

The stabilizer strategy set in motion in 1970 had achieved most of its objectives by 1980. ACE's stabilizer share in Western Europe was nearly 18%. Predictably, the proportion of Barium in total company sales had declined over the years. As of mid-1979, Tin stabilizers were being produced by the company's own facilities in France. In that year, the stabilizer sales force was calling on a total of 170 accounts in the region.

Graaff's first couple of months in the new job were taken up with visits to each of the nine subsidiaries and a review of marketing and sales practices region wide. By December, Graaff had reached a number of conclusions regarding the current Polystab strategy as implemented in the field:

1. *Overreliance on price:* Selling was too price oriented; Barium prices were matched or undercut by 2 to 3 percentage points even for the converted Tin accounts.
2. *Narrow market base:* Price-oriented selling had led to emphasis on those segments where it played an important role, that is, the larger companies and swing accounts.
3. *Low profitability:* Low prices in the region meant low profitability for the stabilizer business. The current regional average contribution margin of $40 per ton was deemed an unsatisfactory return for the recently completed facilities in France.
4. *Price discrepancies:* In the absence of central coordination, differences in subsidiary prices were encouraging the larger geographically diversified clients to buy their entire requirements from cheaper subsidiaries and transfer them for use to other subsidiary markets. Price differentials among subsidiaries were partly due to different average market prices in each country. Traditionally, for example, German stabilizer prices were a few percentage points above those of other European countries.

Graaff commented on the conclusions of his 8-week study:

The picture became rather clear to me. We are a volume-oriented organization, from here all the way down. This is a legacy of the original strategy, which gave us a chance to compete in this market. So, as long as the quarterly sales quotas were met, nobody complained. And to meet the quotas, subsidiaries had a fairly open hand in setting prices. Headquarters price guidelines were only good for the first few days of each month. Afterward, the sales pressure from the field forced the people in Geneva to give in, leading to low average prices for the whole month. This cycle would repeat itself 12 times a year.

Graaff was convinced that a revision of the successful stabilizer strategy was in order. "Product management and top ACE executives have been increasingly concerned with the return on our heavy investment in stabilizer facilities," he explained. "My understanding of this market leads me to believe that improved profitability is possible, provided we have the right segments and selling approach."

In December 1980, Graaff communicated in writing the following elements of the revised stabilizers strategy to the subsidiary sales managers and asked them to incorporate these points into their future sales plans. A summary of the revised strategy follows:

1. *Nonprice selling:* Price to play a subsidiary role in selling; instead, emphasis to be placed on areas where ACE held a competitive edge such as expert sales force, superior technical service, and general corporate reputation for supplier reliability.
2. *New accounts:* Selling aimed at conversion of new accounts to receive added impetus; new accounts to come primarily from small- and medium-sized firms and segments that were less price sensitive such as wire and cable.
3. *Price leadership:* Discounting or merely "meeting Barium prices" will no longer be an acceptable pricing policy for converted accounts; sales management to watch for opportunities to initiate price leadership vis-à-vis other suppliers.
4. *Central coordination:* Geneva was to take a more active part in setting price and volume targets for subsidiaries; the highly competitive low-price markets were to receive less sales emphasis than those enjoying higher average prices; headquarters coordination to aim at regional optimization.

The average price improvement was expected to yield immediate results. For the 1981–1982 planning period, Graaff was projecting a doubling of contribution margins to $80 per ton.

In his communication to the sales organization, Graaff also mentioned that, although he was willing to accept a slight short-term drop in sales due to price improvement, the longer-term objective remained a growth in volume. This, he maintained, was essential if the new stabilizer plant was to operate at an economical utilization rate.

SALES MANAGEMENT RESPONSE

Reactions from the field were not long in coming. Communicating their sentiments to Graaff mostly by phone, sales managers were unanimously against the announced changes in the business strategy. "To speak of price improvement at a time when the whole market is declining is just absurd," was a typical comment from the field. Another manager responded, "Your strategy of improving both price *and* volume is unrealistic and contradictory." Still another commented, "The smaller accounts take the same amount of selling time as the larger ones. If we added them to our customer list, we would be running after more accounts for the same volume of sales. That wouldn't make sense." Another manager labeled the revised strategy as "not market oriented, but rather inward looking."

Sales management also expressed concern about their future relationship with clients. One manager explained,

We have gained our customer base through conversion and the promise of savings to the client. They did not scream when we gradually raised our prices to the Barium level during the past few years. At least they know that they won't be paying more than their Barium-using competitors. Now, if you were a user of Barium for 25 years and I succeeded in converting you, how would you react if I came around a few months later and told you that from now on you will be paying a premium over their prices? You'd probably ask me—whatever happened to the savings you promised? The money is in your pocket not mine!

This executive added that problems of this kind would have a detrimental effect on sales force motivation.

Underlying most managers' complaints was another concern—that the initiative in key decision areas was shifting away from subsidiaries toward Geneva. One subsidiary sales manager explained what was felt by many:

So far, we have succeeded in stabilizers because of local initiative; we knew our markets well enough to have confidence in headquarters marketing. They trusted our best judgment. We are professionals in this field and should be allowed to harmonize our own performance. Headquarters can help by synthesizing and giving broad guidelines. That's all. Rigid rules go against management harmony.

IMPLEMENTATION

Graaff was not surprised by the sales organization's reactions to his proposals. He explained, "I myself was in the subsidiaries for a number of years, so I know how they feel."

Graaff intended to take steps toward implementing the strategy, which he believed was sound and consistent with market realities. "I am convinced the strategy will work," he added in defense of his decisions. "It aims at changing our customer mix, which in turn allows us some pricing leverage in the long run. It also aims at enlarging the base, which reduces our risk with a few large customers and, finally, it takes a regional view of the stabilizer business, where all competitors and a number of customers are operating in more than one national market. A regional strategy gives us the flexibility of shifting our volumes toward those markets where we earn better margins."

Graaff did not minimize the implementation task ahead of him: "The job won't be easy, but I have always been sent into jobs with difficult problems." He added that, although he believed Hansen was in favor of improved profitability, he had not cleared the specifics of his strategy with the director and was certainly not going to ask for his help in implementing it in the field. "I am not the type who would seek advice from the boss on everything," he emphasized. "I have always followed the things I believe in."

Alto Chemicals Europe (B)

In the first 6 months of 1981, Graaff had undertaken a number of steps that he believed were necessary to implement the revised stabilizers strategy. He was reviewing the results to date with the purpose of deciding what to do next.

GRAAFF'S ACTIONS

Between January and June of 1981, Graaff had taken the following measures.

HQ Presentation

Early in January, Graaff invited the subsidiary sales managers to a planning meeting where he made a presentation on the main elements of the revised strategy. Central monitoring on price and volume, in addition to new emphasis on smaller accounts for the less price sensitive segments, was highlighted in the presentation. He also underlined that selling should become more technical in nature, with emphasis on quality and performance arguments. The need for closer collaboration between the sales force and technical service staff was similarly underscored.

Monthly Meetings

Subsidiary sales managers were asked to meet monthly with Graaff at headquarters to set price *and* volume targets and review progress to date. Graaff explained later, "The meetings were necessary to have better control of the business but also to give the subsidiaries a chance to talk to each other and see the whole picture."

Account Targets

Along with price and volume targets, the monthly meetings resulted in a "rolling list" of named accounts for each subsidiary's sales force to pursue. The accounts were segmented by size, end use, and whether they deserved a special effort for conversion. Accounts known for price cutting were left off the list, even the larger ones. Some rules were established for division of the selling effort between old accounts and new ones.

Volume Redistribution

To improve average prices received in the region, lower sales targets were set for historically competitive markets such as Holland. With higher target volumes for less price oriented markets such as Germany, Graaff intended to shift the total volume toward the more profitable subsidiaries.

RESULTS TO DATE

Although Graaff considered the first 6 months too short a time to determine the effectiveness

This case was prepared by Professor Kamran Kashani as a basis for class discussion rather than to illustrate either effective or ineffective handling of a business situation. All names and financial data have been disguised. Copyright © 1986 by IMEDE, Lausanne, Switzerland. The International Institute for Management Development (IMD), resulting from the merger between IMEDE, Lausanne, and IMI, Geneva, acquires and retains all rights. Not to be used or reproduced without written permission from IMD, Lausanne, Switzerland.

of the new strategy, a few results had begun to surface. The company had gained a number of new accounts among the medium-sized and smaller companies. This had been achieved despite the absence of discounts. On the other hand, several medium-sized and large accounts had been lost, some going to competitors and others reverting to Barium.

The overall impact on total volume of changes in the customer base was difficult to assess because industry sales had declined by about 8% during this period. Also, in some markets the contribution margins had increased slightly, in others not.

Meanwhile, the relationship between Graaff and the subsidiary sales managers had deteriorated significantly. The monthly meetings had often turned into shouting matches between Graaff and the more outspoken sales managers. The complaints voiced by the latter centered around the inherent wisdom of the new strategy and its impact on short-term results. Typical among these complaints were the following:

- You show us numbers and ratios to argue why a higher price is better than a lower price. But, the market doesn't have to follow your logic. Our customers don't understand our ratios; they don't even care. What they want is a lower price.
- For every key account I lose, I have to run after several smaller ones.
- You are destroying what took me years to build.

CONCLUSION

Graaff did not enjoy his monthly encounters with the sales managers, but he was not overly concerned. He felt it was part of the job. What was beginning to concern him, however, were signs that his boss was losing patience. On some recent occasions, Hansen had mentioned that sales force motivation should not be sacrificed for the sake of a strategy and that a more consensus-oriented approach might be more effective in winning subsidiary support. Evidently, some subsidiary managing directors had been in touch with him regarding complaints from the field.

Although agreeing with the merits of a consensus approach, Graaff was not totally convinced that it would work in this situation: "Consensus is fine. But, at the end of the day someone has to make a difficult decision and, in this case, that someone is me." Graaff was, however, more profoundly concerned about whether or not Hansen really believed in what he was trying to accomplish. "There are times I think even Hansen doesn't believe the strategy is going to work. It's difficult to change things when people have been around a long time and are used to a different thinking," he complained.

Despite certain signs of unease, Hansen had not tried to stop Graaff. On the contrary, he had given him a free hand to proceed.

6

The Global Challenge

International marketing has been studied as a concept for decades, but only recently has the concept of global marketing been introduced. Although treated by many as a replacement term for international marketing, global marketing represents only the most recent step in the development of concepts for international marketing. Historically, international marketing has been defined as "the performance of marketing activities across two or more countries."[1] This included exporting operations as well as the multicountry activities carried out by many multinational firms. Global marketing, with its emphasis on the simultaneous performance of marketing activities across the world market, is the most recent extension of traditional international marketing concepts.

Popularized first by Levitt, the ideas of globalization began to fascinate executives in many countries.[2] Originally, global marketing was understood as a strategy to offer essentially an identical marketing program to customers worldwide. Two key forces were behind the popularization of global marketing strategies: growing similarities among consumers and the need to achieve economies of scale. Originators of the concept argued that customers in many countries were becoming more similar. Life-style comparisons were made showing that some key demographic trends, such as dual-income households, were converging across many countries. With similarities growing, marketers began to develop similar marketing strategies across the globe. Economies of scale, the other force, forced companies to abandon the tailored marketing programs developed for each market and based on the previous model of multidomestic competition.[3] Many companies were observing the duplication of efforts and reinvention of key ideas. To save on expensive marketing operations, firms began to look into ways to avoid duplication in product design, variations, and advertising and promotional campaigns.

The experiences of early adopters of strict global marketing strategies were not uniformly

---

[1] Jean-Pierre Jeannet and Hubert Hennessey, *International Marketing Management*, Houghton Mifflin, Boston, 1988, p. 7.

[2] Theodore Levitt, "The Globalization of Markets," *Harvard Business Review*, May–June 1983, pp. 92–102.

[3] Thomas Hout, Michael E. Porter, and Eileen Rudden, "How Global Companies Win Out," *Harvard Business Review*, Sept.–Oct. 1982, pp. 98–108.

successful. One of the more celebrated examples was the experience of Parker Pen.[4] The company embarked on a major globalization drive in the early 1980s. Its marketing strategy decision making was centralized, disenfranchising many of the local country managers. Local advertising was replaced by narrowly defined standards worldwide for positioning, slogans, layout, graphics, logo, and even typeface. Finally, all local firms had to work with one centrally appointed advertising agency worldwide. Parker Pen also pruned its large product line and centralized its manufacturing. The experience was poorly received by both the market and the company's managers, so new management was brought in to return to a more locally driven marketing strategy.[5]

Today, it is more accepted that a complete global marketing strategy might work for only a few companies; Coca-Cola is a typical example. More typical are the many companies in between that might find that parts of their marketing strategy might be globalized. This modularization of global marketing is believed to help reduce the tension between a call for globalization due to efficiency reasons and a requirement for localization due to different market requirements.[6] But the experience of Parker Pen showed that successful global marketing requires more than sensitivity to market requirements. Different managerial approaches were also instrumental in bringing about a higher level of commitment by local management. Very important was the early participation in globalization efforts by local management. Success was also enhanced if companies moved to a more horizontal communications flow among participating local organizations, provided flexibility to experiment at the local level, and had champions that believed in the benefit of the globalization process and concentrated on key bottlenecks or barriers inside the organization.[7]

ASSESSING GLOBAL LOGIC

With some firms having successfully adopted global marketing strategies and with others having failed, managers in most international firms are confronted with the task of finding out if such concepts apply to them. Increasingly, it is a question of whether global marketing applies. Since global marketing works only under certain preconditions, marketers must learn to size up the global marketing environment and must test for the presence of such preconditions. When the environment is characterized by conditions that demand a global approach to marketing, we speak of a *global logic*.[8] Global logic is defined as a compelling rationale to approach marketing on a global basis. Disregarding global logic could risk a firm's long-term competitive position under circumstances where competitors have capitalized on global logic.

There are several identifiable sources of global logic.[9] Pressure for global logic could come from the customer base, the market itself, the industry, or competitors. Analyzing the customer brings us closer to the determination of global logic at the customer level. A firm could be a global customer when the nature of its requirements and the reason for purchasing are similar across the world. This form of global customer is actually a rare situation. Instead, customers

[4] "Marketers Turn Sour on Global Sales Pitch Harvard Guru Makes," *Wall Street Journal*, May 12, 1988, p. 1.

[5] Kamran Kashani, "Global Marketing: Pathways and Pitfalls," *IMEDE Perspectives*, No. 1, 1989.

[6] John Quelch, "Customizing Global Marketing," *Harvard Business Review*, May–June 1986, pp. 59–68.

[7] Kamran Kashani, "Beware of the Pitfalls of Global Marketing," *Harvard Business Review*, Sept.–Oct. 1989, pp. 91–98.

[8] Jean-Pierre Jeannet and Hubert Hennessey, *Global Marketing Strategies*, Houghton Mifflin, Boston, 1992, p. 273.

[9] Ibid., pp. 275–277.

may reach various stages of globalization, resulting in different amounts of global logic by segment. At the lowest common denominator are global needs. These are products that satisfy relatively homogeneous needs in many countries, despite the fact that the purchase criteria and features demanded may vary. Personal transportation is such a universal or global need. One step up from this are the motivations or purchasing criteria of customers. Where customers buy worldwide for the same reasons, the basis for global benefits exist. When they even demand or require similar features for products or services, we have reached the level of a global product. When this level has been reached, significant global pressure exists from customers to globalize marketing, and economies of scale can be gained by marketing similar products worldwide.

Analyzing market behavior, or how customers buy, helps us to determine if we have a global market logic. Significant market logic is present when customers go beyond their own domestic markets to purchase products or services. To the extent that they are willing to pursue bargains across the world, we find a global market for these products or services. Global market logic is therefore determined by the purchasing habits of customers, both business to business or individual buyers. When a large international firm starts to source accounting services worldwide from one international accounting firm and is soliciting offers from many firms, we have strong indications of a global logic in the market for such services. Not following through on such global market logic would risk losing business for the accounting firms in question. With more and more firms sourcing internationally, even globally, an increasing number of companies are facing strong global logic from that corner.

Global logic may also emanate from an industry or sector. When the structure of a given industry requires similar approaches across the world, or similar key success factors (KSFs), global industry logic exists.[10] When such logic is present, companies would do well to engage in leveraging such similarities. This requires companies to learn in one market key lessons of how to compete and to apply these lessons elsewhere. Firms that can follow through on such learning would have a substantial advantage in expanding rapidly to other parts of the world and thus obtaining additional leverage from the key lessons learned.

Our final source of global logic comes from competitor analysis. When a firm faces global competitors, the benefit from global marketing is far greater than if the firms face only locally active and always different competitors. Signs of strong global competition are not just in facing off against the same competitors in key markets. More importantly, a company needs to see if it faces consistently the same integrated strategy. When such is the case, strong global competitive logic exists, requiring companies to adjust their marketing strategies to new requirements.

Analyzing the source of global logic is important because global marketing strategies vary depending on the prevalent global logic. It is also necessary to recognize that the sources described here may not be the only ones. However, they have been found to be those most frequently faced by international firms. The four sources may not be equally developed and tend to vary by industry or market sector. It is also conceivable that one company might find very strong global logic from one area but weak pressure from another. Only after having understood the sources and strengths of global logic can a firm proceed to consider global marketing strategies.

---

[10] See Kenichi Ohmae, *The Mind of the Strategist*, McGraw-Hill, New York, 1982, Ch. 3, for an explanation of the concept of KSFs.

SELECTING FROM MANY GLOBAL MARKETING STRATEGIES[11]

As the experience of international marketers with global marketing concepts and strategies has grown, many firms have become aware that the choice no longer lies between a global or international marketing stray, but that the choice increasingly needs to be made among a number of different global strategies.

Integrated global marketing strategies, by which the entire marketing strategy is integrated on a global scale, are not the only types of global strategies available. Appropriate for companies that face a full range of global logic across customers, markets, industry, and competitors, they remain nevertheless appropriate for only a limited number of firms. More likely, the differing patterns of global logic call for partial global marketing strategies. The following additional global marketing strategies can be identified:

Global product category strategies are some of the least integrated forms of global marketing strategies. Adopting such a strategy, companies would attempt to leverage their experience in competing in a certain category of products, which might include several different segments and products and/or brands. In each country organization, the company would stay within the prescribed category, but vary segment, product, brand, and other marketing elements.

Global segment strategies are pursued by firms who integrate their strategies by segment. A company may decide to pursue a particular segment in all geographic markets and, as a result, integrate its approach to that segment. Experience shows that narrowly defined segments often display greater homogeneity across countries than broader marketing strategies. Selecting a global segment strategy, the international firm attempts to capitalize on and leverage its experience with a particular customer group across countries.

Global product strategy would be pursued by a company that wants to offer a relatively standardized or integrated product. Variations may be offered in a modularized fashion. This strategy would be possible when the company faces largely global customers with similar product requirements. Its conceivable that the products offered are very similar, but that branding, segmenting, and other marketing elements are handled on a local basis.

Global communications strategies are pursued by firms that face a strong customer logic with respect to similarity of benefits. Once it has been established that the benefits sought by customers are relatively similar, it can be advantageous for a company to build communications, particularly advertising, on a global scale. This does not mean that all advertising would be identical, which is not possible due to many language and other cultural barriers. Instead, the focus here is on the overall strategy, such as appeal and positioning.

Global branding strategies are adopted by firms that use a common brand name across the world market. The investment in the launch of a new brand is substantial, and many firms want to write off brand creation over many markets. Global branding strategies are appropriate where customers show evidence of shopping or purchasing across borders. This may include business equipment, for which executives might search worldwide for the most appropriate solution. It may also include consumer products for which consumers, by travel or other means, are made aware of the existence of certain brands in other markets.

---

[11] Jeannet and Hennessey, *Global Marketing Strategies*, pp. 277–280.

SUMMARY

One important aspect of building global marketing strategies is the understanding that the above-cited strategies are possible in a number of combinations. A global branding strategy may or may not be supported by a global advertising/communications strategy. A global product strategy may be adopted, but local branding may be chosen. The challenge for global marketers will be to fit the appropriate integrated or modular global marketing strategy to the requirements of the market. This requirement is closely related to the presence or absence of a strong global logic. Finding the ideal combination is a continuous challenge for marketing professionals.

The following cases, drawn from a variety of real situations, will offer the reader a chance to apply some of the concepts described in this section. The Black & Decker case will offer an opportunity to analyze a business for the presence of global logic. The World Robotics Industry case accompanied by the Asea Robotics cases describes the situation of a technology-driven industry facing intensive Japanese competition. Finally, the World Paint Industry case combined with the ICI Paints case deals with both consumer and industrial paints and requires an analysis of the industry, with implications for adapting a global marketing strategy for the industry leader.

Black & Decker International: Globalization of the Architectural Hardware Line

If you don't know where you're going, any road will take you there. . . .

Theodore Levitt

In March 1990, Fred Grunewald was reviewing the presentation he had prepared for top management of the Black & Decker Company. Mr. Grunewald was vice-president of product and market development for the international group (Power Tools and Home Improvement Group); his job was to act as the catalyst for developing the company's businesses from local or regional entities into global players. A perfect opportunity for dramatic changes and profit growth was presented by Black & Decker's recent acquisition of the Emhart Corporation, which brought with it an architectural hardware (locks and locksets) business. Grunewald believed that capitalizing on the opportunity would require both restructuring the way the acquired companies went to market, as well as rethinking how the various parts of the businesses could be integrated on a global scale.

The bottom line of his opening transparency read, "We intend to create a global Black & Decker lock business." Substantial work lay ahead, however, to make this intention a reality—not only in coordinating the management of the acquired entities (with the risk of alienating and losing some key managers), but also in finishing marketing research, simplifying production design and engineering, rationalizing distribution channels, and overcoming regional differences. On top of these tasks, his proposal, which called for the addition of new personnel, would inevitably add to overhead costs at a time when the company's earnings were being squeezed by the costs of financing the Emhart acquisition.

This job would be one of the more challenging jobs Grunewald had faced in his 18 months with the company, but he had developed considerable global knowledge as he had worked with the operating divisions to build strategic plans and to set development priorities. He believed he would also be helped by the globalization momentum that had won the company much favorable publicity in recent times. Because the presentation of his recommendations was scheduled for next week, he set about thinking through the logic and implications of his report one more time.

This case was made possible through the cooperation of the Black & Decker Company. Some of the data are disguised and thus should not be used for research purposes. Case material is intended as a basis for class discussion rather than to illustrate either effective or ineffective handling of an administrative situation. Copyright © 1990 by the University of Virginia Darden School Foundation, Charlottesville, VA. All rights reserved.

BLACK & DECKER[1]

Four years ago, Black & Decker was a struggling industrial also-ran that was in serious trouble. We made a commitment to turn the company around, and we have met that commitment. Today, Black & Decker has been transformed into a global marketing power that has rewritten nearly every performance record in its history.... The company's resurgence has been driven by a four-part strategy that concentrated all of our resources and energies on a set of clear objectives: build core profitability; strengthen management; improve return on equity; and broaden the earnings base. *1989 Annual Report*

Founded in 1917, Black & Decker manufactured and sold a wide line of electric and battery-powered power tools (and accessories), household products, outdoor products, locks and hardware, plumbing products, and mechanical fastening systems. Net sales for fiscal year (FY) 1989 were $3.2 billion, up from $2.3 billion in FY 1988; net earnings were $30 million, down from $97 million. Part of the sales increase and earnings decrease were attributable to the acquisition of Emhart Corporation in 1989.

In 1985, Nolan Archibald became chief executive officer of a Black & Decker company that had disjointed international product lines and policies, dissatisfied customers, and a tarnished reputation. While the Black & Decker name still had a loyal following [in England, a do-it-yourself (DIY) hobbiest would be "Black & Deckering"; a French person who was socially "plugged in" would be "*très Black & Decker*"], the main product lines were losing to Asian global competition (especially Japan's Makita) and to strong local competitors in all parts of the world.

Two of Archibald's key actions had been to develop a worldwide view toward the markets for the company's products and to reduce drastically the number of models needed to fill those global markets. As part of this, the company reverse-engineered its competition's products and established just-in-time, continuous-flow production processes. Archibald hired new top managers, who began an active program of new-product development (60 new or redesigned power tools; 40% of household products less than 3 years old).

As of early 1990, the organization was still in a period of fluid change, an outcome of the shift to looking at global rather than local manufacturing and design opportunities. The organization was a mixture of three forms: functional units, product categories (or strategic business units), and geographical units. Three main divisions, each under a group president, were Power Tools and Home Improvements, Household Products, and Commercial and Industrial Products (see Exhibit 1 for a partial organization chart). Within the Power Tools and Home Improvement Group was a mix of product and geographical divisions; the U.S. Power Tools, Europe, International, Hardware and Home Improvement, and Power Tool Accessories divisions each had a president.

Within the Power Tools Group, the Europe Division, in addition to having full marketing and manufacturing facilities for power tools, was also responsible for sales of the Households Products Group and for the products of the Hardware and Home Improvement Division and the Power Tool Accessories Division. Moreover, the International Division had responsibility for two plants manufacturing household products in Brazil and Mexico, along with sales responsibilities for all company products in the world outside of Europe and the United States. Grunewald, under the president of International, had product and market-development responsibility for all but the North American and European businesses. The Power Tool Accessories Division sold its products in the United States, but also had responsibility for plants and engineering design centers in Europe. Finally, the full-functioned Household Products Group had responsibility for U.S. sales of its own products, for a houseware plant in Singapore, and for sales of all Black & Decker products in Canada.

---

[1] Material for this section comes from "The New Power in Black & Decker," *Fortune*, January 2, 1989, pp. 89–92, and from the company's *1989 Annual Report*.

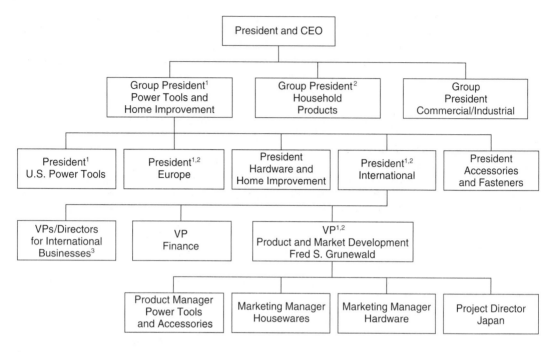

```
                          ┌─────────────────────┐
                          │   President and CEO  │
                          └─────────────────────┘
```

┌──────────────────────┬──────────────────────┬──────────────────────┐
│ Group President[1]   │ Group President[2]   │ Group   │
│ Power Tools and   │ Household   │ President   │
│ Home Improvement   │ Products   │ Commercial/Industrial│
└──────────────────────┴──────────────────────┴──────────────────────┘

| President[1] U.S. Power Tools | President[1,2] Europe | President Hardware and Home Improvement | President[1,2] International | President Accessories and Fasteners |

| VPs/Directors for International Businesses[3] | VP Finance | VP[1,2] Product and Market Development Fred S. Grunewald |

| Product Manager Power Tools and Accessories | Marketing Manager Housewares | Marketing Manager Hardware | Project Director Japan |

[1]Included in the quarterly strategic reviews for the power tools businesses.
[2]Included in the quarterly strategic reviews for the housewares businesses.
[3]"International" included Mexico, Latin America, the Middle East, Africa, and Australasia.

EXHIBIT 1 Partial Organization Chart *Source:* Company documents.

A new position of president under the Hardware and Home Improvement Division had just been established and filled from outside the company. This new president of the Hardware and Security Products Section, a full-functioned marketing/production/finance operation, would be charged with rationalizing the acquired lock companies into one integrated business.

FRED GRUNEWALD

Grunewald had been recruited to Black & Decker in late 1988 to the staff position of vice-president, product and market development, as a key resource in the globalization initiative at Black & Decker. Along with 10 years experience at General Electric in sales, product management, marketing, and strategic planning, Grunewald commented on his credentials:

It seems as if I have the background for international marketing: I was born of German parents, raised in Latin America, nearly completed a Ph.D. in Chinese studies, and got my MBA at Michigan! It helps that my office is located in the same building as those of the group and divisional presidents. That fact, my knowledge about what's going on in the rest of the world (being on the road 25% of the year and constantly asking for information from the field), and an intellectual instinct to view things from a central perspective helps to build a knowledge base and perspective that helps my credibility with the operating managers.

Examples of his job included developing strategic plans, working with field managers to develop market research, and functioning as a critical resource in top-management meetings to set strategic product priorities. As he viewed Black & Decker's "strategy for the 90s," he believed that it was important to leverage the company's solid international base in power tools into housewares and other Black & Decker products that were not as well known. He believed building a global base for housewares—basically a "metal-bending and plastics moldings business"—was especially important to move the company out of the "no-win" box of the middle market in which the low-cost operators won on cost and the high-end niche players won on gross margin. An interesting question to resolve at the international level, he thought, was how well the brand name might transfer from "basement [power tools] to kitchen [housewares]" in non-U.S. cultures. He believed that his part of the world, especially the Pacific rim, was crucial for Black & Decker's future growth: it currently comprised the smallest share of the company's sales (16%), yet was growing the fastest (21% in 1989) and with much larger potential for the future.

He had concluded that the company's businesses would continue to become more diversified—and the complexities increase—as the company pursued its global imperative. Japan remained a particularly elusive market and one that exemplified the different demands that different cultures placed on quality and attention to detail, requiring one to adjust to a myriad of local regulations and customs. He illustrated this as follows:

These two faxes I got from the Far East, just yesterday, are a timely example of what I mean. I had just received this two-page fax from [X country] complaining about the five things that went wrong with a recent product launch. When this message cleared, I got another from our agent in Japan, who had counted our shipment of 3,098 items to find that we had sent only 3,096, and gave us a *credit* of ¥60 [30¢]—the fax cost more than that! You can see the need to be flexible from culture to culture and yet stay above the minutiae of local situations that can threaten to drown you.

Despite such differences, however, the company had succeeded in drastically paring down the number of different product designs. For example, in the case of power tools, the number of motor designs was reduced from over 100 in 1985 to a planned 5 in 1989; the change

was implemented by creating four key design centers for all power tools (DIY tools in the United Kingdom, woodworking tools in West Germany, and similar specialties in Italy and in the United States).

GLOBAL PRODUCT PLANNING AND REVIEW

Black & Decker operationalized its global approach to the identification and development of world products through a process of *strategic, managerial,* and *operational* activities. This approach had developed over the past few years as a way to set priorities for new-product projects and to review their status on a regular basis. In the past, managers tended to look at product-line planning—its depth and breadth—on a purely country-by-country basis, but now a given product line—dubbed by company managers "the product road"—was under a regular cycle of research, evaluation, goal setting, and review.

For the Power Tool and the Household Products groups, *strategic* product-road reviews were held quarterly, attended by key management and engineering/manufacturing personnel (see Exhibit 1). These day-long meetings were held at company headquarters in the United States. Based on extensive research of the market, competitors, and the like, these meetings would set the capital-budgeting priorities for new product types, approve major new-product programs, and review and adjust the progress of previously approved programs. The data for these meetings were developed by product managers in the United States and Europe with input from the international group. Depending on how fast a market seemed to be evolving, a product (for example, a commercial power drill or a cordless screwdriver) would be reviewed on a 12-month, 18-month, or 24-month cycle.

Similar quarterly *managerial* meetings were held at the four design centers in which key engineering and marketing personnel tracked the progress of major product programs. Invaluable by-products of these meetings were exchanges of information and ideas on emerging market trends and on problem solving ("If we could use the 3-meter European cord standard in all markets, look what we would save . . .").

An additional *operational* activity, which Grunewald called "product-road bashing," took place continually among product managers at the same levels in the organization but in different groups in different parts of the world. Under constant encouragement from top management, the product manager for, say, angle-grinders in the Power Tools Division and his or her counterpart in the Europe Division would telephone, fax, and travel to each other's operations to answer the question "How can I reduce my five-item angle-grinder product line, and how can my counterpart reduce his or her eight items, yet still come up with five between us that will produce manufacturing efficiencies but cover even more markets?"

This stream of activity at the operational level was part of the input to the planning documents used at the quarterly managerial and strategy conferences. Once approved, the results of these meetings became the plans and budgets by which each division was measured. In addition, the data developed in these plans were also useful in the preparation of new-product launches. Therefore, as Grunewald pointed out, the headquarters staff were not seen as

information sinks, in which we ask for information—and lots of it—which is never seen again by the field. Our knowledge base, and our use of it, and, more importantly, the actions taken on it by top management are what gives us our credibility. In addition, we have established champions in each of our operating divisions who keep the globalization issues alive at all times. In some cases, these champions happen to be the top managers, which signals the importance of the activity and, of course, makes sure that globalization happens at the local level.

ARCHITECTURAL HARDWARE BUSINESS

The line of door-hardware products that came with the Emhart acquisition included locksets, high-security and electronic locks, door closers and exit devices, and master keying systems. (See Exhibit 2 for basic illustrations of these products.) The eight brands were Kwikset, Russwin, Corbin, Price Pfister, DOM, NEMEF, Lane, and ASTRA. According to Black & Decker executives, Kwikset (California) was the world's largest manufacturer of residential door hardware and the U.S. leader in the retail DIY market. Russwin/Corbin (Connecticut) was another well-known U.S. manufacturer of premium-priced commercial and industrial locksets. The following table summarizes the main products of these eight companies:

Black & Decker Architectural Hardware Companies	
U.S. Based: Kwikset	Tubular[a] locks, residential
Russwin/ Corbin	Cylindrical, mortise, commercial
Europe: DOM (Germany)	Cylindrical, industrial
NEMEF (Holland)	Commercial (all types)
Corbin/(Italy)	Padlocks, commercial locks
Australia: Lane	Residential (Lane), commercial (ASTRA)

[a] "Tubular" and "cylindrical" refer to internal designs related to the lock's security from break-in (cylindrical locks were more secure).

Sales offices for various companies existed in West Germany, France, the United Kingdom, Austria, Italy, Holland, Switzerland, Australia, Hong Kong, and Canada. Each company under Emhart's management had operated as an autonomous unit, with its own design, manufacturing, marketing, and support functions. Manufacturing plants were located in Connecticut, California, West Germany, Australia, the Netherlands, Italy, and Canada. As mentioned earlier, a new president had just been appointed to run the lock companies.

According to Grunewald, the challenge facing the integration of these various companies was not just internal; an equal task was how to conceptualize the global marketing of their products in the various regions of the world. In his view, the door-hardware-products industry was bound by old traditions and complicated by highly fragmented thinking about market opportunities. For example, the man-

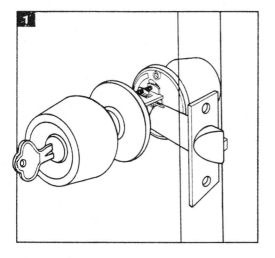

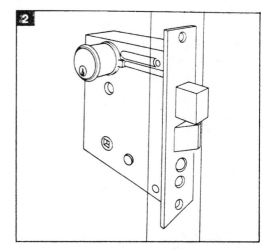

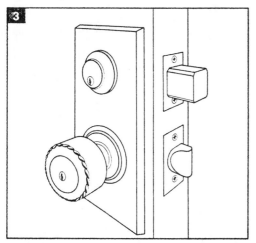

Primary locks There are three main types. **1** Key-in-knob lock: It's standard in new construction, but always vulnerable because the knob can be ripped off. **2** Mortise lock: Often found in older houses, it looks strong, but it actually weakens the door. Also, the cylinder in this type may be easy to pick. **3** Interconnected lockset: The top lock is a dead bolt, but if the knob below is attacked, both locks may be vulnerable.

EXHIBIT 2 Some Lock Types   *Source: Consumer Reports,* February 1990, pp. 98–99.

agers of these companies (and the industry in general) tended to view their markets and products along three major but narrowly constructed continuums: (1) technology (from very simple to electronic); (2) security (from minimal to extremely high); and (3) systems (from providing the internal cylinders only to providing the full trim hardware, electronic circuitry, switches, and so on). Most companies seemed to position themselves at the extremes in one, or perhaps two, of these dimensions. The old companies also tended to specialize at either the high or low ends of the price continuum, allowing competitors to make inroads into the middle, gray areas. No one manufacturer made or offered products to the total market segments (residential, commercial, decorative, and so on).

With regards to international marketing, any one Emhart company tended to think only in terms of expanding its narrow line abroad, without considering the possibility of integrating and sourcing its global production by center of manufacturing expertise, design expertise, or "feeder/eater" systems (manufacturing versus assembly operations). The narrow ap-

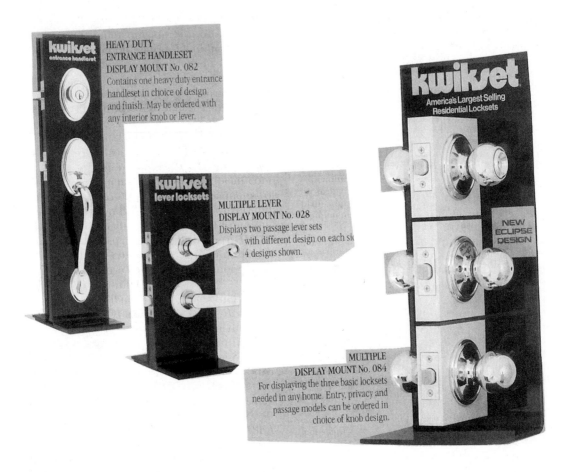

EXHIBIT 2 (*Continued*)   *Source:* Company documents.

proach to overseas business made the companies especially thin in Asia, Latin America, the Middle East, and Africa.

This historical "tunnel" vision was, Grunewald believed, typical for U.S. firms in domestic operations, but it was further exacerbated by the vast differences in distribution, branding preferences, and local-sourcing laws in the various international markets. Some Emhart companies had built a good reputation for service, while others were regarded as "just ok" or "difficult." The companies had developed some strong distributor relationships, however, albeit with low sales volumes and slow growth. The goal of pulling the former Emhart entities into an integrated operation, therefore, would be impeded by the legacies of brand proliferation, marketing inefficiencies, poor market knowledge, and inconsistent merchandising terms and policies.

What was attractive to Black & Decker, on the other hand, was the power that one integrated company could bring to an estimated $15 billion world market ($5 billion in locksets alone), an opportunity for power that would more than offset some of the infrastructural differences. Research indicated that about 60% of the products were sold through builders and original equipment manufacturers and 20% each through wholesale and retail channels. These figures indicated that a great majority of sales were going into new-construction or building-renovation projects. Unfortunately, Grunewald believed that the Emhart companies had not built a strong distribution system with regard to the international bid/contract business. The breadth of the various Emhart lock lines would allow a global approach, however, and Black & Decker's current power-tool presence and distribution abroad promised opportunities for synergies.

RECOMMENDATIONS FOR THE GLOBAL LOCK BUSINESS

Essentially, Grunewald was going to recommend that the International Group establish and take over what he called "on-the-ground" representation in foreign markets, at the same time identifying "local champions" in each lock factory. "On the ground" referred to setting up marketing managers in Belgium, Brazil, Dubai, Japan, Mexico, New Zealand, and Miami (headquarters of the Latin American operations). Reporting to these managers would be a product manager for residential hardware and plumbing, a product manager for architectural hardware, and a technical manager for applications and support. The marketing manager, assisted by the product managers, would be responsible for coordinating marketing and sales activities, including the product road, channel determination, servicing, marketing research, business plans, coordination of assembly and repackaging activities, training sessions with local distributors, and other activities.

Grunewald also saw the need to establish within each lock company a local champion who became for that company the focal point for all activities relating to the business—*as now perceived to be conducted on a global basis.* Among other activities, this person would be the liaison between the company and on-the-ground managers, would serve as project manager for new products (or product modifications required by foreign markets), would represent the international business in establishing product specifications and new-product priorities, and would in general assist the local company in building global opportunities for its business. It would be important that these individuals have senior-level clout and authority,

preferably reporting to the top manager in the company.

Grunewald's recommendation was also to establish at Black & Decker headquarters in Towson, Maryland, a group product manager for hardware products within the International Division; this person would be the central liaison between the global sales and marketing organization and the various hardware businesses. Due to the importance of the Japanese market, the Japanese sales personnel would report directly to this group product manager; however, all other on-the-ground marketing and sales personnel would report to the general managers of the local businesses. Under the group product manager would be product managers for retail locks, construction/architectural, and bid/contract, as well as the sales manager for hardware in Japan.

In Grunewald's mind, the establishment of these new jobs would be meaningless unless there were active "avenues of communication" between headquarters, on-the-ground, and local-champion personnel. He drew a chart to explain what he thought were good avenues of communication, and it was his role to see that the avenues were traveled (see Exhibit 3).

What was also yet to be established was an "intercompany organization" (see bottom of Exhibit 3) to facilitate, across all international organizations, such matters as centralized forecasting, order placement, billing, forwarding, expediting, and processing of export documentation. Additionally, a great many details had to be sorted through to ensure the smooth operation and growth of the hardware business. These details included staffing, training, transfer pricing, and forecasting. Also required was the development of marketing-support documents, such as catalogs, price lists, technical literature, and advertising and sales-support literature.

The advantages of consolidation seemed clear: it would improve market knowledge along the dimensions of competition, consumer segments, product requirements, and the like, and it would give Black & Decker the power to winnow out a complacent distribution base, to instill global quality standards

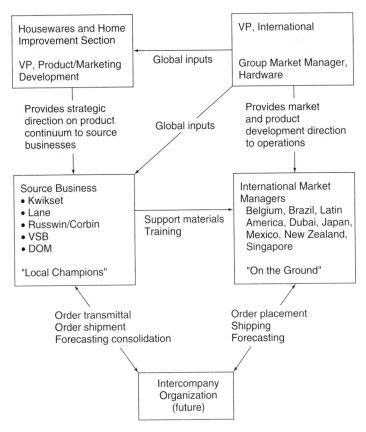

EXHIBIT 3 Avenues of Communication *Source:* Company documents.

throughout the world, to promote product innovation, and in general to bring a unified force and credibility to the now fragmented effort.

Yet to be resolved, according to Grunewald's report, were a number of issues that were generally outside his direct control. How would the new president of the lock business structure the lock companies? Would that business choose to adopt the quarterly planning reviews that characterized the power tools and housewares business? How would the "bashing" of the product roads take place?

What particularly troubled him was the suspicion that Black & Decker was not alone in sensing the global opportunities that existed, and he was hopeful that whatever was decided would not take more than a year to implement.

The Worldwide Robotics Industry, 1987

In the fall of 1987, Stelio Demark, president of ASEA Robotics AB[1] (hereafter referred to as ASEA), was looking back on a period of rapid growth for his company. ASEA had become the leading robot supplier in Europe and was second in the United States, making it one of the world's foremost robot companies. With about 2,000 robots to be shipped, turnover was expected to reach Skr1,300 million for the fiscal year ending December 31, 1987. Despite the company's success, Stelio was concerned about the direction of the business:

We are witnessing an explosion of orders in complete systems at the local subsidiary level. I believe that we have to completely rethink the way we run our business because, despite rapid growth, our profitability has not been satisfactory. Currently, nobody earns a respectable ROI in this industry, and the real question is how to organize a company to achieve that in robotics in the 1990s.

Industry Overview

In 1961, Unimation installed the first industrial robot at a General Motors factory in New Jersey. The following two decades were a time of slow growth in the robotics industry

and, by 1980, only 23,000 robots had been installed worldwide. However, beginning in the early 1980s, sales increased sharply, and by 1985 the worldwide base of installed robots had reached 100,000. Simultaneous to this growth, robots became part of the larger manufacturing automation industry that included CAD (computer-aided design) systems and microprocessor-controlled machinery. (For an overview of automation, see Exhibit 1.) Some industry observers believed that by 1990 the total factory automation industry would have a value of $100 billion, with robots serving as one of the main tools within a completely flexible automation system. By the end of 1986, industry shipments increased the installed base of robots to approximately 130,000. In the same year, total expenditures in the robotics industry reached $1.5 billion, with four-fifths of this value accounted for by unit hardware, or naked robots, and the balance by systems. By 1992, the worldwide robotics market was expected to have a value of $2.5 billion, with industry shipments approaching 47,000 units.

THE ROBOT AS A TOOL

Robots were a logical development in the process of industrial automation, which began in the 19th century. The only real difference between conventional automation systems and

---

[1] ASEA AB, the parent company of ASEA Robotics AB, merged with Brown Boveri & Cie AG of Switzerland on January 4, 1988. Since the merger, the company has operated under the official name of ABB Robotics, or ABB-R for short.

This case was prepared by Research Associate Robert C. Howard under the direction of Jean-Pierre Jeannet, Visiting Professor at IMEDE and Professor of Marketing and International Business at Babson College, Wellesley, Massachusetts. This note was prepared for class discussion and not to illustrate either effective or ineffective handling of an administrative situation. Copyright © 1989 by IMEDE, Lausanne, Switzerland. The International Institute for Management Development (IMD), resulting from the merger between IMEDE, Lausanne, and IMI, Geneva, acquires and retains all rights. Not to be used or reproduced without written permission from IMD, Lausanne, Switzerland.

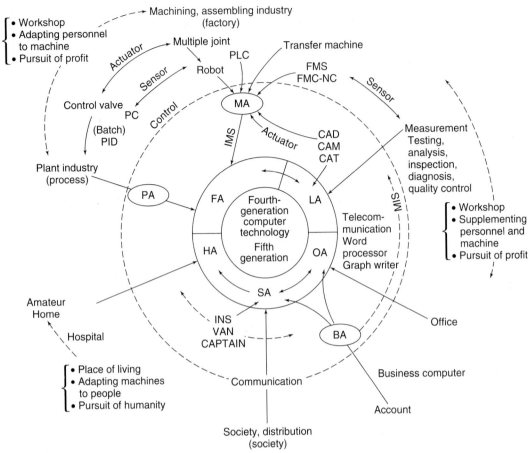

EXHIBIT 1   Genealogical Table for Automation   *Source:* M. Katagiri, in Yokogawa Technical Report No. 2 (1985), p. 3, *FFA and NYPS (Future Factory Automation and New YEW Productivity System).*

Explanation of Abbreviations

BA	Business automation		INS	Integrated network service
CAPTAIN	Character and pattern telephone access information network system in Japan		LA	Laboratory automation
			MA	Mechanical automation
			MIS	Management information system
CAD	Computer-aided design		PA	Process automation (chemical processes but *not* physical automation)
CAM	Computer-aided manufacturing			
CAT	Computer-aided testing		PC	Process control
FA	Factory automation		PID	Proportional integral derivate
FMC-NC	Flexible machining cell-numerically controlled		PLC	Programmable logic controller
			OA	Office automation
FMS	Flexible manufacturing system		SA	Social automation
HA	Home automation		VAN	Value-added network
IMS	Integrated manufacturing system			

robotic automation systems was that the former were designed for a single task, whereas the robot was flexible enough to handle many different tasks on many different workpieces. Because robots were often part of the larger factory automation industry, industry analysts classified robots as machines that could be programmed to do a range of different jobs and did not include less sophisticated and less flexible fixed-sequence manipulators. Typically, robots consisted of a "naked" robot with jointed arms, periphery devices such as sensors and vision systems, and a computer system that served as the controller for specific applications. In addition, robots could be equipped with adaptive controls to detect and correct workpiece imperfections. (See Exhibit 2 for a picture of a robot and accessories.) The term *robotics* included a complete system with one or more robots, peripheries, and computerized controller as used in a flexible production environment.

One way to evaluate robots was to correlate per unit production costs with batch size or order volume. Where the batch size was small, manual labor was usually the most economical production method. On the other hand, for mass production of uniform components, custom-made machines and automated systems were justified. For products in between, a robotics system was often the most advantageous solution, but had to compete with humans and simple machines, depending on the task.

Robot Flexibility

Flexibility was the cornerstone of robot technology. Robots could handle different combinations of workpieces, as well as a variety of shapes, sizes, and materials. Robots were unique in their ability to be programmed for a variety of different work routines according to batch size and requirements. Robots designed for handling components could also perform different process operations. Furthermore, robots often solved environmental problems while lowering costs. A safer working environment combined with manufacturing flexibility resulted in increased quality and productivity gains. When equipped with sensors, vision systems, or adaptive controls, robots compensated for tolerance imperfections in workpieces and fixtures. Furthermore, robots had an advantage over conventional production machines in that they did not need to be replaced or retooled when product design changes were implemented. Alternatively, it was possible to increase the utilization of such standard and often costly production machines by combining them with robots.

Robot Complexity

Robots could be pneumatically, hydraulically, or electrically powered. The advantage of electrically controlled robots was their accuracy, reliability, and low energy requirements. The servo systems of electrically controlled robots allowed movements to be repeated with high accuracy. This made them ideal for complex applications that demanded a high degree of precision. Electrically powered robots were the quietest and had far fewer maintenance requirements than pneumatic or hydraulic robots. Although the latter were often cheaper than electrically powered robots, lower initial costs could be offset by more expensive tooling, higher operating and maintenance costs, and longer downtimes. Electric robots were the newest and, by 1987, the predominant robot type in use, although hydraulic

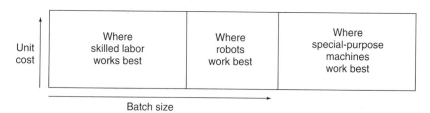

robots could be used for special applications or very high weight applications.

Differentiating Features in Robots

Robots could be classified as nonservo or servo. Nonservo robots were those whose movements were set by manually adjusted stops on each robot axis. Servo robots had their movements totally controlled by computer and therefore had thousands of possible movements in contrast to the nonservo type. Servo robots did not need to have their end stops adjusted, and program changes could be implemented with the mere change of a floppy disk in the control unit.

Robots could be differentiated from one another on the basis of working range, weight-handling capacity, number of axes, speed, and accuracy. Range was the distance a robot could reach and defined a robot's working space. In general, robots used in the automotive industry had longer reaches than for other applications, because the length of a car often determined the length of a corresponding robot arm. In such an application, one robot with a reach of 2 meters might satisfy the demands of two robots with a reach of 1 meter each (see Exhibit 2).

Weight capacity was one criterion for selecting robots. The more sophisticated a robot, the higher the number of axes or degrees of freedom it had. These degrees of freedom covered base rotation, a radial arm movement, a vertical arm movement, a pitching wrist movement, a rolling wrist movement and wrist yaw. Robots with five axes could handle most tasks and represented approximately 80% of the installed base of robots.

Robot speed was measured either in terms of millimeters per second or degrees per second. When describing a robot's speed, it was standard practice to give the maximum operating speed at which a robot could operate with a defined payload. Accuracy or repeatability referred to a robot's ability to return to a given point in space. Repeatability was one of the most important criteria to consider in purchasing a robot because it affected the quality of final products. Repeatability was

measured in terms of millimeters (for example, ±0.10 mm).

Robots offered good solutions to the problems of dull, dirty, and dangerous jobs where the demand for uptime was 95% to 100%. In general, robots reduced labor costs, shortened throughput time, gave more uniform quality, and offered employees a better working environment.

A major consideration in robot selection was the actual work to be done. The ability to be programmed and to store and combine a number of different applications separated robots from other automated production systems. Easy and rapid programming was especially important in small batch operations. Simple robots were acceptable when production involved large batches with little retooling. Sophisticated robots, on the other hand, were more appropriate for tasks such as arcwelding, cleaning of castings, deburring, and grinding/polishing because they involved complex patterns of movement that required robust robots.

THE MANUFACTURING OF ROBOTS

One factor that contributed to a robot's cost was its degree of sophistication. Robot sophistication and cost underwent a number of changes in the early 1980s as robot components changed in price. This was most pronounced for electrical components and microprocessors, particularly ones that had dropped in price due to mass production methods. The larger the microprocessor used in an industrial robot, the more quickly it operated, the more efficiently it functioned, and the broader the range of functions it covered.

Mechanical parts included the robot base, body, arm, wrist, and transmission. These mechanical parts were driven by one of three types of motor (drive): pneumatic, hydraulic, or electric. Electronic parts included the internal workings of direct current (dc) motors, miscellaneous wiring, and other electrical components in the robot body.

Linkages to component suppliers covered a variety of parts. These included parts for CNC

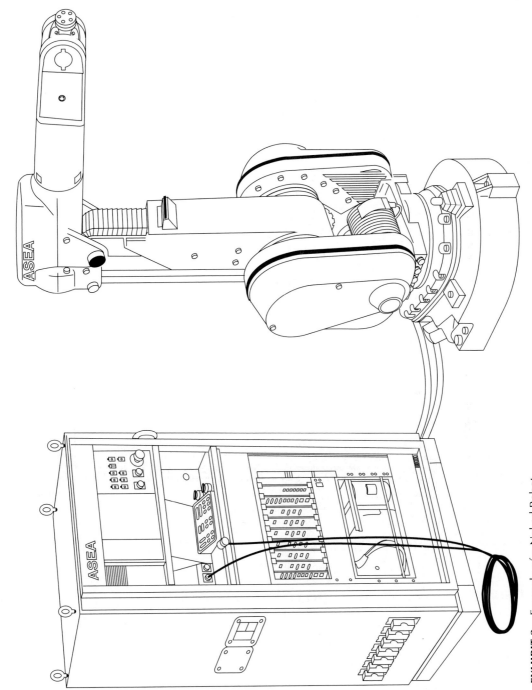

EXHIBIT 2   Example of a Naked Robot

303

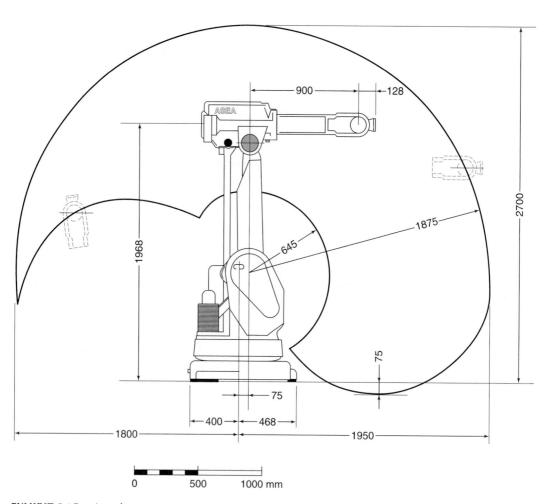

EXHIBIT 2 (*Continued*)

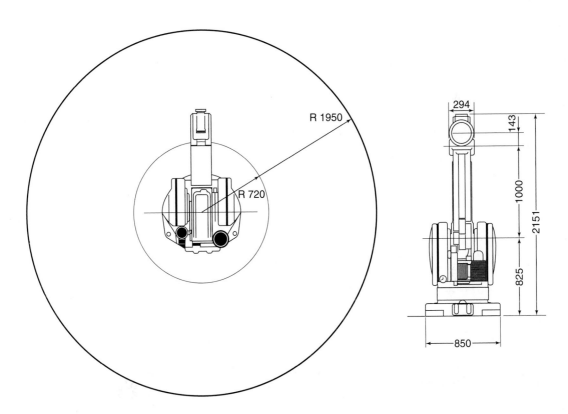

EXHIBIT 2 (*Continued*)

machine tools, machining centers, mechanical devices, and electronic sensing and control devices, as well as programming systems. The extent of backward integration in the robotics industry varies around the world. For example, Japanese component suppliers were responsive to OEM requirements such as quality, cost effectiveness, and timely design changes. Japanese OEMs were also known for providing the smaller component suppliers with financial and technical support.

United States robotics firms, on the other hand, were not as supportive as their Japanese counterparts with respect to backward integration. One exception to this, an area where the United States had a distinct comparative advantage, was in the design and engineering of sensors, control devices, and software. The country with the strongest backward linkages in Europe was Germany, followed by France and Sweden. (For a relative positioning of backward linkages in the robotics industry, see Exhibit 3.)

From a manufacturing viewpoint, industrial robots were specialized products and did not lend themselves to the mass production techniques of other industries. Typical manufacturing volumes per model range were in the low thousands per year. The research and development costs required to bring out one new model (controller and machine) were estimated to be $15 million and were usually recovered over 5 years. One industry analyst commented that although fixed costs had been 50% of sales, the percentage had increased in recent years due to the industry's maturing nature and increasing specialization. This growing specialization translated into steadily increasing research and development costs for robot manufacturers. Consequently, research and development costs, once 10% of sales, had increased over the years to 15%, with no certainty of leveling off in the near future. Remaining cost components (such as selling) accounted for 15%; training, 5%; finance, 5%; and overhead, 10%.

EXHIBIT 3   Comparative Positioning of U.S., European, and Japanese Robot Companies

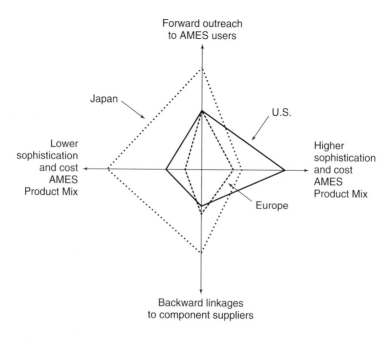

AMES = automatic manufacturing equipment and systems

THE WORLD ROBOT INDUSTRY

Segmenting the Robotics Industry

The worldwide robotics industry could be segmented geographically, by industry sector, or by application. Geographically, robots were concentrated in economically advanced countries where manufacturing and hence automation first appeared. The three main regions with advanced industries that supported the robotics business were Europe, Japan, and North America. These regions contributed to robotics industry revenue as shown in the accompanying table.

Geographic Distribution of Robotics Industry Revenue

Region	Estimated %, 1987	Forecasted %, 1992
Asia	42	36
North America	33	35
Europe	22	25
Rest of world	3	4
Total	100	100

Source: Dataquest.

Asia: Hong Kong, Japan, Korea, People's Republic of China, Singapore, and Taiwan.

North America: Canada and the United States.

Segmentation by Industry

The automotive industry was the largest user of robots, had 55% of the world's installed base, and accounted for 49% of industry sales in 1987. This concentration in the automotive industry had led some automobile manufacturers to start their own robotics businesses to supply themselves as well as other industries and other car makers. Examples included General Motors in the United States, Volkswagen in West Germany, and Renault in France. The volume of robots accounted for by this industry allowed one to segment the robotics market into automotive and nonautomotive users. The automotive segment included both assembly and component manufacturing in the automobile industry.

The major nonautomotive categories included electronics, white goods, and "other."

Examples of applications in the electronics industry included assembly automation, materials handling/machine tending, gluing and sealing, and surface treatment (coating). In addition to the applications found in the automotive and electronics industries, "other" included plastic molding, heat treatment, brick manufacturing, glass manufacturing, inspection/testing, and education/research. In 1987, the electronics and "other" categories accounted for 21% and 30% of industry sales and, by 1992, were expected to grow to 24% and 32%, respectively.

Segmentation by Application

Application segments included spotwelding, arcwelding, gluing and sealing, materials handling/machine tending, final assembly automation, process (deburring, grinding, and polishing), and painting. Spotwelding, which joined metals using electrical resistance heat and an applied pressure, was one of the first applications to be automated using robots.

A common application of spotwelding included car panels, which were tacked together with a line of spot welds. Roboticized spotwelding applications were almost 80% automotive related and one of the first job functions to be automated using robots. The spotwelding segment was characterized by large projects and long negotiation periods. In 1987, spotwelding represented 18% of all robot applications, with 3,691 units shipped worldwide at a value of $264 million. Although sales were forecast to increase to $289 million in 1988, spotwelding was expected to decline as a percentage of all applications to 15% by 1992. In 1987, spotwelding revenues and shipments were as follows:

Region	Automotive ($000)	Units	Nonautomotive ($000)	Units
Asia	76,000	1,312	25,000	452
North America	68,000	783	20,000	234
Europe	53,000	613	13,000	164
Rest of world	7,000	103	2,000	31

Source: Dataquest.

Arcwelding fuses metals by heat when an electric arc bridged an electrode and a workpiece. Arcwelding was used to form continuous seams. This added complexity was more challenging for a robot to control and required continuous path control. Both spot and arcwelding were ideally suited to robots because of their repeatability and accuracy. Welding was normally a heavy task carried out under unpleasant conditions. Experienced welders were also hard to find and expensive, two additional reasons why robots were a success in these segments. At $304 million, arcwelding represented 20% of all applications in 1987, with worldwide shipments of 3,936 units. For 1988, sales were forecast at $339 million, and this segment was expected to grow to 23% of all applications by 1992. Revenues in 1987 for the arcwelding application segment were as follows:

Region	Automotive ($000)	Units	Nonautomotive ($000)	Units
Asia	72,000	1,360	28,000	497
North America	36,000	500	32,000	296
Europe	50,000	609	74,000	534
Rest of world	6,000	90	6,000	51

Source: Dataquest.

Gluing/sealing was an application segment often grouped in "other." With sales of $152 million, "other" represented 10% of applications in 1987 and included processes such as deburring, grinding/polishing, and cutting. This segment was expected to grow to $171 million in 1988 and maintain a 10% share of market into 1992. In 1987, revenues in this category were distributed as shown in Table 1.

Materials handling was often heavy, repetitive, and boring for human operators and included tasks such as palletizing, stacking, and packing. Where hazardous and/or deli-

cate materials were involved, robotization allowed continuous and easy to run operations. Machine tending, or loading/unloading of machines, reduced dead time in a job characterized by a shortage of skilled labor with high wage rates. In 1987 the materials handling and machine tending segments had a combined 23% share of all applications and $345 million in sales, with 6,933 robots shipped worldwide. This segment was expected to have sales of $385 million in 1988 and to maintain its 23% share through 1992. In 1987, revenues for the materials handling/machine tending segment as a function of industry were as shown in Table 2.

Spray painting/coating was also an unpleasant task for human operators because of paint fumes and the associated health risks. The automotive sector represented 72% of the value of the painting segment. The inconsistent quality and low productivity of manual painters in this segment were readily improved with robots that reduced labor and raw material costs. Painting represented 9% of all applications in 1987, with estimated revenues of $135 million and industry shipments of 1,047 robots. Sales in 1988 were expected to increase only slightly to $139 million and, by 1992, this segment was expected to represent only 7% of all applications. Revenues for the painting segment of the robotics industry in 1987 were as shown in the Table 3.

Assembly automation was one of the largest segments in robotics and covered virtually all branches of the industry and all robot sizes. However, the complexity of this segment varied, which contributed to losses for those robotics suppliers who were inexperienced at offering "systems" solutions. This segment represented 20% of the worldwide robotics market in 1987 and had sales of $289 million, corresponding to

TABLE 1 Gluing/sealing applications

Region	Automotive ($000)	Units	Electronic ($000)	Units	Other	Units
Asia	37,000	764	16,000	427	18,000	370
North America	26,000	253	8,000	63	18,000	167
Europe	14,000	173	3,000	33	8,000	81
Rest of world	2,000	32	1,000	11	1,000	16

Source: Dataquest.

TABLE 2 Materials handling application

Region	Automotive ($000)	Units	Electronic ($000)	Units	Other	Units
Asia	39,000	816	71,000	3,069	36,000	501
North America	37,000	476	24,000	450	40,000	424
Europe	45,000	555	11,000	152	30,000	329
Rest of world	6,000	75	2,000	42	4,000	46

Source: Dataquest.

TABLE 3 Painting applications

Region	Automotive ($000)	Units	Electronic ($000)	Units	Other	Units
Asia	12,000	194	1,000	14	3,000	63
North America	58,000	285	3,000	21	22,000	174
Europe	24,000	177	1,000	14	7,000	75
Rest of world	3,000	24	—	—	1,000	8

Source: Dataquest.

TABLE 4 Assembly applications

Region	Automotive ($000)	Units	Electronic ($000)	Units	Other	Units
Asia	15,000	293	104,000	3,962	26,000	345
North America	25,000	394	57,000	1,017	19,000	301
Europe	11,000	149	15,000	223	10,000	120
Rest of world	2,000	23	3,000	55	2,000	22

6,904 robots. In 1988, sales were expected to reach $333 million and by 1992 were forecast to represent 22% of all applications. The spread of revenues in assembly by industry and region in 1987 was as shown in Table 4.

MAJOR PLAYERS IN THE WORLD ROBOTICS INDUSTRY

Viable robot manufacturers had to combine all the technologies on which robots depended, including mechanical, electrical, and software engineering, computers, and communications. In addition to this diverse technology base, robotics firms had to be familiar with their customers' manufacturing processes. This range of technologies and process know-how explained why firms in the industry had such varied origins. Most of the early players in robotics came from other industries where automation brought immediate productivity gains. As such, shipbuilders and automobile manufacturers leveraged their welding expertise into spot- and arcwelding robots, and industrial electric companies used their elec-

trical knowledge to transform robots from pneumatic- or hydraulic-driven tools to electrically powered machines. Once these initial entrants saturated the robotics segments in which they had their expertise, they began linking up with other firms to broaden their overall product offering. As robotics developed into an industry with its own identity, a number of start-up companies entered the business. By the end of 1987, there were an estimated 300 companies worldwide that manufactured and/or marketed robots.

From the middle 1980s onward, the robotics industry showed an increasing trend toward internationalization, as seen by the number of sales and technology agreements among suppliers in the world's three main robot markets. (For an overview of international industrial cooperation in the robotics industry as of 1985, see Exhibit 4.) Worldwide market share data on the robotics industry were available only through 1986. (Company sales by segment and application market shares by revenue for selected robotics companies are summarized in Exhibits 5 through 7.)

One important development in the robotics

industry was the entry of companies such as IBM and Digital Equipment Corporation. As early as 1980, Kenneth G. Bosomworth, president of International Resource Development, Inc., commented that it was only a matter of time before such companies started selling robots. "The mechanics involved have been largely perfected, minimizing the value of machine tool expertise. Now it's becoming increasingly important for a robot company to have electronics and software capabilities." The entry of these large computer companies set the robot industry in perspective as part of the larger factory automation industry, with its 1990 estimated value of $100 billion.

North American-based Players

North America was the second largest geographic market for robots and in 1986 had an installed base of 25,000. Unimation installed the world's first industrial robot in 1961 and had achieved a market share of 40% in 1983 with sales of about $71 million. Shortly after its acquisition by Westinghouse, the market shifted to electrically powered robots and away from Unimation's hydraulically powered ones. Although Unimation responded to the switch in technology, it was felt that the company had lost major market share to GMF, the joint venture formed by General Motors and Fanuc of Japan in 1982.

Westinghouse Electric established itself as a player in the robotics industry when it purchased Unimation in 1983. To speed its entry into the robotics and factory automation markets at home and abroad, Westinghouse established licensing agreements with Olivetti in Italy and with Komatsu and Mitsubishi in Japan. In 1986, Westinghouse Electric had robotics sales of $52 million, an estimated market share of 12.4% in the worldwide machining/other segment, and systems revenue accounted for 54% of sales. Westinghouse Electric manufactured the Puma robot family. In 1983 the company was working on vision, force sensing, and conveyor tracking.

Based on a report that the robotics market would decline by 20% to 30% from 1986 to 1987, Westinghouse chose to change its strategy. Westinghouse turned away from making stand-alone robots on a large scale to supplying integrated automation solutions. Furthermore, Westinghouse closed Unimation and formed an automation division that combined marketing, sales engineering, and other robotics and automated products-related operations. In 1987, Westinghouse also began a factory automation joint venture with Matsushita Electric Industrial. By the end of 1987, Westinghouse robotics had gone through tough times and its continuation was open to question.

General Motors Fanuc Robotics Corp. (GMF) was based in Michigan and was formed in 1982 as a joint venture between General Motors and Fanuc in Japan. From GM's perspective, the deal was aimed at automating GM plants with low-cost hardware from Fanuc. Fanuc, on the other hand, gained access to GM's flexible automation systems (FAS) unit, a group of 60 people with several years of experience in robot systems development. In 1986, GMF had sales of $186 million versus $16 million in its founding year. Its customer base had increased from 20 customers in 1982 to 650 in 1986, and as number 1 in the United States had a 30% share of that market versus 8% in 1982. Eric Mittelstadt, president of GMF, attributed its success to strong customer commitment, with support that ranged from applications engineering to parts and service. On a worldwide basis, GMF had 11% of the 1986 robotics market, with systems sales estimated at 25% of total revenue.

When the automotive market for robotics collapsed in 1986–1987, GMF targeted nonautomotive segments. Hence, GMF signed a contract with DeVilbiss to market electric painting robots. The deal combined the strengths of GMF, the largest overall robot vendor in the United States, with the world's biggest installer of painting robots. Both companies were allowed to market and service each other's products, as well as their own line of painting robots.

In 1987, GMF consolidated its six locations from Troy, Michigan, to a new building at Auburn Hills, Michigan, and established centralized engineering, demonstration, training,

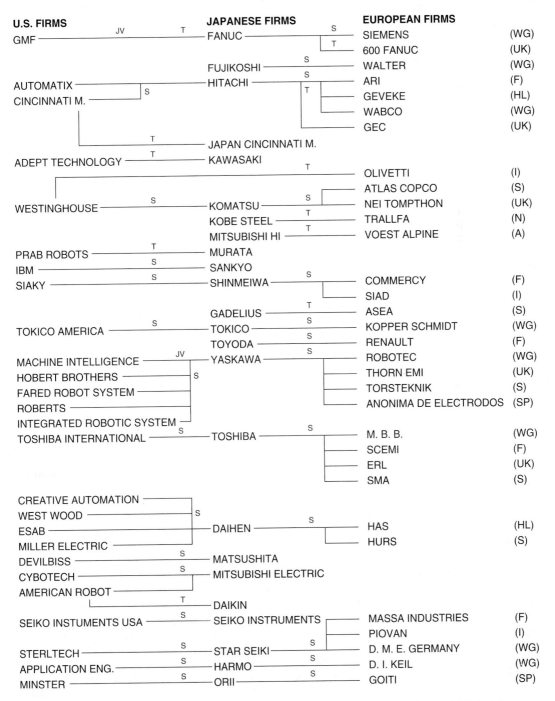

(as of July, 1987)

T, Technical links; S, Sales links; JV, Joint Venture
Arrows indicate the flow of products and technologies

EXHIBIT 4 International Industrial Cooperation on Robots *Source:* Japanese Industrial Robot Assn.

EXHIBIT 5 Company Sales by Application Segment and Application Market Share by Revenue: U.S.-based Vendors

	Sales by Segment ($ millions)	Market Share by Revenue (%)	Units
General Motors–Fanuc			
Assembly	$14	4.7	154
Materials and handling/machine loading	21	5.7	272
Painting	80.1	44.0	162
Spotwelding	40	10.3	527
Arcwelding	8	2.7	140
Machining/other	23.1	14.0	241
DeVilbiss			
Painting	$17.9	9.8	183
Arcwelding	2.1	0.7	21
Machining/other	1.1	0.6	5
Cincinnati Milacron			
Assembly	$2.4	0.8	18
Materials handling/ machine loading	8.2	2.2	81
Spotwelding	65.8	17.0	510
Arcwelding	1.4	0.5	9
Machining/other	1.9	1.2	14
General Electric			
Assembly	$0.5	0.2	6
Materials handling/machine loading	3.2	0.9	32
Spotwelding	0.6	0.2	6
Arcwelding	4.4	1.5	44
Machining/other	1.5	0.9	15
Prab			
Materials handling/machine loading	$14.5	4.0	111
Spotwelding	1.0	0.2	7
Machining/other	3.9	2.3	30

and other services. Also in 1987, GMF secured major European sales with large orders to Peugeot in France and SAAB in Sweden, ASEA's home country. Across Europe, GMF was expected to pursue an aggressive strategy.

In the future, GMF planned to diversify and sell robots to several different industries, including electronics, aerospace, and food processing. To this end, GMF was customizing its standard line of robots to meet the needs of nonautomotive customers. It developed new robots for these markets, some of which could be used in clean-room manufacturing applications. By diversifying along these lines, GMF planned to maintain a 50/50 split in sales between automotive and nonautomotive customers.

Cincinnati Milacron was a world leader in machine tools, systems, and precision measuring equipment and, until 1985, the leading U.S. robot manufacturer. Despite its leading role, Cincinnati Milacron had made a profit in only 1 of the 11 preceding years. In December 1985, this company announced a write-off of $52 million in its robotic and machine tool operations and was still working off a substantial backlog of previous orders. In 1986, 26% of Cincinnati Milacron's $80 million revenue came from systems, and the company had 4.7% of the worldwide robotics market.

General Electric entered the robotics business in the middle 1970s after automating many of its own plants. From 1980 onward, GE entered into a number of licensing agree-

EXHIBIT 6   Company Sales by Application Segment and Application Market Share by Revenue: Japanese-based Vendors

	Sales by Segment ($ millions)	Market Share by Revenue (%)	Units
Fanuc			
Assembly	$9.0	3.0	262
Materials handling/ machine loading	18.0	4.9	512
Painting	3.0	1.6	63
Spotwelding	18.0	4.6	360
Arcwelding	3.0	1.0	63
Machining/other	9.0	5.4	226
Yaskawa			
Assembly	$5.6	1.9	111
Materials handling/ machine loading	6.1	1.7	122
Spotwelding	13.3	3.4	266
Arcwelding	67.2	22.6	?
Machining/other	18.9	11.4	377
Kawasaki			
Assembly	$4.6	1.5	85
Materials handling/ machine loading	3.0	0.8	57
Painting	3.8	2.1	31
Spotwelding	57.8	14.9	737
Arcwelding	1.5	0.5	26
Machining/other	5.3	3.2	39
Nachi–Fujikoshi			
Assembly	$6.4	2.1	115
Materials handling/ machine loading	4.5	1.2	81
Painting	1.9	1.1	17
Spotwelding	43.5	11.2	783
Arcwelding	6.4	2.2	115
Machining/other	1.3	0.8	23

EXHIBIT 7   Company Sales by Application Segment and Application Market Share by Revenue: European-based Vendors

	Sales by Segment ($ millions)	Market Share by Revenue (%)	Units
ASEA			
Assembly	$15.2	5.1	167
Materials handling/ machine loading	70.3	19.2	774
Spotwelding	26.6	6.9	293
Arcwelding	68.4	23.0	753
Machining/other	9.5	5.7	105
KUKA			
Assembly	$0.5	0.2	6
Materials handling/ machine loading	15	4.1	174
Spotwelding	30	7.7	348
Arcwelding	1.5	0.5	17
Machining/other	3.0	1.8	35

ments, joint ventures, and acquisitions to become a one-stop robotics supplier of factory automation systems. Among these moves were licensing agreements with Italy's OEA SpA, Japan's Hitachi, and West Germany's Volkswagen. To try to secure the European market, GE established an automation systems customer training center in Frankfurt, Germany, in 1985.

Despite GE's 1982 announcement to be a lead supplier in the "factory of the future," it lost at least $200 million in 1985 and decided to enter a joint venture with Fanuc. Initiated in January 1987, the $200 million robotics joint venture built on Fanuc's strengths in manufacturing machine tool controls and GE's expertise in robotics technology. In addition to research, the joint venture covered manufacturing and marketing. By the end of 1987, GE–Fanuc had sales of approximately $250 million, but GE planned to stop manufacturing robots. Instead, Fanuc would manufacture all robots in Japan, and GE's extensive distribution channels would be used to market Fanuc products with GE software in the United States.

Prab was based in Kalamazoo, Michigan, and specialized in robots for heavy weights and the materials handling/machine tending segments. In 1987, Prab received nonexclusive rights to market ASEA robots. ASEA also designated Prab as a systems integrator on materials handling and transfer applications. Under the terms of the agreement, ASEA manufactured original equipment robots, and Prab integrated heavy materials systems and parts transfer applications.

An agreement was designed to increase the sales and market penetration of both companies. The sales and service agreement provided for the sale of ASEA robots, controllers, software, and peripheral equipment by Prab's nationwide sales force for integration into Prab automation systems. Prab's initial emphasis for ASEA products was in nonautomotive markets with the intention to expand into other areas. The ASEA–Prab agreement resulted in termination of a previous Prab–GDA (West Germany) agreement. The withdrawal of Prab from robotics production was seen by many in the industry as a move into market-

ing and systems work. Prab sold its robots in Australia and New Zealand through distributors and in South America through an agent. In Japan, Prab had granted an exclusive license to Murata Machines Ltd. to manufacture and sell robots in Japan and other Far East countries. Prab also had a licensing agreement with Can-Eng Manufacturing Ltd. to manufacture and sell robots in Canada. Fabrique Nationale in Belgium was Prab's European licensee, manufacturing and selling robots throughout Western Europe, Africa, and Scandinavia.

In contrast to the five- and 6-axes robots of other manufacturers, Adept built a name for itself using SCARA (selective compliance assembly robot arm) robots with only three axes. Adept had used these robots to penetrate the light assembly and small parts materials handling markets. In 1986, Adept had sales of $25 million, with $16.3 million in assembly and $87 million in materials handling. These sales corresponded to 281 and 151 robots and secured 5.4% and 2.4%, respectively, of the worldwide segments for Adept.

IBM entered the robotics market in 1982 with a system linked to its personal computer. IBM concentrated on the small parts assembly market with SCARA robots imported from Sankyo Seiki in Japan. SCARA robots were invented in Japan and moved only on a horizontal plane. This was suitable for flexible assembly operations where the robot could be changed from one product to another with a mere change in program, eliminating the need for additional robots. In 1986, IBM sold 240 robots valued at $8 million and had an estimated 2.7% of the worldwide assembly market.

Intelledex was almost unheard of in Europe, but in the United States it competed with Adept, Seiko, and IBM. Intelledex concentrated on light assembly in the automotive and electronics industries.

Japan-based Players

Japan was the largest user of robots and had an installed base of 93,000 systems at the end of 1986 by JIRA definitions. By ECE definition, the figure was closer to 50,000. Japan was also at the forefront of robotics hardware and was expected to remain so over the next several years. One example of a hardware advantage was in controls, for which the Japanese tailored control modules to fit particular robotics applications. This was in contrast to Western firms, which tailored robot platforms instead of controls. Another Japanese competitive advantage was a design facility that allowed them to implement changes and offer more products. As a result, Japanese companies had bigger product ranges than Western competitors. With a range of products in each application, the Japanese could provide a more specific robot, usually at a lower price.

Despite their capabilities in microelectronics and hardware, the Japanese were not as sophisticated in software development as many firms in the United States, a disadvantage when attempting total systems integration. And unlike Western firms, where robotics operations were treated as independent profit centers, financing in many Japanese firms came from a parent industrial group. This reflected the Japanese view that robots served a public relations role for the entire industrial group.

Fanuc stood for Fuji Automatic Numerical Control and was formed by Fujitsu in 1955 to enter the factory automation business. Fanuc was the world leader in numerical controls (NC) for machine tools, lathes, and milling machines. It was NC that played a major role in transforming the capabilities of a simple machine into a robot with a range of functions. Fanuc gained access to GM's robot technology with a joint venture in 1982 and sold the robots in Japan at low prices. The joint venture also gave Fanuc an opportunity to better integrate GM's robots with systems in the emerging factory of the future, positioning Fanuc in the systems integration market.

In its 1987 joint venture with General Electric, Fanuc gained access to the large U.S. market, specializing in programmable controllers. One of the more valuable gains was GE's automated production systems, IBM or Digital computers modified to GE specifications. In 1987, Fanuc decided to increase production specialization by producing all hardware in Japan and all software in the United States. Software was produced at Fanuc's two 50/50 joint venture companies: GMF robotics corporation in Michigan and GE Fanuc automation corporation. Both joint ventures imported Fanuc hardware from Japan, added their own software, and sold the finished products as U.S. products. Fanuc licensed to GM in the United States, the 600 group in Britain, and Siemens in Germany.

Yaskawa Electric Manufacturing was established in 1915 and had an excellent reputation for manufacturing motors. One of the parent company's subsidiaries, Yaskawa Electric Data, Inc., specialized in floppy disk drive (FDD) development and combined this expertise with its knowledge of servo-motor technology. This combination gave Yaskawa an advantage in the development of motors for industrial robots. Yaskawa enjoyed a strong home market for arcwelding robots and was continuing to broaden its activities into materials handling and process applications. In 1986, Yaskawa had sales of $111 million, with 20% of its revenues attributed to systems. Yaskawa's world market share was 6.5%, and the company was expected to expand into other applications, broadening its product offering with new robots at a low cost.

Yaskawa claimed to be the first Japanese robot manufacturer to set up an overseas sales network. Yaskawa's distributors included Hobart Brothers, Inc., in the United States and GKN Lincoln in Great Britain. Yaskawa had cooperative ventures with Torsteknik Company of Sweden, Messer Gresheim of West Germany, and Alcas of Italy. Messer Gresheim's welding equipment, power supplies, and welding packs strengthened Yaskawa's position in European welding segments. Yaskawa also had technological agreements with Feado Robot Systems in Japan, Barrons Engineering in South Africa, and A.N.I. Perkins in Australia. Yaskawa sales agreements were with Robotec of West Germany, Thorn EMI in Britain, Torsteknik in Sweden, and Anonima de Electrodos in Spain.

Kawasaki Heavy Industries began operations in 1896 as a shipbuilder and was the company with the longest history in that industry. Kawasaki Heavy Industries was the nucleus of the Kawasaki group, had a broad range of experience in heavy machinery and engineering, and was one of the first to market spotwelding robots. One part of the Kawasaki group specialized in robots and got its start in North America as a licensee to Unimation. More recently, Kawasaki had established a technical link with Adept. In 1986, Kawasaki Heavy Industries had 4.5% of the world robotics market and an estimated 14.9% of the world spotwelding segment, and 34% of its $76 million sales was represented by systems revenue. In 1987, Kawasaki established itself further in the U.S. robotics market with its own organization and a new spotwelding robot.

Matsushita Electric in 1986 had sales of $100 million and a worldwide market share of 5.9%. It was estimated that Matsushita Electric held a 13.7% share of the materials handling/machine tending segment and was number 1 in assembly, with a 16.7% share. Matsushita's stake in assembly was underscored by the fact that, in 1983, 75% of its robot sales were accounted for by robots designed to insert electronic components.

Other important Japanese players were Nachi–Fujikoshi, Toshiba, and Hitachi. Nachi–Fujikoshi was one of Japan's leading bearing manufacturers and ranked first in cutting tools. Nachi–Fujikoshi claimed to be the first to produce heavy-duty robots in Japan and in the past supplied both spotwelding and arc-welding robots to GE. In 1986, Nachi–Fujikoshi held 3.8% of the world robotics market. Toshiba was a world leader in machine tool manufacturing and had agreements to sell robots through Messerschmidt–Boelkow–Bolm in Germany, Switzerland, and Austria, through Scemi in France, and through SMA in Sweden. In 1986, Toshiba had sales of $73 million and about 4.3% of the world robotics market. It was also estimated that Toshiba had market shares of 9.0% in the materials handling/machine tending segment, 9.8% in assembly, and 0.9% in spotwelding. Toshiba revenues for these segments were $33 million, $29.3 million, and $3.7 million, respectively. Hitachi had a technical link and licensing agreement with GE in

the United States and also licensed to GEC and Lansing Bagnall in the United Kingdom. In 1986, Hitachi had total sales of $36 million and an estimated market share of 8.5% in arcwelding that accounted for $25.2 million of its revenues.

European-based Players

Western Europe was the third largest market for robots, with the installed base concentrated in three countries. In 1986 the three countries with the most robots were West Germany with 12,400, France with 7,500, and the United Kingdom with approximately 3,800.

ASEA Robotics was number 1 in the European market with a market share of approximately 25%. ASEA was late in entering the spotwelding market segment and did not have a product in this segment until 1983 versus some competitors with 20 years of spotwelding experience. The United States was ASEA's single biggest market, where it had 200 employees in ASEA Robotics, Inc., by the end of 1987, this area of the company's sales had grown 10% to $45 million despite the downward trend in the industry. With a market share of approximately 12%, ASEA was in second place in the United States behind GMF and expected a market expansion during 1988.

ASEA's start in the robotics industry grew out of a desire to improve its own business. This began in the mid- to late-1970s and followed on the purchase of NC machines and an ASEA climate that favored investment in production engineering. This climate found ASEA executives asking if they could make their own robots. ASEA consequently made and installed its first robots in its own factories, where they were used for handling and tending. Shortly thereafter, ASEA began to sell these robots and approached ESAB to integrate robots with ESAB equipment for welding applications. ESAB marketed welding process equipment to a variety of industries around the world. The arcwelding expertise offered by ESAB expanded ASEA's robot offering into a new application segment. Traditionally, ASEA's expertise had been in electronic control technology, not welding. ESAB provided

ASEA with welding components to be attached to a robot arm and, in a sense, allowed ASEA to offer robotized arcwelding at an early stage.

ASEA's electric drive technology and ESAB's arcwelding expertise were later combined when SAAB figured ASEA into its welding automation plans. SAAB, the Swedish automobile and aerospace firm, gave ASEA the opportunity to develop a spotwelding robot for the automotive industry via on-site testing and refinement. ESAB/ASEA knowledge in welding automation and SAAB's willingness to be a "futuristic" customer helped to establish ASEA in the robotics industry. That these three firms were all within one geographic area, spoke one language, and had the same culture further contributed to ASEA's success.

ASEA robotics had made a number of alliances and several acquisitions over the years. Among these was Trallfa Robot of Norway, partially acquired (51%) in 1985. Trallfa was a leading manufacturer of robots for the painting and surface finishing sector, and its acquisition strengthened ASEA's export operations. Trallfa products consequently filled a void in the ASEA line, previously concentrated on arcwelding and other metalworking applications. The acquisition also saved ASEA from having to modify electric robots for painting and its associated spark hazards.

In 1986, ASEA acquired VS Technology group (Luton, England), a robotics system integrator. VS Technology was known for the design and manufacture of automated welding and assembly lines for European automotive and domestic appliance industries. VS Technology had a history of being a line builder serving the automotive industry. VST's recent moves into machine vision and related areas were directed toward producing smaller parts for the electronics industry. The move gave ASEA the ability to compete more fully on complete and advanced systems.

In 1986, ASEA, Inc., underwent an internal reorganization that created two business divisions. The automotive division focused specifically on that industry, while the industrial automation division focused on a variety of other customers. Each division had total business responsibility for its activities. The restructuring was part of a larger effort to consolidate operations within ASEA, thereby reducing costs and lowering personnel requirements. By the end of 1986, ASEA's product offering was substantially greater than only a few years prior, and the company achieved a worldwide presence with 11.2% of the robotics market. In 1986, 30% of ASEA'S $190 million in revenue was accounted for by systems.

In 1987, ASEA relocated robot production from the United States to Sweden. The move was part of an effort to consolidate robot manufacturing in one plant from six worldwide. The plant manufactured ASEA's entire line of industrial robots and also produced semis for ASEA robotics plants in the United States, Japan, France, and Spain. Also in 1987, ASEA sold its line of pneumatic materials handling robots to MHU Robotics.

In Japan, ASEA was represented by ASEA Robotics/Gadelius (GAR) with a market share of 2% to 3%. ASEA products had an initial reputation of being overpriced in Japan, despite their high quality and precision. ASEA moved to counter this in 1983 by manufacturing in Kobe, a move that reportedly lowered costs by 12% to 13%. In both the United States and Japan, ASEA expanded by setting up large, well-equipped robotics centers that offered customers service and support facilities along with systems engineering and hardware.

Cloos was a family-owned company based in Germany that had developed its reputation as a leader in the arcwelding segments and for delivering turnkey welding systems. Cloos changed its role to a robot manufacturer specialized in arcwelding after it bought Von Jungheinrich in 1986. The acquisition of Von Jungheinrich, which developed and manufactured robot controls, complemented Cloos's previous strengths. In addition to growth by acquisition, Cloos built up its software and engineering departments and was able to target other applications. For the late 1980s and 1990s, Cloos planned to expand its application base to those areas that built upon its traditional arcwelding expertise. Other applications where welding know-how could be leveraged included flame and plasma cutting and laser welding and cutting. Cloos also stated its desire to enter water-jet cutting, gluing and sealing, and possibly the materials handling segments.

With 1986 sales revenues of $70 million, Cloos had a 23.5% market share of the worldwide arcwelding segment. In the United States, Cloos was represented by Cloos International, Inc., established in 1985. In Europe, Cloos worked closely through agents and was represented in Great Britain, Austria, and the USSR. Markets in South America, Africa, and the Far East were cultivated through individual projects. Cloos's vision of the future for the robotics industry was that only a few key players would survive. Management believed that customers would ask robot suppliers to take on more responsibility as applications became more specific and as customers moved to integrate those applications into single systems solutions. For the future, the Cloos team planned to adjust to customer needs as far as its products and market conditions warranted.

Also based in Germany was KUKA, an acronym for Keller und Knappich, Augsburg, founded in 1898 as an acetylene works. KUKA had a successful history as a welding equipment supplier with oxyacetylene welding devices as early as 1905 and the first electric spotwelding gun in Germany in 1936, and supplied the first welding transfer line to Volkswagen in 1956. KUKA's entry into robotics began in 1971 when it supplied the first welding transfer line equipped with U.S.-made robots to Daimler–Benz. From 1980 onward the company's role in robotics grew substantially. In 1981, KUKA was the first to market freely programmable continuous path control systems with sensors for multiaxis robots. In 1982 the firm acquired Expert Automation, Inc., in the United States and a controlling interest in LSW Maschinenfabrik GmbH in Bremen, Germany. These acquisitions complemented KUKA's strengths and helped it to offer fully automated assembly cells with robots and vision systems.

In addition to Germany, where KUKA had an estimated one-half of its sales, the company had subsidiaries in the United Kingdom, Belgium, France, Spain, Denmark, and India. KUKA also had a licensing agreement with the USSR and cooperation agreements with DEA in Italy on assembly robots and Schindler–Digitron in Switzerland on automated guided vehicles. KUKA was organized into four main groups: robots, transfer lines, assembly systems, and special welding systems; the first two represented nearly 90% of the total business. The company's background in welding was represented by its strength in the spotwelding segment, where its application know-how and system capacity were a bonus. These gave KUKA a competitive advantage as a supplier of spotwelding robots and as an automotive line builder and supplier. Unlike other robot companies, KUKA used its robots as a tool for selling systems. To a certain extent, KUKA was a systems house making its own mechanical robot arms. By the end of 1986, KUKA had sales of $50 million and was expecting to increase its presence in gluing and sealing and the materials handling segments.

Two other European competitors were Reis Robot and Comau. Reis Robot had its primary market in Germany, where it concentrated on nonautomotive customers. Reis manufactured robots for general transfer work and for handling tools and workpieces in machining cells and used low prices as a central part of an aggressive strategy. Comau, which specialized in automotive and NC machine tools, started in robotics by working with Fiat. Comau determined design capabilities, limitations of robots, and production lines and, in 1985, was bought by Fiat. In the same year, Comau and Digital announced the formation of a joint venture called Sesam, aimed at the European and world market in computer integrated manufacturing. Sesam combined Comau's strengths in flexible manufacturing systems with Digital's knowledge of computers and concentrated on systems engineering—procuring and setting up equipment for flexible automation systems.

SELECTING A ROBOT SUPPLIER

Variables in Robotics Demand

Factors influencing the purchase of robots at a national level included general economic conditions, financial structures, and government policies such as subsidies. At the level of the firm, demand pull for robotics was determined by the role of manufacturing strategy in company planning policies and an attitude conducive to trying new technology. The purchase of robotics and manufacturing automation in general was favored by firms that sought reduced costs via increases in volume production and/or flexibility in response to market conditions. From a buyer's perspective, this meant being able to make 200X, 500Y, and 300Z, as opposed to only 1,000A. (A summary of user-demand pull and producer-supply push by region is presented in Exhibit 8.)

Installing a Robot System

Robotic systems required considerable investment, not only in capital but also in engineering time, installation, and start-up. In a well-planned installation, a robot system usually paid for itself in 2 to 4 years. A major consideration in robot selection was the actual work to be done. Simple robots were acceptable when production involved large batches with little retooling, such as materials handling/machine tending. Sophisticated robots were more appropriate for such tasks as cleaning castings, deburring, grinding/polishing, arcwelding, and gluing/sealing, because they involved complex patterns of movement.

Robots were sold "naked" (nonengineered, but with a controller) or in conjunction with systems that contained related peripheries, computers, engineering solutions, and software. Naked robots varied in price from $50,000 for simpler models to over $100,000 for the more sophisticated machines. The latter were more easily and economically adapted to different machining requirements, tools, and fixtures.

Systems were often assembled using components from a variety of manufacturers and could have as many as 40 robots. An example of such a system was car body assembly, for which an entire production line was automated. Unlike the relatively easy to design hardware, systems varied in complexity and necessitated a great deal of industrial engineer-

ing expertise. To achieve a satisfactory result, one or more engineers had to design a system based on a customer's particular needs, conduct a feasibility study with robots, and select those robots best suited to the task. When operating across borders, this often required cooperative efforts with foreign manufacturers. This latter point was particularly true for the Japanese where robot companies did not have a systems house capability. Instead, a customer acted on his own behalf by integrating a system himself or by contacting an independent systems house. The Japanese also had to rely on local systems integrators in Europe, but in the United States they tended to bring in their own people.

The Marketing Process

From the customer's viewpoint, a robot could be purchased directly from a manufacturer or a systems integrator. ASEA distribution was characteristic of the larger robotics companies, referring to its sales outlets as robot centers. In addition to hardware sales, robot centers provided the engineering expertise to set up a complete system, including service and training. All robotics companies sold directly to customers. Where robotics companies differed, however, was in the nature of that sale. Aside from selling its own hardware, the larger robotics companies sold their engineering or systems expertise. When that expertise was purchased separately, customers could specify the brand of hardware.

An alternative to buying robots directly from a manufacturer was for customers to go to independent systems integrators. These independents were also known as systems houses; they tended to be local and, in robotics, played the same role as a third-party programmer in the computer industry. Whether owned by a larger robot company or by an independent, integrators sold custom-designed manufacturing solutions. Smaller companies tended to rely more on engineered solutions than larger companies. Systems integrators might select robots and related equipment from several suppliers, competing with robot companies in that they might select a limited number of a robot company's accessory or aux-

EXHIBIT 8 Determinants of Robot Company Performance

User-demand pull	Japan	Europe	United States

General economic conditions:
  Economic growth
  Unemployment levels
  Shortages of skills
  Inflation
  Interest rates
	High growth, low-level unemployment, low inflation, low interest rates, and shortages of industial skills reinforce AMES demand.	Declining growth rates, rising unemployment and inflationary pressures on interest rates undermines AMES demand.	Stagnating growth rates high unemployment, inflationary pressure necessitating high interest rates, mild protectionist forces undermine AMES demand. Foreign competition spurs AMES demand for catch up and survival.

Government–industry relations:
  Industry–trade policies
  Regulatory policies
  Financial support
    mechanisms
	Strong industry–trade policies to reinforce international competitiveness. Focus on AMES as key industry. Tax measures favor "sunrise" industries; leasing systems; permissive, co-operative R&D programs.	Industry–trade tax incentives. R&D subvention and government support strongest in France, weakest in Sweden. Indirectly support R&D.	Industrial policy to maintain competition through antitrust; government–industry relations adversarial; trade policy not focused on reinforcing U.S. enterprise technological parities. Tax policies do not discriminate in favor of technological lead industries. No specific policies to advance AMES industries, other than defense-related procurement.

Capital markets and debt financing:
  Government intervention
  Debt leveraging
  Corporate reserves
  Investor expectations
	Government guidelines to bank lending channel funds into priority areas. High debt leveraging by banks. Investors attuned to long-term growth. Corporate reserves tax sheltered low dividend payout.	Capital markets strongly reinforced by government interventions and tax sheltering of capital expansion funds in France. Swedish government intervention limited. Germany mildly interventionist.	Capital expenditures more heavily dependent upon retained savings (after higher taxes and dividend payout). Debt leveraging much lower than Japan's. Stock investors and financial analysts concerned with next quarter earnings.

Industrial organization and management:
  Strategic planning
    (learning curve)
  Capital budgeting
  Manufacturing in
    corporate strategy
	Global view toward marketing and production; drive toward volume production, high market shares, long-term strategic view toward capital investments, technological growth, and increased flexibility versatility in responding to world market demand shifts.	Industrial management most receptive to AMES introduction in Sweden, followed by West Germany; most conservative in France.	User management over-concerned with quarterly earnings, rather than long-term growth and technological development (aspects of risk aversion). Manufacturing not strategic in corporate planning; low in prestige/pay; managers (narrowly trained specialists) constrain capital budgeting with a strategic view (i.e., rapid movement down learning curve).

EXHIBIT 8   (*Continued*)

Attitudes of labor–management toward introduction of AMES:
  Stake in company performance
  Fear of job displacement
	Labor–Management perceive welfare tied to company performance; broadly experienced managers receptive to AMES.	Comanagement arrangements in Sweden and Germany make labor and managers more receptive to AMES introduction than in France. French labor politically stronger than U.S./Japan (able to exert protectionist pressures and unemployment relief).	Both labor and management feel threatened by new AMES applications. Both fear jobless labor has no stake in improved company performance.

Technical absorptive capabilities of user firms:
  Technical personnel
  Past experience
	High technical absorptive capability among user firms including effective QC circles). Many users have developed and fabricated their own AMES.	Swedish and German user firms work more closely with producers than French enterprises in the design, production, instalation and maintenance of AMES.	U.S. firms highly dependent upon producers for design, manufacturing, installation, and maintenance of AMES (except for a few large firms). Technical adaptive engineering personnel thin at user end.

Competitive structure of user–demand industries:
  Number and product range of AMES producers
  Competitive forces in local economy
	Intensive competition among broad range and large numbers of domestic producers in most user sectors. Foreign competition buffered by difficulties encountered in penetrating Japan.	Protectionist forces in France, much weaker in Germany, and weakers in Sweden (where demand for AMES is most intensive).	Certain user industries (auto, consumer electronics, steel) buffered from foreign competition by import quotas (thereby dulling AMES demand).

Producer-supply push	*Japan*	*Europe*	*United States*

Industrial organization and management:
  Forward outreach to users
  Backward linkages to component suppliers
  Previous AMES-related experience
	Strong forward linkages (customer servicing, aggressive marketing internationally); many producers originally developed and use; backward linkages to suppliers strong in Germany, less so in strong and symbiotic.	Forward linkages strong in Sweden and Germany, less so in France; a few firms experienced in designing/fabricating AMES for own U.S. component suppliers not nearly as responsive to OEM requirements, except France and Sweden.	User–vendor relationship much weaker than in Japan (few firms have strong customer servicing or international marketing network).
			
			in software programs and control/sensor device design.

Sector structural characteristics:
  Number, range, and size of firms
  Types of market segmentation
  Competition facing national industry
	Strong in term of large numbers and wide range of producers, internal competition among domestic producers, and exacting user demand; future export thrust reinforced by aggressive international marketing capabilities and joint international ventures to assist in market penetration and provide product design.	European structure weak relative to both Japan/U.S. in terms of number of competing firms; buffering against foreign competitors (especially in France); a few firms (in Sweden/France) have aggressive international marketing programs, in part through international joint ventures.	Much smaller number of U.S. firms competing in U.S. market, but competition from Japanese, some European firms emerging; U.S. firms not nearly as aggressive in international marketing as Japanese. Major motives for international joint ventures are low-cost component procurement from abroad and earnings from marketing AMES imports.

EXHIBIT 8 (*Continued*)

Government support: Research and development Procurement	Joint funding of research design and engineering of next generation of AMES prototypes for commercial applications. Antitrust does not inhibit joint development programs among competing firms.	French government highly supportive of AMES RD&E (both commercial and military applications); West Germany to a lesser degree, and Sweden less still.	Special funding for compu- terized manufacturing in connection with defense procurement requirements. Antitrust is a de facto inhibitor of intra-industry RD&E programs.

iliary product offerings. Among the independent systems integrators were Thyssen in Europe, Ingersoll Rand in the United States, and Budd & Co. in Canada. (See Exhibit 9 for a summary of the robot distribution process.)

The extent of value added for a naked robot, its package, and the entire system depended on a specific application. An arcwelding system serves as an example. The naked robot, consisting of the platform and controls, would be sold for about $70,000. The required package to make it an arcwelding robot consisted of a power pack ($15,000), an electrode feeder ($15,000), a torch cleaner ($1,000), and arcwelding software and controls ($9,000) for a total of about $40,000. This package was added to the costs of the OEM, such as ESAB of Swe-

den, when that company purchased naked robots from a robot supplier such as ASEA, resulting in a packaged robot price of $110,000. When integrated into a complete manufacturing system, the systems integrator would combine the robot package with the necessary transfer equipment that moved pieces to and from the welding station and performed installation. As part of a complete line, the single robot would cost $300,000 or about four times its naked value. Of the systems integrator's $190,000 added value, about 25% accounted for gross margin; the rest was spent on hardware. Typically, the integrator's margin was 10% for handling and 25% for know-how expressed in engineering worker/hours sold for studies, plans, and the like (see Exhibit 10).

EXHIBIT 9 Distribution Process for ASEA Robots: Trends 1983–1988

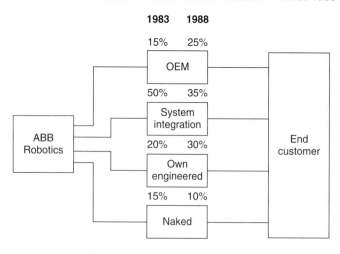

OEM: Mainly ESAB
System integration: Chosen mainly by customer
Own engineered: Value-added deliveries
Naked: Mainly integrated by customer

Robot supplier		OEM supplier		Systems integrator	
Naked robot	M a r g i n	Peripheral equipment for arcwelding	M a r g i n	Transfer and line equipment	Systems integrator margin

$70,000 $110,000 $300,000

Elements

Platform	Power pac
Control	Electrode feeder
Control	Arcwelding controls
Accessories	Torch cleaner

EXHIBIT 10   Value Added for Arcwelding Robot System

The price of a robot varied as a function of application, as seen in the accompanying diagram. Because assembly robots had fewer variations and therefore less flexibility than other robots, they were the most expensive to install when one added system costs to the cost of the naked robot. Of the estimated $1,485 million in robotics sales for 1987, $365 million was accounted for by installation or systems work.

Distribution of Robot Costs (%)

Application	Basic Robot Cost	Accessories	Installation
Welding	55	30	15
Handling	67	22	11
Machining	45	35	20
Machine tending	55	20	25
Painting	70	24	6
Assembly	40	35	25

Source: Le Nouvel Automatisme, June 1982

Training

Training was important for those in robotics because of the need to apply the technology at the shop-floor level. Further objectives of training were to avoid the misuse of robot technology and to minimize faults unnecessarily blamed on the robot. A few robotics companies such as ASEA had been so successful at training that it became a business in its own right, in addition to robot sales. ASEA offered general robotics courses, and it was not uncommon for these courses to be attended by people who purchased competitors' robots.

RECENT DEVELOPMENTS IN THE WORLD ROBOTICS INDUSTRY

From the mid-1980s onward, the robotics industry began to show some of the signs of a mature industry. This was particularly true in the United States, where the number of robots installed peaked in 1985–1986. Among these signs were a decline in the pace of industry sales and the exit from the industry by some of the main robotics players. Manufacturers concentrated in the automotive sector were the hardest hit. Among the reasons cited for declining sales in the mid-1980s was the robot image, a lack of engineering support and cut-backs from the major automotive companies.

With hindsight, insiders in the robotics industry felt that using the term robot had hindered rather than helped the industry's growth. This stemmed primarily from the concept of the word robot generated by science fiction films in which they were depicted as mechanical monsters, not industrial products with a specific business purpose. For this reason, the term *automatic transfer mechanism* was preferred, but it did not gain widespread use in the marketplace. Automatic transfer mechanism was a more accurate term, however, and reflected the changing nature of what robots could do. Specifically, robots were increasingly being used to serve as transfer mechanisms in the automated factory where they connected networks of machine tools turning out products under the direction of computers.

Parallels to the Computer Industry

Ken Johnson, founder and president of Robosoft Corporation, likened trends in the robotics industry to those in the computer industry. The computer industry passed through four stages of market development, starting with custom markets. As custom markets became saturated, vendors sought new and often smaller markets. Smaller market niches were associated with increasing software costs, a problem that was countered with third-generation languages such as FORTRAN. The third cycle in the computer industry began as vendors moved into even smaller niches. These niches were often too small to be economical for vendors and required third-party programmers with existing knowledge of those niches. The need for third-party programmers to work with hardware from different manufacturers pushed the market toward hardware-independent software and made it possible for software to be used over a wide range of hardware. The wider base led to reduced costs, a surge in PC sales, and the emergence of the fourth cycle. Later in the fourth cycle, vendors were divided into large-volume manufacturers of commodity hardware or manufacturers of either systems or applications software.

For the robotics industry, the first growth stage corresponded to the customized spot-welding and spray painting markets, and, just as FORTRAN appeared in the computer industry, KAREL and other languages emerged in robotics. Third-party programmers in the robotics industry were more properly termed *systems integrators*. As of 1988, the robotics industry was just entering the third market cycle with SCARA (selective compliance assembly robot arm) robots, which were expected to play a part analogous to the PC in the computer in-dustry. The emergence of software independent of hardware was expected to ease the job of systems integrators, decrease robotics costs, and contribute to an increase in robotics sales.

Changing Buyer Behavior

Sales in the initial stage of the robotics trade were characterized by naked robots and a few peripheries. Some viewed robots as a sophisticated but nonetheless "commodity" hardware and pressed for fixed pricing. This pressure, in addition to the robotics industry's own changing cost structure, squeezed the profit margins of many robot manufacturers. The changing cost structure in the industry did not facilitate pricing policy. Nick Rizvi, corporate staff special projects at ASEA Robotics, expressed his views on manufacturing in the robotics industry and its effect on pricing.

In the earlier days of the robot industry, manufacturers and Western manufacturers in particular concentrated their manufacturing on a few robots with the same basic control. The end result was a somewhat limited range of robots, one of which could be selected and, if necessary, adjusted to fit an application. The Japanese, on the other hand, had a different philosophy in that they chose to manufacture robots with a variety of controls. This coincides with a Japanese design facility that allows them to implement changes and offer more products. Furthermore, that design facility allows them to do in 4 to 5 months what takes us about 12 months. Consequently, they have a broader product range for a given application that can be marketed as "more specific" for a customer's needs. And, when you add in the Japanese development and finance costs versus those of Western firms, those "more specific" robots can be sold for 10% to 15% less than their competitors' robots.

The Japanese design facility was seen by some in the industry as a major advantage. Given the pressures to manufacture in volume to meet high investment costs, robot makers tried to secure their share of industry shipments using one of two general strategies. The larger competitors sought to be one-stop robotics suppliers and covered virtually all application segments. Consequently, larger firms such as ASEA and GMF had wider product offerings with up to 12 robot models. Smaller firms, however, stressed their expertise in one or two application segments and offered 2 or 3 models. Each model was characterized by a combination of axes, weight-handling capacity, speed, and accuracy. Some firms, such as Adept and Prab, had proved their success using these variables, rather than applications to segment the market.

The Factory of the Future

Whether one used the term robot or not, programmable automation technology was a recent phenomenon for manufacturing industries. From a historical perspective, the more simple custom-made mechanisms predominant only a few years earlier were often expensive, dedicated to one product, and justified only for a large volume of products. Integrating the computer with such devices gave rise to programmable machines that could perform a number of tasks. This flexibility subsequently allowed costs to be spread over smaller batches of several products. As part of automating an entire factory, the next automation step was tying all a factory's activities together. Designs developed on CAD systems could then be transmitted to robotic controllers to turn out parts that in turn could be transported for assembly, using other robots or automated transport vehicles for final assembly. It was the latter stages of automation that proved to be the most difficult, because the complexity of control systems and related software had to be adjusted for each customer's factory. Just as the computer software industry experienced rapid growth with its first packages and slowed with increasingly complex applications packages, the robotics industry had slowed at the stage of factory-wide automation.

Engineering costs had become unpredictable in the robotics industry because people had insufficient knowledge in all the required fields. This made it difficult to move toward systems integration and to justify investments in automation, especially on a short-term basis. One technological advance expected to ease the robotics industry toward systems integration was the call for standards. One such standard was MAP or Manufacturing Automation Protocol. General Motors initiated MAP after realizing that nearly half the cost of an automation project was attributed to the inability of a product from one vendor to talk to a product from another vendor. Each manufacturer of robots, programmable controllers, and data collection systems used different networking systems. To talk with robots and controllers from different manufacturers required special software written explicitly for this task. To ensure that GM's standard was also accepted by non-GM clients, MAP was based on the emerging Open Systems Interconnection (OSI) promoted by the International Standards Organization (ISO).

Other significant technological trends in the robotics industry were the growth of robot intelligence, adaptive control, and load capacity. Robot intelligence included features such as sensory data collection, links to CAM, and supervisory control. Adaptive control allowed one to adapt robot programs to dynamic changes and facilitated off-line programming for specific applications. Load capacity referred to the ability to handle new types of materials as well as greater quantities of material.

Robots for small businesses offered one growth possibility for the future. Eric Mittelstadt, president of Robotic Industries Association, commented in 1988 that as many as 70,000 U.S. companies in the nonautomotive segment could benefit from robots but were not using the technology. Overall, those manufacturers who had software strengths had an opportunity to the extent that they could apply those strengths to different applications. Looking toward the 1990s, analysts believed that systems integration and diversification into nonindustrial segments, such as the military, space, undersea, mining, and medical, were the best growth possibilities.

Nick Rizvi shared his thoughts on the dynamics of the robot industry.

The rules of the robotics game appear to have changed; it is no longer clear what the future rules will be. Where we were once safe selling naked robots, we now need to take bigger risks and sell complete systems. To meet that growing systems demand, we must find sufficient human resources with diverse engineering backgrounds. The financial risks associated with bidding in the systems area are not small either. Yet if we abandon systems work, we will lose our credibility as a robot manufacturer. What do we need to do differently in the future to succeed as well as we have in the past?

CASE 19A

ASEA Robotics AB (A)

In October 1987, Stelio Demark, president of ASEA Robotics AB,[1] looked with satisfaction on a market report just passed to him by Nick Rizvi, head of corporate projects, indicating that in 1986 ASEA Robotics AB had just edged GMF from its leadership position and become the world's largest robot supplier with sales of $190 million and a market share of 11.2% (see Exhibit 1). Reflecting on the challenges still ahead, Stelio Demark commented:

Just like everybody else in this industry,[2] we are still not making a satisfactory return in this business. Our company faces considerable challenges in the next few years. We need to make a number of key decisions as to which market segments and which geographic areas we should emphasize and how we should streamline our business with respect to its product offering, marketing, manufacturing, and R&D. The next 5 years will be crucial with respect to turning this into a profitable business for our company.

---

[1] ASEA AB, the parent company of ASEA Robotics AB, merged with Brown Boveri & Cie. AG of Switzerland on January 4, 1988. Since the merger, the company operated under the official name of ABB Robotics AB, or ABB-R for short.

[2] For background on the robotics industry, see Case 18.

EXHIBIT 1 Worldwide Robotics Industry Market Share, 1986

Company	Total Revenue (million US$)	Market Share by Revenue (%)
ABB Robotics	190.0	11.2
GMF	186.2	11.0
Yaskawa	111.0	6.5
Matsushita	100.0	5.9
Cincinnati	79.7	4.7
Kawasaki	76.0	4.5
Toshiba	73.3	4.3
Cloos	70.0	4.1
Nachi	64.0	3.8
Fanuc	60.0	3.5
Unimation	51.8	3.0
KUKA	50.0	2.9
Hitachi	36.0	2.1
Others	550.7	32.5
Total	1,698.7	100.0

CORPORATE BACKGROUND

The ASEA group, trading under the legal name of ASEA AB (AB stands for Inc. in Swedish), was one of the world's 10 leading electrical equipment companies. Founded in Sweden in 1883, ASEA group sales were $8.95 billion in 1987, with a net income of $641 million. Sales in 1987 were some 12% above 1986 levels. The company employed over 70,000 persons, approximately half of which worked

This case was prepared by Professor Jean-Pierre Jeannet, Visiting Professor at IMEDE and Professor of Marketing and International Business at Babson College, Wellesley, Massachusetts, with the assistance of research associate Robert C. Howard. This case was prepared for class discussion only and not to illustrate either effective or ineffective handling of an administrative situation. Copyright © 1988 by IMEDE, Lausanne, Switzerland. The International Institute for Management Development (IMD), resulting from the merger between IMEDE, Lausanne, and IMI, Geneva, acquires and retains all rights. Not to be used or reproduced without written permission from IMD, Lausanne, Switzerland.

outside Sweden. With its head office located in Vasteras, 60 miles outside Stockholm, ASEA was one of Sweden's largest publicly quoted companies. Shares were traded on the Stockholm, Copenhagen, Helsinki, and London stock exchanges, the OTC in Germany, and NASDAQ in the United States. (For a 5-year summary of the ASEA Group's financial position, see Exhibit 2.)

The ASEA Group was a major producer in the areas of energy, transportation, and industrial equipment. Its major European competitors in those fields were Siemens of Germany, Brown Boveri & Cie. of Switzerland, and General Electric in the United Kingdom. Hitachi, Toshiba, and Mitsubishi were ASEA's major Japanese competitors; General Electric and Westinghouse were the major energy competitors in the United States.

When Percy Barnevik became chief executive officer (CEO) in the early 1980s, ASEA was significantly restructured along nine different industry groups, the largest accounting for some 20% of sales. In the beginning of 1986, ASEA began to incorporate many of its divisions as separate companies, a process that was expected to continue. The following business segments were part of the ASEA Group:

The *power plants* segment consisted of ASEA-Atom, ASEA Generation, ASEA Stal and its subsidiaries, and other foreign subsidiaries. The power plants segment manufactured plants for the generation of hydro, nuclear, and other thermal power, as well as heat-production plants. A number of growth niches existed in this business as a result of new technology and market demands for energy conservation, efficiency, and a cleaner environment. In 1987 this segment accounted for 5.3% of group sales, with nuclear power plants representing 24% of the segment's volume.

Power transmission included ASEA Relays, ASEA Transmission, ASEA Transformers, ASEA Switchgear, and related foreign subsidiaries. This business segment accounted for 13.4% of group volume and constituted one of ASEA's most technology intensive areas. ASEA was a world leader in high-voltage transmission and reactive power compensation, a method used to lower losses in large power networks. The

EXHIBIT 2   ASEA Group Financial Summary

	1983	1984	1985	1986	1987
Order bookings	27,255	35,635	39,358	47,438	56,165
Invoiced sales	30,589	36,600	41,652	46,601	52,271
Earnings after financial income and expense	1,970	2,337	2,413	2,425	2,724
Adjusted stockholders' equity	6,593	7,419	8,635	10,532	11,570
Total capital	32,175	37,087	41,618	47,154	59,040
Capital expenditures for property, plant, and equipment	1,077	1,063	1,427	2,069	2,097
Capital expenditures for acquisitions	358	260	1,009	2,137	2,111
Average number of employees	56,660	58,434	60,979	63,124	72,868
Operating earnings/ invoiced sales (%)	7.9	7.6	6.4	6.1	6.7
Return on capital employed (%)	16.5	17.8	16.8	18.2	16.2
Return on equity (%)	18.3	18.8	16.7	15.0	15.0
Debt/equity ratio	1.07	0.98	1.18	1.01	1.36
Interest coverage ratio	2.80	2.92	2.85	2.40	2.74
Net income per share (50% tax[a])	16.00	18.90	19.60	19.60	22.10
Net income per share, fully diluted (50% tax[a])	—	—	18.70	19.30	21.60
Net income per share according to equity accounting method (paid tax[a])	28.70	32.60	35.60	35.30	29.60
Net income per share according to equity accounting method, fully diluted (paid tax[a])	—	—	34.00	34.70	29.00
Dividend per share[a]	4.00	4.70	6.00	7.00	8.00[b]

[a] Adjusted for stock dividends

[b] 1987: proposed

Note: Translation rates on December 31, 1987: $1.00 = SEK5.84; £1.00 = SEK10.84.

power transmission industry was characterized by worldwide overcapacity and low growth.

Power distribution as a business segment included ASEA Distribution, ASEA Kabel and its subsidiaries, Elektrokoppar, and related foreign subsidiaries. The business segment marketed low- and medium-voltage switchgear and apparatus, cables and capacitors, and manufactured wire, strip, and conductors from aluminum and copper. Power distribution was concentrated on domestic markets and often required local production or adaptation of products to meet local needs. This segment was heavily oriented towards Sweden and represented approximately 9.5% of group volume.

Transportation equipment consisted of ASEA Traction and its subsidiaries, ASEA Truck, Haegglund & Soener, and related foreign subsidiaries. This business segment comprised mass transit systems, electric locomotives, all-terrain carriers, marine deck cranes, hydraulic equipment, and forklift trucks. In railway vehicles, ASEA had a strong position because it was one of the few manufacturers that offered a full range of products from locomotives and railroad cars to electrification systems, all from the same vendor. In 1987, the transportation equipment segment's volume was 7.0% of group sales.

The *industrial equipment* business segment included ASEA Automation, ASEA Drives, ASEA-Hafo, ASEA Metallurgy, Stal Refrigeration, ASEA Robotics, and related foreign subsidiaries. This segment consisted of equipment for improving productivity in the metallurgical and process industries, industrial robots, electronic components, and refrigeration plants. Parts of this sector were undergoing a shakeout, and margins had consequently been under pressure since the early 1980s. In 1987, this segment accounted for 11.7% of group volume.

The *financial services* business segment was formed at the end of 1985 and accounted for 7.7% of group volume. Its purpose was to increase ASEA's return on its liquid assets and provide sales support for ASEA's industrial businesses. Leasing, financing, foreign exchange management, trading, and countertrade were increasingly part of ASEA's industrial sales, and

a presence in these businesses made ASEA's other business segments more competitive.

The *Flaekt group* represented ASEA's largest business segment with 22.6% of group volume. Flaekt AB, in which ASEA had a 51% interest, focused on environmental control, both indoors and outdoors. Flaekt's base was air and energy technology, with flue gas treatment representing an important part of the segment's business. The group's sales depended to a large extent on industrialized countries where sales derived from general investment levels and legislation requirements of public authorities.

Standard finished goods was made up of ASEA Cylinda, ASEA Motors, ASEA Selfa and its subsidiaries, ASEA Skandia, and related foreign subsidiaries. This segment included an electrical wholesale business, electric motors, low-voltage apparatus, and household appliances and, in 1987, represented 10.0% of group volume. *Other operations* included semifinished goods, power utility operations, telecommunications, and service and installation. Most of the companies in this segment were service companies and required a local presence in each country. Low capital expenditures and high margins gave this group a steady cash flow. In 1987, other operations accounted for 12.8% of ASEA's group volume.

DEVELOPMENT OF ASEA ROBOTICS

ASEA Robotics, first established in 1974, had achieved a consolidated sales volume of $250 million in 1987. The company employed some 1,500 persons worldwide, had R&D expenditures of 10% of sales, and was the clear market leader in Europe and a strong number 2 in the United States. ASEA Robotics also maintained sales representations in 20 countries.

ASEA got its start in the robotics business by combining its internal experience in robotics applications with that in electronics to build the world's first all electric robot. ASEA produced approximately 6,000 units of the first robot models, the IRB 6 and IRB 60 (short for Industrial Robot), most of which were still in operation after 70,000 hours of use. The IRB

6 was launched in 1974, the same year that the ASEA Electronics Division designated Robotics as its own profit center in Vasteras, Sweden. Vasteras was ASEA's corporate hometown where Robotics was given considerable freedom in development.

ASEA's start in the robotics industry grew out of the desire to improve its own manufacturing efficiency. This began in the mid to late 1960s and followed on the purchase of NC machines and an ASEA climate that favored investment in production engineering. This climate found ASEA executives asking if they could make their own robots. ASEA consequently made and installed its first robots in its own factories where they were used for handling and tending. Shortly thereafter, ASEA began to sell these robots and approached ESAB to develop a robot for welding applications. ESAB marketed welding process equipment to a variety of industries around the world and was a clear number 1 worldwide for arcwelding applications. ESAB corporate sales amounted to about SKr12 billion ($2 billion). The arcwelding expertise offered by ESAB expanded ASEA's robot offering into a new application segment. Traditionally, ASEA's expertise had been in electronic control technology, not welding. ESAB provided ASEA with welding components to be attached to a robot arm and, in a sense, allowed ASEA to make a robot capable of being integrated with ESAB equipment.

The division grew slowly at first and reached a volume of only 250 robots by 1980. After 1980, new management gave the business added attention and incorporated ASEA Robotics as a separate company in 1985. Thereafter, ASEA Robotics entered a period of rapid growth. From 1980 to 1987, annual output increased from 250 to 2,000 robots; the company expanded aggressively into the United States and Japan and set up production units in France and Spain. ASEA's expertise in robotics continued to grow in this time frame, and by the end of 1987 the company had products for arc and spotwelding, painting/surface finishing, materials handling/machine tending, gluing, assembly, process, and a range of other applications and an installed base of nearly 10,000 robots (see Exhibit 3).

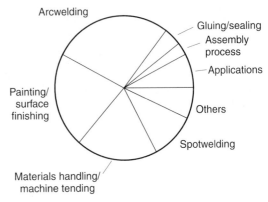

Total: Approximately, 10,000 robots

EXHIBIT 3 ASEA Accumulated Application Experience, 1987

ASEA was late in entering the spotwelding market segment and did not have a product in this segment until 1983, whereas some competitors had 20 years of spotwelding experience. In the United States, ASEA's single biggest market, the company had 200 employees and was in second place behind GMF (see Exhibit 4.)

ASEA Robotics had established a number of alliances and made several acquisitions over the years. Among these was Trallfa Robot of Norway, partially acquired (51%) in 1985. Trallfa was a leading manufacturer of robots for the painting and surface finishing sector, and its acquisition strengthened ASEA's export operations. Trallfa products consequently filled a void in the ASEA line, previously concentrated on arcwelding and other metalworking applications. The acquisition also saved ASEA from having to modify electric robots for painting and its associated spark hazards.

In Japan, ASEA was represented by ASEA Robotics/Gadelius (GAR). ASEA products had an initial reputation of being overpriced in Japan, despite their high quality and precision (*Business Week,* June 27, 1983). ASEA moved to counter this in 1983 by manufacturing in Kobe, a move that reportedly lowered costs by 10% to 15% (*Business Week,* June 27, 1983). In both the United States and Japan, ASEA expanded by setting up large, well-equipped ro-

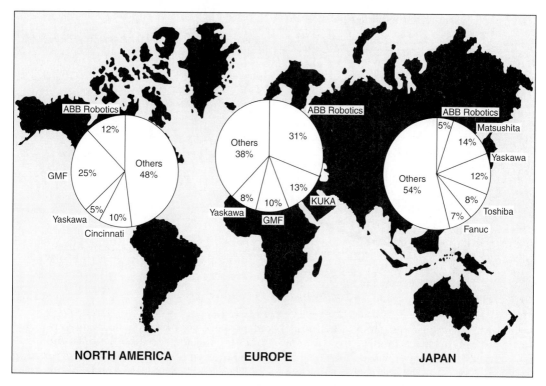

EXHIBIT 4 Robotics Market Shares, 1987

botics centers, offering customers service and support facilities along with systems engineering and hardware (*Business Week*, June 27, 1983).

THE ASEA ROBOTICS PRODUCT LINE

The ASEA product line grew systematically from its original product, the IRB 6, to a full line of seven robot models, the Trallfa paint robot, and a range of accessories to equip robots for their various applications. (Refer to Exhibit 5 for a summary of ASEA's major milestones.)

The IRB 6/2 was ASEA's first industrial robot (IRB) and, at its introduction in 1974, the first electrically powered robot. It handled loads up to 6 kg and had an accuracy of ±0.1 mm. The IRB 6/2 had five axes of rotation and was designed for applications that required great precision and uniform production. As such, the IRB 6/2 was well suited for arcweld-

ing, gluing, polishing, deburring, inspection, and assembly.

The IRB 60/2 was ASEA's heavy-duty industrial robot designed to handle payloads of up to 60 kg with an accuracy of ±0.4 mm. As with all ASEA robots, the IRB 60/2 had an alphanumeric display with a choice of languages, dustproof touch-sensitive buttons, and a logic control. The five-axis IRB 60 was ideal for materials handling, machine tending, and hazardous tasks such as cleaning of castings.

The IRB 90S/2 was a flexible automated spotwelding system suited for severe working environments. The IRB 90S/2 was sold either as a complete 6-axis spotwelding system or in a variety of configurations, from a naked robot on up. The IRB 90S/2 had a unique water, air, and current (WAC) supply inside the robot arm so that cables would not hinder its working space.

The IRB 1000 was a pendular-type robot de-

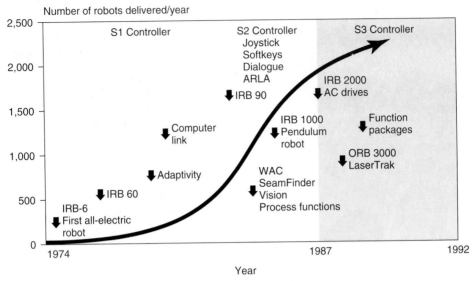

EXHIBIT 5   Milestones in the Development of ASEA Robotics

signed for small parts assembly. This model was a fast and accurate tool for the assembly segment of the robotics market.

The IRB 2000 was a six-axis robot with a payload capacity of 10 kg. This was supplemented by the IRB 3000, also a six-axis industrial robot, with a handling capacity of 30 kg and a reach of up to 2 m. The IRB 2000 and 3000 were ASEA's family of multiapplication robots, ideally suited for materials handling and machine tending. Their extended reach also made them ideal for arc and stud welding, adhesive dispensing, deburring and water-jet cutting, and laser cutting tasks.

The IRB 9000 was a six-axis industrial robot dedicated to spotwelding with a payload capacity of up to 140 kg. Each naked robot included an integrated control unit and was usually sold with a number of accessories. The control unit acted as the digital communications link to the equipment that a robot served. The control unit was compact and easy to use, and its quality reflected ASEA's range of know-how in the diverse robotics industry.

The ASEA Group also sold cell controllers that could be used to control an entire manufacturing cell. In addition to robotics systems and cell controllers, ASEA offered a full range

of grippers, laser-based seam finders and seam trackers, image processing systems, and other accessories that, when combined in a function package, formed ASEA's "solutions" business approach (see Exhibits 7 and 8).

The recent addition of the IRB 2000 and the IRB 3000 had substantially improved ASEA's competitiveness for applications against competition that had already offered a third integrated mechanical wrist movement.

Commented Nick Rizvi, head of corporate projects at ASEA Robotics AB,

When you do not have a robot ideally suited to a specific client application, you often end up designing something from scratch. This is usually more expensive than offering a standard robot solution. Some of our competitors had models of the IRB 2000 and 3000 type that were so specific they drove down the price level for our systems solutions. Consequently, we were competing for systems or turnkey solutions against specifically designed robots, which had a negative impact on our profitability.

Although it was difficult to classify a line of robots on a single dimension, one common approach was to look at weight-handling capacity. Typical weight categories (in kg) were as follows:

0–6	IRB 6, IRB 1000
6–10	IRB 2000
15–25	IRB 3000
30–60	IRB 60
80–100	IRB 90
100+	IRB 9000

For some applications, such as spotwelding, heavy-weight capacity plus reach (that is, big robot arms) were important. ASEA's line was concentrated initially in the lower categories; it was not until 1983 that the IRB 90 came into the market. The recent entry of the IRB 9000 extended ASEA's product range into the heavy handling category.

Essential parts of all ASEA robots were the electronic controllers. As Rizvi commented, "In fact, for us a naked robot always means the robot platform *and* the controller cabinet" (see Exhibit 6). ASEA used the same controllers for all its robots. The present S3 generation had been in use since the mid-1980s, and work on a third-generation controller (S4) was underway.

ASEA's strategy of having the same controller set it apart from its Japanese competitors. "The Japanese offer a modular set of controllers that they can adapt to individual requirements," Rizvi commented. "It puzzles us how they can do this." The advantage of scaling the controller down or up as needed also resulted in cost efficiency.

Japanese competitors of ASEA appeared to have a larger product line with a more limited range in weight-handling capacity for each model. "As soon as you move away from your 'best' range for a robot, the customer usually overbuys and, as a result, has higher acquisition costs. With a product line of, say, 10 rather than 5 robots, you can beat your competitor for the 'in-between' applications. What we have also noticed is that our Japanese competitors can get a new model out in just 4 to 5 months, whereas we need 6 to 8 months for major product changes."

ASEA ROBOTICS MARKET POSITION

By the end of 1987, ASEA Robotics had an installed base of about 10,000 robots, approximately 65% in Europe, 15% in North America, and 10% in Japan and Australia. Corresponding market shares were Europe, 31%; North America, 12%; and Asia, 5%. Growth had been impressive, surpassing 2,000 units in 1986 and $200 million worldwide in consolidated sales in 1987.

ASEA's Position by Application Areas

Of ASEA's 10,000 installed robots, about 8,000 were for automotive applications. Leading applications were arcwelding, painting - and surface finishing, materials handling and machine tending, and spotwelding. Less frequent were applications for gluing and sealing, assembly, and process applications (see Exhibit 7).

ASEA's Competitive Position in Europe

ASEA's market position differed considerably by region (see Exhibit 4). Europe was the company's strongest market, where it was by far the market leader with 31%, followed by Kuka (West Germany) with 13%, GMF with 10%, and Yaskawa of Japan with 8%. Some 10 companies shared the remainder of the market. ASEA's market share varied from country to country, however. For example, ASEA dominated in Sweden with about 60% and was also the market leader in Spain, the United Kingdom, and Germany. ASEA held second place in both France and Italy behind ACMA, a French company, and Comau, an Italian supplier, respectively.

In general, there was a consensus within ASEA Robotics that the company's strength could be rated by application, based on available products, application know-how, and installed base.

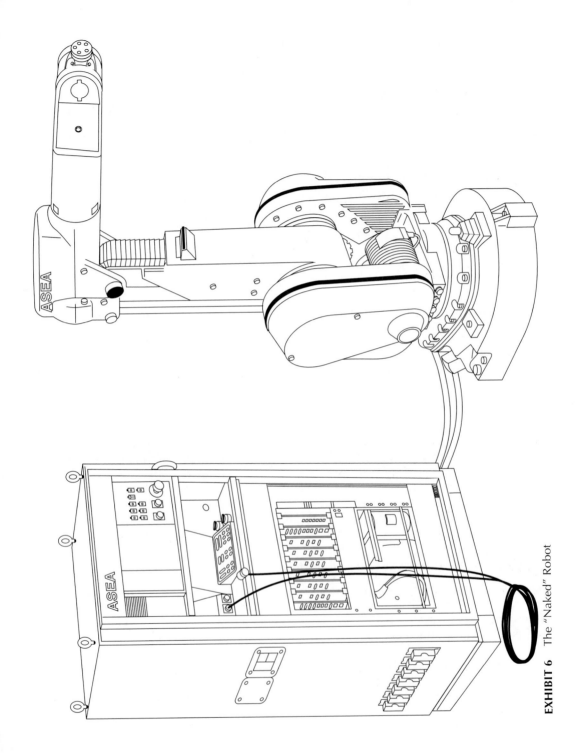

EXHIBIT 6 The "Naked" Robot

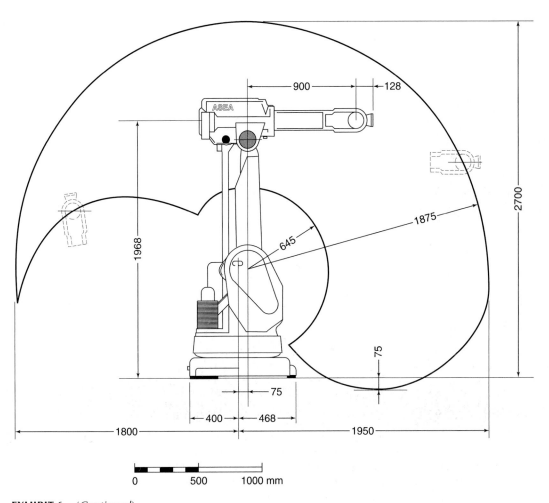

EXHIBIT 6 (*Continued*)

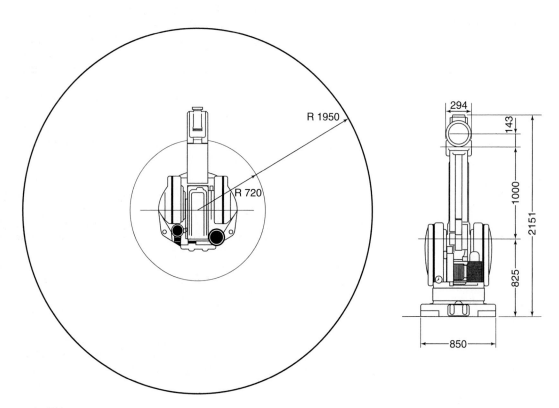

EXHIBIT 6 (*Continued*)

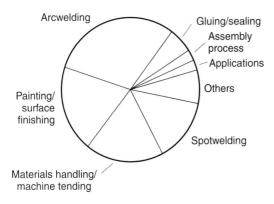

Total: Approximately, 8,000 robots

EXHIBIT 7   ASEA Products Installed Base in Automotive Segment

	First	Second	Third
Arcwelding	ASEA	Yaskawa	Kuka
Spotwelding	Kuka	ASEA	Comau
Gluing/sealing	GMF	Kuka	ASEA
Handling	ASEA	Cincinnati	Unimation
Machine tending	Cincinnati	ASEA	Unim./Yaskawa
Assembly	ASEA	Unimation	Yaskawa
Process	ASEA	Cincinnati	Unimation
Painting	ASEA	GMF/Behr	Graco

Likewise, a consensus existed with respect to customer perceptions and ASEA's position against six key competitors in Europe.

	First	Second	Third
Market image	ASEA	Kuka	Yaskawa
Product technology	ASEA	Kuka	Yaskawa
Application know-how	ASEA	Kuka	Comau
Financial position	ASEA/GMF	Comau	Kuka
Operational resources	ASEA	Yaskawa	Comau
Price levels	Yaskawa	Unimation	Cincinnati/Comau
Price flexibility	Yaskawa	Cincinnati/Comau	Unimation
Nonauto penetration	Yaskawa	ASEA	Unimation
Automotive penetration	Kuka	ASEA/Comau/Cincinnati	—
Local presence	ASEA	Unimation	Kuka
Market share	ASEA	Kuka	GMF

ASEA led in most categories. In price levels and price flexibility, only Kuka was rated below ASEA. Trends indicated that ASEA, Kuka, GMF, and Yaskawa were gaining volume, whereas Cincinnati and Unimation were declining.

ASEA's Competitive Position in the U.S. Market

In the United States, ASEA enjoyed second place with a 12% market share as opposed to GMF with 25%, Cincinnati with 10%, Yaskawa with 5%, followed by Unimation and Kuka. All other manufacturers accounted for 48% of the market but had shares of 2% or less. GMF's share consisted of shipments mainly to GM's own plants.

As with Europe, there was a general belief at ASEA that the company's strength could be rated by application area, as follows:

	First	Second	Third
Arcwelding	Yaskawa	ASEA	Kuka
Spotwelding	Kuka	Cincinnati	GMF
Gluing/sealing	GMF	Cincinnati	Kuka (ASEA 4th)
Handling	ASEA	Cincinnati	GMF
Tending	ASEA	Cincinnati	GMF
Assembly	GMF	ASEA	Kuka
Process	ASEA	GMF	Cincinnati
Painting	GM	ASEA	

And, in comparison to the competition, ASEA employees believed the company's position could be approximated as follows:

	First	Second	Third
Market image	GMF/Kuka	—	ASEA
Product technology	Kuka	ASEA	Yaskawa
Application know-how	Kuka	ASEA	Yaskawa
Financial position	ASEA/GMF	—	Kuka
Operational resources	GMF	ASEA	Cincinnati
Price levels	Yaskawa/GMF	—	Unimation
Price flexibility	Yaskawa/GMF	—	Unimation
Nonauto penetration	Unimation	Yaskawa	GMF

Automotive penetration	GMF/ASEA	—	Cincinnati/Kuka
Local presence	GMF	Yaskawa	ASEA
Market share	GMF	ASEA	Cincinnati

As far as competitive trends were concerned, GMF, ASEA, Yaskawa, and Kuka were all viewed as gaining strength, whereas Cincinnati and Unimation were seen as losing ground.

The United States was ASEA's single biggest market, with a growth rate of 10% in 1987 and an approximate volume of $45 million, despite negative growth trends in the market. Employment had increased to 200 by 1987.

ASEA's Position in the Japanese Market

ASEA's position in the Japanese market, the world's largest robotics market, was number 5 behind four Japanese companies. Matsushita was the leader with 14% followed by Yaskawa (12%), Toshiba (8%), Fanuc (7%), and ASEA (5%). Other manufacturers accounted for 54% of the Japanese market. In Japan, ASEA was represented by Gadelius, another company owned by ASEA Corporation. ASEA products were initially considered overpriced in Japan despite their high quality and reputation. Local manufacturing in 1983 allowed the company to lower costs by about 10% to 15%.

THE ORGANIZATION OF THE ASEA ROBOTICS GROUP

Within ASEA Corporation, the robotics group was organized as a business area. Sales and P&L results were consolidated for the entire group, headed by Björn Weichbrodt. Sales of the business group amounted to about $250 million for 1987. Weichbrodt also acted as president of ASEA Robotics, Inc. (USA). He was assisted by Stelio Demark, who was responsible for the European robot companies and was president of ASEA Robotics AB in Sweden.

The business area management was assisted by an Advisory International Strategy Group consisting of the business area manager (Weichbrodt), head of ASEA Robotics AB in Sweden (Demark), the heads of local robotics sales organizations (Germany, Italy, Japan, and the United States), and the business development manager. A small staff group comprising business development, controlling, and productivity also reported to the business area manager. ASEA Robotics AB (ROB) in Vasteras, Sweden, was the largest single unit in the robotics business group. It comprised the manufacturing organization, engineering, and research. ROB also had sales responsibility for the Swedish market.

ASEA maintained sales units in 11 European countries and in the United States, Canada, Australia, and Japan. Some sales companies (UDBs) were separately incorporated (dedicated sales companies) (United States, Germany, United Kingdom), but for the most part were divisions within country sales organizations maintained by ASEA for the entire corporate product line. In all countries, however, ASEA Robotics had separately identifiable units with a dedicated staff. Reporting was in the form of a matrix, with both the business area management and local country management jointly responsible for the business result. This meant that in, for example, France, the UDB manager reported to the country manager as well as the robotics business area manager for financial results. Although the robotics area management had a considerable amount of control over local divisions, it did not have sole decision-making authority in such issues as personnel.

Marketing Organization at ASEA Robotics

Marketing was essentially in the hands of ASEA's robot centers located in key areas. There were 26 robot centers in existence, 14 in Europe, 5 in the Americas, and 6 in the Pacific Rim countries (see Exhibit 8). Three countries, the United States (with 3), Sweden (2) and Japan (3), had more than one robot center.

The role of the robot center was to project ASEA Robotics customer and sales service

EXHIBIT 8 ASEA Robotics Robot Center Locations

Region	Robot Center	Location
Europe	Austria	Brunn am Gebirge
	Belgium	Zaventem
	Denmark	Odense
	Finland	Espoo
	France	Persan
	Germany	Friedberg
	Holland	Apeldoorn
	Italy	Milan
	Norway	Bryne
	Spain	Sabadell
	Sweden	Gothenburg, Vasteras
	Switzerland	Zurich
	United Kingdom	Luton
The Americas	Brazil	Sao Paulo
	Canada	Toronto, Ontario;
	United States	New Berlin and Milwaukee, Wisconsin; Troy and Detroit, Michigan; Irving, Texas; White Plains, New York
Japan and Australia	Australia	Melbourne
	Japan	Kobe, Tokyo, Nagoya, Hiroshima
	New Zealand	Auckland
	Singapore	

closer to its customer base. They provided full coverage for sales, engineering, training, and service. Engineering services ranged from feasibility studies to systems configuration to on-site installation. Robot Center engineers had to have good knowledge of many manufacturing processes, production engineering, tooling, and related disciplines. A typical robot center had a staff of 15 to 40. Combined employment of all ASEA's robot centers was about 700, including those with complete systems capacity.

The robot centers were a solution to the lack of distribution channels when ASEA started in this field. The company had no contact to the key customer automotive segment. The robot centers were often located in buildings separate from the country sales organization for the corporation. In the United

Kingdom the robot center was in Birmingham near the center of the U.K. car industry.

Nick Rizvi stated:

Other robot manufacturers have solved this differently. The Japanese had a customer in Japan that was sophisticated enough to buy only naked robots and to perform the integration and engineering in-house. In Europe, very few companies could do this. When the Japanese sell in Europe, they use systems houses that provide the package service to their clients locally. We at ASEA are unique in having created our own direct sales channel in all key markets.

The activities at ASEA robot centers covered basic areas. Each center was expected to perform sales, engineering, training, and service to clients in its area.

Systems Engineering at ASEA Robotics

The ASEA robot centers purchased naked robots from ROB in Sweden (platform and control). Based on their own customer contacts, they would equip the robots for the required application by using already existing accessories. If available, accessories were also sourced from ROB in Sweden. The robot centers were in a position to deliver a fully engineered package for a client if needed.

"One of our principal problems," Demark commented, "is the growing tendency to get involved in such engineering efforts at the robot center level. About 50 worker/years, or about one-third of our total engineering effort, is now devoted to customizing robots to client needs. This represents 90% of our systems development effort."

Local tailoring could involve making robots available on a trial basis to clients. "We found that a number of robots were floating around in various places that represented a capital tie-up of about $2.5 million."

Sales to OEMs

About 25% of ASEA's annual unit volume went to the OEMs, such as ESAB who equipped the naked robots with its own application packages. For this segment, no engineering was necessary.

Robot Economics

Although end-user prices varied by application, a typical end-user price for an ASEA robot fully equipped and installed amounted to about $150,000. The robot center would source it to about $75,000 from ROB in Sweden. The rest was value added by the robot center, consisting of about $30,000 for cell engineering and $50,000 for value added.

Training Activities at Robot Centers

Training of customer employees was viewed as an important activity. ASEA offered 1-week courses to customers for operators, programmers, and maintenance engineers at its robot centers. However, instead of selling training as a package only (representing about 1% of product price), ASEA began to sell training as a separate product. By 1987, training revenue represented some 10% of corporate revenue, or $25 million. This service was viewed as important because personnel tended to change and customers always had new employees who needed to be trained. In 1987 alone, about 4,000 people had attended ASEA's courses.

ASEA offered regularly scheduled courses on topics such as operations, basic and advanced programming, safety, mechanical service, electronic service, and preventive maintenance. On special request, courses could be held at a client's site, and seminars on robotics in general could also be offered.

Service

The personnel needs for ASEA's robot service were relatively low. However, spare parts usage was high and had reached 25% of total robotics revenue ($62.5 million). ASEA was in a position to fly in parts and personnel anytime on short notice.

"Imagine that a car manufacturer's line is down because a single robot malfunctions.

Given that a typical production cycle is 3 cars per minute, a 1-minute shutdown will cost a lost value of 3 cars, or easily $30,000," Demark explained. As a result, most robot users needed to stock ample spare parts nearby and to train their own maintenance staff.

Manufacturing Operations

ASEA's manufacturing strategy evolved considerably over time. In its initial phase, all manufacturing of robot platforms and controls took place in Vasteras in Sweden. In the early 1980s, ASEA realized that local acceptance in some markets would be helped if local manufacturing were established. This led to assembly operations in France, Japan, and the United States. However, this was found to be uneconomical and, in a third phase, manufacturing was again centralized in Vasteras, where a completely new plant was built.

The robot manufacturing center was a 15,000-m^2 (165,000-ft^2) area facility with an annual capacity of 3,000 naked robots. It manufactured both platforms and control systems. Delivery was 4 to 6 weeks from the order date. The manufacturing control system allowed a simultaneous release policy, which meant that an order was released for manufacturing only when "all the screws were in."

As a result of the newly adopted manufacturing system, local stocks of naked robots were felt unnecessary. Across the entire business area, inventory and work in process were to be kept at less than 20% of sales.

ASEA emphasized efficiency and had achieved a significant drop in its unit costs in 1987. Labor costs were expected to be reduced further in 1988 and onward. ASEA management expected to be able to offset any inflationary pressures with increased efficiency.

The manufacturing performed at ASEA Robotics in Vasteras largely consisted of assembling robots and systems testing before shipping. This was reflected in a very high content of purchased material, which amounted to more than half of total product costs. Concentrating on assembly alone allowed ASEA to invest its funds into R&D, marketing, and product line expansion without other fixed investments into manufacturing.

Research and Development Activities at ASEA Robotics[3]

For the entire robotics business area, the R&D effort was carried out by about 200 engineers. The total expenditures were estimated at $25 million or about 15% of the volume in naked robots ($75,000 per unit, 2,000 units). About 150 worker/years of engineering were performed at ROB in Vasteras, the remaining at the various robot centers.

Research at Vasteras (ROB) consisted of 120 worker/years in development of new models (IRBs), work on controls, improving the mechanical parts of the existing line, and work on necessary computers and servo drives. Most of these resources went into the development of the IRB 2000, the IRB 3000, and the S3. Whenever a new model was introduced, the maintenance R&D requirements increased correspondingly, having reached about 40% of development worker/years in 1987.

About 80 worker/years were invested into application development, which included the adaptation of a naked robot to a specific task. More than half, or about 50 worker/years, were spent in ASEA's various robot centers in response to special client requests. The bulk of this was carried out, however, in the larger sales companies (Germany, United States, Japan, France, United Kingdom, and Sweden).

Demark considered ASEA's present investment of about 120 worker/years in development as a basic requirement to maintain ASEA's technological standing as a leading robot manufacturer. "A new robot generation/model requires an investment of about SKr100 million. If I want to keep R&D at max. 10% of naked robot sales, I need a volume of at least 2,000 units over the life of the model to cover my initial R&D investment. With an expected life of 10 years, the minimum annual volume is about 200 robots per year."

"Most of our competitors do not have the volume we have. I just cannot see how they can make it given the heavy R&D costs," Demark said. Among the leading Europeans, Kuka (600 to 700 units annually), Comau (200 to 300 units), and Acma (300 units) were below ASEA's level. Although he was not sure, Demark suspected that his Japanese competitors (Yaskawa and others) were able to treat R&D as a corporate expense and did not allocate it directly to the product line. "To them, robotics is a way to show that they were modern and at the edge of new technologies."

Pricing Robots at ASEA

"In general, we are 10% to 15% above the Japanese price level with our robots," Rizvi explained. "Although not all robots delivered the same performance, the Japanese can always beat you on a price/performance basis as they do now in the United States."

Rizvi indicated that some buyers were learning to differentiate between initial acquisition costs and the costs of running and maintaining a robot. In the long term, ASEA robots had demonstrated a higher uptime stability, which, if applied over the total economic life of a robot, would lead to a long-term running cost advantage for ASEA. Despite consistent cost reductions by ASEA, the 10% to 15% price difference vis-à-vis its Japanese competitors had not disappeared.

Currency fluctuations played a role as well. For ASEA, costs were based on the Swedish krona. However, other major competitors had difficulties as well. Kuka of Germany was in the same situation, and the Japanese had seen the yen appreciate substantially during the preceding 2 years. If there were any winners, it was the U.S.-based manufacturers. However, some of those were battered due to a considerable slowdown in new factory orders for the U.S. automobile industry.

ASEA Robotics' Competitive Situation

Management at ASEA Robotics considered several areas of strength when competing in

---

[3] The data in this section have been disguised.

the marketplace. First, ASEA had an orientation toward selling solutions rather than only products. Its broad range of products and accessories gave ASEA the capability to compete for a multitude of applications. Over time, the company had gained diverse application know-how. The company profited from the existence of its robot center concepts, and it also had moderate systems resources to provide the delivery of complete systems fully equipped with robots, accessories, and the necessary software. ASEA had shown an aggressive approach to R&D, had extensive training and service capabilities, and was recognized worldwide for quality and reliability.

At a recent meeting in Sweden, robot center managers developed a ranking system, with different categories and numbers, thought to approximate the importance of key success factors and possible sources of competitive advantage. A score of 0 was an indication of very poor performance in relation to the market and competitors; a score of 5 indicated very good or near perfect performance.

Ranking	Possible Key Success Factors	Ranking	Possible Sources of Competitive Advantage
1	Product costs	1	Exchangeability
1	Distribution costs	1	Exchange of people
2	Efficiency in business	1	Be prepared to take control of EDP opportunities
2	Competitors' knowledge	2	Information exchange
		2	Ease of communications
2	Anticipate market needs	2	Market flexibility
3	Volume	2	Multinational customer handling
3	Profitability	2	Application documentation
3	Professionalism	3	Quick throughout time
3	Market knowledge	3	Selective marketing nucleus
4	Product quality	3	Diversified prodution program
4	Global market	3	Correct organization size
4	Financial strength	3	Control features
3–4	Good management	3	Solutions
		3	Flexible organization
		4	Worldwide organization
		5	Broad range of products

ASEA Robotics AB (B)

"Looking at the next phase of our development, we have to rethink the way we do business in a number of areas," said Stelio Demark, president of ASEA Robotics AB in Vasteras, Sweden.[1] "Our plans for 1988 and 1989 need to reflect first of all a need to improve profitability toward the eventual goal of 20% on invested capital. This means we have to balance the needs for profitability and growth better. Furthermore, we have been pulled into several systems contracts that give me concern about how we tackle this business. At the same time, we have to think how we want to deal with our competitive situation in spotwelding and assembly application, where we have traditionally been weak."

LONG-TERM PROFITABILITY OF ASEA ROBOTICS

"Our corporation expects us eventually to earn 20% on capital employed in our operation," Demark explained. "With $250 million in sales, employed net assets (total assets minus debt) are about $100 million. A return of 20%, or $20 million, amounts to a return of 8% on sales. Right now, most of our competitors are losing money on their robot operations."

---

[1] See Cases 18 and 19A for further background.

Growth at ASEA over the past 5 years had been considerable. The company had moved from about 1,000 units in 1982 to 2,000 units in 1987, requiring a heavy investment in R&D and the expansion of the robot center concept. It was clear to Demark that targeted profitability could not be reached immediately and that progress had to come over time.

OPPORTUNITIES IN ASSEMBLY SEGMENT

Assembly applications, representing a worldwide volume of about 7,000 robots, or about 27% of all installations, was equal in size to materials handling/machine tending. It was made up of robots with a small to very large handling capacity and a wide range of user industries.

To date, ASEA had about 200 installed robots for assembly applications with automotive customers. Annual sales for the entire applications amounted to about 100 units of varying sizes, about 75% of it in Europe. Due to the extensive customization, assembly robots sales tended to involve a large amount of systems design work. These were often complex technical installations that had to be priced before the work was completed. Cost overruns had occurred, partly because solutions tended to be novel.

This case was prepared by Jean-Pierre Jeannet, Visiting Professor at IMEDE and Professor of Marketing and International Business at Babson College, Wellesley, Massachusetts, with the assistance of Robert Howard, research associate at IMEDE. This case was prepared for class discussion only and not to illustrate either effective or ineffective handling of an administrative situation. Copyright © 1989 by IMEDE, Lausanne, Switzerland. The International Institute for Management Development (IMD), resulting from the merger between IMEDE, Lausanne, and IMI, Geneva, acquires and retains all rights. Not to be used or reproduced without written permission from IMD, Lausanne, Switzerland.

The segment itself offered vast potential, and a considerable amount of attention was being spent on it. Experts believed that assembly was going to be the next major investment area for flexible automation. The largest market was the consumer electronics industry, a user segment that was not very familiar to ASEA's robot centers, which were mostly centered on automotive users and applications.

Demark felt that a comprehensive effort aimed at the entire assembly segment would require a large-scale product development effort. Among other things, ASEA would have to develop a SCARA (selective compliance assembly robot arm) robot, get involved in clean-room classifications and communications facilities, and more. Furthermore, ASEA would have to undertake a considerable marketing effort because its contacts with the electronics industry were almost nonexistent. "The electronics industry business culture differs widely from what we are used to with our traditional customers such as the automotive industry."

A second approach consisted of concentrating more narrowly on assembly of products already known to ASEA and on industry segments where contacts existed. This would result in equipping naked robots with the necessary accessories for some clearly identified tasks, but staying away from full-scale design of entire systems or assembly lines. Since the end user would still require robots to be integrated into a system, ASEA would have to work closely with partners. That is, OEMs could buy naked robots from ASEA, adding value by equipping them with needed accessories. Or systems houses could perform the integrating function for customers by buying robots with accessories from various suppliers.

To develop a suitable package of accessories for the various assembly tasks required additional R&D efforts. Each package was estimated to require 5 to 10 worker/years of engineering. ASEA's existing range of robots was considered sufficient for assembly tasks with the exception of micro assembly (very small parts). Leaving the assembly segment all together was a third option, but this would again endanger ASEA's idea of full partnership with the important automotive industry.

EXPANDING INTO SYSTEMS BUSINESS

In the fall of 1986, when orders for robot systems began to expand, Demark became concerned. "We were taking in a lot of systems business in many of our robot centers, exposing ourselves to considerable risks. We needed to become clear on how we wanted to run this to avoid the losses that have occasionally occurred."

ASEA divided the robot business into three elements. The first element consisted of the robot platform, the control cabinet, and the accessories, which together was called a naked robot. A second element consisted of tools, fixtures, magazines to stock parts, and similar items and was referred to as a package. The third element included transfer devices, inspection devices, and all the necessary controls to integrate the robot package into a production process (see Exhibit 1).

The extent of value added for a naked robot, its package, and the entire system depended on a specific application. An arcwelding system served as an example (see Exhibit 2). The naked robot, consisting of the platform and controls, would be sold for about $70,000. The required package to make it an arcwelding robot consisted of a power pack ($16,000), an electrode feeder ($16,000), a torch cleaner ($1,000), and arcwelding software and controls ($9,000) for a total of about $42,000. This package was increased by ESAB when that company purchased naked robots from ASEA, resulting in a packaged robot price of $110,000. When integrated into a complete manufacturing system, the systems integrator would combine the robot package with the necessary transfer equipment that moved pieces to and from the welding station and performed installation. As part of a complete line, the single robot would cost $300,000, or about four times its naked value. Of the systems integrator's $190,000 added value, about 25% accounted for the gross margin; the rest was spent on hardware. Typically, the integrator's margin was 10% for handling and 15% for know-how expressed in engineering worker/hours sold for studies, plans, and the like (see Exhibit 3).

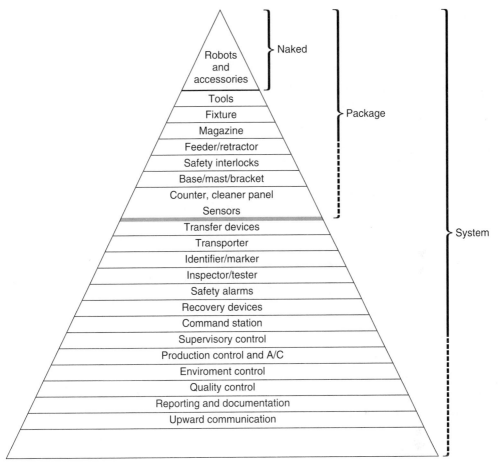

EXHIBIT 1   Robot Systems

"The basic attraction of going into the systems business is the high gross margins due to high value added," explained Nick Rizvi, manager for corporate projects at ASEA Robotics AB in Vasteras. "At the naked robot level, we get a gross margin of about 15%. The systems integrator assumes the role of the general contractor and typically has to deliver the entire robot system according to a prearranged package price. Contracting gross margins were high, but the contractor had to pay for all engineering, planning, and installation expenses, which on average led to net profit margins of only 2%. If there were cost overruns or unexpected events, the extra expenses could easily wipe out the entire profit on a project or even result in a loss."

There were also market factors that pushed companies like ASEA into the systems business. Automotive customers who used to buy naked robots and do their own engineering were increasingly expecting this service from suppliers. Of the major robot companies in Europe, only Kuka and Comau had systems experience because these firms were essentially line builders who integrated backward into robot production. But an entire line of 25 to 80 robots could exceed a price of $10 million, making it risky business for independent systems houses whose financial base was very narrow. As a result, large companies like Kuka and Comau gained a competitive advantage, and they would spec their own robots into a line.

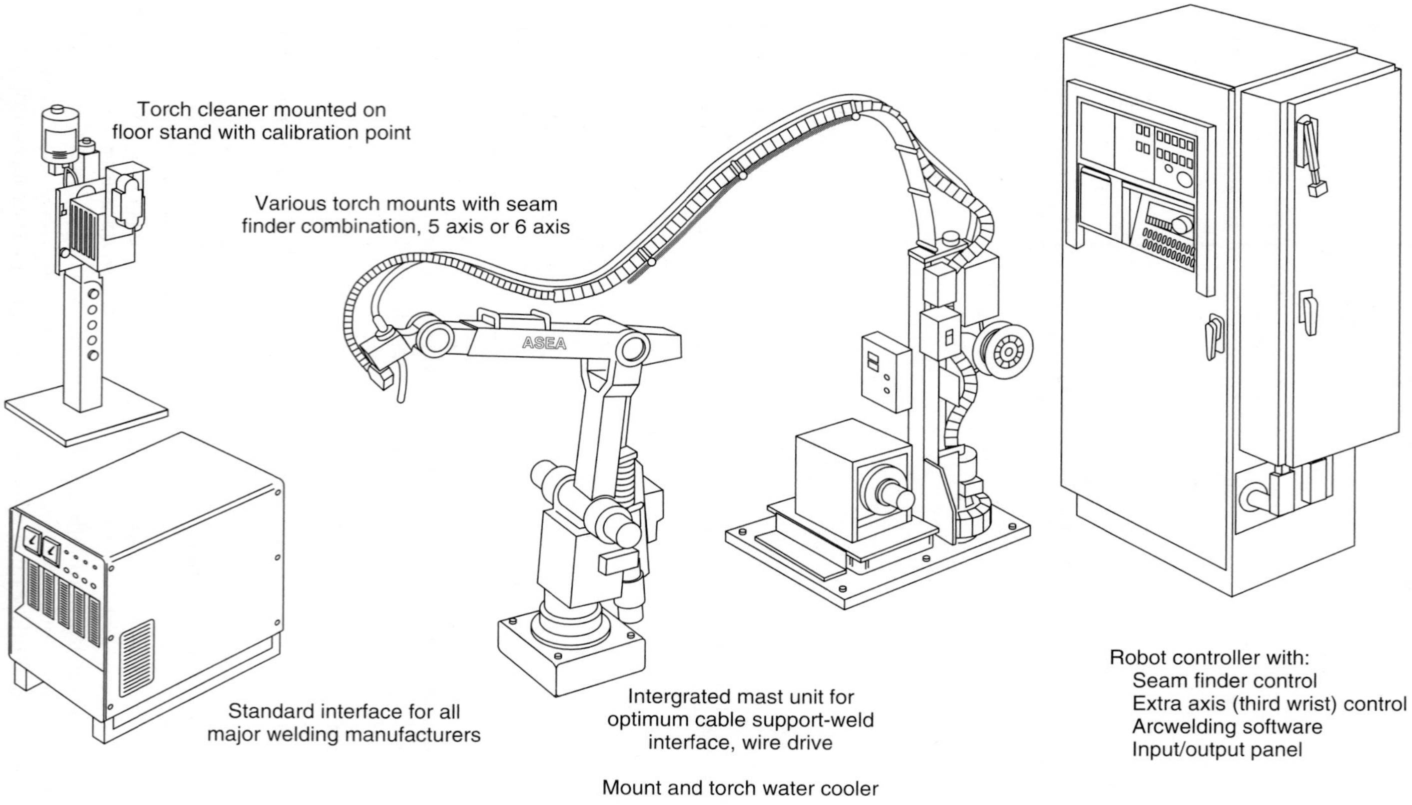

Robot controller with:
Seam finder control
Extra axis (third wrist) control
Arcwelding software
Input/output panel

Intergrated mast unit for
optimum cable support-weld
interface, wire drive

Mount and torch water cooler

Various torch mounts with seam
finder combination, 5 axis or 6 axis

Torch cleaner mounted on
floor stand with calibration point

Standard interface for all
major welding manufacturers

EXHIBIT 2 Arcwelding Function Package

Robot supplier		OEM supplier		Systems integrator	
Naked robot	M a r g i n	Peripheral equipment for arcwelding	M a r g i n	Transfer and line equipment	Systems integrator margin

$70,000 $110,000 $300,000

Elements

Platform	Power pac
Control	Electrode feeder
Control	Arcwelding controls
Accessories	Torch cleaner

EXHIBIT 3   Value Added for Arcwelding Robot System

More recently, automotive clients had realized that a fixed-cost contract could risk financial ruin for its suppliers. They took steps toward a process called *simultaneous engineering*. The entire project was divided into several steps, and release of funds was for one step at a time. "They recognized that they should not kill suppliers," Rizvi explained. "Now they tell suppliers to go ahead with this concept but to report regularly on progress."

The systems business in Europe was dominated by a large number of medium-sized firms. Rizvi believed there were only about a dozen firms in Europe with more than 100 employees. By contrast, Kuka employed 400 and Comau 1,500 in their systems business. However, there were as many reasons for entering as for staying away from the systems business, according to Rizvi. "For a typical system of about DM30 million ($20 million), the robot content can be expected at about 10%, or $2 million, which is the equivalent of about 25 naked robots. The average net profitability of a systems integrator is 2% or $400,000." The low percentage of robots as part of a total system spoke against becoming a systems supplier, whereas the additional feedback gained from client contacts would speak for it. One manager recalled a recent situation in which a German company was rumored to have lost as much as DM100 million on one contract alone due to unanticipated cost overruns.

At the time, ASEA had a number of systems orders. However, Demark considered only ASEA Robotics AB in Sweden and the U.S.

company, ASEA Robotics in New Berlin, Wisconsin, to have real systems strengths. ASEA acquired one systems house in the United Kingdom in 1986, operating in 1988 under the name of ASEA Robotics Ltd. in Luton. All other robot centers were not considered experienced enough to enter the systems business.

Demark believed that ASEA had a number of different alternatives. Based on past experience, he realized that a successful systems business required close monitoring and concentrating on repeat orders to avoid cost overruns on installations not well known. It was still an open question if the present organization should be improved to add systems competence to robot centers or if systems orders should be restricted to those parts of ASEA for which competence already existed. An alternative route was to build a separate organization for the systems business by building or acquiring independent systems houses.

EMPHASIS ON ROBOT PACKAGES

The bridge between the naked robot and the integrated system was the robot package that equipped a naked robot to perform a given task, such as arcwelding, gluing, or deburring. Where ASEA sold through OEMs, the function capability was added by the OEM. However, many times ASEA equipped naked robots for a given task, and in some instances this was done repeatedly.

"The experience has been that our robot centers end up providing the application package. But, frequently, it is done on a one-time basis without regard to what other robot centers may have done when confronted with a similar situation elsewhere," Demark said.

Up to now, ASEA had concentrated its development resources almost exclusively on basic robot development. A push into application packages would represent a redirection. At the robot center levels, however, where approximately 50 worker/years of development took place, this effort was almost exclusively aimed at developing customized solutions for specific applications. However, Demark felt it had occurred in a decentralized way.

When our robot centers sell a naked robot to an OEM or an end user, they often have to explain how the robot might be used to perform a given function. In the process, we give our customers a considerable amount of applications knowledge free of charge because it is so difficult to sell engineering advice as a hardware supplier. However, if we already had tailor-made solutions for given applications, we could sell the robot as a package *and* get paid for it.

The value added of an applications package varied from application to application. A typical range was from 30% to 75% on top of the base robot. ASEA executives believed that the profitability on the packaging elements was about the same as for the naked robot, an approximate 10% to 15% contribution after hardware and engineering.

A preliminary review resulted in a list of some 200 potential function applications. ASEA called these function packages an applications-oriented standard robot system, which was predesigned and tested. It was adapted to a complete solution, including a well-defined basic set of products to fulfill a specified production task on the shop floor with a minimum of systems engineering.

Initially, function packages were based on successful deliveries in installations rather than new applications. They consisted of basic products (robots, controls, accessories), with selected subsupplier products combined with complete sales and engineering docu-

mentation. Furthermore, it was anticipated that marketing and sales tools were included so that all robot centers could use the package and that support tools for applications engineers and systems integrators would be included. Demark also felt that these function packages could generate feedback for product development that might result in a platform for a more complete application oriented product line.

Demark stated:

What bothers me now is the fact that we tailor these function packages to our customer needs on a robot center basis. If the Spanish subsidiary finishes and engineers a press-tending application for a customer, no system exists to ensure that if the Dutch subsidiary meets the same problem next month they will have access to the Spanish solution. In fact, some 50 worker/years of engineering time at our subsidiaries and robot centers is largely devoted to this type of customization, which prevents us from drawing standardized solutions from our experience.

There were a number of key questions still unsolved regarding more function packages. Demark realized that the key lay in complete and thorough documentation for each package that could be put at the disposal of all robot centers. Although required engineering worker/years for each package was expected to vary, Demark considered an average of 5 to 10 worker/years per package realistic.

Implementation of this program depended on a number of variables. Demark needed to consider how important function packages were for ASEA. If he wanted to proceed with this program, how quickly it could be implemented needed to be decided now. Which engineering resources would be made available? Demark had only indirect control over the engineering resources at those robot centers that were part of ASEA Corporation's sales organizations abroad. How much of that 50 worker/years of engineering capacity could be mobilized for the development of function packs?

Nick Rizvi of corporate projects at ASEA Robotics thought about the way the industry had changed during the mid-1980s. Robotics companies were being divided into two camps: the smaller companies that concentrated on selling only robots to specialized customer segments and the larger companies that offered complete system solutions. Amid these changes, Japanese manufacturers were raising the quality of off-the-shelf products and avoiding the systems market. Where the Japanese could not win on robot sophistication, they were expected to compete on price. This placed additional pressure on non-Japanese firms to compete in the less profitable systems side of the robotics business. Nick Rizvi commented on the trend,

Companies have come and gone in this industry. Obviously, the ticket is expensive. What do we do now that we're here and want to stay? How do we focus our efforts to be more profitable? We are profitable in naked robots, but we are being dragged into the systems business to maintain our credibility as a robot manufacturer. How do we protect the profitable side of our business, given our lack of experience in bidding and project management in the systems area?

CONCLUSION

Demark and other senior executives at ASEA Robotics looked at their plans for the next few years. To move toward the expected profitability of about 20% on invested capital would require an additional contribution of $20 million. At the same time, pressures were on ASEA's limited R&D budget and the need to balance short-term with longer-term needs.

The World Paint Industry

OVERVIEW

In 1988, world paint sales were 12,000 million liters, worth $30 billion at suppliers' prices. The paint market was evenly divided between decorative and industrial coatings (*refer to Exhibit 1*). Decorative included the cans of paint or stain purchased at local hardware stores. These products were almost a commodity, produced in high volume and marketed intensively. Industrial coatings, on the other hand, included paint for cars, ships, planes, boats, white goods, cans, and thousands of other applications. Of importance in this market were the paint's properties, for example, protecting from corrosion, abrasion resistance, and ability to withstand high temperature or wet weather.

In 1988, there were about 10,000 producers worldwide. A combination of takeovers, increasingly high technology, rising raw material costs, price wars, and tighter environmental controls were taking their toll, however. The market share of the 10 largest producers rose from 20% in 1980 to 30% in 1987. Some industry observers predicted that the share of the top 10 producers would rise to 50% by 1995. A new hierarchy within the top 10 was emerging, because only four were true global players: ICI, PPG, BASF, and International Paint–Courtaulds, and only the top three were well balanced in terms of geography and market

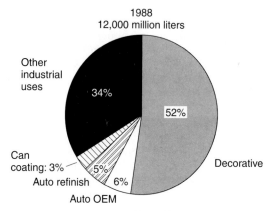

1988
12,000 million liters

Other industrial uses 34%

Decorative 52%

Can coating: 3%

Auto refinish 5%

Auto OEM 6%

EXHIBIT 1   World Paints by Market Sector

sectors served. Others were primarily regional players (*refer to Exhibit 2*).

The paint industry was part of the much larger chemical industry (1988 sales of $1,500 billion). The world's top five chemical companies, BASF, Bayer, and Hoechst (all of West Germany), ICI (United Kingdom), and Du Pont (United States) were important players in paints and coatings or participated indirectly as suppliers of raw materials. Chemical companies, which could make a huge variety of synthetic materials from a small number of basic substances, were in a good position to supply raw materials for the paint industry.

This case was prepared by Arthur Gehring, research assistant, under the direction of Professor Jean-Pierre Jeannet, Professor of Marketing and International Business at Babson College and Adjunct Professor at IMD, Lausanne, Switzerland. Both publicly available material and industry sources were used. Copyright © 1990 by International Institute for Management Development (IMD), Lausanne, Switzerland. IMD retains all rights. Not to be used or reproduced without written permission from IMD, Lausanne, Switzerland.

EXHIBIT 2 World League Table

1988 Approximate Volumes (millions of liters)

1	ICI	United Kingdom	780
2	PPG	United States	460
3	BASF	West Germany	460
4	Sherwin–Williams	United States	360
5	AKZO	Netherlands	350
6	Nippon	Japan	257
7	International	United Kingdom	235
8	Kansai	Japan	231
9	Du Pont	United States	228
10	Valspar	United States	200

EXTERNAL FACTORS

Economic Pressures

The world paint industry was facing the twin pressures of overcapacity and rising costs, particularly in raw materials, in technical service needed to support high-technology industrial coatings, and from increasingly tight antipollution laws.

Some observers suspected that the large paint manufacturers were prepared to live with tight margins, knowing this would speed the rationalization of the industry. Smaller members would be forced to sell if they occupied a desirable niche or close down if they did not. Many smaller companies had long recognized that survival depended on successful international niche marketing of specialty industrial coatings. One alternative for these companies was to start clubbing together, possibly through joint purchasing of raw materials, to have more bargaining clout with suppliers and then use the experience to try to increase cooperation further.

Environmental Factors

Standards of health, safety, and environmental protection were already getting tougher in anticipation of pan-European harmonization in 1992. Some 72 statutory instruments, codes, and safety regulations had been published by various branches of governments in the past 6 months, 15 times as many as in any previous 6-month period. The Germans and French were imposing their standards on the

rest of Europe. Environmental pressures affected what went into paints, how they were made, how effluents were disposed of, and the application methods used by customers. New developments included using water rather than organic solvents, which reduced the emission of organic solvents into the atmosphere. Industrial coatings, which added more value and conferred marketable properties on the surfaces they covered, were more complicated and came under constant and closer scrutiny. Moreover, the pressure was not just from regulators, for the green issue was now being exploited in consumer marketing. This favored big paint makers with deep financial resources. With paint prices depressed, margins under pressure, and industrial customers trying to trim costs further, some medium-sized and smaller paint makers were beginning to get worried, especially with the continuing pressure of raw materials prices. Nonworking capital had to be found for factory improvements, extra research, and compulsory testing to win approvals. As soon as everyone still surviving had met the eventual new standards, the goalposts would be moved to advance them further, shaking out even more companies. In the United Kingdom, "green" capital expenditures had risen to about 10% of total capital investments, or about 0.7% of industry sales. It was estimated that the two largest German paint makers, Hoescht and BASF, were spending 1.4% and 1.2% of sales, respectively, on environmental investments due to the very stringent requirements in Germany.

PAINT MANUFACTURING

Paint was a mixture of several chemical products: solvents, resins, pigments, and additives. These chemical ingredients were typically purchased in bulk, then mixed, packaged by the paint manufacturer, and distributed to the many customer segments.

Raw Materials

The cost of raw materials ranged between 30% and 55% of ex. factory costs depending on application. Resins, accounting for about 40% of raw material costs, were the binding component that resulted in the thick film, or smooth surface, once the paint had dried. Resins gave paint its required durability and other functional properties. Pigments were the elements that gave color to paint. White pigment, a powder largely made of titanium dioxide, gave white its opacity and was widely available. Pigments for other colors were fine chemicals. Overall, pigments accounted for 35% to 40% of raw material costs.

Solvents, accounting for some 10% of raw materials, were commodity chemicals in liquid form. Solvents allowed paint to assume a liquid form before application and evaporated during the drying process. Common solvents were a major environmental hazard, contributing, among other things, to the destruction of the world's ozone layer. As a result, chemical solvents were being more frequently substituted by water. However, the use of water to dissolve paint required different resin formulations, which in turn only came about through intensive research efforts. Additives, accounting for about 15% of raw material costs, included a wide range of items such as metals, catalysts, lead, and chrome, many of which affected the drying process of paint.

The Decision to Make or Buy Raw Materials

Paint manufacturers showed various degrees of integration. Typically, paint companies that were not part of large chemical firms showed less integration. Many small paint firms essentially bought all raw materials in the open market, often from the same chemical firms that also operated paint companies.

Solvents, widely available in the open market, were of no strategic value. The situation for additives was similar, as several hundred suppliers created an open market. At times, the availability of certain additives might be constrained, but for most items, several suppliers existed.

In pigments, titanium dioxide was available from several suppliers, such as Du Pont, SCM,

Finn Titan, Dioxide (ICI), and Ishihara. Prices had been rising over time due to higher raw material prices. Although both Du Pont and ICI had in-house or related suppliers, they also sold on the open market. Color pigments were supplied by specialist open market (or merchant) suppliers, including Ciba–Geigy, Hoechst, ICI, and Bayer. The pigment operations at Hoechst and ICI were separate from the paints businesses and supplied a limited range of pigments to all paint makers. Paint makers typically purchased their pigment from a range of suppliers.

Resins were available from merchant suppliers, captive sources, and a mixture of both. Major merchant suppliers were Rohm & Haas (number 1 worldwide), Union Carbide, Dow Chemicals, and Ciba–Geigy. Among the paint companies, ICI had both in-house capability and operated a merchant house (ICI Resins) independently. In the decorative paint and latex segment, a large number of suppliers existed. In general, paint makers purchased standard resins in the open market while trying to develop some proprietary resins for specialty applications.

The Paint Manufacturing Process

Typically, purchased resins and solvents were supplied by tanker truck and placed into large storage tanks at the plant. The liquids were metered into preliminary mixers and dispersed in a mixing process. Packaging was the final stage and was an important step. Finished paint took up a considerable amount of storage space, as did the containers (labeled, prelabeled, and others).

Larger paint companies used dedicated lines for large-volume paints, such as white, to avoid the time-consuming cleaning operation required when changing color. Low-volume paints were produced in batch mode on different lines. Major manufacturing issues were the appropriate scale of plants, the required range of products, and the range of packaging sizes. Some companies switched to separating low- from high-volume plants because of the different manufacturing philosophies.

Paint Technology and Research

Most paint manufacturers concentrated their research efforts on resin technology. The properties of coatings could only be affected through improvements in resin technology. Over time, several generations of resins had been developed. The older types were solvent borne, whereas the later types were either water or powder borne and had the advantage of reduced emissions. Understanding resin technology was thus considered a necessary core competence for paint makers. The formulation of new resins might result in a technological, and thus competitive, advantage. Although most paint manufacturers worked on some resin developments, standard resins were sourced from merchant suppliers.

Paint development could take place in two forms. Traditionally, paint companies concentrated on the recombination of existing building blocks, or resins, into new formulations. Increasingly, resources were shifted into creating new building blocks, or new resins. While the development of a new variation from existing ingredients might take 2 to 3 worker/months, the development of a new resin would require 25 to 30 worker/years, if successful.

Only those paint manufacturers that were part of major chemical firms engaged in serious resin development work. The others relied on merchant suppliers. Rohm & Haas was believed to have some 300 to 500 scientists working on resin development. But resin suppliers were often removed from paint applications and were thus interested in collaborating with their customers on research projects. Research at major chemical firms was carried out either centrally (Hoechst, Du Pont) or in smaller dedicated groups that were part of the paint organizations (BASF, ICI). Major paint companies were spending about 4% to 5% of sales on R&D, with a trend toward higher levels.

Paint Industry Economics

Paint economics differed considerably by application segment. Raw material costs tended to average 30% to 55% of ex. factory price. Direct labor conversion costs averaged 5% to 10%. Indirect manufacturing costs, which included depreciation for equipment, averaged 15%. Distribution, transportation, and logistics accounted for about 5%. R&D was as much as 7%. Marketing and selling ranged from 5% to 15%, overhead about 10%, and pretax profit 7% to 15% of sales. Successful paint companies experienced an asset turnover of 2.5 to 3.0. Assets tended to be equally split between fixed and working capital. With a 10% return on sales, a company could thus achieve a return on net assets (RONA) of 25% to 30% (*refer to Exhibit 3*).

MARKET SEGMENTS

Although paint was sold for a large number of industrial and decorative uses, some major segments stood out due to their importance. Decorative, which included paints for professional and do-it-yourself (DIY) purposes, was the largest single segment. Industrial paints could be further subdivided into automotive OEM (original equipment manufacturers), automotive refinishes, marine, can coatings, and powder. Each segment had its own particular customer group and usually required its own technology and application base.

Decorative Paints

Accounting for 52% of the 1988 value, about 6.25 billion liters, decorative paint was a major request in most geographic regions. North America accounted for 32%; Western Europe, 31%; Asia–Pacific 20%; and the rest of the world 17%.

Major competitors were, in order of importance, ICI (United Kingdom), Sherwin–Williams (United States), AKZO (Netherlands), and BASF (West Germany). (*Refer to Exhibit 4.*)

Decorative paint had two major segments. The trade segment included sales to professional painters doing both redecoration and new housing, as well as to large professional painting firms. The second segment consisted of individual DIY users, who bought paint

EXHIBIT 3 Paint Manufacturing Cost Structure

	Raw Material (%)	Direct Labor Conversion (%)	Indirect Manufacturing plus Depreciation (%)	R&D and Technical Service (%)	Logistics and Transport (%)	Marketing and Selling (%)	Overhead (%)	PBT (%)	Average Export Price/Liter ($)
Decorative paint	40	5	15	3	5	15	10	7	2.25
Can coating	50	7	15	7	—	5	9	7	2.00
Refinish	30	7	12	7	5	7	6	15	5.00
Automotive OEM	50	5	15	7	—	5	8	10	2.75

through retail stores. This segment had increased its share and now had slightly over half the decorative market.

From the position of a lowly commodity, domestic paint was increasingly being considered a household fashion accessory, adding more value as this concept developed. Women were gaining influence in the selection process because of retailers' efforts to make DIY shopping a pleasurable leisure activity. Most manufacturers had attempted to segment the market by offering special-purpose products, such as anticondensation paint, for specific tasks. Promotion, novel packaging, and seg-

EXHIBIT 4 World Decorative/Architectural Majors by Region

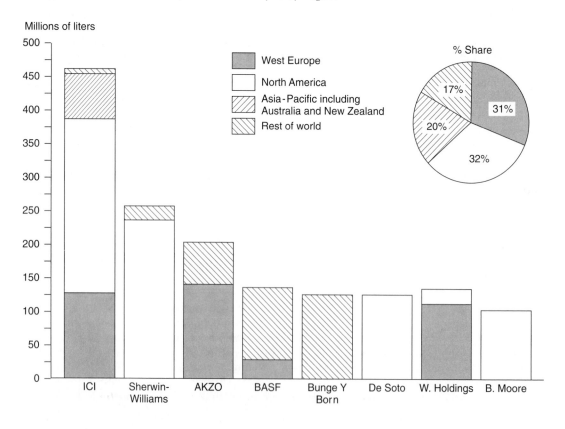

Millions of liters

West Europe
North America
Asia-Pacific including Australia and New Zealand
Rest of world

% Share

31%
32%
20%
17%

ICI Sherwin-Williams AKZO BASF Bunge Y Born De Soto W. Holdings B. Moore

mentation were expected to remain important.

Retail Trade Developments

For paint manufacturers competing in the decorative segment, sales to retailers and DIY customers accounted for about half the volume. The other half was accounted for by the trade or professional market. Professional painters were further subdivided into restoration (mostly indoors), new housing contractors, and commercial contractors. Sales to this segment could be either through small independent stores or branches of manufacturers.

The developments in the retail/DIY segment were significantly changing the retailing process. This fact was most evident in advanced Anglo-Saxon countries such as the United Kingdom, the United States, and Australia, as well as to a lesser degree in such countries as France and Germany, but were considerably less pronounced in countries like Italy and Spain.

Traditionally, paint had been sold in small paint shops or hardware stores. In the late 1960s and early 1970s, specialist store chains like High Street (United Kingdom) and Sherwin–Williams (United States) replaced most of the small shops. In the 1970s and early 1980s, variety department stores and supermarkets took the lead (Woolworth, Sears, J.C. Penney, and Montgomery Ward in the United States and Tesco in the United Kingdom). Sears, partly through private branding, reached as much as 30% U.S. market share at its peak.

In the mid-1970s, large DIY super stores, or sheds, became dominant. In the United States, stores like Home Depot were typical. In the United Kingdom, Texas and B&Q were two leading examples. In the United States, Sears saw its market share cut in half to 15% as a result of this development. The industry was already bracing itself for the next wave, which some experts speculated might lead back to specialty paint stores with enhanced service compared to the simple barn-type DIY stores.

The U.K. decorative market exhibited the trends that were typical of most major decorative markets. The market for household paint, like that for beans, soap, and fish fingers, had become retail led and susceptible to all the pressures that afflicted grocery producers. Price competition had intensified and margins had tightened as major retailers with vast bulk buying orders had demanded ever more advantageous terms. In the United Kingdom, retailers' own-label products had cut through the ranks of established brands, growing 150% since 1981 to claim almost 40% of the market. As in the supermarket trade, the policy of most companies dictated that only leading brands would be stocked.

Persistent promotion had helped ICI's Dulux brand retain its position as the leading paint in the United Kingdom, with a steady 33% share of the market. This market was undergoing a retailing revolution similar to the one that had transformed the grocery trade. The main difference was that, while the supermarket's rise to preeminence in food and packaged goods took 30 years, the storming of the do-it-yourself trade by the superstore brigade happened in only 10 years. The number of DIY specialist stores had shrunk from about 20,000 in 1979 to some 11,000 in 1988. The large DIY chains, led by B&Q, Texas, and Pay Less, accounted for 65% of all sector sales. Advertising expenditures for paint by DIY stores far outweighed paint makers' expenditures. The DIY stores had become brands in their own right.

Throughout this retailing cycle, the marketing task of the paint manufacturer changed at each turn. In the first cycle, independent distributors and wholesalers gave way to manufacturer-owned stores and outlets. When the chains took over, increased buying power led to bargaining over shelf space. The supermarket or departmentalized variety stores brought private labels. Finally, the super stores narrowed the brand choice by typically carrying just one advertised brand and their own private label. The reduced number of brands carried led to the disappearance of many retail paint suppliers and brands.

Automotive OEM

The automotive paint segment consisted of paint sales made to automobile manufacturers for use in their assembly plants. Worldwide, this segment represented 6% of the paint market. Major markets were North America (31%), Western Europe (32%), and Japan (26%). Leading competitors were, in order of importance, PPG, BASF, Kansai, Nippon, Du Pont, Hoechst, and ICI (*refer to Exhibit 5*).

In 1988, the paint sales to car manufacturers amounted to about 720 million liters, averaging $2.80/liter in price or $2.0 billion total. Only PPG with 19% share and BASF with 18% share were true world players. PPG's great strength was its 45% share of the U.S. home market. Kansai was Nissan's paint maker in Japan. In Europe, the race was on to be third in 1992, when the car industry would narrow down its suppliers on U.S. lines. In the running were Herberts, AKZO, and an ICI/Du Pont joint venture.

The customer base, mainly globally operating companies, was technologically very demanding. The technical service requirements of customers required paint suppliers to station technical service personnel permanently on location. As a result, the automotive companies preferred suppliers located at their doorsteps. This led to scattering factories close to assembly plants. In the United States, major paint companies would typically have several plants. The trend had moved away from multiple sourcing, which had kept local players alive, toward single sourcing and worldwide deals. Typically, a customer maintained a major supplier each for top coats and base coats, with a second supplier for smaller volume applications "to keep the big ones honest."

The trend was to build an applied research

EXHIBIT 5   World Auto OEM Majors by Region

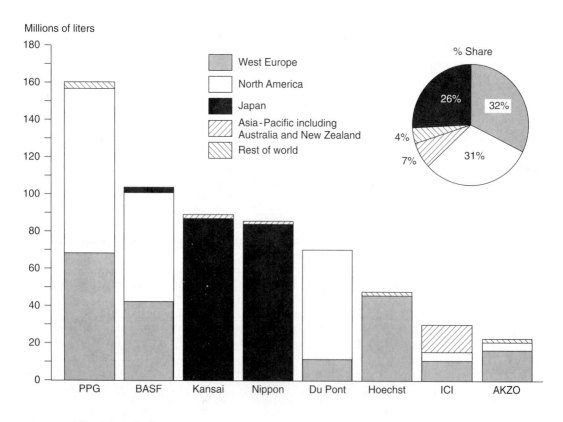

center close to manufacturers. Austin O'Malley, head of PPG/Europe, said, "Ownership of the automotive industry has gone global. Supplies and suppliers must go global, too. We are going for global sales to key customers. Naturally, we are concentrating very hard on the customer. We supply material with high value added to help motor manufacturers cope with their cost and production problems." The trend had already been established on a continental scale in the United States, with only three main suppliers: PPG, BASF, and Du Pont. The arrival of the single European market in 1992 was expected to have a similar effect.

There was a technological dimension to this market. Electrolytic application techniques ensured an even spread of the first coat. This had an important influence on appearance and protection after other coats had been applied. Several paint makers developed this technology. Both PPG and Hoechst licensed their technology to others. Hoechst linked to Du Pont, which linked to Kansai. PPG linked to Nippon, which linked to International Paint. PPG developed a method that produced more stable and rust-resistant coating. In 1988, 83% of the electrolytic tanks in the world used this technology, either supplied or licensed.

Although particular paint applications such as color were developed for each customer, a substantial part of the basic research had worldwide applications. Technical spin-offs were also possible for other paint segments, such as for the refinishing sector (with modifications in formulations due to the different paint application methods) and for industrial components in areas such as the domestic appliance industry. This was one reason why many players stayed in this segment despite low profitability or losses.

PPG had formed a worldwide team for each major manufacturer, so the same people serviced the same customer wherever a car plant was located. PPG was also selling a complete paint shop staffed with PPG employees. An exemplary relationship was in Korea, where General Motors and Daiwoo chose PPG. The specifications for the plant's coating system was designed by Opel in West Germany; pre-treatment chemicals came from the United States, the sealant from Spain, the electrocoat and top coats from France.

Some experts believed the way to get ahead in this business was to develop new products that would leapfrog over competitors, such as water-based paints, which would not emit the organic solvents contributing to acid rain. There was considerable cross-licensing occurring in this market.

Automatic Vehicle Refinishing

The refinish segment included paints and coatings for repairing automobiles. This segment accounted for 5% of world sales, had the highest price per liter ($5.00), and was considered the most profitable paint segment. North America accounted for 36% of the world market, followed by Western Europe (30%) and Asia–Pacific/Japan (25%) (*Refer to Exhibit 6.*)

Only 10 paint manufacturers competed significantly in the refinishing sector. Among those, only Sherwin–Williams of the United States and Rock of Japan did not also compete in the automotive OEM market. No new competitor had entered since the 1950s. The world leader was BASF, due to its recent acquisition of Inmont in the United States. BASF led with 17% of the world market, followed by Du Pont, ICI, and PPG.

Although the volume of paint sold in this market was smaller than the OEM segment, it was a larger segment by value due to its far higher sales price: 480 million liters at an average price of $5.00, making the total market worth $2.4 billion.

Customers were largely small paint shops who needed quick and frequent deliveries, typically on a daily basis. Paint manufacturers supplied their customers with mixing schemes through local distributors who would combine the basic colors and shades with solvents to obtain the correct color match. There were some 10,000 different shades and some 60 different colors to select from.

To compete in this business, a company had to have access to the color and paint shops of the car manufacturers to obtain the needed in-

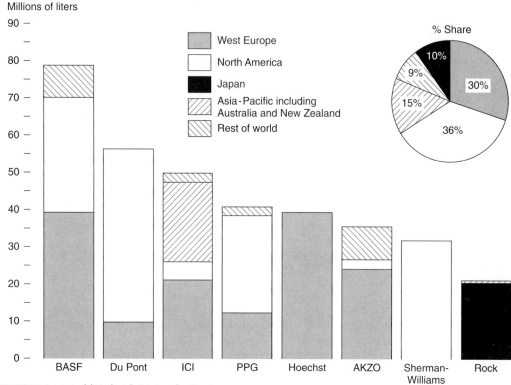

EXHIBIT 6   World Refinish Majors by Region

formation. Automobile manufacturers wanted to make sure that their customers could get their cars repaired wherever they marketed. As an example, a company like Toyota was interested in worldwide coverage. Refinish paint manufacturers profited if they could have access to all car manufacturers wherever they were located so that they could supply the widest possible color range in any geographic market.

Marine Paints

This $800 million market was dominated by a handful of companies. International Paint had 30% of the market. Other important manufacturers were Chugoku, and Nippon Oil and Fats of Japan, Hemel of Denmark, Jotun of Norway, and Sigma Coatings from Belgium. These six companies account for 85% of the paint applied to the world's ships. The for-

tunes of this market followed those of the shipping industry. Outlook for the 1990s looked bright as the aging fleet of merchant vessels would be replaced.

Typically, a ship had at least five outside layers of paint. On top of the primer were two coats of noncorrosive paint and then two coats of antifouling paint below the waterline. Antifoulings released a biocide to prevent barnacles, seaweed, and other marine organisms from growing on the hull. A common ingredient of antifoulings, TBT, was under attack by environmentalists. New tin-free alternatives were being developed, but were not as effective. A new "self-polishing" antifouling released by International Paint had saved the shipping industry $200 million a year in fuel costs. Other important segments of the marine paint industry were coatings for cargo tanks and offshore oil rigs. Tank coatings had to resist a wide range of liquid chemicals. The deck areas of a rig had to survive exposure to seawater, rain, sun, and spillage of oils and chemicals.

Can Coatings

The can coating segment, with worldwide sales of $1.2 million, accounted for only 3% of the world paint market. Some 46% of the market was in North America, followed by Europe (24%) and Asia–Pacific (22%). Major competitors were BASF, Midland, and Valspar (*refer to Exhibit 7*).

The coatings were applied inside the tin and aluminium cans used as food or beverage containers to make them corrosion resistant. This thin layer on the inside of every can was crucial for a successful canning operation. Consequently, this segment of the paint industry was viewed as a high-technology application. Cus-

tomers were concentrated, with major use in the hands of four groups and their licensees: Continental Can, Pechiney–Triangle (included former American and National Can), Carnaud–Metal Box, and Crown Cork and Seal. These can manufacturers operated canning lines all over the world, and they expected the suppliers to follow them everywhere with a consistent product, ensuring the same taste for globally marketed products such as Coca Cola.

Coating products had to be developed for each application, because they depended on the particular food or beverage, as well as on the type of metal or aluminium container used. Customers were increasingly seeking ways to simplify and tended to look for a narrower technology range. In this business, it was important to be able to make the development effort go around. A new product for sardines might be developed in Portugal, but might

EXHIBIT 7   World Can Coatings Majors by Region

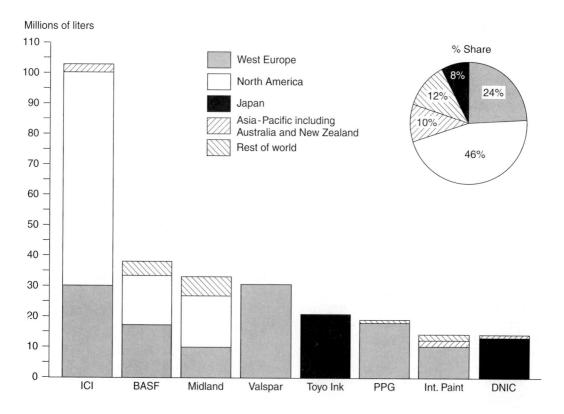

have applications for Norwegian packers as well. Success depended on avoiding duplication of effort in applications development. Although coatings were usually not identical, a considerable part of the concept development could be used again for other customers with the same applications.

Powder Paints

Powder coatings were a precisely formulated mixture of pigment and resin that was sprayed using electrostatic spray guns. The sprayed item, a metal object, was then heated for some 10 minutes to cure the surface. Coatings had been developed for heat resistance or chemical resistance. The major benefits for users were the reduced emissions such as solvents used with wet paints and the reduced need for waste disposal. Major user groups were the automotive component suppliers, metal furniture industry, and domestic appliance manufacturers. Powder paint could conceivably substitute for up to 50% of paint being applied to metal. In Europe, where the product was pioneered, the substitution already amounted to about 20%, compared to about 10% in the United States, an amount that was, however, growing rapidly.

The market for powder coatings was growing between 10% and 20% per year. This had attracted hot competition, resulting in low margins, which were squeezing many medium-sized and smaller companies. International Paint was fighting with Ferro (United States) for the world's number 1 position. DSM (Netherlands) had a dominant position in Europe (*refer to Exhibit 8*).

Potential new markets included car engine blocks, baskets inside automatic washing machines, and the steel reinforcement bars used in concrete. Finally, powder paint was a potential weapon against colored plastics, a big threat to paint makers. There was talk of a powder that could be cured without heat so that it could be used with cheap plastic that had no inherent esthetic properties. Most manufacturers were also experimenting with high-gloss finishes that could eventually be used for car body work.

GEOGRAPHIC MARKETS

The markets of North America (32%) and Western Europe (30%) dominated the world market. The remainder was accounted for by Latin America, Africa, and the Middle East combined (14.5%), Japan (13%), Southeast Asia (9%), and Australasia (1.5%) (*refer to Exhibit 9.*)

Western Europe

The Western European market was dominated by the major economies of West Germany, the United Kingdom, France, and Italy. All major segments were represented in Western Europe, with decorative, automotive OEM, and the refinish portions of the market reflecting their relative importance worldwide. Europe was somewhat ahead of the other regions in powder paints, but can coatings volume was below the representative size of its market, primarily due to the domination of the U.S. market in this area. (*Throughout this analysis, the paint markets of Eastern Europe have been excluded. Representing the equivalent of about 15% of world paint volume, or 1.8 billion liters, this market was not yet open to international competitors.*)

North America

The North American market, consisting of the United States and Canada, was the largest paint market in the world, with 32% of world paint volume in liters. In the decorative and automotive OEM segments, the United States accounted for its typical share of the world paint industry. Both in refinish, and particularly in can coatings, the North American share was relatively higher than the region's share in the entire paint market.

Japan

Although the Japanese market accounted for only 13% of world paint sales, it accounted for 26% of world automotive OEM. As a result, two Japanese companies were among the

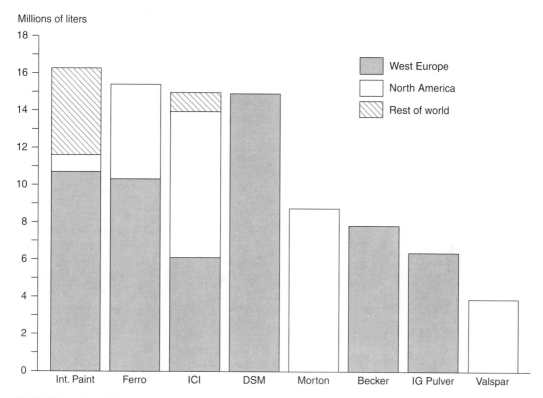

Millions of liters

Legend:
- West Europe
- North America
- Rest of world

Categories (x-axis): Int. Paint, Ferro, ICI, DSM, Morton, Becker, IG Pulver, Valspar

EXHIBIT 8 World Powder Majors by Region

world's top 10 producers. Decorative paint was not a key market. Traditional domestic architecture, with its paper partitions, meant that millions of square feet of walls were not decorated. More modern buildings were being constructed, but decorative still only accounted for 22% of the market. The market's strength came from its industrial base.

Japan's paint industry mirrored the Japanese economy. A large home market was a mixed blessing because it provided little experience in operating outside Japan. The only Japanese paint exported was that already on Japanese goods. Paint production had virtually stopped growing in recent years with the worldwide reaction to trade imbalances with Japan (*refer to Exhibit 10*). Many companies were setting up factories abroad. These were costly and risky, because the race to buy the most promising targets had been won by European and U.S. paint companies. It seemed

likely that cross-licensing of technology would be the most frequently chosen course.

Nippon, the largest paint company in Japan, was also very active in the rest of Asia. Shinto and Nippon Oil & Fats had licenses for ICI's Queens awards winner, Aquabase, the waterborne car paint. "NOF and Shinto are like ICI's children. We have good cooperation with Shinto to develop this product," said Teruji Ogawa, chairman of NOF. Nippon and Kansai were the market leaders in the car factories. Kansai had wanted ICI's technology, but ICI was too "slow moving," so Kansai developed its own alternative by making use of its relationship with Du Pont.

Part of the strength of the Japanese economy was the sheer bulk of intratrading that took place within six major informal corporate groups. The presidents of the 29 companies of the Mitsubishi group met once a month. These social gatherings were reinforced by more for-

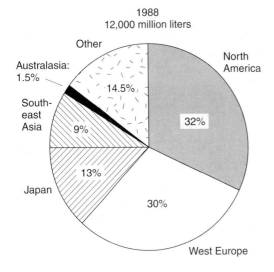

1988
12,000 million liters

Other

Australasia: 1.5%

Southeast Asia

Japan

North America

14.5%

32%

9%

13%

30%

West Europe

Southeast Asia includes China, Southeast Asia, Indian subcontinent. Other includes Latin America, Africa, and Middle East. Excludes USSR and East Europe at 15% of world total.

EXHIBIT 9   World Paint Markets by Region

mal links, such as capital relationships between companies, interlocking directorships, and cross holdings of stock.

Kansai belonged to the Sanwa Group, along with Daihatsu Motor. Dai Nippon Toryo belonged to the Mitsubishi Group, Shinto to the Sumitomo Group, and NOF to the Fuyo or Fuji Group, along with Nissan. There was no motor manufacturer in the Sumitomo Group, but there was no paint maker in the Mitsui Group, in which Toyota Motor had observer status. Shinto had filled the gap with Toyota. Meanwhile, BASF had developed a close relationship with Dai Nippon Toryo, which was inevitably close to Mitsubishi Motors. By going with NOF and Shinto, ICI had an insider's introduction to both Nissan and Toyota, the two Japanese car manufacturers building the most factories abroad. Even in the United States where Nissan's relationship was with Du Pont, there should have been an inside track, since Du Pont and ICI had a joint

EXHIBIT 10   Japanese Paint Production

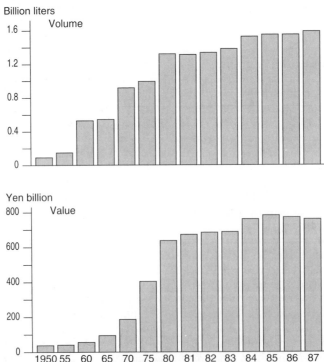

Billion liters

Volume

1.6

1.2

0.8

0.4

0

Yen billion

800

Value

600

400

200

0

1950 55   60   65   70   75   80   81   82   83   84   85   86   87

venture on car paints in Europe. Nippon Paint, which did not belong to any corporate group, was pursuing a strategy of keeping its cross-licensing agreements simple. Nippon had relationships with International Paint and PPG.

The relationships were becoming increasingly confusing: Kansai had a long-standing relationship with both ICI and Hoechst. As a result of their alliance, NOF and Shinto would be attacking Kansai's market share using ICI technology. Kansai's defense would be through its relationship with Du Pont, ICI's partner in Europe. European and U.S. paint makers did not have these problems; they were used to legal watertight agreements about specific technology in specific geographic markets.

Southeast Asia

The battle for the Far East markets was heating up. The prizes were potentially vast; in terms of population the markets compared to Europe. There was continuous, fast economic growth. In developing countries, growth and affluence led to more people painting their homes and to growth in industrial markets as cars and consumer goods were manufactured locally.

Few foreign paint companies were operating seriously in Southeast Asia, as paint markets were just starting to develop. In 1987, the economy of Singapore grew by 10%, Malaysia by 7%, Thailand by 8%, the Philippines by 6%, and Indonesia by 4%. Among the international paint companies, ICI had built factories in Thailand, Malaysia, Singapore, and Indonesia. International Paint had set up in Singapore, where there was a growing market for their marine paints, in Malaysia, where it had targeted the canning industry as a principal customer, and in Bangkok. Nippon Paint was the only other producer approaching the region with the same levels of investment. Early entry into foreign markets was part of its corporate strategy. They had had to follow their customers abroad. The low labor costs of Southeast Asia had encouraged two strategies: first, to develop there ahead of others and, second, to develop low-cost products by making them locally.

Lim Say Chong, managing director of ICI Paints in the region explained,

Don't judge us by European perceptions of risk taking and ways of doing business. Our competition is basically Japanese. They are prepared to make little profit and live with low prices for a long time. They gain in total market share, building up a strong position to give them leverage among distributors and sales outlets, and then start fighting you with better, higher-priced products. We have to make profits acceptable to the city of London year after year. They take a 25-year view of their business. If we stick to the European way, they will walk all over us in the end.

Four-fifths of Malaysia's market was decorative, of which there were three major segments. The quality end comprised about 15%, the middle 52% of the volume, and the cheap market accounted for a third of sales. Lim of ICI stated, "Simple emulsion costs US$1.50 per liter. The Japanese sell it at US$.60 per liter." Nippon quickly established share and then started to bring some better quality paints onto the market. "When the Japanese got into the mid-tier of the market from the bottom tier, we decided to give them some trouble," Lim said. In the early 1980s, ICI moved into the mid-tier from the quality end of the market with a lower-priced brand. The effect was to put a lid on Nippon's march upmarket. In 1988, ICI's share was 27% versus Nippon's 24%. Berger Malaysia and Seasons, two local brands, each had 10%.

A rush of investment was expected during the next 2 years. Foreign companies could set up joint ventures in the region with Asian countries taking a 5% stake and the company keeping a 60% stake as long as the deals were concluded by 1991. Only the makers of industrial paints already there were likely to be able to benefit by supplying coatings for goods made in the new factories, an advantage for ICI, International Paint, and Nippon. "Japanese paint makers will make deals in industrial products because they know now that we will fight and cause them a lot of trouble if they try to come in directly," Lim said.

Australia

Although the Australian market was small, it was a microcosm of things to come. Trends showed up quickly because of the small population. The first two-piece cans outside the United States appeared here. In 1988, there were 116 paint companies in Australia, but the top three controlled 80% of the market. Australia showed the effect of monopoly and duopoly on prices and choice more rapidly than anywhere else, so the world was watching.

ICI was spending A$5 million[1] on Dulux, its decorative brand, equaling the total spent by the entire industry in the past. Taubmans Industries, owned primarily by International Paint, was responding by spending A$6 million. ICI planned to spend A$100 million during the next 5 years to upgrade seven factories. ICI had planned to buy Berger's Australian operations with its two major brands, Berger and British, and then sell one to Taubmans, but Taubmans backed out. As a result, ICI was stuck with too many brands. Although ICI's Dulux had 40% market share compared to Taubmans' 22%, having so many brands was resulting in cannibalization. This gave an advantage to specialist paint shops, which liked receiving three brands from one company. However, big retailers were concerned, as they had limited space and wanted competition among suppliers. ICI Australia had stayed in heavy-duty protective coatings, while ICI Paints had long since abandoned the sector as a core business. The reason for this decision was that Taubmans led this segment, thanks to International Paint, and while Dulux stayed, Taubmans had to keep its prices low. When things settled down, no one expected ICI's Dulux to be anything other than the market leader. It was too far in the lead and too well managed to fall far, if at all, no matter what Taubmans planned to do.

MAJOR PAINT MANUFACTURERS

By 1988, the 10 largest paint companies in the world accounted for almost one-third of the world paint volume. Most of these players had grown by acquisition (*refer to Exhibit 11*). In the process, the ranking by volume was considerably changed. PPG (United States) had lost the number 1 position to ICI (United Kingdom). Hoechst (Germany) and Du Pont (United States) dropped out of the top league, while Inmont and Glidden (both United States) were acquired. Newcomers were Nippon and Kansai (both Japan) and Valspar and DeSoto (both United States). (*Refer to Exhibit 12.*) The leading paint companies tended to be concentrated differently by paint sector (*refer to Exhibit 13*) and by geographic concentration (*refer to Exhibit 14*).

International Paint–Courtaulds

International Paint–Courtaulds' worldwide sales were 235 million liters a year. The company was preeminent in marine and protective coatings. International Paint's (IP) share of profits from the yacht and marine sectors had dropped from 60% to 80% in 1980 to 30%, despite having 40% of the world market. Its profit contribution from Europe was reduced to 35% to 40% from 60% in 1980. Currently, 30% to 35% came from North America, with the rest coming from all over the globe. IP had been aggressively expanding its powder business internationally through acquisitions, despite not being profitable until 1986. Recent acquisitions included Germany (1980); France and Brazil (mid-1980s); Korea, the United States, and Australia (late 1980s); and Spain and Italy (late 1980s). Far East locations included Singapore, Hong Kong, Malaysia, Taiwan, and Thailand. IP led the Australian market in oil and can coatings.

The powder segment was growing significantly for IP due to its industrial marketing skill and global presence in marine coatings. Pragnell of International Paint explained, "Transfer of marketing technology, standards, and operations from marine to powder has

---

[1] US$1.00 = A$0.80.

EXHIBIT 11 Restructuring the World Paint Industry

	Company	Acquisition Year	Sector
AKZO (Netherlands)	Wyandotte (US)	1983	Motors
	Levis (Belgium)	1984	Decorative/motors/industrial
	Bostik (US)	1984	Aircraft
	Blundell–Permoglaze (UK)	1985	Decorative
	Sandtex (UK)	1986	Decorative
	Procolor (Spain)	1986	Decorative/industrial
	Brink Molyn (Netherlands)	1986	Decorative
	Ypiranga (Brazil)	1987	Decorative/industrial
BASF (West Germany)	Valentine (UK)	1984	Vehicle refinishing
	Inmont (US)	1985	Motors/refinishing/can coatings
	Mobil Coatings (Netherlands)	1985	Can coatings
	Lusol (Argentina)	1988	Motors/industrial
Du Pont (United States)	Ford Motor Paints (US)	1986	Motors
	SFDUCO (France)—part	1988	Motors
	IDFAC (joint venture with ICI)	1988	Motors
Hoechst (West Germany)	Renault Paint (France)	1986	Motors
	Ault & Wiborg (UK)—part	1986	Motors/refinishing/industrial
	Divested—part West Germany	1984	Decorative
	Berger (UK)	1987	Decorative
ICI (United Kingdom)	Holdens (UK)	1982	Can coatings
	Valentine (France)	1984	Decorative/refinishing
	Ault & Wiborg (UK)—part	1985	Can coatings
	HGW Paints (Ireland)	1985	Decorative/refinishing/industrial
	Knopp (West Germany)	1988	Powder coatings
	Glidden (US)	1986	Decorative/can coatings/powder
	Bonaval (West Germany)	1986	Refinishing
	Attiva (Italy)	1988	Can coatings
	Du Pont (Spain)	1988	Powder
	Berger (Australasia)	1988	Decorative/industrial
	IDAC (joint venture with Du Pont)	1988	Motors
International–Courtaulds (United Kingdom)	Silap (France)	1982	Powder
	Litoverti (Brazil)	1982	Can coatings
	Oxyplast (Australia)	1985	Powder
	Porter Paint (US)	1987	Decorative/yacht
	Extensor (Sweden)	1987	Marine
	La Minerva (Italy)	1988	Powder
	Suministros (Spain)	1988	Powder
	Epiglass (New Zealand)	1988	Yacht(marine)
PPG (United States)	Cipisa (Spain)	1982	Motors
	IVI (Italy)	1984	Motors/refinishing/industrial
	Wulfing (West Germany)	1984	Motors
	International (UK)—part	1985	Motors

been crucial. Powder is a technology, not a business." IP was expanding Porter Paints, the U.S. decorative manufacturing and marketing company bought for $140 million in 1987. IP was emphasizing technology, marketing, and computerized systems. Shipowners could arrange to have exact quantities of paint delivered at a wide range of ports. IP was determined to defeat ICI in a race to dominate waterborne coating for steel cans.

Sherwin–Williams

The company celebrated its 122nd year of business in 1988 with an increased operating profit of 7.7% of sales, to $101 million. Net sales increased by 8.3% to reach $1,950 million. Sherwin–Williams had 2,000 company-operated paint and wall covering stores across the United States, which accounted for an 8% sales increase over the past year and were the

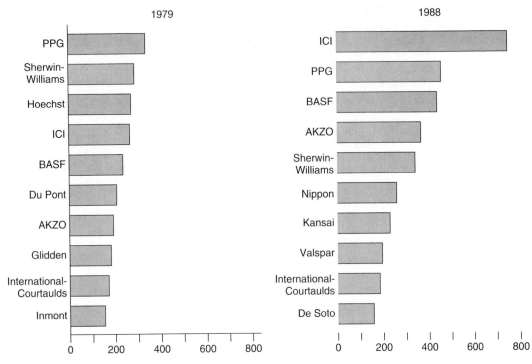

EXHIBIT 12   World Paint Majors: Sales Volume in Millions of Liters

backbone of the company's paint stores segment. The segment's overall operating profit dropped slightly during the year, however, due to provisions established in the fourth quarter for the closing of certain unprofitable stores, as well as to reduced margins caused by the required increase in reserves resulting from the escalating costs of products sold. Sherwin–Williams planned to increase its prices in 1989 to improve operating margins.

In addition to the main Sherwin–Williams brand paint and coatings, the company produced and marketed the brands Dutch Boy, Martin–Semour, and Kem-Tone. Sherwin–Williams also produced private-label brands for sales through independent dealers, mass merchandisers, and home improvement centers, as well as special-purpose coatings for the automotive refinish market, industrial maintenance, and traffic paint.

Sherwin–Williams International Group was divided into four sectors: Canada, Mexico, the West Indies, and Brazil. The company operated 78 of its own stores in Mexico and had 42 stores throughout Jamaica, Trinidad, Puerto Rico, and Panama. Licensing rights had been extended to 25 other countries around the world for production and distribution of decorative coatings, industrial and automotive paint finishes, and a variety of home decorative products. The group's primary markets included dealers, contractors, automotive body shops, commercial and industrial maintenance accounts, original equipment manufacturers, and do-it-yourself customers.

BASF

With corporate sales of $24.4 billion (1988), BASF was the world's largest chemicals company. The company jumped from fifth place ranking in paints to sharing second with PPG by acquiring Inmont, the U.S. paint and inks

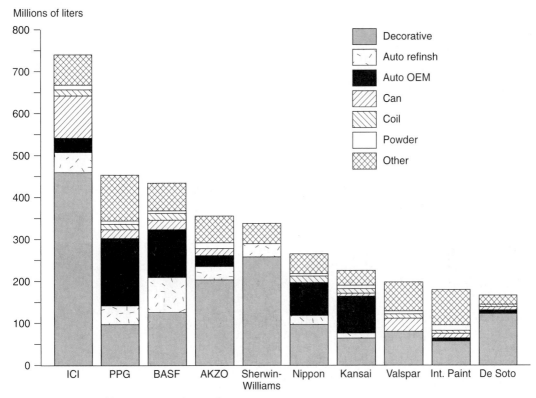

Millions of liters

Legend:
- Decorative
- Auto refinsh
- Auto OEM
- Can
- Coil
- Powder
- Other

Companies (x-axis): ICI, PPG, BASF, AKZO, Sherwin-Williams, Nippon, Kansai, Valspar, Int. Paint, De Soto

EXHIBIT 13   World Paint Majors by Market Sector

giant, for $1 billion in 1985, beating out ICI and AKZO. BASF then had to cope with a different corporate culture, the more North American "can do, profits now" style of management demanded by shareholders wanting ever-better yearly results. Like many German companies, BASF's backers were institutional; they took a longer view of the marketplace and did not burden management with the need to show continuous short-term progress. "Cross- fertilization of research findings has been very beneficial," said Geoffrey Watson of BASF. It had a joint venture with Tanabe in Japan and was close to Dainippon Toryo, which was in the same corporate group as Mitsubishi Motors.

BASF set the pace in minimizing the environmental impact that was driven by ever tighter West German regulations. BASF achieved this goal with a massive capital spend-

ing program. Having spent DM200 million[2] already, it had committed DM1 billion by 1993. Jürgen Kammer, chairman, explained, "In West Germany, we have the highest standards already. What today is a burden, tomorrow will be an advantage." Because of the sophisticated chemistry involved, such things could not be learned overnight or bought. BASF's profile in the industry had been strong on reliable products, high technology, and quality, but less noted for its marketing skills. This area tended to be weak in many German paint companies.

BASF had already spent DM200 million over 4 years on its Munster factory, the largest concentration of paint-making facilities in the world, occupying nearly 100 acres and employing more than 2,800 people. This plant included a new, flexible manufacturing system

[2] US$1.00 = DM1.75.

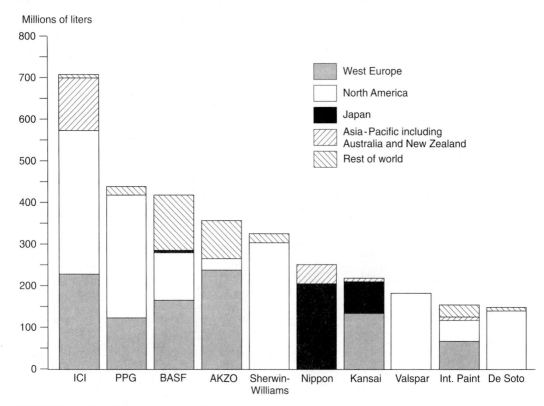

Millions of liters

Legend:
- West Europe
- North America
- Japan
- Asia-Pacific including Australia and New Zealand
- Rest of world

EXHIBIT 14 World Paint Majors by Region

for paint making, a batch process that had previously defied such advances. BASF's engineers realized that the bottleneck was in the blenders where all the ingredients were mixed. Conventionally, they either had to be cleaned out before the next batch was mixed or a less efficient system involving a strict progression from lighter to darker colors had to be followed. BASF's revolutionary solution had been to install movable blenders that could be slotted into line as required. The answer was to convey the several-ton blenders around on hovercraft and hoists. Labor savings had been considerable. The principles were being copied in a new factory in Spain and would be introduced whenever new plants were built on existing sites.

Hoechst

With total sales of $23.4 billion, Hoechst ranked second among all chemical companies.

The group's paint sales were DM443 million. Herberts, its English subsidiary and major paint unit, claimed 36% of the West German vehicle refinish market, 23% in Western Europe, and 7% in the world. It regarded 19 countries in Western Europe as its home market and sold in 24 other countries worldwide.

In 1987, Hoechst decided to leave the decorative segment due to its unenviable third-place position in many markets, as well as escalating promotional costs. The company's decorative arm, Berger, was sold to International Courtaulds of the United Kingdom and merged with another newly acquired company, Crown Paints. Hoechst concentrated on both automotive segments: OEM, where it had leading technology, and refinishing. Hoechst was looking toward North American and Japanese markets for expansion. However, other paint makers had been much quicker to realize that globally based customers wanted globally spread suppliers. Herberts' problem outside Europe was similar to that of leading Japanese paint makers outside Japan; nearly all its major competitors had arrived first, limiting slow starters to their home markets.

ICI

In 1988, ICI had total sales of $20.8 billion and ranked as the world's fourth largest chemicals company. ICI's paint sector was viewed as a laggard within its own group, while being an outstanding performer in the industry. Sales were up £70 million[3] to £1.36 billion; profits rose to £98 million, reaching an ROS of 7.19%. Although twice the level of Japan's paint makers and 50% better than BASF, it was poor compared to ICI's pharmaceutical business of 26% and 12.6% for the entire company. The weakness of ICI's paint sector was compounded by having to satisfy the shareholders year after year.

ICI's marketing of decorative paint was acknowledged as the best in the world. It excelled in highly specialized paints for repairing car bodies and dominated the can-coating sector. The goal for the European joint venture with Du Pont was to have 20% of the Western European market in vehicle refinishing by the early 1990s. ICI manufactured in 29 countries and sold in 50.

ICI had been investing up to 5% of sales in R&D and £525 million for capital projects during the last 3 years. The ICI dilemma appeared to have crystallized into making more of its present strengths and being committed to its customers worldwide so as to build up long-term loyalty. Herman Scopes, principal executive officer of ICI, stated, "We have got to stop being a paint manufacturer and become a service organization that has paint manufacturing as part of its operations."

ICI's corporate goals were (1) to consolidate after the 1986 acquisition of Glidden, (2) to focus growth, and (3) to improve quality so as to achieve better margins and service despite rising costs and static prices. These goals would be pursued utilizing its global spread and balance, very large financial resources, good technological and commercial base, and a general management that competitors acknowledged as being good and having clear strategies. There were problems. Surveys showed that the staff was disquieted about big company bureaucracy, inadequate internal communications, a lack of recognition of people's contributions, and internal rather than customer orientation. Only a large minority of customers rated ICI better than the competition. The bulk opted for the "much the same" category, while a small minority declared ICI worse. These results had sprouted 400 voluntary "customer focus" groups. Benefits so far had been a flow of good ideas, better commitment to the customer at all levels, pinpointing the things that irritate customers, better teamwork, and the identification of training needs.

PPG Industries

With corporate sales of $5.7 billion (1989), PPG had traditionally been the world's largest paint company until ICI acquired Glidden Paints in the United States. Aside from its paints business, PPG was the world's third largest producer of float glass and the second largest producer of fiber glass. PPG was a major global supplier of automotive original equipment glass. PPG also operated a chemical division that sold a range of products to several user industries.

PPG's paint and resins sales of $2.07 billion (1989) resulted in operating earnings of $287 million. PPG was the world's leading supplier of automotive and industrial finishes and a major supplier of trade paint (decorative) and stains. In automotive (OEM), PPG offered a wider range of services and products compared to competitors, ranging from finishes to metal pretreatments, electrodeposition prime coats, top coats, sealants, and adhesives. PPG was able to expand its OEM business in North America by supplying "transplants" of Japanese car manufacturers and through acquisitions of paint suppliers in Europe. Major R&D work had been undertaken to make top coats chip resistant, including the development of a top coat from powder paint. PPG gained from

_____
[3] US$1.00 = £0.70.

specific development centers in Flint, Michigan, and Cordstonn, Ohio, as well as a new corporate automotive technology center near Detroit, Michigan, housing fiber, glass, and coatings specialists to serve automotive clients' needs.

Automotive refinishes continued to be a high-profit growth segment for PPG. The company maintained a 17,000 color library. The market grew due to longer manufacturers' warranties, which enticed customers to hang on to their cars longer. In Europe, PPG consolidated its marketing under the PPG brand name, as it had done previously in the United States. In 1969, PPG acquired a major Swedish supplier. The European refinish segment was managed out of the United Kingdom with other technical color teams in France. National refinish marketing managers were maintained in all major European markets. In industrial coatings, PPG continued to build on its electrodeposition technology by expanding into the appliance sector in Europe and into container coatings.

The decorative segment, where PPG competed with its Pittsburg Paint products in the United States, acquisitions of Olympic (leading stains in the United States) and Lucile strengthened its channel position into home centers and mass merchandisers. Due to its size and volume stability, PPG considered the decorative sector important. PPG particularly emphasized its finishes for building claddings. Applied to pretreated metal and then oven-cured, PPG's Duranar coatings protected more area of architectural metal worldwide than any other formulations.

AKZO

AKZO was Holland's largest chemical company with sales (1989) of G18.7 billion,[4] operating income of G1.39 billion, and net income of G954 million. Originally strong in fibers, the fibers and polymer group accounted for 29% of sales. Other sectors were chemical products (35%), coatings (22%), and health care and

[4] US$1.00 = G2.00.

miscellaneous (22%). AKZO ranked twelfth among the world's largest chemicals companies.

AKZO's coating division achieved sales of G3,659 million (1989), up from G2,794 in 1988. Operating value for 1989 was G281 million, or 7.7%. The coating division reported an operating income of 18.7% of average invested capital based on a net sales/average capital ratio of 2.44. Of the total sales increase of 31%, 19% were due to acquisitions, 3% to higher value, and 6% to price increases.

In the decorative sector, which included decorative, do-it-yourself, and architectural paints, AKZO introduced its color consultancy system with the installation of computers for color research in the Netherlands and Germany. In car refinishes, AKZO made progress everywhere, particularly in the United States. AKZO was working on an integrated system for the color mixing process, calculations, and management and was introducing this system in its training courses in car refinishing information centers around the world. A new plant in Pontiac, Michigan, came on stream in 1989.

In industrial coatings, volume was up and margins were slightly down. The automotive OEM sector yielded inadequate returns in 1989. For some of its major customers, AKZO operated on-line and offered water-based finishes, particularly primers. Of increasing importance were coatings for plastics. AKZO also competed in coatings for aircraft. A major development in 1989 was AKZO's acquisition of Reliance Universal (United States). This company was a major producer of industrial coatings for wood, metal, plastics, metal packaging, paper, and coil coatings. Reliance was integrated with AKZO's other operations in the United States.

To enhance its operations, AKZO had started to consolidate manufacturing in fewer plants. The company was streamlining its product range, which had grown as a result of various acquisitions. AKZO had major operations in Europe (the Netherlands, Germany, Belgium, Austria, Denmark, Spain, the United Kingdom, and Greece), in North America (the United States and Canada), Latin America

(Brazil, Mexico, and Argentina), and Asia (Indonesia, Malaysia, and Thailand).

Nippon Paints

With a total volume of 257 million liters, Japan's largest paint company, Nippon Paint, had 1989 sales of about US$1 billion. Operating profit was about $40 million and net profit $25 million. This was the highest net profit earned during the last 10 years. Synthetic resin paints represented 80% of its volume. Thinners, lacquers, and other chemicals represented the rest (resin printing plate materials).

Nippon Paint was the leader in Japan in electrodeposition paint and number 2 in metal surface treatment. Paint for automobiles was about 40% of sales, while strong developments in paint for exteriors and industrial machinery were taking place. Nippon's R&D expenditures amounted to $41 million. Total employment stood at 2,700. The company had plans to expand its European operations based in Germany.

Kansai Paint

As Japan's second largest paint company, with a volume of 230 million liters worth $1 billion, Kansai Paint's operating profits amounted to $45 million, with a net profit of $28 million. Some 81% of sales were in synthetic resin paints. The rest was accounted for by lacquers, thinners, oil paints, and other chemicals. About 40% of sales were in the automobile industry. Also represented were paints for construction, building materials, and other metals. The company had recently built a new paint technology center and was spending $26 million on research.

ICI Paints (A):
Strategy for Globalization

"We at ICI Paints aspire to the number 1 position globally in the paint business. Our goal is to make ICI Paints the first choice among paint suppliers to whom a customer anywhere in the world would turn if he were seeking a long-term supply relationship," said Herman Scopes, PEO of ICI Paints. "Now, we are already the world's leader if measured in market share, sales volume, or liters of paint produced. However, we have not yet been able to translate this position into superior financial performance. To get there, we will have to become much better at learning from each other and at transferring best practice from one operation to another."

INDUSTRY PROFILE

The world paint market was estimated at some £20[1] billion at ex. factory level and some 12 billion liters. Growth was expected to average 2% to 3% through the next decade.

North America accounted for 31% of the market by volume, followed by Europe (29%), Japan (13%), Asia–Pacific (11%), and the rest of the world (16%). In the more mature paint markets of North America and Europe, annual growth was expected to be below GNP growth, whereas in the newly industrializing countries

[1] In 1988, £1.00 = $1.50.

growth was expected to be in line with GNP growth. Long term, the three principal paint user areas of Europe, North America, and Asia–Pacific were expected to become of equal size and account for 75% of the world market (*refer to Exhibit 1*).

Major application segments included decorative uses (50%), industrial uses (37%), coatings for cans (3%), automotive OEM (6%), and car repair/refinishing (4%).

There were approximately 10,000 paint manufacturers worldwide. Leading paint companies, aside from ICI, PPG, and BASF, were Sherwin–Williams (United States), AKZO (Netherlands), Nippon (Japan), International–Courtaulds (United Kingdom), Kansai (Japan), Du Pont (United States), and Valspar (United States). The top 10 companies shared 30% of the world paint market in 1988. That share was expected to increase over the next decade.

COMPANY PROFILE

ICI Paints was the world's largest paint manufacturer with a sales volume of £1.5 billion, or 8% of the world market, and an annual output of 800 million liters, or 7% of world volume. The company operated 64 manufacturing plants in 29 countries. Licensees operated in another 14 countries (*refer to Exhibit 3*). ICI was

This case was prepared by Jean-Pierre Jeannet, Professor of Marketing and International Business at Babson College and Adjunct Professor at IMD, as a basis for class discussion rather than to illustrate either effective or ineffective handling of a business situation. Copyright © 1990 by the International Management Development Institute (IMD), Lausanne, Switzerland. IMD retains all rights. Not to be used or reproduced without written permission directly from IMD, Lausanne, Switzerland.

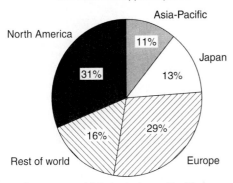

12,000 million liters worth
$35 billion at suppliers' prices

EXHIBIT 1 World Paint Industry Profile by Region

EXHIBIT 3 ICI Paints Territorial Spread

ICI Paints Manufacturing Companies

Australia	Malaysia	Taiwan
Canada	Mexico	Thailand
Fiji	New Zealand	United Kingdom
France	Pakistan	United States
India	Papua New Guinea	Uruguay
Ireland	Singapore	West Germany
Italy	Spain	
Madagascar	Sri Lanka	

ICI Minority Holdings

Botswana	Malawi	South Africa
Indonesia	Nigeria	Zimbabwe

Companies Manufacturing under License

Columbia	Korea	Turkey
Cyprus	Portugal	Venezuela
Japan	Saudi Arabia	Yemen
Jordan	Sudan	
Kenya	Trinidad	

about 70% larger than its next biggest competitor, PPG Industries.

ICI Paints was part of the consumer and specialty products sector of ICI. The division accounted for about 12% of total ICI turnover and 7% of its trading profit. Sales in 1988 (excluding sales by related companies) had reached £1.363 billion with a trading profit of £98 million, resulting in a return of 7.2% of sales. ICI Paints' profitability was on a par with BASF, its leading European competitor, and about twice that of its Japanese competitors. ICI Paints had been a consistent performer in an industry that had been characterized by considerable restructuring (*refer to Exhibit 4*).

EXHIBIT 2 World Paint Volume by Market Segment

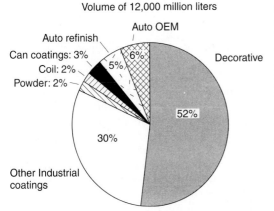

Volume of 12,000 million liters

ICI's market position varied considerably by market segment. The company was the world leader in the decorative and can-coatings areas, a major player in automotive refinishes, and one of the smaller automotive OEM players, and it also held positions in powder, coil coatings, and other industrial coatings. ICI was absent from the marine paints sector (*refer to Exhibit 5*).

Decorative Paint Segment

About 57% of ICI Paints' business was accounted for by the decorative segment, which included paints and coatings used for the protection and decoration of industrial, commercial, and residential buildings. ICI was the world's largest producer of decorative paints, both for professional and do-it-yourself (DIY) users. The company marketed its Dulux brands in the United Kingdom, Australia, New Zealand, and a few other Asian markets, the Valentine brand in France, Ducolux in Germany, and Glidden Spred in the United States, which was acquired as part of the acquisition of Glidden in 1986. Glidden was the inventor of waterborne latex paints for popular emulsions. Although trading under different brands, ICI was the leader in most of these markets, particularly in the premium end of the market.

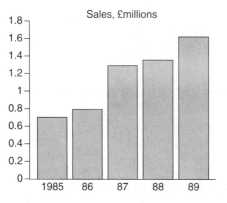

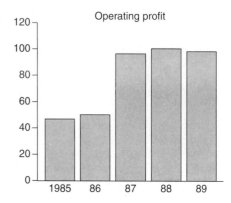

EXHIBIT 4 ICI Paints Financial Performance, 1985–1989

Most decorative paint was used where produced with little cross-shipping due to its low value. ICI tended to meet different local players country by country.

The wholesaling structure and retailing industry, as well as the role of the DIY market, varied considerably from one country to another. Furthermore, there was little economy of scale effect in this business. Some 500 paint companies competed in this segment in Italy alone. Paint formulations used also had to be adjusted to local use conditions, such as prevailing surfaces, building materials, and climate.

Despite these local differences, some commonalities existed. "Attitudes to what consumers want are far more common than different," commented John Thompson, ICI Paints planning manager. "We have done market research in Turkey, Italy, and Columbus, Ohio, and the same overall pattern emerges: the woman in a household determines when a surface is to be painted and she determines the color. The husband selects the brand, usually on the basis of price and technique, although women are increasingly also making this decision. In terms of paint application, it is about evenly split between husbands and wives."

Can-coating Segment

Although the can-coating segment with worldwide sales of £800 million accounted for only 3% of the world paint market, it accounted for 11% of ICI business, or £165 million, representing about 28% market share and giving it world leadership. Some 46% of the market was in North America, followed by Europe (24%) and Asia–Pacific (22%). Major competitors were BASF, Midland, and Valspar.

The coatings were used on the inside of tin or aluminium cans for food or beverage containers, making them corrosion resistant. This thin layer on the inside of every can was a crucial part of a successful canning operation. Consequently, this part of the paint industry was viewed as a high-technology application.

Customers were concentrated, with major use in the hands of four groups and their licensees: Continental Can, Pechiney–Triangle

EXHIBIT 5 ICI Volume by Market Segment

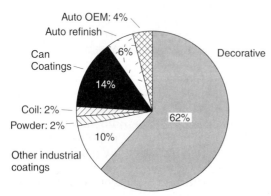

Volume of 800 million liters

(included former American and National Can), Carnaud–Metal Box, and Crown Cork and Seal. These can manufacturers operated canning lines all over the world, and they expected the suppliers to follow them everywhere with a consistent product, ensuring the same tastes for globally marketed products such as Coca Cola.

Coating products had to be developed for each application and depended on the particular food or beverage, as well as on the type of metal or aluminium container used. Customers were increasingly looking for simplifications and tended to look for a narrower technology range.

In this business, it was important to be able to make the development effort go around. A new product for sardines might be developed in Portugal, but might have applications for Norwegian packers as well. Success depended on avoiding duplication of effort in applications development. Although coatings were usually not identical, a considerable part of the concept development could be widely applicable to other customers with the same applications.

ICI had acquired 11 coatings companies over the years, including Holden (Birmingham) with operations in Europe, Marsden (United Kingdom), Wiederhold (Germany), Attivilac (Italy), and Glidden (United States). In Europe, ICI had strong operations in Rouen, France, where its Holden operation was located near the Carnaud company. The French operation had thus always been strong in food applications. Glidden, on the other hand, enjoyed an 80% market share in the United States for beverage cans.

ICI had targeted the can-coating segment for major growth and planned to increase its market share to 40% of the world market, up from 28% currently. A new production facility was planned for Taiwan. As part of this expansion strategy, the company combined all its various can-coating businesses under the same leadership in a single packaging group. Prior to that change, can coatings had been part of the larger group for general industry coatings.

Major changes were also contemplated for development. Work was conducted to transfer Glidden's aluminium can-coating technology to steel and tin plate. Also under review was a decision whether or not to site a new development center in Singapore or Malaysia to service the growing Asia–Pacific markets. Other research initiatives were considered on basic background chemistry and how to develop this for the canning industry.

Automotive OEM Paint Segment

The automotive paint segment consisted of paint sales made to automobile manufacturers for use in their assembly plants. Worldwide, this segment represented 5% of the paint market. Major markets were North America (31%), Europe (32%), and Japan (26%). Leading competitors were PPG, BASF, Kansai, Nippon, Du Pont, Hoechst, and ICI, in order of importance.

ICI's market share was about 6% worldwide, ranking it number 7 out of 8 international players. Most of its sales were in Europe, followed by the Asia–Pacific area (exclusive of Japan) and North America, with major local markets in Malaysia, Australia, and Canada. ICI was considered technically good but commercially weak in this segment. The company was a leader in the initial development of electrolytic paint and in the development of water-based top coat paints (Aquabase) for automotive users. The latest product was first introduced by GM in Canada and was now being introduced by Volvo in Sweden. Other European manufacturers were testing it, and ICI had granted a license to a Japanese company.

"This is an incestuous industry," remarked John Thompson, ICI Paints' planning manager. The customer base was largely globally operating companies and technologically very demanding. The technical service requirements of customers required paint suppliers to station technical service personnel permanently on location. As a result, the automotive companies preferred suppliers located at their doorsteps. This led to scattering factories close to assembly plants. In the United States, major paint companies would typically have several plants. Trends were away from multiple sourcing, which had kept local players alive, toward single sourcing and worldwide deals. Typically, a customer maintained a major supplier each for top coats and base coats, with a second supplier for smaller volume applications "to keep the big ones honest."

This segment was technically very demanding. PPG had reached segment leadership by developing electrolytic techniques that were key for the important base coating of car bodies. The initial development was actually made by ICI, but it was PPG that had made a commercial success out of the invention. At that time, PPG occasionally achieved single-source status through the installation of "hole-in-the-wall" plants where the company was producing adjacent to the paint shops of the assembly plant.

Although the particular paint applications such as color were developed for each customer, a substantial part of the basic research had worldwide applications. Technical spin-offs were also possible for other paint segments such as the refinish sector (with modifications in formulations due to the different paint application methods) and for industrial components in areas such as the domestic appliance industry. This was one reason why many players stayed in this segment despite low profitability or losses.

ICI had a very narrow geographic base in this segment and currently lacked platforms for major expansion. As a result, ICI engaged in a joint venture with Du Pont called IDAC on a 50:50 basis to supply the Western European automotive market. Du Pont had most of its automotive paint business in the United States and was therefore relatively weak in Europe. Du Pont's area of strength was in the top coat business, with GM and Ford as major customers in the United States. The IDAC goal was to reach a 20% market share in Europe during the early 1990s.

Automotive Refinish Paint Segment

The refinish segment included paints and coatings for repairing automobiles. The segment accounted for 4% of world sales and had the highest price per liter (£3.34). It was considered the most profitable paint segment. North America accounted for 36% of the world market, followed by Europe (30%), and Asia–Pacific (25%).

Only 10 paint manufacturers competed significantly in the refinish sector. Among those, only Sherwin–Williams of the United States and Rock of Japan did not also compete in the automotive OEM market. No new competitor had entered since the 1950s.

The world leader was BASF as a result of its recent acquisition of Inmont in the United States, followed by Du Pont and ICI. ICI was the largest refinish supplier outside the United States. Its Autocolor brand led in the United Kingdom and was well known in Europe. In France, the company was the leader with its Valentine brand. ICI had a color inventory of some 30,000 formulas to match the stock colors of virtually all vehicle manufacturers. ICI's matching capability was developed in the U.K. market where a wide variety of car models was on the road following the decline of the local U.K. car industry.

Customers were largely small paint shops who needed quick and frequent deliveries, typically on a daily basis. Paint manufacturers supplied their customers with mixing schemes through local distributors who would combine the basic colors and shades with solvents to obtain the correct color match. There were some 10,000 different shades and some 60 different colors to select from. For ICI, this resulted in some 30,000 different formulas, partly as a result of different application techniques for the same shades and colors. A recent trend was in the direction of color mixing at the end-user location using color systems supplied by the paint manufacturer. Recently, ICI had placed a computerized management system at the disposal of its customers.

To compete in this business, a company had to have access to the color and paint shops of the car manufacturers to obtain the needed information. Automobile manufacturers wanted to make sure that their customers could get their cars repaired wherever they were marketed. As an example, a company like Toyota was interested in worldwide coverage. Refinish paint manufacturers profited if they could have access to all car manufacturers, wherever they were located, so that they could supply the widest possible color range in any geographic market.

Powder Paint Segment

Powder paint was the fastest growing segment and represented an alternative technology for traditional wet paint, rather than a particular application segment. Growing 10% to 20% annually, the segment had attracted many large companies as well as smaller suppliers. Leaders were International–Courtaulds (United Kingdom), Ferro (United States), ICI, and DSM (Netherlands).

Powder coatings were a precisely formulated mixture of pigment and resin, which was sprayed using electrostatic spray guns. The sprayed item, a metal object, was then heated for about 10 minutes to cure the surface. Coatings had been developed for heat resistance or chemical resistance. The major benefits for users were the reduced emissions such as solvents used with wet paints and the reduced need for waste disposal. Major user groups were the automotive component suppliers, the metal furniture industry, and domestic appliance manufacturers. Powder paint could conceivably substitute for up to 50% of the paint being applied to metal. In Europe, where the product was pioneered, the substitution already amounted to about 20%, compared to about 10% in the United States, an amount that was, however, growing rapidly.

While the technology itself had become basic, there was room to develop many applications. ICI had selected some specific applications for further development, such as domestic appliances and architectural components. ICI had concluded a joint venture with Nippon Oil & Fats of Japan in Malaysia. About half of ICI's powder volume was in the United States, about 40% in Europe, and the rest spread over many countries. In the United States, ICI was tied for first place with Morton, but was only sixth in Europe.

General Industrial Paint Segment

Some £250 million of ICI Paints' business was part of the general industrial paint category, which included general industrial liquid paints, wood finishes, adhesives, ink, and others. Two-thirds of this segment was allied in some way to its four core business areas, such as adhesives in the United States or metal can printing. Another part consisted of stand-alone businesses, not necessarily connected to core sectors, such as inks for screen printing in Germany. In these segments, ICI did not compete consistently throughout the world and had only selected local pockets of excellence.

STRATEGY

ICI Paints aimed at world leadership and profitable growth. The company intended to concentrate on its key paint businesses on a global basis and wanted to exploit particular regional opportunities in the EC and Asia–Pacific regions. ICI believed that a commitment to R&D and innovation was an essential part of industry leadership.

Organizationally, ICI aspired to become a marketing-driven organization that was quality and customer focused, health and safety conscious, and environmentally responsible.

Organization

ICI management believed it was essential to have a global organization and management structure that would be both global and territory centered, support R&D centers of excellence in certain locations, and maximize resources and synergy among businesses, operations, and locations.

ICI Paints was organized both along geographic and business lines (refer to Exhibit 6). Reporting to the principal executive officer (PEO) were three regional heads (chief executives) for Europe, North America, and Asia–Pacific. Each chief executive had P&L responsibility for the entire paint business in his area. The North American chief executive was

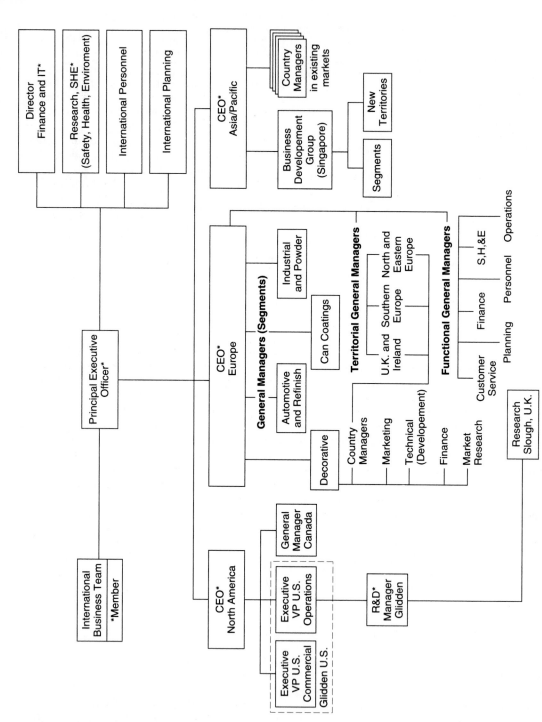

EXHIBIT 6 Organization Chart

also the head of Glidden, ICI Paints' major U.S. operating unit.

Reporting to each chief executive were several managers with country or territorial responsibility, called TGMs (territorial general managers) and BAGMs (short for business area general managers), for the four core sectors: decorative, can, automotive refinish and OEM, and powder. In some situations, BAGMs were identical with TGMs. In general, P&L results were a joint responsibility of BAGMs and TGMs.

At the territory or country level, BAGMs existed for the core business areas to the extent that each country had business in each of the four core sectors. Each territory also had other paint businesses. The percentage of sales in the latter category varied across territories, with higher percentages reported for some developing markets in Asia and lower percentages in the developed markets of Europe and North America.

Decision Making

Major decisions were always discussed and decided on by the International Business Team (IBT) chaired by Herman Scopes, its PEO. Eight executives were members of the IBT, including the PEO and the three chief executives. The ICI Paints Group was led by Herman Scopes as its PEO and the seven members of the IBT. Part of the IBT were the three chief executives for North America, Europe, and Asia/Pacific/Australia regions, as well as four other executives with either functional or segment responsibility (*refer to Exhibit 7*). The IBT met six to eight times per year at various locations.

Executives were nominated to the IBT because of their ability to contribute broadly to the development of the ICI Paints Group, rather than for their specialties or specific skills. Once part of the IBT, members were assigned portfolios based on their own talents and experience, occasionally resulting in changes when the personnel constellation changed in the IBT.

An important aspect of the way ICI Paints operated was its use of international leaders (ILs). These positions existed for each of its four core business areas (decorative, can coat-

EXHIBIT 7 Members of the International Business Team (IBT)

Herman Scopes	PEO ICI Paints
John Dumble	Chief Executive North America, President Glidden
Doug Curlewis	Chief Executive Europe International Leader Decorative Paint
Richard Stillwell	Chief Executive Asia–Pacific/Australia
John Danzeisen	Finance Director International Leader Powder International Leader Finance Function International Leader IT Function
Alex Ramig	International Leader R&D
Brian Letchford	International Leader Automotive Refinish and OEM (designated International Leader Can)
Quintin Knight	International Leader Can Coatings (retiring in March 1990)

Other International Leaders Not Part of the IBT:

June Thomason	Operations Manager, Glidden International Leader Operations
Ian Cope	International Leader Management Development

ings, automotive, and powder), as well as for five functional areas: finance, information technology, operations, R&D, and management development. The ILs for three of these five areas were members of the IBT.

The ILs of the core sectors had the roles of facilitators or coordinators. These international leaders did not have P&L responsibility. However, they were responsible for the development of global strategies for each of their assigned core sectors. Powder was coordinated out of the United States, decorative out of Europe (by the chief executive Europe), and automotive and can coatings from Europe (head of that sector for Europe).

Strategies were developed at the business level by the international leaders and their teams and were then proposed to the International Business Team.

COORDINATING CORE BUSINESS SEGMENTS

The strategy-making and coordination process differed considerably across the four core business areas.

The *decorative world strategy* consisted of three major elements. First, ICI Paints was to pursue quality leadership in all markets where the company was competing. It was understood that this meant setting the pace in the sector and pursuing a premium price. Second, there was to be a drive toward running a world brand, Dulux, the only world consumer paint brand in existence. This goal included having a consistent role for Dulux as the aspirational brand in all ICI decorative paint markets. Third, ICI was to use the fact that it was the largest paint producer worldwide and should thus be able to maximize its resources in key functional areas.

Coordination was hampered by the fact that local operating companies considered their competitive situations to be unique. Glidden in the United States did not compete in the premium sector at all and its market share was only about 10%, compared to 40% in the United Kingdom, or the three-brand product line in Australia. To launch Dulux as a premium brand in the United States would entail a marketing investment of about $50 million over 4 to 5 years with a 7-year payback period for a required 5% market share. Glidden executives were not convinced that this strategy would be successful in the United States.

Due to the differences encountered, the IL for the sector had pursued a "consultative mode," meeting about twice annually with the key executives from the various operating companies. In addition, the IL had frequent individual meetings with operating executives and territorial managers.

In the *automotive sector*, the IL positions for the OEM and refinish segments were combined. For refinishes, where ICI had major positions in Europe and Australia only, the strategy was fairly heavily led from the center. Involved were key managers from Europe and Australia with others "mostly along for the ride." A major point of discussion was ICI's future strategy in the United States where it had no position at that time. Glidden executives were very interested in entering the refinish sector. However, a "greenfield approach" (that is, starting up with no previous capability) was considered

difficult and, as yet, no ready candidates for acquisition existed.

In the automotive OEM segment, the IL role consisted largely of outside contacts with Du Pont, ICI's partner for Europe, and frequent negotiations with Japanese companies on technology transfers that might result in obtaining business for ICI from Japanese transplant operations in Canada, Australia, Southeast Asia, India, and Pakistan, all countries where ICI was active in the OEM business.

Coordination in the *can-coatings sector* was very close and involved a formal business area review team under the leadership of the IL for can coatings. The team consisted of the key players worldwide in ICI Paints, who met several times each year. A major challenge here was to devise a strategy in view of the increased concentration among customers. Despite ICI's leading market position, the company could not dictate prices. The resulting squeeze on margins had reduced profitability, and a new strategy would have to be devised to lead the company out of this "commodity hole."

For the *general industrial paint sector*, no IL had been appointed. These businesses were led in various ways. Businesses that were closely affiliated with one of the four core areas were attached to the IL teams of those areas. Others were left under the direction of the territorial management. Some businesses not directly tied to the paint business were kept as long as they were meeting required profitability targets.

Coordinating at the Functional Level

The ILs for the five key functions undertook their roles in different ways. For all functional ILs, however, the objectives were similar. ICI wanted to transfer skills, experience, and best practice around its group operating companies. It also wished to accelerate the innovation process (as distinctly different from the invention process). Finally, the desire, as elsewhere in the business, was to simplify and focus on operational aspects, not just "spin wheels."

For the finance area, this largely involved

the enforcement of corporate guidelines and practice around the Paint Group. For information technology (IT), the mission was still vague. One job was to encourage and promote the use of IT where appropriate, often convincing chief executives to make the necessary investments. The coordinating activities had led to a policy of using DEC equipment for technical applications and IBM for commercial and operational tasks.

In operations, efforts were undertaken to spread efficient production procedures across the group. Here, ICI relied on Glidden's skill as a low-cost producer.

In the R&D area, there had been a long-held conviction that technology was driven by the automotive and industrial market, such as coil coatings. ICI Paints was now moving the emphasis of its R&D brainpower to new fields such as decorative, can coatings, and powders, which was beginning to yield exciting results.

Coordinating the various functions was a challenging task since many of its operating companies had different corporate origins, were acquired from various sources, and represented different nationalities and cultures.

Current Organizational Issues for ICI Paints Worldwide

Over the past years, ICI's organization had undergone considerable changes. Aside from its territorial focus, it introduced the idea of ILs for segments and functions. However, the company encountered a major obstacle in the fact that much of its production assets were shared. It was believed that some 50 of its 64 plants were common sites for a number of paint products and segments. This meant that the business segments were largely responsible for business volume, but the BAGMs did not have full asset responsibility. At this time, not more than 75% of the company assets could be clearly attributed to individual business lines.

Aside from the organization issues and the challenges faced by each of the four core sectors, ICI Paints needed to leverage the benefit of its being the largest global player into a superior financial performance.

OPPORTUNITIES FOR ICI PAINTS

ICI Paints faced a number of opportunities in different geographic areas and various paint segments. These opportunities had to be seen in relationship to its own resources. "Although ICI is a very large corporation with considerable financial resources, it is not realistic to expect that we can do everything," said Thompson. "We still need to keep in mind that our profitability, while on a par with the best paint competitors, is below average for ICI as a whole." Some typical opportunities (not an exhaustive list, however) follow.

ICI Paints' Opportunities in Japan

ICI Paints, despite its world leadership, did not have a direct presence in the Japanese market. For some time, the company had been considering an opportunity to go beyond licensing, but was unsure about the appropriate entry strategy. Considered were approaches ranging from exporting to joint ventures, making an acquisition, or even a greenfield start-up. Furthermore, which paint business to launch first in Japan was an unresolved question. Another question was how to relate any operation to the rest of ICI's business in Japan.

ICI Paints had virtually no direct sales in Japan. From time to time, decorative paint had been supplied by its Southeast Asian factories for sale as Japanese brands. Dulux Australia had supplied solid emulsion to be sold by Nippon Paints in the small Japanese DIY market.

The company's current presence in Japan consisted of two full-time ICI Japan employees, one long-serving and performing a liaison job with licensees plus providing a color standards collection from Japanese automakers for ICI's refinish business, and the other recently appointed as a technical coordinator for submission of can-coatings products for approval by the can manufacturers.

ICI had also concluded a series of licensing agreements, some granting technology to Japanese companies and others gaining access to Japanese technology. ICI granted automotive OEM licenses to Kansai, NOF, and Shinto, while obtaining licenses in the same area from Kansai and NOF. Furthermore, a powder coatings license was granted to Shinto while an industrial electrocoat license was obtained from the same company. A flexible packaging refinish license was granted to Rock, which in turn granted ICI a refinish license. A can coatings license, due to expire in 1991, was also granted to Dai Nippon Inks.

ICI Paints considered it inopportune to enter the general paints business. Instead, an entry through one of its key segments was viewed as more promising. Best opportunities appeared in can coatings and powder paints.

Powder paints were viewed as having a major opportunity in Japan due to the high concentration of metal-based industries (automobile, appliances) dominated by firms such as Matsushita, Hitachi, and Mitsubishi.

The market for powder coatings was estimated at about 18,000 tons, or 8% of the world market. This was equal to the U.K. market but smaller than the market for powder coatings for Italy. The cost of building a factory was estimated at about $3 million with break-even volume of about 1,500 tons annually. Some $500,000 to $750,000 of the original investment might be saved if the investment could be made together with ICI Films, another ICI international business, because the same buildings could be used. However, there were no production or marketing synergies between films and powder coatings.

In the can-coatings sector, the opportunity was also tempting. Japan was a major market for metal cans, particularly in the beverage sector with three leading brewers, Kirin, Ashahi, and Sapporo, as well as international soft drink firms such as Coca-Cola and Pepsi Cola. The soft drink firms were global companies that were already indirect customers of ICI Paints elsewhere.

The Japanese can-making market was dominated by Toyo Seikan, the second largest can maker in the world, Mitsubishi, and Daiwa. They supplied coated cans directly to major users. Can users, such as beverage companies, often looked for suppliers who could serve them on a worldwide basis. Can coatings were typically formulated to the specific requirements of a customer.

The Japanese market for can coatings was estimated at some 70 million liters, or about 17.5% of the world market. A greenfield investment would cost about $15 million. The annual break-even point depended considerably on the particular product mix achieved. However, annual operating costs would be about $4 million, with another $1 million required for technical support. This would result in a break-even volume of about 5 million liters. On the other hand, licensing fees averaged about 3% of sales, with a minimum annual payment of $150,000.

ICI Paints needed a presence in Japan as part of its strategy to reach its goal of 40% market share worldwide in the can-coatings sector. Major risks were a drain on critical resources such as human resources and capital funds and the need for "patient money" to do well in Japan.

Present suppliers for can coatings included Dainippon, an old ICI Paints licensee of an earlier generation of coatings technology. Market leaders were Toyo Ink and Dainippon (DNIC), which accounted for about 50% and 40% of the Japanese market, respectively. In the present Japanese market, ICI Paints could compete with superior technology. No other foreign company maintained a base in Japan for can coatings.

The major question remained on how to proceed. A joint venture with Toyo Sekan appeared possible. It was not clear, however, how to develop a local technology base or how to do the manufacturing and staffing. Another issue was how fast to proceed.

ICI Paints' Decorative Opportunities in the United States

ICI Paints had undertaken a recent attempt to investigate the possibilities of entering the premium paint segment in the United States. The difficulty of this strategy was underlined by the fact that such a premium segment was very small in the United States, amounting to about 12% of the market for DIY paint compared to the United Kingdom, where it represented almost 40% of the decorative paint market. In the United States, regional companies such as Benjamin Moore and Pratt & Lambert were leaders in that segment.

Glidden, acquired in 1986, had pursued a low-price strategy that had resulted in enormous success. Sometimes described as "pile it high and price it low," Glidden was able to expand its business from just 4% market share to 17% currently in the DIY market, expanding its brand into national distribution and reaching the leading brand position in the U.S. market. By contrast, Sears (supplied by De Soto) had dropped from 30% to just 16% market share in the same 15-year time period. Furthermore, Glidden also achieved a 10% share in the contractor market aimed at painters and professionals.

At first, ICI Paints in the United Kingdom believed it might pave the way for a launch of a premium decorative brand in the United States by sending one of its own people to the U.S. operation. The assignment was to investigate if ICI's premium brand Dulux might be launched in the United States at some time in the future. Actually selected by Glidden, this British executive was soon isolated and "cocooned," which rendered his situation untenable, and no progress was achieved in resolving the issue of whether a premium strategy might work in the United States. "It was like sending a 'Brit' to the 'Colonials'," commented Herman Scopes, ICI Paints PEO. "This experience taught us that some other approach would have to be chosen."

ICI Paints set up a study team consisting of both Glidden and ICI Paints executives. Scopes thought it might be helpful to "park" the idea of a position on global branding around Dulux and to look at the market more objectively. The output of the study was to be fed into a global review of ICI's decorative paint business. In the meantime, ICI's Canadian operation had agreed to launch a premium brand under the Dulux name.

Automotive Refinish Opportunity in the United States

The automotive refinish segment was a very stable market with only four major players: Du Pont, BASF/Inmont, PPG, and Sherwin–Williams. These top four accounted for 90% of the market. This segment was highly profitable, with return on sales ranging from 18% to 24% and return on net assets (RONAs) of around 40%. The market consisted of some 60,000 body shops supplied through local jobbers via company-owned warehouses. Warehouse distributors played a decreasingly important role because they were usually not specialized enough.

The refinish segment in the United States was subject to a number of changes. One major factor was the increase in car imports into the United States, which tended to increase the range of products requiring refinishing. New top coat technologies adopted by car manufacturers required new refinishes and continued technological improvements on the part of the paint manufacturers. More sophisticated body shop equipment, such as controlled environments to counter solvent emission into the air, constantly forced adjustment in the refinish formulas. Furthermore, there was a trend toward supplying body shops with color mixing schemes rather than factory-packaged colors, shifting the mixing forward into the body shop as each job required it.

In the opinion of John Thompson, ICI Paints planning manager, key to success in this segment was color performance, followed by technical service to body shops, then environmental friendliness, training opportunities for paint sprayers, and, finally, delivery service. Price was viewed as much less important than any of these five criteria.

Several theoretical entry options existed. The first was through a major acquisition. "Who would sell such a beautiful business?" John Thompson asked. Acquisitions of a smaller player would not be big enough to make a difference. A greenfield entry was likely to be slow. AKZO, the large Dutch paint manufacturer, had been working at it for 10 years and had still only achieved a 3% market share. There was an opportunity to enter regionally with expansion to national distribution later.

The financial resources required to develop this segment were considerable. Depending on the approach chosen, the pace of expansion, and the company's skill and success, a maximum negative accumulated cash flow of about $30 million to $50 million for a national introduction would have to be considered. Thompson considered the necessary volume for break-even to be 5% market share of a significant regional market and 4% market share nationally.

SELECTING A COURSE FOR THE FUTURE

ICI Paints management approached the future with some confidence. 1989 had been another good year for the paints business with total sales of £1,628 million and a trading profit of £100 million. Volume in the major decorative DIY markets of the United States and United Kingdom were affected by the depressed housing markets in both countries. Competitively, however, Glidden was able to assume clear brand leadership for decorative paints in the United States. Dulux Australia enjoyed record profits following the integration of an acquisition. Sales in Southeast Asia achieved strong growth with the successful introduction of new paint product lines and a joint venture in Hong Kong to develop business with China PRC.

In the can-coatings segment, ICI was able to increase its world market share. Its position in Europe was strengthened through an acquisition in Spain (Quimilac SA). Powder paint continued to experience strong growth in Europe.

7

The Managerial Challenge: Implementing International Marketing Programs

The challenge for international marketing managers is to focus all their efforts to combine separate elements of their international marketing programs into a single, well-balanced, and well-adapted marketing program. The principal elements of this program are the four elements of the marketing mix: product, place, promotion, and price.[1] In this section, we will focus on some ideas and concepts that help in the development of an appropriate marketing mix as a company moves abroad.

The development of a good marketing mix always depends on careful evaluation of the environment. Managers must determine which elements of that environment they can truly change and which are completely beyond their control, but within which they must shape the marketing program. In international marketing especially, this process also involves looking at three more "p's" related to the foreign environment: people, profits, and politics. Analysis of these must support decisions about the four P's. In fact, this is a continuing iterative process, with the three p's of the environment shaping the marketers' thinking about the four P's, and the result, including the reactions to their marketing plan, in turn further sharpening their analysis of the environment.

The evaluation of the first factor, people, stresses the importance of *consumer analysis* in all marketing planning. The determination of needs and wants becomes more difficult in international marketing to the extent that they are affected by cultural differences (see Section 2). In fact, "people" should really be expressed as "persons" in order to emphasize that a market can be segmented into groups of persons and does not consist of an undifferentiated, homogeneous mass.

Profit, in an international context, however, may differ from profit as it is understood in a purely domestic marketing situation, as will be seen in some of the case studies. In some situations, a foreign government will not allow funds to be transferred out of its country or will require that a certain percentage of the company be owned by local parties. In these cases, it will not be possible to repatriate dividends or income to the parent organization, so corporate goals for return on investment will have to be modified or different goals adopted. It will still usually

---

[1] Philip Kotler, *Marketing Management: Analysis, Planning & Control*, 7th ed., © 1991.

be possible, however, to calculate a return on investment for the company's operations internally within the foreign country, so this important analysis is still undertaken.

No marketing plan makes sense unless it can bring in more money than it costs—an obvious observation, but one that unfortunately is too often overlooked. Even though it might not be possible to repatriate profits, many corporations continue building their operations in a country in the expectation that there will be opportunities to get their investment back, or that the exposure to that market is advantageous for political reasons, or that there are opportunities for lowering worldwide costs, or for all these reasons.

Increasingly, profits will not be available as hard currency at all, but will be offered in goods or other payments in kind through the mechanism of countertrade. *Countertrade* involves various kinds of transactions (with such names as barter, buyback, or counterpurchase) that may or may not involve cash in some part of a multifaceted deal. According to one survey, 88 countries had asked for countertrade terms, and another survey reported that all 55 multinational firms surveyed had been involved in countertrade. There is agreement that this will be an increasing force involving manufacturers directly, as well as banks and world trading companies, especially in deals involving more than two partners.

A government's pressures for countertrade or other concessions reflect the p factor of politics, which in some cases will alter the marketing mix in a foreign environment. Other political demands or laws affecting the marketing mix might prescribe the amount of added value that must be produced in the local country (*local content* laws), or might require that citizens of the local country hold a certain percentage of management jobs, or require that all advertisements be produced locally, or impose very high import tariffs on certain items to encourage local sourcing. Finally, some countries can be described as inherently more or less stable politically; assessment of a country's political risk will not only affect a decision whether to enter (or remain in) a country, but will also affect whether managers wish to take a relatively short or long term view in their marketing plan.

Having assessed the problems and opportunities in a foreign environment in terms of the three p's in the target country, managers can plan their strategy—the classic four P's—in more detail. Their analysis is then not materially different from that which would be done at home, but there are important added dimensions that we now consider.

PRODUCT LINE DECISIONS

A product can be described in two fundamental ways. The more common way is to list its physical characteristics, much in the way that the product design engineer might draw up a set of technical specifications for the manufacturing department; in the same vein, a typical sales brochure for a product might describe its attributes and special features in technical terms to give the reader a good idea of how the product is made. We call this product orientation the *clipboard approach,* since it views the product much as a factory quality-control engineer would as he or she walks up and down the manufacturing line, clipboard in hand. The product's worth is measured according to quality of materials, soundness of construction, special features, and ability to live up to its functional standards, all dimensions that can scientifically be described and measured. This is the essence of a product as it can be captured in concrete terms and written down, let's say, on the specification sheet taped to the back of the package. The clipboard approach means that the product, not the consumer, is the center of attention. This all too common point of view probably explains why most new product introductions have not been successful.

The other fundamental way to describe a product is to view it from the perspective of the target consumers; here the product is really a *bundle of perceptions* that may or may not correspond to what is physically built into the product. The chemist in the coffee factory can precisely measure the proportions of three different kinds of coffee beans in a particular blend, its acidity, and at least 10 other characteristics of the brand. One consumer, however, may perceive the brand as one that causes extreme tension, while another buyer may regard that brand as the only one suitable to serve when entertaining important clients at home. In both cases, it is the same coffee in the cup, but quite a different product in the mind.

A consumer segment can be described according to the product attributes—the bundles of perceptions—that are most important to it. The marketer can then promote and advertise the product to this segment by emphasizing how well the product delivers on those perceived attributes. When a marketer selects the consumer segment and specifies the special product attributes and image to be emphasized, he or she is positioning that product. *Positioning* can be accomplished both in terms of the physical attributes built into the product or by the emphasis that the advertising places on certain of those attributes.

In taking a product abroad, it is important to reexamine both its clipboard specifications and its positioning. Considerations of the former may seem obvious, but are, unbelievably, often overlooked. For example, a large part of the world uses 220-volt and 50-hertz power systems (versus 110 volts and 60 hertz in the United States), and the legal codes of each country place different safety and health requirements on a product. Moreover, overt or covert attempts by a country to discourage imports may lead to standards that discriminate against a product design, and redesigning it may lead the firm to lose its cost competitiveness or distinctive product superiority. Some redesign may also be necessary in order to tap the largest global market. A product designed for the German market, for example, may be overdesigned for much of the developing countries of the world, and the potential demand in those countries could far surpass the German market.

Positioning the product with the correct bundle of perceptions is even trickier. The elephant traps described in Section 2 are waiting for the insensitive marketer, and several kinds of mistakes can be made. Some well-documented problem areas involve local tastes and preferences for certain colors, materials, product qualities, and "feel," but even less obvious are built-in prejudices found in many nations for the homegrown product. In some cases a product with a foreign label can connote prestige and quality and, in other cases, can be perceived as cheap and having low status. Finally, a true measure of the need for one's product and whether it really fills a hole in the market requires marketing research, and often such research has been defective due to ignorance or insensitivity toward certain aspects of the local culture.

To avoid mistakes, good marketing research should precede any product introduction, whether in the home country or in the foreign environment. There seems to be even less research commissioned in foreign countries, however, due to skepticism that good marketing research firms exist in those countries or due to the marketer's lack of confidence that he or she will be able to evaluate the results being reported. Many times, marketers feel they are under time pressure, which is exacerbated in the foreign environment by the need to line up new distributors, for example, and the inefficiencies of having to communicate and negotiate and then operate at great distances from the home office. Under these adverse circumstances, the marketer seems to be willing to take the word of one or two local distributors or agents. Once again, this seeming carelessness actually boils down to fear and avoidance of the unknown and negative assumptions that are simply unwarranted, since there is in fact an increasing supply of well-trained and sophisticated suppliers of marketing research throughout the world. A few inquiries made through local advertising agencies or through the U.S. International Trade Administration offices abroad can locate these sources.

Product decisions that result from analysis of the marketing research can involve minor modifications in the product's clipboard specifications or positioning or might call for major modifications in one or both. If the product requires substantial redesign, the question becomes one of whether the manufacturing personnel possess the expertise and commitment to succeed with an essentially new product concept. If the product requires substantial consumer repositioning, the question is whether the marketing personnel have the insights and instincts and management has the desire to communicate the new positioning effectively. The level of commitment to major changes may depend on the prospect of large profits that would allow for hiring personnel who have experience with that market or those marketing or manufacturing changes. As usual, there should be good economic reasons for introducing products or strategies that depart from management's areas of expertise; such moves are difficult to do well in a domestic market, and the problems are only multiplied in a foreign environment. The extent of product adaptation required tends to vary by the type of market target segment. It has been the experience of most multinational corporations that product changes and positioning adaptations are more sweeping for consumer products than for industrial products. Many industrial products are used around the globe in very similar ways, requiring only superficial changes in electric wiring, for example, while the basic configuration remains identical; the same experience goes for office equipment or computers. For industrial marketers, the real challenge is more in providing adequate service or maintenance rather than product design.

PRICING DECISIONS

As in product line decisions, determination of the proper price starts with an analysis of the values and needs of your target consumer segment. Experience has shown, however, that many executives start at the wrong end of the analysis—with product costs—and therefore set cost-plus prices. This thinking is similar to the clipboard delineation of product benefits: It ignores the fact that it is not the tangible bill of materials in the product that determines its value. Rather, value comes from people, who with their own perceptions of a product's worth will determine the ultimate market price. It is true that many customers will have an opinion or some knowledge about what it costs to make the product and will consequently have an opinion concerning what constitutes a fair price. When this knowledge or belief is widespread and when there are many competitors with products perceived to be similar (a typical situation late in the product life cycle), the market price will in fact be close to the production cost.

Many segments of the market put a value on a product that is relative to other products or services that they may have to sacrifice when buying the product; if the value is right or the sacrifice is relatively small, then the price is right. This concept of *value pricing* allows the marketer to optimize profits from a product, since it is usually some price above a minimum cost-plus figure that allows a product to achieve its highest profit potential.[2] In a sense, cost-plus pricing is antimarketing; it assumes that the worth of a product rests with its cost of materials plus some arbitrary profit target, not with what the customer thinks.

Pricing analysis in international markets, then, should begin with this question: What value does the target segment place on this product category, and how do the differences in the product add or subtract from that value? In practice, this is a difficult question to research, probably because most consumers don't know what they are actually willing to pay until they are ready to reach into their pockets. Price–demand curves are a very useful way to conceptualize how much a marketer should charge, but few practitioners have been able to construct these curves in their own markets.

The international environment complicates the pricing analysis in several ways. Local laws may constrain maximum prices, or a country may enforce antidumping laws to control the minimum prices that an imported product must carry. Rampant inflation in certain countries, serving to drive up product costs, make pricing a continual headache; structural differences between countries may lead to multiple price lists around the world, thus setting up conditions for *parallel* or *gray market* importing. Certain countries also have laws regulating how transfer pricing between subsidiary companies may operate. The growing importance of countertrade, in which no cash at all may change hands but a value for the product must still be determined, requires the marketer to be creative and flexible. You will see many of these complicating factors in the cases contained in this section, but the fundamental approach is the same: One must determine a target consumer segment; consider which relevant products are in competition for the consumer's attention; and calculate, in light of consumers' perceptions of value, the price that can produce the most contribution to one's fixed, or committed, costs. While the international dimension may complicate this reasoning, it should not prevent a thorough job of consumer analysis.

Regarding transfer pricing, a company may try to price a product that is sold by one subsidiary to another subsidiary in a different country so that the greatest reportable profits exist in the country that charges lower corporate income tax. However, most countries have passed laws effectively preventing a company from avoiding taxes by this practice. In the same way, competitors are extremely sensitive when they suspect that a company is dumping a product in their country, in effect subsidizing lower prices abroad by higher factory prices at home. As in all other aspects of exporting, a firm must be fully aware of the law in other countries, and it is equally true everywhere that the cost of defending the company in a lawsuit, including the time it consumes, is considerable.

When a product is exported to another country, many costs are added to the product that most domestic marketers don't face. Added to the larger freight and shipping insurance costs (which go to make up what is commonly known as C.I.F., cost plus freight plus insurance) are tariff or import duties, usually assessed on the C.I.F. cost. Since distributors and retailers who handle the product in the local country usually work on a percentage markup of the total delivered cost, the markups are substantially larger than the same percentage markups in the home country. If several levels of distribution are involved, these multiplicative factors can easily increase the final retail price by a factor of two to three times over the factory price in the home

---

[2] Readers not familiar with profit maximization on the price–demand curve are encouraged to refer to any basic economics textbook. The major point is that as prices rise, demand will probably fall, but that for mathematical reasons there will be one price that will provide the greatest profit contribution; this price will usually be between the cost-plus price and the maximum price that some customers will pay.

country. If the value of the currency in the foreign country is subject to constant devaluation or revaluation relative to the exporting country, the retail price in the foreign country and the value of the profits remitted to the parent company are also affected. In addition, a country may protect certain industries by imposing stiff import duties on certain classes of products.

The resulting price disparity between imported and local products may force the exporting company to consider setting up a local manufacturing operation or licensing local manufacturers for the product in order to be competitive. Local manufacturing may add to the company's fixed costs and exposure to risk, and licensing may involve giving up certain secrets or proprietary information. One challenge is to develop products that are distinctive enough or that fit the needs of a given segment well enough to command a price that covers its higher costs; another challenge is to find sources of the least expensive supplies and labor in the world so that an imported product can still possibly be priced at a level with locally made products. The first step involves thorough consumer analysis of the country's market segments, and the second step involves close coordination with the operations and manufacturing people in the company. Both of these are good marketing practices that become much more important in international marketing in overcoming the inherent disadvantages of selling products at a distance from their source of manufacture.

Although some companies face only the difficulty of pricing their products for another market while adding extra costs, many firms compete in dozens of markets simultaneously. If prices are set with only local market conditions in mind, substantial variations from one country to another can occur. Such price differentials can cause difficulties and force companies to design procedures that allow them to approach pricing as a process across many countries to prevent large differences between markets.

DISTRIBUTION DECISIONS

Unless a product is made available for sale, customers won't have the opportunity to buy it. We make this seemingly obvious statement simply because many students of marketing don't fully appreciate the importance of channels in the marketing mix. Likewise, too many international marketers don't appreciate how the differences in foreign market structures will destroy what looks like an otherwise intelligent marketing plan.

In some countries, the innumerable layers of wholesalers, distributors, agents, subagents, and local distributors seem both incomprehensible and unnecessary. The number of retailers per thousand citizens varies tremendously from one country to another, and the physical appearance and functions of the merchant, who is sometimes vastly different from American conceptions of "the retailer," also reveal major differences in customers' buying behavior and in their expectations concerning the goods a shop should carry. Finally—and this cannot be stressed too strongly—the importance of *personal relationships* between the various buyers and sellers from one channel to the next can overwhelm the rest of the marketing strategy; this also varies by country and by product category. The international marketer's challenge is to uncover all these aspects and differences and to incorporate them correctly into the marketing plan.

For many of the cases in this book, you will have to make decisions regarding which products to introduce into a new country and how to position them through the selection of product features and advertising. In the analyses, you must take into account what competitors are offering and whether there might be an unfilled need in the market. Yet you may not realize that in this country the retailer for the segment you are targeting might be a small family-run operation, located in a tiny space of 3 meters by 10 meters, its narrow shelves and counters loaded up not only with a hodgepodge of competitors' products but also with a bewildering array of seemingly unrelated products, all confusingly displayed. This shop might serve only a few tens of families in a small radius around the outlet, and while there may be hundreds or thousands of similar stores in the market area, it faces almost no competitive threat from any of them, since it has built its business on close relationships with its clientele, often carrying many of them on the cuff over the years. From this retailer's point of view, why should he or she take your product? Where will it fit on the shelf (or what product will have to be dropped)? Will he or she make more money with your product, especially since satisfactory credit terms have already been established with current suppliers? If some of the clients ask for the product as a result of seeing advertising or hearing a friend talk about it, the retailer can very likely "unsell" your product by his or her own sales pitch and established credibility with customers. You may have imagined by now that the shop being described here is in a less-developed country, but in fact similar descriptions can apply to a significant segment of the market in some European countries, especially in the rural areas that still contain a large portion of the population.

Retail stores that seem more similar in appearance to those at home may, on closer inspection, be found to carry quite a different assortment of products. The U.S. drug store, for example, is just as confusing for a foreigner who expects to find mostly medicines, but instead finds an assortment of goods that would only be found in many different specialty stores at home. You may find that a sizable portion of your proposed product entry is sold through street vendors or direct door-to-door salespersons. While it is true that many large retail outlets in the larger cities are becoming more similar the world around, the differences are still present and important. These differences exist because historical and cultural factors have resulted in unique patterns of shopping behavior; your target segment will have definite, deeply rooted expectations concerning where certain goods should be found and what services the dealer should provide.

The key to using retail distribution well is to avoid the most common trap in international marketing analysis—unwittingly using one's home experience when thinking about the structure and behavior of retailers in the target country. By forcing yourself to ask explicit questions about the nature and quantity of the outlets, you will simultaneously be asking questions about the needs of your consumer segments, which is the fundamental marketing analysis you need to do in any event.

Just as the small retailers described can prove to be most influential with their clients, likewise the distributors, brokers, or salespeople who deal with them might also prove to be their most reliable and trusted sources of information. In some cultures, personal relationships among the various intermediaries are vital. Japan is often cited as the premier example of fragmented and confusing distribution that can only be unraveled by the knowledge and personal contacts of a Japanese partner. However, the role of personal contacts is also very important in such countries as Brazil and Italy. The new marketer on the scene cannot expect to break into such markets easily without relying on the established networks of current players. Many marketing plans have failed because the marketer underestimated the time and effort required to establish links with a portion of the market large enough for profitable operation.

When a firm decides to enter international markets, channels of distribution are often its first consideration, since most firms new to international business are reluctant to make fixed commitments to sales offices or factories abroad until they have developed some experience and tangible sales results. The least commitment involves using a domestic exporting firm that may or may not take title to the goods, but that effectively takes over full responsibility for finding sales abroad. The exporter may be a relatively passive vehicle or may work with the firm's marketing department to suggest product modifications for the foreign market. The next level of commitment is for the producing firm to set up its own export or international department, using its own employees to locate attractive foreign markets. The export department can decide to license its technology abroad, thus leaving most production and marketing decisions to the discretion of the foreign licensee. Or the department can find sales companies in the target country to become agents who will obtain distribution. Advertising and product decisions are often retained in the export department at home. With increasing sales and commitment, the exporting firm may find it more profitable to set up a wholly owned sales subsidiary in the foreign country and eventually to set up manufacturing as well under a foreign subsidiary complete with its own marketing, operations, and finance departments.

Marketers of industrial products face one of their greatest challenges in gaining adequate distribution for their products. Companies in industrial fields often have to make major commitments to service and repair centers, spare parts warehousing, and other support functions. Industrial marketers must find ways to gain a local presence that is credible to the local market; this can go as far as building a local plant.

Given the importance of variations in distribution patterns and the resulting necessity for securing local intermediaries who are sensitive to local customs and practices, the international marketer must be prepared to take the time and expend considerable effort to develop lists of names, to visit prospective distributors in person in order to establish their level of ability and interest in the assignment, and to negotiate arrangements that will be both profitable to the company and sufficiently interesting to the distributor to get the extra effort needed for successful introduction. There are various ways to develop a list of prospective names, but, as mentioned in Section 2, the International Trade Administration (ITA) of the U.S. Department of Commerce and its associated offices abroad can do some of the preliminary screening. In particular, the ITA offers an agent distributor service; its U.S. commercial officers in the foreign country conduct a search and then forward a report on as many as six prospects who have examined the company's proposal and have expressed interest in representing it in that country.

Too often in securing a distributor, and indeed in investigating a foreign opportunity, American executives have left too little time for personally visiting the prospective agent to establish interest, to travel through the country with the agent in order to gather evidence firsthand about the possible opportunities, to establish links with retail or industrial customers, and to observe how well the prospective agent deals with these ultimate customers. Reasons for this failure may include a lack of appreciation of how important the international differences are; a fear of the unknown, perhaps augmented by not being able to speak the language; or a simple lack of commitment to the venture. Success depends on the exporter developing strong relationships with the agents, in continuing to nurture those relationships over time, or—if the decision turns out to be a bad one—in having the knowledge and courage to terminate the relationship. Successful international marketing requires a strong commitment on the part of the exporting firm, even if it decides to leave most of the spadework and selling to its agents overseas. Without that commitment, the marketer must either hope for good luck or expect to be very disappointed with the results.

PROMOTION DECISIONS: ADVERTISING AND PERSONAL SELLING

You have the product or service, and your target consumer group will want it. But how do you get the right information about this fact to the right people at the lowest cost? That is the role of the communications part of the marketing mix, commonly referred to as *promotion*. Promotion usually refers to the activities of advertising and personal selling, but it also can include public relations, direct-mail solicitation, point-of-purchase displays, and any other effort to get people to talk about the product. In addition, the promotion effort can be subdivided according to whether the intended audience is the ultimate buyer or some member of the intermediate channels of distribution.

If the intention of the promotion is to persuade the ultimate buyer directly, this is referred to as *pull communication*. Presumably, demand created at the consumer level is sufficient to require an outlet to carry a product; the outlet requires that its distributor stock the item; the distributor in turn orders the product from its wholesaler or from the factory, depending on the levels of distribution. Thus the product has been effectively pulled through the channels of distribution by the success of promotion in generating interest directly at the consumer level. If, on the other hand, the promotion is geared to persuading the various levels of the channels to stock the product, and it is also expected that, by virtue of its stocking the product, each channel will undertake vigorous efforts to sell it to its clients, the promotion is known as *push communication*. The marketer is relying on its channels to move, or push, the product along to the ultimate buyer. A communications strategy is never purely push or pull, but is characterized as being one or the other based on the major thrust of the campaign. One way to gauge a competitor's intentions is to estimate the amount of money it is directing toward each level as a percentage of its total communications budget.

In general, a pull strategy is associated with heavy consumer advertising, whereas the push strategy involves efforts spent on personal selling usually geared to persuading a distributor to stock. In addition to using sales calls, a marketer may provide other incentives for a dealer to stock, including higher margins or a relatively exclusive sales territory.

The concepts of push and pull communications are most useful for a marketing planner when evaluated in conjunction with the product life cycle (PLC). Consideration of where a product is in the PLC in a foreign environment is vital to avoiding insensitive international marketing errors. Early in the product life cycle, because the majority of target consumers know little about the product, they tend to view it as a riskier purchase: Either they risk spending their money on a product that may fail to perform as they expected or to fill a real need, or they risk looking foolish in the eyes of their peers. Both types of risk—*problem solving* risk and *psychological-social* risk—may induce a customer to spend some energy and time gathering more information. The greater the risk as perceived by the customer, the more he or she feels the need to obtain more information.

On the other hand, not all sources of information are considered equally reliable; they can be ranked according to credibility. Friends might be the most credible information source, especially if the friend or acquaintance is an acknowledged "expert" in the product category.

For example, you might ask one friend what kind of tires you should get for your car, but you might ask another friend—a camera buff—what telephoto lens to buy. Next in reliability might be objective reporting in magazines or newspapers, and then might come your own observations as you shop around and talk to sales personnel. Last and least in credibility comes paid advertising. In fact, it is a wonder that advertising works at all, given the low opinion most people express when asked about it in surveys!

Yet advertising works, a fact that has been documented by practitioners and researchers in almost every economy. Advertising works best when other sources of more credible information are either not available or a buyer is unwilling to spend the effort to get it. Since advertising is ubiquitous, it can thus provide information almost by default. The more self-assured buyers are, the more likely they are to rely on their own judgments and experience, and they can effectively use advertising to supplement that information. Thus they can be willing to take more risks—to buy the advertised product—without worrying about whether it will work well, since the risk of failure is now lower. Or they firmly believe that most products are "pretty much alike" and that the differences, mostly minor, can accurately be described by advertising. Or their basis of choice is on attributes that relate more to the image of the product than to its clipboard specifications, and they pick up these positioning differences through the advertising. Advertising seems to work more effectively in the later stages of the product life cycle, since this is when the segment has acquired a great deal of accumulated experience with the product. This is also when products, in the mature phase of the cycle, seem to be differentiated more by advertising (marketing positioning) than by major product differences (product positioning). Conversely, in the earlier stages of the cycle, more information and reassurance on the product's features and performance are required, and the role of the sales force is more important. Despite the relative inefficiency of the sales force in reaching many ultimate consumers, the marketer is willing to spend this money in order to gain distribution, thus pushing the communications effort through the channels of distribution.

In using advertising in other cultures, two major considerations affect the international marketer's thinking. The first, already described, is where the product or service is on the product life cycle in the foreign environments. If enough of the markets abroad are in similar stages and if the product appeals are not much affected by cultural differences, the marketer may have the opportunity to enjoy economies of scale through similar copy points and even the same advertising execution. The second major consideration is how legal and infrastructure differences may affect the opportunities to use the same advertising or the same media plan.

The infrastructure and legal constraints are more obvious than those of the PLC. In some countries, TV is unavailable to much of one's target segment. TV advertising is restricted to a period or two per day, or there are too many advertisers for the time available. Advertising copy that may seem humorous in France may seem frivolous in Switzerland. British advertising has subtle humor and sophisticated tone; many English are offended by the "blatant" TV advertising in the United States. Many countries have strict laws that advertising must be locally produced (in order to protect the local film industry). For these reasons, TV advertising may have to be ruled out and other readily available media used, such as radio, newspapers and magazines, outdoor posters, pamphlets, and movie houses (a medium used more commonly abroad than in the United States).

Some product categories seem to lend themselves more than others to a global approach in advertising. Commonly cited examples of these products are high-priced cosmetics and liquors, watches, and automobiles; here the appeals are to status, which is important to certain segments that can be found in almost any economy. Soft drinks, which in the past have been differentiated more on image connotations than on taste appeals, have been another area where advertising appeals can be standardized. Increasingly, marketers are also discovering another universal segment, the value segment, which is looking for a good quality product at an excellent price. Finally, many industrial products, as opposed to products sold to individual consumers, tend to be sold on clipboard attributes more than on psychological qualities. A purchasing agent in any culture might be looking for the best buy for a product that satisfies basic product specifications; thus there might be an opportunity to use the same product literature with a minimum of translation effort. However, studies of industrial purchasing behavior question the assumption that psychological or social factors are not important and imply that cultural differences may be as important in writing industrial advertising as in consumer advertising.

In looking for opportunities to standardize the basic advertising appeal, an international marketer does not expect to be able to produce a video advertisement at home, for example, and then dub in the local language. Often the copy, the shooting, and other aspects of the execution must be tailored to fit local customs or to take advantage of local competitive strengths and situations. However, all advertising abroad can be reviewed in the central headquarters for its consistency with the global strategy. This allows the company to use the best research and copy talent to develop the basic advertising platform and to use these same resources to evaluate the job being done by the local managers and agencies. Since all languages are rich in nuance and all cultures are unique, it makes sense to let the local agencies develop the actual copy, given that the local manager can find talented and hard-working agency people.

CONCLUSION

The four P's of the marketing mix and the three p's of people, profits, and politics are as useful in international marketing analysis and execution as they are at home. The differences in implementation are due to differences in the culture, infrastructure, and legal environment. Thus international marketers must be careful to devote as much effort to researching these differences as they usually spend in analyzing consumer motivations and market segmentation.

There is one common pitfall in the analysis: forgetting to take into account the differences. When reading these cases, be sensitive to those differences mentioned by the case writer, but also question data or behaviors that don't seem to make sense to you. And it's a good idea to state your own assumptions out loud or in writing. For example, when the case mentions "grocers," be sure that you aren't unwittingly thinking in terms of the Safeway down the street. When the case mentions TV advertising, are you thinking about half-minute spots scattered throughout the program, all in full color? When the case mentions "market," are you thinking about the enclosed mall out in the suburbs, or are you thinking about a row of small specialty shops, with merchants selling similar products, all clustered together? If you remember to ask specific questions about the marketing infrastructure in some detail, then you have most likely avoided the trap and advanced toward intelligent international marketing analysis.

Pakkasakku Oy:
Communicating with Customers

In the words of Mauri Hattunen, managing director of Pakkasakku, the "starter battery business is not a fancy business." He was referring to the management challenges of operating in a fairly stagnant, competitive, and low-margin business such as that of Finland's domestic starter batteries. Nonetheless, in this tough environment the management was aiming for improved profitability through a combination of productivity improvement and cost-cutting measures, in addition to innovative marketing strategies.

In recent months, two issues related to the domestic replacement market had caught the management's attention. One had to do with the productivity of Pakkasakku's domestic sales force, which some in the management believed was below acceptable levels. The other issue dealt with the role of media advertising in the company's marketing strategy. Early results from the first extensive TV advertising campaign ever undertaken showed relatively high awareness and recall rates for the advertised product, the new Super Power battery. Reviewing these results, Hattunen was wondering if some of the funds now devoted to the sales force should not be channeled to media advertising or sales promotion in order to strengthen the company's standing in the market.

BACKGROUND

Pakkasakku was a division of Neste Corporation, the largest industrial firm in Finland. The parent's other divisions operated in diverse sectors of energy, chemicals, and shipping. Among products produced by Pakkasakku's sister companies were refined petrochemicals, automative lubricants, liquid gas, and basic industrial chemicals. Pakkasakku's product line included, in addition to starter batteries, a variety of industrial batteries for electric vehicles (such as lift trucks), stationary sources of electricity (such as for standby emergency systems), and submarines.

The domestic market in Finland for replacement starter batteries was estimated to be around 400,000 units or approximately FM 95 million at retail prices. Like other lead–acid battery markets in Western Europe, the Finnish market was stagnant and highly competitive. Pakkasakku and Salama, the other local manufacturer and subsidiary of Germany's Varta, each accounted for approximately 35% of the market. In addition, low-priced imports from as far away as Japan and Korea were responsible for a rising share of sales in the replacement market, reaching an estimated 30% of total units in recent years.

Pakkasakku was believed to have a respectable level of manufacturing productivity due to

This case was prepared by Professor Kamran Kashani as a basis for class discussion rather than to illustrate either effective or ineffective handling of an administrative situation. Copyright © 1986 by IMEDE (International Management Development Institute), Lausanne, Switzerland. The International Institute for Management Development (IMD), resulting from the merger between IMEDE, Lausanne, and IMI, Geneva, acquires and retains all rights. Not to be used or reproduced without written permission from IMD, Lausanne, Switzerland.

its flexible production process and modern facilities. Low production cost was becoming increasingly a critical factor for success in the competitive starter battery market. Hence some observers believed that a restructuring of the European industry was imminent. Furthermore, a long-term threat to the industry came from new concepts (including nickle–cadmium, bipolar, and other batteries) replacing the old but low-cost lead–acid technology.

Pakkasakku's total unit production was divided between starter (two-thirds) and industrial (one-third) batteries. Of the company's annual production of 170,000 starter batteries for the domestic market, close to 130,000 were destined for replacement and the rest for the original equipment manufacturers. Exports accounted for approximately 30% of Pakkasakku's overall unit production.

According to management, an average starter battery selling to consumers at FM 250 had the following approximate breakdown of costs and contribution margins:

	Consumer retail price	FM 250[1]
less:	Sales tax (15%)	40
	Retail margin	60
	Manufacturer selling price	150
less:	Unit production cost	95
	Sales force and distribution	30
	Manufacturer margin	FM 25

The manufacturer margin had to cover all administrative overhead, including advertising, and profits. Retail margins for imports were believed to be less, while importers' margins were about the same.

In the replacement market, where batteries were bought by car owners, brand reputation was thought by some to play an important role. Equally important to the success in this market was believed to be the intensity and support of the distribution channel. Cost of production and consumer prices were considered by these executives to be of secondary importance in the domestic replacement market.

---

[1] One Finnish markka = 0.21 U.S. dollar = 0.33 Swiss franc.

As with the rest of Europe, the retail distribution channels for starter batteries in Finland were undergoing gradual change. The role of specialists was declining in the total sales of batteries, while those of gas stations, mass merchandizers (including farmers' cooperatives), and hardware stores were on the rise. This continual move away from specialist retail outlets, where consumers received "expert" advice on different batteries, was thought to have a lasting impact on marketing of starter batteries.

Both Pakkasakku and its Finnish rival sold through an intensive retail network covering all channels and about two-thirds of all outlets, estimated at around 3,500 locations. The two companies charged similar prices for their batteries and offered approximately the same retail margins.

PERSONAL SELLING

For the domestic replacement market, Pakkasakku employed 22 people in its sales force, consisting of 11 field and 2 phone salesmen and 9 branch and administrative personnel. In the past, the geographically organized sales force was the primary vehicle for communicating with the company's immediate customers, the members of the trade, and the distribution channel. The field force's functions included customer visits, usually to familiar accounts estimated at around 1,500. These visits allowed salespeople to check on inventories, help with promotional displays, and take orders. The selling of starter batteries was concentrated primarily in the last half of the year. Salama, the company's only Finnish rival, was thought to maintain a sales force slightly larger than that of Pakkasakku.

Last year, the 22-person sales force cost Pakkasakku a total of FM 3.5 million. Of this, salaries accounted for 73%, traveling expenses for 16%, and branch expenses for the rest. The amount spent on personal selling compared with FM 1 million spent on media advertising and FM 200,000 on sales promotion, including dealer conferences, contests, and posters.

SUPER POWER AND MEDIA ADVERTISING

Last year's advertising campaign for the Super Power battery was Pakkasakku's first departure from its past strategy of not utilizing mass advertising in its communication strategy. The other local manufacturer had also refrained from using advertising extensively.

Super Power was first introduced 2 years ago with a modest advertising budget of FM 200,000 spent primarily on roadside billboards. The product was an addition to Pakkasakku's starter battery line, and the first to be based on the American SAE standards. The company's other batteries followed the European DIN standards promoted heavily by the Varta group. The SAE standard batteries had a lower capacity when measured in hours of discharge, but a higher cold cranking power. "Super Power is a standard battery, but its higher starting power in cold weather allowed us to differentiate it from competitive products," explained one executive. Compared with other batteries, Super Power cost approximately FM 10 less per unit to produce because it required less lead in manufacturing.

According to management, improved profitability was the main motivation behind Super Power's addition to the line. The product's higher ex-factory price allowed Pakkasakku a better contribution margin than the other starter batteries. The margin averaged about FM 80 per unit after production costs, but before sales force and distribution costs. Although consumer retail prices varied among outlets, it was believed that retail margins were also somewhat higher on Super Power.

The first year's initial advertising for Super Power was judged inadequate after a postcampaign survey of replacement battery consumers. The survey, covering male adults between 20 and 40 years of age, showed that Pakkasakku trailed Salama in consumer brand awareness. Only 50% of respondents recognized Pakkasakku versus 60% for Salama. In the survey, merely 6% could identify Super Power.

Last year's campaign was designed with the double objectives of (1) informing the target buyers that Pakkasakku was a part of NESTE, which, it was felt, stood for quality in the public's eyes and (2) promoting Super Power as a battery that "started any car in any climate." It was also decided to use TV as the main medium for the campaign, which had now an expanded budget of FM 1 million. A commercial was prepared showing a car stalling in the cold while another one, a small Citroën 2 CV, started quickly thanks to the Super Power battery. The 30-second spot was accompanied by a famous melody with the words "We only come here to visit and not to stay . . ." (in Finnish, the word *visit* also means *start*). Exhibit 1 shows the storyboard for the commercial.

The campaign's budget was spent on 20 spots that were broadcast between mid-October and mid-November last year. It was felt that a concentrated broadcasting schedule had much more impact than one spread over several months. The early results from the TV campaign were encouraging. In particular, awareness and recall rates achieved were judged as excellent. Exhibit 2 shows highlights of the results measured at the end of the campaign.

MANAGEMENT DISCUSSION

Although the Super Power campaign was Pakkasakku's first experiment with mass media advertising, a number of people in management believed that the practice should be continued. They pointed out that advertising had a high impact when it was most needed, that is during the peak of battery-buying season. It also gave the company an edge over the other local manufacturer, who abstained from heavy advertising because of poor profitability. Thus, these managers argued, advertising was a more effective competitive weapon than price, which was expensive and often not very effective. In fact, the company's recent price increases on all of its starter batteries had been matched closely by the other firm.

Advocates of media advertising also argued that in promoting starter batteries the company's sales force was not doing a satisfactory job. One executive explained this point of view as follows:

The new Super Power Hybrid battery from Pakkasakku

Superior Pakkasakku

Starting again and again, the melody stops quickly....

Another car is starting success-fully, and the melody starts again, now with a song.

Snow and howling of the cold wind

Starting sound which changes into the melody "we only come here to visit and not to stay..."

Starting as in the summer

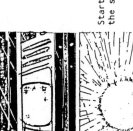
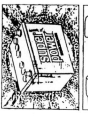
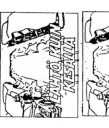

EXHIBIT 1 Super Power Commercial Storyboard

EXHIBIT 2 Highlights of Postcampaign Survey Results (%)

1. *Recall of Advertising*

	Super Power Campaign	Average of Neste TV Campaigns	Average of Other Campaigns	Range of All Campaigns
Spontaneous	53	34	26	0–65
Total awareness	87	62	54	10–93

2. *What Campaign Communicated:* Among those aware of the commercial, the name of the product was remembered as follows:

Pakkasakku	32
Nesteen Pakkasakku	20
Nesteen Akku	7
Nesteen Super Power	7
Pakkasakkun Super Power	3
Salama	1
Others	8
Could not remember	22

Of those who recalled the commercial, 77% mentioned correct product name or NESTE, 62% thought it gave a positive impression of the battery, 9% gave negative feedback, and 10% mentioned that the battery is Finnish.

Source: Advertising agency.

Personal selling is an expensive luxury that we can't afford when our profits are under pressure and every effort is being made to increase productivity and reduce overhead. The problem is partly due to the fact that the sales force is practically idle for half of the year because the selling season is only 6 months long. Besides, I think we don't have a highly motivated sales force to begin with. They are for the most part old timers with traditional attitudes toward selling. A smaller, more aggressive sales force would free up funds that can be spent on consumer advertising.

These opinions were not shared by others in the management. One advocate of maintaining a large sales force explained his reasons as follows:

It is true that selling is concentrated in a few months, but that's an opportunity not a problem. We could use our sales force to sell other products such as those produced by sister companies, like liquid gas or lubricants, to the same channels during the rest of the year. The low level of performance is less of a sales force problem than a management issue. We don't have the right people, because our salaries don't attract highly skilled salespeople. Nor do we have the right sales incentives. Right now, incentives account for about a month's salary per year. That's not much of an incentive; it should be more like 30% to provide sufficient motivation for high performance. Advertising can't replace good trade selling, which only a highly motivated sales force can do.

An unresolved issue in the management discussion on the relative emphasis of media advertising versus personal selling was the role of dealer influence on consumer decision about what type and brand of a battery to buy. While admitting that dealers did exert some influence on the final decision, advocates of more advertising believed this influence was not absolute. One executive explained: "I think the consumer asks the dealer for his opinion, but given a choice among equal alternatives, he or she will buy the one with the most recognizable name and features. And that's the job of advertising." Some also thought that, with the trend away from the specialist dealers, the consumer would be relying more on his or her own assessment of different batteries. Hence, they argued, the opportunity for consumer education through advertising.

Others in the management thought it risky to put too much emphasis on consumer advertising because the dealer was still the most important source of influence. They believed a personal relationship between the sales force and the dealer was the best guarantee of dealer loyalty for the company and its products.

CONCLUSION

Hattunen was keenly interested in the ongoing discussions regarding the company's communication strategy. He felt this was an important issue for Pakkasakku's standing in the domestic market. He also felt that both sides of the debate had certain valid arguments. For example, he agreed with those who saw a "sleepy atmosphere" in the company's sales organization. He wanted to see a vibrant, performance-oriented sales force "in spite of the fact that we at NESTE have never been good at direct selling." On the other hand, he believed a good name and product image were important to successful marketing of starter batteries. He pointed to the results of the recent campaign, which showed more than 60% of those who recalled the Super Power TV commercial thought positively of the battery. Nevertheless, he sensed some resistance to the idea of media advertising among the old-timers in the company.

For Hattunen, the issue of Pakkasakku's strategy for communicating with its customers boiled down to how much should be spent on sales force relative to advertising or sales promotion. He was wondering if the current level and division of the FM 4.7 million budget among the three communication elements was an appropriate one. He was keenly aware that any savings here could help the company's drive for improved profitability.

Mediquip S.A. (R)

On December 18, Kurt Thaldorf, a sales engineer for the German sales subsidiary of Mediquip, S.A., was informed by Lohmann University Hospital in Stuttgart that it had decided to place an order with Sigma, a Dutch competitor, for a CT scanner. The hospital's decision came as disappointing news to Thaldorf, who had worked for nearly 8 months on the account. The order, if obtained, would have meant a sale of DM 2,370,000 for the sales engineer.[1] He was convinced that Mediquip's CT scanner was technologically superior to Sigma's and, overall, a better product.

Thaldorf began a review of his call reports in order to better understand the factors that had led to Lohmann University Hospital's decision. He wanted to apply the lessons from this experience to future sales situations.

BACKGROUND

At the time, the computer tomography (CT) scanner was a relatively recent product in the field of diagnostic imaging. This medical device, used for diagnostic purposes, allowed examination of cross sections of the human body through the display of images. CT scanners combined sophisticated X-ray equipment with a computer to collect the necessary data and translate them into visual images.

When computer tomography was first introduced in the late 1960s, radiologists had hailed it as a major technological breakthrough. Commenting on the advantages of CT scanners, a product specialist with Mediquip said, "The end product looks very much like an X-ray image. The only difference is that with scanners you can see sections of the body that were never seen before on a screen—like the pancreas. A radiologist, for example, can diagnose cancer of the pancreas in less than 2 weeks after it develops. This was not possible before CT scanners."

Mediquip was a subsidiary of Technologie Universelle, a French conglomerate. The company's product line included, in addition to CT scanners, X-ray, ultrasonic, and nuclear diagnostic equipment. Mediquip enjoyed a worldwide reputation for advanced technology and competent after-sales service.

"Our competitors are mostly from other European countries," commented Mediquip's sales director for Europe. "In some markets they have been there longer than we have, and they know the decision-makers better than we do. But we are learning fast." Sigma, the subsidiary of a diversified Dutch company under the same name, was the company's most serious competitor. Other major contenders in

---

[1] For the purposes of this case, use the following exchange rates for the deutsch mark (DM): DM 1.00 = SF 0.85, $0.60, Ecu 0.50, £0.35.

This case was prepared by Professor Kamran Kashani as a basis for class discussion rather than to illustrate either effective or ineffective handling of a business situation. All names and financial data have been disguised. Copyright © 1991 by the International Institute for Management Development (IMD), Lausanne, Switzerland. IMD retains all rights. Not to be used or reproduced without written permission from IMD, Lausanne, Switzerland.

the CT scanner market were FNC, Eldora, Magna, and Piper.

Mediquip executives estimated the European market for CT scanners to be around 200 units per year. They pointed out that prices ranged from DM1.5 to DM3.0 million per unit. The company's CT scanner sold in the upper end of the price range. "Our equipment is at least 2 years ahead of our most advanced competition," explained a sales executive. "And our price reflects this technological superiority."

Mediquip's sales organization in Europe included eight country sales subsidiaries, each headed by a managing director. Within each country, sales engineers reported to regional sales managers who, in turn, reported to the managing director. Product specialists provided technical support to the sales force in each country.

BUYERS OF CT SCANNERS

A sales executive at Mediquip described the buyers of CT scanners as follows:

Most of our sales are to what we call the public sector, health agencies that are either government-owned or belong to nonprofit support organizations such as universities and philanthropic institutions. They are the sort of buyers that buy through formal tenders and have to budget their purchases at least one year in advance. Once the budget is allocated, it must then be spent before the end of the year. Only a minor share of our CT scanner sales goes to the private sector, profit-oriented organizations such as private hospitals or private radiologists.

Of the two markets, the public sector is much more complex. Typically, there are at least four groups that get involved in the purchase decision: radiologists, physicists, administrators, and people from the supporting agency—usually the ones who approve the budget for purchasing a CT scanner.

Radiologists are the ones who use the equipment. They are doctors whose diagnostic services are sought by other doctors in the hospital or clinic. Patients remember their doctors, but not the radiologists. They never receive flowers from the patients! A CT scanner could really enhance their professional image among their colleagues.

Physicists are the scientists in residence. They write the technical specifications that competing CT scanners must meet; they should know the state of the art in X-ray technology. Their primary concern is the patient's safety.

The administrators are, well, administrators. They have the financial responsibility for their organizations. They are concerned with the cost of CT scanners, but also with what revenues they can generate. The administrators are extremely wary of purchasing an expensive technological toy that will become obsolete in a few years.

The people from the supporting agency are usually not directly involved with decisions as to which product to purchase. But, since they must approve the expenditures, they do play an indirect role. Their influence is mostly felt by the administrators.

The interplay among the four groups, as you can imagine, is rather complex. The power of each group in relationship to the others varies from organization to organization. The administrator, for example, is the top decision maker in certain hospitals. In others, he is only a buyer. One of the key tasks of our sales engineers is to define for each potential account the relative power of the players. Only then can they set priorities and formulate selling strategies.

The European sales organization at Mediquip had recently started using a series of forms designed to help sales engineers in their account analysis and strategy formulation. (*A sample of the forms, called Account Management Analysis, is reproduced in Exhibit 1.*)

LOHMANN UNIVERSITY HOSPITAL

Lohmann University Hospital (LUH) was a large general hospital serving Stuttgart, a city of 1 million residents. The hospital was part of the university's medical school. The university was a leading teaching center and enjoyed an excellent reputation. LUH's radiology department had a wide range of X-ray equipment from a number of European manufacturers, including Sigma and FNC. The radiology department had five staff members, headed by a senior and nationally known radiologist, Professor Steinborn.

Thaldorf's Sales Activities

From the records he had kept of his sales calls, Thaldorf reviewed the events for the pe-

Key Account: _____

ACCOUNT MANAGEMENT ANALYSIS

The enclosed forms are designed to facilitate your management of:

1   A key sales account
2   The *Mediquip* resources that can be applied to this key account

Completing the enclosed forms, you will:

- Identify installed equipment, and planned or potential new equipment
- Analyze purchase decision process and influence patterns, including:
  —Identify and prioritize all major sources of influence
  —Project probable sequence of events and timing of decision process
  —Assess position/interest of each major influence source
  —Identify major competition and probable strategies
  —Identify needed information/support
- Establish an account development strategy, including:
  —Select key contacts
  —Establish strategy and tactics for each key contact, identify appropriate *Mediquip* personnel
  —Assess plans for the most effective use of local team and headquarters resources

KEY ACCOUNT DATA

☐ Original (Date:_____)   Account No.: _____   Type of Institute:_____

☐ Revision (Date: _____)   Sales Specialist: _____   Bed Size: _____

                                     Country/Region/District: _____   Telephone: _____

1. CUSTOMER (HOSPITAL, CLINIC, PRIVATE INSTITUTE)

Name: _____

Street Address: _____

City, State: _____

2. DECISION MAKERS — IMPORTANT CONTACTS.

INDIVIDUALS	NAME	SPECIALTY	REMARKS
Medical Staff			
Administration			
Local Government			
State Government			

EXHIBIT 1   Account Management Analysis Forms (condensed version)

3. INSTALLED EQUIPMENT

TYPE	DESCRIPTION	SUPPLIED BY	INSTALLATION DATE	YEAR TO REPLACE	VALUE OF POTENTIAL ORDER
X-ray Nuclear Ultrasound RTP CT					

4. PLANNED NEW EQUIPMENT

TYPE	QUOTE NO.	QUOTE DATE	% CHANCE	EST. ORDER DATE 1980	EST. ORDER DATE 1981	EST. DELIVERY 1980	EST. DELIVERY 1981	QUOTED PRICE

5. COMPETITION

COMPANY/PRODUCT	STRATEGY/ TACTICS	% CHANCE	STRENGTH	WEAKNESS

6. SALES PLAN Product:_____ Quote No: _____ Quoted Price: _____

KEY ISSUES	*Mediquip's* PLAN	SUPPORT NEEDED FROM:	DATE OF FOLLOW-UP/REMARKS

7. ACTIONS – IN SUPPORT OF PLAN

SPECIFIC ACTION	RESPONSIBILITY	DUE DATES ORIGINAL	DUE DATES REVISED	COMPLETED	RESULTS/REMARKS

8. ORDER STATUS REPORT

REVISION DATE	ACCOUNT NAME AND LOCATION	ISSUES/COMPETITIVE STRATEGY	ACTIONS/ STRATEGY	RESPON- SIBILITY	% CHANCE	EXPECTED ORDER TIMING	WIN/LOSE

EXHIBIT 1 Account Management Analysis Forms (condensed version)

riod between May 5, when he learned of LUH's interest in purchasing a CT scanner and December 18, when he was informed that Mediquip had lost the order.

May 5

Office received a call from a Professor Steinborn from Lohmann University Hospital regarding a CT scanner. I was assigned to make the call on the professor. Looked through our files to find out if we had sold anything to the hospital before. We had not. Made an appointment to see the professor on May 9.

May 9

Called on Professor Steinborn who informed me of a recent decision by university directors to set aside funds next year for the purchase of the hospital's first CT scanner. The professor wanted to know what we had to offer. Described the general features of our CT system. Gave him some brochures. Asked a few questions, which led me to believe other companies had come to see him before I did. Told me to check with Dr. Rufer, the hospital's physicist, regarding the specs. Made an appointment to see him again 10 days later. Called on Dr. Rufer, who was not there. His secretary gave me a lengthy document on the scanner specs.

May 10

Read the specs last night. Looked like they had been copied straight from somebody's technical manual. Showed them to our product specialist, who confirmed my own hunch that our system met and exceeded the specs. Made an appointment to see Dr. Rufer next week.

May 15

Called on Dr. Rufer. Told him about our system's features and the fact that we met all the specs set down on the document. He did not seem particularly impressed. Left him with technical documents about our system.

May 19

Called on Professor Steinborn. He had read the material I had left with him. Seemed rather pleased with the features. Asked about our upgrading scheme. Told him we would undertake to upgrade the system as new features became available. Explained that Mediquip, unlike other systems, can be made to accommodate the latest technology, with no risk of obsolescence for a long time. This impressed him. Also answered his questions regarding image manipulation, image processing speed, and our service capability. Just before I left, he inquired about our price. Told him I would have an informative quote for him at our next meeting. Made an appointment to see him on June 23 after he returned from his vacation. Told me to get in touch with Carl Hartmann, the hospital's general director, in the interim.

June 1

Called on Hartmann. It was difficult to get an appointment with him. Told him about our interest in supplying his hospital with our CT scanner, which met all the specs as defined by Dr. Rufer. Also informed him of our excellent service capability. He wanted to know which other hospitals in the country had purchased our system. Told him I would provide him with a list of buyers within a few days. He asked about the price. Gave him an informative quote of DM 2,850,000—a price my boss and I had determined after my visit to Professor Steinborn. He shook his head saying, "Other scanners are cheaper by a wide margin." I explained that our price reflected the fact that the latest technology was already built into our scanner. Also mentioned that the price differential was an investment that could pay for itself several times over through faster speed of operation. He was noncommittal. Before leaving his office, he instructed me not to talk to anybody else about the price. Asked him specifically if that included Professor Steinborn. He said it did. Left him with a lot of material about our system.

June 3

Went to Hartmann's office with a list of three hospitals similar in size to LUH that had installed our system. He was out. Left it with his secretary who recognized me. Learned from her that at least two other firms, Sigma and FNC, were competing for the order. She also volunteered the information that "prices are so different, Mr. Hartmann is confused." She added that the final decision will be made by a committee made up of Hartmann, Professor Steinborn, and one other person whom she could not recall.

June 20

Called on Dr. Rufer. Asked him if he had read the material about our system. He had, but did not have much to say. I repeated some of the key operational advantages our product enjoyed over those produced by others, including Sigma and FNC. Left him some more technical documents.

On the way out, stopped by Hartmann's office. His secretary told me that we had received favorable comments from the hospitals using our system.

June 23

Professor Steinborn was flabbergasted to hear that I could not discuss our price with him. Told him about the hospital administration's instructions to that effect. He could not believe this, especially when Sigma had already given him their quote of DM 2,100,000. When he calmed down, he wanted to know if we were going to be at least competitive with the others. Told him our system was more advanced than Sigma's. Promised him we would do our best to come up with an attractive offer. Then we talked about his vacation and sailing experience in the Aegean Sea. He said he loved the Greek food.

July 15

Called to see if Hartmann had returned from his vacation. He had. While checking his calendar, his secretary told me that our system seemed to be the "radiologists' choice," but that Hartmann had not yet made up his mind.

July 30

Visited Hartmann accompanied by the regional manager. Hartmann seemed to have a fixation about the price. He said, "All the companies claim they have the latest technology." So he could not understand why our offer was "so much above the rest." He concluded that only a "very attractive price" could tip the balance in our favor. After repeating the operational advantages our system enjoyed over others, including those produced by Sigma and FNC, my boss indicated that we were willing to lower our price to DM 2,610,000 if the equipment were ordered before the end of the current year. Hartmann said he would consider the offer and seek "objective" expert opinion. He also said a decision would be made before Christmas.

August 14

Called on Professor Steinborn, who was too busy to see me for more than 10 minutes. He wanted to know if we had lowered our price since the last meeting with him. I said we had. He shook his head and said with a laugh, "Maybe that was not your best offer." He then wanted to know how fast we could make deliveries. Told him within 6 months. He did not say anything.

September 2

The regional manager and I discussed the desirability of inviting one or more people from the LUH to visit the Mediquip headquarter operations near Paris. The three-day trip would given the participants a chance to see the scope of the facilities and become better acquainted with CT scanner applications. This idea was finally rejected as inappropriate.

September 3

Dropped in to see Hartmann. He was busy but had time to ask for a formal "final offer" from us by October 1. On the way out, his secretary told me there had been "a lot of heated discussions" about which scanner seemed best suited for the hospital. She would not say more.

September 25

The question of price was raised in a meeting with the regional manager and the managing director. I had recommended a sizable cut in our price to win the order. The regional manager seemed to agree with me, but the managing director was reluctant. His concern was that too big a drop in price looked "unhealthy." They finally agreed to a final offer of DM 2,370,000.

Made an appointment to see Hartmann later that week.

September 29

Took our offer of DM 2,370,000 in a sealed envelope to Hartmann. He did not open it, but he said he hoped the scanner question would soon be resolved to the "satisfaction of all concerned." Asked him how the decision was going to be made. He evaded the question but said he would notify us as soon as a decision was reached. Left his office feeling that our price had a good chance of being accepted.

October 20

Called on Professor Steinborn. He had nothing to tell me except that "the CT scanner is the last thing I want to talk about." Felt he was unhappy with the way things were going.

Tried to make an appointment with Hartmann in November, but he was too busy.

November 5

Called on Hartmann, who told me that a decision would probably not be reached before next month. He indicated that our price was "within the range," but that all the competing systems were being evaluated to see which seemed most appropriate for the hospital. He repeated that he would call us when a decision was reached.

December 18

Received a brief letter from Hartmann thanking Mediquip for participating in the bid for the CT scanner, along with the announcement that LUH had decided to place the order with Sigma.

Club Med España

Jean-Michel Landau, the newly appointed managing director of Club Med España, was eager to proceed with his plans to launch a full-scale marketing and sales effort for the Spanish market. It was February 3, 1992, and in less than 2 weeks Club Med would be holding a press conference in Madrid to announce its first major communications campaign aimed at Spanish holiday travelers. With vacation spending rising at an annual rate of 32%, Spain was one of Europe's fastest growing markets for package holidays. In fact, some managers at "The Club" feared that they had waited too long to exploit the Spanish market and that sales opportunities had been lost; consequently, there were high expectations that, once a formal communication campaign was launched, sales in Spain would quickly blossom.

Jean-Michel's communications budget for the Spanish market was limited. Jean-Michel knew that he would have to employ an effective mix of communication techniques in order to promote the product, while at the same time generating enough sales over the next few seasons to continue funding his marketing efforts. Should he emphasize the unique Club Med concept through media advertising? Or should he focus directly on his distributors and target customers? What was the most effective means of reaching his target audience? How

effectively would he be able to measure the results as the season progressed so that he could modify his strategy appropriately for the next season?

As he considered these issues, Jean-Michel thought back on his successful years as marketing manager for Club Med's biggest market—France. "Spain is a different kind of challenge," he said, "but here in Spain, I have a brand new market, and there are no constraints on how I operate. I can build this organization from the bottom up."

BACKGROUND

Club Mediterranée was founded in 1950 by Georges Blitz who, along with a group of friends, developed the Club as an association devoted to sports and seaside vacations. Originally, the Club was a nonprofit organization, and during their travels the members adhered to a set of principles encompassing rustic, communal life. By 1954, as the organization grew increasingly popular, Blitz asked Gilbert Trigano, whose family business supplied the Club with tents, to take over management of the Club. Trigano accepted, and sensing the commercial potential of the Club's concept, he transformed the organization into a profitable enterprise.

This case was prepared by Research Associate Alex Bloom, under the supervision of Professor Dominique Turpin, as a basis for class discussion rather than to illustrate either effective or ineffective handling of a business situation. Copyright © 1993 by the International Institute for Management Development (IMD), Lausanne, Switzerland. IMD retains all rights. Not to be used or reproduced without written permission from IMD, Lausanne, Switzerland.

The Club Med Concept

The Club's venue began to evolve when, in 1954, Club Med under Trigano's management opened its first straw hut village. Social life at the village also took its formal shape; customers were named *gentils membres* (GMs) or "nice members," and staff were referred to as *gentils organisateurs* (GOs) or "nice organizers." The GO's role in the village was, in the words of the Club, that of a "friend rather than a servant." Much of the Club's appeal stemmed from the daily games and sports activities that the GOs would organize and the nightly amateur entertainment that the GOs would perform, often with the GMs themselves participating. Each resort was run by a *chef de village* who was responsible for village operations, as well as for hosting and entertaining the GMs. These *chefs de village*, who would move from village to village each season, soon attained fame both within Club Med and among its loyal GMs.

The Club Med vacation was sold as an all-inclusive package, including transportation, food, entertainment, sports, and activities. This was integral to the Club's principles of egalitarianism and communal interaction at the village. For example, instead of using money, GMs would pay for any extras (usually drinks) with beads taken from a necklace; and at mealtimes, GMs and GOs alike would sit together at tables of eight. Furthermore, the hassles of modern civilization—such as telephones, televisions, and even newspapers—were not provided or allowed in the villages.

Globalization

As Club Med's unique vacation concept attained fame and success, the company expanded its operations by opening new villages at prime locations around the world. The first snow village was opened in Switzerland in 1956, and over the next decade villages were opened throughout Europe and North Africa. In 1968, a village was opened in Guadeloupe in the Caribbean; in 1979, villages opened in South America, New Caledonia, and Malaysia. The first village in the United States was opened in 1980, and the first one in Japan was opened in 1987. By 1990, Club Med operated over 100 villages in 33 countries around the world and employed over 24,000 people.

Sales had also expanded around the world. Countries like Belgium, Italy, and Germany had provided strong customer bases from early on in the Club's history; North and South American markets were cultivated during the 1970s, and, more recently, sales had been growing rapidly in Japan and the Far East. Club Med's target in Japan was ambitious: 200,000 members by 1999 from 50,000 in fiscal year 1989. By 1990, with sales offices in 26 countries, Club Med's global revenues had reached FF 8.2 billion.[1] Sixty-two percent of their customers came from Europe, 20% from North America, and 12% from Japan and the Far East. France, with 431,700 GMs, was still the Club's largest single market, providing over 35% of its total customer base.

Global expansion was not painless, however. As sales grew outside France, it became apparent that village operations had to be modified to accommodate the demands of non-French GMs. Consequently, GOs were hired from different nationalities in order to address any cultural or language problems that might arise, menus were modified to cater to non-French tastes when necessary (Japanese GMs, for example, expected seaweed for breakfast rather than croissants), and bookings were controlled in order to balance the mix of nationalities at the villages. GOs and GMs from around the world mixing together in Club Med villages gave the product an "international" character, but created a complex logistical tangle between marketing and operations.

Sales and Marketing

New markets were typically launched by opening a Club Med agency (or "boutique") that would sell directly to the public while serving as a base for operations. In the larger, more highly penetrated markets, the bulk of the sales were made through independent travel

---

[1] 1990 average market exchange rate: 1US$ = FF 5.4453.

agents; the boutiques continued to play an important role, however, serving as information outlets and reinforcing the Club's image through their presence in metropolitan centers. Besides, sales made through the boutiques normally yielded better margins than those made through travel agencies.

Club Med focused on providing outstanding service to its GMs. A sophisticated customer feedback survey, known internally as the *baromètre* (or "barometer"), was used to monitor GM satisfaction, and the results of the survey were used to measure the performance of the village managers and their GO teams. Consequently, the repeat purchase rate for Club Med products was typically high (the repeat purchase rate in France, for example, was 70%), and many GMs returned to the Club year after year for their holidays.

Product Evolution and Diversification

While much of the early Club Med concept remained as an integral part of the village experience, attention to GM satisfaction and changing tastes had led to an evolution of the product. Upscale activities (such as golf) were added, special facilities were created to accommodate children, and the product line now ranged from straw-hut villages and bungalows to luxury resorts. Most villages now had locks on the rooms, and the Club had become sensitive to criticisms of being "overorganized."

In addition to its village holidays, Club Med had begun to diversify into other, related activities. Club Med villages were marketed to corporate customers for seminars, conferences, and incentive trips through the Club Med Business program; luxury yachts (the Club Med One and Club Med Two) offered cruise packages in the Mediterranean and the Caribbean or the Pacific. A City Club was opened in downtown Vienna, and Club Med subsidiaries operated time-share holiday villas.

CLUB MED IN SPAIN

Club Med's presence in Spain began in 1962 when the company opened a hut village in

Cadaquès on the Costa Brava, a resort area on the Mediterranean Sea. Since then, four more villages were opened, bringing total capacity to over 4,000 beds. The most recent village, an upscale resort hotel in Ibiza, was opened in 1990. Two of the villages were operated during both the summer and winter seasons, while the remaining three operated as summer villages only.

Club Med began selling its holiday packages to Spanish vacationers in the mid-1970s through Club de Vanguardia, a local tour operator. In 1982, the Club opened a boutique in Barcelona, where most of its customers were concentrated. The boutique sold Club Med holidays directly to the Spanish public, while at the same time serving as a base for managing village operations in Spain. Parallel to the opening of the Barcelona boutique, Club Med made its products available for distribution by most leading travel agencies in Spain. Promotion of the product was left to word of mouth and to the travel agents, who received a standard commission (5% to 8% on the retail price) for every sale.

Sales during the 1990–1991 season alone totaled 7,000 bookings, representing about 8,000 customers with revenues reaching Pta 450 million.[2] Thirty-nine percent of these revenues were from group sales to companies using Club Med villages for conferences, seminars, or incentive trips. Awareness of the product (1.5% in 1990) remained low in Spain, but the unfostered growth in sales led Club Med management in Paris to conclude that the Club Med vacation should be marketed more actively to the Spanish market. Italy was cited as an example of a country where, some years earlier, conditions had been similar to those currently existing in Spain; Italy had since grown to become Club Med's largest market in Europe outside France.

Jean-Michel Landau

Jean-Michel Landau, 42, was a veteran Club Med manager. Born in Southern France, he

---

[2] 1990 average market exchange rate: 1US$ = Pta 10.19.

grew up in North Africa where he joined Club Med at the age of 19. He soon became a *chef de village* and eventually moved into management, heading Club Med country offices in Mexico, Tunisia, Italy, and Canada. Prior to taking over the Spanish office in October 1991, he had spent 6 years as head of marketing and sales activities in France. Under Jean-Michel, sales in France were the highest they had ever been for Club Med, reaching revenues of FF 2.3 billion in 1989.

"As marketing manager in France," explained Jean-Michel, "you are not allowed any mistakes. One percent loss of market share in France represents a tremendous amount of money to the Club." In contrast to the 300-person organization he managed in France, Club Med's office in Spain employed only 25 people; but Jean-Michel felt this gave him the freedom and flexibility he needed to tackle a new market launch. Because of his success in France, Club Med senior management felt that Jean-Michel was ideal for building up the marketing organization in Spain. Sales potential in Spain was felt to be high, and Paris wanted to develop the Spanish market as quickly as possible. Christian Remoissenet, who had been with Club Med in Spain since 1989, was appointed sales and marketing manager by Jean-Michel, and together the two of them would oversee the day-to-day activities of marketing the product (*refer to the organization chart in Exhibit 1*).

THE SPANISH TOURIST INDUSTRY

By 1990, more than half of Spain's population of 39 million traveled on holiday each year. While this figure had not changed dramatically through the 1980s, holiday spending had increased at an average yearly rate of 32%, with 1989 expenditures (excluding international transportation) reaching Pta 365 billion. Spaniards were thus among the fastest growing holiday spenders (average growth around the world was only 18% for the same period), and by 1990 Spain ranked fifteenth among nations in terms of overall vacation spending.

Most Spaniards spent their holidays in Spain. By the late 1980s, however, the number of Spaniards traveling abroad for their holidays began to increase rapidly, growing from 7% of vacationers in 1985 to 19% by 1990. (*Exhibit 2 shows a breakdown of foreign destination by geographical origin for Spanish travelers and lists the key travel incentives for Spanish holiday makers.*)

Club Med's Spanish GMs represented the upper end of the vacation market. An analysis of the 1987 season showed that over 75% of Spanish GMs were professionals or executives, most were between the age of 30 and 50, and most traveled as singles or couples, with less than 20% of the bookings consisting of families. In contrast to the overall market, Club Med customers preferred to vacation abroad, with nearly two-thirds of the GMs choosing non-Spanish destinations (although only one-third chose destinations outside the Mediterranean basin; *refer to Exhibit 3*). The Club also achieved a higher than average volume of low-season sales, with 26% of its GM's traveling during the winter.

In preparation for the marketing campaign, Jean-Michel commissioned a customer satisfaction study with Metra-Seis, a market research firm in Barcelona. The study, which was based on interviews with selected GMs, indicated that certain aspects of Club Med's products conflicted with Spanish expectations. Complaints focused on the quality of accommodations, the inflexibility of time schedules, the high degree of organization, and the fact that French was the principal language of the Club; some also felt that the Club concept was not adequately explained in either the brochure or at the point of sale. However, overall satisfaction with the Club was high. Positive comments particularly emphasized the sports activities, the children's activities, and the food.

Competitive Package Holiday Products

Club Med's principal competitors in Spain were the major tour operators who developed and sold inclusive package holiday products.

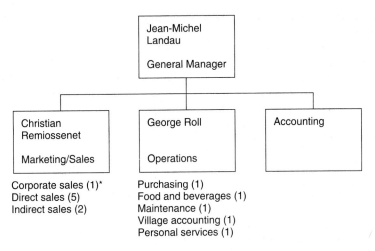

*Numbers in parantheses denote number of employees

EXHIBIT 1 Organization Chart of Club Med Spain

Sales of package holiday products had been growing in Spain, from 900,000 packages sold in 1985 to 1.5 million packages in 1990.

EXHIBIT 2 Excerpts from a Survey of the Spanish Tourist Market

Motivations for tourist travel within Spain:	
Diversion and change of environment	41.6%
Visit family and friends	31.5%
Health and relaxation	16.1%
Visit new places	13.6%
Motivations for tourist travel to foreign countries:	
Tourism	49.3%
Tourism and other	31.5%
Visit family	13.8%
Cultural curiosity	10.5%
Preferred activities:	
Cultural activities	86.0%
Relaxation	49.4%
Night life	27.4%
Cuisine	25.6%
Rural tourism	14.0%
Principal foreign destinations (some respondents listed two destinations, so total is greater than 100%):	
France	30.3%
Italy	19.0%
Portugal	17.8%
Andores	14.0%
Germany	7.2%
Switzerland	6.1%
United Kingdom	6.0%

Source: Le Marché Touristique Espagnol—Guide Pratique (Maison de la France, 1990).

(Travel agent revenues for 1990, *including* transportation, reached Pta 900 billion, with nearly one-third of this amount estimated to be attributed to package holiday sales.) The typical package holiday was comprised of transportation and accommodation, often including one or more meals and sometimes consisting of excursions to multiple destinations. The most common package holiday products sold to Spanish vacationers were to local sun/sea destinations in Spain, followed by European and North African sun/sea destinations during the summer and winter seasons and European snow destinations during the winter; less common were excursions to the Americas and the Far East.

By 1990, there were 284 tour operators developing package holiday products in Spain. Tour operators distributed their products through independent travel agencies, which operated more than 3,000 travel agency outlets throughout the country (an "independent" typically owned an average of one to three outlets, all in one particular city or region, and sold holiday packages on behalf of the tour operators on a commission basis). The larger tour operators, however, generally operated their own outlets as well. Wagons-Lits and Viajes Melia, the two largest such compa-

EXHIBIT 3   Customer Profile

Sales by destination (individuals):

1. Club Med Spain customer profile, summer 1989 season

Spain	35%
Mediterranean basin (Morocco, 19%; Tunisia, 7%; Turkey, 5%; Greece, 4%; others)	35%
Nearby destinations (France, 6%; Portugal, 4%; Italy, 3%)	13%
Exotic islands (Caribbean, 6%; Polynesia, 2%; Mauritius, 1%; Maldives, 1%; Phuket, 0.7%; Bali, 0.7%)	13%
Long-distance destinations (Mexico, 2.5%; Brazil, 1%; Malaysia, 0.25%; Senegal, 0.25%)	4%

2. Survey of current and potential customers who contacted the Barcelona boutique, November 1989

First heard of Club Med through:

Friends, acquaintances	70%
(80% for potential customers)	
Brochure	22%
Media	4%
Mailing	4%

Principal motivations for purchase of Club Med:

Sports activities	35%
(40% for potential customers)	
Meet new friends	19%
Rest/relaxation	16%
Social activities	16%
Destination country	11%
Exoticism	3%

Travel status:

Couple	30%
Family	26%
Couple with children	18%
Friends	15%
Alone	11%

3. Club Med Customer analysis, 1987 season

Profession:

Heads of enterprises	36%
Executives	19%
Liberal professions	27%
Employees	11%
Students	5%
Other	2%

Departure status:

Alone	44%
Couple	38%
With family friends	18%

Source: Evaluation du Marché du Tourisme Espagnol et Stratégie de Développement (Charles Riley Consultants International).

nies, operated 150 and 120 outlets, respectively. Both of these companies were typical of the large international travel groups that had been expanding globally, primarily through acquisition of local travel agent chains. Wagons-Lits, a French conglomerate, had worldwide revenues of FF 16.1 billion in 1990, while Viajes Melia, a Spanish company that had been bought by an Italian group in 1987, had revenues of Pta 33.9 billion.

Jean-Michel estimated that the retail price of Club Med holidays averaged 30% higher than those of available package holidays to comparable destinations. Club Med believed that this premium price reflected the unique characteristics of the product and that the organized activities, the entertainment, and the GO spirit at a Club Med village were features that were not to be found in the standard inclusive packages. In other countries, Club Med often justified its higher prices by claiming that the additional activities at the Club yielded higher value for money and that just the transportation, accommodation, food, and activities would cost the consumer much more if purchased separately than through a Club Med package.

CLUB MED'S STRATEGY FOR SPAIN

Jean-Michel's goal was to build up the GM customer base in Spain from the current 8,000 customers to 50,000 customers and to raise national awareness for the Club from 1.5% to 40% over a 5-year period. According to Club Med España's estimates, a target of 50,000 customers represented about 10% of the 500,000 Spaniards who took package holidays comparable in value to the average Club Med product. Jean-Michel expected marketing efforts to result in a doubling of both group and individual sales for the 1991–1992 season and for growth to continue steadily over the next few years as the product gained recognition.

An advertising and public relations campaign would be launched within the month. This, along with the Club Med brochure, would be critical in building the Club's image in Spain. An effective distribution network would also have to be created. Selected travel agencies would have to develop a good understanding of the product, and incentives would have to be provided to sell Club Med over other package holiday products.

Target

Club Med España aimed at targeting the most affluent segment of the Spanish population, particularly liberal professionals—doctors, lawyers, property owners, business people, and the like. Charles Riley Consultants International had estimated Club Med's potential market in Spain in 1990 to be 375,000 customers.

Product Offering

In 1991, Club Med España wanted to offer its Spanish customers a whole range of products and destinations through three versions of the Trident:

- The winter ski catalogue offered nine destinations to French ski resorts, one in Italy, and nine in Switzerland.
- The winter sun catalogue destinations introduced 12 destinations in Europe and Africa—Spain, France, Israel, Ireland, Morocco, Portugal, Senegal, Tunisia, and the Caribbees (Antilles); 13 in the Caribbean or America—Bahamas, the French Caribbean, Haiti, Brazil, Mexico, and the United States; 8 in Asia, Polynesia, and other faraway places—Indonesia, Malaysia, the Maldives, Tahiti, New Caledonia, Mauritius, and Thailand.
- The summer catalogue introduced 32 villages in Europe and Africa—4 each in Spain and Turkey, 5 each in France and Morocco, 3 each in Greece, Tunisia, and Italy, 1 each in Ireland, Israel, Portugal and Senegal; 16 destinations in the Americas—5 in Mexico, 3 in the French Caribbean, 2 each in Brazil and the Bahamas, 1 each in the United States, the Turks and Caicos, and Haiti; and 6 destinations in Asia and Polynesia—Indonesia, Malaysia, the Maldives, Mauritius, Thailand, and Tahiti.

Communication

A poll conducted by Dym S.A. (a market research organization that had developed a holiday and travel-oriented omnibus) found that only 1.5% of the population in Spain had heard of Club Med. (In contrast, the awareness level for France was 90%; *results of the Spanish survey are shown in Exhibit 4.*)

Advertising would be developed by the local offices of RSCG, an international advertising agency based in Paris that handled all of Club Med's advertising for Europe. RSCG planned to use existing Club Med material from its archives in Paris, but to design advertisements specifically targeted to a Spanish audience. (*Exhibit 5 shows preliminary advertisements developed by RSCG for the Spanish campaign.*) Jean-Michel had run two series of trial tactical advertisements in Barcelona's daily *La Vanguardia* in December 1991. The test, which was timed to coincide with the Christmas holidays, seemed to have produced successful results, with more bookings requested than could be accommodated.

RSCG would also be used to produce the Club Med brochure the "Trident," as it was called within the company in reference to the Club's logo. The Trident was distributed to travel agents, who displayed it on shelves, redistributed it to customers, and used it as a reference to the Club's products. Brochures were also distributed to customers directly by Club Med, both at the boutique and, when new brochures were printed, through direct mailings to previous GMs. Historically, Club Med gave away four brochures for every direct booking and 10 brochures for every indirect booking. A total of 50,000 brochures had been printed and distributed in Spain during the two 1990–1991 seasons, and another 30,000 brochures had already been printed for the winter season of 1991–1992.

A major decision that Jean-Michel had to make was to determine the size of the communications budget. Since Club Med España was spending almost nothing on communications before he took over his new position, Jean-Michel had to start from scratch to figure out an appropriate budget for the Spanish market. He knew that his major local competitor had spent Pta 300 million on communications during the past year. However, such a budget was well over what he could afford. In any case, any budget he would present to the Paris headquarters had to be fully justified.

EXHIBIT 4   Results of the DYM Survey, November–December 1991

Question 1: Have you ever had the occasion to hear about Club Med?
Question 2: If "yes," tell me please, what is the principal activity of Club Med?
Results:

	Total	Age			Status[a]				Sex	
		16–30	31–45	46–50	A + B	C1	C2	D	M	F
Q1:										
Yes	1.5	1.3	2.1	1.1	3.3	0.8	1.6	0.9	1.5	1.5
No	98.5	98.7	97.9	98.9	96.7	99.2	98.4	99.1	98.5	98.5
Q2:										
Vacation club	10.6	—	25.3	—	12.9	53.7	—	—	13.2	8.0
Travel agency	3.7	11.6	—	—	12.1	—	—	—	—	7.5
Club Méditerranée[b]	3.3	—	7.9	—	10.7	—	—	—	6.6	—
Residences w/activities	—	—	—	—	—	—	—	—	—	—
Conglomerate	2.5	—	—	9.5	—	—	6.4	—	—	5.0
Sports facilities	11.9	26.8	7.9	—	27.8	—	8.6	—	6.6	17.3
Sports/football	4.3	13.4	—	—	13.9	—	—	—	—	8.6
Food company	9.7	9.5	9.7	10.0	8.4	24.9	10.5	—	13.3	6.1
Other	26.9	11.0	33.2	36.4	7.9	21.4	48.1	17.8	12.3	41.5
Don't know	31.3	41.0	15.9	44.0	20.4	—	26.4	82.2	47.8	14.7

[a] The socioeconomic status classification is defined as follows:

	Social Status	Head of Household's Occupation
A	Upper middle class	Higher managerial, administrative, or professional
B	Middle class	Intermediate managerial, administrative, or professional
C1	Lower middle class	Supervisory, clerical, junior managerial, administrative, or professional
C2	Skilled working class	Skilled manual workers
D	Working class	Semi- and unskilled manual workers
E	Others	

[b] Club Med had recently changed its name in Spain from Club Méditeranée to Club Med.

Distribution

By 1990, only one-third of Club Med's individual sales in Spain were made through 40 travel agents. Club Med España expected that agents would make about two-thirds of its sales by 1995–1996. Jean-Michel's objective was to obtain national coverage by increasing this number to 150 to 200 agents. Travel agents would be key to a successful marketing effort, however, and because of his experience as marketing manager for France, Jean-Michel was particularly concerned about developing the distribution channels properly in Spain. "In France," he explained, "99% of our indirect sales are made by one agency—a competitor of ours, Havas Voyages. We account for 30% of their gross turnover, and they account for 30% of ours. We fight a lot, but we can't live without them, and they can't live without us. I don't want a situation like this in Spain—it leaves you with no control over the distribution."

Consequently, Jean-Michel planned to spread the risk of indirect distribution over several of the more prestigious independent travel agents in Spain, which would be selected based on gross turnover (candidates should average about Pta 400 million per year), geographical location, and their previous track record selling Club Med. Selected agents would be groomed as Club Med Experts. Employees from Expert agencies would be sent to Club Med villages, would receive extensive training on Club Med's products and selling techniques, and would eventually be granted more favorable commissions than normal travel agencies.

The boutique was still the most critical point of sale with two-thirds of the GMs currently booking their trips directly through Club Med. Jean-Michel was preparing to open

VENGA A MARRAKECH, QUEDARÁ ENCANTADO.

EL ENCANTO DE MARRAKECH

Imagínese el encanto de una de las plazas más famosas del mundo. La de Djemaa-El-Fna, llena del color berebere, donde retumba el bullicio del zoco, con la magía del Atlas y las Kasbah fundiéndose en este centro vital de Marrakech.
Justo allí, en este ambiente, en esta plaza, está el Hotel Club Med.

UN HOTEL ENCANTADOR

Club Med tiene un precioso hotel con confortables habitaciones de inspiración morisca y un sinfín
de servicios a su disposición: Boutique, Discoteca, Piscina, Hammam, alquiler de coches y restau-

rante-barbacoa donde podrá degustar el sabor de Marrakech en forma de cus-cus, mechui o Kabah. Puede usted también jugar al golf, tenis, balonvolea, tiro al arco o simplemente petanca en las instalaciones del Club Med y asesorado por nuestros organizadores.

UNA OFERTA QUE LE ENCANTARÁ

Aprovechando el puente de la Inmaculada, con salida de Barcelona la noche del jueves 5 de Diciembre y vuelta el Domingo 8 a última hora, Club Med ha preparado una oferta única que incuye:

—————— **IDA Y VUELTA EN AVIÓN** ——————
BARCELONA-MARRAKECH-BARCELONA
———— **ESTANCIA EN HOTEL CLUB MED**————
EN RÉGIMEN DE PENSIÓN COMPLETA
—————————— **TRASLADOS** ——————————
AEROPUERTO-HOTEL-AEROPUERTO

69.500 Ptas.
POR PERSONA, TODO INCLUIDO
Llámenos, quedará encantado.
INFORMACIÓN Y RESERVAS

ClubMed
Diagonal, 503 Tel. 439 57 02 Fax 405 33 46

EXHIBIT 5 Tactical Advertisements Developed by RSCG for Club Med, Spain (published in *La Vanguardia*, December 1991)

EXHIBIT 5 *(Continued)*

a second boutique in downtown Madrid by the end of February, in time for the beginning of summer bookings. Start-up costs for the Madrid boutique had been budgeted at Pta 36 million, of which Pta 25 million represented a one-time rental rights payment, while the remaining Pta 11 million had been used for construction and decorating. With a rent of Pta 300,000 per month, Jean-Michel estimated that the direct costs of operating the Madrid boutique would amount to about 5% of its gross sales within 2 years of operation. A third boutique was planned for Valencia, the third largest city in Spain, but no time frame had been set; boutiques located outside Madrid, however, were expected to incur significantly lower rental and rights costs.

OPTIONS

Commercial activity for Club Med Spain was measured by headquarters in Paris on a sales-driven system whereby the Spanish office received a 15% commission for each booking. Profitability of the office was then effected by two main factors: transportation margins and the cost of sales. Since transportation was included in every Club Med booking, the office bought seats on charter flights and resold them to its GMs; profit margins from this activity averaged 20% to 25% for the Spanish office, and Jean-Michel estimated that transportation would soon be accounting for 35% to 40% of gross revenues. Cost of sales were comprised of travel agent commissions, overhead for boutiques, and the cost of advertising and promotion. (Village operations for Spain, which also fell under Jean-Michel's management, did not represent a factor in measuring the commercial activity of the Spanish office; Spanish villages were booked worldwide, and Jean-Michel was only responsible for their cost of operations.)

The communications budget would be based on loss-making sales during the initial years of the marketing plan. As a budgetary guideline, Jean-Michel had agreed with Club Med headquarters in Paris to maintain gross operation costs (not including village operations) at 30% to 35% of revenues for about 3 years, beginning with the 1991–1992 season, until operations could become profitable.

While Spain showed every indication of providing Club Med with a strong market, Jean-Michel faced the dilemma of allocating his limited budget between promoting the product and pushing it through the distribution channels. Furthermore, the right products had to be sold to the right customers; otherwise, the initial marketing effort could backfire through client dissatisfaction.

The Cost of Advertising

Advertising represented the most expensive component of the communications campaign. RSCG proposed an advertising schedule that focused on print media in Barcelona and Madrid and would cost the Club an estimated Pta 34 million, including Pta 2.3 million for design and layout. (*The schedule and a summary of advertising rates are shown in Exhibit 6.*) The RSCG proposal was for a series of double-page, color advertisements to be run in selected daily and weekly newspapers during the summer season. The proposal also included periodic tactical advertisements for promoting specific destinations and included advertisements in two travel-oriented specialty magazines. Lead times for reserving advertising space limited the extent to which advertising could be mod-

EXHIBIT 6   RSCG Proposed Advertising Schedule

| *Double-page, color, image advertisements, newspapers:* | | |
Sunday Supplements	Weeks of:	Total Cost (pta '000,000)
La Vanguardia	16/3, 4/5, 18/5, 1/6	10.0
El Periodico	16/3, 22/5	4.5
ABC	18/5, 1/6	5.3
El Mundo	16/3, 25/5	4.0
El Pais	4/5	6.4

| *Double-page, color, image advertisements, magazines:* | | |
Periodical	Month of:	Total Cost (pta '000,000)
GEO	May	1.5
Viajar	June	1.2

| *Quarter-page, tactical advertisements, newspapers:* | | |
Leading Dailies	No. Ads	Total Cost (pta '000,000)
La Vanguardia	8	3.3
El Pais	8	3.9

ified as the season progressed. Jean-Michel also planned to repeat the Dym survey at least once per year (at a cost of Pta 200,000 per poll) in order to monitor the awareness level as the advertising campaign proceeded.

The advertising campaign would be coordinated with public relations activities, including a press conference scheduled for mid-February to announce the launch of Club Med's advertising campaign. A public relations firm, Gene Associates, had been contracted to manage all of Club Med's public relations activities in Spain for a fee of Pta 500,000 per month; the firm's responsibilities included organizing press conferences and feeding stories to the press, as well as organizing any special events. Jean-Michel was considering sponsoring some events (such as golf tournaments) that would promote the Club and generate news coverage; in addition to the public relations firm's fee, such activities typically cost the Club about Pta 400,000 per event.

A New Brochure

Since Spaniards were unfamiliar with the Club, the Trident would play a critical role in promoting the product and generating sales. The current Spanish Trident was similar to the European Trident produced every season in Paris and translated into the appropriate languages for Club Med's other marketing organizations in Europe. A brief introduction described the Club, after which the villages were listed by country, with one to two pages and a few photographs used to describe each village; a separate insert listed the prices of each destination (*refer to Exhibit 7*).

Three decisions had to be taken on the Trident: the number of different Tridents, the number of copies, and the content. RSCG estimated the cost of producing three separate brochures (summer, winter-sun, and winter-ski) to be Pta 3 million for layout and design, plus Pta 173.7 per copy for printing. As with advertising, RSCG would use photographs from Paris in the production of the new Spanish Tridents. Layout and text would be different, however, with the aim of targeting Spanish GMs and better explaining the Club concept.

Targeting included the emphasis placed on the individual villages; popular Club Med destinations for Spaniards, for example, could be displayed more prominently, and the least visited villages would have their description omitted entirely (although the full product line would be included in the price list).

Finally, direct mailings to previous customers were conducted to distribute newly published brochures and to announce special offerings. A direct mailing to the current customer base cost approximately Pta 600,000; several mailings would have to be conducted during the 1991–1992 season.

Prices and Quotas

Each village had a basic price that was set by Club Med's headquarters in Paris. Jean-Michel could adjust the price seasonally as long as the basic price remained the annual average. In addition to setting prices based on time of year, special promotions were often used to fill certain destinations or if bookings were slow (promotions could be in the form of price discounts, special deals such as free accommodation for children, and the like).

Price setting, however, had to be balanced between Spanish seasonal holiday patterns and a complex quota system imposed by Paris, which limited the bookings that Jean-Michel

EXHIBIT 7 Summary of the Introduction from the Club Med Spanish Trident *Sol-Invierno 91/92* (Sun-Winter 91/92)

The introduction consists of seven pages of text, interspersed with pictures of scenes from Club Med villages. The text is divided into the following subtitled sections:

Life in the Club

   The Village
   Freedom
   The GOs
   The Food
   The Necklace Bar
   Entertainment

The Best Sports School in the World
The Paradise of Children
Enrich Your Knowledge, Discover
Club Med One

EXHIBIT 7 (*Continued*)

INDICE

EUROPA - AFRICA

AMERICA - OCEANIA

ASIA - OCEANO - INDICO

Club Med Diagonal, 503 - 08029 Barcelona
Tel. (93) 439 57 02 - Fax (93) 405 33 46

EXHIBIT 7   (*Continued*)

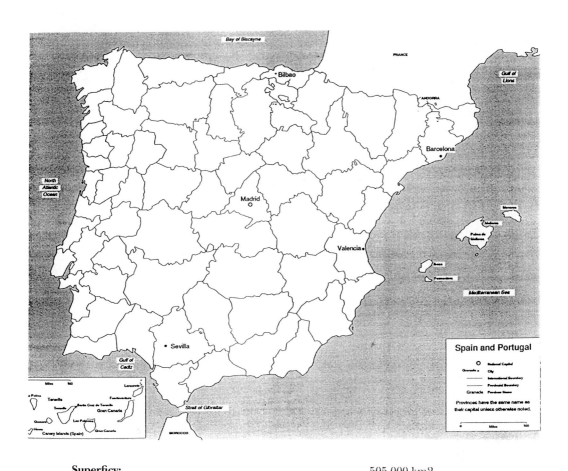

Superficy:		505,000 km2
Population:	Total	39,217,000
	Active	14,700,000
	Working	12,000,000
	Uenmployed	2,700,000
	Unemployment Rate	18%
Major Cities:	Madrid	3,400,000 inhabitants
	Barcelona	1,900,000
	Valencia	800,000
	Sevilla	660,000
	Bilbao	400,000

EXHIBIT 8   Basic Information on Spain

could make for each village. Club Med attempted to manage the mix of GMs at the villages by assigning each country a fixed number of booking slots for each destination, and countries like Spain did their best to fill these slots by adjusting their marketing efforts. These quotas were primarily in place to ensure adequate supply for France, Club Med's biggest market; consequently, quotas during the high-season months were rarely adequate for the other countries. Jean-Michel did not expect this to affect 1991–1992 sales, but he did expect the quota system to become problematic relatively soon, since Spanish holiday patterns were heavily concentrated in the month of August.

The Travel Agent Network

The standard travel agent commission in Spain was 5% to 8% of the retail price. Club Med Experts were expected to promote the Club because of the training they received and because of the expected volume that Club Med sales would generate for them (Jean-Michel expected Experts to eventually reach 10% of their gross turnover through Club Med sales). Initial training costs were minimal—about Pta 5,600 per agent. Commissions could be adjusted, however, either temporarily as an incentive to fill specific destinations or on a permanent basis to push the Club through specific agencies (above-average commissions were typically set at 10%).

While travel agent incentives were particularly critical during the initial stages of the marketing strategy, the demand for Club Med could be expected to increase on its own once the product gained reputation. Thus, Jean-Michel had to determine the optimal number of agencies to include in the Club Med Expert program and set an incentive policy that would generate sales effectively until the advertising campaign began to pay off. Furthermore, to maximize selling margins, Jean-Michel wanted to maintain a 65% direct-sales ratio (including group sales); the direct-sales ratio was currently much higher than 65%, but an increase in demand for the product combined with a successful travel agent program was expected to increase the level of indirect sales over the next few years.

The next 3 years, then, would be a busy time for Jean-Michel and his staff as they faced the intricacies of growing their customer base as quickly as possible with a limited budget and within the constraints imposed by Club Med headquarters. Would the advertising campaign be successful in conveying a positive image of the Club? What should Jean-Michel's communications budget be? Would awareness increase fast enough? Would distribution be effective? The upcoming season's sales—by which Paris would ultimately judge them—would go a long way in answering these questions.

EXHIBIT 9 Pro Forma Income Statement

	A	B	C	D	E	F	G
1							
2							
3		90/91	91/92	92/93	93/94	94/95	95/96
4	Number of Customers (GM)						
5	Number of Bookings						
6							
7							
8	**Revenues (Millions Ptas)**						
9	Of Which:						
10	Transport. (35%)						
11	Transport. Margins (23%)						
12							
13	Villages (100%-35%)						
14	Villages Margins (15%)						
15							
16	Total Gross Margins						
17	Cost of Sales (%)						
18	Cost of Sales						
19	**Net Profit/(Loss)**						

	A	B	C	D	E	F	G
20							
21							
22							
23							
24		90/91	91/92	92/93	93/94	94/95	95/96
25	Bookings						
26							
27	**SALES (Million Pta.)**						
28	Of Which:						
29	Boutique (%)						
30	*Of Which:*						
31	*Barcelona (%)*						
32	*Madrid (%)*						
33	Total Boutique (Mill. Pta)						
34	Travel Agency (Mill. Pta.)						
35							
36	**EXPENSES (Million Pta.)**						
37	Overheads Boutique Barcelona						
38	Overheads Boutique Madrid						
39	Indirect Commissions (8%)						
40							
41	PR Agency (Fees/year)						
42	No. of PR Events/Year						
43	Cost/Event						
44	Total PR						
45							
46	Advertising Layout (Pta)						
47	Advert. Space (Summer)						
48	Advert. Space (Winter)						
49	Total Advertising						
50							
51	No. of brochures/year						
52	Brochure Layout (Pta.)						
53	No. of copies						
54	Printing cost/brochure						
55	Total Printing						
56	Total Cost for Brochures						
57							
58	Market Survey (once/year)						
59							
60	No. of Direct Mailings						
61	Cost of Direct Mailings						
62	Total Direct Mail						
63							
64	Other Expenses:						
65							
66							
67							
68							
69							
70	**Total Expenses**						
71	Budgeted Cost of Sales (%)						
72	Budgeted Cost of Sales						
73	Budgeted Surplus (Overrun)						

EXHIBIT 10   Budget

Libby's Beverages:
Um Bongo Fruit Drink

Um Bongo is a success story in the UK, Portugal and Spain and we think the US market should also be ready for it. *A headquarters beverage executive at Nestle, Vevey, Switzerland.*

Um Bongo has a strange flavor, unfamiliar to the American child's taste buds, and a very unusual commercial with jungle drums and animals and lots of activity all over the place. . . . In tests it lost to Hawaiian Punch, a leading competitor, so the project died right there." *A Libby's executive, Purchase, New York, USA.*

In 1989, managers at Libby's American operation and its parent Nestle were debating the future of Um Bongo in the United States. Um Bongo was a fruit-based drink with 25% juice content specifically developed for children. It was originally introduced by Libby's U.K. company, but later also marketed by the Spanish and Portuguese organizations. Nestle executives considered the Um Bongo concept of combining "fun and health" a significant product and marketing innovation with broad international appeal. As proof, they pointed to the success of the brand in three different European markets.

Libby's U.S. managers were less convinced about Um Bongo's general appeal. Initial consumer tests had indicated potential problems with its taste and the TV commercials used in Europe. Besides, they claimed they were busy with another children's brand, Juicy Juice, a 100% fruit juice product. Juicy Juice had been relaunched 2 years earlier with great success. United States management now intended to consolidate Juicy Juice's gains for further growth

and improved profitability. The addition of Um Bongo to the product line, these managers argued, would only detract from the tasks ahead.

BACKGROUND

Libby's was a division of Nestle, the world's largest food company. With more than $24 billion in sales and 428 factories on five continents, Nestle and its wholly owned divisions marketed a large variety of products, including evaporated milk and infant foods, chocolate, coffee, beverages, culinary products (such as sauces, mixes, and soups), and refrigerated and frozen products. Nestle's flagship products, such as its 50-year-old Nescafe, were sold in more than 100 countries.

Since the early 1970s, Nestle had pursued an active acquisition policy in the international food business. In 1970, Nestle acquired Libby's, one of the largest fruit and vegetable processors in the United States. Other major acquisitions that followed were Stouffer (US: 1973), Chambourcy, (France: 1978), Carnation (US: 1985), Buitoni–Perugia (Italy: 1989), and Rowntree (UK: 1989). In most cases, the acquired companies, including Libby's activities around the world, were integrated into Nestle's local operations.

In 1989, less than 3% of the company's total turnover came from nonfood activities, including cosmetics and pharmaceuticals. (*Refer*

This case was prepared by Professor Kamran Kashani, with assistance from Research Associate Robert C. Howard, as a basis for class discussion rather than to illustrate either effective or ineffective handling of a business situation. All names have been disguised. Copyright © 1992 by the International Institute for Management Development (IMD), Lausanne, Switzerland. IMD retains all rights. Not to be used or reproduced without written permission from IMD, Lausanne, Switzerland.

to Exhibit 1 for a breakdown of sales by product category and geographic region.)

Each Nestle country operation was run by a country manager who had full responsibility for profitability and for overseeing all functions, including marketing, manufacturing, and finance. Many country managers were local nationals who had risen through the marketing function.[1]

Nestle's corporate structure was organized along five geographic zones and nine product groups. The zones were Europe; Asia, Australia, and New Zealand; South and Central America; the United States and Canada; and Africa and the Middle East. The product groups consisted of beverages (including coffee, mineral water, fruit juices, and drinks); cereals, milks, and dietetic; culinary; frozen foods and ice cream; chocolate and confectionery; refrigerated products; pet foods; pharmaceuticals and cosmetics; and food services.

Zone managers who were located in the company's headquarters in Vevey, Switzerland, worked with individual country managers for setting overall sales and profit targets and monitoring performance. Product directors and their teams of product managers reporting to them were also in Vevey. They interfaced with their respective country product managers, who reported to their local executives, to implement global or regional product strategies, to search for new products, and to maximize cross-fertilization of marketing practices internationally. In the beverages group, for example, four product managers looked after Nestle's worldwide activities in roasted and ground coffee, instant coffee, chocolate and malt drinks, and tea and liquid beverages, including fruit juices and drinks. In Nestle's matrix of staff product groups and line geographic zones, zone management wielded considerably more influence on local matters. (Refer to Exhibit 2 for a partial organization chart.)

Nestle had traditionally been run as a decentralized organization giving much autonomy to country management. Country heads, evaluated on overall results, were thought of as

EXHIBIT 1   NESTLE'S 1988 Sales Breakdown: Sales of 40 Billion Swiss Francs

	Product Category (%)	Geographic Regions (%)	
Beverages	27	Europe	46
Dairy	15	N. America	26
Chocolate/confectionary	12	Asia	12
Culinary	12	L. America	10
Frozen foods/ice cream	10	Africa	3
Refrigerated products	9	Oceania	3
Infant foods	6		
Pet foods	5		
Pharmaceuticals/cosmetics	2		
Others	2		
	100		100

Source: Company records.

"pillars of the organization" and allowed freedom to run their "one-man shows." Marketing, more than other functions, was considered to be a local activity aimed at capitalizing on the particularities of each market.

Recently, more attention was being paid to global branding and looking for marketing opportunities that cut across traditional market boundaries. Helmut Maucher, Nestle's CEO, was explicit on this point:

[Our] aim is to identify market groups and build global brands. These can be sold to the same groups of people all over the world—single households, the health conscious, old people, oriental food lovers, instant coffee drinkers. The idea is to target these segments clearly for maximum sales, and hence become the lowest-cost producer.[2]

Nevertheless, Nestle believed there were limits to how far a food company could go global and satisfy consumers on five continents. The company aimed to stay close to local markets.

WORLD FRUIT AND JUICE MARKET

In 1988, the world's total consumption of fruit juices and juice-based drinks[3] amounted to an estimated 27 billion liters, representing a value of $23 billion at manufacturers' prices.

---

[1] Certain data pertaining to Nestle's organization are based on the Harvard Business School case study, Nestle S.A.

[2] Management Europe, January 16, 1989.

[3] "Drinks" was a term used to refer to fruit-based beverages whose juice content was less than 100%. Most drinks contained 10% to 50% fruit juices, with the rest consisting of water, sugar, color, and flavoring.

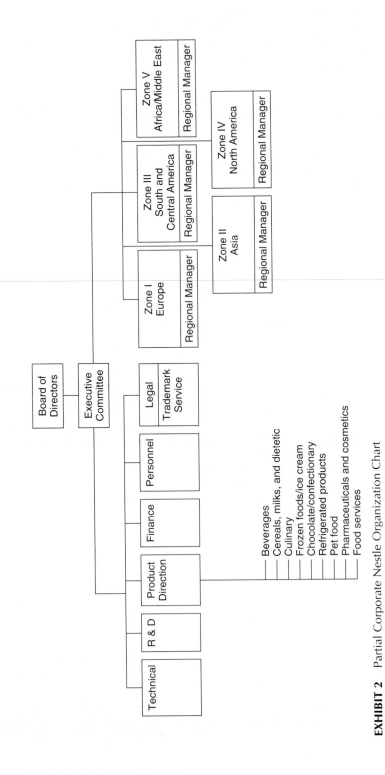

EXHIBIT 2 Partial Corporate Nestle Organization Chart

These figures included all forms of industrially processed juices and drinks, including nectars, ready-to-drink preparations, concentrates, and frozen. Orange juice and orange-based drinks were the best selling flavors, accounting for nearly one-half of all consumption. Apple was the second most popular flavor with 15%, followed by grapefruit, pineapple, and grape. Fruit juice and drinks consumption had grown by about 8% per year since the early 1980s.

Unlike soft drinks, the world market for fruit juices and drinks was fragmented. No competitor appeared dominant internationally, although Coca-Cola held the leading position with an estimated worldwide share of 15%. Coca-Cola's brands were Hi-C, Minute Maid, Five Alive, and Sprite, a carbonated soft drink with 10% of fruit juice content. Other major competitors were Pepsi Cola (Slice), P&G (Citrus Hill), Seagram's (Tropicana), U.K.-based Cadbury Schweppes (Sunkist), and Melitta (Granini) headquartered in Germany.

Three countries accounted for more than 60% of the world's volume of juices and drinks: the United States, 41%; Japan, 13%; and Germany, 9%. Consumption volumes and patterns differed internationally. For example, one study showed that, while per capita consumption in the United States surpassed 70 liters annually, in the other Anglo-Saxon countries the volume was in the 20- to 25-liter range, and in the Latin countries it was below 10 liters. The same study highlighted other differences in how juices and drinks were consumed:

Amounts of Consumption

	Anglo-Saxon (%)	Latin (%)
Breakfast	35	10
Lunch/dinner	25	10
During the day	40	80
At home	70	55
Outside the home	30	45

Source: Company records.

Despite national and cultural differences, Nestle management identified a number of trends that were influencing the juice and drinks industry worldwide:

Health: Among the industrialized countries, consumers were paying unprecedented attention to their own and their family's health and diet. Fruit juices and drinks were benefiting from this trend as "healthy" alternatives to modern soft drinks or traditional coffee and tea.

Quality: In major markets internationally, a growing number of consumers were turning to the premium-quality fruit juice segment. This factor explained the growth of premium-priced ready-to-drink brands marketed under taste platforms like "freshly squeezed."

Value: In large markets, the low-priced "value for money" segment accounted for an increasing percentage of fruit juices and drinks. The rise in the number and volume of private brands marketed by large food chains in Europe and North America had helped this trend.

Advertising: Media advertising for fruit juices and drinks was on the rise. In some markets it had already surpassed relative expenditure levels of soft drinks, historically a media-intensive category. In 1987, for example, the U.S. media expenditure for fruit juices approached $200 per 10,000 liters versus $100 for soft drinks.

THE U.S. FRUIT JUICE AND DRINKS MARKET

Overview

In 1988, the U.S. market for fruit juice and drinks was approximately $9.4 billion at manufacturers' prices. This volume represented only a small portion of a much larger beverage market estimated at more than $112 billion in that year. (*Refer to Exhibit 3.*)

Libby's management divided the juice and drinks products into frozen, shelf-stable, and refrigerated segments. The ready-to-drink shelf-stable products were by far the largest segment, accounting for close to one-half of the market. The refrigerated products—typi-

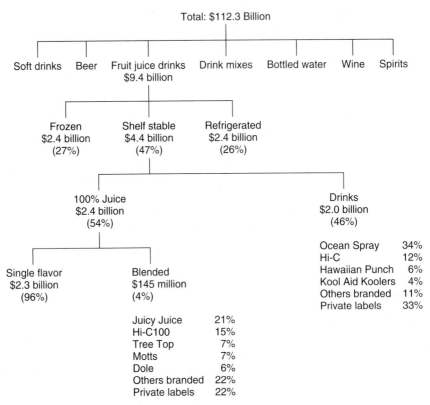

Total: $112.3 Billion

Soft drinks   Beer   Fruit juice drinks   Drink mixes   Bottled water   Wine   Spirits
                       $9.4 billion

Frozen   Shelf stable   Refrigerated
$2.4 billion $4.4 billion $2.4 billion
(27%)   (47%)   (26%)

100% Juice   Drinks
$2.4 billion $2.0 billion
(54%)   (46%)

Ocean Spray	34%
Hi-C	12%
Hawaiian Punch	6%
Kool Aid Koolers	4%
Others branded	11%
Private labels	33%

Single flavor   Blended
$2.3 billion $145 million
(96%)   (4%)

Juicy Juice	21%
Hi-C100	15%
Tree Top	7%
Motts	7%
Dole	6%
Others branded	22%
Private labels	22%

EXHIBIT 3   Segmentation of the U.S. Beverage Market, 1988 *Source:* Company records.

cally citrus flavors—accounted for 26% of the market in 1988. These products had increased their market share by nearly 10 points over the last 5 years at the expense of the frozen segment.

The juice and drinks market was also segmented by flavor. In the shelf-stable category, blended juices and drinks were leading with about two-thirds share of the dollar volume, followed by apple (17%), grapefruit (5.2%), grape (5.6%), and orange (3.3%). Orange juice was the dominant flavor in both frozen and refrigerated segments, with 61% and 72%, respectively.

A variety of packaging was used for fruit juices and drinks. Glass was by far the most dominant form among shelf-stable products, accounting for 47%, followed by cans (31%), aseptic brik packs (16%), and plastic containers (6%). In recent years, both glass and brik packs had grown relatively, while cans had declined. In the refrigerated and frozen segments, paper and plastic cartons were the most common forms of packaging.

The overall fruit juice and drinks market had grown by nearly one-third since 1982 and was projected to reach $11 billion by 1990. The annual growth rates had doubled since the mid-1970s, reaching 7% by 1988. Since 1982, the dollar sales in the refrigerated segment had grown 104%, while the frozen product sales had actually declined 6%. With 36% growth during this period, the shelf-stable segment had slightly overtaken the industry average. Among the flavors, orange and blended flavors were the fastest growing varieties in the refrigerated and shelf-stable segments, respectively.

Industry analysts attributed the continued U.S. market growth to the concern with health and fitness by consumers, the growing popularity of new aseptic packaging, and the impact of new products such as blended fruit juices. These combined factors had contributed to a rise in annual per capita juice and drinks consumption from 11.5 gallons (52 liters) in the mid-1970s to 15.7 gallons (71 liters) in the mid-1980s.[4]

Competition

Three firms dominated the U.S. fruit juice and drinks market: Coca-Cola Foods, Seagrams, and Ocean Spray. Coca-Cola Foods was the largest juice and drinks marketer with a total 1988 sales of $1.3 billion and a market share of 14%. The company's Minute Maid brand, an orange juice in shelf-stable and frozen forms, accounted for slightly more than $1 billion of sales. Another major brand was Hi-C, a shelf-stable fruit drink with sales of $203 million. Seagrams was the second largest producer in the industry. The firm's 10% market share came almost entirely from its highly successful and fast growing Tropicana brand of refrigerated and shelf-stable orange juice. Ocean Spray, the industry's third largest, had sales of $700 million and a market share of 9%. The company's wide variety of cranberry-based and other fruit drinks made it the largest player in the shelf-stable segment.

Besides the three largest, more than 10 other producers, including divisions of such large firms as P&G, Campbell Soup, RJR/Nabisco, and Nestle, competed in the industry. Private labels represented a growing segment of the U.S. juice and drinks market, accounting for an estimated 16% in 1988. (*Exhibit 4 provides data on competitors and products in the shelf-stable segment, including Libby's brand, Juicy Juice.*)

According to Libby's management, a number of juice and drinks companies had recently entered the 100% blended fruit juice segment, where Juicy Juice was the leading brand. The newcomers had been attracted by the segment's growth, which was estimated to be the highest in the industry. Starting with a modest size of $10 million in mid-1970s, the blended juice market had reached $145 million by 1988. Among the new entrants were

Coca-Cola Food's Hi-C100, Seagram's Tropicana Twisters, Motts, and Dole. However, in the opinion of Libby's management, despite "strong introductions and megabuck expenditures," none of the "big boys" had seriously damaged Juicy Juice's leadership in the segment. Nevertheless, the management believed that all fruit-based beverages competed with one another directly or indirectly, and Juicy Juice's competition came not only from the 100% blended juice products, but also from the single-flavor juices and the lower-priced fruit drinks. (*Refer to Exhibit 5 for sales and market shares of major brands.*)

JUICY JUICE BY LIBBY'S: "100% REAL FRUIT JUICES"

We turned a corporate dog into a success story and we did it by following the good old recipe of effective product management. *A Nestle fruit juice and drinks executive in Vevey, Switzerland.*

We went to market at a time when the juice content of products was becoming important in parents' minds. . . . A lot of people thought Hi-C and Hawaiian Punch were good products; they felt they were giving their kids something that was healthy. Well, we came along and said "no"; they have only 10% juice, whereas we have 100%. And a lot of people were not aware of that fact. . . . *A Libby's executive in Purchase, New York.*

History

The preceding comments refer to the turnaround of Juicy Juice, a brand acquired by Libby's in 1984 from Fruitcrest, a regional producer. The brand had been launched by Fruitcrest in 1978 and was distributed in the eastern part of the United States. With five different blended flavors[5] targeted at children, from "Real Red" and "Yummy Yellow" to "Golden Good," Juicy Juice enjoyed a sales level of $34 million in 1984.

Each product was made up of a blend of 100% fruit juices—including apple, grape,

---

[4] U.S. population in 1989 = 247 million.

[5] A blended flavor was a mixture of concentrates from different fruits. In manufacturing, only water and natural fruit flavor were added to restore the juices to their original strength.

EXHIBIT 4   U.S. Competitive Overview: Who Is Who in Shelf-stable Juice

Manufacturer/ Brand	1988 Sales[a] ($Million)	Positioning	Product	Retail Price	Packaging	1988 Ad Spending[a] ($Millions)
Ocean Spray (all brands)	695	Refreshment for adults (cranberry juice and grapefruit)	Line of cranberry cocktails (27% juice) including concentrates	$1.89–$2.29 (48 oz)	92% glass; 8% brik	21.9
cranberry line	562					
Mauna Lai	41	Exotic taste (Mauna Lai)	grapefruit juice cocktail	$0.99–$1.29 (brik)		
grapefruit juice	51		Mauna Lai drinks			
Splash	1		Crantastic			
concentrate	40		Testing Splash (carbonated juice drink)			
Coke Foods	239					
Hi-C	203	Fun and good taste targeted to kids	10% fruit juice	$0.79–$0.99 (46 oz) $0.79–$0.99 (brik)	34% cans; 61% brik 4% glass	2.8
Hi-C100	14	Family and kids	100% fruit juice brik pak is only shelf-stable item. Offer 100% juice and drinks	$1.19	100% brik	
Minute Maid	22	Wholesome juice for kids		$0.99–$1.29 (brik)	brik	N/A Part of $25 million umbrella campaign
RJR/Nabisco	195					
Hawaiian Punch	114	Great taste for kids	10% juice	$0.79–$0.99 (46 oz) $0.79–$0.99 (brik)	60% cans; 23% brik 14% glass; 3% plastic	1.8
DelMonte fruit blends	81	Great tasting fruit drink for adults	50% juice	$1.79–$1.99 (48 oz)	glass brik	0.1
General Foods	73					
Kool-Aid Koolers	57	The wacky, "cool" juice drink for kids	20% juice	$0.79–$0.99 (brik)	100% brik	4.6
Tang	16	100% Natural with great taste and variety targeted to kids	10% juice	$0.79–$0.99 (brik)	100% brik	2.5
Nestlé	73					
Juicy Juice	38	100% Juice and they're not	100% juice for kids	$1.59 (46 oz) $1.19 (brik)	76% can 21% brik 3% glass	2.5
Other Libby's	35					
Tree Top	177	100% Pure fruit juices targeted to adults	100% juice blends based largely on apple juice, product inferior due to the absence of natural flavors	$1.79–$1.99 (48 oz) $1.39–$1.49 (cans) $0.99–$1.29 (brik)	glass, brik, can	3.2
Seagrams Tropicana Twisters	13	Unusual taste	Line of 6 citrus-based juice drinks with 30% to 40% juice	$1.79–$1.99 (46 oz)	100% glass	7.9
Welch's	268	Heritage campaign (100 years)	50% juice	$1.79–$2.09 (40-oz glass)	glass, brik	2.7, umbrella campaign
Welch's	200					
Welch's Orchard	58			$0.99–$1.19 (brik)		
All others	10					

Source: Company records.

[a] A. C. Nielsen, 1988.

Manufacturer	Brand	1988 Volume	Versus Last Year (%)	Share	% National Distribution
Coke Foods	Total company	$1,255	+6.7	16.5	
	Minute Maid	1,038	+7.3	13.7	100
	HI-C	203	+4.6	2.7	100
	HI-C100	14	−10.8	0.1	89
Seagrams	Total company	$748	+24.2	9.8	
	Tropicana	735	+22.5	9.7	99
	Tropicana Twisters	13	+++	0.1	71
Ocean Spray	Total Ocean Spray	$696	+4.8	9.2	100
Procter and Gamble	Total Citrus Hill	$342	+36.1	4.5	98
Campbell Soup	Total Company	$268	+20.4	3.5	
	Campbells	50	+3.3	0.7	100
	V-8	218	+25.3	2.8	100
Welch Foods	Total company	$268	+9.9	3.5	
	Welch's	200	+12.5	2.6	100
	Welch's Orchard	58	−2.0	0.8	84
	All other	10	+45.3	0.1	
Quaker Oats	Gatorade	$221	+36.0	2.9	100
RJR/Nabisco	Total company	$195	+7.7	2.6	
	Hawaiian Punch	114	+0.6	1.5	100
	DelMonte	81	+19.9	1.1	99
Tree Top	Total Tree Top	$177	+12.5	2.3	78
Nestle	Total company	$73	+28.1	1.0	
	Juicy Juice	38	+51.3	0.6	45
	Libby Nectars	25	+7.5	0.3	63
	Hearts Delight	10	+17.5	0.1	34
General Foods	Total company	$73	+10.2	0.9	
	Kool-Aid Koolers	57	−12.6	0.8	99
	Tang	16	+++	0.1	89

Source: A. C. Nielsen, 1988.

and cherry—to give it a distinctive taste and color. Libby's management believed the brand would not be profitable for Fruitcrest.

Libby's own products in 1984 included Libby's Nectars, a range of drinks with 50% juice content, and Hearts Delight, a private label drink with less than 50% juice. Both were targeted at adults and families. In the opinion of many Nestle executives, prior to the launch of Juicy Juice, Libby's beverage range was "imbalanced" toward the price-oriented segment of the market. "Libby's was trying to fight the big brands like Del Monte and Minute Maid in the volume business," explained an executive in Vevey. "But, with such a small share, the company had no chance." In the early 1980s, Libby's annual losses amounted to nearly 10% of sales.[6]

---

[6] By 1984, Nestle had sold off Libby's other operations and had kept only the beverages.

In 1985, Libby's launched Juicy Juice nationally with a "100% juice" taste platform, spending $2.5 million on media (70%) and promotions (30%) targeted at children. But, a year later, due to what management diagnosed as "inferior" taste and a "weak marketing program," the line was withdrawn from national distribution. Juicy Juice continued to be marketed in its core market, the eastern states (representing 48% of the United States). By the end of 1986, the brand's sales were $13 million, or 60% below 1985 level.

In 1986, Juicy Juice was given to Robert Mead, the newly appointed group vice-president for beverages, and his management team to turn around. (*Refer to Exhibit 6 for Libby's partial organization chart in the United States.*) The appointment came when, in Mead's words, "the whole damn Libby's beverage business was going to hell." In his opinion, the product had failed because of poor taste, its "1950s image" labels, and a positioning that did not differentiate it from competition. Although constrained by limited funds, Mead's team was expected to put new life into Juicy Juice and relaunch it initially in its core markets and later nationally.

Juicy Juice was relaunched in 1987 following a number of changes. First, with help from Nestle's research facilities in the United States and outside, the formulation and taste of the product were improved dramatically. Consumer research showed that Juicy Juice had a taste superior to the major blended juice brands, Tree Top and Hi-C100. Next, labels were changed to show real fruits on the package and to substitute fruit names (for example, "Cherry") for what had been color names ("Real Red"). The new labels clearly identified Libby's as the parent behind Juicy Juice. Also, while the number of flavors was expanded from four to six (cherry, grape, punch, tropical, berry, apple), the pack sizes were reduced from four to two (a 1.4-liter can and a new 0.250-liter brik pack).[7] (*Refer to Exhibit 7 for sample labels.*)

According to Libby's management, the most important change from the past was repositioning Juicy Juice from good taste and "100% juice" to "We are 100% juice and they're not." (*Exhibit 8 shows a positioning map used by management for locating the repositioned Juicy Juice and its competitors.*) As Dennis Scott, the general manager for beverages, explained:

There is a lot of confusion out there. Some say they are "100% natural," or "a blend of ten different juices." Yet they all contain 50% or less of real fruit juice. So when we come along and say "we are 100% and they are not," that stays in the consumer's mind. Juicy Juice became a point of reference for the consumer against which to compare all others.

The brand carried a significant price premium over drinks, leading to relatively higher trade margins. Juicy Juice's $1.59 retail price for its 1.4-liter can, for example, compared

---

[7] An option for glass packaging was dropped, initially because of its higher costs.

with the $.79 to $.99 price range for similar sizes of Hi-C and Hawaiian Punch. Management believed that the premium prices reinforced the superior quality positioning. "When you offer something that's unique or with high value added, you ought to be able to get a price for it," argued Mead.

In 1987 the company spent $3 million on advertising in the media to relaunch the product in its core market, but stayed away from excessive price-oriented promotions common in the industry. (*Exhibit 9 shows 15-inch TV commercial storyboard for Juicy Juice and Hawaiian Punch, a leading drink.*)

Juicy Juice's positioning was thought to have contributed to its strength against recent competitive entries such as Coca-Cola's Hi-C100, a 100% blended juice brand extension from Hi-C. "They came at us with all kinds of ad dollars," recalled Mead. "But, when they raised their prices for the juice, the consumers refused to pay. They said 'you are a drink, a price brand, and I won't buy what you are selling.' "

Results to Date

"With this improved product, improved label, improved positioning, and improved everything else," Mead recalled, "we went to war."

The results of the relaunch were dramatic. By the end of 1987, a full year later, Juicy Juice sales in its core market had increased by 82% to $23 million. In 1988, when the product was reintroduced to new markets representing an additional 21% of the United States sales increased by another 32% to $31 million. (Between 1986 and 1988, the total shelf-stable blended segment had grown by 20% to $145 million.) Currently, Juicy Juice was being sold in cans (73% of dollar shipment) in addition to brik packs (24%) and the newly introduced glass (3%). It was distributed through more than 28,000 grocery stores in 42 states, representing 80% of national market. Libby's management projected sales of nearly $50 million nationwide in 1989. (*Refer to Exhibit 10 for a consumer profile drawn by management for the relaunched Juicy Juice. Exhibit 11 shows highlights of the brand's 1989 marketing plan.*)

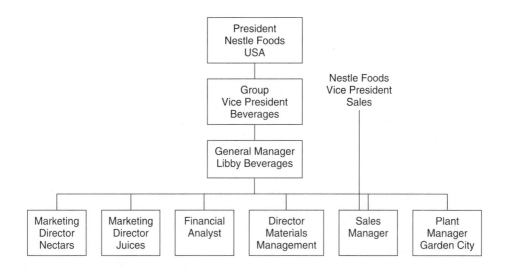

EXHIBIT 6   Libby's U.S. Division Reporting Structure   *Source:* Company records.

UM BONGO BY LIBBY'S: THE "JUNGLE JUICE"

The success of Um Bongo is due to its concept—a product developed specifically for kids. It's not a me-too this or a me-too that which anybody can imitate. It's UM BONGO from nose to tail!   A Nestle beverage executive in Vevey, Switzerland.

Um Bongo was one of the few juice drinks targeted at children with a fun overtone; its advertising was very instrumental in getting the product off to a good start.   *A Libby's marketing manager in Croyden, United Kingdom.*

History

Um Bongo was introduced in 1984 by Libby's U.K. beverages division. It was the company's newest entry in a growing but also highly competitive local market for fruit juices and drinks where price-oriented private brands held more than 50% share. Libby's other products included a line of fruit and vegetable juices and drinks targeted primarily at adults. The company was also producing under private labels. In the early-1980s, the U.K. company was annually losing approximately

2% on a stagnating turnover of about $15 million. (*Refer to Exhibit 12 for data on the U.K. market and shares.*)

Before Um Bongo's introduction, company-sponsored research had shown that, while annual per capita consumption of traditional beverages such as tea (290 liters), milk (110 liters), and beer (100 liters) had declined over the years, consumption of soft drinks (100 liters) and fruit juices and drinks (14 liters) had risen constantly. Research also showed that 45% of all soft drinks was consumed by children aged 15 years or younger, a segment accounting for only 20% of the population.[8] Furthermore, focus group discussions revealed that fruit juices and drinks, though considered by children as "good for you," suffered from having an old traditional image compared to the younger and more contemporary soft drinks. Mothers indicated that they wanted a healthier alternative to soft drinks, which they thought to be artificial and "not good for you."

"All those facts led to the conclusion that there was a marketing opportunity for a prod-

[8] Population of the UK in 1989 = 57 million.

EXHIBIT 7   Juicy Juice: Sample Labels

436

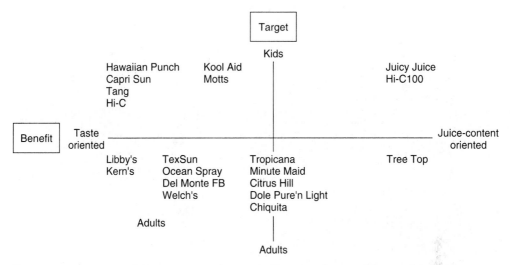

EXHIBIT 8   Juicy Juice Positioning (Based on 1987 Creative)   *Source:* Company Records.

uct especially developed for children," re-called Paul Lawrence, the U.K. marketing manager for Libby's beverages. "Thus was born Um Bongo."

Um Bongo was a blended drink with 25% juice content. It was launched under Libby's umbrella with one flavor, a mixture of nine juices, and in two brik pack sizes (1 liter and 0.2 liter). Its extraordinary "jungle name" and its "jungle juice" positioning were decidedly unique, helping the brand to stand out with its offer of a "balance of fun and health." Almost every aspect of the product, including its tropical flavor, color, packaging, and cartoon advertising, had been designed for and tested with children and their mothers. The "jungle juice" concept had been developed by Libby's advertising agency to project the "fun overtone," which management considered important. (*Refer to Exhibits 13 and 14 for samples of packaging and TV commercial storyboard, respectively. Exhibit 15 shows U.K. consumer research data on Um Bongo.*)

Um Bongo carried a premium price that was 32% over private brand drinks, but 10% below equivalent volumes of 100% fruit juices. The launch was supported in its first year by $1.5 million in advertising and $1 million in consumer and trade promotions. New flavors

(Apple Um Bongo and Orange Um Bongo) were introduced subsequently, thus capitalizing on the largest flavor segments in the juice and drinks category. The company also added a new package incorporating three single-serve briks. In 1988, $230,000 was spent on advertising and $152,000 on promotions.

Results to Date

Um Bongo's factory sales in its first year of introduction were $2.1 million. The brand had grown to $3.9 million by 1988, accounting for 20% of Libby's total sales in beverages. In 1989, sales were expected to grow by about 40%. Um Bongo's performance was a key factor behind the U.K. division's growth in total sales and the significantly improved profitability since 1984.

Um Bongo's success had led to the entry of what management considered to be imitative drinks—brands such as Kia Ora by Cadbury Schweppes in 1986 and Fruit Troop by Del Monte, a division of RJR/Nabisco, in 1989. Both brands had targeted children and their mothers and, like Um Bongo, had used cartoon characters on packaging and in TV commercials. In mid-1989, Libby's management carefully watched Del Monte's launch of Fruit

"Trick Glass"

KID #1: You'll never get more than 10% real juice out of those drinks.

No matter how much you pour.

But Juicy Juice from Libby's is 100% real fruit juice.

KID #2: Wow.

ANNCR: Juicy Juice is a juicer juice.

KID #1: It's 100%.

EXHIBIT 9 Juicy Juice Storyboard

EXHIBIT 10 Juicy Juice Consumer Profile

1. *DEMOGRAPHICS*
   Heavy users
      Income: +$25M/yr.
      Female head under 35 and full-time
         housewife/mother
      Household size: 3+
      User's age: 2–11
2. *PURCHASING PATTERNS*
   Juice purchase cycle is short.
      Purchased every 2 weeks
      Comparatively, coffee is purchased every 9 weeks
   Juice is a high impulse item.
      Planned purchase for juice: 39%
      Planned purchase for coffee: 64%

Source: Company records.

EXHIBIT 11 Highlights of 1989 Marketing Plan:
Juicy Juice

1. Long-term strategy: Increase sales to $100 million
   plus via expansion of product into multiple store locations (shelf-stable and refrigerated) and through multiple distribution outlets (grocery stores, nonfood,
   convenience stores, vending, food service).
2. Short-term strategies
   • Increase household penetration
   • Increase product usage
   • Continue to steal share from juice drinks and 100%
     juices
   • Continue to improve profitability
3. Target sales: $39 million
   Target spending: $9   million (+13% over 1988)
      Ads   3   million
      Consumer promotion   1.3 million
      Trade promotion   4.7 million
4. Pricing: Price at significant premium to kid's 10%
   drinks, but not at a premium that risks volume. Parity
   with other 100% juices.
5. Advertising: To create awareness in new markets;
   maintain awareness in core markets.
6. Positioning: Juicy Juice is the 100% juice blend alternative to kids' 10% juice drinks.
   Target audience: Moms ages 25 to 49 with kids 2 to
   11, $20,000+ household income
7. Promotions:
   • Consumer: To maintain current heavy-user base
                To increase household penetration
   • Trade: To increase listings in core market and new
            expansion markets
            To focus on gaining displays at reduced price
8. New products: continue work on new flavors, packaging, and form (concentrate).

Troop, which was being supported with heavy
advertising.

Um Bongo's performance in the United
Kingdom had not gone unnoticed by Libby's
other European divisions. Since 1987 the
Spanish and Portuguese companies had introduced Um Bongo in their markets. The brand
concept, including its communication, had
been kept intact, and only the product's taste
and the language on the label were adapted locally. The drinks were produced from imported concentrates. Both countries had used
the U.K. TV commercials dubbed in the local
language.

In Spain, the per capita consumption of
processed fruit juices and drinks (less than 2
liters) had traditionally been limited due to
the availability of freshly prepared varieties at
relatively low prices.[9] The market was also characterized by low marketing activities and poor-
quality products. (*Refer to Exhibit 16 for data on
the Spanish market.*)

Libby's produced a line of fruit juices and
drinks targeted at families. Sales had declined
by about 25% in volume since the early 1980s
to $3.5 million in 1986, or less than 3 million
liters. Nestle executives attributed the decline
to poor packaging, unfocused positioning,
and the absence of advertising support.

Libby's beverage sales in Spain received a
boost with the 1987 test introduction of Um
Bongo in the Valencia region, which represented 25% of the national market. Supported
by $100,000 in TV advertising, the brand's
sales reached $110,000 dollars in the test area,
a level several times higher than its target. In
1988, sales in the region had grown to
$350,000 and 300,000 liters. The increased
marketing activities related to Um Bongo had
helped to pull the rest of Libby's business up
to a total of $4.5 million and 4.2 million liters
in 1988. The management projected an additional 90% growth for Um Bongo in 1989 after national introduction.

In Portugal, a smaller market than Spain
but with similar features, Um Bongo had been
introduced nationally in the spring of 1988.[10]
Nestle's local management had recently con-

---

[9] Population of Spain in 1989 = 39 million.

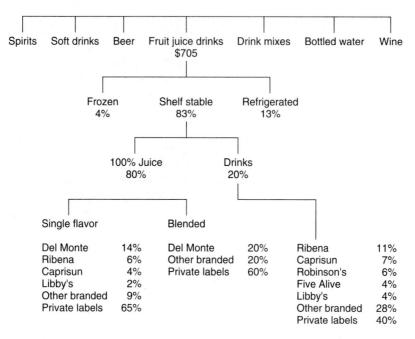

| Spirits | Soft drinks | Beer | Fruit juice drinks $705 | Drink mixes | Bottled water | Wine |

Frozen 4% **Shelf stable** 83% **Refrigerated** 13%

100% Juice 80% **Drinks** 20%

Single flavor

Del Monte	14%
Ribena	6%
Caprisun	4%
Libby's	2%
Other branded	9%
Private labels	65%

Blended

Del Monte	20%
Other branded	20%
Private labels	60%

Ribena	11%
Caprisun	7%
Robinson's	6%
Five Alive	4%
Libby's	4%
Other branded	28%
Private labels	40%

EXHIBIT 12 Segmentation of the U.K. Beverage Market, 1988 (million $)

cluded that significant growth opportunities existed in the beverages sector where Libby's had not been present. Previously, sales had been limited to only Nestle's dry grocery products such as coffee and cereals. (*Exhibit 17 provides data on the Portuguese juice and drinks market.*)

In the words of Patrick Martin, the Nestle headquarters product manager for juices and drinks, Um Bongo's introduction in Portugal "blew up the market." With an advertising support of $1.2 million, Um Bongo's national sales for the year reached $4.7 million or 4.8 million liters. The first year sales were 240% of budget. By early 1989, with less than 1 year in the market, Um Bongo had reached what management believed was a significant market position and accounted for close to 5% of total Nestle sales in the country. The company expected a doubling of Um Bongo sales in 1989.

———
[10] Population of Portugal = 10.5 million.

REACTIONS IN THE UNITED STATES TO UM BONGO

Convinced that Um Bongo was a global concept with a universal appeal, executives at Vevey had prodded Libby's U.S. management to examine the opportunities for the brand's introduction in the American market. According to one headquarters executive, "We have a winner and it would be a pity if we couldn't transfer it to the world's largest market—the United States."

Research Results

Recently, Libby's U.S. management had commissioned a study to test the acceptance of Um Bongo by the American consumer. The research consisted of a taste test and interviews with 300 children between the ages of 8 and 18 in four states—Ohio, New York, Arizona, and Florida. Um Bongo imported from the United

EXHIBIT 13 Um Bongo Brik Packs

Kingdom was tested against the leading drink, Hawaiian Punch. The research also aimed to evaluate the effectiveness of Um Bongo's "jungle" commercial used in the United Kingdom, Spain, and Portugal.

The study's overall conclusion stated that "Um Bongo could be a viable entry in the U.S. fruit juice/drinks market, given certain refinements." The refinements primarily were making the flavor less "sour/tangy" and changing the commercial so that the product concept would be more clearly communicated. The product was rated equal to Hawaiian Punch in everything except "purchase interest" and "taste," where the latter's ratings were significantly higher. (*Refer to the Appendix for a summary of the study's findings and conclusions.*)

Management Priorities

"It's hard for Um Bongo to make the jump to the U.S. marketplace because food habits are so culturally dependent," Dennis Scott explained his reactions to the brand's performance in the test. "To give you a fresh example on how cultural food is, we tested a 1-liter (32-oz.) brik pack, which is so popular in Europe but doesn't exist here. We thought it made inherent sense for the American consumer. We

put Juicy Juice into it, made big supermarket displays with special prices, but the American consumer said, 'I don't know what that is, so I am not going to venture out.' People are just resistant to change."

A change in Um Bongo's flavor had been considered by U.S. management. But, according to Scott, "We just don't have the time or personnel to focus on it right now. We have our hands full."

Currently, Scott and his colleagues were preoccupied with Juicy Juice's performance on a national level. "Our aim is to make Juicy Juice a $100 million business in 5 years," explained Jean Graham, Juicy Juice's marketing director. Among short- and medium-term actions being planned were completion of the national roll-out, introduction of new concentrated and refrigerated forms, expansion into nongrocery outlets, and the addition of glass packaging. Improved household penetration was a prime medium-term objective. With 7.8% penetration, Juicy Juice was trailing Hi-C (16%) and Ocean Spray (34%).

Profitability remained another issue of immediate concern. "Our biggest challenge is to make this business profitable," explained Graham. "We have high costs in a low-margin industry. Our current gross margin is 35%, which is the number off the production line,

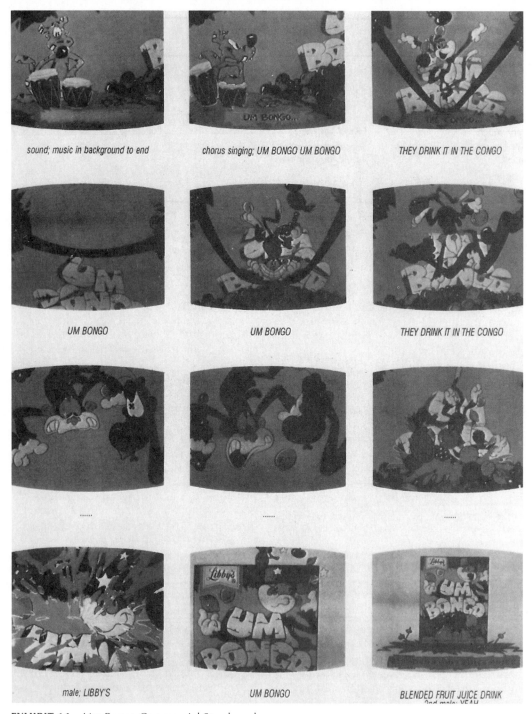

EXHIBIT 14   Um Bongo Commercial Storyboard

EXHIBIT 15 U.K. Consumer Data on Um Bongo[a]

Children's Opinion (%)		Children's Agreement with Attributes[b] (%)		Mothers' Agreement with Attributes[b] (%)	
Like a lot	53	Fun	81	Fun	93
Quite like it	34	Something I would buy	79	Children would ask for it	92
		Exciting flavor	84	High quality	80
Don't like it very much	7	Good for me	86	Full of goodness	70
Don't like it at all	3	Something mother would	65		
No opinion	3	buy for me			
	100				

[a] Responses given after product trial and exposure to video of TV commercial.

[b] Percentages do not add up to 100 due to multiple responses.

before any distribution costs or marketing expenses. That's pitiful compared to other grocery categories such as 65% on tea or 85% on corn chip snacks."

In 1989, management was looking at ways of reducing the raw material and packaging costs. A target date of 1990 was set for breaking even on Juicy Juice.

Other projects preoccupying Libby's management included a new children's beverage product made from a combination of milk and fruit juices. "We are looking at 'Moo Juice' or some such brand name for a milkshakelike product that means fun to kids and health to moms," explained Graham. The product was in an early phase of development.

Management believed that timing was an-

other factor in favor of innovative new products such as milk–juice mix and against a drink like Um Bongo. "The Um Bongo idea has severe competition today in the United States from companies like Coca-Cola, General Foods, Ocean Spray and RJR/Nabisco," argued Scott. "If we had introduced such a product a few years ago, it might have had a chance. But Um Bongo would be entry number 5 at this point."

CONCLUSION

Vevey was aware of the U.S. management's views on Um Bongo. "There is no secret about our different views concerning Um Bongo's potential in the United States," confirmed Pa-

EXHIBIT 16 Spanish Fruit Juice and Drinks Market, 1988[a]

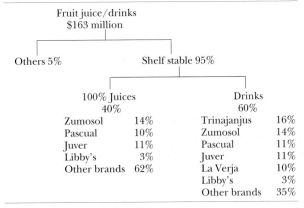

100% Juices 40%		Drinks 60%	
Zumosol	14%	Trinajanjus	16%
Pascual	10%	Zumosol	14%
Juver	11%	Pascual	11%
Libby's	3%	Juver	11%
Other brands	62%	La Verja	10%
		Libby's	3%
		Other brands	35%

Source: Company records.

[a] Excludes fresh juices.

EXHIBIT 17 Portuguese Fruit Juice and Drinks Market, 1988[a]

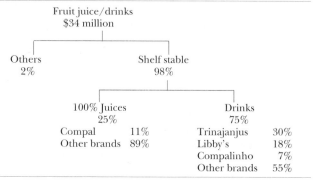

Source: Company records.

[a] Excludes fresh juices.

tricia Martin, the worldwide juice and drinks product manager. "While we are totally convinced that it's a good product concept, we also understand their hesitation to take on ideas from outside. It's natural. Even the management in Portugal were initially resistant to the Um Bongo idea, and look what happened there when they tried it. So our attitude is: 'Give it a try and prove the idea wrong.' Meanwhile, all we could do from here is to build confidence in the product by telling them what is going on elsewhere."

Martin and his colleagues in Vevey advocated a test marketing of Um Bongo as the next step in the United States. "We would like to see a real market test and not just a consumer taste test," Martin explained. Estimated costs of undertaking such a test ranged from $500,000 to $1 million per city, including advertising and promotional expenses. A minimum of two major cities representing at least 2% of the U.S. consumption was considered necessary for representative results.

On the U.S. side, meanwhile, the attention was focused on the future of Juicy Juice. Mead described his views on the next steps: "My challenge is to identify the three biggest ideas and make sure we execute them. Therefore, I tell my people I don't want to hear about product extensions. You've got big, big opportunities still with Juicy Juice that need to be fulfilled. Once you've the important piece in place, we can always add another. We can always circle back."

APPENDIX
UNITED STATES UM BONGO RESEARCH: INTERPRETATIVE SUMMARY AND SELECTED FINDINGS

Background and Purpose

The ready-to-drink fruit juice and fruit drink markets continue to be among the fastest segments of the overall U.S. beverage market.

Nestlé has offered Libby USA the opportunity to market Um Bongo, a ready-to-drink fruit juice-drink presently being successfully marketed by Libby in the United Kingdom.

Management wishes to evaluate the acceptability of the product to the American consumer. Specifically to determine:

1. The acceptance of the Um Bongo product versus Hawaiian Punch (the market leader) on a blind taste basis

2. The incremental value of the Um Bongo concept (in video form) in heightening the appeal of the product

3. How well the Um Bongo product lives up to the expectations generated by the concept

4. The communication ability of the Um Bongo commercial

Conclusions/Recommendations

Based on the research results, it appears that Um Bongo could be a viable entry in the

U.S. fruit juice/drink market given certain refinements.

The strength of the Um Bongo product itself lies in the specific fruit flavors and the strength of those flavors. However, a "sour/tangy" taste seems to pull down the product's acceptance and would need to be reduced to improve acceptance.

From a conceptual standpoint, the current commercial enhances the product's acceptance and the perception that the product is unique—definitely a plus in the vast sea of fruit juice/drink beverages. However, the commercial needs to communicate the concept in a clearer manner. It is hypothesized that after viewing the commercial consumers are not sure of what to expect and when they taste it they are pleasantly surprised. A more focused and clear explanation of the product in the commercial without diminishing the uniqueness would aid in enhancing the product's acceptance overall.

Key Findings

1. The Um Bongo commercial generated limited interest in trying the product. After trial, however, consumers were more receptive to the product.
2. Positioning the product prior to trial enhanced the product's perception of being unique as well as its acceptance overall.
3. On a blind basis, Um Bongo performs similarly to Hawaiian Punch in terms of overall rating and total purchase interest. However, when directly compared, Hawaiian Punch is significantly preferred.
4. Um Bongo's product advantages are seen in its specific fruit flavors and the strength of those flavors. However, its "sour/tangy" aspect was the major focus for rejection.

Summary of Findings

I. Video Impact
1. Within the context of a single viewing, the Um Bongo video produces limited enthusiasm for product trial.
2. The video succeeds in communicating the brand name and places the product squarely in the fruit juice-drink market.

3. Consumers who are reluctant to try Um Bongo have ill-defined concerns apparently based on their difficulty in understanding words in the commercial.
4. Despite these reservations, concept positioning via the video ultimately appears to aid in the actual product's acceptance.

II. Product Acceptance after Commercial Exposure
1. The product fosters significantly greater buying interest than was considered before trial; it was better than expected.
2. Um Bongo is judged best in terms of its uniqueness; providing a good overall taste through a combination of strong, tangy fruit flavors.
3. Acceptance/rejection, although often expressed in terms of sweetness/tartness levels, ultimately translates into the impact of these physical attributes on beverage benefits, that is, taste satisfying, refreshing.

III. Blind Acceptance of Um Bongo versus Hawaiian Punch
1. In absolute terms, the Um Bongo product produces ratings approximate to those given the Hawaiian Punch.
2. They are not equal however:

   • Purchase interest in Hawaiian Punch is significantly higher.
   • When directly compared, Hawaiian Punch is overwhelmingly preferred to Um Bongo.

3. The sweeter, not too tart flavor of Hawaiian Punch is the dominant reason for its preference.
4. Tanginess is the major point of focus in rejecting Um Bongo.

IV. Selected Tables
A. Impact of Video
1. *The Um Bongo commercial*, albeit after a single exposure, *produces only limited enthusiasm for product trial.*

Just 5% of children 8 to 18 years of age express a definite commitment to buy. The overwhelming reaction appears to be one of cautious reserve, with 81% indicating a "probably buy" to "might or might not buy" purchase interest.

	Postvideo Purchase Intent
Base: Total respondents	(150)
Definitely would buy	5
Probably would buy	50
Might or might not buy	31
Probably would *not* buy	7
Definitely would *not* buy	7

2. *The video succeeds in communicating the brand name and places the product squarely in the fruit juice-drink market.*

- 86% recall Um Bongo as the brand name.
- 84% believe product will be most similar to other fruit juice-drinks, particularly Hawaiian Punch.

	One Beverage Most Similar
Base: Total respondents	(150)
Hawaiian Punch	45
Juicy Juice	22
Hi-C	17
Orange juice	7
Kool-Aid	4

3. *Commercial also positions Um Bongo as most appropriate for preteenage children at other than the formal meal occasions of dinner and breakfast.*

- Regardless of age, Um Bongo is perceived as most suitable for young chil-

Use/Occasions Appropriateness

		Age	
	Total	8–13	14–18
Base: Total respondents	(150)	(76)	(74)
	%	%	%
Would be likely to use:			
Children under 8	89	88	89
Children 8–12	73	67	78
Teenagers 13–19	21	24	19
Adults 20 and over	13	17	10
With breakfast	47	51	42
"On the go" occasions	58	54	62
Drink at home	79	**87**	**70**
With a snack	79	83	76
With lunch	64	68	60
With dinner	23	29	16
Away from home	60	66	54

Boldface indicates significant difference at the 90% level of confidence.

dren, particularly those under 8. Few teenagers (19%) see the product directed at them, while 2 of 3 (67%) preteens indicate they would be likely to use.

- Nonmeal at-home occasions are considered best for Um Bongo.

4. *In spite of these reservations, the video, as the tool for presenting the Um Bongo concept, appears to favorably alter ultimate product acceptance.*

Actual product ratings and interest in buying Um Bongo are uniformly higher when consumers are previously shown the video than when tasting the product occurs without concept positioning.

Video Impact on Product Evaluation

	Um Bongo		
	With Video	Without Video	
	(150)	(75)	Difference
Base:	%	%	(+/−)
Purchase intent			
% Definitely would buy	**25**	**15**	−10
Total positive	67	60	−7
Overall rating			
% Excellent/ extremely good	44	33	−11
Mean	3.97	3.80	−17
Attribute ratings (% excellent/extremely good)			
Is tangy	**50**	**36**	−14
Is refreshing	47	39	−8
Has a strong fruit taste	56	49	−7
Is sweet tasting	46	43	−3
Is satisfying	44	40	−4
Is bitter tasting	27	20	−7
Is a good combination of flavors	49	45	−4
Has a good overall flavor	51	41	−10
Leaves a pleasant taste in your mouth	46	43	−3
Has an appealing color	45	43	−2
Is different	59	56	−3
Is a beverage for me	44	41	−3
Is fun to drink	43	33	−10

Boldface indicates significant difference at the 90% level of confidence.

B. **Product Acceptance after Commercial Exposure**

With product trial, the uncertainties that existed

after only concept exposure are clarified, producing a significantly broader base of favorably disposed purchasers.

Tasting the product engenders significantly greater buying interest than was considered before trial.

Purchase Intent

Base:	Postvideo Exposure	Post Product Trial	Difference
Total respondents	(150)	(150)	(+/-)
	%	%	
Definitely would buy	**5**	**25**	**+20**
Probably would buy	50	42	−8
(Total Positive)	**(55)**	**(67)**	**+12**
Might or might not buy	31	15	−16
Probably would *not* buy	7	7	±
Definitely would *not* buy	7	11	+4

Boldface indicates significant difference at the 90% level of confidence.

C. Product Acceptance Blind versus Hawaiian Punch

Um Bongo overall and specific product characteristics ratings closely parallel those elicited by Hawaiian Punch. Only in the specific area of fruit taste does Hawaiian Punch garner a higher satisfaction rating.

Nevertheless, in spite of this seemingly similar level of acceptance, purchase interest is significantly greater for Hawaiian Punch.

Blind Test: Um Bongo and Hawaiian Punch

Base: Total respondents	Um Bongo (75) %	Hawaiian Punch (75) %
Purchase intent		
% Definitively would buy	**15**	**29**
Total positive	60	72
Overall rating		
% Excellent/extremely good	33	36
Mean	3.80	4.04
Attribute ratings (% excellent/extremely good)		
Is tangy	36	27
Is refreshing	39	43
Has a strong fruit taste	49	48
Is sweet tasting	43	49
Is satisfying	40	45
Is bitter tasting	20	11
Is a good combination of flavors	45	45
Has a good overall flavor	41	41
Leaves a pleasant taste in your mouth	43	41
Has an appealing color	43	56
Is different	56	43
Is a beverage for me	41	44
Is fun to drink	33	37
Directional Ratings (% just right)		
Sweetness	77	80
Color	79	79
Fruit taste	**68**	**84**
Too strong	17	11
Too weak	15	5

Boldface indicates significant difference at the 90% level of confidence

Alliance ANDIV

One day in early July 1988, Stephen Kenyon closed his briefcase and prepared to head home. Kenyon, senior product manager for companion animals (dogs and cats) in Alliance's ANDIV Division, had completed analyzing the outstanding second-quarter 1988 sales figures for his product, Lung-Check, a parasite preventive for dogs. Lung-Check had been launched successfully in the United States, Canada, and Japan in 1987, and by the end of the year, was the number 2 product for the prevention of canine lungworm disease (CLD). ANDIV expected it to attain the top position in 1988.

Despite the success of the past year, Kenyon faced a difficult marketing challenge in devising a strategy for the launch of Lung-Check in Europe. Unlike in the product's current markets, CLD prevention and consumer education about the disease were virtually nonexistent among Western European veterinarians, although the incidence of this devastating (and fatal) disease had increased rapidly in recent years in many areas of Western Europe.

The potential for sales based on the number of dogs in Western Europe approached 60% of the existing $83 million U.S. market, but the reluctance of European veterinarians to participate in CLD prevention troubled Kenyon. To compound the problem, ANDIV had no presence among companion-animal veterinarians in Western Europe; all previous sales efforts had been in the production-animal market (sheep, swine, poultry, and cattle). Moreover, the approaching 1992 Economic Unity among Western European countries could affect the competitive structure of the industry. Nevertheless, ANDIV's senior management remained committed to marketing Lung-Check globally and to using this product as a cornerstone to develop a global presence in the companion-animal market.

Kenyon realized he needed to address several fundamental questions before developing a marketing plan for Lung-Check. First, could he transfer his marketing strategy from the United States and Canada (mature, growing markets) to Western European countries (infant markets)? Did consumer segments vary among European countries, or did global market segments exist among dog owners? What factors motivated the veterinarians in Western European countries, and how did they perceive the threat of CLD? What pricing strategy should he consider? What were the near-term and long-term competitive threats for the CLD-preventive market?

ALLIANCE, INC., AND THE ANDIV DIVISION

Alliance was one of the world's largest and most successful health-care companies. Its core business was the discovery, development, and manufacture of products to improve the health

This case was prepared by Stephen M. Kelley, under the supervision of Professor Christopher Gale, through the cooperation of a company that prefers to remain anonymous. Some data have been disguised. Copyright © 1989 by the University of Virginia Darden School Foundation, Charlottesville, VA. All rights reserved.

and quality of life for humans and animals. Market analysts cited Alliance as a research-intensive company, devoting the highest percentage of its funds to research (16%) of any major company in the health-care industry. In 1987, Alliance planned to devote over $600 million to research activities and, based on future sales projections, anticipated increasing this amount to over $1 billion in the early 1990s. In addition to Alliance's research success, the company was admired throughout corporate America for its overall success.

Alliance Research Laboratories Division (ARLD) was charged with conducting all research and development for new products of the various operating divisions of the organization. The ANDIV Division's mission (with ALRD's support) was to discover, develop, and market specialty products to improve the health and productivity of animals. The division generated over 80% of its revenues from the production-animal market. This segment was profitable, but historically sales and profits rose and fell with the strength of the highly cyclical agricultural economy.

Alliance ANDIV marketed products specifically for various animal species; the common link among its products was that they were derivatives of a core, patented compound—Pneumectrin. All Pneumectrin-based products were designed for the prevention of internal parasites that crippled the health and productivity of animals. Alliance had developed Pneumectrin at an estimated cost of $75 million in the late 1970s. Despite the high development costs, the many products derived from Pneumectrin and marketed to the animal-health industry far exceeded the company's original sales expectations for the compound. (Exhibit 1 lists 1987 sales by species.)

In an effort to lessen dependence on the production-animal segment, ANDIV management had charged ARLD with developing a Pneumectrin-based product for the prevention of CLD; after spending $18 million in development costs, ARLD produced Lung-Check. Alliance ANDIV launched Lung-Check in the United States and Canada in April 1987. First-year sales exceeded $19 million. Alliance expected to sell $53 million of Lung-Check in 1988 (including new sales in Japan and Australia) and to replace Fisher's Carterets as the market leader. The advantage of Lung-Check was that the pet owner had to administer the product (a pill) only once every 30 days (compared with once each day for Carterets).

ANDIV believed Lung-Check and the companion-animal industry in general represented an excellent product to establish a global presence in the portion of the companion-animal market in which ANDIV was interested. ANDIV wanted to pursue business only in the ethical (prescription) segment of the companion-animal industry and avoid the highly competitive over-the-counter market.

THE COMPANION-ANIMAL MARKET

The companion-animal market was, for the most part, confined to the United States and other developed countries. In 1988, industry analysts estimated that the global market for companion-animal health-care products approached $685 million, of which 60% were sold in the United States (see Exhibit 2). The percentage of global dollar sales of animal-health-care products in the United States (60%) exceeded the U.S. share of the worldwide population of companion animals.

EXHIBIT 1 Pneumectrin Sales by Species, 1987

	Millions	Percentage
Cattle	$217	71
Sheep	12	4
Swine	25	8
Horses	34	11
Dogs	19	6
Total	$307	100

Source: Company records.

EXHIBIT 2 World Companion-animal Health Market, 1988 Sales (millions of dollars)

Endoparasiticides		$105
Ectoparasiticides		250
	Total parasiticides	$355
Biologicals		155
Other pharmaceuticals		175
	Total pharmaceuticals	$685

Source: Company records.

Products manufactured for companion animals' health covered a broad spectrum of ailments or potential ailments. Alliance focused its efforts on developing products to fight or prevent ectoparasites (internal parasites), because management believed the ectoparasiticide segment of the market offered the highest dollar share; the most opportunity to develop highly differentiated, patent-protected product(s); and the greatest opportunity for future growth.

Within the ectoparasiticide segment, ARLD researchers had focused on a product for the prevention of CLD, because sales of products to prevent this disease had risen at a 32% annual rate in the United States during the 1982–1986 period. Furthermore, ARLD strongly believed it could develop a unique product based on the existing Pneumectrin chemistry and thus minimize research and development costs to the corporation. In essence, the companion-animal segment represented the logical next step for ANDIV's species-diversification effort.

The Role of the Veterinarian

As of July 1988, in the United States there were approximately 30,000 licensed veterinarians. Of this total, about 18,000 veterinarians participated exclusively in companion-animal practice.

Generally, veterinarians were businesspersons as much as they were animal-health-care professionals. According to *Vet Economics*, the average salary of U.S. veterinarians was $37,000 a year, substantially less than their counterparts in the human side of the business. Industry experts expected the supply of new veterinarians to exceed future demand, however, and thus create competitive economic pressures among veterinarians.

Veterinarians differed from human doctors in that they enjoyed the right to pharmacy (resell) animal-health-care pharmaceuticals to their clients. In the United States, industry experts estimated that companion-animal veterinarians generated 30% to 40% of their clinic revenues through dispensing companion-animal pharmaceuticals. On the sale of these

pharmaceuticals, the veterinarian typically enjoyed a 35% to 40% markup (based on selling price = 100%). Industry analysts expected the dispensing of animal-care pharmaceuticals to play an increasingly important role in the economics of the companion-animal health-care industry as competitive pressures increased.

The role and economic profile of the veterinarian in Canada and Australia paralleled those in the United States. Western European veterinarians also enjoyed the right to pharmacy, but industry experts contended they were much less active in the various preventive markets. Focus-group interviews with veterinarians in Italy, Spain, and France (Appendix A) suggested that the older veterinarians tended to treat existing ailments and were less interested in preventives. Younger veterinarians with recent exposure to current disease patterns were more receptive to advocating the use of preventives to protect dogs.

In addition to these findings, of particular concern to ANDIV management was the fact that most Western European veterinarians lacked the simple but critical blood-testing kit to test for CLD. Alliance executives recognized that supplying this test kit to veterinarians would be an important part of its sales strategy for Western Europe.

Market Segments by Types of Dog Owners

Market research indicated that about 35% of U.S. households owned canine pets. After extensive research, ANDIV's market research department had established five distinct market segments of dog owners in the United States (although whether these segments applied in Europe was unknown). Using focus groups, ANDIV developed profiles for the five market segments and used these profiles to determine the likelihood of dog owners to purchase a CLD preventive.

Qualitative analysis of the U.S. focus-group interviews indicated that those segments willing to purchase veterinary care viewed it as expensive, but, in practice, they were willing to spend large sums of money to care for their pets. In essence, pet owners who purchased pet care perceived this care as an emotional decision, not an economic one. Industry experts estimated that total expenditures on veterinary care (prescriptions and services) in the United States approached $5 billion in 1987. Of this care, dogs received $3 billion, cats about $1 billion, and production animals and horses about $850 million. Because these consumers who purchased preventive products did so on the basis of "perceived value" rather than straight economics, veterinarians had little trouble convincing pet owners to purchase canine lungworm preventives based on two factors. The first factor was emotional—to preserve the animal's health and prevent it from suffering a destructive disease. Second, the costs of prevention were substantially less than the costs of treatment for the disease ($25 for a 6-month supply of a preventive versus $200 for eradication of the disease from an infected animal).

The five distinct dog-owner segments developed by ANDIV management were as follows:

Suburbanite

This group considered the dog to be a member of the household. The owners tended to be married, with one or two children, and lived in affluent suburbs. Dog ownership was considered a necessary element of their image. Their active life-styles limited trips to the veterinarian, but they would likely administer any preventive recommended by the veterinarian for their dogs. This target segment represented 20% of all dog owners, and ANDIV estimated approximately 50% of Lung-Check sales to come from this segment.

Joe Average

This segment also considered the dog an important part of the family. Owners generally were blue-collar workers, often owned more than one dog, and had extremely close attachments to their pets. They were concerned about their pets' health and regularly took them to the vet. This target segment represented 30% of all dogs and 40% of ANDIV's sales.

Lonely Lady

This group considered the dog a substitute child and was composed of divorced, widowed, or maiden women who had no children or no children living at home. They treated their dogs with great affection and concern, as if the dog were a newborn baby. They represented 20% of all dog owners and approximately 10% of ANDIV's sales. ANDIV executives believed the most trouble existed in penetrating this market because of the Lonely Ladies' subtle perceptions that competitive products (particularly, Carterets) were daily "treats" for their dogs and because of the false perception that a once-a-day product would be more effective in preserving health than one administered monthly.

Country and Western Man

This segment considered the dog nothing special. The owner was likely to be a married man with children and to reside in rural areas. His income was generally below average, and he only owned a dog to please the children. These owners showed little interest in the pet and generally did not visit the veterinarian. If the dog got very sick, a shotgun and a shovel would solve the problem. This segment represented 25% of all dog owners and accounted for virtually no Lung-Check sales.

Poor Folk

Economics was the limiting factor in this segment. These people were emotionally attached to their dogs and considered the dog a good friend, but lack of money usually prevented them from seeking veterinary care. They often resided in rural areas and had low incomes. Like their Country and Western counterparts, they often ended a dog's illness with their own hands. This segment accounted for 5% of all dog owners and virtually none of ANDIV's sales.

Major Canine Lungworm Disease Markets

CLD was a debilitating and potentially fatal disease to dogs. The presence of adult lungworms caused many major respiratory problems, the most important of which was chronic congestive lung blockage.

Dogs contracted lungworm disease through infected mosquitoes, whose bite transmitted lungworm larvae into the dog's bloodstream. The larvae circulated through the dog and congested in the arteries and veins around the dog's lungs. As the lungworms grew, they gradually debilitated and eventually killed the dog. Infected dogs were also carriers of the disease; mosquitoes that bit an infected dog could transmit that blood to other dogs.

To treat canine lungworm disease, veterinarians administered a blood test to detect the presence of the lungworm larvae. If the tests were positive, the veterinarian had to administer a series of highly toxic and painful injections to the dog to remove the lungworm larvae. Therefore, veterinarians usually advocated the use of a lungworm preventive in areas of high disease incidence. Until Lung-Check, preventive products were administered daily and ensured that the dog would not contract the disease.

Active CLD prevention existed in the United States, Canada, Japan, and Australia. In those markets, diagnosis, treatment, and prevention procedures were firmly established, and many veterinarians considered revenues from prevention important to their practice.

The CLD risk was in direct proportion to the length of the mosquito season; thus the incidence of lungworm disease varied regionally. In the southern United States and northern Australia, where mosquitoes were active throughout the year, the risk of a lungworm infection lasted year round. In the northern United States and Canada, the mosquito season extended from 6 to 9 months.

In recent years, the incidence of lungworm disease had increased throughout North America (see Exhibit 3). Previously, low-incidence regions such as the Pacific Coast, the Rocky Mountain states, and southern Ontario reported dramatic growth in the disease. Reasons for this increase were the expanded mobility of the North American population and the appearance of (or the existence of) more durable mosquitoes that could survive in colder climates. Virtually all metropolitan areas of North America were reporting increased incidence of canine lungworm disease, often at an alarming rate.

The disease also existed in Western Europe, where it had increased dramatically throughout the 1980s along the coastal areas of Spain, France, Italy, and Portugal to a degree of incidence close to the interior Mid-Atlantic region of the United States (12% to 15% of the dog population). All countries in Western Europe reported cases of canine lungworm disease (see Exhibit 4 for a list of incidence rates on the macro level in various European countries, as well as dog populations, dog populations under veterinary care, and percentage of households owning dogs). Veterinary health-care experts expected CLD to expand rapidly throughout Western Europe.

Daily-administered carbamazine was the only competitive product to Lung-Check for use in the prevention of canine lungworm disease. As of 1987, the existing technology for this product no longer fell under patent, and three companies competed in this market. Of these companies, only Fisher approached Lung-Check sales estimates for 1988 ($38 million versus $53 million).

Despite the current limited competition, field reports indicated that two potential competitors were working on a once-a-month formulation for the prevention of CLD. Ciba-Geigy, a Swiss company, reportedly intended to launch its product in the fourth quarter of 1991. Sankyo, a Japanese company with a reputation for introducing products with low efficacy (safety-test) levels, also planned to pursue this market in Japan.

Ciba-Geigy represented a substantial threat. It had a broad line of companion-animal products and a global sales force for them, including a strong presence in the Western European market. Thus ANDIV management considered a successful launch of Lung-Check in Europe a year ahead of Ciba-Geigy essential—not merely to ensure Lung-Check's success in Europe, but also to position Alliance ANDIV as a viable participant in the European companion-animal market.

1960s

From its original area in the eastern half of the United States, lungworm disease has spread throughout the United States and into Canada. Experts say reasons for the spread include increased mobility of dogs, carrying the infection into areas where it previously was not found; increase in stray dogs, serving as reservoirs of infections; decreased mosquito control measures; and the parasite's adaptability to colder climate.

1980s

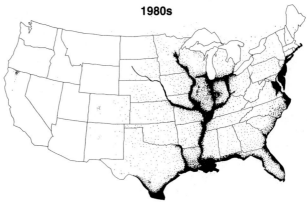

EXHIBIT 3 Spread of Lungworm Disease *Source:* Company records.

EXHIBIT 4 Selected Statistics on Dog Ownership and Care, 1987

	Dog Population (millions)	*Households Owning Dogs (%)*	*Under Vet Care (millions)*	*(%)*	*CLD Incidence (%)*
United States	70	37	49.7	71	7
Canada	8	35	5.2	65	2
Total North America	78	37	54.9	70	7
France[a]	11	25	7.7	70	7
France[b]	3	26	2.0	67	14
United Kingdom/Ireland	6	22	3.5	58	1
Italy[a]	8	18	5.1	64	3
Italy[b]	2	14	1.1	55	17
West Germany	4	8	3.0	75	1
Spain[a]	7	19	2.8	40	2
Spain[b]	2	21	0.8	40	11
Benelux	3	28	1.7	57	1
Portugal	0.5	9	0.2	40	6
Other Western Europe	3	16	2.0	67	1
Total European	49.5	20	29.9	60	4

[a] Except Mediterranean.

[b] Mediterranean.

Source: Company records.

LUNG-CHECK STRATEGY IN THE UNITED STATES

Pricing

Considerable debate among Alliance marketing and sales managers had preceded the launch of Lung-Check as to the proper pricing strategy for the product. Marketing managers supported a premium price for Lung-Check based on a dose equivalent to Carterets (that is, the cost to the veterinarian of one Lung-Check tablet would equal the cost to the veterinarian of 30 Carterets tablets). Thus the effective coverage to the pet owner for his or her animal would cost the same under either method. Fisher sold Carterets by the jar, with 180 tablets in each jar. Lung-Check was sold in packages of six tablets. With either brand, a pet owner would always receive a 6-month supply. Marketing managers had argued that the added convenience of a once-a-month pill supported a premium pricing strategy.

The sales managers, however, had contended that Alliance's lack of presence in the companion-animal market argued against expecting a price premium from veterinarians. They advocated an equivalent-per-dose price with Carterets (one Lung-Check dose would cost the same as one Carteret dose). In addition, preliminary market research indicated consumers were reluctant to spend more than $25 on their pets for one veterinarian visit (including a visitation charge of $12 to $15). Given the usual distribution and veterinarian markups, the suggested retail price of $10 to $12 for a package of Lung-Check (plus the veterinarian's visitation charge) could result in a total cost to the pet owner of $22 to $27.

Senior management elected to follow the recommendation of the sales executives and launched the product at a $1.00-per-dose price (30-day protection) to distribution. After the typical distributor mark-up (20%), the Lung-Check price would approximate the market price of Carterets to veterinarians of $1.25. The suggested retail price would be $1.75 to $2.00 per dose, or about $10 to $12 per pack.

Alliance's cost to manufacture a Lung-Check tablet (dose) was $0.03 for raw material, $0.02 in manufacturing expense, and $0.07 in packaging.

Selling

Alliance used the existing ANDIV sales force to sell the product through 44 appointed professional distributors located throughout the country. Alliance's distributors stocked a broad range of veterinary pharmaceuticals, surgical supplies, veterinary hospital equipment, and other products used, dispensed, and prescribed by veterinarians. Because of their extremely broad lines, distributors acted essentially as order takers, allocating little time to direct promotion of products.

To stimulate sales, Alliance required its direct sales force to call on companion-animal veterinarians to persuade them to purchase Lung-Check from their local distributors. In 1988, Alliance expected to have the 44 full-time sales representatives selling Lung-Check and 10 product specialists pushing the product to companion-animal veterinarians. Alliance executives recognized the margin advantages of selling direct to companion-animal veterinarians, but could not justify this strategy because of the company's dependency on the one Lung-Check product in the companion-animal market segment.

LUNG-CHECK'S FUTURE

Much to their elation, ANDIV executives saw Lung-Check sales in 1988 begin to exceed original expectations, and they increased the product's global sales predictions (including Japan and Canada) for 1988 from $43 to $53 million (90% to be in the United States). Thus, in one and a half years, Alliance would have captured close to 58% of the CLD-preventive market.

Moreover, Alliance executives contended that ANDIV was barely scratching the surface in potential Lung-Check sales. They estimated that, at an average price of $1.00 per dose, the total world market for CLD preventives approximated $92 million. The 1987 industry data indicated that only 70% of dogs in the United States received veterinarian care. Of them, only 45% of the dogs received a CLD preventive. And of those animals receiving the preventive, compliance with the recommended regime averaged only 3.6 months a year, a level substantially below that considered safe to ensure effective prevention of the disease. In fact, some 7% of dogs tested were found positive for CLD (see Exhibit 4).

To tap the tremendous upside potential in the market, ANDIV management believed that, although they could not increase the number of dogs under veterinarian care in the United States and Canada, their marketing strategy could expand the total market for CLD preventives and thus substantially increase Lung-Check sales. ANDIV management analyzed strategies designed to (1) commit a greater percentage of veterinarians to testing for and advocating prevention of CLD, and thus increase the percentage of the dog population receiving a CLD preventive, and (2) expand the compliance of dog owners who administered a CLD preventive (with such gimmicks as a refrigerator magnet that rang every 30 days to remind Lung-Check users to administer the product).

Furthermore, Alliance executives now recognized that the $25 pricing threshold for consumers was a myth; they had priced Lung-Check too low. Thus, they decided to increase the price per dose of Lung-Check by 50%.

In early 1988, Kenyon launched a two-pronged promotional strategy to increase Lung-Check sales in the United States and Canada. First, promotional efforts to veterinarians were designed to strengthen the once-a-month image of Lung-Check and to detail the economic incentive for veterinarians to participate in the CLD-preventive market. Kenyon used point-of-purchase advertising (veterinarian office posters and educational pamphlets) to inform dog owners of a convenient once-a-month CLD preventive. Second, using major media (*People* magazine and cable television), Kenyon launched an advertising/public-awareness campaign to increase public knowledge of the risks of canine lungworm disease and the need to administer a preventive.

The sales success over plan appeared to vindicate this strategy, and, as a result, Kenyon decided to ask for a $9 million global promotional/advertising budget for 1989, up from $3.5 million in 1988.

THE EUROPEAN CHALLENGE

Kenyon believed that the launch campaign for Lung-Check in Europe had to increase veterinarian awareness of the disease, its dangers, and methods for routine testing of the disease, and it had to demonstrate Lung-Check as a highly effective, safe canine lungworm preventive that could expand the veterinarian's practice. For dog owners, the plan had to introduce CLD and its dangers and communicate the reasons to administer a preventive medication throughout the mosquito season. Kenyon had allocated $2 million for promotional/marketing expenditures in the first year of launch (1989) and planned to increase this amount by $1 million a year as sales increased and marketing strategy for Lung-Check shifted.

The company was considering supplying the European market with a filter kit for each carton of Lung-Check purchased; a carton sold to distributors would contain 10 packages (six doses/package). Distributors generally resold Lung-Check by the carton to veterinarians. The filter would contain adequate supplies to test 100 animals for the presence of CLD. The cost of one filter kit would be $5.00 for the kit, $0.50 for its shipping, and $0.25 for assembly of the carton (wrapping) in the local country.

Kenyon was uncertain about *how* to carry out the launch campaign and develop the sales objectives for Europe, however. He planned to study the results of European focus groups and market-research surveys conducted recently with veterinarians (Appendix A) and consumers (Appendix B) in Spain, France, and Italy in an effort to answer the following questions about the European market:

- Did pet owners in each of these countries cluster into market segments similar to those in the United States, and did they demonstrate the same degree of emotional attachment to dogs as U.S. owners?

- What was European veterinarians' knowledge of CLD, and did they perceive the disease as a threat to their clients? Would they consider a CLD-preventive program for their clients?
- Did economics motivate European veterinarians to the degree seen in the United States?
- Based on the existing information about variations in disease incidence across European countries, what were logical sales estimates for the present and future European markets?
- What price should ANDIV charge (shipping and import duty would add about 10% to Alliance's manufacturing costs)?

Kenyon was considering several options for his sales force: (1) hiring six Lung-Check sales specialists (at $80,000 each), (2) obtaining 5% of the existing production-animal European sales force's time (at an absorption cost of $200,000), or (3) some combination of these two forces. The overriding question, however—could he transfer the marketing strategy of Lung-Check in the United States to individual European countries—lingered in Kenyon's mind as he began to prepare the European marketing plan.

APPENDIX A

EUROPEAN VETERINARY FOCUS GROUPS AND SURVEYS

ANDIV conducted six of these discussions to determine attitudes and market trends among European veterinarians in countries of relatively high incidence of CLD. Alliance conducted these interviews among veterinarians throughout each country (Spain, Italy, and France) and then conducted specific-region focus groups with veterinarians in the Mediterranean region of each country. ANDIV's reasons for focusing on the Mediterranean region stemmed from the high-incidence data from there. Management believed that an understanding of the disease in areas of high present incidence would provide insights for developing strategies for marketing Lung-Check to all European veterinarians.

Veterinary Focus Groups (Summary Figures)

I. Italy (27 non-Mediterranean veterinarians, 29 Mediterranean veterinarians on the panel)

- 83% of the veterinarians indicated an increasing awareness among pet owners about monitoring and improving the health of their dogs.
- 94% of the non-Mediterranean veterinarians felt the general dog-owning public was unaware of the dangers of CLD. In the Mediterranean region, this figure fell to 79%, and these veterinarians predicted greater public awareness of the disease as incidence continued to increase.
- 63% of the non-Mediterranean veterinarians indicated they had treated (eradicated) CLD from at least one client's dog. In the Mediterranean region, this figure was 91%.
- Asked if their clients would purchase a preventive ($60/year) for their dogs if recommended by them, 72% believed their clients would accept their recommendation. In the Mediterranean region, this figure was 84%.
- Asked if they viewed CLD as a threat to the dog population, 34% felt it was or would be in the next 5 years. In the Mediterranean region, this figure was 95%.
- Asked to evaluate the percentage of their clinic revenues derived from various prevention programs (rabies, distemper, and so on), 95% of all the veterinarians believed such programs accounted for at least 25% of their revenues.
- Asked if they saw potential for a CLD preventive, 41% said they would consider recommending a CLD preventive to their clients. In the Mediterranean region, this figure was 84%.
- In both regions, qualitative assessment of the discussion revealed younger veterinarians (less than 7 years in practice) appeared much more interested in the spread of CLD and developing a CLD-preventive program among their clients.

II. Spain (31 non-Mediterraneans, 23 Mediterraneans on the panel)
- 64% of all veterinarians believed there was an increasing awareness among dog owners about monitoring and improving the health of their pets.
- 97% of the non-Mediterranean veterinarians believed the dog-owning public was unaware of the dangers of CLD. In the Mediterranean region, this figure approximated 82%, and the veterinarians expected the figure to decline in the near future.
- 74% of the non-Mediterranean veterinarians indicated they had treated (eradicated) CLD from at least one client's dog. In the Mediterranean region, this figure was 84%.
- Asked if their clients would consider purchasing a CLD preventive ($60/year) if recommended by them, 60% believed their clients would. In the Mediterranean region, this figure was 66%.
- Asked if they believed CLD was a threat to the general dog population, 22% felt it was or would be in the next 5 years. In the Mediterranean region, this figure approximated 81%.
- Asked to evaluate the percentage of their clinic revenues derived from various prevention program (rabies, distemper, and so on), 95% of all veterinarians estimated that such programs accounted for at least 25% of their revenues.
- Asked if they saw potential in their clinic for a CLD preventive, 34% indicated they would consider recommending a CLD preventive to their clients. In the Mediterranean region, this figure was 67%.
- In both regions, qualitative assessments of the conversation revealed that younger veterinarians (less than 7 years in practice) appeared more interested in the latest incidence figures on CLD and in developing CLD-prevention programs for their clients.

III. France (46 non-Mediterraneans, 29 Mediterraneans on the panel)
- 80% of all veterinarians indicated an increasing awareness among pet owners about monitoring and improving the health of their dogs.
- 83% of the veterinarians believed the general pet-owning public was unaware of CLD and its dangers. In the Mediterranean region, this figure declined to 50%, and those veterinarians anticipated public awareness of CLD would continue to increase.
- 70% of non-Mediterranean veterinarians indicated they had treated (eradicated) CLD from at least one client's dog. In the Mediterranean region, this figure was 94%.
- Asked if their clients would purchase a CLD preventive ($60/year) for their dogs if recommended by them, 79% believed their clients would accept their recommendation. In the Mediterranean region, this figure was 81%.
- Asked if they perceived CLD as a threat to the general dog population, 47% believed it was or would be in the next five years. In the Mediterranean region, this figure was 95%.
- Asked to evaluate the percentage of their clinic revenues derived from various prevention programs (rabies, distemper, and so on), 100% of all veterinarians believed that such programs accounted for at least 25% of clinic revenues.
- Asked if they saw sales potential for a CLD preventive in their clinic, 40% indicated they would definitely consider recommending a preventive to their clients. In the Mediterranean region, this figure was 80%.
- Again, younger veterinarians (from qualitative assessments of the conversations) appeared more interested in participating in the CLD-prevention market.

APPENDIX B

CONSUMER MARKET RESEARCH AND FOCUS-GROUP RESULTS

ANDIV used focus groups and market surveys to develop an understanding of European dog owners and to determine if a market existed among these pet owners for preventive products. The market surveys attempted to allocate by percentage the European consumer segments into those established for North America (for example, Lonely Lady and Joe Average). Preliminary research had supported that European dog owners fell into these basic segments, although in substantially different allocations. As with the veterinarian studies, ANDIV conducted research among the general population in Italy, Spain, and France and among the Mediterranean areas of high CLD incidence.

ANDIV asked its market-research staff to address four questions in developing segment profiles: (1) the percentage of the population of dog owners in each market segment, (2) the percentage of each dog-owner market segment that used a veterinarian once a year, (3) the percentage in each market segment of dog owners who were aware of canine lungworm disease, and (4) those dog owners in each segment who would purchase a CLD preventive if recommended by a veterinarian.

Focus groups were designed to measure the emotional attachment of each country's dog owners to their pets. In particular, the focus groups attempted to distinguish notions among each country's dog owners about disease prevention in their dogs. (No effort was made to subdivide the focus-group results by geographic region, as ARLD was concerned with attitudes toward disease prevention for pets in general, not CLD specifically.)

The information in the following tables was obtained from company records.

Italy: Market Survey of 142 Dog Owners (%)

	Suburbanite	Average Giuseppe	Lonely Lady	Rural Man	Poor Giuseppe	Total Italian
1. Percentage of population	11	30	20	24	15	100
2. Use a veterinarian (once a year)	78	76	90	1	0	50
3. Aware of CLD	8	7	11	0	2	5
4. Would use CLD preventative if recommended (only those in each segment who visit vet)	87	87	94	0	0	44

Italy (Mediterranean): Market Survey of 112 Dog Owners (%)

	Suburbanite	Average Giuseppe	Lonely Lady	Rural Man	Poor Giuseppe	Total Italian
1. Percentage of population	10	36	23	13	18	100
2. Use a veterinarian (once a year)	77	72	83	3	1	53
3. Aware of CLD	29	24	31	3	6	20
4. Would use CLD preventative if recommended (only those in each segment who visit vet)	94	92	98	1	0	50

Italy: Focus-group Analysis[a]

1. All owners claimed an emotional attachment to their pets.
2. Discussion indicated approximately 80% of pet owners accustomed to prevention for their pets (rabies, distemper, birth control). Other dog owners usually visited the veterinarian for pet sickness or birth-control procedures.
3. Discussion revealed that approximately 85% of dog owners generally purchased products recommended by veterinarians.
4. After being briefed on the dangers of CLD to their dogs and the costs to eradicate the disease versus prevention, 89% of the dog owners indicated they would purchase a preventive for their pet. Reasonable cost appeared relatively irrelevant to maintaining the pet's health.

[a] 29 dog owners; 2 groups; all owners used a veterinarian.

Spain: Market Survey of 109 Dog Owners (%)

	Suburbanite	Average Juan	Lonely Lady	Rural Man	Poor Juan	Total Spanish
1. Percentage of population	13	32	20	16	19	100
2. Use a veterinarian (once a year)	59	52	79	0	0	40
3. Aware of CLD	6	5	6	0	1	4
4. Would use CLD preventative if recommended (only those in each segment who visit vet)	91	83	94	0	0	36

Spain (Mediterranean): Market Survey of 99 Dog Owners (%)

	Suburbanite	Average Juan	Lonely Lady	Rural Man	Poor Juan	Total Spanish
1. Percentage of population	13	30	21	15	21	100
2. Use a veterinarian (once a year)	62	52	83	0	1	41
3. Aware of CLD	17	19	29	2	1	15
4. Would use CLD preventative if recommended (only those in each segment who visit vet)	84	76	92	0	2	35

Spain: Focus-group Analysis[a]

1. Ninety percent of all dog owners claimed an emotional attachment to their pets.
2. Discussion indicated that 70% of dog owners accustomed to prevention (rabies, distemper). Like Italy, the balance generally used veterinarian for evaluation of a sick animal or birth control.
3. Eighty-five percent of dog owners generally adhered to veterinarian recommendations for their pets.
4. After a briefing on the dangers of CLD to the dog and the costs of eradication versus prevention, 80% of dog owners indicated they would purchase a preventive if available. Reasonable cost not an important factor in maintaining the animal's health.

[a] 41 total dog owners who used a veterinarian; combined results of two groups.

France: Market Survey Conducted with 171 Dog Owners (%)

	Suburbanite	Average Pierre	Lonely Lady	Rural Man	Poor Pierre	Total French
1. Percent of population	23	33	19	14	11	100
2. Use a veterinarian (once a year)	96	91	92	2	0	70
3. Aware of CLD	10	5	10	1	3	6
4. Would use CLD preventative if recommended (only those in each segment who visit vet)	90	89	96	0	0	63

France (Mediterranean): Market Survey of 165 Dog Owners (%)

	Suburbanite	Average Pierre	Lonely Lady	Rural Man	Poor Pierre	Total French
1. Percentage of population	19	35	20	11	15	100
2. Use a veterinarian (once a year)	96	88	93	3	0	68
3. Aware of CLD	35	35	38	9	5	28
4. Would use CLD preventative if recommended (only those in each segment who visit vet)	94	95	98	1	0	65

France: Focus-group Analysis[a]

1. All dog owners claimed an emotional attachment to their dogs.
2. Discussion yielded the clear consensus (95%) that dog owners who use a veterinarian are accustomed to prevention for their animals (rabies, distemper).
3. General consensus (90%) of pet owners: usually approved of recommendations by veterinarian and would purchase dog-care products or veterinarian services for reasonable sums.
4. After a briefing on the dangers of CLD to the dog and the costs to eradicate the disease versus prevention, 84% of dog owners indicated they would purchase a preventive for their pet. Generally, cost was irrelevant to providing a healthy life for their pets.

[a] 37 total dog owners; 2 groups; all owners used a veterinarian once a year.

CHESTER COLLEGE LIBRARY